THE COOKBOOK
THAT □ **W9-COY-786**

This is America's bestselling basic cookbook of all-time—the one indispensable cookbook that includes a complete range of recipes in every category: every-day, classic, foreign, and de luxe. Everything needed for the success of a recipe is clearly explained and illustrated, and recipes within a recipe are cross-referenced at the point of use by volume and/or page number. For example, in this volume a recipe to be found in Volume 1, Page 275 will be cross-referenced as (I, 275).

JOY OF COOKING, now being published for the first time in two convenient-to-use volumes, has added over 1,200 new recipes, new menus, and new chapters on ingredients and entertaining to the trusted, well-loved material that has made it first among the basic cookbooks for more than a quarter of a century.

JOY OF COOKING
The encyclopedia of cooking know-how

"A masterpiece of clarity."
—Craig Claiborne, author,
NEW YORK TIMES COOKBOOK

"As essential as the kitchen range."
—Clementine Paddleford,
THIS WEEK Food Editor

VOLUME 2

APPETIZERS, DESSERTS & BAKED GOODS

JOY OF COOKING

IRMA S. ROMBAUER

MARION ROMBAUER BECKER

ILLUSTRATED BY

Ginnie Hoffmann

AND

Beverly Warner

A SIGNET BOOK

NEW AMERICAN LIBRARY

TIMES MIRROR

CONTENTS

	PAGE
DEDICATION	
Foreword and Guide	ix
Entertaining	1
Menus	14
Drinks	25
Canapés and Tea Sandwiches	49
Hors d'Oeuvre	66
Fruits	85
Pancakes, Waffles, Croquettes and Fritters	111
Know Your Ingredients	129
Yeast and Quick Breads and Coffee Cakes	239
Pies, Pastes and Filled Pastries	292
Cakes, Cup Cakes, Torten and Filled Cakes	334
Cookies and Bars	386
Icings, Toppings and Glazes	418
Desserts	436
Dessert Sauces	473
Ice Creams, Ices and Frozen Desserts	483
Candies and Confections	499
The Foods We Keep	527
Canning, Salting and Smoking	530
Freezing	547
Jellies, Jams, Preserves and Marmalades	570
Pickles and Relishes	584
Index	595

*"That which thy fathers have bequeathed to thee,
earn it anew if thou wouldst possess it."*

Goethe: Faust

DEDICATION

In revising and reorganizing "The Joy of Cooking" we have missed the help of my mother, Irma S. Rombauer. How grateful I am for her buoyant example, for the strong feeling of roots she gave me, for her conviction that, well-grounded, you can make the most of life, no matter what it brings! In an earlier away-from-home kitchen I acted as tester and production manager for the privately printed first edition of "The Joy." Working with Mother on its development has been for my husband, John, and for me the culmination of a very happy personal relationship. John has always contributed verve to this undertaking, but during the past ten years he has, through his constant support and crisp creative editing, become an integral part of the book. We look forward to a time when our two boys—and their wives—will continue to keep "The Joy" a family affair, as well as an enterprise in which the authors owe no obligation to anyone but themselves —and you.

MARION ROMBAUER BECKER

FOREWORD AND GUIDE

"The cook," said Saki, "was a good cook, as cooks go; and as cooks go, she went." Indeed she did go, leaving us, whether in charge of established or of fledgling families, to fend for ourselves. We are confident that after you have used this book steadily for a few months, paying due attention to our symbols ✳, ▲, (), ❂, ⋏, ☰, ★, and to our "pointers to success" ▶—as identified at the end of the Foreword—you will master the skills the cook walked off with. What is more, we believe that you will go on to unexpected triumphs, based on the sound principles which underlie our recipes, and actually revel in a sense of new-found freedom. You will eat at the hour of your choice. The food will be cooked and seasoned to your discriminating taste. And you will regain the priceless private joy of family living, dining and sharing.

For a number of years, manuscript in hand, I have lunched with friends to whom the preparation and presentation of food is a major interest. At these meetings this text, as it grew, came in for lively critical evaluation. I wish you could have been part of the proceedings, as the chefs, food chemists, processors and artists piled in on the problems which arose, searching for the simplest, the most practical and the most comprehensive approaches to this fresh version of "The Joy" and pored over our new illustrations.

The nucleus of this group included Chef James E. Gregory, American-trained and French-finished, with his flair for making food as appetizing to look at as it is delicious, and Chef Pierre Adrian, at whose restaurant we gathered. Pierre grew up in the Vosges, and has a down-to-earth understanding of food as it comes from the land, coupled with a mastery of the *haute cuisine*.

Other "regulars" were Lolita Harper who, as chief home economist for Cincinnati's utility company, has made a career of rescuing frantic housewives from one dilemma after another; and Luella Schierland, a well-traveled, knowedgeable and skilled hostess. Always present through their handiwork, and sometimes in person, were Ginnie Hofmann and Beverly Warner, whose sensitive response to our layouts resulted in the spirited drawings which make our cooking techniques come alive.

What fun we have had talking out and resolving culinary questions—which I brought back for further scrutiny to the staff at home: to Jane Brueggeman who headed it, and whose unerring common sense and devotion have been invaluable; to Dorothy Wartenberg, our consultant for the English edition; and to Odessa Whitehead, who kept the stove warm and the kitchen bright.

As you can guess, we are also indebted to uncounted friends and "fans" of "The Joy," and to any number of technical consultants, both private and governmental, who have given generously of their time, experience and special competence. Of course, any expression of indebtedness does not discharge us from responsibility for the entire contents of the book—a responsibility which rests with Mother and me as its sole authors.

We have assumed that in buying this book you intend to use it daily. For this reason every effort has been made, space permitting, to provide information at the point of use. Whenever emphasis is needed, when an important principle is involved, we have inserted a "pointer." "Pointers" are vital, friendly reminders which guide you through more exacting processes—beating egg whites, heating delicate food over— not in—hot water, the proper temperatures for holding and storage.

There are also the seven other graphic symbols mentioned in the first paragraph. Among these we have retained from the previous edition the parentheses to indicate that an ingredient is optional: its use may enhance, but its omission will not prejudice, the success of a recipe.

You will notice too that we have attached to certain words, phrases and categories special meanings. For example, any meat, fish, or cereal, unless otherwise specified, is *raw*, not cooked. Again, eggs are the 2-ounce size; milk means fresh whole milk; butter means sweet, unsalted butter; chocolate means bitter baking chocolate; flour denotes the all-purpose variety; spices are ground, not whole; condensed canned soup or milk is to be used undiluted. Recipes which have the word "BLENDER" in their title are only successful when an electric blender is used. Many dishes made with cooked, canned and frozen cooked food are grouped in the chapter BRUNCH, LUNCH AND SUPPER DISHES.

Also, for greater clarity, we defined culinary terms for which there are no generally accepted meanings: see the Index for "parboil," "simmer," and "casserole." Finally, in response to many requests from users of "The Joy" who ask "What are your favorites?", we have added to some of our recipes the word "Cockaigne", which signified in medieval times "a mythical land of peace and plenty," and also happens to be the name of our country home.

There are two other parts of the book with which we hope you will quickly acquaint yourself: KNOW YOUR IN-GREDIENTS, and THE FOODS WE HEAT. Both are brand new. INGREDIENTS will tell you in detail about the prop-erties of the materials you commonly combine in cooking, how and why they react as they do and, when feasible, how to substitute for them. To us, the chapter on HEAT is one of the most important. When you become familiar with its contents you will understand why we assign a high priority to it. And do read the ABOUTS for special information.

We have tried to correlate the entire text so that you can readily find your way around in it. But, as in the past, we have kept in mind the tremendous importance of a detailed Index. Not the least of its virtues is the stimulus it gives to the cook's aspiring eye.

New, too, in this edition is a far more conscious emphasis on interpreting the classic cuisine—those dishes whose circu-lation is worldwide, and whose traditional language, like that of love and diplomacy, is French. We propose clearing up once and for all the distinctions between terms like *printa-nière, bonne femme, bordelaise, allemande,* and *polonaise,* while giving at the same time authentic descriptions of such national culinary enthusiasms as *couscous,* Devonshire cream, *strudel, zabaglione* and *rijsttafel.* Actually, the experienced cook will recognize many of these exotics as intimates whom she has known for years in her own kitchen under other names.

Ever since the last revision, a decade ago, we have been refashioning "The Joy" into a handbook which will more faithfully and flexibly meet your needs. How do we know these needs? From the hundreds and hundreds of heartwarming letters which have set out in detail your own experiences with our book, and reflected new tastes and trends in American living. Many of your messages reflected not only the revolution in transport which has made available distant and previously unobtainable foods, but showed a reawakened interest in the cookery of far-off lands.

Most important to us are all of you, both at home and abroad, who are preoccupied every day with that old yet ever-new question, "What shall we have for dinner?" This revision, we hope, is the inclusive and effective answer.

WATCH FOR THESE SYMBOLS

 POINTERS TO SUCCESS

 FROZEN FOODS

 OPTIONAL

 PRESSURE COOKING

 BLENDER

 OUTDOOR COOKING

 CHRISTMAS

 ALTITUDE COOKING

JOY

OF COOKING

ENTERTAINING

When you are entertaining, try not to feel that something unusual is expected of you as a hostess. It isn't. Just be yourself. Even eminent and distinguished persons are only human. Like the rest of us, they shrink from ostentation; and nothing is more disconcerting to a guest than the impression that his coming is causing a household commotion. Confine all noticeable efforts for his comfort and entertainment to the period that precedes his arrival. Satisfy yourself that you have anticipated every known emergency —the howling child, the last-minute search for cuff links, your husband's exuberance, your helper's ineptness, your own ill humor. Then relax and enjoy your guests.

If, at the last minute, something does happen to upset your well-laid plans, rise to the occasion. The mishap may be the making of your party. Capitalize on it, but not too heavily.

The procedures below present simple, dignified, current practice in table service. If you plan to serve cocktails before a meal, have glasses for drinks and non-alcoholic beverages ready on a tray. With these, you may pass some form of cracker, canapé or hors d'oeuvre. If you and your guests are discriminating diners, you will keep this pick-up light. Too generous quantities of food and drink beforehand will bring jaded palates to the dinner on which you have expended such effort. Should you have the kind of guests who enjoy a long cocktail period and varied hors d'oeuvre, be sure to season your dinner food more highly than usual. Cocktail preliminaries, which have a bad habit these days of going on indefinitely, may be politely shortened by serving a delicious hot or cold consommé or soup, either near the bar area or from a tureen on a cart. Your guests are apt to welcome this transition heartily.

No matter for whom your preparations are being made, careful forethought and arrangement contribute greatly to the pleasure that results. Never forget that ◗ your family is really the most important assembly you ever entertain. Whether for them or for friends ◗ always check the freshness of the air, the temperature of the dining area and the proper heat or chill for plates, food and drinks—especially hot ones. If warming oven space is limited, use the heat cycle of your dishwasher or, if you entertain often, you may wish to install an infrared heating unit which can be raised or lowered above a heatproof counter. Be sure that each diner has plenty of elbow room, about 30 inches from the center of one plate service to the center of the next.

Formal meals, given in beautifully appointed homes, served by competent, well-trained servants—who can be artists in their own right—are a great treat. We cannot expect to have ideal conditions at all times in the average home. However, no matter what the degree of informality, always be sure that the table is attractive and immaculately clean—and always maintain an even rhythm of service.

ABOUT TABLE DÉCOR

As to the table itself, a top that is heat- and stain-resistant lends itself to the greatest ease of service and upkeep. You can expose as much or as little of its surface as you like. If you have a tabletop of natural hardwood, you must protect it against heat at all times with pads.

For versatility and effective contrast, keep your basic flatware and dishes simple in form and not too pronounced in pattern or color. Then you can combine them, without fear of clashing, with varied linens, fruits and flowers and—most importantly—varied foods. You will find that changes in décor and accessories stimulate the appetite, as much as do changes in seasoning.

Serve soups sometimes in covered soup bowls, and other times from a tureen or in cups. Serve salads on plates, in bowls or on crescent-shaped "bone plates" which are made to fit at the side of dinner plates—giving a less crowded feeling to the table. For variety, replace vegetable dishes with an outsize platter holding several vegetables attractively garnished. Also, small raw vegetables and fruits may substitute for garnishes of pars-

ley and cress to give a meat platter a festive air. Instead of using pairs of matching dessert dishes, try contrasting bowls of glass or bright pottery. For a rustic effect, serve a hearty menu on your everyday dishes and use bright linens and wooden salad bowls with a centerpiece of wooden scoops filled with pears and hazelnuts in the husk.

For a more elegant effect, serve a dainty meal on the same dishes, against a polished board decorated with fragile glasses and flowers. See sketch.

Whatever your decorative scheme, flower arrangements should be low or lacy. Tall arrangements that obstruct the view discourage across-the-table conversation. There is nothing more distracting than dodging a floral centerpiece while trying to establish an intimate relationship among your guests. For the same reason, candles should be placed strategically. On a formal buffet or tea table, which is viewed from above, the decorations may be as tall as you wish. In fact, food or flower accents that are elevated on epergnes or stemmed dishes add a note of drama.

Table decorations need not be costly, and they can always express your own personality. In-

genious hostesses can confect stunning arrangements of vegetables, fruits, flowers—alone or in combination—or can use handsome man-made objects and leaves. Several harmonious small containers of flowers or fruit—similar or varied—can be effectively grouped around a central element or placed along the length of a table to replace a single focal point. Use one of these small units of long-needled pine tufts and snowdrops, or clematis, illustrated in the semiformal luncheon service, above.

A piece of sculpture of a suitable size for your table makes a charming base for a centerpiece. Surround it with an ivy ring and vary the décor from time to time with other greenery or any elements that suggest borders or garlands. If the sculpture is slightly raised on a base, it can be enjoyed to great advantage. Whatever you use, don't overcrowd the table. One of the most important things to remember is that ◗ no matter what the decoration, it should be suitable in color and scale with the foods served to enhance it. Don't make your effects so stagey that your guests' reactions will be, "She went to a lot of trouble." Make them say, rather, "She had a lot of fun doing it!"

ABOUT PLACING SILVER AND DISHES

There are certain time-honored positions for silver and equipment that result from the way food is eaten and served. So keep in mind these basic placements. ◗ Forks to the left except the very small fish fork, which goes to the right. ◗ Spoons, including iced-tea spoons, and knives to the right, with the sharp blade of the knife toward the plate. There is, of course, a practical reason for placing the knife at the diner's right, since

right-handed persons, who predominate, commonly wield the knife with their favored hand, and do so early in the meal. Generally, having cut his food, the diner lays down his knife and transfers his fork to the right hand. Formal dining makes an exception to this rule; and with left-handed or ambidextrous persons the transfer seems to us, on any occasion, superfluous. ◗ Place silver that is to be used first farthest from the plate. It is also better form never to have more than three pieces of silver at either side. Bring in any other needed silver on a small tray as the course is served. The server is always careful to handle silver by the handles only, including carving and serving spoons and forks, which are placed to the right of the serving dish.

If you look at some of the place settings illustrated, you can, with a few exceptions, practically predict the menu. Let's consider the semiformal luncheon setting above. Line the base of the handles up about one inch from the edge of the table. Some people still consider it important to serve a knife at luncheon, even if that knife is not needed for the actual cutting of meat. Others omit the knife if a typical luncheon casserole is passed—or served in individual containers. For a formal luncheon, a butter plate is placed to the left on a level with the water glass. The butter knife is usually placed as shown and a butter ball or curl, page 56, is already in place before the guests are seated. Later, the butter plate is removed simultaneously with the salad plate. Both are taken from the left side. The butter plate is picked up with the left hand, the salad plate with the right. At semiformal luncheons, you may have the dessert spoon and fork in place above the plate, as sketched. This indicates that no finger bowl will be served. Or you may, as in the dinner service, bring the dessert silver to the table with the finger bowl, as sketched on page 8.

Water and wine glasses are in place as sketched above. The water is poured in the former to about ¾ capacity; the wine glasses are left empty. ♦ Glasses, filled from the right, are never lifted by the server when pouring. Goblet types are always handled by the stem by the diner and by the server when he replaces or removes them. Tumbler types are always held well below the rim.

When it is time to serve coffee, empty cups and saucers are placed to the right. There is a spoon on the saucer, behind the cup and parallel to the cup handle, which is turned to the diner's right. After all the cups are placed, they are filled by the server and afterward sugar and cream are offered from a small tray from the left. But the entire coffee service may be served, even for luncheon, in the living room, after the dessert.

Individual ash trays and cigarettes may be placed on the table. Although smoking between courses is frowned on by all epicures because it lessens the sensitivity of the palate, guests must be permitted to do what pleases them. If you are a strong-willed hostess, you may prefer to have the ash trays and cigarettes placed on the table just after the dessert is served.

If your party is not formal, place cards may be omitted. If the party is to be for six, ten or fourteen, the host is at one end of the table, the hostess at the other. If the guests number eight or twelve, the host is at

one end and the hostess just to the left at the other end.

The honor guest, if a woman, is seated to the right of the host; if a man, to the left of the hostess. At a formal meal, food is presented, but ♦ not served, to the hostess first. Food is actually offered first to the woman guest of honor. The other women are then all served. Finally, the men are served, beginning with the guest of honor. If there is no special guest of honor, you may want to reverse the direction of service every other course, so that the same people are not always served last.

While it is not the best form, some people prefer to have the hostess served first. She knows the menu and by the way she serves herself sets the pace for the other guests. This is a special help if the guest of honor is from another country. In America, it is customary for guests to wait until everyone is served and the hostess begins to eat. In Europe, however, where each individual service is usually complete in itself, it is permissible to start eating as soon as one is served.

♦ Plates are usually removed from the right and placed or passed from the left. Service and dinner plates are frequently of different patterns. For the purpose of clarity in the illustrations following, service plates, as a rule, are sketched with a solid banding, hot plates or plates on which cold food is being served are shown with a thin double-banded edge.

ABOUT FORMAL ENTERTAINMENT

Most of us moderns look with amazement, not to say dismay, at the menus of traditionally formal dinners. Such meals are a vanishing breed, like the bison —but, like the bison, they manage here and there to survive. They begin with both clear and thick soups. Then comes an alternation of relevés and removes, each with its accompanying vegetables. The relevés are lighter in quality than the hefty joints and whole fish which make up the removes. Any one of the rather ironically titled removes could count as the equivalent of what, in current parlance, is called an entrée, or main dish.

However, in the classic formal menu, the term entrée has a quite different significance. Classic entrées occur immediately after a final remove and consist of timbales, sea foods and variety meats, served in rich pastes and with delicate sauces —trifles distinguished for their elegance.

A salad takes next place in this stately procession, and is usually made of a seasoned cooked vegetable, such as asparagus, with greens doing garnish duty only. After this, the diner may choose from a variety of cheeses.

Entremets—hot or cold sweets —succeed the cheese course and these are topped off, in turn, by both hot and cold fruits. We now have completed the major framework of a classic formal menu, in which, it goes without saying, each course is accompanied by a sympathetic wine.

We marvel at the degree of gastronomic sophistication required to appreciate so studied and complex a service—to say nothing of the culinary skills needed to present the menu in proper style. But, more critically, we ask, "Where do the guests stow away all that food?" Granted that a truly formal dinner lasts for hours and that each portion may be a dainty one, the total intake is still bound to be formidable. Such an array is seldom encountered in this casual and girth-conscious era. But a semiformal dinner with traces of classic service still graces the privileged household.

When the guests come into the dining room, the table is all in readiness. ♦ The setting forecasts the menu through the first three courses. Should more silver be required, it is always brought in separately later. The water glasses are about ⅔ full; the wine glasses, though empty, stand in place, see illustrations, page 6.

At formal and semiformal dinners, butter plates are seldom used. Melba toast or crackers are served with the appetizer or soup, and hard rolls later, with the roast. The next setting sketched indicates a seafood cocktail, a soup, a meat course, a salad course, water and two wines. Water and wine are poured from the right. The glasses may stay in place throughout the meal, but it is preferable to remove each wine glass after use. A third wine glass may be strung out on a line with the others or placed to form a triangle slightly forward toward the guest and just above the soup spoon. However, if more than three wines are to be served, fresh glasses replace the used glasses as the latter are removed.

Once the guests are seated, the server's steady but unobtrusive labor begins. ♦ There is a plate, filled or unfilled, before each guest throughout the meal. The server usually removes a plate from the right and replaces it immediately with another from the left, so that the courses follow one another in unbroken rhythm. At such a dinner, second helpings are seldom offered.

When a platter is presented, it is offered from the left to the guest by the server who holds it on a folded napkin, on the palm of his left hand and may steady it with the right. The server should always make sure that the handles of the serving tools are directed toward the diner.

The passing of crackers, breads, relishes, the refilling of water glasses and the pouring of wines take place during, not between, the appropriate courses. When the party is less formal, the host may prefer to pour the wines himself from a decanter or from a bottle. If the wine is chilled, he will wrap it in a napkin and hold a napkin in the left hand to catch any drip from the bottle. The hostess on such occasions may pass relishes to the guest at her right and the guests may continue to pass them on to one another. Also, relishes may be arranged at strategic places on the table, but must be removed with the soup. However, even with these slight assists, the work of the server is one that calls for nicely calculated timing. It is easy to see why ♦ one server should not be called on to take care of more than six or eight guests— at the most—if smooth going is expected.

Let us go back to our dinner, which begins—as forecast by the setting sketched below—

with a sea-food cocktail and goes on to the soup. For this dinner, the sea food, served in a specially iced glass, is in place when the guests are seated.

When the sea food has been eaten, the empty cocktail glasses are removed—leaving the service plate intact. The soup plate is now placed on it—served from the left. Crackers, melba toast and relishes are now presented.

The service plate is removed along with the empty soup plate, from the right. Now, if a platter of hot food is to be passed, an

empty hot plate is placed before the guest—from the left.

However, if the meat course is to be carved and served in the dining room, the soup plate only is removed, leaving the service plate before the guest. The meat platter has been put before the host and he carves enough meat for all the guests before any further serving takes place. The server, who has replaced the host's service plate with a hot one, stands to the left of the host, holding an extra hot plate on a napkin. When the host has filled the one before him, the server removes it and replaces it with the empty hot plate he has been holding. Then, after taking the service plate before the guest of honor from the right, the server gives him the filled hot plate from the left. He then returns to the host, and waits to replace the hot plate being filled by the host for another guest.

When all guests have been attended to, the server passes the gravy and then the vegetables —with a serving spoon and fork face down on the platter and the handles directed toward the guest. The hot breads come next. During this course, the server replenishes water and wine.

The menu we have been serving has consisted of three courses: sea-food cocktail, soup, meat-and-vegetable. A salad and dessert course will follow; but first let us consider a different menu—one that omits the cocktail and introduces a fish course.

Obviously, a different setting of silver is in order for this alternate menu. The illustration will show that it consists of soup, first. After that, there is a fish course, followed by meat, salad and so on. You will notice

For the second menu, plates of soup are passed from the left and placed directly on the service plates—after guests have removed napkins and place cards. Should sherry be served with the soup course, both glass and plate are removed, along with service plate. Now the fish course arrives. It has been arranged on individual plates in the pantry. This is given from the left—just as the soup and service plates have been taken from the right.

After the server has removed the empty fish plate from the right, a hot plate is put before the guest from the left, as shown next.

that there are one water and two wine glasses. Because no sea-food cocktail is included, the napkin is placed on the service plate, with a place card on top. For this setting, cigarettes, matches and an ash tray, as well as individual salt are placed on the right, with pepper on the left. No food is on the table when the guests are seated.

The meat course follows—either carved by the host, or previously arranged in the pantry. A separately served vegetable or the salad course, as sketched, may follow. With such vegetables as asparagus and artichokes or salads with vinegar dressings no wines are served.

Each guest places the fork and spoon to each side of the plate and then puts the doily, with finger bowl on it, to the upper left side of his place setting— opposite the water glass.

A handsomely arranged fruit compote, passed during the meat course, can be used as an alternate to a salad. Crescent-shaped plates suit either of these courses. If a compote is substituted for a salad, a spoon is put on the right of the setting, instead of a salad fork on the left, as illustrated.

After the salad course is removed, the table is denuded for a short time. Any unused silver, salts and peppers and relishes are taken away. The table is crumbed. The server uses a folded napkin and brushes the crumbs lightly onto a plate.

Now, the dessert setting is placed in front of each guest.

The finger bowl, partially filled with water, may have a scented geranium leaf, a fragrant herb or flower or a thin slice of lemon floating in it.

An exception to this finger bowl rule is made when fruit is to be served after dessert. In this case, the dessert plate complete with silver is placed in front of each guest. After the dessert has been passed and eaten, the dessert plate is removed. Next comes a fruit plate with doily, finger bowl, fruit knife and fork.

Now, if coffee is to be served at the table, empty demitasse cups and saucers are placed to the right of the diners. Demitasse spoons are on the saucers, behind the cups and parallel to the handle. Coffee is poured from the right and cream and sugar are passed on a small tray from the left. Liqueur may be served with the coffee or passed on a tray later, in the living room.

Men often like to loiter at the table, for strictly male conversation, over a glass of port or brandy. In England, before the port, a savory, page 472, is served. The hostess may retire to the drawing room with the women guests and later, pour coffee for her reassembled guests there. By this time, good food, wine and conviviality have usually broken down the minor social inhibitions, and the serving of coffee may be completely informal.

ABOUT INFORMAL
ENTERTAINMENT

Your chances for a successful party are much greater if you key your efforts to your own belongings and service rather than struggle to meet the exacting demands of the kind of dinner which has just been described. Your standards need not be lowered in the least. ▶ Plan a menu which will simplify last-minute preparation and subsequent serving. Offer fewer courses and put several kinds of food on one platter. But please do not let your guests sit, trying to make conversation, with a gradually congealing slice of meat before them, while waiting longingly for the vegetables and the reluctant gravy boat to follow.

If you must rely on indifferent service, or if your harassed cook is trying to pinch-hit as a waitress, plan to serve the main course yourself from an attractively arranged platter. For informal meals, when the hostess may be both waitress and cook, it pays to spend lots of time planning menus that can be prepared in advance and served with little fuss. Here again, in order that food will reach the table at the right temperature, it is wise to choose cooperative equipment such as covered dishes—but do remember to allow a place to put hot lids—double dishes with provision underneath for ice or hot water, and a samovar arrangement for hot drinks.

For both service and removal, a cart may facilitate matters, especially if there are no children trained to help unobtrusively. Deputizing your guests invites chaos, and should, except in extreme emergencies, be avoided.

When service is completely lacking, it is sensible to decide well in advance what concessions will achieve the most peaceful and satisfying conditions for everyone. Plates, already prepared and garnished, can be brought into the dining area on a tray or cart. If the meal is a hot one, we find this scheme impractical for more than four people. For a larger number of guests, attractive platters and casseroles of food may be placed at each end of the table, so that serving responsibilities are divided ▶ but whatever the meal, be sure to serve hot foods hot and cold foods cold.

There are many devices for keeping foods hot during a meal and while it is true that food is always best when served just as it comes from the stove, the informal hostess should not scorn such heating aids as electric trays, candle warmers, chafing dishes or electric skillets. Be sure, though, that none of these devices allows the food to boil or permits steam to form. If it does, crusty foods go limp and sauces may become either too thick or too thin.

Try iced platters or an ice tray, page 40, for chilled foods. For a buffet, serve dramatic-looking meats en croûte (I, 458) and chaud-froid (I, 388). Both are "insulators" which will keep foods from drying out.

ABOUT BUFFET SERVICE

This is the most satisfactory service for large groups. However, plan your table placement so the guests are routed from tables to buffet without crowding.

For a buffet, plan a menu of foods that hold well—and the best way to keep an attractive buffet looking that way is to concentrate on individual portions. These can be replenished

easily, thus keeping the table always intact. For instance, rather than a large aspic, use individual fancy molds—even paper cups. Use sea shells or vegetable cups (I, 39), as individual containers for sea food or other mixtures. And cut turkey, ham and salmon in individual portions. Also see About Stuffed Vegetables (I, 256) and Cases for Food (I, 208). For garnishes see (I, 39) and (I, 38).

If the servings are not individual, cater generously, as guests are apt to take larger portions at buffets. The following layouts show typical buffet settings. The first one represents a dinner at which the host or hostess serves the guests, who then proceed to tables which are already set. The menu includes duck with orange cups, wild rice, podded peas and a green salad. The serving platters are later removed and replaced by the dessert; or individual desserts may be served at table.

The drawing above shows a buffet at which the guests serve themselves and proceed to sit at small tables. If there are no tables, individual trays may be used. For tray service, plan food that does not call for the use of a knife.

Note also that height in candles and flowers is often a dramatic asset in buffet service as is the use of tiered dishes.

Shown on page 11 are a meat or fish casserole dish, artichokes vinaigrette filled with devilled eggs, relishes and rolls. A dessert may be on the table at the beginning of the service. If the serving table seems too crowded, place the water and hot drinks on another serving surface.

ABOUT TEA SERVICE

What is more hospitable than afternoon coffee or tea, whether served on a tray in the living room or on a lavish table in the dining room? For an informal tea, the hostess pours and serves. However, when the tea is formal, friends of the hostess sit at each end of the table and consider it an honor to pour.

The drawing on the next page shows a large, formal tea table, with a coffee service at one end. Tea may be served at the other. It is wise to instruct a supplier to keep in frequent touch with the pourers to anticipate their need for additional hot water, coffee or cups. It is also canny to have additional platters ready to replace those at the table that have become rather ragged-looking. Medium-size rather

than large platters are easier to keep in trim.

ABOUT CASUAL ENTERTAINING FOR ONE OR FOR MANY

Tray meals can be a delightful stimulant if they include a surprise element in the form of a lovely pitcher, a small flower arrangement or some seasonal delicacy. Make sure, especially if the recipient is an invalid, that all needed utensils are present, that the food is hot or cold as required, sufficient in amount and fresh and dainty looking.

A cookout, whether a mere wienie roast or a luau, can be— although it seldom is anymore —one of the least complicated ways to entertain. We suggest, unless your equipment is equal to that of a well-appointed kitchen and you can ensure your guests of comparably controlled cooking, that you choose menus which are really enhanced by outdoor cooking procedures, page 24.

Have enough covered dishes on hand to protect food from flies. Give your guests a tray or a traylike plate if there are no regular place sets or normal seating arrangements. And pre-

pare an alternate plan of accommodation, in case of bad weather.

We remember a successful informal party that was really too big for our quarters and whose pattern might provide a substitute in case of a weather-beleaguered barbecue. The guests arrived to find no evidence of entertaining, only the most gorgeous arrangements of colchicum—those vibrant, large fall blooms which resemble vast, reticulated crocus. After drinks were served and hors d'oeuvre passed, a cart with soup tureen and cups circulated. This was followed by tray baskets containing white paper bags, each completely packaged with individual chicken salad, olives, endive filled with avocado, cocktail tomatoes, cress and cheese sandwiches, bunches of luscious grapes and foil-wrapped brownies. Coffee was served, again from the circulating cart.

In order to get an informal after-supper party rolling, young hostesses are often so eager to present the fruits of their labors that solid food is served too early for the comfort of the guests, most of whom have rather recently dined. If the party gets off to an early start, it sometimes seems too soon to start drinking alcoholic or carbonated drinks or punches. Why not suggest a tisane (I, 20), to engender sociability at the takeoff of an evening. Tisanes can also prove a pleasant variation for older people, who frequently refuse coffee when food is to be served later.

Here are a few parting shots —as we close this chapter on entertaining. In cooking for more people than you are normally accustomed to, allow yourself enough extra time for both food preparation and heating or cooling of food. Please

read the comments on the enlarging of recipes, page 228. Be sure that your mixing and cooking equipment is scaled to take care of your group, and, ♦ most important of all, that you have the refrigerator space to protect chilled dishes and the heat surface to maintain the temperature of the hot ones. Don't hesitate to improvise steam tables or iced trays. Utilize insulated picnic boxes or buckets either way, and wheelbarrows or tubs for the cracked ice, on which to keep platters chilled.

If you entertain this way frequently, it may be worthwhile to make—as one of our friends did—a large rectangular galvanized deep tray, on which the dishes of a whole cold buffet can be kept chilled. Or try confecting an epergne-like form, such as that shown on page 40, for chilling sea foods, hors d'oeuvre or fruit.

For camping trips or boating parties, consider the safety factor in choosing the menu. No matter what the outing ♦ don't transport perishable foods in hot weather in the even hotter trunk of a car.

Not all types of entertaining —formal or casual or in between —can be detailed here. But, whatever the occasion, assemble your tried skills in menu planning so as to reflect the distinctive character of your home. Flavor the occasion with your own personality. And keep handy somewhere, for emergency use, the cool dictum attributed to Col. Chiswell Langhorne of Virginia: "Etiquette is for people who have no breeding; fashion for those who have no taste."

ABOUT COOKING FOR LARGE PARTIES

Most of the recipes in this book are for from 4 to 6 servings and will double satisfactorily for 8 to 12. But all of us are called on, at times, to produce meals for larger groups and this is when we must be on our guard. For unexpected surprises are apt to pop up just when we want everything to go particularly well. No matter how rich or how simple the menu, remember, first, that it is preferable to cook recipes with which you are familiar for special occasions. Secondly, cook in several moderate-sized batches rather than in one big chunk. Because, mysterious as it sounds—but true, even for the experts—quantity cooking is not just a matter of indefinite multiplication, page 228. If you overexpand, too, you may run into a number of other problems.

Take into account the longer time needed in preparation—not only for paring and washing of vegetables or drying salad greens, but for heating up large quantities. Even more important, you may be confronted with a sudden pinch of refrigerator space—discovering that the shelves are needed for properly chilling large aspics or puddings just when they should be doubling to keep other sizable quantities of food at safe temperatures. ▶ This warning is of great importance if you are serving stuffed fowl, creamed foods, ground meat, mayonnaise, cream puffs, custards or custard pies. These foods spoil readily without showing any evidence of hazard. Before planning the menu for larger groups, assess equipment for mixing, cooking, refrigerating and serving.

Plan, if the meal is a hot one, to use recipes involving both the oven and top burners. Increase your limited heating surfaces with the use of electric skillets, steam tables or hot trays to hold food in good serving condition. Make sure, if you plan individual casseroles, that you have enough oven space; or if the casseroles are large, that they will fit. In fact, stage a dress rehearsal—from the cooking equipment requirements right through to the way the service dishes and table gear will be placed. Then, satisfied that the mechanical requirements are met, plan the actual work on the menu so enough can be done in advance to relieve the sink and work surface of last-minute crowding and mess.

Stick not only to those dishes you are confident you can handle without worry, but to those that make sense for the time you can spare for them. If one dish is going to require much last-minute hand work and fiddling, balance it against others that can be preassembled or are easy to serve: casseroles, baked or scalloped dishes, gelatin or frozen foods. See Menus for further suggestions, page 20.

One of the hardest things in mass cooking is to give the food that personalized and cherished look that is achieved in intimate dinners. Do not hesitate to serve simple foods for company. Choose seasonal ingredients and cook them skillfully. Then wind up with a home-baked cake or pastry—nothing is more delicious or more appreciated. Guests are really captives, so build a menu, in any case, that is not too restrictive. If you decide on Octopus Pasta, be sure you know the guests are adventurous enough or have sophisticated enough palates to enjoy it—or that they know you well enough to be able to ask for an egg instead.

MENUS

ABOUT MENU MAKING

When to eat what is a matter of ever-changing habit and custom. Think of an epicure's diet in pre-Communist China: the constant nibbling of small rich confections, interspersed with light, irregularly spaced meals. Think of the enormous breakfast, dinner and bedtime repasts of early 19th Century England, with a little sherry and biscuit served at lunch-time to guarantee survival. And, if you imagine for a moment that we have triumphantly freed ourselves from the excesses of the Groaning Board, think of the multitude of strange hors d'oeuvre that are downed during a typical big cocktail party in the Age of Anxiety.

Present-day nutritionists are divided. One group advises us that at least ⅓ of our daily intake should be consumed at breakfast, and that breakfast proteins are more completely utilized by the body than those eaten at any other time of the day or night. Another school, meanwhile, advocates something like a return to the traditional Chinese dietary—that is, scrapping our 3-square-meal schedule altogether in favor of intermittent snacks. ◗ For the sheer amounts of food that will suffice to hold the average American body and soul together, see page 527.

Whichever menu practice we decide to follow, there is in the combining of foods a perennial fascination; and we can still on all occasions respond sympathetically to Brillat-Savarin's dictum: "Menu mal-fait, diner perdu." Below are some suggestions for assembling successful meals. They are suggestions only. Your tastes, your girth, your circumstances, your market—and, we hope, your imagination—will considerably modify them. ◗ For service suggestions please read the chapter on Entertaining, page 1. ◗ Note also that individual recipes nearly always carry recommendations for suitable accompaniments.

BREAKFAST MENUS

Banana Slices and Orange Sections, p. 102
Eggs Baked in Bacon Rings (I, 193)
Hot Biscuits, p. 283

Chilled Canned Pears with Jelly Sauce, p. 475
French Omelet (I, 188)
Bacon in Muffins, p. 279, 280

Orange and Grapefruit Sections, p. 101, 102
Smoked Salmon with Scrambled Eggs (I, 191)
Brioches, p. 258
Apple Butter, p. 578

Orange and Lime Juice (I, 24)
Pecan Waffles, p. 120, with Brown Sugar Butter Sauce, p. 479

Poached Plums, p. 88
A hot cereal (I, 153–156)
Soft-cooked Egg (I, 183)

Stewed Rhubarb and
Pineapple Compote, p. 109
Sautéed Bacon (I, 492)
Fluffy or Soufflé Omelet with
Cheese (I, 189)
Toast

Pork Scrapple or Goetta (I, 533)
Hot Applesauce, p. 95, or
Rhubarb, p. 109
Corn Sticks, p. 277

Dry cereal of wheat or bran biscuit type covered with Baked
Custard, p. 437
and garnished with
Sugared Strawberries, p. 98

Baked Eggs (I, 192), with
Sautéed Sausage Meat Patties
(I, 532)
Croissants, p. 260
Black Cherry Conserve, p. 582

Broiled Grapefruit Cups, p. 101
Chipped Beef in Sauce (I, 222)
Squares of Corn Bread, p. 277
Guava Jelly, p. 576

Fresh Fruit Compôte Composée,
p. 86
French Toast Waffles, p. 121
Blueberry Jam, p. 577

Blueberries and Cream, p. 98
Sautéed Ham or
Canadian Bacon (I, 492), and
Eggs (I, 491)
Whole Grain Muffins, p. 281
Paradise Jelly, p. 575

Fresh Pineapple, p. 106
Broiled Fresh Mackerel (I, 413)
Vienna Rolls, p. 262
Currant Jelly, p. 574

Sliced Rounds of Honeydew
Melon filled with Raspberries,
p. 104
Ham and Potato Cakes (I, 220),
with
Eggs (I, 183)

Sliced Peaches
Broiled Kidneys (I, 543)
Whole-Grain Toast
Lime Marmalade, p. 582

Ripe or Stewed Cherries, p. 88
Baked Brains and Eggs (I, 541)
No-Knead Yeast Coffee Cake or
Panettone, p. 264

LUNCHEON MENUS

Below are listed some complete
luncheon menus. But if you turn
to Brunch, Lunch and Supper
Dishes (I, 208), Pastas (I,
153), and Eggs (I, 183), you
will find many combination
dishes that need only a simple
salad or a bread to form a complete menu. If speed is your object ◗ remember, too, that many
fish and ground meat dishes are
very quickly prepared.

LUNCHEON MENUS

Pilaf (I, 166)
Tossed Green Salad (1, 33)
Chutney Dressing (1, 344)
Melba Toast, p. 290
Banana Pineapple Sherbet, p.
497

Jellied Ham Mousse (I, 60)
Fresh Corn Pudding Cockaigne,
(I, 285)
Sliced Fresh Cucumbers and
Basil, p. 203, 204
No-Knead Refrigerator Rolls, p.
263
Fruit Soup Cockaigne, p. 91

Eggs in Aspic Cockaigne on
Water Cress (I, 163)
Brioche Loaf Cockaigne, p. 245
Macedoine of Fresh Fruits, p.
86
Molasses Crisps Cockaigne, p.
400

Tomato Aspic Ring II (I, 66),
filled with Chicken Salad (I, 51)
with Curry Mayonnaise (I, 348)
Corn Dodgers, p. 278
Chocolate Bombe, p. 490

Frog Legs in Mushroom Sauce
(I, 446)
Melon Salad (I, 55)
Biscuit Sticks, p. 285
Cream Meringue Tart Cock-
aigne, p. 372

Chicken Soufflé (I, 200) with
Mushroom Sauce (I, 367) and
Cress Garnish (I, 31)
Deep Fried Okra (I, 258)
Filled Pineapple III, p. 107
Pecan Drop Cookies, p. 412

Turkey Divan (I, 228)
Popovers, p. 283
Flambéed Peaches, p. 90
Curled Cookies, p. 409, with
Chocolate Cream Cheese Filling,
p. 428

Garnished English Mixed Grill
(I, 484)
Tomato Pudding Cockaigne
(I, 335)
Asparagus Salad (I, 41)
Hard Rolls, p. 262
Baked Fruit Compote I, p. 88

Cold Sliced Roast Beef (I, 463),
or Smoked Tongue (I, 546)
Tomato Stuffed (I, 48), with
Russian Salad (I, 40)
Sour Dough Rye Bread and
Cheese, p. 250
Flan with Fruit, p. 324

ONE PLATE LUNCHEON MENUS

Plate service is awkward at best
for anyone in a crowded room,
but it's the most convenient way
to serve food easily to a large
number of people, especially if
the food is of the type that requires no knife. ▶ Be sure if hot
and cold things are to be on the
same plate that the hot food is
in ramekins or the cold food in
a container that will not be affected by the heated plate.

Beef Stroganoff I (I, 476)
Rice Ring or Mold (I, 161)

Grilled Tomato (I, 333)
Water Cress Garnish (I, 31)

Eggplant Stuffed with Lamb or
Ham (I, 292)
Garlic Bread, p. 289
Molded Vegetable Salad (I, 63),
with Boiled Salad Dressing II
(I, 350)

Ham Timbales (I, 203), or
Croquettes, p. 121, 122, with
Mushroom Sauce (I,367)
Molded Pineapple Ring (I, 69)
Hot Buttered Muffins, p. 279–
283

Quick Chicken Pot Pie (I, 212)
Romaine or Cos Salad (I, 30)
Lorenzo Dressing I (I, 342)

Molded Filled Fillets of Fish
(I, 405), with Hollandaise Sauce
(I, 368–369)
Fresh Asparagus (I, 260)
Hard Rolls, p. 262

Blanquette of Veal (I, 504), on
Noodles (I, 172)
Panned or Sicilian Spinach (I,
326)

Creamed Eggs and Asparagus
Cockaigne II (I, 194)
French Tomato Salad with
Bibb Lettuce (I, 47)
Biscuit Sticks, p. 285

Honeydew Melon or Cantaloupe
filled with Creamed Cottage
Cheese garnished with
Seedless Green Grapes (I, 55)
Nut Bread, p. 271

VEGETABLE PLATTERS

Spinach Ring Mold (I, 205)
filled with Buttered Parsley
Carrots (I, 279)
Baked Winter Squash II (I, 331)

Creamed Onions au Gratin in
Casserole (I, 301), surrounded
by Dauphine Potatoes (I, 320),
and Carrots in Bunches (I, 280)

Celery Root Ring Mold filled
with Peas (I, 205), surrounded
by New Potatoes with Parsley
(I, 310)

Cauliflower with Buttered
Crumbs (I, 281)
surrounded by Snap Beans
(I, 262)

Wild Rice Ring (I, 160), filled
with Brussels Sprouts Hollandaise (I, 273)
surrounded by Broiled Mushrooms (I, 297)

Baked Macaroni (I, 170), or
Baked Noodle Ring (I, 173),
filled with a vegetable of your
choice

MEATLESS MENUS

Vegetable Soup or Soup Pay-
sanne (I, 116)
Cheese Soufflé Cockaigne (I,
198)
French Bread, p. 245
Avocado Fruit Salad (I, 54),
with French Dressing (I, 341)

Cold Bulgarian Cucumber Soup
(I, 128)
Curried Eggs (I, 193)
Cracked Wheat Bread Toast,
p. 249
Fresh Cherry Pie, p. 312

Quiche Lorraine (I, 214)
Tomato Aspic (I, 65)
Strawberries with Kirsch, p. 98,
on Meringues, p. 309

Creamed Eggs and Asparagus
Cockaigne (I, 194)
Cheese Bread, p. 244
Ambrosia, p. 86
Anise Drop Cookies, p. 394

Shrimp in
Seafood Curry (I, 230), in a
Rice Ring (I, 162), with
Chutney, p. 592
Spinach Salad (I, 32), with
French Dressing (I, 341)

Chocolate Custard or
Pot-de-Creme I, p. 441

Jellied Beet Consommé (I, 114)
Cold Stuffed Tomatoes II (I, 48)
Swedish Rye, p. 249
Angel Pie, p. 330

Crab Louis (I, 50), garnished
with Avocado Slices (I, 53)
Parkerhouse Rolls, p. 254
Lemon and Orange Ice, p. 494,
with Cherry Heering

Clam Broth (I, 431)
Cheese Popovers, p. 283
Butterfly Shrimp (I, 442)
Celery Salad (I, 32)
Boiled Salad Dressing I (I, 350)
Chocolate Charlotte, p. 375

Jambalaya with Fish (I, 164)
Oakleaf Lettuce (I, 30), with
Chutney Dressing (I, 344)
Melba Toast, p. 290
Orange Cream Pie, p. 326

Leek Potato Soup (I, 130)
Fillets of Sole Florentine (I, 418)
Corn Sticks I, p. 277
Spiked Honeydew Melon, p. 104

Cheese Casserole I (I, 238)
Waldorf Salad (I, 53)
Bread Sticks, p. 246
Raspberry Parfait, p. 492

Tomato Bouillon (I, 111)
Fish Fillets Baked in
Sea Food Sauce Marguery
(I, 403)
Baked Green Rice (I, 159)
Crêpes, p. 114, with
Tutti Frutti Cockaigne, p. 583

Quick Onion Soup (I, 141)
Deviled Eggs in Sauce (I, 196)
Snap Bean Salad (I, 42), with
Vinaigrette Sauce (I, 341)
Rye Rolls, p. 258
Florentines, p. 414

Hot Double Consommé (I, 109)
Stuffed French Pancakes I, p.
113, with

Creamed Oysters (I, 424)
Celery and Olives, p. 76, 77
Fruit Brûlé, p. 90

Waffles, p. 118, with
Seafood à la King (I, 229)
French Tomato Salad (I, 47)
Lemon Ice with Rum, p. 495
Pecan Puffs, p. 414

Broiled Stuffed Mushrooms
Cockaigne (I, 297), on
Puréed Peas (I, 306)
Bibb Lettuce Salad (I, 29), with
Green Goddess Dressing (I, 348)
Overnight Rolls, p. 256
Lime Sherbet, p. 496

Sautéed Shad Roe (I, 416), with
Braised Endive (I, 292)
Podded Peas (I, 307)
Corn Zephyrs Cockaigne, p. 278
Frozen Orange Surprise, p. 495
with Marzipan Leaf Decoration,
p. 505

Melon Baskets, p. 104
Artichokes Stuffed with Crab
Meat (I, 40)
Buttermilk Corn Bread, p. 277
Pineapple Snow, p. 456

Quick Tomato Corn Chowder
(I, 141)
Cucumbers Stuffed with Tuna
Fish, Shrimp or Shad Roe Salad
(I, 51)
Sour Dough Rye Bread, p. 250
Cream Meringue Tart Cock-
aigne, p. 372

Smelts III (I, 418)
Buttered Peas and Carrots (I,
306)
New Potatoes with Dill (I, 310)
Poached Apricots, p. 88
Sand Tarts, p. 402

Scalloped Scallops or Mornay,
(I, 433)
Corn Creole (I, 286)
Quick Blender Slaw (I, 37), with
Mayonnaise (I, 345)
Bran Muffins, p. 281
Coffee Tarts, p. 325

Sea Food à la King (I, 229)
Grilled Tomatoes II (I, 333)
Water Cress (I, 31), with
Sour Cream Dressing (I, 351)
Rhubarb Pie, p. 315

Poached Quenelles (I, 181), with
Sea Food Spaghetti Sauce (I,
379)
Green Peas with Mushrooms (I,
307)
Clover Leaf Rolls, p. 253
Wilted Cucumbers I (I, 43)
Velvet Spice Cake, p. 352

Chilled Spinach Soup (I, 124)
Made-in-Advance Cheese Souf-
flé (I, 197)
Avocado and Fruit Salad (I, 54),
with Curry Dressing (I, 352)
Rich Roll Cookies, p. 402

Tomatoes Stuffed with Crab
Meat VI (I, 48–49)
Pepper Slices with Cream
Cheese Filling (I, 45)
Whole Grain Bread Plus, p. 248
Orange Fruit Soup, p. 92

SUGGESTIONS FOR AN AFTERNOON TEA

Serve tea, coffee or chocolate
accompanied by cinnamon toast
or a light sandwich: marmalade,
pecan, water cress, etc., or nut,
prune, fig or orange bread
spread with cream cheese. You
may follow this with a cup cake
or other small cake or cookie.
Serve a sandwich without nut
meats if you plan to have a nutty
cake, and vice versa. See Tea
Sandwiches, page 49, Cup
Cakes, page 358. ◗ For more
formal teas, see menus below,
which begin with a very formal
tea indeed!

AFTERNOON TEA MENUS

Spiced Tea (I, 19)
Coffee (I, 15–18)
Dry Sherry
Mixed Seafood Newburg (I, 231),
in Timbale Cases (I, 209)
Puffed Roquefort Sticks, p. 59

Homemade White Bread Plus, p. 244
spread with Seasoned Butters, p. 56 and (I, 383)
Orange Tea Rolls, p. 262
Tortelettes, p. 392
Small Babas au Rhum, p. 371

Sweet Tea Spreads I on Assorted Breads, p. 60
Deviled Eggs (I, 195)
Canapé Snails, p. 55
Stuffed Choux or Puff Paste Shells, p. 54
filled with Chicken Salad (I, 51)
Orange or Lemon Ice, page 494
Glazed Fruits, p. 523
Hazelnut Torte, p. 367
Peppermint Cream Wafers, p. 504
Molasses Crisps Cockaigne, p. 400

Flower Canapés, p. 51
Pineapple Biscuits with Cream Cheese, p. 286
Small Choux Paste Shell II filled with a Large Strawberry, p. 54
Orange Marmalade Drops, p. 397
Caramel Curled Cookies, p. 411 filled with Cream Cheese Icing, p. 427
Toasted Seeds, p. 71

Mushroom Canapés, p. 61
Bouchées filled with Sea Food à la King, p. 304
Cucumber Lilies, p. 76
Toasted Cheese Logs, p. 59
Filled Cookies, p. 406
Coconut Macaroons, p. 398
Bourbon Balls, p. 517
Rolled Sandwiches, p. 51
Small Chicken and Cream Cheese Sandwiches (I, 246)
Cheese Puff Canapés, p. 58
Thin Ham on Beaten Biscuits, p. 287
Peach, p. 486, or Strawberry Ice Cream, p. 486
German Honey Bars, p. 390
Small Mohrenkoepfe, p. 370
Candied Citrus Peel, p. 524
Salted Nuts, p. 189

COCKTAIL PARTY SUGGESTIONS

Cocktail parties, the favored mode of entertaining today, are of different kinds. In large metropolitan areas, when you are invited for cocktails, this may be strictly a prelude to dinner and the party does not last through the night. In the "provinces," you have to have the assurance that there will be adequate heavier foods to sustain you if you are going on to the theatre. In the first type of party, choose rich delicate small tidbits which are drink-inducers and appetite-stimulators, see Hors d'Oeuvre, pages 66–84, and Canapés, pages 49–65. The other kind of party calls for some blander types of food which may include large joints or fowl and even salads, and turns into a light buffet. See Buffet Suggestions, below. In choosing your cocktail menu, be sure to include something that is rich enough to cut the impact of the alcohol —something heavy in cheese, butter or oils.

BUFFET SUGGESTIONS

Cold Fillet of Beef (I, 472)
Cold Baked Ham (I, 490)
Tongue in Aspic (I, 546)
Cold Glazed Salmon (I, 415)
Mousseline of Shellfish (I, 61)
Standing Rib Roast of Beef (I, 463)
Cold Fried Chicken (I, 576, 577)
Jellied Chicken or Veal Mousse, (I, 60)
Sliced Turkey (I, 575)
Terrines (I, 528)

HOT BUFFET ENTRÉES

Seafood in Creole Sauce (I, 230)
Lobster or Seafood Curry (I, 230)
Spiced Beef (I, 498)
Lasagne (I, 176)
Mushroom Ring Mold with Sweetbreads or Chicken (I, 206)

Chicken or Turkey à la Campagne (I, 586)
Gaston Beef Stew (I, 496)
Beef Kabobs (I, 476)
Welsh Rarebit in Chafing Dish (I, 237)

PARTY MENUS

That, somehow, when we go to a dinner party, the excitement lies most in the unusual was demonstrated to us years ago by our younger child. His brother was sick and unable to attend a Thanksgiving feast to which our family had been invited by a great gastronome. We made our way through an impressive sequence of delicacies—from oysters Rockefeller, served at just the right temperature on their bed of hot salt, to a fabulous mince pie. Questioned on his return by the drooling invalid, the five-year-old ecstatically ticked off the highlights: "Ice water"—which we seldom serve at home, since we regard our well water as having just the right degree of coolness, "salt crackers," and "candles"—two other accessories which rarely grace our table. These, to him, summed up the only really memorable items on that Lucullan menu. Try, then, serving as a dish for occasions a true "spécialité de la maison"—something you do particularly well, or something your guests are not so likely to prepare themselves, or find at the homes of their more convention-bound friends. Below we list a few more menus—this time for company dinners.

PARTY DINNER MENUS

Stuffed Veal Roast (I, 478)
Casserole Green Beans (I, 262)
Cold Beef Cups (I, 42)
Rice Flour Muffins, p. 282
Profiteroles, p. 307

Prosciutto and Fruit, p. 78
Olives, p. 77, Fennel (I, 292)
and Marinated Carrots, p. 75
Lasagna (I, 176)
Tossed Salad (I, 32), with French Dressing (I, 341)
Zabaglione, p. 439
Bel Paese Cheese with Crackers, p. 470
Dry Red Wine, p. 32

Marinated Herring with Sour Cream, p. 81
German Meat Balls (I, 518)
Noodles au Gratin II (I, 172)
Carrots Vichy (I, 280)
Tomato Aspic (I, 65)
Linzertorte, p. 316

Fruit Cup, p. 86
Braised Sweetbreads (I, 538)
Caesar Salad (I, 35)
English Muffins, p. 261
Sour Cream Apple Cake Cockaigne, p. 447

Chicken Bouillon with Egg (I, 110)
Small Tomatoes filled with Cole Slaw de Luxe, VI (I, 49)
Squab (I, 590), stuffed with Dressing for Cornish Hen (I, 564)
Purée of Green Beans (I, 263)
Hard Rolls, p. 262
Strawberry Bombe, p. 490
Dry White Wine, p. 35

Lobster Parfait (I, 232), and thin salt wafers
Crown Roast of Lamb (I, 482), with Bread Dressing (I, 560)
Asparagus II (I, 261)
Belgian Endive (I, 31), with S...c. Vinaigrette (I, 341)
Fruit Soup Cockaigne, p. 91

Tomatoes Stuffed with Crab Meat Salad (I, 48, 49)
Fillet of Beef (I, 472), with Marchand de Vin Sauce (I, 367)
Franconia or Browned Potatoes (I, 314)
Stuffed Baked Artichokes (I, 260)

Ricotta Cheese Pie or Cake, p. 329

Bouillabaise (I, 135, 136)
Mixe l Salad Greens (I, 32), with French Dressing (I, 341)
French Bread, p. 245
Assorted Fruit, p. 86

Shrimp (I, 442), in Hot Snail Butter (I, 384)
Pheasant in Game Sauce (I, 595)
Wild Rice (I, 160)
French Bread, p. 245
Gooseberry Preserves, p. 581
Strawberries Romanoff, p. 98
Dry Red Wine, p. 32

Onion Soup (I, 113)
Roast Wild Duck (I, 593)
Poached Oranges, p. 101
Kasha (I, 156)
Creamed Lettuce (I, 294)
Almond Tart Cockaigne, p. 366
Dry Red Wine, p. 32

EVERYDAY DINNER MENUS

Braised Lamb Shanks with Vegetables (I, 508)
Boiled Noodles, (I, 172)
Cucumber Salad (I, 43)
Jelly Tot Cookies, p. 407

Pork Roast (I, 485)
Celery and Carrot Stick Garnish
Sauerkraut Baked in Casserole (I, 279)
Mashed Potatoes (I, 311)
Sour Cream Apple Cake Cockaigne, p. 447

Veal Pot Roast (I, 505)
Kohlrabi (I, 293)
Wilted Greens (I, 35)
Riced Potatoes (I, 310)
Mocha Gelatin, p. 454

Beef Pot Roast (I, 495)
Spatzen or Spaetzle (I, 179)
Glazed Turnips (I, 338)
Glazed Onions (I, 302)
Pickled Beet Salad (I, 42)
Brown Betty, p. 460

Leg of Lamb Roast (I, 482)
Lemon Sherbet, p. 496
Grilled Tomatoes (I, 333), on Broiled Eggplant Slices (I, 290)
Individual Shortcakes, p. 376, with Strawberries, p. 97, 98

Sauerbraten (I, 497)
Potato Dumplings (I, 180)
Green Bean Casserole I (I, 262)
Apple Pie, p. 311

Roast Chicken (I, 574), Stuffed with Apricot Dressing (I, 565)
Creamed Spinach (I, 326)
Escarole (I, 30), with Roquefort Dressing (I, 343)
French Chocolate Mousse, p. 441

Chicken Braised in Wine or Coq Au Vin (I, 579)
Rice Cooked in Chicken Stock (I, 159)
Molded Cranberry Salad (I, 67)
Angel Cup Cakes, p. 359, with Sauce Cockaigne, Whipped Cream, p. 474

Chicken Stew (I, 577), and Dumplings (I, 178)
Asparagus (I, 260), with Polonaise Sauce (I, 386)
Mixed Green Salad (I, 32), with Green Goddess Dressing (I, 348)
French Apple Cake, p. 320

Raw Smoked Ham Loaf (I, 524)
Canned Baked Beans with Fruit (I, 266)
Cole Slaw (I, 36)
Rombauer Jam Cake, p. 365

Baked Ham (I, 489)
Snap Beans with Butter (I, 262)
Crusty or Soft Center Spoon Bread, p. 279
Pear and Grape Salad (I, 56)
Angelica Parfait, p. 492

Rice Ring, (I, 162), filled with Creamed Oysters (I, 424)
Belgian Endive (I, 31), with French Dressing (I, 341)
Pineapple Sponge Custard, p. 441
Pecan or Benne Wafers, p. 413

Steak Au Poivre (I, 475)
Grilled Tomatoes (I, 333)
Boston Lettuce (I, 30) with
Roquefort Dressing (I, 343)
Refrigerator Potato Rolls, p. 263
Fresh Fruit Soufflé, p. 446

Roast Beef (I, 463)
Franconia or Browned Potatoes
(I, 314)
Quick Creamed Broccoli (I, 273)
Marinated Carrots, p. 75
No-Knead Refrigerator Rolls, p.
263
Chocolate Soufflé, p. 445

Lentil Soup (I, 120)
Broiled Steak (I, 474), with
Sauce (I, 367)
Never-Fail French Fries (I, 318)
Sautéed Cauliflower (I, 281)
Applesauce Cake, p. 354

Shrimp Bisque (I, 134)
Chicken Tarragon with Wine
(I, 580)
Green Peas and Lettuce (I, 306)
Beaten Biscuits, p. 287
Grape Jelly, p. 575
Pecan Pie, p. 318

Broiled Sausage Patties (I, 532),
with Sautéed Mushrooms (I, 296)
Summer Squash Casserole
Cockaigne (I, 330)
Boiled Noodles with Poppy
Seeds (I, 172)
Prunes in Wine, p. 108
Molasses Nut Wafers, p. 413

Sweetbreads on Skewers with
Mushrooms (I, 540)
Boiled New Potatoes (I, 310)
Grilled Tomatoes (I, 333)
Cheese Straws (I, 152)
Coffee Chocolate Custard, p.
437

Liver Lyonnaise (I, 534)
Shoe String Potatoes (I, 318)
Sweet Sour Beans (I, 263)

Tomato and Onion Salad (I, 49)
Fresh Fruit, p. 85

FORMAL LUNCHEON MENU

Quick Clam and Chicken Broth
(I, 143)
Refrigerator Cheese Wafers or
Straws (I, 152)
Cooked Fish Soufflé with Lob-
ster (I, 200)
Broiled Lamb Chops (I, 483),
garnished with
Stuffed Baked Artichokes (I, 260)
Tomato Olive Casserole (I, 334)
Bibb, Water Cress and
Endive Salad (I, 30, 31), with
Avocado Dressing (I, 342)
Assorted Cheeses, p. 470
French Bread, p. 245
Sweet Butter, p. 171
Cabinet Pudding, p. 450
Coffee (I, 15, 16)
Dry Champagne served
throughout, p. 36, 37

FORMAL DINNER MENU

Aperitifs, p. 25
Bread Sticks or Grissini, p. 246
Lobster Parfait (I, 232); Dry
Sherry, 35
Consommé (I, 109), with
Royale (I, 146)
Peach or Mango Chutney, p. 591
Seeded Crackers (I, 152)
Chicken Kiev (I, 582), Dry
White Wine, p. 36
Raspberry Sherbet, p. 497
Filet Mignon (I, 475), with
Béarnaise Sauce (I, 370); Red
Bordeaux or Burgundy, p. 36
Soufflé or Puffed Potatoes (I,
316)
Creamed Spinach (I, 326)
Belgian Endive (I, 31), with
Vinaigrette (I, 341)
Hard Rolls, p. 262
Assorted Cheeses, p. 470
French Bread, p. 245
Fruit Mousse, p. 490; Dessert
Wine or Champaigne, 36
Madeleines, p. 359
Fresh Fruits, p. 85
Coffee (I, 15, 16); Liqueur, p.
36, 38

**THANKSGIVING OR
CHRISTMAS DINNER
MENUS**

Christmas Canapés, p. 52
Clear Soup (I, 109), with
Marrow Balls (I, 150)
Celery, p. 76
Goose (I, 588), Stuffed with
Sweet Potatoes and Fruit (I, 324)
Turnip Cups filled with Peas II
(I, 339)
Parkerhouse Rolls, p. 254
Fruit Cake Cockaigne, p. 356
German Cherry Pie, p. 313

Oysters Rockefeller (I, 425)
Chicken Broth (I, 110)
Roast Stuffed Turkey (I, 575),
with
Chestnut Dressing (I, 562)
Glazed Onions (I, 302)
Brussels Sprouts with
Hollandaise (I, 273)
Celery, Radishes, Olives, p. 76,
77
Filled Pimientos or
Christmas Salad (I, 45), on
Water Cress (I, 31)
Mince Pie Flambé, p. 315, or
Pumpkin Pie, p. 318, 319
Dark Fruit Cake II, p. 357

Mushroom Broth with Sherry
(I, 112)
Roast Suckling Pig (I, 485), with
Onion Dressing (I, 562)
Duchess Potatoes I (I, 319)
Red Cabbage (I, 277)
Escarole and Romaine (I, 30),
with
Thousand Island Dressing (I,
349)
Hazelnut Soufflé, p. 446

**NEW YEAR'S EVE
BUFFET MENU**

Champagne, p. 36, 37
Pâté De Foie De Volaille (I, 525)
Boned Chicken (I, 585)
French Bread, p. 245
Hot Consommé (I, 109)
Hot Standing Rib Roast of Beef
(I, 463)
Casserole of Green Beans (I, 262)

Tossed Salad (I, 33), with
Roquefort Dressing (I, 343)
White Fruit Cake, p. 356
Brandy Snaps, p. 411
Pulled Mints, p. 512

WEDDING BUFFET MENU

Dry Champagne, p. 36, 37
Mushrooms in Batter (I, 296)
Rolled Sandwiches, Cress and
Cucumber, p. 51
Pastry Cheese Balls, p. 73
Hot Consommé Brunoise (I, 109)
Galatine of Turkey (I, 529)
Hard Rolls, p. 262
Lobster Newburg (I, 231), in
Patty Shells, p. 304
Bibb and Water Cress Salad
(I, 30, 31), with
Sour Cream Dressing (I, 351)
Stuffed Endive and Olives, p.
76, 77
Macedoine of Fruits with Kirsch,
p. 86
Wedding Cake, p. 346
Petits Fours, p. 360
Spiced Nuts and Mint Wafers,
p. 516, 504

HUNT BREAKFAST MENU

Bloody Marys, p. 31
Hot Buttered Rum, p. 48
Café Brûlot or Diable (I, 17)
Blended Fruit Juice (I, 25)
Baked Fresh Fruit, p. 88
Steak and Kidney Pie (I, 502), or
Pheasant in Game Sauce (I, 595)
Broiled Bacon (I, 492)
Pan Broiled Sausage (I, 532)
Scrambled Eggs (I, 191)
Grilled Tomatoes (I, 333)
Chestnuts and Prunes in Wine,
p. 108
Toasted English Muffins, p. 261
Croissants, p. 260
Red Strawberry Jam, p. 576
Orange Marmalade, p. 581
Scandinavian Pastry, p. 267

ABOUT PICNIC MEALS

Picnics are fun; but picnic food
is subject to hazards, and they
are not all ants. Transport per-

ishables in the coolest part of
your car, covering them against
the sun. If you have no cold
box or insulated plastic bags
carry frozen juices. Use them
en route to cool your mayonnaise
and deviled eggs. Or fill a plastic bag with ice cubes and put
it in a coffee can to improvise a
chilling unit that will last out
transportation time. Or insulate
the sandwich boxes with damp
newspapers. ♦ Should you use
dry ice be sure the container
and the car windows are partially open to allow the gas
to escape. ♦ To wrap sandwiches for easy identification,
see page 50. ♦ To mix picnic
salads conveniently, see (I,
33).

Most important of all, if it's
a basket picnic ♦ plan the kind
of food which holds well and is
easily served, so everyone can
enjoy every minute of the outing. If it's to be a ♦ cookout,
please read About Outdoor
Cooking (I, 89), and check
your menu against recipes
marked 目 which are suitable
for outdoor preparation. Check
also Clam Bake (I, 428).

Sandwiches, salads, fruits and
cookies are naturals for picnics.
Consult these sections; or for
slightly fancier combinations, see
the menus below.

PICNIC MENUS

Barbecued Frankfurters (I, 220)
Bread and Butter Pickles, p.
587
Versatile Rolls, p. 257

Cheddar Cheese, p. 176
Gingerbread, p. 364
Pears and Grapes, p. 105, 103

Beef Kabobs (I, 476), with
Canned Potato Sticks
Tossed Salad (I, 33), with
Thousand Island Dressing (I,
349)
Pickled Watermelon Rind, p.
591
Parkerhouse Rolls, p. 254
Pound Cake, p. 349

Beef Hamburger or Lamb
Patties (I, 516, 517, 518)
Potato Salad Niçoise (I, 46)
Corn Relish, p. 589
Health Bread, p. 252
Marble Cake, p. 347

Fried Fish (I, 400), or
Barbecued Chicken (I, 576)
Campfire Potatoes (I, 254)
Grilled or Roasted Corn (I, 285)
Cole Slaw (I, 36)
Quick Oatmeal Cookies, p. 396
Peaches, p. 105

Sautéed Eggs (I, 184), with
Bacon or Sausages (I, 491, 530)
Baked Beans (I, 266)
Pickles, p. 585, 586, 587
Toasted Buttered French
Bread Loaf, p. 289
Apples, p. 93
Gold Layer Cake, p. 348, with
Caramel Icing, p. 425

Baked Ham (I, 489)
Picnic Tossed Salad (I, 33, 34)
Rye Rolls, p. 258
Nut Creams Rolled in Chives,
p. 73
Chilled Melon, p. 104

DRINKS

Now and then we look into the work of our fellow cookbook authors and are usually surprised to discover how little attention they pay to liquor. In past editions we, too, have approached this subject rather apologetically —after all, there was a time when selling or serving alcoholic refreshment was considered disreputable in America. But here and now we drop all subterfuge, frankly concede that "something to drink" is becoming with us an almost invariable concomitant of at least the company dinner, and have boldly enlarged this section of the book. Always in the back of our minds, spurring us on, is the memory of a cartoon which depicted a group of guests sitting around a living room, strickenly regarding their cocktail glasses, while the hostess, one of those inimitable Hokinson types, all embonpoint, cheer, and fluttering organdy, announces, "A very dear friend gave me some wonderful old Scotch and I just happened to find a bottle of papaya juice in the refrigerator!"

COCKTAILS AND OTHER BEFORE-DINNER DRINKS

The cocktail is probably an American invention, and most certainly a typically American kind of drink. Whatever mixtures you put together—and part of the fascination of cocktail making is the degree of inventiveness it seems to encour-

age—hold fast to a few general principles. ◗ The most important of these is to keep the quantity of the basic ingredients —gin, whisky, rum, etc.—up to about 60% of the total drink, never below half. ◗ Remember, as a corollary, that cocktails are before-meal drinks—appetizers. For this reason they should be neither oversweet nor overloaded with cream and egg, in order to avoid spoiling the appetite instead of stimulating it.

If you mix drinks in your kitchen, your equipment probably includes the essential strainer, squeezer, bottle opener, ice pick, and sharp knife. Basic bar equipment also includes a heavy glass cocktail shaker; a martini pitcher; an ice bucket and tongs; a bar spoon; a strainer; a jigger; a muddler; a bitters bottle with the dropper type top; and—for converting cubes to crushed ice—a heavy canvas bag and wood mallet. We also show a lemon peeler guaranteed to get only the colored unbitter part of the rind, and the only corkscrew that doesn't induce complete frustration.

A simple syrup is a useful ingredient when making drinks. Boil for 5 minutes 1 part water to 2 parts sugar, or half as much water as sugar. Keep the syrup in a bottle, refrigerated, and use it as needed.

In addition to various liquors, it is advisable for the home bartender to have on hand a stock of: bitters, carbonated water;

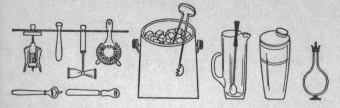

lemons, oranges, limes, olives, cherries. For Garnishes see page (I, 27). See also the chapters on Canapés and Hors d'Oeuvre for suitable accompaniments for cocktails—besides a steady head.

Note the two types of cocktail glasses illustrated below. Both are so designed that the heat of the hand is not transferred to the contents of the glass. These hold about 3 ounces each. The old-fashioned glass featured next holds about 6 ounces and retains its chill by reason of a heavy base. The next two drawings show typical sour and daiquiri glasses. Each holds about 4 ounces. Champagne cocktails, also about 4 ounces each, are often served in the saucer-bowl footed glass used for daiquiris. The small glass shown last is for straight whisky.

▶ Mix only one round at a time. Your stock as a bartender will never go up on the strength of your "dividend" drinks. The cocktails which follow are some fundamental ones, listed according to their basic ingredients. ▶ Each recipe, unless otherwise noted, makes about 4 drinks. When cracked—not crushed—ice is indicated, use about ¾ cup. ▶ All "shaken" cocktails

should be strained into the glasses just before serving.

ABOUT MEASUREMENTS FOR DRINKS

1 dash	= 6 drops
3 teaspoons	= ½ ounce
1 pony	= 1 ounce
1 jigger	= 1½ ounces
1 large jigger	= 2 ounces
1 standard whisky glass	= 2 ounces
1 pint	= 16 fluid ounces
1 fifth	= 25.6 fluid ounces
1 quart	= 32 fluid ounces

ABOUT GIN AND GIN COCKTAILS

Gin is a spirit—that is, a distilled liquor. Much of its distinctive flavor comes from the juniper berry. Victorian novelists tended to assume that only the lower classes—footmen, scullery maids and the like—had a taste for gin; just as they implied that rum was an equally vulgar tipple and might be relegated to the common seaman. The "bathtub" concoctions of the Roaring Twenties did nothing to enhance gin's repute. Recent generations, however, have

recognized the fact that this liquor, regardless of its shady past and its possibilities as a straight drink, is probably the best mixing base ever invented.

Of the three general gin types, Geneva and Holland are somewhat bitter and highly aromatic. They appeal to a small minority and should be taken "neat." By far the most popular kind of gin is the dry London type, which can be found in all liquor dispensaries. More perhaps than is the case with most other liquors, the quality of commercial gin varies; its cost is a rough measure of its worth. Certain brands of gin, which we happen to prefer, are aged for a time in sherry casks, a process which imparts a golden color.

ALEXANDER

Shake with ¾ cup cracked ice:
   1 jigger sweet cream
   1½ jiggers crème de cacao
   5 jiggers gin
Strain into chilled glasses.

BRONX

Shake, using ¾ cup cracked ice:
   1 jigger dry vermouth
   1 jigger sweet vermouth
   1 jigger orange juice
   5 jiggers gin
Strain into chilled glasses. Add a twist of orange peel to each glass.

GIMLET

Shake, using ¾ cup cracked ice:
   1 tablespoon sugar syrup
   2 large jiggers lime juice
   5 jiggers gin
Strain into chilled glasses. Substituting orange juice for ½ the lime juice changes a Gimlet into an Orange Blossom. Vodka is becoming increasingly popular as a base for both.

GIN BITTER   [1]

With bourbon or rye whisky this becomes a Whisky Bitter.
Half fill an old-fashioned glass with cracked ice. Shake, using ¾ cup cracked ice:
   2 jiggers gin
   2 dashes angostura or
      orange bitters
Pour into glass. Top with twist of orange peel.

GIN OR WHISKY SOUR

This recipe becomes a Whisky, Rum or Brandy Sour if the base is changed.
Shake, using ¾ cup cracked ice:
   1 jigger sugar syrup
   2 jiggers lemon or lime
      juice
   5 jiggers gin or whisky
Strain into chilled glasses.

PERFECT MARTINI

Stir well, using ¾ cup cracked ice:
   1 jigger dry vermouth
   1 jigger sweet vermouth
   6 jiggers gin
Add to each drink:
   1 dash orange bitters
Serve with olive in bottom of glass.

MARTINI

With a small onion in each glass, this cocktail becomes a Gibson. Try also a hazelnut and name it yourself. Changing the base makes a Vodka Martini.

In the last edition of "The Joy" we told the story of a bartender who was proffered so much advice on how to make a mint julep that he retired in complete frustration. Purism still seems to run rampant in drinking circles; and this time we should like to substitute the experience of still another hapless barkeep who just couldn't seem to produce a martini dry enough for his customer. Finally, after the vermouth content had been reduced to what the bartender regarded as absolute minimum, the customer snarled: "Try it again! This time only a whisper." The barkeep tried again; the customer took a wary sip, set down his glass, glared furiously at him and shouted, "Loudmouth!"

Stir well, using ¾ cup cracked ice:

  1 to 2 jiggers dry vermouth
  6 to 7 jiggers gin

Twist over the top:
  Lemon peel
or add:
  A small seeded olive

PINK LADY

Shake, using ¾ cup cracked ice:
  ½ jigger grenadine
  1 jigger lemon or lime juice
  1 jigger apple brandy
  2 egg whites
  4½ jiggers gin
Strain into chilled glasses.

WHITE LADY

Shake, using ¾ cup cracked ice:
  1½ jiggers lemon juice
  1 jigger Cointreau
  2 egg whites
  4½ jiggers gin
Strain into chilled glasses.

ABOUT WHISKY AND WHISKY COCKTAILS

There are, as everyone knows, several kinds of whisky; but two in particular, bourbon and Scotch, far outrank all others in popularity. Bourbon is chiefly —and we believe preferably— of American, and by American we mean United States, manufacture, distilled from corn. Scotch is made, as might be expected, in Scotland, of barley. Its distinctive taste is achieved by smoking the barley malt be-

fore distillation on a porous floor, over peat fires.

Bourbon and Scotch differ again in that Scotch is always sold blended, several varieties being combined before bottling whereas only bourbon of lower quality is blended. It is important to note in this connection that Scotch blends are invariably blends of whisky alone, but that bourbon blends may be either combinations of straight whiskies or of whisky and so-called neutral spirits, i.e., alcohol. The nature of the contents is always indicated on the label. Even if you must economize, we recommend buying only straight blends.

High quality or bonded bourbon, again always so labeled, is a straight whisky with certain important guarantees of quality: first, as we have said, it is straight liquor; second, it is all of the same age, never less than 4 years; third, it contains no additives, except for the amount of water necessary to bring it down to 100 proof, the legally required minimum. A word about proof, which simply means the alcoholic content, by volume, of a given spirit: 100-proof liquor is one which has an alcoholic content of 50%; 90-proof of 45%; and so on. Age in whisky is important. Remember, however, that aging takes place only in the cask to which whisky is transferred after distillation —never subsequently in the bottle. Moreover, bourbon whisky is matured in charred casks; and since, after 10 or 12 years, the spirit penetrates the char and is adversely affected by the raw wood underneath, bourbon older than a decade or so becomes increasingly less acceptable.

Which is "better," bourbon or Scotch? This is a little like asking whether a peach or a pear is better. It depends, like the appreciation of a good many other kinds of liquor, on one's personal taste. It can certainly be said, however, that in concocting mixed drinks—cocktails, old-fashioneds, sours, etc.— bourbon, or if you happen to prefer it, rye, is immeasurably superior to Scotch, the smoky taste of which tends to inhibit successful mergers. This situation is reflected in the formulas which follow.

Incidentally, a fourth kind of whisky, Irish, which makes a rather off-beat choice—except in Irish Coffee, see (I, 18)—is now being manufactured in both smoky and non-smoky types. If you are inclined to use Irish in cocktails, the same kind of discrimination as with Scotch should apply.

PERFECT MANHATTAN

Scotch may replace the bourbon or rye in this formula and the one following; in which case the cocktail is called a **Rob Roy.** When a dash of Drambuie is added, a **Rob Roy** becomes a **Bobbie Burns.** Try substituting Peychaud bitters as a variation. Stir well with ice cubes:

    1 jigger dry vermouth
    1 jigger sweet vermouth
    6 jiggers bourbon or rye
Add to each drink:
    1 dash angostura bitters
    (maraschino cherry)

MANHATTAN

Stir well with ice cubes:

    1 to 2 jiggers dry vermouth
    6 to 7 jiggers bourbon or rye
Add to each drink:
    1 dash angostura bitters
    A twist of lemon peel

OLD-FASHIONED   [1]

Put into an old-fashioned glass and stir:

    ½ teaspoon sugar syrup
    2 dashes angostura bitters
    1 teaspoon water
Add:
    2 ice cubes
Fill glass to within ½ inch of top with:
    Bourbon or rye
Stir. Decorate with a twist of lemon peel, a thin slice of orange and a maraschino cherry. Serve with a muddler.

The above formula, like that for the Julep, which follows, page 40, is a rock-bottom affair. Some like their old-fashioneds on the fancy side, adding a squeeze of lemon juice, a dash of curaçao, kirsch or maraschino liqueur or a spear of fresh pineapple; or substituting a fresh ripe strawberry for the time-honored cherry. Try also, if you care to, a Scotch old-fashioned.

SAZERAC

Stir with ice cubes:

    4 teaspoons sugar syrup
    4 dashes Peychaud bitters
    4 dashes anisette or Pernod
    7 jiggers bourbon or rye
Pour into chilled glasses. Add a twist of lemon peel to each glass.

ABOUT RUM AND RUM COCKTAILS

Another spirit, this, as blithe and potent as whisky and gin and, next to gin, perhaps the most versatile of "mixers." Rum is distilled from sugar cane—or, rather, molasses. Generally the rum available to the American consumer is of two fairly sharply differentiated types: Puerto Rican, or light-bodied, and Jamaican, a heavier-bodied, darker and quite dissimilar tasting product. Only the light type and of the highest quality should be used for cocktails: that marked "white label" for dry drinks, "gold label" for sweeter ones. Save the heavier, more pungent types of rum for long drinks, punches, nogs, colas and shakes.

Some people like the taste and look of a frosted glass and consider it the final fine touch to cocktails of the rum type.

To frost a cocktail glass: cool the glass and swab the rim with a section of lemon from which the juice is flowing freely or dip it in grenadine. Swirl the glass to remove excess moisture, then dip the rim to a depth of ¼ inch in powdered or confectioners' sugar. Lift the glass and tap it gently to remove any excess sugar.

BENEDICTINE

Shake with ¾ cup cracked ice:
    1½ jiggers lime juice
    1½ jiggers Benedictine
    5½ jiggers rum
Strain into chilled glasses.

CUBANA

Shake with ¾ cup cracked ice:
    ½ jigger sugar syrup
    1½ jiggers lime juice
    2 jiggers apricot brandy
    4 jiggers rum
Strain into chilled glasses.

DAIQUIRI

With grenadine substituted for sugar syrup, this cocktail becomes a Pink Daiquiri or Daiquiri Grenadine.
Shake well with ¾ cup cracked ice:
    ½ jigger sugar syrup
    1½ jiggers lime juice
    6 jiggers rum
Strain into chilled glasses.

⅄ BLENDER FROZEN DAIQUIRI

Spectacular and delicious frozen cocktails may be made by using an electric blender. In the Dai-

quiri recipe, for instance, by increasing the amount of crushed ice to between 2 and 3 cups, substituting 2 tablespoons confectioners' sugar for each jigger of syrup and blending the ingredients until they reach a snowy consistency, you will achieve a hot weather triumph. Serve it in champagne glasses. This is a formula which can be interestingly varied. For a group, try using more ice, more rum and instead of the lime juice and sugar, a chunk of frozen concentrated limeade, fresh out of the can.

EL PRESIDENTE

Shake with ¾ cup cracked ice:
    1½ jiggers dry vermouth
    1½ jiggers lemon juice
    2 dashes grenadine
    2 dashes curaçao
    5 jiggers rum
Strain into chilled glasses and decorate with a twist of orange peel.

KNICKERBOCKER

Shake well with ¾ cup of cracked ice:
    ½ jigger raspberry syrup
    ½ jigger pineapple syrup
    1½ jiggers lemon juice
    5½ jiggers rum
Strain into chilled glasses and serve with a twist of orange peel.

ABOUT BRANDY AND BRANDY COCKTAILS

Here is a spirit distilled from fruit, most commonly from grapes. Except for apple brandy, known in America as applejack and in France as calvados, brandy is a scarce commodity on these shores. Most other alleged fruit brandies in this country are cordials, not true distillates or true brandies. In the formulas which follow, references always apply to grape brandy, although experimentation with a superior grade of applejack is encouraged. Incidentally, the name "cognac" does not by any means apply to all grape brandies—only to the best.

Aging is of great importance in the quality of this liquor but, due to a variety of circumstances, most brandies sold over American counters neither boast of nor confess to their true age. The only sure signs, in order of increasing seniority, are these: Three-Star, V.O., V.S.O., V.S.O.P., and V.V.S.O.P. While we firmly adhere to the belief that "the better the liquor, the better the drink," no one in his right mind and of sound palate should use brandies more venerable than V.O. for any purpose other than reverential sipping.

Brandy cocktails, too, may be served in frosted glasses, see page 30, with grenadine substituted for the lemon juice in preparing the glass for frosting.

CHAMPAGNE [1]
COCKTAIL

Pour into large champagne glass:
    ½ teaspoon sugar syrup
    ½ jigger chilled brandy
Fill glass almost to top with:
    Chilled dry champagne
Add:
    2 dashes yellow Chartreuse
    2 dashes orange bitters

CURAÇAO COCKTAIL

Shake well with ¾ cup cracked ice:
    1½ jiggers curaçao
    ½ jigger lemon juice
    6 jiggers brandy
Add to each drink:
    1 dash angostura bitters
Strain into chilled glasses and add a twist of lemon peel.

SIDECAR

Sometimes this drink is served in a frosted glass, page 30. The use of apple brandy changes a Sidecar into a Jack Rose.
Shake with ¾ cup cracked ice:
    ½ jigger Cointreau
    1½ jiggers lemon juice
    6 jiggers brandy
Strain into chilled glasses and serve with a twist of lemon peel.

STINGER

Shake with ¾ cup finely crushed ice:
    1½ jiggers white crème de menthe
    6 jiggers brandy
    (½ jigger lime juice)
Strain into chilled glasses.

ABOUT VODKA, AQUAVIT, TEQUILA AND THEIR COCKTAILS

The spirits mentioned above just about complet the roster of those normally obtainable in the American market. They are strikingly different in character. Vodka and aquavit look—deceptively, we hasten to add—like branch water. But whereas vodka is almost tasteless while going down and almost odorless afterwards, aquavit has a strong aroma of caraway. It follows that while vodka is often used instead of gin or whisky in mixed drinks —particularly sours—aquavit is almost invariably drunk straight and very cold. Occasionally, it is combined with tomato juice as a cocktail. Tequila, which a friend of ours has dubbed "the Gulp of Mexico," appeals to a very limited number of aficionados. Try it before you buy it.

BLOODY MARY

Shake well or blend with ¾ cup crushed ice:
    3 jiggers vodka or aquavit

6 jiggers or 1 cup chilled
tomato juice
1 teaspoon lemon juice
1 teaspoon Worcestershire
sauce
2 drops hot pepper sauce
¼ teaspoon celery salt
¼ teaspoon salt
Pinch garlic salt

Serve without straining in
whisky sour glasses.

MARGARITA

Stir well with ¾ cup cracked
ice:

5 jiggers tequila
2½ jiggers lime or lemon
juice
½ jigger triple sec

Pour into glasses, the rims of
which have been rubbed with
citrus rind and then spun in salt.

ABOUT SHERRY AND
OTHER FORTIFIED WINES

True sherry—the "sack" so es-
teemed by Falstaff—comes from
a relatively small area around
the town of Jerez in Spain. Its
extraordinary qualities are the
result of a continuous, elaborate
and unique method of blending,
called the "solera" system. Like
port and Madeira, sherry is a
fortified wine, bolstered, so to
speak, with brandy. It is interesting to know that sherry, the
Spanish kind—with its so-called
domestic counterpart—is the
most popular American wine.

Sherries fall into two basic
types: "fino," or dry and "oloroso," more or less sweet. The
imported product appears under
these further subclassifications:
for the finos, manzanilla—very
dry, very pale, light body; fino
very dry, very pale, medium
body; amontillado—dry, pale,
full-bodied; for the oloro-
sos, amoroso—medium sweet,
golden, full-bodied; oloroso—
sweeter, golden-brown, full-
bodied; cream—sweet, deep gold,

full-bodied; brown—very sweet,
dark brown, full-bodied. Most
Spanish sherries, except the
very dry ones, are distinguished
by an elusive and delightful
"nutty" taste.

Sherry, in its drier manifesta-
tions, is a pleasant substitute
for the more insistent cocktail,
as well as a favorite wine for
cooking. Along with the less
frequently encountered port and
Madeira, it makes an excellent
late-afternoon tranquillizer or
an after-dinner drink. Never, we
counsel, serve any of these three
fortified wines as accompaniments to a meal—at least not
later than the soup—for they are
simply too substantial for the
symphonic effects required of
table wines.

A good deal of dispute, it
seems, can be sparked over
whether or not to serve sherry
at room temperature. On this,
as in several other similar controversies, we are latitudinarians
rather than fundamentalists and
happen to prefer sherry cooled
to about 50°. Extreme chilling
often results in temporary but
unattractive cloudiness.

Sometimes, for a preprandial
pickup, a host or hostess will
prefer to switch from sherry to
other types of aperitif wines: a
medium-dry vermouth, for example, Cinzano, Byrrh, Pernod,
Positano, or Dubonnet of either
the dark imported or the blond
domestic variety. The temperature of these, again, we like
lowered to about 20° below that
of the room.

ABOUT WINES

A French general is reputed to
have ordered his troops to present arms every time they
marched past his favorite vineyard. Alexander Dumas père,
himself a famous cook, declared
that certain wines should only

be drunk kneeling, with head bared. In this exceedingly complex and mystique-haunted preserve we can only, like the fools of the aphorism, rush good-naturedly in, make what points we regard as basic and rush even more quickly out again, before the sticklers take us apart.

First—to clear the air of a few widely held misconceptions—wine does not improve invariably or indefinitely with age. It is true that no wine whatever should be drunk until a year or so after it is made. White wines, except sweet ones which can live for a generation, should be drunk before they are ten years old, preferably earlier. Red wines, if properly stored, may go on getting better and better for many years. We say "may" because whether they do or not depends on the superiority of the original product and on the amount of alcohol and certain organic acids it contains—the more alcohol, by and large, the better maturation. Again, while it is true that red wines seem to consort well with certain kinds of food and white with others, it is pretty absurd to deprive yourself of wine with a meal just because the kind you have on hand does not traditionally match the entrée.

We should state categorically, however, that wine is ♦ never served with courses that include asparagus, artichokes, salads made with vinegar, vinaigretted foods, curries or oranges. We might also warn that fish with a fishy flavor, strongly flavored sauces like Diable, Remoulade, Poivrade, Chasseur, Provençale and mayonnaise, do much to destroy the subtleties of the wine which is served with them.

There is also this matter of temperature. We grant that, by and large, whites, including rosés, should be served chilled, 45° to 50°, and reds at room temperature. We confess, however, that we have known occasions when, like Kurt Stein's German-American concert-goer, "Wir haben uns by mistake entchoyed" a supper claret or an equally humble chianti served at 55° or so. Remember, too, if you like dry wine, to buy varieties that are naturally dry. Don't look for dryness in such wines as sauterne, Barsac, or Vouvray, which are inherently and characteristically sweet. See Wine Chart for usage and temperature, page 35, 36. All wines should be stored in a dark, cool place, 55° to 60°, with the liquid contacting the cork.

For a quarter of a century, the French Government, to bring order out of what had been a chaotic situation, has rigorously defined which vineyards had the rights to which names. As a corollary, they induced the growers of the Burgundy region to bottle their own wines, label them accurately, and personally vouch for their authenticity—a practice which before 1930 had been systematically followed only in the other chief center of French viniculture, Bordeaux. As a result, it is possible to buy the world's greatest wines with considerable confidence.

If you pick up a bottle of French wine at your vintner's, you may be sure that it comes to you, without admixture or adulteration, directly from the vineyards whose name it bears, if you read any of the following: "Mise en bouteilles au chateau," "Mise en bouteilles par le propriétaire," "Mise à—or de—la propriété," "Mise au—or du—domaine," "Mise en bouteilles au domaine" or the name of the vineyard followed by "propriétaire," "propriétaire-récoltant," "vigneron" or "viticulteur."

Among French vintners another reform is a century past due—that of reclassification. Many of the traditionally great vineyards have gathered to themselves over the years lesser "crus" unworthy of their names. And a number of first-rate vineyards have been developed which are not yet listed even among the "honorable" ones. When these injustices are corrected—and there is increasing support for reclassification—we shall indeed be living in the Golden Age of Wine.

We have, of course, been speaking of the more important French wines—the "estate" wines. But these are not by any means the only palatable ones. Many lesser French wines are well worth enjoying. Nor, of course, is France the only country from which good wines come. Surprisingly enough, more white wines of German than of French origin are today being sold in the United States. And entirely acceptable imports are available from Italy and Spain—to say nothing of the domestic varieties produced in California, New York and Ohio.

Only a few of the comments which apply to still white wines apply also to champagne. Like other wines, it should be drunk before it rounds out its first decade, or as soon as possible. Unlike them, except for rosés, champagne is usually considered fit to drink with any sort of food, as well as before and after a meal. Types range from dry to sweet, in the following order: brut, extra dry, sec, demi-sec and doux. A good many experts prefer the first, because its low sugar content permits the taste of the original wine to come through.

◆ Never open a bottle of champagne until it has been thoroughly chilled. In opening it, hold it away from you or anyone else in the room, at an angle of about 30° from the vertical. Then untwist the wires and gently ease out the cork.

To dispose of one more misconception about wine: sparkling Burgundy is definitely not a substitute for champagne. It is an inferior product.

A word of caution about purchasing wine. We have implied that you will deal best with an established vintner; not necessarily because he alone carries superior merchandise, but because he is likely to know more about it and consequently to handle and store it with greater care. It is amazing, in some sections of the country, how much fine wine has found its way into the corner grocery store and neighborhood delicatessen. But considering its preciousness and fragility, it is even more amazing to discover that the proprietors of these establishments, almost to a man, know absolutely nothing about the wines they sell, except their price, and that they are perfectly content to hustle them about as if they were so many cans of pork and beans.

It would take a bold connoisseur, indeed—and a foolish one —to undertake a listing of the world's wines in order of their excellence. As a matter of fact, many are excellent—inimitably so. Familiarity with acquaintances often breeds contempt; never with wines. To become discriminating, it is necessary to taste many varieties; and discrimination brings greater and greater enjoyment.

ABOUT SERVING WINES

Here are a few suggestions to guide the inexperienced host.

All wines respond favorably to a "resting period" of 24 hours or so before being brought to the table. With few exceptions, wines are served at 45° to 60°. Champagne is always served cold—35° to 40°. It should be cooled gradually in a refrigerator and placed in ice shortly before being used. The younger vintages of champagne call for 35°, the older for 40°. ◆ If champagne is not chilled, you may get an explosion instead of the characteristic "pop."

Except for bottles of sparkling wine, which must be drunk at one sitting, partly filled bottles of table wine may be "held over" for another occasion—as long as that occasion occurs within a week or so and provided the wine, if chilled, remains chilled.

We are aware that wrapping the wine bottle in a napkin, as it makes its rounds, is regarded by restaurateurs as poor practice—apparently because it may be used to disguise a poor-vintage label. We contend that different standards prevail at home. After all, you don't suspect your host of serving an inferior soup if he ladles it from a tureen! We still much prefer the napkin to the serving basket—it is simpler and provides better insulation.

Below are shown various types of glasses for wine. From left to right: a tall tulip glass for champagne, which is preferable to the rather outmoded saucer type, as it keeps the drink colder and preserves the fizz; a traditional Rhine wine römer; an all-purpose tulip glass, suitable for red and white wines generally; a bubble glass for sparkling Burgundy; a pipe-stem sherry glass; a balloon brandy snifter; a glass for liqueurs. All are shown filled to the proper levels at the initial pouring. All, except the brandy glass, are held by the stem when drinking. The brandy glass is held cradled in the hand, both before and during drinking, to warm the liquor and release its aroma.

Remember, in handling wine, to disturb the contents of the bottle as little as possible. At table, wine is poured from the right, since the glass occupies a top right location in the table setting.

DINING WITH WINE

COURSE	WINE	HOW TO SERVE
SHELL-FISH OR HORS	Chablis Graves Rhine Moselle	Cold—40° to 45°
SOUP	Sauterne	Cold—40° to 45°
	Dry Sherry	Room Temp.
	Madeira	Cool—50°

DINING WITH WINE Cont.

COURSE	WINE	HOW TO SERVE
FISH	White Bordeaux White Burgundy Rhine Moselle Other Whites	Cool—50°
ENTREES	White Wine Champagne	Cold— 40° to 45°
	Red Wine	Room Temp.
ROASTS Red Meats	Red Burgundy Red Bordeaux Other Reds	Room Temp.
	Sparkling Burgundy	Cold— 40° to 45°
ROASTS White Meats	White Bordeaux White Burgundy	Cold— 40° to 45° Cool—50°
	Champagne	Cold— 40° to 45°
FOWL OR GAME	Red Burgundy Red Bordeaux Rhone Other Reds	Room Temp.
CHEESE	Red Burgundy Red Bordeaux Other Reds Port Sherry Madeira	Room Temp.

COURSE	WINE	HOW TO SERVE
DESSERT	Madeira	Room Temp.
	Sherry Champagne	Cold— 40° to 45°
COFFEE	Cognac Port Sherry Madeira Liqueur Red Wine	Room Temp.

Note: Champagne—cold—may be served with any course.

The average serving of dinner wine or champagne is 3 to 3½ fluid ounces; of cocktail or dessert wine, 2 to 2½ ounces. The chart below gives volumes and servings:

SIZE		DINNER WINE— CHAMPAGNE		COCK-TAIL— DESSERT WINE
	OUNCES	SERVINGS		SERVINGS
Fifth ⅘ qt.	25.6	8		8–12
Tenth ⅖ pt.	12.8	4		4–6
Split	6.4	2		
Quart	32	10		10–14
Pint	16	5		5–7
½ Gallon	64	20		20–30
Gallon	128	40		40–60

ABOUT VINTAGES

Domestic wines and those produced abroad in similar mild or temperate climates do not vary greatly in quality. Differences between them, however, are due chiefly to predictable and more or less constant differences in selectivity and manufacture.

None of these fair-weather wines can approach French and German wines at their best. But climatic extremes and certain other individual factors introduce into the production of the vintages of France and of the Rhine a strong element of chance. As a consequence, they are not by any means always at their peak. Yet, even in a so-called poor vintage year, some of the many North European wines may be exceptional.

In view of this rather complicated situation we have resisted the temptation to draw up a detailed vintage guide for French and German wines. We do venture to note that, during the past couple of decades, the following years are generally regarded as having produced, in these regions, excellent wines: '59, '61, '62, '66, '69, '70, '71. Average or better were '64 and '67. '60, '63, '65, and '68 were poor.

There are events in life which should be celebrated with a gala! A single pouring from a jeroboam takes care of 34 glasses placed in fountain form. Whether you pour champagne or punch, the effect is memorable. Better practice first, though, with tap water! See this page.

living quality of his brew. Even today's pasteurized beer is still full of living organisms, subject to deterioration and shock. So, if he wants to savor beer at its height, he looks at the date to make sure it won't be over 2 months old when it is served. He keeps it stored in a dark place. He chills it slowly before serving and once cold he does not allow it to warm up again and be rechilled, nor does he ever allow it to freeze.

Like the wine connoisseur, the beer expert is most particular about the temperatures at which he serves his brew. Forty degrees is favored as producing the fullest flavor, a not too great contrast between the temperature of the drink and that of the taste buds.

A slightly higher serving temperature is suggested for ale.

ABOUT SERVING BEER AND ALE

The beer connoisseur, like the wine fancier, never forgets the

This drink is made from the same ingredients as beer, except for the strain of the yeast. It is fermented rapidly and at room temperature rather than at the almost freezing temperatures modern beer demands, in its long, slow and intricately controlled processing.

Beers vary greatly in alcoholic and sugar content, depending on how they are brewed. Bock, which appears at Eastertime, is frequently advertised by a picture of a monk—for Shrove Tuesday was the traditional tasting and testing day in the old monasteries. This brew is dark and is usually higher in alcoholic content than beer set in the spring. Beer is light and tart, or dark and sweet—depending on whether the barley is processed with low, slow heat or with high, swift heat. Which to serve is a matter of personal taste.

Here are the traditional beer and ale glasses or mugs.

Steins, heirloom and everyday, the Pilsener glass for light beer and an ale glass and mug are shown on page 37. The true connoisseur is probably happiest drinking beer from an opaque container. It does not allow him to see the small imperfections in the appearance of the beer, which are visible when it is served in improperly washed glasses. Grease is the natural enemy of beer, for it kills the foam. So wash glasses with soda, not with soap. The glasses should never be dried, but

should be allowed to drain on a soft cloth washed with a detergent.

Glasses may be chilled before using, but, in any case, they should be rinsed in cold water just before using and the beer should be poured into a tilted, wet glass.

You may like a high or a low collar, but the usual size is one-fourth the height of the glass or mug. A bottle of beer, despite popular superstition, is not so caloric as the average cocktail, but since it lacks the disembodied quality of table wines it is usually served with snacks and suppers.

ABOUT LIQUEURS AND CORDIALS

A common characteristic of almost all liqueurs and cordials is their sweetness. This quality relegates them as straight drinks to the after-dinner hour, along with a second demitasse. With some, such as kümmel, curaçao, Cointreau, Grand Marnier, anisette, crème de menthe or crème de cacao, a single flavor predominates. In others—Chartreuse, Benedictine, Vieille Curé, Drambuie, for example—the flavor is more intricate. Still a third class of liqueurs of which falernum and orgeat—almond, kirsch—wild cherry, crème de cassis—currant, grenadine—pomegranate, and maraschino—cherry are perhaps the

best known, are used almost entirely as components of mixed drinks. However, do not overlook this potentiality with all other liqueurs: a few drops, experimentally added, have touched off many a brave new cocktail. By themselves, serve liqueurs at room temperature or a little below, and in small quantities.

ABOUT MIXED DRINKS

In the foregoing pages of this chapter we have dealt with our material on the "basic ingredient" principle and have attempted a chronological résumé of the drinks, simple or compound, which are likely to precede, go along with or follow meals—from the ceremonious to the completely informal. The following sections describe a number of between-meal or special-occasion drinks of such variety as to defy systematic listing—at least as far as their components are concerned.

Glasses and cups for mixed drinks vary greatly in size and shape. Collins glasses, lemonade and highball glasses, shown at the left, are similar in shape and vary in content from 8 to 16 ounces.

Silver cups with a handle, so that the frost remains undisturbed, are highly favored for such drinks as mint juleps. Some persons dislike drinks served in metal, but if straws are used no metallic taste is noticeable. Juleps without straws should be served in very thin glassware. To frost the glasses, see page 40.

Tom and Jerry mugs, shown next, hold about 8 ounces; punch glasses or cups, 3 or 4 ounces. These are frequently made of porcelain, an advantage when serving mulled or flaming drinks.

ABOUT TALL DRINKS

King-size drinks are commonly served in glasses holding 8 ounces or more. When mixers such as carbonated water—seltzer, club soda, Vichy, etc.—or ginger ale are used, refrigerate them if possible before adding them to the drink. To make decorative ice cubes for tall drinks, see (I, 23).

HIGHBALLS AND RICKEYS

[Individual Servings]
Use bourbon, Scotch, rye, or gin.
Into a 6-oz. glass, put 2 large ice cubes and add:
       1 jigger of liquor chosen
Fill the glass with:
       Carbonated water
Stir lightly with bar spoon and serve.

For a rickey, add, before the carbonated water:
       Juice of ½ large lime
With dry liquors, you may add:
       ½ teaspoon sugar syrup
Interesting effects in the two drink categories above are possible by further varying the basic ingredient. Try an applejack highball or one made with Dubonnet. The three following drinks are classic results of using one's imagination freely in this area: **Vermouth Cassis,** with a base consisting of 1 pony crème de cassis and 1 jigger dry vermouth; **Horse's Neck** or **Cooler,** with a long spiral of lemon peel draped over the edge of the glass and ginger ale substituted for carbonated water; and **Spritzer,** with half Rhine wine and half carbonated water. A luxurious rickey can be concocted by adding a teaspoon or so of liqueur to the lime juice.

TOM COLLINS   [1]

Collinses, like rickeys, are a

large family. But this one is the granddaddy of all the rest. Combine in a 14- or 16-oz. glass, with 4 ice cubes:

> 1 tablespoon sugar syrup
> Juice of medium-size
>   lemon
> 2 jiggers gin

Fill glass with:

> Carbonated water

Stir and serve immediately.

GIN FIZZ   [1]

Combine in a bar glass:

> 1 tablespoon sugar syrup
> Juice of medium-size
>   lemon or lime
> 1½ jiggers gin

Shake well with ½ cup crushed ice and strain into prechilled 8-oz. glass. Fill with:

> Carbonated water

Stir and serve.
A Silver Fizz is made by beating into the above Gin Fizz ingredients:

> 1 egg white

Fizzes may be made with whisky, rum or brandy as a base.

MINT JULEP   [1]

This drink can be superlative. And it is well, at this point, to remember that, as the French say, "The good is the enemy of the best." Use only bonded bourbon, tender, terminal mint leaves for bruising and very finely crushed or shaved ice. Chill a 14- or 16-oz. glass or silver mug in refrigerator. Wash and partially dry:

> A long sprig of fresh
>   mint

and dip it in:

> Powdered sugar

Combine in a bar glass:

> 2 teaspoons sugar syrup
> 6 medium-sized mint
>   leaves
> (1 dash angostura bitters)

Bruise leaves gently with muddler and blend all ingredients by stirring together. Pour into bar glass:

> 1 large jigger bourbon
>   whisky

Stir again. Remove serving glass from refrigerator, pack it with ice and strain into it the above mixture. With a bar spoon, churn ice up and down. Add more ice to within ¾ inch of top. Add:

> 1 pony whisky

Repeat churning process until glass begins to frost. Decorate glass with:

> Sprig of mint

Insert long straws and serve.

When making a number of mint juleps, a less nerve-racking way to frost the glasses is to omit prechilling them. After churning, instead of waiting for them to frost in the open, place them in the refrigerator for 30 minutes. ◗ Be careful throughout this whole process not to grasp glasses with bare hands.

The stand illustrated, with its tiers of ice and carrying ring, makes a julep server par excellence. If the number of glasses required is not enough to fill all the shelf space, use the ones at the top for hors d'oeuvre. A deep tray, packed with finely crushed ice, will make an acceptable substitute for the julep stand.

CUBA LIBRE [1]

Combine in bar glass:
        Juice of 1 lime
    ½ squeezed lime
    1 large jigger rum
Put ingredients into 12- or 14-
oz. glass. Fill glass with 3 large
ice cubes. Add:
        Cola
Stir and serve.

RUM PUNCH [1]

Combine in 10-oz. glass:
        Juice of 1 lemon or lime
    1 tablespoon pure maple
        syrup
    1 jigger rum
    2 dashes grenadine
Fill glass with finely crushed ice
and churn up and down with
bar spoon. Have ice within ¾
inch of top. Add:
    1 pony rum
Churn again, insert straws and
decorate before serving with:
        Pineapple stick
        Slice of orange
        Cherry

ZOMBIE [1]

Combine in bar glass:
    1 teaspoon sugar syrup or
        falernum
    1 pony lemon juice
    1 pony pineapple juice
    1 large jigger light rum
    1 large jigger dark rum
    2 teaspoons apricot liqueur
    (1 pony papaya juice)
Shake with ¾ cup crushed ice
and pour into a 14- or 16-oz.
glass. Float on top:
    1 teaspoon Demerara rum
Decorate with:
        Orange slices
        Pineapple stick
        Green and red cherries
        Sprig of mint
Sprinkle over top:
        Powdered sugar
Insert straws and serve.

PLANTER'S PUNCH [1]

Combine in bar glass:
    2 teaspoons sugar syrup
        Juice of ½ lemon
    2 jiggers dark rum
    2 dashes angostura bitters
    1 dash grenadine
Shake well. Pour into a 12- or
14-oz. glass. Pack glass to top
with crushed ice and fill to
within ½ inch of top with:
        Carbonated water
Churn contents with bar spoon
until glass begins to frost. Insert
straws and decorate before serving with:
        Orange slice
        Cherry
        (Sprig of mint)

TONIC [1]

Into a 12-oz. glass place 3 ice
cubes and add:
    1 large jigger gin or vodka
Fill glass with:
        Quinine water
        (Lime or lemon juice to
        taste)

ABOUT PLUGGED FRUIT

We had no luck when, much
younger, we plugged a watermelon and cautiously tried to
impregnate it with rum. We
never quite solved the problem
of distribution. Later we discovered we had been too impatient. Time does the trick—
about 8 hours. For those fortunate ones who can easily
come by an abundance of other
kinds of fruit, we give the following formulas for a couple of
picturesque and delightfully refreshing drinks.

COCONUT [1]
EXTRAVAGANZA

To hold a coconut upright, see
page 194. Cut or saw off the top
of:
        A coconut
This should produce a hole

about 1 inch in diameter. Drain
and reserve the milk and add to
it that of a second coconut. Pour
into the hollow:
>1 large jigger light rum
>3 teaspoons apricot liqueur
>or Cointreau
>3 teaspoons coconut cream
>The coconut milk

Add ¾ cup finely crushed ice,
shake, insert straws and serve.

PINEAPPLE TONIC   [1]

Slice off the top of:
>A ripe pineapple

Hollow out a cavity about the
size of a highball glass. Pour
into it:
>1 large jigger light rum
>3 teaspoons Benedictine

Fill cavity with finely crushed
ice; stir well, bruising the inside of the pineapple and decorate with:
>Fresh fruit

Insert straws and serve.

SHORT DRINKS

"Some like it hot, some like it
cold." The drinks which follow
are of both varieties, in that
order.

TODDY   [1]

In an 8-oz. mug, place:
>1 teaspoon sugar syrup
>1 stick cinnamon
>1 jigger whisky, rum or
>brandy

Fill mug with:
>Very hot water

Impale over edge of mug:
>½ lemon slice

studded with:
>3 cloves

To serve cold, add cold water
instead of hot with an ice cube.

GROG   [1]

In an 8 oz. mug, stir together:
>1 teaspoon sugar syrup
>1 tablespoon strained
>lemon juice

>1 jigger dark rum

Fill mug with:
>Very hot tea or water

Garnish with a twist of:
>Lemon peel

Try this drink using molasses
instead of sugar syrup. Dust top
with a little:
>Ground nutmeg or
>cinnamon

★ HOT TOM AND   [4]
JERRY

Beat to a stiff froth:
>3 egg whites

Beat separately until light in
color:
>3 egg yolks

Beat into yolks gradually:
>3 tablespoons powdered
>sugar
>½ teaspoon each ground
>allspice, cinnamon and
>cloves

Fold yolks into whites and pour
2 tablespoons of this mixture
into each of four 8-oz. china
mugs. Add to each mug:
>½ jigger lukewarm brandy
>1 jigger lukewarm, dark
>rum

Fill mugs with very hot water,
milk, or coffee. Stir well and
sprinkle the tops with:
>Grated nutmeg

SYLLABUB OR MILK   [4]
PUNCH

Beat together in bar glass:
>1 tablespoon sugar syrup
>1 jigger top milk
>1 large jigger heavy cream
>½ cup sherry, port,
>Madeira or bourbon
>whisky

Serve at once in punch glasses.

POSSET OR HOT MILK   [6]
PUNCH

Blanch and pound in a mortar:
>5 or 6 bitter almonds

Heat:
>1 quart milk

1 teaspoon grated lemon
rind
½ cup sugar

Add the almonds and when the milk begins to scald, page 137, remove the mixture from the heat. Beat and add:

2 egg whites

Add and combine lightly, until the whole drink is frothy:

½ cup dark rum
1 cup brandy

Serve in punch cups.

FLIP [1]

Shake in bar glass with cracked ice:

1 whole egg
1 teaspoon sugar
1 jigger sherry, brandy
or port

Strain into 6-oz. glass. Sprinkle over top:

Grated nutmeg

★ EGGNOG [1]

If you are preparing this drink for an invalid, see note on uncooked eggs on page 453.

In a small bowl, beat until light:

1 egg yolk

Beat in slowly:

1 tablespoon sugar
¼ cup cream
⅛ to ¼ cup rum, brandy or
whisky
A few grains salt

Whip separately until stiff:

1 egg white

Fold white lightly into other ingredients. Transfer mixture to punch glass. For eggnog in quantity, see About Party Drinks, following.

ABOUT PARTY DRINKS

Most of the formulas in this section are of the punchbowl variety. In each instance, the ▶ quantity of liquid will amount to approximately 5 quarts and will serve about 20 persons—each one having two 4-oz. cups.

When the word "bottle" is used, it means a fifth of a gallon or 25 oz.

Fruit juices used in the concoction of party drinks should preferably be fresh; but frozen, unsweetened concentrates are quite acceptable, as long as you dilute them only about half as much as the directions on the container prescribe. Canned and bottled juices vary in quality—the best, in our opinion, being pineapple, apricot, cranberry, raspberry and grape. Ideally, punch mixes should be allowed to blend for an hour or so and, if served cold, chilled in the refrigerator before carbonated water or ice are added. With cold punches, be on the alert for dilution. Ice only ⅔ of the liquid at the outset and add the remainder just before the guests come back for seconds. Speaking of ice, avoid small pieces. At the very least, remove the cube grid from your ice trays and freeze a full unit. However, the two chilling devices illustrated are a lot more fun.

DECORATIVE ICE MOLDS

Set aside in a bowl the amount of water to be frozen. Stir it well 4 or 5 times during a 10 to 15 minute period to break up and expel the air bubbles with which newly drawn tap water is impregnated. Otherwise, the ice mold you build will be cloudy instead of crystal clear.

Have at hand such decorative ingredients as: whole limes, lemons, oranges, slices of citrus fruit, large fresh cherries or strawberries, clusters of grapes, sprigs of mint, sweet woodruff, lemon thyme or other herbs and a few handsome fresh grape or bay leaves, etc.

Select a decorative metal mold of the tubular or ring type. Avoid vessels which are so deep as to induce top-heaviness in your final product and risk its turning turtle, later.

Begin operations by partially freezing a layer of water in the container—proceeding much as you would in making a fancy gelatin salad, see page 185. In this case, of course, successive hardenings are frozen, instead of being chilled. On the first slush-like layer, arrange a wreath of fruit and greenery. Cover the decoration carefully with a sec-

ond layer of very cold water, returning the mold to the freezer, so that with renewed freezing the decoration is completely surrounded by clear ice. Repeat this procedure if the depth of the mold permits. Allow the contents to become thoroughly frozen. When the refrigerated drink has been transferred to the punch bowl, reverse the ice mold container, wrap a hot wet towel around the metal until the ice is disengaged, and float it in this position on the drink.

To make decorative ice cubes for individual drinks, see (I, 23).

ICE PUNCH BOWLS

Next, we show a punch bowl which is ice itself—particularly useful if you wish to dilute a cold drink as little as possible. Place in the kitchen sink a 50 lb. cube of ice. Choose a round metal bowl of at least 3 qt. capacity. Chip out a small depression in the center of the ice block and set the bowl over it.

Fill the bowl with boiling water, being careful not to spill any on the ice beneath. As the heat of the bowl melts the ice, stir the water. As the water cools, empty and refill the bowl each time, bailing out the depression in the ice, until the desired volume is displaced. Now, move the ice block onto a square "tray" of aluminum foil. Set it where you wish to dispense the drink. The tray should be a couple of inches larger than the block, constructed of heavy-duty material in leak-proof fashion, the edges turned up about 1½ inches all around to form a gutter. Any crudities can be masked by greenery or flowers. The "ice bowl" may, of course, be utilized equally well for serving sherbets and mixing cocktails.

However you serve party drinks, go easy on solid fruit trimmings; launching too much of this sort of thing makes for a very ramshackle-looking bowl. Work for larger decorative effects. A subtle flavor can be

DRINKS

45

imparted to punches by steeping in the basic mix, during the lagering period, slices of peeled seeded cucumber, then removing them before the drink is further processed. Sometimes a few dashes of bitters will confer "the old one-two" on an otherwise flabby punch.

FISH HOUSE PUNCH

Mix in punch bowl:

    1 cup sugar syrup
    1 cup lemon juice
    1 bottle dark rum
    1 bottle light rum
    1 bottle brandy
    7 cups water
    ½ cup peach brandy

If peach liqueur is used instead of peach brandy, the amount of syrup should be reduced to taste. Some recipes for this famous punch use strong tea instead of water.

BOWLE

A German favorite which may be made with any of a variety of fruits.

Slice and place in a large bowl one of the following fruits:

    6 ripe unpeeled peaches or
    8 ripe unpeeled apricots
    or 1 sliced pineapple or
    1 quart strawberries

Sprinkle over the fruit:

    1 cup powdered sugar

Pour over mixture:

    1½ cups Madeira or sherry

Allow to stand 4 hours or longer. Stir, pour over a block of ice in a bowl. Add:

    4 bottles dry white wine

CHAMPAGNE PUNCH

Most punches are traditionally mixed with plain, rather than carbonated water. When carbonated water is a component, the drink becomes a cup. Champagne Punch, sacred to weddings, occupies middle ground.

Peel, slice, crush and place in a large bowl:

    3 ripe pineapples

Cover pineapple and juice with:

    1 lb. powdered sugar

Let mixture stand, covered, for 1 hour. Add:

    2 cups lemon juice
    ½ cup curaçao
    ½ cup maraschino
    2 cups brandy
    2 cups light rum

Stir and let stand for 4 hours. Place in a punch bowl with a block of ice. Stir to blend and chill. Just before serving, add:

    4 bottles chilled
    champagne

WHISKY OR BRANDY CUP

Slice, place in a large bowl and crush:

    2 cups fresh pineapple

Add:

    1 quart fresh strawberries

Sprinkle over the fruit:

    ¾ lb. powdered sugar

Pour over mixture:

    2 cups dark rum

Allow mixture to stand, covered, for 4 hours. Add:

    2 cups lemon juice
    1½ cups orange juice
    1 cup grenadine
    2 bottles bourbon or
    brandy

Place in punch bowl with block of ice. Stir to blend and chill. Just before serving, add:

    2 quarts chilled carbonated
    water or dry ginger ale

If you like a predominant rum flavor, substitute for the fruit-steeping ingredient above:

    1½ cups brandy

and for the basic ingredient:

    2 bottles light rum

In this, as in other punch bowl drinks, it is wise to test the mix for flavor and sweetness before adding the diluent.

RUM CASSIS CUP

Mix in a punch bowl:

2½ bottles light rum
2½ cups dry vermouth
2½ cups crème de cassis
Add block of ice. Pour over the ice:
2 quarts carbonated water

CLARET CUP

Slice, place in large bowl and crush:
1 cup fresh pineapple
Peel, halve and add:
4 ripe peaches
4 peach stones
½ cup brandy
Sprinkle over mixture:
1 cup powdered sugar
Let stand for 4 hours. Add:
1 cup lemon juice
2 cups orange juice
½ cup maraschino
½ cup curaçao
2 bottles claret or other red wine
Chill the mixture for 1 hour; remove peaches and stones and pour over a block of ice in a punch bowl. Stir and add:
2 quarts carbonated water

RHINE WINE CUP

Mix in punch bowl:
1 cup sugar syrup
2 cups lemon juice
1 cup brandy
2 cups dry sherry
1 cup strong tea
3 bottles Rhine wine or other dry white wine
2 cups thinly sliced, peeled, seeded cucumbers
After 20 minutes, remove cucumber. Add a large block of ice and pour over it:
1 quart carbonated water

MAY WINE

Another German drink, dedicated to springtime and featuring fresh Waldmeister or sweet woodruff. This highly decorative plant may be grown in a shady corner of your herb garden.
Place in a bowl:
12 sprigs young Waldmeister
1¼ cups powdered sugar
1 bottle Moselle or other dry white wine
(1 cup brandy)
Cover this mixture for 30 minutes, ♦ no longer. Remove the Waldmeister. Stir contents of bowl thoroughly and pour over a block of ice in a punch bowl. Add:
3 bottles Moselle
1 quart carbonated water or champagne
Thinly sliced oranges, sticks of pineapple and, most appropriately of all, sprigs of Waldmeister, may be used to decorate the "Maitrank."

★ EGGNOG IN QUANTITY

I. A rich and extravagant version that is correspondingly good. Some people like to add a little more spirit to the following recipes, remembering Mark Twain's observation that "too much of anything is bad, but too much whisky is just enough." Beat separately until light in color:
12 egg yolks
Beat in gradually:
1 lb. confectioners' sugar
Add very slowly, beating constantly:
2 cups dark rum, brandy, bourbon or rye
These liquors may each form the basic ingredient of the nog or may be combined to taste.
Let mixture stand covered for 1 hour to dispel the "eggy" taste. Add, beating constantly:
2 to 4 cups of liquor chosen
2 quarts whipping cream
(1 cup peach brandy)
Refrigerate for 3 hours. Beat until stiff ♦ but not dry:
8 to 12 egg whites

Fold them lightly into the other ingredients. Serve the eggnog sprinkled with:

Freshly grated nutmeg

II. Less powerful, less fluffy than the preceding nog, and a boon to the creamless householder.

Beat until light in color:
12 eggs
Beat in gradually:
1 lb. confectioners' sugar
½ teaspoon salt
¼ cup vanilla
Stir in:
8 cups evaporated milk
diluted with:
3 cups water
Stir in:
4 cups dark rum, brandy, bourbon or rye

Cover the nog closely and permit it to ripen in the refrigerator for 24 hours. Stir it again and serve it sprinkled with:

Freshly grated nutmeg

Before taking leave of cold party drinks, we want to remind you that any of the "sour" type cocktails—those made of an alcoholic base plus fruit juice—may serve as the foundation for delectable punches and cups. See Cocktails, pages 25–32.

In preparing the following hot drinks, bring the liquid almost to a boil ◗ but not to the boiling point.

★ **TOM AND JERRY IN QUANTITY**

Beat until stiff ◗ but not dry, cover and set aside:
1 dozen egg whites
Beat separately until light in color:
1 dozen egg yolks
Into the yolks, beat gradually:
¾ cup powdered sugar
2 teaspoons each ground allspice, cinnamon and cloves

Fold seasoned yolks into whites.

Into each of twenty 8-ounce china mugs, place 2 tablespoons egg mixture and:
½ jigger lukewarm brandy
1 jigger lukewarm dark rum
Fill each mug with:
Very hot water, milk or coffee
Stir vigorously until drink foams. Dust top with:
Grated nutmeg

★ **MULLED WINE OR NEGUS IN QUANTITY**

Make a syrup by boiling for 5 minutes:
2½ cups sugar
1¼ cups water
4 dozen whole cloves
6 sticks cinnamon
3 crushed nutmegs
Peel of 3 lemons, 2 oranges
Strain syrup. Add to it:
4 cups hot lemon or lime juice
Heat well and add:
4 bottles red wine
Serve very hot with slices of:
Lemon and pineapple

These proportions may be varied to taste. Sometimes Madeira, port or sherry is used in this formula.

★ **WASSAIL**

The best time to "come a-wassailing" is, of course, Christmas week.

Core and bake, see page 95:
1 dozen apples
Combine in a saucepan and boil for 5 minutes:
1 cup water
4 cups sugar
1 tablespoon grated nutmeg
2 teaspoons ground ginger
½ teaspoon ground mace
6 whole cloves
6 allspice berries
1 stick cinnamon
Beat until stiff ◗ but not dry:

1 dozen egg whites

Beat separately until light in color:

1 dozen egg yolks

Fold whites into yolks, using large bowl. Strain sugar and spice mixture into eggs, combining quickly. Bring almost to boiling point separately:

4 bottles sherry or Madeira
2 cups brandy

Incorporate the hot wine with the spice and egg mixture, beginning slowly and stirring briskly with each addition. Toward the end of this process, add the brandy. Now, just before serving and while the mixture is still foaming, add the baked apples.

Wassail can also be made with a combination of beer and wine, preferably sherry; in which case the proportion should be roughly 4 of beer to 1 of sherry.

HOT BUTTERED RUM

[Individual Serving]

Place in a hot tumbler:

1 teaspoon powdered sugar

Add:

¼ cup boiling water
¼ cup rum
1 tablespoon butter

Fill glass with boiling water. Stir well. Sprinkle on top.

Freshly grated nutmeg

This is an old-time New England conception of an individual portion. It may be modified. Curious, isn't it, that the Pilgrims made rum—especially a drink like this one, which has been said to make a man see double and feel single.

CANAPÉS AND TEA
SANDWICHES

Canapés and hors d'oeuvre are appetizers offered with drinks.
▶ The canapé has a built-in bread or pastry. The hors d'oeuvre is served alone and may be accompanied by, but not served on, a pastry or bread base. For more details, see page 53. Canapés often resemble very small tea sandwiches and since the making of both of these is so similar they are discussed together. Additional fillings for sandwiches served as luncheon entrées and heartier, larger sandwiches will be found on (I, 240).

Since gay and festive presentation of canapés and tea sandwiches is so essential, we suggest ways in which breads and pastries can be made to look their best, either by fast and furious or by more leisurely and amusing methods.

It is often easier to make small sandwiches in quantity ▶ by working with a whole loaf rather than with individual slices. A number of ways to cut and combine different breads are illustrated. In several instances the crusts have been removed and the bread cut horizontally. It is possible to get six or seven long slices from the loaf and then spread the entire surface before stacking and shaping. A variation of forms that is economical of area is sketched below. Particolored sandwiches can be produced by combining white and whole wheat or white and brown bread. Rolled sandwiches can be made quickly by rolling long horizontal slices. A number of other shapes are illustrated on the next page. On the upper left are two-layer sandwiches, in which the top layer is doughnut-shaped to allow the color of the filling to show through. On the lower right, successive bread or sausage slices are shown bound with a filling and cut in pie-wedge ribbon slices.

In making sandwiches of any kind in quantity ▶ time is saved by setting up an assembly line and using mass-production techniques. Place bread slices in rows. Place dabs of seasoned butters or mayonnaise on one row, filling on the next. Then do the final spreading by bringing the fillings and butters well

out to the edges. Put hard butter or mayonnaise twice through a grinder with other ingredients and use a coarse blade. For closed sandwiches, do all the assembling, stacking, cutting and packaging in turn. For open-faced sandwiches, have garnishes cut shortly in advance and keep them from drying out by placing them in foil, damp wrung-out towels or plastic bags—then refrigerate. After the base is spread, do all the garnishing of one type, then of another, before arranging for serving.

throughout, and is a particularly good technique in preparing rolled shapes, which should be very thin and made of very fresh bread. Other sandwiches are easier to make if the bread is one day old. Cut fresh or frozen bread with a very sharp hot knife. Remember, though, that all bread which has been frozen dries out very quickly after thawing and that precautions should be taken to keep the sandwiches as moist as possible. Have spreads at about 75° to protect bread from pulling or tearing.

ABOUT BREAD FOR SANDWICHES

The number of sandwiches to a loaf of bread is hard to gauge because of shape variations, but from a 1-lb. loaf of sandwich bread you can expect at least 20 slices. Allow about 1 lb. butter for 3 to 4 lbs. of sandwich loaf. Do not have the loaf pre-sliced, but slice it thin yourself. The number of sandwiches to allow for each guest is even harder to judge, although 8 to 10 small snacks, either sandwiches or hors d'oeuvre, are not too much to count per person, if drinking is protracted.

♦ To avoid raggedy sandwiches, use a finely textured bread. If not available, try chilling or freezing ordinary bread before cutting. Freezing before cutting and then spreading makes for easier handling

ABOUT KEEPING SANDWICHES

Preparations should be made ahead of time in order to serve sandwiches in prime condition. Have ready foil or wax paper and moistened, wrung-out cloths, transparent self-sealing tissue or plastic bags. Refrigerate double sandwiches, wrapped, without delay. Open-faced sandwiches, if made of suitable materials, page 564, are often quick-frozen and can then be wrapped without damage to their decorations or surfaces. Store them wrapped and in boxes to keep them free from the weight of other foods. Also place them away from the coils of the freezer, page 548. ♦ It is often preferable to freeze the fillings alone and make up these fancy sandwiches shortly before serving.

Be sure that any moist or juicy filling is put on bread well spread with a firm layer of butter or of heavy mayonnaise, so that the bread will not get soggy. If tomato or cucumber slices are used, see that they are cut and allowed to drain well on a rack before putting them in the sandwiches.

It is sometimes suggested that bread be rolled with a rolling pin to compress it, so it will not be too absorptive when the butter is put on, but we find that this rolling gives the bread a dense and rather horrid texture.

♦ Toasted canapés, if served immediately after their preparation, should be on bread that is toasted on one side only—then spread and heated. If serving is to be delayed, the bread should be toasted on both sides—or use Melba toast or croutons. Then reheat when the filling is applied.

ABOUT SANDWICH SHAPES

It is surprising how a few fancy sandwiches with attractive garnishes (I, 39), will help to perk up a platter. If the platters are kept small, they are easier to replenish. A combination of open and closed sandwiches gives variety to the tray. But sometimes medium oblong trays, filled with alternating rows of similarly spread open-faced sandwiches—placed closely together—make a quick and pleasant change from the large platters more sparsely filled with fancy sandwiches. To give variety to your tray, plan both open and closed types.

Rolled sandwiches, especially with a sprig of cress or parsley protruding, make a charming intercepted wreath around the edge of the platter—if they are placed like spokes on a round tray. For other garnishes for platters, see illustrations on (I, 39).

ROLLED SANDWICHES

Freeze:
        Fresh sandwich bread
Remove crusts and slice as thin as possible with a sharp hot knife. Spread the bread with:
        A softened filling
We particularly enjoy as a filling:
        (Cream cheese mixed
        with cucumber and onion
        juice with cress)
Be sure the filling goes out to the edge, so the roll will be well scaled. When the bread is well thawed, roll the sandwiches. Tuck into the ends, but allow to protrude:
        Cress or parsley sprigs
♦ Wrap firmly and refrigerate, so they will hold their cylindrical shape when served.

RIBBON SANDWICHES

Cut the crust from:
        White bread
        Dark bread
Spread the slices with:
        Butter or Cream Cheese
        Spreads, page 58
Place 3 to 5 slices of bread alternately in stacks. Cut them into bars, squares or triangles, see illustration, page 49.

FLOWER CANAPÉS

If you have an herb garden, many enchanting sandwiches can be made from the small-scaled leaves and blossoms. Or in winter try cutting:
        Small rounds or squares
        of bread
Spread them with:
        Soft cream cheese
Place across each sandwich a very narrow:
        Strip of green pepper or
        a stem of chive or parsley

This represents a stem. Place at the top of the strip to form the flower:

A slice of stuffed olive or a fancy cut of carrot or radish

Cut into lengthwise slices to form leaves:

Small sour-sweet pickles

Place the pickle slices opposite each other on the green pepper stem.

★ CHRISTMAS CANAPÉS

I. Cut into 2-inch rounds:

Thin bread slices

Spread the rounds with:

A cream cheese mixture, page 58

Cut into tiny rounds, about ⅛-inch:

Maraschino cherries, pimiento, cranberries or use tiny red decorettes

Chop until fine:

Parsley

Make a narrow ring of the parsley around each piece of bread. Dot it at intervals with the red rounds to make it look like a holly wreath.

II. Or, use:

A sprig of parsley

shaped like a tree and dot it with the small red "balls" described above.

ZOO SANDWICHES

For very young children's parties, make closed double or triple sandwiches in animal shapes using fancy cookie cut-

ters. Triple-layered sandwiches can be made to stand upright on the plate.

SANDWICH LOAVES

These can even be a meal by themselves—an excellent luncheon dish with coffee and a dessert, and—when made in individual size—real charmers. If you want a decorative sandwich center for a birthday buffet, make an individual loaf for each guest and group the loaves around a pile of gaily wrapped gifts.

I. Cut the crusts from:

A loaf of white or whole wheat bread

Cut the loaf into 3 or 4 lengthwise slices. Butter the inner sides of the slices and spread them with a layer of:

Chicken, shrimp, egg or salmon salad

a layer of:

Drained crushed pineapple and cream cheese

a layer of:

Drained sliced tomatoes, lettuce or watercress

or with any good combination of salad or sandwich ingredients. If it fits with your filling, add some:

Anchovy paste

to the cream cheese. Be sure to cut the bread thin enough and spread the fillings thick enough, see illustration, to keep the bread from dominating. Wrap the loaf firmly in a moist towel, chill well, unwrap and place on a platter. Cover with:

Softened cream cheese, smooth cottage cheese, or Mayonnaise Collée (I, 387)

An individual slice, cut from the finished loaf, is shown.

II. This holds well if prepared in advance. Cut the top and bottom from:

A large round rye loaf and reserve them as the base and lid for a crust container. Carefully cut out in one piece a straight-sided cylinder from the soft center. Then slice this cylinder of bread horizontally into 6 thin slices. Spread the upper surfaces of the first, third and fifth slices with not too moist:

Seasoned fillings

Cover the spread slices with the second, fourth and sixth slices. Keeping the shape of the large cylinder orderly, cut it into narrow wedges. Now, carefully place the cut cylinder on the bottom crust. Insert toothpicks around the edge of the crust bottom and impale the crust ring on the picks to form a container for the sandwich wedges. Cover with the top crust as a lid. Wrap and refrigerate until ready to serve.

ABOUT BREAD BASES FOR CANAPÉS

Use coarse ryes, whole wheats, cheese breads from the Yeast and Quick Bread Chapter, page 239, and suggestions from the Uses for Ready-Baked Breads, page 288. There are good cracker suggestions in Soups (I, 151), and various pastries in the Pie Chapter, pages 297, 298, 299.

Or use small versions of Luncheon Sandwiches (I, 240); Ravioli (I, 177); Bouchées, page 304, or Tarts or Barquettes, below.

TARTS AND TARTLETS FOR CANAPÉS

I. Prepare:
Biscuit Dough, page 284, or
Pie Dough, page 293
Roll or pat it until it is about ⅛-inch thick. Cut it into 3-inch squares. Place in the center of

each square one of the fillings listed under:
Fillings for Pastry Canapés, page 55
Moisten the corners of the dough lightly with water. Fold up the sides of the dough and pinch the corners to make a tart shape. Bake the tarts in a 425° oven for about 10 minutes.

II. Or, fill the tart with:
A thin slice of cheese,
1½ x 2 inches
Top this with:
½ slice tomato
Season the tomato with:
A grating of pepper
A little salt
(A sprinkling of brown sugar)
Sprinkle the top with:
Cooked diced bacon
Bake as in I, above.

III. Fill with:
Hot spicy puréed spinach
Lay on it:
A smoked oyster
Brush with:
A little Cream Sauce (I, 359, 360)
to which has been added:
Grated Swiss cheese
Bake as in I, above.

RICH COCKTAIL TART OR QUICHE

A physician in our family once took to task a scandalously obese patient. "But, doctor," said the patient plaintively, "one must offer the stomach something from time to time." This is a favorite offering in our family. Prepare any unsweetened:
Pie Dough, page 293
Shape as for tartlets and bake for only 5 minutes in a 400° oven. Remove from the oven. ◗ Lower the heat to 325°. Place in the bottom of each tart 1 tablespoon of the following mixture:

1 beaten egg
¾ cup cream
½ teaspoon grated
   Parmesan cheese
(2 tablespoons sautéed
   mushrooms or crab meat)
½ teaspoon salt
   A small pinch coriander
Bake the tarts for 15 minutes or
until the quiche has set. Keep
them hot and toasty in an electric skillet. For other Quiche
recipes, see (I, 214)

BARQUETTES FOR CANAPÉS

I. Prepare:
   Biscuit Dough, page 284,
   or Pie Dough, page 293
Roll it until it is about ⅛ inch
thick. Since barquettes are
shaped like a scow or flat-bot-
tomed boat, but with pointed
ends, use either a barquette
mold or something similarly
shaped to form the pastry. Place
in the barquettes a:
   Filling for Pastry
   Canapés, page 55
Bake for about 10 minutes in a
425° oven.

II. Line the bottom of the bar-
quettes with a coating of:
   Mayonnaise
Make a pattern of:
   Chilled caviar
   Pearl onions
Coat the top with:
   Aspic Glaze (I, 387)
The aspic should be based on
fish or chicken stock. Flavor
with:
   Lemon
Refrigerate several hours before
serving.

STUFFED CHOUX, PUFF PASTE OR PÂTÉ SHELLS

I. Bake:
   1-inch Choux Paste Shells,
   page 305, or Bouchées,
   page 304
Split them on one side. Fill

them with one of the softer
fillings, see:
   Fillings for Pastry
   Canapés, page 55
Reheat the puffs in a 425° oven.

II. For a marvelous tea-teaser,
put into the base of a small
cream puff shell a layer of:
   Whipped cream
Lightly insert with the pointed
end up:
   A flawless ripe
   strawberry

III. Or, fill the puffs with:
   Soft cream cheese
   A dab of bright jelly

TURNOVERS, RISSOLES OR FRIED PIES

These triangular or crescent-
shaped pastries make attractive
canapés. If baked, they are turnovers. If deep fat fried, you may
apply the homely title of fried
pies or the fancy one of rissoles.
Roll to the thickness of ⅛ inch
any:
   Pie Crust, page 293 or
   Puff Paste, page 300
Cut it into 2½-inch rounds or
squares. Place in the center of
each round any of the:
   Fillings for Pastry
   Canapés, page 55
Brush the edges of the rounds
lightly with water. Fold the
dough over into crescents. Be
sure to seal the rissoles very
firmly if you are deep fat frying,
so that none of the filling es-
capes into and ruins the frying
fat. The tops of the turnovers
may be brushed with:
   1 egg yolk, diluted with
   2 tablespoons cream
Bake them in a 400° oven until
brown or fry them in deep fat
heated to 360° to 370° (I,
75). Serve them around a large
garnish of:
   Fried parsley or chervil

CANAPÉ SNAILS

If the approval of guests is to be taken as a criterion of excellence, this is the prize-winning canapé, reminiscent of the guest who hesitated to help himself, saying, "Well, I shouldn't, I've had two already." Which remark was capped by his hostess' brisk and crushing reply: "You've had six, but who's counting?"
Roll into very thin oblongs any:

Pie Crust, page 293, or
crustless soft bread

The bread will be easier to cut if wrapped in foil and chilled thoroughly. Spread the oblongs with:

Fillings for Pastry
Canapés, below

Roll them like a jelly roll. Chill; cut in ½-inch slices and bake on a greased pan, in a 425° oven, until light brown.

TACOS

This popular Mexican treat is called by many names in different parts of the country. They are toasted tortillas cut into thirds and filled with hot or mildly seasoned ingredients. This one is fairly mild. Sauté until golden brown:

1 finely chopped onion

in:

2 tablespoons butter

Add and simmer for about 3 minutes:

½ cup tomato juice
3 peeled minced green chilis
1 cup shredded cooked chicken or pork sausage meat
⅛ teaspoon thyme
1 teaspoon salt
Dash of cayenne

Set this filling aside. Now fry in deep fat at 380° until crisp:

1 can tortillas: about 18

Remove them from the fat and drain. Cut into thirds. Place 1 teaspoon of the above filling on each piece. Fold in half, secure with a toothpick and bake until crisp in a 450° oven.

GLAZED CANAPÉS AND SANDWICHES

Small glazed canapés are very showy for cocktail service and in larger sizes make a lovely luncheon plate when garnished with a salad. ♦ But they must be kept refrigerated as they have a natural tendency to sogginess. Use:

Choux paste shells,
tartlets or fancy-shaped thin toasts

Coat these canapé bases first with:

Mayonnaise

Then spread them with:

Well-seasoned fish paste,
turkey, tomato slices,
ham strips, asparagus
tips

or any combination suitable for open-faced sandwiches. Cover with a ¼-inch to ⅜-inch layer of:

Well-seasoned aspic
glaze

using 1⅛ cups stock or vegetable juice, 1 tablespoon gelatin and 1 tablespoon lemon juice. Place the canapés on a rack. The aspic should be jelled to the thickness of heavy cream partially beaten. Allow it to coat the surface of the tart or envelop the canapé. Refrigerate at once and allow the gelatin to set 1 to 2 hours. Then serve as soon as possible.

FILLINGS FOR PASTRY CANAPÉS

Place in the center of the preceding pastry cases 1 teaspoon or more of one of the following ingredients:

Cheese Spreads, page
58

Anchovy paste and soft
cream cheese
Well-seasoned or mari-
nated oysters
Mushrooms, heavily
creamed and seasoned
Chicken or other
croquette mixtures,
highly seasoned
Chicken, lobster, crab or
fish salad
Caviar and soft cream
cheese
Liver sausage or
braunschweiger,
seasoned with catsup
Sausage meat, seasoned
with mustard
Link sausages, seasoned
with stuffed olives
Deviled ham, cream
cheese and catsup
Minced clams or crab
meat
Calf brains with
Hollandaise sauce
Curried shrimp or
poultry

ABOUT BUTTER SHAPES

Such a delicious staple deserves
attractive presentation. Try
using a butter curler, our favorite because the light ⅛-inch-
thick shell forms are such decorative assets and just the right
texture for spreading. Dip the
curler into warm water before
pulling it lightly over firm butter.
If the butter is too cold, the
curls will crack. Put the curls at
once into cold water and store
in the refrigerator until ready to
drain and serve. Keep butter
balls or molds described later in
good form the same way until
ready to use.

The easiest molds to handle
are those with a plunger. Both
the molds and the paddles for
butter balls must be conditioned
for use by pouring over them a
generous stream of boiling water.
Then plunge them at once into

ice water. Cut butter for molds
into ⅓-inch thick slices. The
mold will determine the size of
the squares. For an easy way to
make butter balls, use various-
sized melon ballers. Dip them
first in hot water. Scoop out the
butter ball and drop it into a
dish of ice water. Serve them
piled in a small pyramid or cone
in a covered, sliding-domed,
ice-racked butter dish.

Another attractive way to
serve butter is in small clay
crocks. Our favorite is one that
fits into a base which holds cold
water. Squares of butter can be
made attractive by even cutting.
For a smooth cut, sheath your
knife trimly in the butter
wrapper before you make a cut.
Decorate with tiny herb leaves
and/or flowers, lightly pressed
into the squares of butter.

BUTTER SPREADS

There are many ways of preparing good, quick sandwich
spreads with a butter basis. Beat
butter until soft. Add other ingredients gradually. Chill the
butter mixture until it is of a
good consistency to be spread or
make it into a shape.

Use one of the simple suggestions in this recipe or the more
elaborate Seasoned Butters that
follow. Also see (I, 383–385).
Beat until soft:

　　¼ cup butter
Add to the butter slowly one or
more of the following:

　　½ teaspoon lemon juice
　　½ teaspoon Worcestershire
　　　　sauce or ½ teaspoon dry
　　　　mustard
　　½ teaspoon grated onion or
　　　　minced garlic
　　(⅛ teaspoon lemon rind)
Good additions to the butter
mixture are a choice of the following—either chopped or made
into a paste by using your mortar and pestle:

2 tablespoons chopped
    parsley
2 tablespoons chopped
    chives
1 tablespoon chopped dill
1 tablespoon chopped
    mixed herbs: basil,
    tarragon, burnet and
    chervil
2 tablespoons chopped
    watercress
¼ cup soft or grated cheese:
    Parmesan or Romano
1 tablespoon anchovy or
    or other fish paste
1 tablespoon horseradish
1 tablespoon olive paste
2 tablespoons catsup or
    chili sauce
1 tablespoon chutney
¼ teaspoon curry powder
    Correct the seasoning

⋏ SEAFOOD BUTTER

For a more economical form, see
(I, 385). Put through a sieve
or blender or chop:

1 cup cooked shrimp,
    lobster, lobster coral,
    etc.
¼ lb. butter
1 teaspoon or more lemon
    juice
    A fresh grating of white
    pepper

Mold and chill to serve on an
hors d'oeuvre platter or use as
a spread.

DRIED HERBS IN WINE
FOR BUTTER SPREADS

Combine:

2 tablespoons crushed
    dried herbs: thyme, basil,
    tarragon, chervil
½ cup dry white wine or
    lemon juice

Permit the herbs to soak for 2
hours or more. Follow the above
recipe for Butter Spreads, using
a little of this mixture. Keep the
rest to use combined with
melted butter as a dressing for
vegetables.

⋏ BLENDER MUSHROOM
BUTTER

Sauté until golden brown:

½ lb. sliced mushrooms

in:

¼ cup butter

Put the mushrooms and butter
into an electric blender and add:

½ cup soft butter
¼ teaspoon black pepper
¼ teaspoon salt
3 tablespoons dry sherry
    or brandy

Blend until smooth.

NUT BUTTERS

I. Cream until soft enough to
stir:

½ cup butter

Stir in:

1 cup ground pecans or
   walnuts
2 tablespoons Worcester-
   shire sauce

II. ⅄ In an electric blender
combine:
   · 1 tablespoon salad oil
   1 cup salted nuts: peanuts,
      cashews or pecans

CREAM CHEESE SPREADS

What would we do without
cream cheese? The perfect emergency binder for the many taste-
provokers below.
Rub a bowl with:
   (Garlic)
Mash until soft and combine:
   1 package cream cheese:
      3 oz.
   1 tablespoon cream
Add one or more of the following:
   ½ teaspoon onion juice
   1 teaspoon chopped onion
      or chives
   1 tablespoon lemon or lime
      juice
   1 tablespoon finely chopped
      Fines Herbes, page 220
   1 tablespoon finely chopped
      parsley
   1 tablespoon finely chopped
      celery
   ¼ cup chopped stuffed
      olives
   1 tablespoon horseradish
   3 tablespoons crisped
      chopped bacon or
      minced chipped beef
   ½ tablespoon anchovy or
      fish paste
   ½ cup shredded salted
      almonds
   1 tablespoon caviar
Season with:
   Salt, paprika or red
      pepper, if needed
For a tea canapé, use a:
   Bar-le-Duc mixture, page
   472

CUCUMBER CREAM CHEESE SPREAD

Mash with a fork:
   2 packages cream cheese:
      6 oz.
Into a fine sieve or cheesecloth
bag, grate:
   1 medium-sized cucumber
   1 onion
Press out the juice and combine
with the cream cheese. Add:
   Salt to taste
   ⅛ teaspoon hot pepper
      sauce
Now add until of spreading
consistency:
   Mayonnaise

CHEESE PUFF CANAPÉS

Preheat Broiler
Beat until very stiff:
   2 egg whites
Fold in:
   1 cup grated American
      cheese
   1 teaspoon Worcestershire
      sauce
   ½ teaspoon paprika
   ½ teaspoon dry mustard
Toast on one side:
   Small rounds of bread or
      crackers
Spread the untoasted side with
the cheese mixture. Place the
canapés under a broiler for
about 6 minutes, until the cheese
is well puffed and brown.

ROQUEFORT SPREAD

This delicious spread keeps well
and improves with age—better
when 1 week old than when
newly made.
Combine to a paste:
   ½ lb. Roquefort cheese
   2 packages soft cream
      cheese: 6 oz. or use an
      8-oz. package
   2 tablespoons soft butter
   (1 small grated onion)
   1 tablespoon Worcester-
      shire sauce
   2 tablespoons dry sherry
   Salt as needed

Keep the spread in a closely covered jar in the refrigerator. May be spread on crisp potato chips, crackers or on toast rounds. Decorate with:

    Radish slices and capers

PUFFED ROQUEFORT STICKS

Have ready:

    4 slices bread

The bread should be several days old. Coat with:

    Butter

Prepare:

    ¾ cup Béchamel Sauce (I, 359, 360)

Combine with:

    2 oz. Roquefort cheese
    1 beaten egg
    Correct the seasoning

Spread the sauce on the bread and run under the broiler for 5 to 8 minutes. Serve at once.

CHEESE SPREADS FOR TOASTED SANDWICHES OR CHEESE DREAMS

I. This practical sandwich spread will keep for a week or more. Scald in a double boiler:

    ½ cup milk

Add:

    1 beaten egg
    ¼ teaspoon dry mustard
    ½ teaspoon salt
    ¾ lb. diced American cheese

Cook these ingredients over hot water for 15 minutes. Stir constantly. Cool the mixture and keep it in a closed jar in the refrigerator. When ready to use, spread it between:

    Rounds of bread

Place on each side of the canapés or sandwiches a generous dab of:

    Butter

Toast them in a 350° oven or under a broiler until they are crisp.

II. ⚘ This filling is more quickly made, but not as bland as the preceding one. Combine and stir to a smooth paste or blend in the electric blender:

    2 cups soft sharp cheese, grated if necessary
    ½ teaspoon salt
    A few grains cayenne
    1 teaspoon prepared mustard
    3 tablespoons cream or 1 to 2 tablespoons soft butter

Cut the crusts from:

    Thin slices of white bread

Spread and roll the slices. Toast as in I. Serve the rolls very hot.

CHUTNEY AND CHEESE CANAPÉS

Preheat Broiler

Cover:

    Round crackers or toast

with:

    Chutney
    A thin slice of American cheese

Broil the crackers to melt the cheese.

TOASTED CHEESE LOGS OR ROLLS

Preheat Oven to 350°

Trim the crusts from:

    Thin slices of bread

Place on each slice, not quite covering it:

    A thin slice of cheese

or, place on each slice of bread:

    An oblong block of cheese

Spread the cheese lightly with:

    Anchovy paste, prepared mustard or horseradish

Gather up 2 opposite corners and fasten them with a toothpick or roll the bread. Seal the ends, using:

    Butter

Brush the outside of the logs with:

    Melted butter

Toast them until light brown. Serve piping hot on toothpicks.

SWEET TEA SPREADS

For those of us afflicted with a "sweet tooth," it is always a welcome sight to behold on the canapé tray something less acid, spicy or tart than the usual fare. And don't forget those good Nut Butters, page 57, and Cinnamon Toast, page 289.

I. Moisten:
    Cream cheese
with:
    Rich milk
Add:
    Chopped ginger
    Chopped almonds
This is very good spread on:
    Brown bread

II. Spread on small toasts:
    Bar-le-Duc, page 472

III. Combine:
    1 package soft cream
        cheese: 3 oz.
    Rind of 1 orange or 2
        tablespoons orange or
        ginger marmalade
    ¼ teaspoon salt
    ⅛ teaspoon paprika
Spread:
    Thin slices of bread
with:
    Mayonnaise or butter
Cover them with the cheese and:
    Toasted chopped pecan
        meats

IV. Combine:
    Equal parts soft butter
        and honey

V. Spread toast with:
    Butter
    Apple butter
Sprinkle with:
    Grated cheese
Run under the broiler until the cheese is toasted.

HARD-COOKED EGG SPREADS

I. Combine and mix to a paste with a fork:
    2 hard-cooked eggs
    1 tablespoon or more thick
        cultured sour cream
    ¼ teaspoon salt
    ⅛ teaspoon paprika
    1 tablespoon chopped
        chives
    (1 teaspoon lemon juice)
Garnish the canapé with a row of:
    (Sliced stuffed olives)

II. Combine:
    4 chopped hard-cooked
        eggs
    1 cup chopped pecan
        meats
    2 dozen chopped stuffed
        olives
    Well-seasoned
        mayonnaise

III. Shell, then chop:
    Hard-cooked eggs
Combine them with:
    Minced anchovies
    Minced celery
Moisten these ingredients with:
    Mayonnaise

IV. Marinate for 30 minutes:
    Shrimp or crab meat
in:
    French dressing or lemon
        juice
Drain and combine, by making into a paste with:
    Mayonnaise
    A dash Worcestershire
        sauce
    Hard-cooked eggs

V. Combine:
    Finely chopped
        hard-cooked eggs
    A liver pâté (I, 524)

ROLLED ASPARAGUS CANAPÉS OR SANDWICHES

Cut the crust from:
    Thin slices of bread
Spread them thinly with:
    Butter and mayonnaise
Sprinkle lightly with:

Chopped chives

Place on each slice a well-drained:

Asparagus tip

Roll the canapés. Wrap the rolls in waxed paper until ready to serve. These sandwiches may be toasted.

AVOCADO SPREAD OR GUACAMOLE

★ A good holiday touch is a bit of pimiento or a slice of stuffed olive.

I. Pare:

1 or 2 ripe avocados

Mash the pulp with a fork. Add:

Onion juice and lemon juice

Salt

(Tomato pulp—a very small amount)

Heap this on small crackers or toast. Garnish with:

Paprika and parsley

II. Have ready a combination of:

1 peeled, seeded, chopped ripe tomato

1 finely chopped scallion: 2 inches green

(½ seeded, chopped green pepper)

½ teaspoon chili powder

1 teaspoon olive oil

1 tablespoon lemon or lime juice

½ teaspoon coriander

Salt and pepper

Add to the above, just before spreading:

2 mashed ripe avocados

MUSHROOM CANAPÉS

Sauté, see (I, 79)

Mushrooms

Mince the mushrooms. Prepare:

Cream Sauce II (I, 359)

Make ½ as much sauce as mushrooms. Season it with:

Salt and paprika

Freshly grated nutmeg

Combine sauce and mushrooms. When cold, add a little:

Whipped cream

Heap these ingredients on:

Small rounds of bread or toast

Garnish the canapés with:

Paprika and parsley

Serve immediately or run under the broiler.

ONION AND PARSLEY CANAPÉS

Parsley has the power to neutralize onion odors. Use it profusely in this decorative sandwich, so no one will know you have indulged.

Make a filling of:

1 drained grated onion

1 cup heavy mayonnaise

¼ teaspoon Worcestershire sauce

A few drops hot pepper sauce

⅛ teaspoon turmeric

Put the filling between small rounds of:

Brioche-type bread

or a bread that will not become soggy. Spread the outside edge of the sandwich with:

Mayonnaise

and roll these edges in:

Finely chopped parsley

BLACK RADISH CANAPÉ

Peel and mince:

2 black radishes

Combine with:

1 small minced onion

2 tablespoons cultured sour cream or yogurt

1 tablespoon lemon juice

⅛ teaspoon salt

Just before serving, spread on thin slices of:

Pumpernickel bread

TOMATO OR CUCUMBER SANDWICHES

These sandwiches are very attractive for a spring tea party. Cut:

Small rounds of bread
Spread them lightly with:
Butter
Place on each round, covering it completely:
Small round of sliced tomato or a large round of pared sliced cucumber or both
Decorate each sandwich with a generous:
Dab of mayonnaise
For daintiness, but not for food value, slice tomatoes, then drain them for 2 hours to keep the sandwiches from being soggy.

CAVIAR AND ONION CANAPÉS

I. Sauté in butter:
Rounds of thin toast
Combine and spread on the toast equal parts of:
Caviar
Finely chopped onion
Season with:
Lemon juice
Garnish the edges of the canapés with:
Riced hard-cooked egg yolks
Top with:
(Tiny shrimp or prawns)

II. Sauté:
Chopped onions
in:
Butter
Make a mound of the chopped onions on a round of:
Pumpernickel bread
In the scooped-out center, put some:
Cultured sour cream
and a dab of:
Caviar

CAVIAR AND CUCUMBER CANAPÉS

Dip:
Slices of cucumber
in:
French dressing
Drain them. Prepare:

Small rounds of buttered toast
Peel, then slice crosswise:
Mild onions
Separate the slices into rings. Place a ring on each round of toast, so that it will form a wall. Place a slice of cucumber in each ring. Cover the cucumber with:
Small mounds of caviar, seasoned with lemon and onion juice or chives
Garnish the canapés with:
Capers
Riced hard-cooked eggs

TENDERLOIN AND CAVIAR CANAPÉ

Trim half-frozen:
Tenderloin of beef
to fit small squares of:
Melba toast
Spread the toast first with:
Onion Butter, page 56
then with a layer of the tenderloin and some:
Caviar

CHICKEN OR HAM SALAD SPREAD

Chop until fine:
1 cup cooked chicken or ham
Add:
2 tablespoons finely chopped celery
¼ cup chopped blanched almonds or other nut meats
(¼ cup chopped pineapple or ½ cup finely chopped green olives)
Combine these ingredients with sufficient:
Highly-seasoned mayonnaise
to make a paste that will spread easily.

SMALL PIZZA CANAPÉ

Good with cocktails, tea and for late evening or barbecues.

Tear in two, fairly evenly, but do not cut:

> Small English muffins
> or biscuits

Toast on flat sides only, at least 5 inches below broiler heat. On the broken sides, spread:

> 1 teaspoon chili sauce
> (¼ teaspoon spaghetti sauce)
> Strips of sharp Cheddar
> or grated mozzarella or
> Gruyère cheese
> ⅛ teaspoon oregano

Top with an:

> Anchovy fillet

and drizzle over all:

> A little olive oil

Return to the broiler and toast until the cheese is thoroughly melted. For a different flavored pizza, see (I, 213, 214).

FOIE GRAS AND
LIVER PASTES

You may serve pâté in the classic manner (I, 526); cut it into rondelles on toast; or incorporate it into Brioches, page 258, Bouchées, page 304, pastry, barquettes or turnovers. Use it for stuffing olives, artichoke hearts or mushrooms; or roll it up like small cheroots, in the thinnest slices of prosciutto. Use also in individual molds, glazed with port wine or aspic jelly. See (I, 524–525) for a number of versions of liver pastes, soufflés and pâtés—both simple and complex.

LIVER SAUSAGE CANAPÉS

I. Combine and mix to a paste:

> ¼ lb. liver sausage
> 1 or more tablespoons
> cream

Add:

> ¼ cup or more chopped
> watercress

Serve on rye bread or toast.

II. Make a paste of:

> ½ cup mashed liver sausage

> 2 tablespoons tomato paste
> (A few drops
> Worcestershire sauce)

Spread on thinly-cut crustless bread, then roll and toast.

CLAM PUFFS

Try some of the "Dips" on page 83, in this same manner.
Combine:

> 1 package cream cheese:
> 3 oz.
> 2 tablespoons heavy cream
> 1 cup minced clams
> ¼ teaspoon dry mustard
> 1 tablespoon
> Worcestershire sauce
> ¼ teaspoon salt
> ½ teaspoon grated onion
> or onion juice

Heap the mixture on toast rounds and broil.

CRAB OR LOBSTER
PUFF BALLS

Serve these only if you have time to whip the cream and fill the puff shells at the last minute. The charm of this canapé lies in the bland creaminess of the filling and the dry crunchiness of the casing.
Shred or dice:

> Cooked crab or lobster
> meat

Combine lightly 2 parts of the chilled seafood with:

> 1 part stiffly whipped
> seasoned cream

Put the mixture into:

> Small cream puff shells,
> page 305

Sprinkle the tops with:

> Chopped parsley and
> basil

Serve open or put puff lid on top after filling. Good hot or cold, but serve at once—and we mean at once.

MARINATED HERRING
AND ONIONS ON TOAST

Drain:

> Marinated herring

Place the fillets on:
>Squares or rounds of
>toast
Cover with:
>Thin slices of Bermuda
>onion
Sprinkle with:
>Chopped parsley or
>watercress

LOBSTER SPREAD

Combine:
>Chopped cooked lobster
>meat
>Chopped hard-cooked
>eggs
>Chopped cucumbers
>Well-seasoned
>mayonnaise

HOT LOBSTER, CRAB
OR TUNA CANAPÉS

Combine:
>½ lb. cooked lobster, crab
>or tuna meat
>½ lb. Sautéed Mushrooms
>(I, 296)
>1 cup rich Cream Sauce
>II (I, 359)
>1 tablespoon finely
>chopped green pepper
>1 tablespoon chopped
>pimiento
>¼ teaspoon curry powder or
>1 teaspoon Worcester-
>shire sauce
>3 tablespoons dry white
>wine
>Salt and pepper
Heap the mixture on rounds of:
>Toast
which may be spread with:
>Anchovy paste
Sprinkle the tops with:
>Au Gratin II (I, 389)
Heat the canapés under a broiler
until slightly brown. Serve at
once.

HOT CREAMED OYSTER
CANAPÉS

Messy but good little things!
Prepare:

>Creamed Oysters (I,
>425)
Place the pan containing the
oysters over hot water. Toast
and butter lightly:
>Small rounds of bread
Place a coated oyster on each
round. Sprinkle with:
>Chopped parsley
Serve the canapés at once.

ANGELS ON HORSEBACK

May also be served as a savory,
see page 472.
Toast lightly and butter:
>Small rounds of bread
Wrap:
>Large drained oysters
with:
>Thin pieces of bacon
Secure with toothpicks and
place the canapés in a pan. Bake
at 400° for about 3 minutes or
long enough to crisp the bacon.
Remove the toothpicks and serve
on the rounds of toast.

SMOKED SALMON
CANAPÉS

If the salmon you are served is
pale pink and not salty, it has
been truly smoked; but if it is a
strong red in color and very
salty, smoke salt extract, page
197, has been used in the processing. Salmon for canapés
should be sliced across the
grain. It is delicious served garnished with cucumber or egg
and, when thinly sliced, it makes
an ideal lining for tarts or barquettes.

I. Place on round waffle wafers
or crackers:
>Squares of smoked
>salmon
Top them with a slice of:
>Stuffed olive
Brush the canapés with:
>Mustard or Aspic Glaze
>(I, 387)

II. Or, top the salmon with:

Guacamole, page 61 and serve on toasted rounds.

SARDINE CANAPÉ ROLLS

Mash with a fork:
    12 skinless, boneless
        sardines
Add:
    ½ teaspoon Worcestershire
        sauce
    ½ teaspoon tomato catsup
    1 tablespoon finely cut
        celery or onion
    1 tablespoon chopped
        stuffed olives
Moisten these ingredients until they are of a good consistency to be spread with:
    Mayonnaise or French
        dressing
Season with:
    Salt and pepper
Cut the crusts from:
    Thin slices of white
        bread

Spread the sardine mixture on the bread. Roll the slices and secure them with toothpicks. Toast the canapés in a 400° oven and serve very hot.

SHRIMP PUFFS

[24 Puffs]
Preheat Broiler
Clean, then cut in half:
    12 shrimp
Whip until stiff:
    1 egg white
Fold in:
    ¼ cup grated cheese
    ⅛ teaspoon salt
    ⅛ teaspoon paprika
        A few grains red pepper
    ½ cup mayonnaise
Heap these ingredients lightly onto crackers or rounds of toast. Garnish each one with ½ shrimp. Broil the puffs until light brown. Serve hot.

HORS D'OEUVRE

Hors d'oeuvre and canapés are appetizers served with drinks. The canapé sits on its own little couch of crouton or pastry tidbit, while the hors d'oeuvre is independent and ready to meet up with whatever bread or cracker is presented separately. Many hors d'oeuvre are themselves rich in fat or are combined with an oil or butter base to buffer the impact of alcohol on the system. If, during preprandial drinking, the appetizer intake is too extensive, any true enjoyment of the meal itself is destroyed. The palate is too heavily coated, too overstimulated by spices and dulled by alcohol. A very hot, light soup is a help in clearing the palate for the more delicate and subtle flavors of the meal. The very name "hors d'oeuvre," literally interpreted, means "outside the main works." These hold themselves aloof as do the famed Russian Zakuska or the Italian antipasto, the so-called "dry" soup of southern countries. But hors d'oeuvre and antipasto, in spite of their separatist quality, may even replace the soup course when the portions offered are somewhat more generous in size or amount.

♦ Allow about 6 to 8 hors d'oeuvre per person.

Serve imaginative combinations, but remember that, unlike the opera overture the hors d'oeuvre course should not forecast any of the joys that are to follow in its train. Never skip hors d'oeuvre or canapés when you are serving drinks, for they play a functional role, but there is no harm in keeping them simple—just olives, salted nuts and one or two interesting spreads or canapés, so the meal that is to follow can be truly relished.

Should you serve—either in the living room or at the table—caviar in pickled beets or anchovy eggs on tomatoes, forget the very existence of beet and tomato when planning the flavors of the dinner. This is not a superfluous caution, for one encounters many unnecessarily repetitious meals. ♦ Choose for living-room service bite-size canapés or hors d'oeuvre, unless you are furnishing plates. ♦ If hors d'oeuvre are meant to be hot, serve them fresh from the oven. If they are the type that will hold, use some form of heated dish. ♦ Have cold offerings right out of the refrigerator or on platters set on cracked ice. Cheeses should be presented at a temperature of around 70°.

There are recipes given in other chapters of this book that are suitable for hors d'oeuvre. It is difficult to assign certain dishes to a single course, as they may be as versatile as Alec Guinness. So, be sure to look in Salads, Fruits and Luncheon dishes, as well as in the Index. The Index may not be literature but a careful perusal of it will sometimes produce a poem.

Set hors d'oeuvre off with plenty of attractively-cut vegetables (I, 38), and garnishes of fresh herbs and greens (I, 39).

Here are a few types of food

which are particularly appropriate for the hors d'oeuvre course: caviar, pâté and terrines, vegetables à la grecque, stuffed artichoke hearts, mushrooms, beets, Brussels sprouts and cherry tomatoes. You may also use spreads and dips; deviled, pickled, truffled or chopped eggs; skewered or bacon wrapped tidbits; smoked, sauced or mayonnaised seafood; quenelles and timbales; choice sausages, both hot and cold; glazed or jelled foods; nuts, olives or cheeses. And, from the Salad chapter, choose individual aspics, a filled ring of aspic (I, 57), one of the mousses (I, 62), or an Italian Salad (I, 40).

ABOUT WAYS TO SERVE HORS D'OEUVRE AND CANAPÉS

Food often looks more dramatic if some of it can be presented on several levels. This old dodge has been manifested in some really frightening ways. Look at the complex, inedible architectural underpinnings by which the glories of ancient chefs used to be supported and still are today, on celebratory occasions, in some large hotels and restaurants. Artificial coloring, rigid aspics, fussy detailing abound. These techniques for presenting food in fancy form are unpleasantly obvious and eating quality is sacrificed. Don't torture the food. Instead, play up its gustatory highlights and allow its natural subtle colors and textures to shine. Keep in mind what the platter will look like as it begins to be demolished. For this reason, it is often wiser to arrange several small plates which are easily replaced or replenished than one big one which may be difficult to resurrect to its pristine glory.

First described are some mechanical aids to give platters a lift. Here are a few of the simplest: cut a grapefruit in half or carve a solid base on an orange or apple, place cut-side down on a plate, stud with hors d'oeuvre—and surround with a garnish of canapés, as upper left, page 68. You may also cut a melon or use a small, deep bowl or a footed bowl as a receptacle for hors d'oeuvre and surround it with canapés, as shown on the right and center.

Stud a pineapple, cut as shown page 68, or see other ways, page 106, to make this highly decorative fruit a focal point.

Try cabbages, especially savoys, among whose beautiful curly-veined, velvety leaves small shrimp can cascade down onto the plate surface. The center can be hollowed out to hold invisibly a glass container for a dip, or use red cabbages, whose color can be picked up with stuffed beets and modified with artichokes and pâté slices. Even plain, everyday cabbages can be made interesting if you persuade your green-grocer to let you have one from which the outer leaves have not been hacked or if you can get one direct from a garden. Then curl the leaves back carefully, so as not to bruise them and cut a cavity into which you can insert a sauce bowl, deep enough so the curled leaf edges will conceal its rim as shown right below.

Just by the placement of food on the platter you can bring about height variations and attractive color relationships. On an oblong plate, center some dainty triangular sandwiches, peaks up like a long mountain range. Alternate sandwiches of a fine ham spread or thinly sliced ham with others made of caviar or mushroom spread or

with thin buttered bread. Place small, well-drained marinated shrimp along the base of the range, on either side, and accent the water cress garnished edge of the platter with French endive or celery filled with Guacamole, page 61, and smoked salmon, wrapped around asparagus tips.

Try to choose edible garnish for hors d'oeuvre trays. You may want to use beautifully cut vegetables, see (I, 39). ◆ Should the vegetables for garnish or hors d'oeuvre be watery, like tomato or cucumber, be sure to rid them of excess moisture by draining well.

If platters are not passed and you want a table accent, place hors d'oeuvre directly on crushed ice, on a layered tray similar to the one shown on page 40 or on a simple epergne. ◆ If you use a silver or metal tray, you may want to protect it from food acids by an undergarnish of lettuce, grape leaves or croutons.

We saw a chef friend rapidly arrange a tray almost entirely from stored foods—a gala quickie if you feel suddenly convivial when an unexpected mob descends on you with short warning. Garnish a large platter with lettuce. For the center,

make a large mound of Russian salad (I, 40), using canned drained vegetables, of shrimp salad or of Spiced Cabbage Mound, page 75. Garnish it with slices of tomato with hard-cooked egg slices on them—topped with a tiny tip cluster of tarragon, thyme or parsley; or, cut the eggs and tomatoes into wedges and border the mound by placing the wedges against it, with the yolk side against the salad, see page 74.

If you want something less rich, you might use a mound of cottage cheese decorated with tender stalks of burnet pressed into the mound to resemble coarse fern fronds and accented with borage blossoms. You may also make a double spiral of overlapping radish discs and fill the interspace with chopped chives. Place at each end of the platter sardines or asparagus tips held by onion or lemon rings (I, 39). Prepare onion cups (I, 39), to hold caviar and surround them with lemon slices. Use a crock of cheese, a good cheddar or Liptauer, page 472, or Cucumber-Cheese Spread, page 58. Even a can of good white meat tuna, unmolded and coated with mayonnaise and attractively garnished with ripe olives or capers,

looks well with canned drained artichoke hearts or hearts of palm. Fill in with shrimp or mussels. Sprinkle vinaigrette sauce, sour cream, mayonnaise or even catsup over one or another of these items; or place small bowls of sauces on the platter. Green pepper, cucumber or onion cups (I, 39), also make attractive containers for the dips.

Don't forget an occasional garnish of anchovy or pimiento strip and even the ubiquitous radish or gherkin, see (I, 39). And remember that a plate of interesting breads and crackers is a tremendously attractive foil to all of this rich, highly seasoned food.

ABOUT ANTIPASTO

This ever-present constituent of Italian menus is a great snack bar of fine hard sausages; prosciutto with melon or figs; fish, such as anchovies, sardines and Mediterranean tuna; pickled onions, beets, peppers, artichokes, cauliflower and mushrooms; highly seasoned Garbanzos; and cold eggplant in tomato purée. It also includes fresh tomatoes, fennel, cheeses —the hard types, as well as mozzarella and ricotta, fine crusty breads, and deep-fat fried fish, meat, fowl or game, which go under the name of Fritto Misto when encased in a light batter.

Like hors d'oeuvre, antipasto —or "what comes before the pasta course"—can be a snack with drinks or the base of an entire luncheon.

Some recipes in this book, which are suitable for antipasto, are listed below. Serve them on platters or make them up on individual plates.

Tomato slices cut lengthwise

Vegetables à la Grecque (I, 257)
Anchovies
Seviche, page 80
Smoked Salmon Rolls, page 81
Rollmops, page 81
Pickled Oysters, page 82
Marinated Mushrooms, page 76
Stuffed Celery, page 76
Pickled Beets and Caviar, page 75
Eggplant Casserole (I, 291)
Sardines
Slices of salami
Hard-cooked eggs
Masked Eggs (I, 194)
Garlic Olives, page 77
Cucumber and green pepper sticks
Stuffed Leeks, page 76
Black Radishes, page 77

ABOUT SMORGASBORD

This Scandinavian spread has been in this country so thoroughly adapted to the casual cocktail hour that some of us have lost sight of its original importance. Smorgasbord in its original country is a square meal in itself, not the prelude to one. Its mainstays of meat and fish —and the aquavit which washes them down—are climatic imperatives when subarctic weather hovers for months outside the door. Like all native dishes, smorgasbord closely reflects a country's ecology and its people's way of life.

The foods of which a smorgasbord is traditionally composed are sufficiently dissimilar to require at least three plates and silver services per person, so that the flavors of one course do not disturb those of the next. Typical of those first presented are herring, hot and cold, smoked eel, salmon or shellfish —all served with small boiled potatoes, seasoned with dill—and at least three kinds of bread with small mountains of butter balls. In fact, it is bread and butter that gives this kind of meal its name.

With the first change of plate come cheeses, deviled eggs, pancakes and omelets with lingonberries, sausages, marinated and pickled vegetables and aspics.

With the next, hot foods follow, such as meatballs, ham with apples, goose with prunes, tongue and baked beans. Although many of these foods are prepared in advance, their true charm lies in the freshness of their garnish and arrangement. Do not leave the platters with their cut meats exposed too long to air on the buffet table.

To assemble a smorgasbord from some of the recipes in this book, see Herring, page 81 and (I, 411), Swedish Limpa Bread, salmon hors d'oeuvre, page 81, Salmon in Aspic (I, 415), Swedish Meat Ball (I, 519), Crêpes with Lingonberries, page 114, shrimp dishes, Swedish Roll Cookies.

ABOUT CRACKERS AND BREADS TO SERVE WITH HORS D'OEUVRE

Bought crackers and breads can be dressed up into delightful additions to the hors d'oeuvre table with the cut of a knife, a few aromatic seeds, a bit of cheese and an oven. See About Fancy Breads and Crackers for Soup (I, 151), and Uses for Ready-Baked and Leftover Breads, page 288.

You can also bake small Biscuits, page 284, Beaten Biscuits, page 287, Corn Meal Crackles, page 278, and Corn Zephyrs Cockaigne, page 278. Bake Grissini, page 246, or some good rye, cheese or French breads.

Make Potato Chips (I, 319), and don't forget Cheese Straws (I, 152), and unsweetened pastries in variety, page 292–297.

NUTS AS HORS D'OEUVRE

These can be roasted or deep-fat fried.
I. Preheat oven to 250° to 300°.
To roast, put in a greased shallow pan:

> Blanched or unblanched
> nuts, page 189

Bake until golden, about 20 minutes. Sprinkle during baking with:

> (Melted butter)

seasoned with:

> (Celery salt, onion salt,
> cayenne or paprika)

II. Preheat deep fryer to 360°.
Have ready:

> Blanched or unblanched
> nuts, page 189, almonds,
> pecans, peanuts,
> pistachios or cashews

For every cup of nuts, allow:

> ½ cup cooking oil

Cook the nuts in the hot oil until golden. Pecans and Spanish peanuts will need about 2 minutes. Skim off and drain nuts on absorbent paper. After salting store tightly covered.

NUTS TOASTED IN THE SHELL

These are delicious served hot with cheeses or as snacks.
Preheat oven to 425°.
Roast in the shell, in a shallow pan, in the oven for about 15 minutes before serving:

> English walnuts

CURRIED NUTS

Combine in a skillet:

> ¼ cup olive oil
> 1 tablespoon curry powder
> 1 tablespoon Worcestershire sauce
> ⅛ teaspoon cayenne

When this mixture is very hot, add:

>   2 cups nuts: walnuts,
>   almonds, etc.

Stir until well coated. Now line a baking pan with brown paper, pour in the nuts and bake at 300° for about 10 minutes or until crisp.

TOASTED SEEDS

Separate the fiber from:

>   Melon, pumpkin, squash,
>   sunflower or watermelon
>   seeds

Cover with:

>   Salted water

Bring to a boil and ♦ simmer for 2 hours.

Drain and dry on brown paper. Then:

I. Deep-fat fry as for Nuts, above.

II. Spread the seeds in a shallow pan. Coat with:

>   Cooking oil
>   (Salt)

Bake in a 250° oven until golden brown. Stir from time to time.

PUFFED CEREALS FOR COCKTAILS

Melt in a skillet, over low heat:

>   1½ cups butter

Stir in lightly:

>   2 packages crisp small
>   cereals
>   1 tablespoon curry
>   Garlic
>   Celery salt
>   1 teaspoon Worcestershire
>   sauce
>   (1 cup pumpkin seeds or
>   nuts)

Mix gently until the cereal has absorbed the seasoned butter. Serve at once.

SEASONED POPCORN OR POPPED WILD RICE

Prepare:

>   Popcorn, page 517 or
>   wild rice as for popcorn

Season with:

>   Melted butter
>   (Squeeze of garlic or
>   onion juice)
>   (Grated sharp cheese)

STUFFED DRIED FRUIT APPETIZERS

Prepare well in advance, as described in Prunes in Wine, page 108:

>   Apricots, dates or prunes

Drain the fruit and reserve the liquor for sauces, gravies, etc. Place in each cavity 1 or 2 of the following:

>   A walnut or other
>   nutmeat
>   A canned water chestnut
>   A sautéed chicken liver
>   Chutney
>   Cheddar or Roquefort
>   cheese

The fruit may be served cold or hot. You may also wrap each piece with:

>   A narrow strip of bacon

Secure it with a toothpick and bake in a 375° oven until the bacon is crisp.

COLD SKEWERED TIDBITS

Alternate on small toothpicks:

>   Small onions with pieces
>   of cocktail sausages and
>   burr gherkins
>   Squares of cheese with
>   pickle slices, stuffed
>   olives or small onions
>   Slices of raw carrot and
>   blocks of tongue or ham
>   Shrimp, lightly flavored
>   with mustard and pieces
>   of celery
>   Squares of cheese and
>   slices of green onion,
>   topped with a ripe olive
>   Chilled balls of cream
>   cheese, sprinkled with
>   paprika or mixed with
>   chopped olives and pieces
>   of herring or anchovy
>   Pieces of ham or bacon
>   and watermelon pickle

Cubes of cooked turkey,
honeydew melon and
pistachio nut
Pieces of kippered
salmon or herring and
onions

In short, use your imagination
and your leftovers.

FILLED EDAM CHEESE

Fine for a buffet meal. Hollow:

An Edam or Gouda
cheese

Crumble the removed part:

I. Combine it with:

2 teaspoons or more
Worcestershire sauce or
red wine
1 tablespoon prepared
mustard
A few grains cayenne
1 or 2 tablespoons fresh or
dried minced herbs

II. Or, to preserve its lovely
characteristic flavor, blend just
enough:

Heavy cream

with the cheese to make it easy
to spread. Refill the cheese shell.
Serve it surrounded by toasted
crackers.

EDAM NUGGETS

[About 16]
Grate:

1 cup Edam cheese

Add:

2 tablespoons finely
chopped celery
⅛ teaspoon dry mustard
2 tablespoons cream or ale

Make into small balls and roll
in:

Finely chopped parsley

VICKSBURG CHEESE

Blend with a fork until smooth:

⅓ Roquefort cheese
⅓ Cheddar cheese
⅓ soft cream cheese

Sprinkle thickly a large piece of
waxed paper with:

Paprika

Roll the cheese mixture into a
sausage shape on the paper until
it has a generous coating of
paprika. You can cut it into
slices later. You may also roll
the mixture into a large ball,
which can be coated with:

(Chopped nuts)

Place in refrigerator to chill.

NUT CHEESE BALLS

Work to a paste:

½ cup Roquefort cheese or
part Roquefort and part
cream cheese
1 tablespoon butter
½ teaspoon Worcestershire
sauce or 1 tablespoon
brandy
½ teaspoon paprika
A few grains cayenne

Shape into 1-inch balls. Roll
them in:

¼ cup ground nutmeats
Chopped herbs or
watercress

Chill them. This is also effective
made into one large cheese ball.

GELATIN CHEESE MOLD

Dissolve:

1¼ teaspoons gelatin

in:

¼ cup cold water

Add, when melted and mixed
over hot water:

¾ cup American cheese
2 packages Neufchatel
cheese
1 teaspoon paprika

Beat well and add:

1 cup whipped cream

Beat until light and put in buttered mold. Ice for several hours
before serving. Unmold and garnish with:

Fresh burnet sprigs

ANCHOVY CHEESE OR
KLEINER LIPTAUER

Work until smooth:

2 packages cream cheese:
6 oz.

Work in:
    3 tablespoons soft butter
    2 minced anchovies
    1½ tablespoons grated onion
       or 1 minced shallot
    1½ teaspoons capers
    ½ teaspoon caraway seed
    ¾ teaspoon paprika
    2 drops Worcestershire
       sauce
       Salt, as needed
Shape the mixture into small
patties. Chill thoroughly.

NUT CREAMS

Roll into ¾-inch balls:
       Soft cream cheese
       (Squeeze of garlic or
       lemon juice)
Flatten them slightly between:
    2 salted English walnuts or
       pecans

CHEESE CARROTS

Grate:
       Yellow cheese
Moisten it, until it is of a good
consistency to handle, with:
       Cream or salad dressing
Shape it into small carrots. In
the blunt end, place:
       A sprig of parsley

ABOUT DEEP-FAT FRIED
HORS D'OEUVRE

If you can lick the service problem and get to your guests this
type of hors d'oeuvre while hot
and just out of the fryer, nothing
is more delicious. Consider the
many suggestions in this chapter
and also both the Japanese Tem-
pura (I, 258), and the Italian
Fritto Misto (I, 258), which
are deep-fat fried.

CHEESE BALLS
FLORENTINE

◗ Please read about Deep Fat
Frying (I, 75–79).
Preheat deep fryer to 375°.
Measure by packing closely:

    1 cup cooked, well-drained
       spinach
Put it through a purée strainer
or chop in the ⅄ blender until
fine. Stir in:
    2 beaten eggs
    1½ cups fine dry bread
       crumbs
    1 tablespoon grated onion
    ½ cup grated cheese
    1 teaspoon salt
    1 tablespoon lemon juice
Shape this mixture into 1½-inch
balls. Fry them in deep fat until
brown and crisp. Drain them on
absorbent paper. Serve with:
       Thickened Tomato
       Sauce (I, 376)
Spoonfuls of this mixture may
be sautéed in hot butter. Good
with Hollandaise Sauce (I,
368). The balls may be rolled in
1 egg, beaten with 2 tablespoons
water, then in sifted, seasoned
bread crumbs and again in the
egg mixture before being fried
or sautéed. Permit the crumbs to
dry for 20 minutes before frying.

FRIED CHEESE DREAMS

◗ Please read about Deep Fat
Frying (I, 75–79).
Preheat deep fryer to 375°.
Mix:
    ½ lb. grated Swiss cheese
    3 well-beaten eggs
    1 teaspoon double-acting
       baking powder
    1 tablespoon sherry
    ⅛ teaspoon paprika
Put some flour in a narrow glass
or cup. Drop a tablespoon of
the mixture into the flour and
swirl it until it is coated with
flour. Fry until a golden brown.

PASTRY CHEESE BALLS

[About 24]
Preheat oven to 400°.
Cream together:
    ½ cup sharp spreading
       cheese or grated
       American cheese
    3 tablespoons butter

Sift, then add:
> ¾ cup all-purpose flour
> ½ teaspoon salt
> ¼ teaspoon paprika
> ¼ teaspoon curry

When well blended, pinch off pieces of dough and form them into ¾-inch balls. They should be chilled for 2 hours but they may be baked at once. Bake for about 10 minutes. Serve hot or cold.

ABOUT EGGS AS HORS D'OEUVRE

Perhaps no other single food plays such a varied role in hors d'oeuvre as do eggs. You find them plain hard-cooked as a bland foil for the many spicy items surrounding them; deviled in the most complex ways, with anchovies, curry, capers, caviar; truffled and En Gelée (I, 63), or pickled (I, 195). They are particularly useful cut into fancy shapes as garnishes for other hors d'oeuvre—or with the whites chopped fine and the yolks pulverized, to add fresh color in decorating all kinds of foods.

Overlap slices of hard-cooked egg as shown at the top on the right, or pink the whites with an hors d'oeuvre cutter as shown second from the top on the left. Garnish egg slices with herbs, caviar, small shrimp or rolled anchovy fillets as shown on the bottom left and on the far right in the second row. Deviled or plain hard-cooked eggs may be similarly garnished and the deviled ones may be further decorated by using a pastry tube filled with the softened yolk. On the bottom right are 3 cuts for deviled egg cups. Shown second on the left is a molded salad garnished with sliced sections arranged in a pinwheel around a center of parsley or chervil. Another mold to the right shows a center of sieved egg and shreds of white which form a casual chrysanthemum motif. To make the egg and tomato wedge border on the top left, see page 68.

EGG APPLES
Prepare:
> Hard-cooked eggs

While they are warm, shell them and press them gently between the palms of the hands until they are round. Color them by placing them in beet juice or red vegetable coloring. Place in 2 sides of each egg, to represent the blossom ends and the stems:
> Cloves

Or shape the eggs, add the cloves and paint the cheeks of the eggs with a dash of red and a dash of green color.

CRAB-APPLE GARNISH

Roll into 1-inch balls:
> Coarsely grated yellow cheese

Place in one side of each ball:
> A whole clove

Place in the opposite side:
> The stem of a clove

Sprinkle one cheek of each ball with:
> Paprika

GARNISH ASPARAGUS SPEARS

Drain:
> Canned white asparagus tips

Wrap around the base of each spear:
> Thinly sliced ham

Serve chilled.

AVOCADO AND CHUTNEY

Peel just before serving and slice lengthwise into 4 to 6 thick slices:
> Avocado

Fill the hollow at the base of each slice with:
> Chutney

MARINATED BEANS

Drain:
> 2 cups canned Garbanzo beans or freshly cooked haricots blancs

Prepare the following marinade and soak the beans in it for four hours:
> 2 tablespoons lemon juice
> 2 tablespoons red wine vinegar
> ½ cup olive oil
> Garlic clove
> Various herbs

Drain and serve chilled.

STUFFED BEETS COCKAIGNE

I. Prepare, leaving them whole, very small shapely Beets (I, 270) or canned beets. If small beets are not available, shape large ones with a melon scoop. Hollow the beets slightly. Fill the hollows with:
> Caviar

sprinkled with a very little:
> Lemon juice

Garnish with:
> A sprig of parsley or lemon thyme

II. Fill the beet cups with:
> Frozen Horseradish Sauce (I, 343)

III. Or fill them with a combination of:
> Chopped hard-cooked eggs
> Mayonnaise
> Herbs, preferably chives and tarragon

IV. You may also fill them with:
> Chopped vinaigretted cucumbers

and garnish with:
> Anchovy

STUFFED BRUSSELS SPROUTS

Drain well:
> Cooked or canned Brussels sprouts

Cut a small hollow in each one, preferably from the top. Drop into each hollow:
> ½ teaspoon French dressing

Chill them. Fill them with any good:
> Sandwich spread

Use liver sausage and tomato paste, cream cheese and chives or anchovy, adding the chopped center portion of the sprouts to the spread. Garnish with:
> A sprig of parsley, savory, basil, etc.

Serve several as a salad or use as hors d'oeuvre.

SPICED CABBAGE MOUND

A decorative platter for a buffet or first course.
Shred:
> White cabbage

Dress it with equal parts of:
> Mayonnaise
> Chili sauce

Arrange it in a mound. Cover the top with:
> Marinated shrimp

Surround the mound with:
> Deviled eggs, topped with caviar

MARINATED CARROTS

Slice as thin as soup noodles:
> Carrots

Marinate the slices in:
> Lemon or orange juice
> A little sugar

Serve well chilled.

CELERY CURLS

Separate, then wash:
> A stalk of celery

Trim leaves, cut several long gashes into each rib. Soak in ice water until curled, as sketched.

STUFFED CELERY OR FRENCH ENDIVE

I. Combine:
> 1 tablespoon butter
> 1 tablespoon Roquefort cheese
> 1 package cream cheese: 3 oz.
> Salt
> (1 teaspoon caraway, dill or celery seed)

Place this mixture in:
> Dwarf celery ribs or French endive

If you want them to look very elegant, force the mixture through a large pastry tube. Sprinkle with:
> Paprika

Chill.

II. Or, fill celery with:
> Guacamole, page 61

III. Another wonderful filling is:
> Caviar and cultured sour cream, with a little lemon juice

CUCUMBER LILY

Have ready:
> Thinly sliced unpeeled cucumber rings
> 3-inch carrot sticks

Gently fold the cucumber slice around the base of the carrot stick. Fold a second slice around the stick from the other side. This forms the lily petals, with a carrot stamen in the center. Fasten with a toothpick, being careful to catch all four lapped edges of the cucumber as well as piercing the carrot stick. Wrap flowers lightly in a moistened paper towel and refrigerate until ready to use as garnish for the hors d'oeuvre or salad tray.

STUFFED LEEKS

[18 to 24 Pieces]

Cut into 1½-inch cross sections the white portions of:
> 3 large cooked leeks

When chilled, cut the cross sections in two, lengthwise. Stuff the leeks with Shrimp or Shad Roe Salad (I, 51). Coat the top with more:
> (Mayonnaise)

or garnish with a tiny sprig of:
> (Fresh lemon thyme)

MARINATED MUSHROOMS

Be sure to include in your repertoire Stuffed Mushrooms (I, 297–298).

The ranchers of the West frequently resort to a repast of raw mushrooms. Here is a variation. Cut into thin vertical slices:
> Large firm mushrooms or use very small button mushrooms

Marinate them for 1 hour or more in:
> French dressing
> (Dash herb vinegar)
> Chopped chives or onion juice
> Chopped parsley

Serve the mushrooms on:

Lettuce or water cress
or on toothpicks.

ABOUT OLIVES

So much fuss is made about
commercial grading and typing
of olives! The thing to remember
is that size is not always a matter of quality. You don't have to
be a connoisseur to know that
the big dull-green woody Queen
Olives can't compare in flavor
or in texture with the Manzanil-
las fines—those small, succulent,
yellowish green fruits.

Try various types in making
up your hors d'oeuvre tray. The
green ones, picked unripe, are
treated with a potassium or ash
solution and then pickled in
brine. Since they have not been
heat treated, a film sometimes
forms after opening the bottle. If
this happpens, you may float
olive oil on the surface of the
liquid in the bottle before re-
storing or rinse the olives in cold
water, drain, place in a clean jar
and recover with a solution of 1
teaspoon salt and 1 tablespoon
white vinegar to a cup of water.

The black ones are picked
ripe, put in a boiling brine and
sold dried, pickled or in oil. To
reduce the saltiness of dried or
pickled olives, store them in
olive oil that you can later use
for dressing.

The ripe olives found on an
hors d'oeuvre tray have usually
been oil treated. There are many
ways to stuff them. For a real
treat, put in a little foie gras
and close with a pistachio nut.

GARLIC OLIVES

Drain the liquid from:
      Green or ripe olives
Add:
      12 peeled cloves garlic
Cover with:
      Olive oil
Permit to stand for 24 hours or
more under refrigeration. Drain.

Use the oil for salad dressing.
You may dust the olives with:
      Chopped parsley

MARINATED ONIONS

Skin, then slice:
      Bermuda onions
Soak them for 30 minutes in:
      Brine: ⅔ cup water to
      1 tablespoon salt
Drain. Soak them for 30 minutes
in:
      Vinegar
Drain, then chill them. They are
then ready to be served side by
side with celery, radishes, olives,
etc.

PEPPER HORS D'OEUVRE

Remove skin from:
      Peppers
by roasting under the grill until
burned. Remove the core and
seeds. Marinate in:
      Olive oil
      Lemon juice
for 15 minutes. Slice the peppers
into thirds. On each strip, put:
      1 tablespoon tuna salad or
      anchovies with capers
Roll the strips like small sausages. Garnish with the marinade and:
      Chopped parsley

RADISH HORS D'OEUVRE

I. Dip whole or strips of:
      White or red radishes
in:
      Whipped cream
seasoned with:
      Salt
      Vinegar

II. Or serve red radishes cut in
rose shapes, filled with:
      Anchovy Butter or
      Other Seasoned Butters
      (I, 383)

III. Remove the rind from and
slice thinly across the grain solid
black radishes. Soak them covered in a little salted water for

about 15 minutes. Drain, marinate in a mixture of:
>   Oil
>   Vinegar
>   White pepper

Serve chilled.

TIDBITS IN BACON OR HAM

Surround any of the following:
>   Pineapple chunks
>   Spiced cored crabapples
>   Prunes, stuffed with almonds
>   Watermelon pickles
>   Dates, stuffed with pineapple
>   Skinned grapefruit sections
>   Large stuffed olives
>   Pickled onions
>   Smoked oysters or mussels
>   Raw scallops or oysters
>   Cooked shrimp
>   Sautéed chicken livers

with:
>   Thin strips of ham or bacon

Secure them with picks. Broil until the meat is crisp.

PROSCIUTTO AND FRUIT

On small toothpicks alternately interlace:
>   Prosciutto or Virginia ham slices

around:
>   Melon balls
>   Pineapple, pear or peach chunks
>   Fresh figs

The fruit may be marinated in:
>   (Port wine)

At the very tip of the toothpick, impale a clustered tip of:
>   Mint leaves

MARROW HORS D'OEUVRE

Bake:
>   Beef marrow bones

Serve the marrow with long spoons. It is delicious.

CANNIBAL MOUND OR STEAK TARTARE

Combine:
>   2 lbs. raw, scraped or finely chopped, fresh, lean steak

with:
>   2 raw egg yolks
>   ½ cup finely chopped onions
>   4 mashed anchovies

and the following, to taste:
>   Capers
>   Chopped parsley and herbs
>   Worcestershire sauce
>   Olive oil

Serve in a mound, garnished with whole anchovies and sprigs of parsley and surrounded by small squares of pumpernickel bread, or shape small balls of the above mixture and roll in:
>   chopped parsley

MEAT BALL HORS D'OEUVRE

Prepare:
>   Tiny Meat Balls, Hamburgers, Nutburgers, Koenigsberger Klops (I, 518), or small size Dolmas (I, 522)

Season them well. Serve them very hot on toothpicks or between small biscuits.

TONGUE, CHIPPED BEEF OR BOLOGNA CORNUCOPIAS

Prepare one of the following spreads:
>   Seasoned Cream Cheese, page 58
>   Hard-Cooked Egg Spread, page 60
>   Piccalilli, page 588
>   Cultured sour cream and horseradish

Spread the mixture on very thin slices of:
>   Smoked boiled tongue, chipped beef or bologna

Roll into cornucopias. Or stack

6 slices. Wrap them in waxed paper. Chill. Cut into 6 or more pie-shaped wedges.

TINY BROILED SAUSAGES

Heat on a hibachi or broil:
>   Very small sausages

Serve them hot on toothpicks with:
>   Mustard Sauce (I, 363)

RUMAKI

Cut into bite-size pieces:
>   Chicken livers

sprinkle with:
>   (Soy sauce)

Prepare an equal number of:
>   ¼-inch canned water chestnut slices

Marinate the chestnuts in:
>   (Port wine)

Wrap a slice of liver and one of water chestnut together in:
>   ½-inch-wide slice of bacon

Secure with a wooden toothpick and broil slowly, until the bacon is crisp. Serve hot.

SHERRIED CHICKEN BITS

Stew and place while still warm into a large jar:
>   Breasts of fat stewing hens

Leave the meat on the bone and cover with:
>   Sherry

Cover the jar closely and refrigerate for 10 days before using. To serve, skin, bone and cut the meat into bite-size pieces. Serve cold on toothpicks.

CHOPPED GOOSE OR CHICKEN LIVERS

For other liver hors d'oeuvre, see (I, 524 and 528).
Drop into boiling seasoned water and simmer until barely done:
>   1 lb. chicken livers

Drain them and cool. Cook until hard, shell, chop and add:
>   2 eggs

Chop coarsely, then sauté:

>   2 medium-size onions

in:
>   2 tablespoons butter

Chop or blend these ingredients until they are a fine paste.
>   Correct the seasoning

Add:
>   (2 tablespoons chopped parsley)
>   (1 oz. cognac or brandy)

TURKEY AND OLIVE HORS D'OEUVRE

Roll:
>   Thin slices of turkey

around:
>   Large pitted green olives

ABOUT CAVIAR AND OTHER ROES

A lady was once moved to ask plaintively why caviar is so expensive; to which a quick-witted maître d' replied: "After all, madam, it is a year's work for a sturgeon." The word caviar applies only to salted roe, but the best caviar is the roe of the sturgeon. The most sought-after form comes from Russia or Iran where highly-skilled workers prepare it. It is neither fishy nor briny in taste, as 2% of salt is enough to hold it. The eggs should be shiny, translucent, gray and large grained. ◆ As it spoils in a few hours in temperatures of 40° or above, always serve on ice. Its high oil content keeps it from freezing. To prepare caviar, see page 546.

To serve individual portions attractively, heat the back of a metal spoon, press it into an ice cube and fill the depression with the caviar—using a plastic spoon. ◆ Never allow the caviar itself to touch metal or to be served on it. If you spread it on canapés or in barquettes, see page 54, or stuff beets with it, page 62, be careful not to bruise the eggs. The classic accompaniments are lemon wedges, parsley, black bread or not-too-dry toast. Although egg whites, yolks and onions—all very finely minced and separately arranged —are more frequently served as the garnish, they are not considered by connoisseurs as suitable as the simpler lemon and parsley. Other favored ways of service are in Blinis with Sour Cream, page 116. or simply mixed half and half with sour cream and served with pumpernickel.

Other types of roe used as caviar are those of the salmon, cod, herring, tuna and gray mullet. Serve, as suggested for sturgeon roe, with slightly iced white wines, never red ones. To cook roes, see (I, 416). An ideal accompaniment to caviar dishes is champagne or vodka.

ABOUT SEA TIDBITS

When you go collecting at the shore, you can often find edible treats. Sketched are shellfish that can be eaten raw as hors d'oeuvre. Shown on the left are first 2 kinds of cockles, then an oyster. A sea urchin appears next to the right above the oyster. Known as a sea egg, it can be cooked just like soft boiled eggs and eaten with buttered toasted bread or puréed for tart filling. If cooked, cut the urchin on the concave side. The easiest way is to use scissors and remove the gut which surrounds the edible tangerine-like sections. In flavor it is not unlike

brains. To eat out-of-doors, simply throw them on the rocks to crack them open. ◗ Just be certain to use gloves when handling sea urchins. Directly below the urchin is a clam, next 2 kinds of mussels and a razor clam. Following in the upper row, are first a limpet. You eat the foot and discard the visceral hump. Then you see a tiny winkle which can be extracted with a pin. Below the winkle is a bay scallop, and on the far right a sea scallop. In these the hinge muscle is edible. For other sea tidbits try small shellfish (I, 421), in spicy sauces. Serve hot or cold. Due to red tides, mollusks may be poisonous during the summer months. Be sure to check local conditions.

SEVICHE

Marinated raw fish is very popular in South America as an hors d'oeuvre. If you are squeamish, you may prefer, as the Spaniards do—for a similar effect in their Escabèche—to poach the fish lightly and pour over it a hot marinade, based on olive oil and vinegar, rather than rely on the acid of lime juice. Refrigerate, covered, for 24 hours and serve cold; or,

I. Skin, remove bones from lemon sole, pompano or red snapper or use flaked crab meat. Dice:

  2 lbs. very fresh,
    firm-fleshed fish

Marinate in a glass dish, covered,

and refrigerate for 3 to 4 hours, entirely immersed in:

    2 cups lime juice
    ½ cup finely chopped onions
    ¼ cup chopped green chilis
    1 cup chopped, peeled and
      seeded tomatoes
    2 teaspoons salt
    A few grains of cayenne
    ⅛ teaspoon oregano

Serve in small scallop shells. Garnish with:
    Hot chili peppers
Serve with:
    Cornmeal Crackles,
    page 278
    tortillas or hot red
    peppers

II. Cut into quarters:
    1 cup raw scallops
Cover with:
    ½ cup lime juice
and marinate refrigerated overnight. Drain. Add:
    2 tablespoons finely
      chopped onion
    1 tablespoon finely
      chopped parsley
    2 tablespoons finely
      chopped green pepper
    3 tablespoons olive oil
    Correct the seasoning
Serve as a garnish in a bowl with individual toothpicks.

FISH BALLS

Prepare very small:
    Codfish Balls (I, 408)
Serve them hot on toothpicks with:
    Tartar Sauce

HERRING, ANCHOVY OR SMOKED SALMON ROLLS

I. Cut into ½-inch strips:
    Pickled herring, smoked
    salmon or anchovies
Roll the strips around tiny:
    Sour-sweet or other
    gherkins

Secure and serve the rolls with picks.

II. Cut into very thin slices:
    Smoked salmon
Spread them with:
    Cream cheese, seasoned
    with cucumbers,
    horseradish, chopped
    chives or parsley
Roll the strips. Secure and serve them with toothpicks.

HERRING OR SARDINE HORS D'OEUVRE

Place on plates:
    Lettuce leaves
Build up into a cone:
    Finely shredded onion
    or pickled pearl onions
    Finely shredded cole
    slaw, topped with pieces
    of pickled herring,
    sardine or anchovy
Pour over the cone:
    Cultured sour cream
The cream may be thinned with a few tablespoons of the liquor from the pickled herring. Have all ingredients very cold.

ROLLMOPS

On a:
    Herring fillet
place a layer of:
    Capers
    Chopped shallots
    Chopped gherkins
    A little prepared mustard
Roll the fillet and fasten with a wooden toothpick. Place the rolled herrings in jars and cover well with:
    Wine vinegar
to which you add:
    Slivers of lemon peel
    Mustard seed
    Sliced onion
    Peppercorns
Allow the rollmops to steep for 10 days in the refrigerator. Drain and serve cold, lightly brushed with:
    Olive oil

COLD OYSTERS OR MUSSEL HORS D'OEUVRE

Mix together carefully:
 Sour Cream Dip, page 83
Coat with this sauce:
 18 oysters or mussels in the
  half shell
Decorate tops with:
 Red caviar
Serve on a bowl of ice.

PICKLED OYSTERS

Combine in the top of a double
boiler:
 1 quart oysters
 1 quart oyster liquor
Heat until the oysters are plump.
Drain and wipe the oysters. Reserve the liquor and simmer it
for 15 minutes with:
 1 tablespoon peppercorns
 1 tablespoon whole allspice
 1 thinly sliced lemon
 2 tablespoons vinegar
  Dash of hot pepper sauce
  Correct the seasoning
Pour the sauce over the oysters
and refrigerate at least 24 hours
before serving.

ASPIC-GLAZED SHRIMP

Clean and devein (I, 441):
 1½ lbs. boiled shrimp
Cut them lengthwise down the
center, as shown on (I, 441).
Prepare:
 Aspic Glaze (I, 387)
Chill the glaze until it begins to
set. Spear the shrimp on tooth-
picks. Dip them into the glaze.
When partly set, dip them again.
Chill well. Serve cold.

PICKLED SHRIMP

Warn your guests about these—
they're hot!
Cover:
 5 lbs. shrimp
with:
 Flat draft beer or ⅔
  vinegar and ⅓ water
Add:
 1 tablespoon bruised
  peppercorns

 ¼ cup salt
 3 bay leaves
 1 teaspoon hot pepper
  sauce or ⅛ teaspoon
  cayenne pepper
 ¼ cup chopped celery tops
Bring to a boil and simmer for
15 minutes. Remove from the
heat and let shrimp stand in the
liquor for at least 1 hour in the
refrigerator. Drain and serve on
a platter of crushed ice.

☰ BROILED SHRIMP

Without cutting into the meat,
shell, clean and devein (I,
441).
 2 lbs. jumbo shrimp
Be sure to leave the tails on.
Marinate the shrimp in the refrigerator for several hours in:
 1 clove pressed garlic
 1 cup olive oil
 ½ cup sauterne wine
  Juice of ½ lemon
 3 tablespoons parsley and
  basil, chopped together
 1 teaspoon salt
 ¼ teaspoon pepper
Grill or broil the shrimp for
about 10 minutes, being careful
not to scorch them. Serve at
once with:
 Lemon Butter Sauce
  (I, 384)
flavored with:
 1 large pressed clove of
  garlic

FRIED SHRIMP BALLS

Mix and shape into balls:
 1¼ lbs. shelled, deveined,
  minced shrimp
 6 finely chopped canned
  water chestnuts
 1 piece finely chopped
  ginger
 1 small chopped onion
 1 egg white
 1 teaspoon cornstarch
 3 teaspoons wine
 1 teaspoon sesame or
  cooking oil
  Dash of pepper

Fry in deep fat, heated to about 360°, until golden brown.

ABOUT DIPS

Maybe overused, they are still the most popular type of hors d'oeuvre and the easiest to prepare. Good before dinner or for afternoon and late evening snacking. However, we feel that dips are not good for large groups, as it is too difficult to hand them around often enough. Don't forget to use some of the fine spreads listed earlier in Canapés. Make them juicier ▶ but still on the firm side, with a little cream, lemon juice or mayonnaise and choose additional seasonings to your own taste.

Try putting your favorite dip in this kind of bowl: a hollowed-out red cabbage, grapefruit or eggplant or a lovely scooped-out pineapple which, on fern or grape leaves, delights the eye and tantalizes the palate.

FOODS TO BE DIPPED

Crackers
Potato chips
Small wheat biscuits
Toast sticks
Corn chips
Fried Oysters (I, 423)
Cooked shrimp
Iced cucumber strips
Iced green pepper strips
Cauliflower florets
Carrot sticks
Radishes
Celery sticks
Peeled broccoli stems, etc.

SOUR CREAM DIPS

I. Combine:
  2 cups thick cultured sour cream
  2 tablespoons chopped parsley
  2 tablespoons chopped chives
  1 teaspoon dried herbs

⅛ teaspoon curry powder
½ teaspoon salt
¼ teaspoon paprika

II. Combine:
  1 cup cultured sour cream
  1 or more tablespoons horseradish
  ½ teaspoon salt
  ¼ teaspoon paprika

CHEESE DIPS

The mania for cheese dips, cold, has replaced that for cheese dips, hot—without which no party used to be complete. But don't forget those old favorites, Welsh Rarebit, made with beer, and Cheese Fondue (I, 239).
I. Combine:
  ¾ lb. cheddar cheese
  ¼ lb. Roquefort cheese
  2 tablespoons butter
  ½ teaspoon Worcestershire sauce
  ½ teaspoon mustard
  ¼ teaspoon salt
  ½ pressed clove of garlic
and melt over heat with:
  1 cup beer

II. Beat until smooth:
  2 packages cream cheese: 6 oz.
  1½ tablespoons mayonnaise
  1 tablespoon cream
  ¼ teaspoon salt
  1 teaspoon grated onion or chives
  1 teaspoon Worcestershire sauce

LONG-KEEPING CHEESE SPREAD OR DIP

[About 1½ Cups]
This keeps well and makes excellent toasted cheese sandwiches or a sauce. Thin it as needed with a little milk in a double boiler.
Cut into small pieces and stir over very low heat, or in a double boiler, until melted:
  ½ lb. cheese
We find a soft cheese or a proc-

essed one preferable for this recipe. Add:

1 cup evaporated milk
¾ teaspoon salt
¾ teaspoon dry mustard
¼ teaspoon curry powder
¼ teaspoon dried herb

Remove from the heat and stir in:

1 beaten egg

Stir and cook the cheese mixture very slowly until the egg thickens slightly. Remove from the heat. Pour it into a dish. Cool it slowly. Beat it as it cools, to keep a crust from forming, cover and chill.

ORIENTAL DIP

Good with raw mushrooms and raw cauliflower.
Combine:

½ cup finely chopped green onions
½ teaspoon fresh coriander
¼ cup chopped parsley
2 tablespoons chopped fresh ginger
1 tablespoon soy sauce
2 tablespoons canned chopped water chestnuts
1 cup cultured sour cream
2 tablespoons mayonnaise

CAVIAR DIP

Whip:

½ cup whipping cream

Fold in:

2 to 3 tablespoons caviar
1 to 2 tablespoons finely chopped onion

Place in the center of a dish and garnish with:

Sliced hard-cooked eggs and small toast rounds

CLAM DIP

Drain:

1 cup minced clams

Combine them with:

1 package soft cream cheese: 3 oz.
1 tablespoon

Worcestershire sauce
A pinch of dry mustard
Salt, as needed
1 tablespoon, more or less, onion juice
¼ cup heavy cream

CRAB MEAT OR TUNA DIP

Flake:

1 cup crab meat or tuna

Stir in:

2 tablespoons mayonnaise
1 to 2 tablespoons tomato paste or catsup
Juice of 1 lemon
Seasoning, as needed
(Chopped celery or olives)

SHRIMP DIP

I. Combine:

1 can cooked shrimp: 5 oz.
1 cup large curd creamy cottage cheese
3 tablespoons chili sauce
½ teaspoon onion juice
2 teaspoons lemon juice
1 to 2 tablespoons cream, if needed

II. Put through a coarse food chopper:

1½ lbs. cooked, cleaned shrimp
2 tablespoons capers
1 very small onion

Combine the above ingredients in a mixing bowl with:

¼ lb. soft butter
¼ cup heavy cream
¼ cup Pernod or dry white wine

Season with:

Salt
Hot pepper sauce
Tarragon
Chopped parsley

Mix well until of the consistency of whipped cream. Pack in a pretty mold which has been rinsed in cold water and refrigerate, covered, for 3 or 4 hours. Unmold and garnish with:

Cherry tomatoes

FRUITS

Too often the menu-builder takes herself too seriously and tops off a rich edifice with a disastrously rich dessert when fresh fruit with, perhaps, a cheese would be a far happier conclusion of the meal for all concerned. Well worth exploiting are the virtues of fruit—in either cup, compote, salad or sherbet form—as a "lightener" during, as well as after, a big meal.

If fruits lack flavor, serve them or prepare them with candied peels, ginger, zest or spices; or add a little lemon or lime juice to cooked fruits and fruit fillings. Vary the flavor of a particular fruit by processing it in the juices of other fruits, or in wine, or by blending it with other fruits in a purée. You may glaze poached fruit with contrasting fruit jellies, especially those of apple and quince, which are high in pectin. Also combine canned, frozen and fresh fruits—cold or slightly heated—in what the French call a compôte composée. Try presenting your "composed compôte" in a giant lidded snifter, laced with brandy or liqueur and serve it to your guests in smaller individual snifters.

Serve Fruit Soups, pages 91 and (I, 114); Fruit with Custards, page 436, or Creams, page 377–378; Fruit Brûlé, page 90, or Flambé, page 90. For dried or preserved fruits used as garnishes, see About Candies and Glazed Fruits, page 522. For fresh fruit combinations, see below and also consult the chapter on Salads, pages 101–104.

ABOUT FRESH FRUITS

Andrew Marvell, the Puritan poet, wrote these lines:

> What wondrous life is this I lead!
> Ripe apples drop about my head;
> The luscious clusters of the vine
> Upon my mouth do crush their wine;
> The nectarine, the curious peach,
> Into my hands themselves do reach;
> Stumbling on melons, as I pass,
> Ensnared with flowers, I fall on grass.

Like Marvell, we have a passion for fruit. Like him also, we have encountered, in acquiring it, a few pitfalls.

Be wary of "fruit specials." Such produce may include pieces which are below standard in either quality or size. Therefore, they could prove to be no bargains at all. U. S. Government standards are of necessity variable, but you can judge for yourself as to size by the units packed to the box ♦ the smaller the number of fruits per box or basket, obviously, the larger the individual fruit.

If purchased underripe, fresh fruits should be kept at room temperature in a dark place. Place them loosely so the fruits are separated in partially closed paper bags. Examine them twice daily, keep from bruising and, as soon as ripened, chill in the refrigerator before serving.

Most fresh fruits lose their flavor rapidly when soaked in water, so always ◗ wash them quickly in gently flowing water and dry at once. Below are some recipes for fresh fruit combinations.

FRUIT CUPS

Use attractive small bowls or glass cups. ◗ To frost them, see page 30. Use seedless grapes, citrus sections, watermelon, green and yellow melons, cut into balls with a French potato cutter, see (I, 39). Queen Anne cherries and cubed fresh pineapple combine well.
Chill and prepare for serving.
Fresh fruit
Five minutes before serving, sprinkle lightly with:
Powdered sugar
Immediately before serving, flavor with:
Lime juice, lemon juice, sherry or lightly sweetened fruit juice
Garnish with:
Candied Mint Leaves

AMBROSIA   [4]

This is a versatile old favorite, especially popular in the South. Peel carefully removing all membrane:
2 large Valencia oranges
Peel and cut into thin slices:
3 ripe bananas
Pineapple is sometimes added, as are other fruits. Combine and stir:
¼ cup confectioners' sugar
1½ cups shredded coconut
Arrange alternate layers of oranges and bananas in individual serving dishes or in a bowl. Sprinkle each layer with part of the coconut mixture, reserving some for the top. Chill well before serving. Instead of coconut, try a garnish of:
(Crushed mint and a cherry or a strawberry)

MACÉDOINE OF FRESH FRUITS

The following fruit and wine or liqueur combinations should be composed of ripe, perfect, pared, seeded and sliced seasonal fruits. Favorites for this dessert are strawberries, raspberries, peeled seedless green grapes, peaches, apricots, avocado slices, orange and grapefruit sections, melon balls, cherries and nectarines. Be sure to prick the fruits to allow the marinade to soak in. If you use raw apples or pears, marinate the slices for several hours in wine or liqueur or they will be too hard.
Some good marinating combinations are:
Cognac with oranges
Brandy with cherries and clove-studded peaches
Port with melon balls
A macédoine is usually served cold, but you may flambé it, see page 90, if the fruit is at room temperature—and if you add extra liqueur, slightly warmed. Place in layers in a crystal bowl:
Prepared fruit, see above
Sprinkle each layer with:
Powdered sugar
Stir the fruit gently until the sugar is almost dissolved, then add for each quart of fruit:
2 to 4 tablespoons cognac, brandy, rum or kirsch
Serve very cold over:
Vanilla ice cream, page 484
or with:
Cake

FRUIT FOOLS   [4]

Long ago the word "fool" was used as a term of endearment. We have an old-fashioned fondness for the recipes in which fruit is combined with cream.

I. With Fresh Fruit

Prepare:

> Raspberries or
> strawberries

Add to taste:

> Powdered sugar

Let the mixture stand for 10 minutes. Now combine with an equal amount of:

> Thick cream

Flavored with:

> (3 tablespoons kirsch, port
> or Madeira wine)

Chill well before serving.

II. With Cooked Fruit

Whip until stiff:

> 1 cup heavy cream

Fold in:

> 1 cup applesauce, rhubarb,
> berry, apricot, currant or
> other fruit purée
> 1½ teaspoons grated lemon
> rind or ¼ teaspoon
> almond extract

Place the mixture in the bowl from which it is to be served. Sprinkle the top with:

> Crumbled macaroons

Chill thoroughly. Serve with:

> (Ladyfingers, page 359)

ABOUT COOKED FRUITS

A good reason for serving fruits uncooked is to retain fully their high vitamin content. But we can minimize the loss of vitamins and of natural sugars by using as little water as possible and by cooking briefly. Fruits may be poached, puréed, baked, broiled, sautéed or pickled, see Spiced Sirup, opposite.

Fruits should always be poached rather than stewed. ♦ Drop them into a boiling liquid ♦ reduce the heat at once and simmer until barely tender. Remove them from the heat and drain them immediately afterwards, so that they will not continue to cook in the pan and get mushy. Soft, very juicy fruits, like ripe peaches, are best poached if they are put, for a few moments, into heavy boiling sirup and if the pan is then plunged into a larger pan of cold water to arrest the cooking. Apples and other hard fruits should be poached in simmering water. Watch closely, so that they do not overcook. If necessary, add sugar, but only after poaching. A baked fruit compote or a mixture of cooked fruits makes a refreshing addition to a meat course, provided that fruit juices have not been used in basting the meat. Always pare fruit with a ♦ stainless knife to keep from discoloring.

SIRUPS FOR FRUIT

Thin Sirup

For apples, grapes and rhubarb.

Combine and heat:

> 1 cup sugar
> 3 cups water
> ⅟₁₆ teaspoon salt

Medium Sirup

For apricots, cherries, grapefruit, pears and prunes.

Combine and heat:

> 1 cup sugar
> 2 cups water
> ⅛ teaspoon salt

Heavy Sirup

For berries, figs, peaches and plums.

Combine and heat:

> 1 cup sugar
> 1 cup water
> ⅛ teaspoon salt

SPICED SIRUP FOR FRESH FRUITS

[Enough for 1 to 1½ Pints Fruit]

Tie in a cheesecloth bag:

> 1½ teaspoons each cloves,
> allspice and cinnamon

Add and boil for 5 minutes:

> 1½ cups white or brown
> sugar or 2 cups honey
> 1 cup cider vinegar
> 1 cup water

Remove the spice bag and discard. Drop the prepared fruit into the boiling sirup. Cool and serve.

SPICED SIRUP FOR CANNED FRUITS

Drain and reserve the sirup from:

> Canned peaches, apricots, pears or pineapple

Measure the sirup and ▶ simmer until slightly reduced with:

> ¼ to ½ as much wine vinegar

Allow for every 2 cups of juice and vinegar:

> 1 stick cinnamon
> ½ teaspoon cloves without heads
> (2 or 3 pieces gingerroot)

After simmering for about 10 minutes, add fruit. Remove the pan from the heat and allow the fruit to cool in the liquid. Serve hot or cold with meat.

POACHED OR "STEWED" PARED FRUIT

Boil for 3 minutes:

> Any sirup for Fruit, page 87

Drop, into the boiling sirup, about:

> 1 quart prepared fruit

▶ Reduce the heat at once. Poach gently until tender. You may season the sirup with any of the following:

> Spices
> Crème de Menthe
> Wine
> Stick cinnamon
> Slice of lemon

Drain fruit and reduce sirup. Pour sirup over fruit and chill before serving.

POACHED OR "STEWED" THIN-SKINNED FRUIT

By adding the sugar late in the cooking as suggested here, you will need less of it to sweeten

the same quantity of fruit than if you had used it from the start. This method will also keep the skin soft.
Boil:

> 2 cups water

Prepare and add:

> 1 quart unpared fruit: peaches, pears, apricots or nectarines

Reduce heat at once. Simmer fruit until nearly tender. Add:

> ½ to ¾ cup sugar

During the last few minutes of cooking, add:

> (A Vanilla Bean, page 201)

POACHED OR "STEWED" THICK-SKINNED FRUIT

Use whole or cut into halves and remove the seeds from:

> 4 cups thick-skinned fruit: plums, blueberries or cherries

Drop them into:

> 1 to 1½ cups boiling water

Reduce heat at once. ▶ Simmer until nearly tender. Add:

> ½ to 1 cup sugar

Cook a few minutes longer.
▶ After cooking blueberries, to which lemon juice is a good addition, shake the container to avoid clumping.

BAKED FRESH FRUIT COMPOTE   [4]

Use as is or as a garnish for custard or blancmange.
Preheat oven to 350°.
Pare:

> 8 small peaches, apples or pears

Place them whole or in thick slices in a baking dish. Combine, heat but do not boil, stir and pour over them:

> ⅔ cup red wine or water
> ⅔ cup sugar
> ½ stick cinnamon
> 4 whole cloves
> ⅛ teaspoon salt

½ thinly sliced seeded
lemon or lime

Bake the fruit either covered or
uncovered until tender when
tested with a fork. If cooked uncovered ♦ it must be basted
every 10 minutes. For more
rapid and even cooking, some
people prefer to turn the fruit
over after the first two bastings.

ADDITIONS TO
BAKED FRUITS

I. To be served with meats. Fill
centers of fruits with:

Mint, currant or
cranberry jelly or
Roquefort cheese

II. Add:

Pearl onions and
shredded candied ginger

PURÉED FRUITS

Puréed fruits are most delicate
if cooked covered over gentle
heat. ♦ We do not recommend
pressure cooking of any fresh
fruits. Apples, rhubarb and cranberries, especially, tend to sput-
ter and obstruct the vent during
cooking. However, should you
be tempted to use a pressure
cooker, do not remove the cover
until all steam is exhausted. ♦ If
you want to purée canned fruit,
you should know that a No. 2½
can will yield 1¼ to 1½ cups.

GARNISHES FOR
PURÉED FRUITS

Serve puréed fruit hot or cold,
with one of the following toppings:

Grated lemon rind,
cinnamon or nutmeg
and cream
Chestnuts and marmalade
6 crushed dry macaroons
to 1 cup whipped cream
Cultured sour cream,
sugar, rum and nuts
Bread or cake crumbs

browned in butter with
slivered chopped
almonds
Freshly chopped mint

BROILED FRUITS

Drain:

Poached or canned
peaches, pears or
pineapple

Place them, hollow side up, in
a shallow pan. Place in each
hollow:

A dab of butter

Sprinkle each piece of fruit
lightly with:

Salt and cinnamon

Broil the fruits under moderate
heat until light brown. You may
fill them with:

(Cranberry or other jelly)

FRESH FRUIT KEBABS

Serve with meat course or as a
dessert. Marinate for about 30
minutes:

6 canned peach halves—
drained and cut in half
3 thickly sliced bananas
2 apples, cut in sections
1 cubed fresh pineapple
3 sectioned grapefruits

in:

1 cup grapefruit juice
½ cup honey
2 tablespoons Cointreau
(1 teaspoon chopped mint)

Broil on skewers for about 5
minutes, basting often with the
marinade.

ABOUT FLAMBÉING
FRUITS

For a good effect, use at least 2
oz. of alcoholic liquor and remember that ♦ unless the temperature of the fruit is at least
75°, you may not get any effect
at all. For best results, heat the
fruit ♦ mildly in a ♦ covered
chafing dish or electric skillet.
♦ Warm the liquor, too, but do
not boil it. Sprinkle the fruit

lightly with sugar and, after pouring the warm liquor over the warm fruit, re-cover the pan for a moment before lighting. Stand back—be careful.

FLAMBÉED FRUITS

This recipe makes 6 servings as a sauce, but only 3 if used as a main dish. Caramelize, page 169, lightly over low heat:

> 3 tablespoons sugar

Add:

> 3 tablespoons butter

or, if you are lazy, melt the butter first and substitute brown sugar, stirring until dissolved. Cook over very low heat for 4 to 5 minutes. Add 2 of the following:

> 3 split bananas, peaches or pears or 3 slices pineapple

Simmer until tender, basting occasionally. Since the banana will cook more rapidly than the rest of the fruit, it should be added later. Flambé the fruit, see above, with:

> 2 oz. cognac, dark rum or liqueur

FRUIT BRÛLÉ

[4 to 5]

This recipe is most often made with seedless green grapes, but it lends itself equally well to strawberries, raspberries and peaches.
Preheat broiler.
Fill the bottom of a 9-inch oven-proof baker or glass pie pan with an even layer of one of the above-mentioned:

> Fruits

Cover the fruit with:

> 1 cup cultured sour cream

mixed with:

> 1 teaspoon vanilla

The cream should then be dusted very evenly with:

> About 1 cup light brown sugar

so that none of it shows through.

Place the filled pan over a pan of equal size filled with:

> Cracked ice

Put the stacked pans under the hot broiler until the sugar caramelizes, page 439. This is a moment of watchfulness, as the sugar must fuse but not scorch. Refrigerate, covered, for 5 hours before serving.

SAUTÉED FRUITS

Core and slice or cut in rings:

> 6 tart, well-flavored apples, peaches, apricots or pineapple slices

Melt in a skillet over quick heat:

> 2 tablespoons butter or bacon drippings

When the fat is hot, to the point of fragrance, fold in the fruit. Cover until steaming. Sprinkle with:

> ½ cup sugar or brown sugar
> ⅛ teaspoon salt

Cook, uncovered, over gentle heat until tender. Add, if needed:

> (Butter)

Serve with a meat course or with:

> Bacon

To serve with meat, you may begin making this dish by placing a layer of onions, about 1 cup, in the butter. Cook slowly for 5 minutes. Season with salt and paprika. Add the fruit, as directed.

CURRIED FRUIT

Fruit in season may be dipped into or served in a two-way hot sauce—hot with both spice and heating. Cut into cubes or finger-size sections:

> 4 doz. pieces of fruit— pineapple, tropical mangoes, bananas, melons and papaya

Combine and simmer, covered, for ½ hour:

> 1 cup chicken broth
> 1 cup dry white wine

1 tablespoon curry

Add:

1 tablespoon quick-cooking tapioca

dissolved in:

3 tablespoons water

Stir the sauce until thickened. Add:

1 cup freshly grated coconut

1 cup slivered, toasted almonds

½ cup white raisins

Keep the sauce hot in a chafing dish and add the fruit pieces or place them alongside as dippers.

ABOUT COOKED DRIED FRUITS

Do not wash or soak dried fruits unless it is called for on the package. The less water used, the more natural sugars will be retained within the fruit. If you must soak fruit such as dried apples, cover with water for about 12 hours and then use the soaking water in further preparation. Allow 1 pound dried for 3½ to 4 pounds fresh apples and proceed as for any apple recipe. In using dried dates, raisins and currants, see Ingredients, page 191.

Fine quality dried dessert fruits are an elegant note on the cheese platter, especially dried Malaga grapes. Only a few are needed, as they are nutritively rich, see page 191. Should any of the fruits have become unpleasantly dried out, steam them lightly—sprinkled with wine or water—in the top of a double boiler ▶ over—not in—hot water; or, prepare them for stuffing by steaming 10 to 15 minutes in a colander ▶ over boiling water, until tender enough to pit. Stuff with a hazelnut or with fillings suggested under confections, page 520. If you would like to use some of the smaller, drier types, do not wash or soak them

unless it is called for on the package. The less water used in steaming—either for eating uncooked or processing for compote—the more natural sugar will be retained. Often no further sweetening is necessary.

ABOUT FRUITS FOR MEATS AND ENTRÉES

Fruit Compotes, page 86, Fruit Kebabs, page 89, Sautéed Fruits, page 90, or Pickled Fruits, pages 592, 593, served with meat are neglected delights. Consider using as occasional decorative fruit garnishes:

Apple Rings
Glazed Filled Apricots
Kumquats
Orange Slices with Cranberry or other jelly
Ornamental Cranberries
Filled Apples and the Filled Fruit Cases, page 208, stuffed with Farces (I, 564)

ABOUT FRUIT SOUPS

Soups of cooked fruit juice combinations with cherries, orange slices or puréed fruits added, are delightful at the beginning or end of a summer meal. If served at the beginning, go easy on the sugar. Fruit soups are also refreshing when made from frozen fruits, in winter, as a dessert.

FRUIT SOUP [4] COCKAIGNE

This good German fruit pudding, Rote Gruetze, long popular in our family, is usually made with raspberry juice. It is designed to end a meal, not, like the less sweet Fruit Soups (I, 114), to begin it. Strawberries, cherries or black currants may be used, but our favorite base is a combination of raspberry and strawberry juice, which may be strengthened with raspberry

jelly or red wine. A wonderful fresh taste may be obtained in winter, if you cook frozen raspberries and strawberries and strain off the juice.
Bring to a boil:
> 2 cups fruit juice

Sweeten it palatably with:
> Sugar

Season with:
> ⅛ teaspoon salt

Stir into the boiling juice:
> 2 to 2⅔ tablespoons tapioca

Cook this mixture in the top of a double boiler ◗ over—not in —hot water for about 20 minutes. Stir until it thickens. Pour into individual serving dishes. Chill. Serve very cold with:
> Heavy cream

ORANGE FRUIT SOUP   [6]

Scrub and remove the orange-colored peel in shreds from:
> 1 Valenica or navel orange

Add these peelings to a sirup of:
> 1 cup sugar
> ½ cup currant jelly
> ¼ cup water

◗ Simmer for about 15 minutes. Meanwhile, section the peeled orange, page 104, and also:
> 5 more peeled Valencia or navel oranges

◗ Cool the sirup to about 85°. Pour it over the orange sections. Add:
> 2 tablespoons brandy

◗ Refrigerate, covered, for about 12 hours, before serving with:
> A crisp thin Ice Box Cookie, page 399, or a Curled Cookie, page 409

Also good with:
> Cinnamon toast

INDIVIDUAL FRUITS

In the following pages we list various kinds of fruits, describing their particular charms and various ways to store and handle them. The exotic fruits shown on this page include, reading from left to right: the pomegranate, avocado, papaya, tropical mango and the oriental persimmon.

Opposite are sketched from left to right: figs, tamarind pods, akees, two forms of cherimoya, a guava, lichee nuts and a mangosteen.

PURÉED AKEE   [3]

Blighia sapida, named after the infamous Colonel Bligh, is one of the most strikingly beautiful, delicious and demanding of fruits for, unless it has ripened to the point of voluntary opening, it is a deadly poison. No fallen, discolored or unripe fruit dare be eaten and the greatest care must be used to ◗ remove all seeds before cooking, as these are always poisonous. When picked ripe, hulled and completely seeded, the akee is parboiled for use hot or cold. See illustration, above.
Remove the white pods from:
> 6 firm unbruised open akees

Discard every seed. Place the pods in:
> Boiling water

to cover. ◗ Reduce the heat at once and simmer gently until soft. Strain and mash them until coarsely crushed. Season with:
> Salt and pepper

(Grated Parmesan cheese)
(Toasted chopped cashews)

Although akee is technically a fruit it is served hot or cold with meats or fish like a vegetable.

ABOUT APPLES

Although apples are in the market the year around, they are not at their peak from January to June. The best month-to-month varieties are listed below. Check them and then turn to the next paragraphs which will tell you how to use the available apples at their prime. There is probably no flavor superior to that of the Greenups or Transparents, that fleetingly initiate the harvest. If you plan canning or freezing, do try to get the first picking for prompt preservation of this unusual tart flavor.

July to August: Early McIntosh, Gravenstein, Yellow Transparent
August to November: Wealthy
September to December: Grimes Golden
September to January: Jonathan, Late McIntosh
October to April: Red Delicious, Golden Delicious
October to January: Courtland, York Imperial, Rhode Island Greening
November to April: Newtown Pippin, Baldwin, Rome Beauty
December to March: Northern Spy, Stayman, Winesap
December to May: Winesaps

All-purpose apple varieties—good for eating, salads and for most cooking—are Yellow Transparent, Baldwin, Jonathan, Stayman, Winesap, Northern Spy, Wealthy, McIntosh, Gravenstein, Grimes Golden, York Imperial and Rhode Island Greening, which cooks best of all. So-called dessert apples—the firm types, most desirable for eating uncooked—are Delicious, Gold and Red Delicious and Newtown Pippin. Northern Spys, Wealthys and McIntoshes are not good bakers. ◗ Best for this purpose are Courtlands, Staymans, Winesaps, Baldwins and Rome Beautys, unless they are overripe. In that condition they become mealy.

Mealiness in apples may also denote too long or improper storage. Large apples tend to acquire greater mealiness during storage. If browning occurs near the core, the fruit has been stored at too low a temperature.

If you wonder why the apple in commercial pies has a firmer texture than yours, it is due to added calcium. If you notice also a more powerful apple flavor, this may be caused by the addition of a rather new product, made from the apple itself. If the flavor of your apples is poor, add lemon juice—but remember that nothing can really compensate for natural tartness. After paring, should apples seem dry, simmer their cores and skins, reduce the liquid and use it to moisten them during cooking.

If you receive a windfall from

a friend's orchard and want to reserve some of it, let it stand in a cool, shady place for 24 hours. Inspect for blemishes. Wrap each fruit in paper and store in slotted boxes in a cool, dark, airy place.

The old saw about the doctor and the daily apple has been reinforced by recent discoveries. Raw apple, we now learn, has properties which help the digestive juices kill germs in the stomach; and dentists like apples as a tooth-cleaning aid. So keep them around for family munching.

For Fried Apples, see below. For other apple recipes, see below and the Index.

APPLE RINGS

Wash, core and cut crosswise into slices:
    3 large perfect cooking
        apples
Heat in a skillet:
    3 tablespoons bacon fat or
        butter
Place in it a single layer of apple rings. Sprinkle lightly with:
    Powdered sugar
Add to the skillet:
    2 tablespoons water
Cover the skillet and ◗ simmer the apples until tender. Remove cover and brown rings on both sides. Serve hot, the centers filled with:
    Bright red jelly
or dust the rings with:
    Cinnamon

HONEY APPLES

An excellent way to use a dull-flavored apple. Heat in a small porcelain or stainless steel pan:
    1 cup honey
    ½ cup vinegar
Peel, core and slice thinly:
    2 cups apples
Drop the apples a few at a time into the simmering, bubbling honey mixture. Skim them out when transparent. Serve chilled or hot as a relish with pork, a tart filling, or a dessert with cream.

★ CINNAMON APPLES   [4]
    OR PEARS

Pare and core without cutting through the stem end:
    4 baking apples or pears
Stir and boil in a saucepan until dissolved:
    ½ cup sugar
    1 cup water
    ¼ cup cinnamon drops
Add the fruit slowly, one at a time. ◗ Simmer gently until tender. Test with a straw. Remove from sirup. Fill hollows with:
    (Blanched almonds or
        other nut meats and
        raisins)
Boil the sirup until it falls heavily from a spoon. Pour it over the apples. Chill.

SAUTÉED APPLES   [4]
AND BACON

A fine breakfast or luncheon dish.
Pare:
    Tart winter apples
Cut them into cubes. There should be about 4 cups. Sauté in a heavy skillet, see (I, 79):
    8 slices bacon
Remove the bacon when crisp. Keep it hot. Leave about 2 tablespoons of grease in the skillet.
Add:
    2 tablespoons cooking oil
Add the apples. Sauté uncovered over high heat until translucent. Sprinkle them with:
    2 tablespoons white or
        brown sugar
Place them on a hot platter. Surround them with the bacon. Serve garnished with:
    Parsley

BAKED APPLES [4]

I.

Preheat oven to 375°.
Wash, remove core to ½ inch
of bottoms, then cut a strip of
peel from the hollowed ends of:

 4 large tart apples

Combine:

 ¼ cup sugar or brown sugar
 (1 tablespoon cinnamon)

If the apples are bland, add:

 (⅛ teaspoon grated lemon
  rind)

Fill the centers with this. Dot
the tops with:

 Butter

Put in an 8 x 8-inch pan with:

 ¾ cup boiling water
 (2 tablespoons sugar)

Cover and bake forty to sixty
minutes—or until tender but not
mushy. Top the core holes
with a:

 (Marshmallow)

After removing from the heat,
baste the apples several times
with pan juices. Serve hot or
chilled.

II.

Obviously a richer dish than
that produced by recipe I.
Preheat oven to 425°.
Peel and core:

 6 apples

Fill the cores with a mixture of:

 ½ cup chopped blanched
  almonds or pecans
 ½ cup sugar
 2 tablespoons raisins
 (1 egg white)

Make another mixture of:

 ½ cup fine bread crumbs
 2 tablespoons sugar
 1 teaspoon cinnamon

Coat the apples with:

 6 tablespoons melted
  butter

Roll them in the bread crumbs.
Bake the apples in individual
buttered bakers for about 25
minutes. Serve hot, covered
with:

 Caramelized Sugar,
 page 169

or cold with:

 Cream

APPLES STUFFED [4]
WITH SAUERKRAUT

Preheat oven to 375°.
Pare the tops of:

 4 large baking apples

Remove the pulp and discard
the core, leaving a ½-inch shell.
Chop the pulp, add to it:

 2 cups drained canned or
  cooked sauerkraut
 ⅛ teaspoon pepper
 ¼ teaspoon caraway seeds
 Salt, as needed

Fill the shells. Place them in a
dish with ¼ cup water or dry
wine. Bake until tender. Baste
frequently.

BAKED APPLES [6]
FILLED WITH SAUSAGE
MEAT

A 3-star winter dish.
Preheat oven to 375°.
Wash:

 6 large tart apples

Cut a slice from the tops. Scoop
out the cores and pulp, leaving
shells ¾-inch thick. Cut the
pulp from the cores and chop
it. Combine it with:

 1 cup well-seasoned
  sausage meat or sausage
  links

Sprinkle the shells with:

 1 teaspoon salt
 (2 tablespoons brown sugar)

Fill them heaping full with the
sausage mixture. Bake until
tender. Serve with:

 Potatoes or rice

or place them around a mound
of:

 Boiled Noodles (I, 192)

APPLESAUCE

♦ Please read About Puréed
Fruits, page 89.
Wash, cut into quarters and
core:

 Apples

Place them in a saucepan and partly cover them with water. Old apples require more water than new ones. ♦ Simmer the apples until tender. Put them through a purée strainer or ricer or ↲ blend, skin and all. Return the strained apple pulp to the saucepan. Add enough:

    Sugar

to make it palatable. Cook gently for about 3 minutes. Add to tasteless apples:

    Sliced lemon or lemon
      juice

Canned applesauce may be seasoned in the same way. Sprinkle it, if desired, with:

    Cinnamon

Serve hot or cold. If served hot, add:

    1 or 2 teaspoons butter

If served cold, add:

    ½ teaspoon vanilla or a few
      drops almond extract

If it is to be served with pork, add:

    1 or 2 tablespoons
      horseradish

You may also combine:

    2 cups applesauce
    1 cup puréed apricots or
      raspberries

or:

    2 cups applesauce
    1 cup crushed pineapple
    1 teaspoon finely crushed
      preserved ginger

CRANBERRY APPLESAUCE

Combine and stir:

    2 cups cranberries
    2 cups quartered apples
    ¾ cup water

Cook these ingredients slowly until the fruit is soft. Put them all through a colander. Add:

    1 cup sugar

Cook and stir the purée until the sugar is dissolved. Sprinkle with:

    Grated orange rind

ABOUT FRESH APRICOTS

Fresh apricots have a beautiful blush and should be firm in texture. If they appear wilted or shriveled, they lack flavor and will decay quickly. Eat apricots raw or cook them in a very light sirup and serve them flambéed in Meringues, page 310.

DRIED APRICOTS   [10]

Place in a heavy pan:

    1 lb. dried apricots
    3 cups water

Simmer the fruit for about 35 minutes. Add:

    (½ to 1 cup sugar)

Heat until the sugar is dissolved, about 5 minutes longer.

ABOUT AVOCADOS

A native of America, this valuable fruit harbors no less than 11 vitamins, including large quantities of vitamin C. Buy it slightly underripe and mature it at 70°, hastening the process, if you like, by enclosing it in a paper bag. The high and perishable vitamin C content causes rapid discoloration when the flesh of the avocado is exposed. To forestall browning, sprinkle it with citrus or pineapple juice. If using only half an avocado, keep the unused part unpeeled, with the seed still embedded in it, wrap it in foil and store at a temperature between 40° and 70°. When combining avocado with cooked foods ♦ add the last moment, away from heat.

BAKED AVOCADOS
STUFFED WITH
CREAMED FOOD

Preheat oven to 375°.
Cut into halves:

    Avocados

Place in each half:

    1 tablespoon Garlic
      Vinegar, page 151

Permit to stand for ½ hour.

Empty the shells. Fill them with hot creamed, well-seasoned:

> Crab, lobster, shrimp, chicken, ham, etc.

Use ¼ as much sauce as filling. Place them on waxed or buttered paper. Cover the tops with:

> Grated cheese, buttered crumbs or cornflakes

Bake until just heated through.

ABOUT BANANAS

Cook all bananas called plantains (I, 309). Others, picked green, are matured by special moist processing, before reaching the point of sale. They make beautiful arrangements while green, but should not be eaten until further ripened by holding them at 70° in a closed paper bag until yellow in color. Once cut, they darken rapidly and should be sprinkled with citrus or pineapple juice.

As a rule use slightly underripe bananas for cooking, except in Banana Bread.

☰ BAKED BANANAS

I. Preheat oven to 375°.
Bananas may be baked in their skins in oven or on outdoor grill for about 20 minutes. On opening, sprinkle with:

> Lemon juice
> Confectioners' sugar
> Salt

II. [2]
This is a candied version.
Preheat oven to 375°.
In a small saucepan, melt together and boil for about 5 minutes:

> ½ cup dark brown sugar
> ¼ cup water

Peel, slice in half the long way and then laterally and place in a shallow buttered dish:

> 1½ to 2 slightly underripe bananas

Sprinkle with:

> Salt

Add to the cooled sirup:

> Juice of ½ lemon or 1 lime

Pour the sirup over the bananas and bake for about 30 minutes, turning the fruit after the first 15 minutes. Serve on hot dessert plates, sprinkled with:

> Rum
> Chopped candied ginger

BANANAS IN BLANKETS

Good as a breakfast dish or served with a meat course.
Preheat broiler.
Cut into lengthwise halves:

> Firm, ripe bananas

Place between the halves:

> Canned pineapple sticks

Wrap the bananas with:

> Slices of bacon

Broil in a pan, turning frequently until the bacon is crisp.

CARIBBEAN BANANA

For each serving, melt in a skillet:

> 1 tablespoon butter

Peel and split lengthwise:

> A moderately ripe banana

Simmer the banana gently in the butter, first on one side, then on the other. Baste with:

> 2 tablespoons Sauce Cockaigne, page 474
> (A dash of lime juice)

Serve on a hot plate, flambé (I, 80), with:

> Rum

and garnish with:

> (A kumquat and sprig of lemon thyme)

or, after flambéing the bananas, garnish with:

> Vanilla ice cream

ABOUT BERRIES

Strawberries, when ripe, keep their green cap intact, but all other berries, when mature, come loose from the hull. Good color is usually a test of prime condition, except for cranberries, which differ in color, depending on variety. Currants, in their dried form, taste delicious when used as a garnish in or on sweet breads. Otherwise these fruits, along with barberries and gooseberries, are of interest chiefly for preserving. Gooseberries, when ripe, are a light amber in color. Remember in preserving, see page 572, that the less ripe berries contain more pectin. Store ripe berries immediately in the refrigerator, covered, unwashed and unstemmed. Do not crowd or press.

For an attractive way to serve out of doors, make some berry cones. We saw them first in the shadows of the rain forest in Puerto Rico, where we were greeted beside a waterfall by children with wild berries in leaf cones, held in punctured box tops. Glorify your box top with foil.

FRESH SELF-GARNISHED BERRIES

Clean:
> 1 quart berries

Reserve ⅔ and chill. Rub the remaining ⅓ through a sieve or blend, if using strawberries. Sweeten the pulp and juice with:
> Powdered sugar

and stir until well dissolved. Serve the whole berries chilled and garnished with the sweetened pulp.

BERRIES WITH CREAM

Serve:
> Unhulled berries

Arrange them on the plate around mounds of:
> White or brown sugar or shaved maple sugar

Pass a dish of:
> Cultured sour cream, yogurt or whipped cream

FRESH STRAWBERRY VARIATIONS

Place in fruit cocktail glasses:
> Sliced strawberries

Simmer for 10 minutes equal parts of:
> Orange juice
> Strawberry juice

with:
> ¼ as much sugar or as much as is palatable

Chill the sirup. Season it well with:
> Sherry or kirsch

Add:
> Shaved ice

Or cover:
> Chilled strawberries

with:
> Chilled pineapple juice

Add, if needed:
> Confectioners' sugar

Or, sprinkle berries lightly with:
> Lemon juice
> Confectioners' sugar

Decorate fruit with:
> Mint leaves

STRAWBERRIES ROMANOFF

Prepare:
> 2 quarts sugared strawberries

Whip slightly:
> 1 pint ice cream

Fold into the ice cream:
> 1 cup whipped cream

Add:
> 6 tablespoons Cointreau

Blend the cream and the strawberries ♦ very lightly. Serve immediately.

BLUEBERRIES OR HUCKLEBERRIES

Pick before the dew is off:
> Huckleberries

which are richer in flavor than blueberries. To cook, see:
> Poached Thick-Skinned Fruit, page 88

CRANBERRY SAUCE OR JELLY

New England sea captains were early aware of the cranberry's worth as a preventive against scurvy. Cranberries are so packed with vitamin C that they may retain a high degree of nutritive value even after being stored fresh for a year or more. If you are a vitamin buff, you may actually find more of it in the canned version, for this fruit will probably have been processed very soon after picking. Color differences in fresh cranberries have to do with variety, not with relative age. Wash and pick over:
> 4 cups cranberries: 1 lb.

Place them in a saucepan. Cover with:
> 2 cups boiling water

As soon as the water begins to boil again, cover the saucepan with a lid. Boil the berries for 3 to 4 minutes or until the skins burst. Put them through a strainer or ricer. Stir into the juice:
> 2 cups sugar

Place the juice over heat and bring it to a rolling boil. If you want cranberry sauce, remove at once. If you want to mold the cranberry jelly, boil for about 5 minutes, skim, then pour it into a wet mold. The cooking periods indicated are right for firm berries. Very ripe berries require a few minutes longer.

SPICED CRANBERRY JELLY

Prepare:
> Cranberry Jelly, above

adding to the water:
> 2 inches stick cinnamon
> 2 whole cloves
> ¼ teaspoon salt

WHOLE CRANBERRY SAUCE

Place in a saucepan and stir until the sugar is dissolved:
> 2 cups water
> 2 cups sugar

Boil the sirup for 5 minutes. Pick over, wash and add:
> 4 cups cranberries: 1 lb.

Simmer the cranberries in the sirup ▶ uncovered, very gently without stirring, until the sauce is thick, about 5 minutes. Skim. Add:
> (2 teaspoons grated orange rind)

Pour the cranberries into 1 large or several individual molds which have been rinsed in cold water. Chill until firm. Unmold to serve.

UNCOOKED CRANBERRY RELISH

This relish is to be served like a compote. Grind:
> 4 cups cranberries

Remove the seeds, then grind:
> 1 whole orange

You may prefer to use only the yellow portion of the orange skin, as the white is often bitter. Stir into the cranberries the orange and:
> 2 cups sugar

Place these ingredients in covered jars in the refrigerator. Let them ripen for 2 days before using. Serve the relish with meat or fowl or on bread.

ABOUT CHERIMOYA

The nineteenth century traveler, Humboldt, who left his scientific imprint over South America and Mexico, declared that this fruit is worth a trip across the Atlantic. It must be tree-ripened but still firm when picked and should be handled carefully so as to avoid bruising. Sometimes called custard apple, sherbet fruit or sweetsop, this fruit shows on its light green skin jacquarded engravings or longish bumps. Discard the hard black seeds which occur at random in the pulp, see illustration on page 93.

ABOUT CHERRIES

Mark Twain claimed that we women could, if given enough time and hairpins, build a battleship. Hairpins, also mighty useful as cherry-pitters, are growing scarce. You may then prefer to substitute a fresh, strong pen-point, inserted in a clean holder. Whether pitted or not, cherries remain great favorites, especially the dark Bing and Queen Anne, both sweet, and the incomparable Tartarian pie cherries.
I. For Stewed Cherries, see page 88.

II. Cook until tender but still shapely, page 88:
    Pitted sweet cherries
To each pound, allow:
    ½ cup currant jelly
melted in:
    ¼ cup kirsch or other
    liqueur
Drain the cherries. Reserve the juice for pudding sauce or use it in basting meats or in baking. Shake the drained cherries in the jelly mixture until well coated. Chill and serve.

ABOUT CITRUS FRUITS

ORANGES

The day, for many of us, begins with oranges, which we often casually classify as "juicers" or "eaters." Valencias, Temples, Kings and blood oranges yield

the sweetest juice. For eating straight, try navel oranges, one of the many tangerine types, or tangelos, which are a cross between tangerine and grapefruit. For meat and fish cooking, for garnishes, marmalades or drinks, use Aurantium Seville, the bitter orange, if available. For other garnishes, watch the market for kumquats and calamondins. Although these smaller orange types are more popular preserved, page 525, they are charmingly decorative when fresh. Do not be misled by the color of orange skin. Some of the best-flavored fruit is green or russet, unless specially dipped.

GRAPEFRUIT

The main types are whitish or pink-fleshed. Late in the season, the skin may change in tint from yellowish to greenish, a sign of real maturity and high sugar content. But beware of the late season grapefruit if it seems unduly light in weight or if the skins are puffy, for the flesh may then be dry. ◗ Always chill grapefruit at once. It will not ripen after picking and keeps better at lower temperatures.

To section grapefruit, remove the outer skin, pull into halves, and split the membrane as shown. Pull the membrane parallel with the outer edge to the base of the section. The segment may break but virtually none of the juice is lost. You may prefer the method shown for oranges, page 102.

SWEETENED GRAPEFRUIT [4]

Peel, section and chill:

 2 large grapefruit

Place the fruit in cocktail glasses. Fifteen minutes before serving, sprinkle it lightly with:

 Confectioners' sugar

Immediately before serving, add to each glass:

 (1 tablespoon Cointreau)

or fill each glass ¼ full of:

 Chilled orange juice

GRAPEFRUIT CUPS

I. Chill:

 Grapefruit

Cut in halves. Loosen the pulp from the peel with a sharp-toothed, curved grapefruit knife or remove the seeds and cut out the tough fibrous center with a grapefruit corer. Five minutes before serving, sprinkle the grapefruit with:

 Confectioners' sugar

Add to each half immediately before serving:

 1 tablespoon curaçao or a
 Crystallized Mint Leaf

II. Preheat broiler to 350°.
Prepare:

 Grapefruit Cups, above

When grapefruit is very ripe it is inadvisable to loosen the pulp from the peel, as it makes the fruit too juicy. Sprinkle each half with:

 1 tablespoon or more sugar

Run the fruit under the broiler. When the grapefruit is hot, pour over each half:

 1 tablespoon dry sherry

Serve the fruit at once.

KUMQUATS AND CALAMONDINS

These citrus fruits, oval in shape and a little less than two inches long, have largish seeds and a distinctively bittersweet flavor. Calamondins are a cross between a kumquat and a tangerine. They may be eaten raw, without

paring. Use them as a garnish for meat. Parboil, unpeeled, for 5 minutes:

 Kumquats

Drain and cool. Slice the top off of each. Remove seeds and fill each fruit with:

 ½ teaspoon sugar

Stand upright in a shallow buttered pan. Bake for about 15 minutes in a preheated 350° oven, basting frequently with:

 Pineapple juice

For Preserved Kumquats, see page 525.

LEMONS

How could we ever get on without this versatile and delicious fruit? Many uses for juice and rind are indicated in individual recipes. For Beverages, see (I, 14), for flavoring suggestions and for use against the discoloration of fresh fruits and vegetables, see page 555. To cut it for use as a garnish, see below. For Limes, see page 331.

POACHED ORANGES [6]

Wash and cut into halves or thick crosswise slices:

 3 navel oranges

Place them in a saucepan. Pour over them:

 Boiling water to cover

▶ Simmer for 1 hour. Drain well. Discard the water. Cook for 5 minutes:

    1 cup sugar
    1¼ cups water
    3 tablespoons lemon juice

Place the oranges in the sirup. Cook until tender, for about 1 hour. Place in a jar with the sirup. Keep in a cold place until ready to use. The centers may be slightly hollowed and filled with:

    Crushed pineapple,
    chopped nut meats,
    maraschino cherries
    or a dab of tart jelly

Good served with baked ham, spoon bread and a green salad.

TO SECTION AN ORANGE

Wash and dry:
    An orange

Hold the fruit over a bowl to catch all the juices and use a sharp knife to remove the rind

and the white skin. Pare it around and around like an apple so that the cells are exposed. Loosen the sections by cutting down along the membrane. Lift out the segment in one piece and remove any seeds. If the sections are large, use the method described for grapefruit, page 100.

ABOUT FIGS

When Cato advocated the conquest of Carthage, he used as his crowning argument the advantage of acquiring fruits as glorious as the North African figs, specimens of which he pulled from his toga as exhibits in the Roman Senate. These fruits have become so popular in America that many varieties—purplish, brownish and greenish—are grown in profusion. Even when shipped, they must be vine ripened. We grow a few ourselves; and every year we wonder how many will be spared us by the chipmunks and the frost, for making Antipasto with Prosciutto, page 78.

Fresh figs are very different from the dried ones we get from Smyrna and our South. They are ripe when soft to the touch and overripe when sour in odor, indicating a fermentation of the juice. See illustration, page 93. For dried fig confections, see page 521.

STUFFED FRESH FIGS

Fill stemmed fresh or canned:
    Figs
with:
    Cultured sour cream or
    Devonshire Cream
flavored with a touch of:
    Grated orange peel

DRIED FIGS

Wash and remove the stems from:
    1 lb. dried figs
Add:
    Cold water to cover well
    1½ tablespoons lemon juice
    A piece of lemon rind
    (A large piece of
    gingerroot)
Stew the figs, covered, until they are soft and drain. Sweeten to taste with:
    Sugar: about 1 cup
Simmer the sirup until thick. Add:
    (1 tablespoon dry sherry)
Chill and serve with:
    Cream

ABOUT GRAPES

For us, clusters of grapes, with their inimitable plastic charm, put the finishing touch to decorative fruit arrangements. Be sure to choose table varieties for eating raw. Best known of these are the pale green Thompson seedless, the white Malagas and Niagaras, the red Tokays, and Emperors. The latter feel quite hard, even when ripe. The blue Concords, the olive-shaped Cornichons and the late black Ribieros also look luscious. The fruits should be plump and have a bloom, the stems should not be brittle. When ripe for eating, grapes are highly perishable and should be stored refrigerated. Frost them, page 523, and serve in a fruit bowl or as a salad (I, 54), or use seedless types as the foundation for a Brûlé Dessert, page 90.

GUAVAS

These fruits, when ripe, vary in color from white to dark red and in size from that of a walnut to that of an apple. They may be served puréed, baked or fresh, alone or in combination with other fruits such as bananas or pineapple. They have an exceptionally high vitamin content, much of which lies near the skin. Sprinkle:

Peeled and sliced guavas
lightly with:
Sugar
Chill and serve with:
Cream

or bake in a 350° oven for about 30 minutes and then serve with the cream. See also Apple Cake Cockaigne page 319, and guava jelly with cream cheese, as for Bar le Duc, page 472.

TROPICAL MANGOES

These delicious flattish oval fruits are of a yellowish-green color, sometimes freckled with red or black and about 8 inches long. When chilled and eaten raw, they are as good as any peach-pineapple-apricot mousse you can concoct—rich and sweet but never cloying. If unchilled, they sometimes have an overtone of turpentine. The seed, which extends the length of the fruit, makes eating somewhat awkward, and special holders, not unlike those which bring corncobs under control, may be used. Pare, slice and serve mangoes on vanilla ice cream. Sauté ripe fruits. Use them when just mature in chutneys and when unripe for poaching or baking. If you want to freeze mangoes, see puréed fruits, page 556.

MANGOSTEEN

This 2- to 3-inch-diameter fruit has a most exquisite milky juice. Its sections—5 to 6 in number—may be easily scooped out and eaten with a spoon, see illustration on page 93.

MEDLARS

In Southern Europe these 2-inch fruits, which resemble crabapples, are eaten fresh-picked; but in England they are mellowed by frost and not attractive to look at, although the flavor is desirable, especially for jellies.

ABOUT MELONS

Melons are being developed into so many delicious strains that it is difficult to list them all by name. These fruits are usually eaten raw. The varieties can be served singly or in combination. Try a palette ranging from the pale greens of the honeydews, through the golden peach tones of the cantaloupes or cranshaws, to the blue-reds of the watermelon. They can be served from one end of a meal to the other in many attractive ways.

In order to be genuinely sweet—and this is one's perennial hope, as he bites into each fresh melon—the fruit must have matured on the vine. If it did, you will see that the scar at the stem end is slightly sunken and well calloused. The more fragrant the melon, the sweeter it will be. A watermelon, if truly ripe, will respond by giving up a thin green skin if scraped with a finger nail.

If you want to store melons for several days, keep them at 70°, away from sunlight and chill just before serving. To protect other food in your refrigerator from taking on a melon taste, cover the fruit with plastic or foil. Melons can be cut into highly decorative shapes. For an aspic-filled melon, see (I, 70), or cut Melon Baskets, as shown on this page.

MELON BASKETS OR   [8]
FRUIT CUPS

Cut into halves and remove the seeds from:

    4 cantaloupes or other
       melons

Scallop the edges. Chill the fruit. Combine the following ingredients:

    2 cups peeled, sliced
       oranges
    2 cups peeled, sliced, fresh
       peaches
    2 cups peeled, diced
       pineapple: fresh or
       canned
    1 cup peeled, sliced
       bananas
    (1 cup sugar, dissolved in
       the various fruit juices)

Chill thoroughly. Just before serving, fill the cantaloupe cups with the fruit. Pour over each cup:

    (1 tablespoon Cointreau
      or rum)

Top with:

    Orange and Lemon Ice,
    page 494, or Sherbet,
    page 496

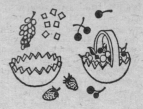

MELON ROUNDS FILLED
WITH RASPBERRIES
OR STRAWBERRIES

Cut into 1- to 2-inch crosswise slices:

    Chilled honeydew melon
      or cantaloupe

Allow 1 slice for each person. Remove seeds. Fill the centers with:

    Chilled, sugared
      raspberries or
      strawberries

Serve on individual plates with:

    Lime or lemon wedges

Melons are good sprinkled with ginger and served with limes. Also see Melon Baskets, above, for a decorative way to use melons.

SPIKED MELON

Cut a plug in the upper side of a:

    Melon

Dig out seeds and pulp with a long handled spoon. Pour in:

    ¾ to 1 cup port wine

Chill melon in ice in the refrigerator. Slice and serve with rind removed and use the marinating wine as a dressing.

ABOUT NECTARINES

This happy half-breed of plum and peach can be used in any recipe calling for peaches. It comes in both freestone and cling types, but lacks the peach "fuzz."

PAWPAWS

These small native fruits should be picked after the first heavy frost, individually wrapped in tissue paper and stored in a cool place until soft. A taste for them, we feel, is an acquired one.

ABOUT PAPAYA

These fruits grow up to 20 inches in length. When fully ripened, the flesh develops orangey tones and the greenish rind turns soft and yellow. They are eaten like melons. Their milky juice, when chilled, makes a pleasant drink. Their black seeds, which contain pepsin, are used for garnish, eaten raw or used as for capers. Many of us know this plant only by its derivative papain, the tenderizer made from the enzymes of its leaves (I, 452).

Use underripe fruits for cooking. Process as for summer squash types (I, 328). If serving papaya raw, chill and sprinkle with lime or lemon juice. See sketch, page 92.

ABOUT PEACHES

Choose firm but well-colored fruit—not green ones. When plucked green peaches will not ripen. They merely soften and wither, gaining nothing in flavor.

In cooking, a few seeds are sometimes added to strengthen the flavor, but the inner almond-like nut should never be eaten, as it is high in prussic acid.

FILLED PEACHES   [6]

Peel and halve:
    4 chilled peaches
Place them in a bowl. Combine and stir:
    2 cups chilled berries
    6 tablespoons sugar

1½ tablespoons lemon juice
If you live in a semi-tropical climate, try adding a few fresh green almonds. Pour the berries over the peaches. Serve with:
    Whipped cream

ABOUT PEARS

All pears seem to keep congenial company with cheese. Follow the season, beginning with the tiny sugar-sweet Seckels, good straight or pickled. By late summer the Bartletts are prime, but they do not keep well. With fall, come the buttery Comices and, in midwinter, the russet-skinned Boscs and the green-skinned Anjous. Kiefers, too, are acceptable winter pears, but need a special approach in cooking, so that the fruit is softened and the sugar absorbed.

Pears are best if picked green and ripened at 70° until soft for eating, but if you plan to cook them, make sure to use them while still firm. To store for eating, wrap the fruit in paper and put it away in a slotted box, in a cool place. If you wonder why pears which look sound have become brown inside, it is because they have been held too long at a too-low temperature.

STUFFED PEARS   [4]

Preheat oven to 350°.
Peel, core and halve:
    4 firm pears
Mix together and stuff into the hollows:
    ¼ cup raisins
    2 tablespoons chopped walnuts
    2 tablespoons sugar
    1 tablespoon lemon juice
Place the pears in a baking dish with:
    2 tablespoons water
Pour over them:
    ½ cup light corn sirup
Cover and bake for 1½ hours. Baste during the cooking with:

(Pineapple juice and
brown sugar)
or remove the cover and sprinkle
the fruit lightly with:
(Granulated sugar)
(A light dusting of
cinnamon)
then place under the broiler
until golden brown and serve
immediately.

PEARS IN LIQUEUR   [4]

Combine:
1 cup chilled orange juice
1 tablespoon powdered
sugar
Before serving, add to the orange
juice:
(2 tablespoons curaçao)
Pare, quarter, core and prick
lightly:
4 pears
Cover them with the juice. Chill
until ready to serve.

ABOUT PERSIMMONS

Be sure, in the recipes, to distin-
guish between our native Diospyros virginiana and Kaki, the
oriental type. Ours are small,
full of seeds and inedible until
after frost. In fact, we wonder
how we survived the many we
consumed as children, because
the skins resist digestion and can
form obstructive waddy balls, as
hard as the hair balls of animals.
Both native and oriental persimmons sometimes tend to be
puckery, even when ripe—depending on variety. The ori-
entals lose their astringency if
stored for 2 to 4 days in a plastic
bag with a ripe apple. The natives do not always prove so
amenable. Eat both as fresh
fruit; or puréed, fresh or frozen,
combined in ice creams, custards
or sherbets. See illustration on
page 92.

ABOUT PINEAPPLE

So beloved was this fruit that on
many Southern mansions it was

carved above the door as a symbol of hospitality. In fact, the
first fruits grown in England in
a nobleman's "stove-house" were
graciously rented to his friends
for their table decorations. To
be fully appreciated, the pineapple must be savored where
the fruit is field-ripened, for it
does not increase in sweetness if
picked green. If field-ripened,
even the core is tender and can
be eaten. ◆ A small compact
crown usually denotes prime
condition. When one of the
inner leaves of the crown pulls
out easily, the eyes are protruding and the whole fruit has developed a delightful aroma, it is
apt to be ripe.
Store at 70° temperature
away from sunlight. Pineapple
lends itself magnificently to all
kinds of combinations, but watch
for one thing ◆ be sure to cook
fresh pineapple before combining with any gelatin mixture, see
page 183.

PINEAPPLE TIDBITS

I.   [8]
This dish is alluring in appearance, but needs very ripe pineapple. Trim ⅔ from the leafy
top of:
1 chilled ripe pineapple
Cut the fruit into 8 lengthwise
wedges. Cut off the core and
place each part so that it will
resemble a boat, as sketched.
Pare the skin in 1 piece, leaving
it in place, and cut the pulp
downward into 5 or 6 slices,
retaining the boat shape. Serve

each boat on an individual plate, with a small mound of:

> Confectioners' sugar

Add:

> 5 or 6 large unhulled strawberries for each serving

II. A Texas girl taught us to prepare a pineapple this way. Loosen each section of a chilled pineapple by cutting it down to the core with a sharp knife. When all sections have been loosened, serve the pineapple, a toothpick stuck into each eye. Let the guests serve themselves.

III. Pineapple can make an attractive edible centerpiece. Cut off the top and bottom of a ripe pineapple and reserve them. Insert a long, sharp knife about ½ inch from the outer edge so the fruit is entirely loosened. Leaving the fruit in this cylindrical shell, cut it in about 12 long pie-shaped wedges. Set it back on its base and use the top for a lid.

FILLED PINEAPPLE

Cut in half, hollow out and chill:

> A fresh pineapple

Cube the cut-out pineapple and also some:

> Slices of melon

Fill the chilled pineapple shells with the cubed fruit and add:

> A few raspberries

Sprinkle the tops with:

> Chopped mint leaves
> (2 tablespoons liqueur)

FRESH PINEAPPLE   [6]
CUP

Peel, core and dice:

> 1 fresh pineapple

Chill it. Boil for 1 minute:

> 1 cup sugar
> ⅓ cup water

Chill this sirup. Add:

> ½ cup chilled orange juice

> 3 tablespoons lime juice

Place the pineapple in glasses and pour the sirup mixture over it.

GRILLED PINEAPPLE   [4]

Drain:

> 8 pineapple spears

Wrap around them:

> 8 slices bacon

Fasten the slices with toothpicks and broil the bacon under moderate heat.

QUICK-GLAZED PINEAPPLE

Drain:

> Canned pineapple slices or spears

Brown them by simmering for about 3 to 5 minutes on each side in hot:

> Bacon drippings, pan drippings or butter

You may also dust them with:

> Grated cheese
> A few grains red pepper

and broil or bake them in a moderate oven to melt the cheese.

ABOUT PLUMS AND PRUNES

There are many varieties of plums, some for eating, some for cooking and some, like the very firm Damson, strictly for jellies and sauces; and then, of course, there are sugar plums.

Plums are best when soft but not mushy, shrivelled or brownish. Store them refrigerated. Two unusual varieties of plums are the Loquat and the Carissa Grandiflora. The Loquat, or Japanese Plum, has a downy fuzz over a smooth, thin, yellow-gold skin. Its pulp is juicy like a cherry and contains 4 or 5 large brown seeds. Use it as a garnish for salads or fresh, straight. The Carissa or Natal Plum is a thin-skinned crimson fruit with white mottling, which contains 12 small brown seeds. It has a mild flavor, slightly astringent, and a granular texture. The Natal is fine for jelly, a good vitamin C source, but does exude a harmless white latex which sticks to the cooking pan. Remove it by rubbing with a cloth soaked in salad oil.

DRIED PRUNES

◗ If the label calls for soaking, please read About Cooked Fruits, page 87. Otherwise, cover with cold water:

      1 lb. dried prunes

Bring to the boiling point. ◗ Reduce the heat and simmer gently for about 20 minutes. Add:

      (¼ cup or more sugar)

Cook about 10 minutes longer. You may add to the prunes, during this second cooking period:

      (½ sliced lemon)
      (1 stick cinnamon)

PRUNES IN WINE   [4]

Cook by the above method until almost tender:

      ½ lb. prunes

Add:

      3 tablespoons sugar

Cook 5 minutes longer. Remove from heat and add:

      ½ cup or more dry sherry or
         ½ to ¾ cup port wine
      (6 very thin slices lemon)

Place in a screw-top jar. Chill thoroughly. Shortly before serving, the prunes may be pitted and filled with:

      Halves of walnuts or
         blanched almonds

PRUNES AND   [4 to 6]
CHESTNUTS

Drain and place in a casserole:

      1½ cups canned chestnuts
      ¾ cup pitted canned prunes

Combine, heat and pour over the above:

      1 tablespoon butter

      ¼ teaspoon salt
      (1 tablespoon sugar)
      ½ cup dry white wine

Heat thoroughly and serve as the compote in a meal in which the entrée is ham or fowl.

PICKLED PRUNES

Keep this delightful compote on hand, for it makes a decorative meat garnish and may be used drained in Stuffings (I, 565). Place in a heavy pan:

      3 cups water
      1 cup cider vinegar
      2 cups brown sugar
      2 cups dried prunes
      1 teaspoon whole cloves,
         with heads removed
      1 teaspoon whole allspice
      1½ sticks cinnamon

◗ Simmer about 1 hour or until prunes are plump. Place the prunes in a jar and drain the liquid over them to cover, straining out the spices.

ABOUT POMEGRANATES

The shiny ruby seeds of this sophisticatedly-shaped fruit make a most beautiful garnish. Use them in small cream cheese balls. When eating pomegranates fresh or when making jelly do not bruise the seed kernels, for then an unpleasant flavor develops. See illustration, page 92.

ABOUT PRICKLY PEARS

Also known as Indian fig, barbary fig or tuna, the prickly pear is now as much at home on the shores of the Mediterranean as in its native America. The red and yellow fruits, which are eaten raw, have sharp spines which can be removed by singeing before peeling.

BAKED QUINCE

Preheat oven to 350°.
Wash:

Large whole quinces

Rub with:

Butter

and bake for about 45 minutes, until about ⅔ done. Hollow out about ⅔ and mix the pulp with:

Bread crumbs
Chopped nuts
Brown sugar
Grating of lemon rind
Salt

Return mixture to hollow rind and bake about 15 minutes longer or until tender. Serve hot or cold.

STEAMED RHUBARB

Rhubarb is tenderer and needs no peeling if hothouse grown. If the hardy, greenish type is used, young shoots are preferred. If you find it tough, peel it back like celery and remove the coarsest strings before cooking. In either case, use as little water as possible. Never cook the leaves, as they are heavy in oxalic acid.
Wash and cut, without peeling, into 1-inch blocks:

1 lb. rhubarb

Place in the upper part of a double boiler over boiling water or in a low oven. Cover closely. Steam for 20 to 30 minutes until nearly tender. Do not stir at any time. Dissolve:

½ to ¾ cup sugar

in:

¼ cup hot water

Pour this over the rhubarb and steam it for about 2 minutes longer.
Dot with:

Butter
Cinnamon or ginger

BAKED RHUBARB
AND JAM

Preheat oven to 350°.
To give color to rhubarb and keep it whole, have ready:

¼ cup seedless red jam

Coat a small baker with ⅓ of

the jam. Cut into 2-inch slices:

1 lb. rhubarb

Lay the slices in the jam base, in close patterns. Sprinkle with:

**(½ teaspoon powdered
    ginger)**

Add another layer of rhubarb and cover with the rest of the jam. Bake covered for about ½ hour.

ROSELLE SAUCE

A substitute for cranberries. To prepare a sauce, cut off the red part and discard the green pod of:

2 cups well-washed roselles

▶ Simmer them ▶ uncovered, for about 10 minutes in:

1 cup water

Add:

1½ cups sugar
2 tablespoons cornstarch

Cook about 5 minutes longer or until the cornstarch cannot be tasted. Serve cool with meat or dessert.

SAPODILLAS

The rough brown skin looks like that of a potato. Remove the seeds. It has a sweet, grainy but tender pulp—like brown sugar. Use it raw, for puddings and for desserts. A little lemon juice helps bring out the flavor.

WHITE SAPOTAS

This "peach of the tropics," a greenish-yellow fruit, can be used as a peach.

SOURSOPS

Annona muricata is a heart-shaped fruit, weighing up to 5 lbs. It has a heavy, green, rough, spiny rind and a wet, soft, cottony interior. Press the pulp through a colander to remove the many shiny blackish-brown seeds. Used mostly for iced drinks and sherbets.

TAMARINDS

The 2- to 6-inch pods of this graceful tree, known as St. John's Bread, are fuzzy and cinnamon colored, see illustration, page 93. When fresh and tender, they can be either cooked with rice as "tamarind fish" or sucked raw for their spicy pulp, with its date-apricot kind of flavor. The leaves are used in curries and the dried, shiny, polished pods are ground into a meal called carob flour. To cook with this meal, see page 158. To keep the pulp, remove the seeds and pack it into jars with alternate layers of sugar and pod. Keep in a cool place.

PANCAKES, WAFFLES, CROQUETTES AND FRITTERS

ABOUT PANCAKES, GRIDDLE OR BATTER CAKES

No matter what your source of heat, a hot rock or an electric skillet, no matter how fancy the name, blintzes, crêpes or Nockerl, all these confections are easily mixed and made from simple batters.

There are three equally important things to control in producing such cakes: the consistency of your batter, the surface of your griddle or pan and its even heat. Mix the liquid ingredients quickly into the dry ingredients. ◗ Don't overbeat. Give just enough quick strokes to barely moisten the dry ingredients. ◗ Ignore the lumps. Superior results are gained if most pancake doughs are mixed and ◗ rested, covered, for 3 to 6 hours or longer before cooking. This resting period does not apply to recipes which include separately beaten egg whites or to yeast-raised cakes that have the word "raised" in the title. Variation in moisture content of flours, see page 152, makes it wise to test the batter by cooking one trial cake first. Adjust the batter ◗ if too thick, by diluting it with a little water ◗ if too thin, by adding a little flour.

If your griddle is a modern one or is of soapstone, you may not need to use any type of grease. Nor should you need to grease any seasoned pan surface if you have at least two tablespoons of butter for every cup of liquid in the recipe. If you are using a skillet or crêpe pan, you may grease it lightly and continue to do so between bakings. ◗ Before baking, test the griddle by letting a few drops of cold water fall on it. If the water bounces and sputters, the griddle is ready to use. If the water just sits and boils, the griddle is not hot enough. If the water vanishes, the griddle is too hot.

◗ To assure a well rounded cake, don't drop the batter from on high but let it pour from the tip of a spoon. After you pour the dough from the spoon, it will be two to three minutes before the cakes are ready to turn. When bubbles appear on the upper surfaces, but before they break, lift the cakes with a spatula to see how well they have browned. ◗ Turn the cakes only once and continue baking them until the second side is done. Cooking this second side takes only about half as long as cooking the first side. The second side never browns as evenly as the first. Serve the cakes at once. If this is not possible, keep them on a toweled baking sheet—well separated by a tea towel—in a 200° oven. Or fold for yourself a sort of cloth file in which to store them. ◗ Never stack one on the other without the protection of cloth—for the steam they produce will make the cakes flabby.

▲ In high altitudes, use about

¼ less baking powder or soda than indicated in the following recipes.

Several egg dishes approximate pancakes, see Egg Foo Yoong (I, 190), and Italian Frittata (I, 190).

Pancakes are delicious stuffed, rolled or glazed with a sauce and run under the broiler. Try filling with prunes and cinnamon or with creamed seafood (I, 229). You may incorporate in the doughs chopped nuts, candied fruits or currants; or wheat germ, flaked bran or corn. To do this, let the cereal or fruit rest in the liquid called for in the recipe for about half an hour before making it up. For additional garnishes and sauces, see Dessert Sauces.

PANCAKES, GRIDDLE OR BATTER CAKES

[About Fourteen 4-Inch Cakes]
Sift before measuring:
  1½ cups all-purpose flour
Resift with:
  1 teaspoon salt
  3 tablespoons sugar
  1¾ teaspoons double-acting
    baking powder
Beat lightly:
  1 or 2 eggs
When using 2 eggs, you may separate them. Add the yolks to the milk mixture. Beat the whites until ♦ stiff, but not dry and fold them lightly into the blended batter, after adding the milk and butter. Add:
  3 tablespoons melted butter
  1 to 1¼ cups milk

♦ To test griddle and bake, see About Pancakes.

WHOLE-GRAIN GRIDDLE CAKES

Prepare:
    Griddle Cakes, above
Use in all:
  ¾ cup cake flour
  ¾ cup whole-grain flour
Add to the liquid ingredients:
  2 tablespoons molasses
Serve the cakes with:
    (Sausages and sirup)

GRAHAM GRIDDLE CAKES

[About Fourteen 4-Inch Cakes]
Sift before measuring:
  ½ cup all-purpose flour
Resift with:
  2 tablespoons sugar
  ½ teaspoon salt
  ½ teaspoon double-acting
    baking powder
  ¾ teaspoon soda
Stir in:
  1 cup graham or finely
    milled wholewheat flour
Combine and beat:
  1 egg
  2 cups sour milk
  2 tablespoons melted butter
    or bacon drippings
♦ To test griddle and bake, see About Pancakes, page 111.

FRENCH PANCAKES

[About Fourteen to Sixteen 5-Inch Cakes]
Sift:
  ¾ cup all-purpose flour
Resift with:
  ½ teaspoon salt

1 teaspoon double-acting
    baking powder
2 tablespoons powdered
    sugar

Beat:

2 eggs

Add and beat:

⅔ cup milk
⅓ cup water
½ teaspoon vanilla or ½
    teaspoon grated lemon
    rind

Make a well in the sifted ingredients. Pour in the liquid ingredients. Combine them with a
few swift strokes. Ignore the
lumps; they will take care of
themselves. Heat a 5-inch skillet.
Grease it with a few drops of
oil. Add a small quantity of
batter. Tip the skillet and let the
batter spread over the bottom.
Cook the pancake over moderate
heat. When it is brown underneath, reverse it and brown the
other side. Use a few drops of
oil for each pancake. Spread the
cake with:

Jelly

Roll it and sprinkle with:

Confectioners' sugar

STUFFED FRENCH
PANCAKES OR CRÊPES

I. With Seafood

Prepare but omit the sugar:

French Pancakes

Prepare:

Creamed Oysters
    (I, 424)

or use any available canned or
frozen seafood. Spread the pancakes with the creamed mixture.
Roll them. Cover with the remaining sauce. Sprinkle with:

(Grated cheese)

Brown them lightly under a
broiler.

II. With Meat or Vegetables

Follow the above recipe, filling
the pancakes with:

Hash with gravy or
    creamed vegetables,
    chicken, ham, chipped

beef or other precooked
    meat

The cream sauce may be made
from a condensed cream soup.

III. Roll in the pancakes:

Precooked pork sausages

Serve very hot with:

Applesauce

GÂTEAU CRÊPE

[10-Inch Skillet]

An unusual way to make a Torte.
Prepare batter for:

French Pancakes

Make four or five large pancakes.
Cool them.

Spread between the layers:

Lemon, Orange or Lime
    Sauce, page 473, or
    Lemon or Orange Filling,
    pages 379, 389

You may spread over the top
layer:

Caramelized sugar, see
    Dobos Torte, page 367

or simply sprinkle the top with:

Powdered sugar

FRUIT PANCAKES

Prepare batter for:

French Pancakes

Melt in a skillet:

1 tablespoon butter
1 tablespoon shortening

When the fat is hot, pour in ½
the batter. Sprinkle it with:

1 cup or more pared, cored,
    thinly sliced apples,
    peaches, bananas or
    blueberries, or ½ cup
    elderberry blossoms,
    stripped from the stem

Pour the remaining batter over
the fruit. Turn the cakes when
they are brown underneath.
Brown the other side. After
browning the cakes on both
sides, you may keep them on a
rack in a preheated 250° oven
for about 5 minutes to assure
that the center is sufficiently

cooked. Serve the pancakes hot with:

Powdered sugar

BLINTZES OR COTTAGE CHEESE PANCAKES [4]

Prepare:
French Pancakes
Use a 5-inch skillet. Cook very thin cakes on one side only, until the top is bubbly. Place them on a damp tea towel, cooked side up. Prepare the following filling. Mix well:

1½ cups smooth, rather dry, cottage cheese: 12 oz.
1 egg yolk
1 teaspoon soft butter
1 teaspoon vanilla or grated lemon rind

Place about 2 tablespoons of filling on the center of each cake. Roll the edges up and over from either side. At this point the blintzes may be placed seam side down in a closely covered dish and chilled for several hours or they may be cooked at once. Melt in a large skillet:

½ tablespoon oil
½ tablespoon butter

Place several blintzes in it, seam side down. Fry them to a golden brown, turning them once. Repeat, adding more oil or butter to the skillet, until all are done. Serve them hot, sprinkled with:

Sugar and cinnamon

You may pass:
Cultured sour cream

CRÊPES SUZETTE [4]

At the age of 14 the famous Franco-American cook, Henri Charpentier, invented crêpes Suzette—a glorified French pancake. His patron was Albert, Prince of Wales, whose penchant for all that was bright and gay seemed a defense against his incredibly dull upbringing. In "Life à la Henri," he tells amusingly of his delight in tempting the jaded palate of the royal gourmet.

One day he was composing a crêpe sauce—a most complicated affair—a blend of orange and lemon peel, sugar, butter, maraschino, curaçao and kirsch. By accident the cordials caught fire and the poor boy thought that both he and his sauce were ruined. The Prince was waiting. How could Henri begin all over? He tasted the sauce—it was delicious. Quickly he plunged the crêpes into the boiling liquid, added more of the cordials and let the sauce burn again. The dish was a triumph. Asked by the Prince what he called these fabulous cakes, Henri stammered, "Crêpes Princesse." The Prince, acknowledging the compliment to himself, answered gallantly that there was a lady present. There was, a very small girl—would Henri consent to changing the name to Crêpes Suzette? Henri would and did. Later he received from the Prince a jeweled ring, a hat and a cane, but best of all he had put his foot on the first rung of the ladder to his future success.

This is Henri's recipe, condensed and put into what approximates American form. It makes 8 cakes—"enough for 4 people," says Henri.

Combine and stir until the ingredients are the consistency of thin cream:

3 eggs
2 tablespoons all-purpose flour
1 tablespoon water
1 tablespoon milk
A pinch of salt

We recommend keeping this batter 3 hours to overnight, covered and refrigerated. Place in a skillet:

Butter "as one joint of your thumb"

When this bubbles, pour in

enough paste to cover the bottom of the pan with a thin coating—"almost like the white of an egg." Keep the pan moving, for this is a delicate substance. A minute of cooking and the job is ¾ done. Turn the cake. Now again and again and again until the cake is well browned. Fold the cake twice. It will be triangular in shape "like a lady's handkerchief." The crêpes may be stacked, with foil or waxed paper in between, and reheated much later in sauce. Reheating and freezing are often suggested and, while possible, the crêpes are not improved.

Henri's Butter Sauce for Crêpes Suzette

This may be made in advance and kept for months refrigerated. Cut into very thin strips pieces of:

>   Lemon rind, ¾-inch
>   square
>   Orange rind, ¾-inch
>   square

"Enough to put a patch on the ball of your thumb." Use only the thin yellow rind. Add:

>   1 teaspoon Vanilla Sugar,
>   page 170

We say—not Henri—you may substitute a few drops of vanilla and 1 teaspoonful of sugar. Permit these ingredients to stand closely covered for 12 hours or more. Melt in a large thin skillet:

>   ½ cup sweet butter

When it starts to bubble, add:

>   1 pony maraschino
>   1 pony curaçao
>   1 pony kirsch

Put a lighted match to the sauce. As the flame dies down, add the lemon and orange mixture. Place the sauce in a cool place until ready to use, if you wish. Make the crêpes. Plunge the cakes in boiling sauce. Turn them. Add:

>   1 pony maraschino
>   1 pony curaçao
>   1 pony kirsch

Put a lighted match to the sauce. Permit it to flame. Serve the cakes at once. The final performance—plunging the folded crêpes into the hot sauce, adding and burning the liquor—is done in the presence of the one to be feted.

PFANNKUCHEN OR   [2]
GERMAN PANCAKES

Henriette Davides, the German counterpart of the fabulous English Mrs. Beeton, says that the heat under this pancake must be neither "too weak nor too strong," that it is advisable to put "enough butter in the skillet, but not too much" and that the best results are obtained in making this simple great pancake with not more than 4 eggs. Henriette's recipes make mouthwatering reading. But only a strongly intuitive person on speaking terms with his imagination has a chance of success. Firming up Henriette's rule, will you try our version of this large pancake?
Combine and stir until smooth:

>   4 beaten egg yolks
>   2 tablespoons cornstarch
>   ¼ cup lukewarm milk
>   ¼ cup lukewarm water
>   ¾ teaspoon salt
>   1 tablespoon sugar
>   Grated rind of 1 lemon

Beat until stiff:

>   4 to 5 egg whites

Fold them into the yolk mixture. Melt in a heavy 10-inch skillet:

>   2 tablespoons butter

When the skillet is hot, pour in the pancake batter. Cook it over low to medium heat, partly covered with a lid, for about 5 minutes. Or the batter may be cooked until it begins to set and then be placed in a preheated 400° oven until it is puffed and firm. Cooking time in all is about 7 minutes. It should puff up well, but it may fall. So serve it at once with:

> Confectioners' sugar and cinnamon or lemon juice, covered with jam or jelly and rolled, or with wine, fruit or rum sauce

AUSTRIAN PANCAKES OR NOCKERLN

[Four Small Servings—If You Are Not Very Hungry]

In Salzburg few visitors failed to indulge in one or more of these fluffy globular puffs between the delights of the Annual Musical Festival. This rich souffléd pancake is good as a breakfast, a supper dish or a dessert with rum or fruit sauce. Make it immediately before serving, as it has very little body and shrinks quickly.

Melt in a 9- or 10-inch skillet:
> 1 tablespoon butter

The butter should be hot when the soufflé mixture is put into it. Beat until very light:
> 4 egg yolks
> 2 to 4 tablespoons sugar

Add:
> ⅛ to ¼ teaspoon vanilla

Whip until stiff:
> 4 to 6 egg whites

Fold the yolk mixture lightly into the egg whites. Heap the soufflé into the hot skillet by the spoonful. Allow about 5 minutes in all for cooking. Brown the underside lightly, turn the puffs and brown the other side—also lightly. The center should remain soft. If you are serving the Nockerln without fruit or sauce, sprinkle them with:
> Confectioners' sugar

RUSSIAN RAISED PANCAKES OR BLINI

[About Twenty-Four 2-Inch Cakes]

Dissolve:
> ½ cake compressed yeast

in:

> 2 cups scalded milk which has cooled to 85°

Stir in, until well blended:
> 1½ cups sifted all-purpose flour
> 2 tablespoons sugar

Set this sponge to rise in a warm place for about 1½ hours. Cover the bowl with a cloth. Beat until well blended:
> 3 egg yolks
> 6 tablespoons soft butter

Stir in:
> 1½ cups sifted all-purpose flour
> ¾ teaspoon salt

Beat these ingredients into the sponge. Permit the sponge to rise again for about 1½ hours or until almost double in bulk. Whip until stiff, but not dry:
> 3 egg whites

Fold them into the batter. After 10 minutes bake the batter, a very small quantity at a time, in a greased skillet or on a griddle. See About Griddle Cakes, page 111. Turn to brown lightly on the other side. Serve each blini filled with:
> 1 tablespoon caviar

Garnished with:
> Cultured sour cream

SOUR MILK PANCAKES

[About Ten 4-Inch Cakes]

Sift before measuring:
> 1 cup cake flour

Resift with:
> 1 teaspoon sugar
> ½ teaspoon salt
> ¾ teaspoon double-acting baking powder
> ½ teaspoon soda

Beat until light:
> 1 egg

Add:
> 1 cup buttermilk

Combine the sifted and the liquid ingredients with a few swift strokes. Beat in:
> 1 to 2 tablespoons melted butter

To bake, see About Pancakes, page 111.

CORN MEAL PANCAKES

[About Twelve 4-Inch Cakes]
Delicate and good.
Measure:

    1 cup white or yellow
       corn meal

Place it in a bowl. Add:

    1 teaspoon salt
    1 to 2 tablespoons sirup or
       sugar

Stir in slowly:

    1 cup boiling water

Cover these ingredients and permit them to stand for 10 minutes. Beat:

    1 egg
    ½ cup milk
    2 tablespoons melted butter

Add these ingredients to the corn meal. Sift before measuring:

    ½ cup all-purpose flour

Resift with:

    2 teaspoons double-acting
       baking powder

Stir the sifted ingredients into the batter with a few swift strokes. To bake, see About Pancakes, page 111.

▤ CRISP CORN FLAPJACKS

[About Twenty Thin 2-Inch Cakes]
A distinguished botanist friend had as visitors on a field trip a Parisian confrére who traveled accompanied by his gifted Indonesian chef. To amuse the chef, our friend cooked his favorite corn cakes for him over a campfire. As he tossed the flapjacks, the chef cried out in delight, "Crêpes Sauvages!"
If you make this version up without the eggs, the pancakes become lacy.
Place in a bowl:

    1⅓ cups white corn meal
    1¼ teaspoons salt
    ½ teaspoon soda

    ¼ cup sifted all-purpose
       flour

Cut into this with a pastry blender:

    ¼ cup butter

Combine and beat:

    2 cups buttermilk
    (1 to 2 eggs)

Stir the liquid into the sifted ingredients with a few swift strokes. Make the cakes small for easier turning. The batter settles readily, so beat it between spoonings. To test griddle, bake and serve, see About Pancakes, page 111.

RICE CORN MEAL GRIDDLE CAKES

[Twelve 4-Inch Cakes]
Sift before measuring:

    ½ cup all-purpose flour

Resift with:

    1 teaspoon salt
    ½ teaspoon soda
    1 tablespoon sugar

Add:

    ½ cup water-ground corn
       meal
    1 cup cold boiled rice

Combine, beat, then stir into the sifted ingredients with a few swift strokes:

    2 cups buttermilk
    2 egg yolks
    2 tablespoons melted,
       cooled shortening

▶ Beat until stiff, but not dry:

    2 egg whites

Fold them into the batter. To test griddle and bake, see About Pancakes, page 111.

OATMEAL GRIDDLE CAKES

[About Twelve 4-Inch Cakes]
Sift before measuring:

    ½ cup all-purpose flour

Resift with:

    1 teaspoon double-acting
       baking powder
    ½ teaspoon salt

Beat:

    1 egg

Stir in:
    1½ cups cooked oatmeal
    ½ cup evaporated milk
    ¼ cup water
    2 tablespoons melted butter
      or bacon drippings
Stir this mixture into the sifted
ingredients. To bake and serve,
see About Pancakes, page 111.

BUCKWHEAT CAKES

[About Forty 3-Inch Cakes]
This batter is so light that it
makes a lot of cakes. It keeps
well covered in the refrigerator
for several days. Sift before
measuring:
    ½ cup all-purpose flour
Resift with:
    ½ teaspoon double-acting
      baking powder
    ½ teaspoon salt
    1 teaspoon soda
    2 teaspoons sugar
Two teaspoonsful molasses may
be substituted. Add it to the
milk.
Add:
    1½ cups buckwheat flour
Pour into a bowl:
    3¼ cups buttermilk
Add:
    2 tablespoons melted
      shortening
Add the dry ingredients. Beat
the batter until it is blended
only. To bake and serve, see
About Pancakes, page 111.

RAISED BUCKWHEAT
CAKES

[About Eighteen 2½-Inch
Cakes]
Scald, then cool to about 85°:
    2 cups milk
Add and stir until dissolved:
    ¼ crumbled cake
      compressed yeast
Add and stir to a smooth batter:
    1¾ cups buckwheat flour
    ½ teaspoon salt
Cover the batter with a cloth
and permit it to rise at room
temperature for 12 hours. Stir in:

    1 tablespoon molasses
    ½ teaspoon soda, dissolved
      in ¼ cup lukewarm
      water
    1 egg or ¼ cup melted
      shortening
To bake, see About Pancakes,
page 111.
Serve with:
    Maple sirup

ONION GRIDDLE CAKES

[About Fourteen 4-Inch Cakes]
Serve these filled with seafood,
Creamed Sweetbreads, or chick-
en. Use a tomato or other suit-
able sauce and a green salad.
Prepare:
    Griddle Cakes, page 111
using only:
    1 tablespoon of butter
Sauté until tender and golden:
    1½ cups finely chopped
      onion
in:
    2 tablespoons butter
Add them to the batter. To test
griddle and bake, see About
Pancakes, page 111.

RICE FLOUR GRIDDLE
CAKES

[About Eighteen 4-Inch Cakes]
Mix, then sift:
    2 cups rice flour
    4½ teaspoons double-acting
      baking powder
    2 teaspoons maple sugar
    2 teaspoons salt
Beat the mixture while adding:
    2 cups milk
Add and barely blend:
    1 beaten egg
    1 tablespoon melted butter
To bake and serve, see About
Pancakes, page 111.

ABOUT WAFFLES

You don't have to be told how
good these are with sirup,
honey, marmalade and stewed
fruit. But you may not realize
what attractive cases they make
for serving creamed foods, left-

overs and ice creams. You can even cook raw bacon directly into the dough, as illustrated, and have it come out crisp and nut brown. But be sure to treat your iron with care. Manufacturer's directions should be followed exactly in seasoning a new electric waffle iron. Once conditioned ◆ the grids are neither greased nor washed. You may brush the iron out to remove any crumbs. ◆ The iron itself is never immersed in water. After use, merely wipe down the outside with a cloth well wrung out in hot water.

Heat a waffle iron until the indicator shows it is ready to use. If it has been properly conditioned, it will need no greasing, as most waffle batters are heavy in butter. Have the batter ready in a pitcher. Cover the grid surface about ⅔ full, as sketched on the left. Close the lid and wait about 4 minutes. When the waffle is ready, all steam will have stopped emerging from the crack of the iron. If you try to lift the top of the iron and the top shows resistance, it probably means the waffle is not quite done. Cook about 1 minute more and try again.

You may think our waffle recipes heavy in fat. But the richer the waffle dough, the crisper it becomes. With the butter flavor baked in, there is then no reason for ladling butter on top of it. We also suggest ◆ beating egg whites separately for a superbly light waffle. Since waffles are made from a batter ◆ keep them tender by not overbeating or overmixing the dough. See About Muffin Batters, page 279.

▲ In high altitudes, use about ¼ less baking powder or soda than indicated in our recipes.

WAFFLES

[6 Waffles]
If used with savory foods, omit the sugar.
Sift before measuring:
   1¾ cups cake flour
Resift with:
    2 teaspoons double-acting
      baking powder
   ½ teaspoon salt
   1 tablespoon sugar
Beat well:
   3 egg yolks
Add:
    2 to 7 tablespoons melted
      butter or salad oil
   1½ cups milk
Make a hole in the center of the sifted ingredients. Pour in the liquid ingredients. Combine them with a few swift strokes. The batter should have a pebbled look, similar to a muffin batter. ◆ Beat until stiff, but not dry:
   3 egg whites
Fold them into the batter until they are barely blended. To bake, see About Waffles, above.
Good served with:
   Maple sirup or Honey
   Butter
   Sweetened strawberries
Be sure to check under Dessert Sa.. s page 473, for other toppings.

FRUIT WAFFLES

[6 Waffles]
Prepare:
    Waffles
Add to the sifted ingredients:
    1 tablespoon sugar
    1 teaspoon grated lemon
        rind
Beat in with the last few strokes
before adding the egg whites:
    1 cup thinly sliced ripe
        bananas, or ½ cup
        drained crushed pine-
        apple, or ¾ cup puréed
        apricots or prunes or 1
        cup blueberries

RAISIN, NUT OR
COCONUT WAFFLES

[6 Waffles]
Prepare:
    Waffles
Add to the sifted ingredients:
    ½ cup chopped seeded
        raisins and ½ cup
        chopped nut meats or
        ¾ cup shredded coconut
        or ¾ cup broken pecans

CHEESE WAFFLES

[6 Waffles]
Prepare but omit the sugar:
    Waffles
Use in all:
    2 tablespoons butter and
        ½ cup grated sharp
        cheese
    (1 cup finely diced cooked
        ham)

GOLDEN YAM   [6]
WAFFLES

Prepare:
    ½ cup boiled mashed yams,
        page 298
Add:
    3 well-beaten eggs
    1½ cups milk
    2 tablespoons melted
        shortening
Sift together and add to the yam
mixture:
    1 cup sifted flour

    ½ teaspoon salt
    2 teaspoons double-acting
        baking powder
    2 tablespoons sugar
◗ Stir only enough to moisten.
To bake, see About Waffles,
page 118. Serve with:
    Honey and butter or
    Sauce Cockaigne,
        page 474
The sauce makes this a dessert
waffle.

BUTTERMILK WAFFLES

[6 Waffles]
Sift before measuring:
    2 cups all-purpose flour
Resift with:
    ¼ teaspoon soda
    1⅓ teaspoons double-acting
        baking powder
    1 tablespoon sugar
    ½ teaspoon salt
Beat in a separate bowl until
light:
    2 egg yolks
Add and beat:
    1¾ cups buttermilk
    6 tablespoons melted butter
Combine the liquid and the dry
ingredients with a few swift
strokes. ◗ Beat until stiff, but
not dry:
    2 egg whites
Fold them into the batter. To
bake, see About Waffles, page
118.

SOUR CREAM WAFFLES

[About 4 Waffles]
These waffles are superlative.
Sift before measuring:
    1 cup cake flour
Resift with:
    1⅓ teaspoons double-acting
        baking powder
    ⅛ teaspoon salt
    1 teaspoon sugar
    1 teaspoon soda
Beat in a separate bowl, until
light:
    3 egg yolks

Add:

2 cups thick cultured sour
cream

Combine the liquid and the dry
ingredients with a few swift
strokes. ◗ Beat until stiff, but
not dry:

3 egg whites

Fold them into the batter. To
bake, see About Waffles, page
118.

BACON CORN MEAL WAFFLES

[6 Waffles]

Don't worry about too much
grease from the bacon, as this is
all absorbed in the cooking of
the waffles.

Beat slightly

2 eggs

Add:

1¾ cups milk

Sift:

1 cup cake flour or ⅞ cup
all-purpose flour

2½ teaspoons double-acting
baking powder

1 tablespoon sugar

½ teaspoon salt

Add:

1 cup yellow water-ground
corn meal

Combine these ingredients with
the eggs and milk in a few quick
strokes. Add:

5 tablespoons melted bacon
fat or other shortening

Cut into halves or quarters:

6 to 12 very thin slices
bacon

Place a piece of bacon on each
waffle iron section after pouring
the batter, see illustration, page
119. To bake, see About Waffles, page 118.

CHOCOLATE WAFFLES

[6 Waffles]

Delectable with ice cream.

Sift before measuring:

1½ cups cake flour

Resift with:

2 teaspoons double-acting
baking powder

1½ teaspoon salt

(¼ teaspoon cinnamon)

(¼ teaspoon nutmeg)

Cream:

½ cup butter

with:

1 cup sugar

Beat in, one at a time:

2 eggs

Add:

1 teaspoon vanilla

Melt, cool and add:

2 oz. chocolate

Add the sifted ingredients in
about 3 parts, alternately with:

½ cup milk

To bake, see About Waffles,
page 118.

FRENCH TOAST WAFFLES

Combine:

1 beaten egg

¼ cup milk

2 tablespoons melted
butter

⅛ teaspoon salt

Cut into pieces to fit a waffle
iron:

Sliced bread

Coat the bread well in the
batter. Toast it on a hot waffle
iron.

ABOUT CROQUETTES

While croquettes are frequently
made with freshly cooked ingredients—minced chicken, mushrooms, sweetbreads, lobster,
oysters—these breaded deep-fat
fried delicacies are also a good
means for utilizing leftover food.
◗ Use about ¾ cup of heavy
cream or brown sauce to 2 cups
of ground or minced solids,
meat or fish and vegetables. ◗
The solids should not be watery
—always well drained. You may
add to the hot sauce 1 to 2 egg
yolks and let them thicken
slightly off the heat. Add enough
sauce to the solids so they are

well bound, but still of a rather stiff consistency. There is a good deal of leeway in this relationship, provided—after chilling—the mixture can be easily handled. Spread it in a greased pan and chill thoroughly. You may also brush the top of the mixture lightly with butter to avoid crusting. When cool, form into shapes not larger than 1 x 1 x 2½ inches or in small balls or cones. Roll in flour, then coat carefully in a bound breading, page 160. Allow them to dry on a rack for an hour, if possible. To avoid bursting, if the mixture is a soft one, you may coat as described. Then dry for about 10 minutes, recoat and dry for 1 hour before frying. ◗ Please read About Deep-Fat Frying (I, 75–79). Preheat deep-fat fryer to 375° to 385° and immerse the croquettes, not too many at a time, in a basket, so they will have exactly the same amount of cooking time. They will be golden in 2 to 4 minutes, unless otherwise indicated. Drain on absorbent paper. You may hold them briefly before serving on a rack in a 350° oven. ◗ To reheat croquettes, use a 400° oven.

CROQUETTES OF COOKED FOOD

[About 12 Croquettes]
◗ Please read About Croquettes, page 121, and About Deep-Fat Frying (I, 75–79).
Prepare:
    Cream Sauce III
    (I, 359)
When the sauce is smooth and hot, remove from heat and add:
    1 to 2 egg yolks
allowing them to thicken slightly. Add to the sauce until it binds:
    2 cups minced solid food:
    cooked meat, fish or
    vegetables

    1 tablespoon chopped
    onion
    2 tablespoons chopped
    parsley
Return the pan to very low heat and season the food well with a choice of:
    Salt, pepper or paprika
    Freshly grated nutmeg or
    celery salt
    2 teaspoons lemon juice
    1 teaspoon Worcestershire
    sauce
    ½ teaspoon hot pepper
    sauce
    2 teaspoons cooking sherry
    ½ teaspoon dried herbs
    ½ teaspoon curry powder
Cool and, in shaping, place in the center of each croquette either:
    A sautéed mushroom
    A piece cooked chicken
    liver
    A pimiento olive
    A well-drained, seasoned
    or marinated oyster
Bread, dry and deep-fat fry the croquettes as directed. Drain on absorbent paper.
You may serve the croquettes with one of the following if suitable to your croquette mixture:
    Onion Sauce (I, 363)
    Mushroom Sauce
    (I, 367)
    Tomato Sauce (I, 376)
    or leftover gravy, etc.

HAM AND CORN CROQUETTES

[8 Croquettes]
◗ Please read About Croquettes, above, and About Deep-Fat Frying (I, 75–79).
Combine and mix well:
    1¼ cups cream-style corn
    2 tablespoons chopped
    green pepper
    1 cup ground or minced
    ham
    1 beaten egg
    ½ cup dry bread crumbs

Chill these ingredients. Shape them into 8 croquettes. Bread, dry and deep-fat fry as directed. Drain on absorbent paper. Serve the croquettes with:

Tomato Sauce (I, 376)

RICE CROQUETTES

[About 8 Croquettes]
♦ Please read About Croquettes, page 121, and About Deep-Fat Frying (I, 75–79).
Place in a double boiler:
2 cups cooked rice
Soften with:
2 or 3 tablespoons hot milk
Add:
2 tablespoons butter
¼ teaspoon nutmeg
1 or 2 beaten eggs
(1½ tablespoons chopped parsley)
Correct the seasoning
Cook and stir the rice until the egg thickens. Cool the mixture. In shaping, imbed in center:
Small pieces of ham or cheese
Bread, dry and deep-fat fry as directed. Drain on absorbent paper and serve.

CHEESE AND RICE CROQUETTES

[About 10 Croquettes]
♦ Please read About Croquettes, page 121, and About Deep-Fat Frying (I, 75–79).
Combine:
2 cups Boiled Rice (I, 158)
½ cup grated sharp cheese
½ cup Cream Sauce III (I, 359)
1 tablespoon chopped parsley
½ teaspoon paprika
A few grains cayenne
Salt
Cool and shape these ingredients into cones or croquette balls. Bread, dry and deep-fat fry as directed. Drain on absorbent paper and serve at once.

SWEET RICE CROQUETTES

[About 12 Croquettes]
♦ Please read About Croquettes, 121, and About Deep-Fat Frying (I, 75–79).
Combine:
1 cup chopped walnuts
½ cup toasted white bread crumbs
2 cups Boiled Rice (I, 158)
1 teaspoon sugar
½ teaspoon salt
1 beaten egg
1 teaspoon grated lemon rind or vanilla
Cool, if necessary, shape, bread, dry and deep-fat fry as directed. Drain on absorbent paper. Serve them with:
Tart jelly

MUSHROOM CROQUETTES

[About 6 Croquettes]
♦ Please read About Croquettes, page 121, and About Deep-Fat Frying (I, 75–79).
Prepare:
½ cup Cream Sauce III (I, 359)
Remove it from the heat. Add:
½ teaspoon Worcestershire sauce
⅛ teaspoon curry powder
1 slightly beaten egg
2 tablespoons cracker crumbs
1 cup chopped mushrooms
½ teaspoon salt
¼ teaspoon paprika
Cool, shape into croquettes or cones. Bread, dry and deep-fat fry the croquettes as directed. Drain on absorbent paper. Serve at once.

CHEESE CROQUETTES

[12 Croquettes]
♦ Please read About Croquettes, page 121, and About Deep-Fat Frying (I, 75–79).
Melt:
¼ cup butter

Stir in:

> 5 tablespoons flour

Stir in gradually until thickened:

> 1 cup milk
> ⅓ cup cream

Stir in, over low heat:

> ½ lb. grated Swiss cheese

Cool slightly. Stir in:

> 3 beaten egg yolks
> ¾ teaspoon salt
> ⅛ teaspoon paprika

Pour the custard into a well-greased pan, about 6 x 9 inches. Chill well. When ready to use, immerse pan for a moment in hot water, reverse it and turn the custard onto a flat surface. Cut into shapes. Bread and dry twice and deep-fat fry as directed. Drain on absorbent paper. Serve with:

> Hot Tomato Sauce
> (I, 376)

CHICKEN OR VEAL CROQUETTES

◗ Please read About Croquettes, page 121, and About Deep-Fat Frying (I, 75–79). Try adding poached sweetbreads or brains.

Combine:

> 1½ cups minced chicken
> or veal

with:

> ½ cup sautéed mushrooms, minced celery or minced nuts

Add, until these ingredients are well bound:

> About ¾ cup hot Velouté Sauce (I, 362)

Cool, shape, bread, dry and deep-fat fry the croquettes as directed. Drain on absorbent paper. Serve them with:

> Mushroom Sauce
> (I, 367), or Poulette
> Sauce (I, 362)

OYSTER AND CHICKEN CROQUETTES

[About 12 Croquettes]
◗ Please read About Croquettes, page 121, and About Deep-Fat Frying (I, 75–79).
These whole oysters in a chicken croquette mixture are very good. Heat in their liquor until they are plump:

> 1 pint oysters

Drain them. Reserve the liquor. Dry them. Melt:

> 2 tablespoons butter

Sauté slowly in the butter until golden:

> (3 tablespoons minced onion)

Stir in, until blended:

> ¼ cup flour

Slowly add:

> 1 cup oyster liquor and
> Chicken Stock, page 142
> Correct the seasoning

and add:

> A few grains cayenne
> A few grains nutmeg

Stir in:

> ½ cup cooked minced chicken

Reduce the heat and add:

> 3 beaten egg yolks
> 1 tablespoon minced parsley

Allow mixture to thicken. Whip until stiff and fold into the chicken mixture:

> ½ cup heavy cream

Spread the mixture on a platter. Cool. Dip the oysters one at a time in the chicken mixture until they are well coated. Shape, bread, dry and fry the croquettes, as directed. Drain them on absorbent paper. Serve them garnished with:

> Lemon slices
> Parsley or water cress

SALMON CROQUETTES

[About 12 Croquettes]
◗ Please read About Croquettes, page 121. Mix:

> 2 cups flaked cooked or canned salmon
> 2 cups mashed potatoes
> 1½ teaspoons salt or anchovy paste

⅛ teaspoon pepper
1 beaten egg
1 tablespoon minced
parsley
1 teaspoon lemon juice or
Worcestershire sauce

Shape, bread, dry and fry the croquettes as directed. Drain on absorbent paper before serving.

ABOUT FRITTERS

The term fritter is rather confusingly used to cover three quite different types of food. We think of a truly light, good fritter as a delicately flavored batter, heavy in egg and deep-fat fried. While they are not called fritters, crullers and doughnuts, see pages 466–470, are very closely related to them—the crullers usually richer in fat, the doughnuts heavier in flour. The success of these simple batters depends on the care and skill with which they are mixed and fried, so please read About Deep-Fat Frying (I, 75–79).
◗ Don't confuse the texture of any of these fritters with certain pan-fried mixtures like corn fritters (I, 286). The term fritter also applies to bits of meat, fish, vegetable or fruit dipped in a batter and dried before deep-fat frying. In this last type, the fritter batter acts as a protective coating and we prefer to think of these delicacies as frittered foods. Examples are Deep Fat Fried Vegetables (I, 258).
Variations of this completely encased food are rosettes and timbale cases or cassoulettes in which the deep-fat fried casing is a free-standing affair, so shaped that it may be filled. ◗ Be sure to choose fillings that are rather on the stable side with these types and put them in just before serving so the fritterlike casing will stay crisp.
To prepare frittered vege-

tables, use almost any leftover or raw vegetables. Tomatoes or seafood are also delectable served this way. ◗ But veal, pork and pork products should always be cooked and brains must be parboiled before frying. ◗ To cook, please read About Deep-Fat Frying (I, 75–79).
▲ Doughs for deep-fat fried fritters and doughnuts have to be adjusted and the temperature of the fat usually has to be lowered when cooking at high altitudes.

ABOUT FRITTER BATTERS

These are really much like simple pancake mixtures, but they ◗ must have the consistency that makes them stick to the food to be fried. As in all recipes involving flour, measurements can only be approximate, see page 152. But don't despair. There is an easy test. And if the surface of the food you are frying is as dry as possible, the dough will adhere. ◗ Take a generous spoonful of batter and hold it above the mixing bowl. Instead of running from the spoon in a broad shining band that the French call "en ruban," the batter should start to run for about a 1½-inch length, then drop in successive long triangular "splats." When the batter is this consistency, ◗ beat it until very smooth. ◗ Cover it refrigerated for at least two hours. It may even be stored this way overnight. This resting period allows a fermentation which is even greater if beer or wine forms part of the liquid used and any rubberiness in the batter is broken down.
◗ If you do not have time to let the dough rest, mix it to smoothness with as few strokes as possible so as not to build up the gluten in the flour. Batters heavy in egg yolk resist fat pen-

etration during frying. Use whole eggs if you wish, but if you separate them and plan to rest the dough, fold in the whites beaten ◗ stiff, but not dry, at the last minute before coating the food. ◗ To fry, see about Deep-Fat Frying (I, 75–79). Either cooked or uncooked foods may be fried in batter, although uncooked meats are more satisfactory if minced. Time depends on the size of the fritter. If slightly smaller than doughnut size, precooked food requires only about 2 to 3 minutes at about 375°. Uncooked food in larger units is better at around 350° to 360° and will need from 5 to 7 minutes. This allows more time for thorough cooking of the interior.

FRITTER BATTER FOR VEGETABLES, MEAT AND FISH

◗ Please read About Fritter Batters, above.
[Enough to Coat About 2 Cups Food]
Put in a bowl and mix well:
   1⅓ cups all-purpose flour
   1 teaspoon salt
   ¼ teaspoon pepper
   1 tablespoon melted butter or cooking oil
   2 beaten egg yolks
Add gradually, stirring constantly:
   ¾ cup flat beer
Allow the batter to rest covered and refrigerated 3 to 12 hours. Just before using, you may add:
   (2 stiffly beaten egg whites)
To coat food and fry it, see About Fritter Batters, page 125.

ABOUT FRUIT FRITTERS

Fritter batter for fruit, like any other batter, profits by resting at least 2 hours after mixing.
◗ Please read About Fritter Batters, on page 125.
It is very important that fruit

used in these desserts be ripe but not mushy. Keep fruit slices about ½-inch thick. Use apples —cored and cut crosswise— pineapple and orange wedges, halves of canned or stewed apricots or bananas cut in 3 or 4 diagonal pieces. In season, even try fuzzy white elderberry blossoms. Dusted with powdered sugar and sprinkled with kirsch, they are dreamy.

The fruit is often marinated in advance in a little wine, kirsch, rum or brandy. This marinade may also be used in the batter, but in this case you must marinate and drain prior to mixing the batter and adjust the amount of liquid to that called for in the recipe. Even beer can be used as a liquid. Both beer and wine help to break down the gluten and make a tender batter. After marination of about 2 hours, be sure to ◗ drain the fruit well and dust it with confectioners' sugar just before immersing it in the batter. To cook, please read About Doughnuts, on page 466. Fritters are good either dusted with sugar or served with a sauce like Sabayon, see page 475.

If a variety of fruits are served in this way, they are called a Fritto Misto.

FRITTER BATTER FOR FRUIT

[About 8 to 10 Servings]
This batter can be used either to encase about 2 cups diced fruit or to hold the same amount of small fruits and berries that are mixed directly and gently into it. See About Fruit Fritters, opposite.
Heat deep fat to 375°
I. Beat together:
   2 egg yolks
   ⅔ cup milk or the liquid from the fruit marinade
   1 tablespoon melted butter

Sift before measuring:

1 cup all-purpose flour

Resift with:

¼ teaspoon salt

1 tablespoon sugar

Combine liquid and dry ingredients. If you have the time, rest the dough at least 2 hours, covered and refrigerated. Then beat this mixture well, until smooth. Otherwise, stir until just blended. Just before using the batter, whip ▶ until stiff, but not dry:

2 egg whites

Fold them into the dough. Dip into the batter or mix with it the well-drained sugared fruit. To cook, please read About Deep-Fat Frying, on (I, 75–79). The fritters will take from 3 to 5 minutes to brown. Drain them on absorbent paper. Dust with:

Confectioners' sugar

II. Prepare:

Fritter Batter for Vegetables, above

omitting the pepper and adding:

1 to 2 tablespoons sugar

To coat food and fry it, see About Fritter Batters, page 125.

III. Mix together and beat until smooth:

1¼ cups sifted all-purpose flour

1 cup white wine

1 tablespoon sugar

½ teaspoon grated lemon rind

¼ teaspoon salt

Rest the batter refrigerated and covered 3 to 12 hours. Just before using ▶ whip until stiff but not dry:

1 egg white

To coat food and fry it, see About Fritter Batters, page 125.

UNSWEETENED CHOUX PASTE FRITTERS

Prepare:

Choux Paste, page 305

Omit the sugar. Shape dough with greased spoons or a small greased self-releasing ice cream scoop. Fry in 370° deep fat for about 6 minutes. For sweetened choux paste fritters, see Beignets, page 469.

PURÉED VEGETABLE [3] FRITTERS

Preheat deep fryer to 375°.

Beat until light:

1 egg

Add and beat well:

1 cup cooked mashed or puréed carrots, parsnips, butter beans, etc.

Stir in:

¼ teaspoon salt

1½ tablespoons melted butter

1½ tablespoons flour

6 tablespoons milk

1 teaspoon Worcestershire sauce or 2½ teaspoons onion juice

½ teaspoon dried herb, or 2 tablespoons chopped parsley

Spread these ingredients on a greased platter. When they are cold, shape them into 1-inch balls. Flour and roll the balls in:

Bound Breading, page 160

Fry the balls in deep fat (I, 75–76).

EGGPLANT FRITTERS [6]

Preheat deep fryer to 365°.

Pare and slice:

A small-sized eggplant

Cook it until it is tender in:

Boiling water to cover

Add:

1 teaspoon vinegar

Drain the eggplant. Mash it. Beat in:

1 egg

½ teaspoon salt

3 tablespoons flour

½ teaspoon any baking powder

◗ To fry, see About Fritter Batters. page 125.

Serve the fritters with a meat course.

CALF BRAIN FRITTERS [3]

Preheat deep fryer to 375°.
◗ Please read About Deep-Fat Frying (I, 75–76).
Prepare and blanch:
    1 set Calf Brains (I, 540)
Dry them between towels. Pull them into small pieces. Sift:
    1 cup all-purpose flour
    1 teaspoon double-acting baking powder
    ¼ teaspoon salt
Beat until light:
    2 egg yolks
Beat in the sifted ingredients until blended. Beat in:
    1 tablespoon melted butter
    1 teaspoon grated lemon rind
    A grating nutmeg
    ½ cup milk
    (1 tablespoon wine or brandy)
Beat until stiff ◗ but not dry:
    2 egg whites
Fold them into the batter. Add the brains. Drop the batter into hot deep fat. Serve when golden.

COOKED MEAT FRITTERS

Prepare as for:
    Calf Brain Fritters
substituting for the brains about:
    1½ cups chopped cooked meat
Add to the meat, if desired:
    2 tablespoons chopped parsley
    1 tablespoon lemon juice or
    1 teaspoon Worcestershire sauce
Serve the fritters with:
    Gravy, Tomato Sauce (I, 376), or Horseradish Sauce (I, 362)

CORN AND HAM FRITTERS [6]

Preheat deep fryer to 375°.
Beat until light:
    2 egg yolks
Add and combine with a few swift strokes:
    ½ cup milk
    1½ cups sifted flour
    2 teaspoons double-acting baking powder
    ¾ teaspoon salt
    ¼ teaspoon paprika
Fold in:
    2 tablespoons minced parsley or onion
    ¼ cup drained cream-style corn
    ¾ cup cooked minced ham
    2 stiffly beaten egg whites
To fry the fritters, see Deep-Fat Frying (I, 75–79).

BLOOMS IN BATTER

There is a chichi revival of the age-old custom of eating flowers. If you are an organic gardener and if you know your flowers, all is well. A lily of the valley which always looks good enough to eat is very poisonous and the sprays used on roses are not only lethal to pests, but to you. From sprayed gardens, save petals for fragrance only—not eating. Wash well any kind of blooms and leaves you use for garnish.

◗ To make fritters of blossoms, please read About Fritter Batter, page 125, and About Deep-Fat Frying (I, 75–79). Pick with the dew on them and dry well:
    Unsprayed elderberry, squash or hemerocallis blooms
Dip them in:
    Fritter Batter for Fruit II, page 126
Fry them in deep fat preheated to 350°.

KNOW YOUR INGREDIENTS

Oddly enough, many of the very basic cooking materials—those that go into ninety-nine out of a hundred recipes—are so familiar, or rather so constantly used, that their characteristics are taken for granted even by experienced cooks. And this is to say that, by beginners, their peculiarities are often simply ignored. Yet success in cooking largely depends on one's becoming fully aware of how grass roots ingredients react. Here and now we put them all —from butter to weather— under the enlarging glass and point out just what it is that they contribute to the cooking process. With the knowledge gained in this chapter and the chapter on Heat, plus the information keyed by symbol and reference into our recipes at the point of use, we assure you a continuous and steady development from would-be to sure-fire cook.

ABOUT MILKS AND CREAMS

"Drink your milk" is an admonition less and less frequently heard in this generation. Many of our children lazily and almost automatically pour "down the hatch" considerably in excess of the 1½ to 2 pints they need every day, instead of mustering enough energy to chew other equally nourishing foods, as they should. Beware, incidentally, of assuming that chocolate milk is the nutritional equivalent of whole milk, see (I, 20).

Most adults, including the middle-aged and their seniors, are well aware of the value of milk in their diet and manage to ingest their daily pint, if not as a drink, in soups, sauces or puddings. Sometimes they may prefer to substitute with cheeses. But if they do, they must be sure to get adequate B vitamins in the rest of their diet; for in cheese-making more B vitamins are lost in the whey than can be subsequently recreated in the final product.

Milk is as perishable as it is valuable and everything possible should be done ◗ to keep it constantly refrigerated at about 40° ◗ to protect it from sunlight, which robs it quickly of vitamin B content and ◗ not to hold milks of any type longer than three days before using. Milks vary in color, even when the animals from which they are taken have all been pastured in the same fields, on the same fodder. The milk of Jersey cows will be yellower than that of Holsteins and Holstein milk, in turn, yellower than the almost white milks of ewes and goats. Yellow coloring reveals the presence of a provitamin A factor called carotene, which some individuals can convert better than others into vitamin A—itself almost colorless. ◗ In this book the word milk means pasteurized fluid, whole milk unless otherwise specified. Such milk contains about 87% water, 4% fat, 3% protein, 5% carbohydrate and 1% ash, which includes its minerals and vitamins.

PASTEURIZATION OF MILK AND CREAM

Milks sold in interstate commerce must by law be pasteurized and most communities have enacted the same regulation for milk sold within their limits. Some people oppose pasteurization because of certain changes that occur in the milk as a result, such as losses of vitamin C and enzymatic changes affecting fermentation. But pasteurization, a mild, carefully controlled heating process, effectively halts many dreaded milk-borne diseases that the sanitary handling and certification of raw milk—no matter how scrupulously carried out—cannot achieve. Raw milk or cream may be pasteurized at home in one of the three following ways. The first two require the use of a dairy thermometer and all demand a ♦ quick cooling of the processing water or processing pan, so that the milk does not take on a "cooked" taste.

I. This is the preferred method. Arrange empty, sterile, glass, heatproof jars on a rack, in a deep kettle. Allow an inch or two of headroom when you pour the raw milk or cream into the jars. Fill the kettle with water until it comes above the fill line of the milk in the jars. ♦ Put the thermometer in one of the jars. ♦ Heat the water and, when the thermometer registers 160°, hold the heat at that temperature for 15 to 30 minutes. ♦ Cool the water rapidly to between 50° and 40°. ♦ Refrigerate, covered, at once.

II. This method is more apt to leave a cooked taste, as the heat is harder to control than in I. Heat milk or cream slowly over direct heat to ♦ 143° and keep it there for 30 minutes. Plunge the pan at once into ice water and reduce the heat to between 50° and 40°. ♦ Refrigerate, covered, at once, in sterile jars.

III. This method should be used only in emergencies, as the milk flavor is definitely altered. Place the milk to a one-inch depth in a wide pan and bring it quickly to a rolling boil, stirring constantly. ♦ As soon as the boiling reaches its full peak, reduce the heat by plunging the pan into ice water. When the bottom of the pan is cool enough to touch, ♦ refrigerate the milk at once in covered sterile jars.

If any pasteurized milk develops an "off" or bitter flavor, it has been held too long after processing. Unpleasant flavor may also appear in milk when cows eat wild garlic or other strongly scented herbage. "Cowy" or cardboardy tastes are also due to improper feeding and a fishy taste may be the result of processing in the presence of copper.

SWEET MILK

Milk is sold in many forms, some with added vitamins—especially D—to make its calcium and phosphorous more available to the body. Much milk is "standardized," which simply means that it comes from a milk pool covering a wide area and has cream or skim milk added to make it conform to the prevailing legally required balance between these two elements. If milk is marked as follows, it has a definite composition.

WHOLE MILK

This is a fresh, fluid milk containing 4% butterfat. The fat accounts for a cream line that forms above the milk when the fat particles rise. The cream is plainly evident if the milk has been left undisturbed for some time.

HOMOGENIZED MILK

Also a fresh, fluid milk, this has the same percentage of fat as whole milk. However, it has no cream line, as during preparation the fat particles are broken up so finely that they remain uniformly dispersed throughout. Its finer curd is more easily digested than that of whole milk. Processors appreciate homogenization because it allows them to mix older and newer milks without the tell-tale evidence of curdling which tends to characterize milks beginning to stale.

Fresh homogenized milk produces a different texture in cooking than does whole milk. Sauces are stiffer and fat separation is greater. Cornstarch puddings are more granular and soups, gravies, cooked cereals, scalloped potatoes and custards tend to curdle. This texture change is not present, however, when homogenized milks are evaporated.

SKIM MILK

This has all the protein and mineral value of whole milk but, because the fat is removed, only half its caloric value. It is also deprived of the valuable fat-soluble vitamins A, D, E and K.

EVAPORATED MILK

This is whole milk which is freed of half its moisture content and canned. It can be reconstituted by adding ½ cup water to the same quantity of evaporated milk and used to replace 1 cup fresh whole milk in any recipes except those calling for junket. Because it can be preserved during times of excess production, it is sometimes less expensive than whole milk. It has a slightly caramelized taste, due to the processing. The cans, which come in 6 oz. and 14½ oz. sizes, should be reversed every few weeks in storage to keep solids from settling. Do not hold condensed milk over 6 months before using. Once opened, the milk should be stored and treated as fresh milk. To make it flow easily from the can, punch two holes near the rim at opposite sides of the top.

SWEETENED CONDENSED MILK

This process was used as early as Civil War days. It is milk in which the water content has been reduced about 60%. The 15-oz. can contains the equivalent of 2½ cups milk and 8 tablespoons sugar. It, too, settles during storage. The can should be reversed about every 2 weeks and not held longer than 6 months before using. Once opened, the can should be refrigerated. Because of the high sugar content, the milk will keep somewhat longer than regular condensed milk after opening.

DRY MILK SOLIDS

These are pasteurized milk particles, air dried to eliminate all but about 5% moisture. They come in both whole and skim milk form and should be free of any rancid, tallowy, scorched or soapy odors or flavors. Milk solids should always be stored in a lightproof, airtight container, in a cool place. Once opened, it is best to refrigerate the package.

◆ To reconstitute whole dry milk solids or skim milk solids, use 3 to 4 tablespoons of powdered milk to 1 cup water. Or follow the instructions on the package. This quantity will equal 1 cup fresh milk. For the best flavor, reconstitute at least 2 hours in advance of use. Dry milk solids are useful in enriching the diet, but need special handling. They scorch easily, requiring a lower temperature in baking meat loaves or similar mixtures to which dry milk solids have been added. To avoid scorching gravies and sauces made with dry milk, use a double boiler or very low heat. Do not add more than 3 tablespoons of milk solids to each cup of liquid in preparing sauces. To avoid lumping, mix the milk solids first with the flour and then with the melted fat, off the heat, and then add the warm, but not hot, liquid gradually.

In cooked cereals, add 3 tablespoons dry milk solids to each ½ cup of the dry cereal—before cooking—then use the same amount of water or milk called for in the regular recipe.

For cocoas, custards and puddings, add 3 tablespoons of dry milk solids for each cup of liquid.

In baking, mix dry milk solids with the flour ingredients, see Cornell Triple Rich Formula, page 243, but be careful never to add more than ¼ cup of milk solids for each cup of flour or the result will be too dense a crumb.

SWEET CREAMS

Cream is that fatty part of whole milk which rises to the surface on standing. The longer the milk stands, the richer—up to a point—it gets. There are few dishes which do not improve with a slight addition of cream, if it is properly incorporated.

The following terms are used throughout this book:

HALF-AND-HALF

This is 12% cream and often suggested as a drink in fattening diets.

CREAM

Cream is just "cream," without further qualification. It has between 18% and 20% butterfat and reaches this stage after about 12 hours of standing. It is sometimes referred to as Coffee or Cereal Cream.

WHIPPING CREAM

This is skimmed from milk after 24 hours' standing. It has between 32% and 40% butterfat. When containing 32%, it is referred to as Light Cream and when 40%, Heavy Cream.

WHIPPED CREAM

This is whipping cream, at least a day old, which is expanded from 1 cup to 2 cups by the incorporation of air. To get the right texture, the bowl, beaters and cream should all be chilled in a refrigerator at least 2 hours before whipping, so that the milk fat stays firm during whipping rather than becoming oily from the friction involved. In warm weather beat over ice, see illustration (I, 180). If the cream is warmer than 45°, it will, on beating, quickly turn to butter. ◗ Never overwhip. We like our cream whipped just to the point where it falls in large globs and soft peaks, but still carries a gloss. This is a state almost comparable to the ◗ stiff, but not dry, of Beaten Egg White, see page 180. It is possible to use it in this desirable delicate state only if it is prepared the last split second before serving.

If whipped cream is to be used decoratively, bring it to the point where the cream molecules are about to become buttery. Should the cream really threaten to turn into butter, whip in 2 or more tablespoons of "top" or evaporated milk or cream and continue to beat.

Cream at this stage may also be forced through a pastry tube for decorating. ◗ To freeze small decorative garnishes, shape them on foil. Freeze them uncovered on the foil, wrap when firm and return to the freezer for future use.

◗ To beat cream with an electric beater, turn to medium high speed until the chilled cream begins to thicken, then lower the speed and watch like a hawk. Do not try to whip cream in a blender. If whipped cream is to be held for 24 hours or so, it sometimes is suggested that a small amount of gelatin be incorporated for stiffening, but we have never found this technique to be an advantage. It does help, if the cream is to be flavored, to mix in a small quantity of confectioners' sugar, as the cornstarch in the sugar forms a stabilizer. For interesting ways to flavor whipped creams, see page 377.

CRÈME CHANTILLY

This is the French equivalent of our Sweetened Whipped Creams, page 377.
Unsweetened, it is called "Fleurette."

WHIPPED CREAM SUBSTITUTES

First, let us say there are really no very satisfactory substitutes for whipped cream, but the following makeshifts are sometimes used. It is often wise to add vanilla, 1 teaspoon per cup, or one of the other flavors suggested in Sweetened Whipped Creams, page 377, to mask both the inferior flavor and texture of these substitutes.
I. If you allow 20% cream to stand refrigerated for 48 hours and skim it, the skimmed portion will sometimes—not always —whip. Handle as for whipped cream, above.

II. Soak:
    1 or 1½ teaspoons gelatin
depending on heaviness of cream desired, in:
      2 tablespoons cold water or fruit juice
When it is clear, dissolve it well in:
    ½ cup scalded 20% cream
Add:
    1 cup 20% cream
    1 tablespoon powdered sugar
Refrigerate. Stir from time to time. During the early part of the 4 to 6 hours needed to chill properly, add:
    ½ teaspoon vanilla
Then beat as for whipped cream, about 5 to 7 minutes.

III. Chill for 12 hours:
    1 can evaporated milk
For each 13-oz. can, add:
    1 teaspoon lemon juice
Whip until stiff.

MILK AND CREAM SUBSTITUTIONS

Sometimes it is convenient to substitute milk for cream. But, if the substitution is made for baking, a different texture will result—unless the fat content of the cream is compensated for. ◗ To substitute for 1 cup 20% cream, use ⅞ cup milk and 3 tablespoons butter. To substitute for 1 cup 40% cream, use ¾ cup milk and ⅓ cup butter. This substitution, of course, will not whip.

SWEET AND SOUR MILK SUBSTITUTIONS

If recipes for baking specify sour or buttermilk when you have only sweet milk on hand, you may then proceed as follows: interchange sweet milk and baking powder with sour milk and soda. ◗ Use the same amount of liquid as is called for in the recipe. ◗ To sour the sweet milk, have the milk at 70°. Place in the bottom of a measuring cup:

 1 tablespoon lemon juice or distilled white vinegar

Then fill the cup with:

 Fresh sweet milk or the equivalent amount of reconstituted evaporated or dried whole milk solids

Stir and let the mixture stand about 10 minutes to clabber. It should have the consistency of cultured buttermilk or yogurt. ◗ If the leaven is baking powder or soda, be sure that it is added to the dry, not the liquid, ingredients. Make the following adjustments: for every teaspoon baking powder indicated in the recipe, use ¼ teaspoon baking soda plus ½ cup sour milk or ¼ teaspoon baking soda and ½ teaspoon vinegar or lemon juice plus ½ cup sweet milk.

SOUR AND FERMENTED MILKS
AND CREAMS

The long life of the Arabs, Bulgars and other Eastern peoples is often attributed to their diet of fermented milks. The friendly bacteria in these milks settle in the intestines where they break down the sugar in the lactic acid and where some, like yogurt and koumis, are reported to manufacture B vitamins. Soured milks and creams also play an important part in cooking. The presence of lactic acid gives them all a tenderer curd and this, in turn, makes for a tenderer crumb in baking and a smoother texture in sauces. In sauces, too, they contribute a slightly acid flavor which is highly prized.

Milks and creams may be allowed to sour naturally, but yogurt and some other similar varieties are processed by means of specially introduced bacterial cultures. When pasteurized dairy products are used, they never sour naturally

and must always be cultured to do so. In this book, for reasons of safety, we recommend only sour milks and creams that have been pasteurized and cultured. In cooking ◗ be sure to add these milks and creams at the very last and off the heat or over very low heat, or they will curdle. And in breadmaking, don't scald, just heat until warm.

Should a recipe—like the clssic Smitane Sauce (I, 364) —call for the addition of sour cream or milk at the start of the cooking process, be sure to use naturally soured dairy products, and no other, to prevent curdling. ◗ In either case, after adding the sour milk ingredient, the mixture should never be allowed to boil. In any sour cream recipes, use salt sparingly, as salting also tends to cause curdling.

BUTTERMILK

Originally this was the residue from the butter churn. Today it is usually made from pasteurized skim milk. A culture is added to develop flavor and to produce a heavier consistency than the skim milk from which it is made. Buttermilk differs nutritionally from skim milk mainly in its greater amount of lactic acid. As its protein precipitate is in the form of a fine curd, it is also more quickly digested than skim milk. Commercial buttermilk frequently has added cream or butter particles. Try making buttermilk yourself: Combine:

 1 quart 70° to 80° skim milk
 ½ cup 70° cultured buttermilk
 ⅛ teaspoon salt

Stir well and cover. Let stand at 70° until clabbered. Stir until smooth. Refrigerate before serving. Store as for fresh milk.

SOUR MILK

This is whole or skim milk that is allowed to sour naturally. It is good only if it is made from unpasteurized or unscalded milk. Pasteurized or scalded milk will not sour, but simply spoil. In this book, therefore, recipes which formerly called for sour milk now call for buttermilk.

YOGURT

If you have ever eaten good, naturally flavored yogurt, you will try, as we have, to make it. We hope these directions will spare you some of our exasperating failures. Eastern yogurts are made with milk reduced by about ⅓. Our commercial yogurts have the same value as the milk from which they are made. This is also true of the yogurt you can make yourself.

Like yeast, the activator in yogurt is a living organism sensitive to temperatures. Test the milk with a thermometer for consistent results. Use milk from skim to half-and-half richness. Yogurt has the added idiosyncrasy that it doesn't care to be jostled while growing, so place all your equipment where you can leave it undisturbed for 8 hours. However, there are electric devices which can produce yogurt in 3 hours. If you use one of these, follow the directions carefully. Failure may result if milk or utensils are not absolutely clean.

We make yogurt regularly without the use of any heat other than that retained in the milk—using either an insulated cooler or the "snug nest" described next.

For this very satisfactory contraption, you will need a lidded vessel like a deep-well liner. Acquire enough inch-thick foam rubber and plastic wrapping or bags to cover the foam rubber —thus insuring a sanitary, well-insulated lining for your pan. Cut the foam rubber into 3 pieces. Make one round to fit the bottom, one overlapping, long, narrow piece for the side wall and a small round that will fit snugly into the top of the side wall. This smaller disk will be held in place between the top of the cups and the lid. Fit into this insulated space any heat-resistant cups or jars that fit your vessel. Also have ready a piece of foil to go between the cups and the top pad.

For the first batch, you will need a starter. Buy a jar of yogurt, get a small quantity from a friend or buy a package of yogurt culture from a health store. If you use the culture, heat a pint of milk to 180°. Cool it to 110°. Stir into this milk very thoroughly a package of the culture. Do not allow the milk to register less than 106° when it is in the jars. Then place them in the insulated equipment. Cover the jars at once and check in 7 to 8 hours to see if the contents have reached a thick, custardy consistency. Then check every half hour. Refrigerate when ready. Reserve from this first batch a small quantity to use for the second batch. Preferably, this should be not older than 5 days when used as a starter. The yogurt will keep for about 6 to 7 days.

When you are ready to start the second batch, have the equipment where you will be able to leave it for the next 8 hours. Measure the contents of your jars or cups. Heat that amount of milk. Bring it to 180° and pour it directly into the clean jars that are in place, except for the foil closures. Cool the jars until the milk reaches between 109° and 106°. When this state has been reached, it is important to work quickly. Take one tablespoon of milk from each pint. Add to the combined amount, for each tablespoon, ½ teaspoon of starter yogurt. Distribute the yogurt and milk mixture evenly into the bottles, stirring it in gently. Cover the jars with foil, pad and lid. Let it set 7 to 8 hours.

You may wonder why so little starter is used and think that a little more will produce a better result. It won't. The bacillus, if crowded, gives a sour, watery product. But if the culture has sufficient Lebensraum, it will be rich, mild and creamy. If the yogurt should not have thickened in 8 hours, you may start all over again and have success by reheating the same yogurt slowly to 180°, cooling to 109°–106° and adding a fresh starter. Should you not succeed, it may be due to too great heat in the mixing so that you have killed the culture; it may be that your culture was a poor one or that there were antibiotics in the milk. Always remember ◗ don't eat every drop of your most recent batch. Keep those few teaspoons to form the starter for the next one.

CULTURED SOUR CREAM

The mention of sour cream may bring from the uninitiated a disdainful sniff and a vision of a yellowed mass of decomposed solids swimming on a bluish whey. But the seasoned cook responds to the term with delight, for she sees the culinary possibilities of this smooth semiplastic and rolls her tongue in anticipation of its promise. Many uses for sour cream are suggested in this book and if your dairy does not carry it, try making it yourself.

Place in a quart glass jar:

    1 cup pasteurized 20%
        cream
◗ The cream must be at least this heavy and may be heavier —the heavier the better for the texture of the end product. Add:
    5 teaspoons cultured
        buttermilk
The commercial type which is 1% acid and has carefully controlled bacteria is suggested rather than the less acid and less controlled home product. Cover the jar and shake these ingredients vigorously. Stir in:
    1 cup pasteurized 20%
        cream
Cover the jar and allow this mixture to stand at about 75° to 80° for 24 hours. The sour cream may then be used at once, although storage under refrigeration for another 24 hours makes a finer product.

It is possible to "stretch" sour cream. Use half a jar and fill with 20% cream.

DEVONSHIRE OR CLOTTED CREAM

One of those regional specialties we always wish we could make locally. If you have a cow, you might try! In winter, let fresh cream stand 12 hours; in summer, about 6 hours, in a heatproof dish. Put the cream on to heat—or on the back of a peat or well-insulated iron coal stove—the slower the heat the better. It must never boil, as this will coagulate the albumen and ruin everything. When small rings or undulations form on the surface, the cream is sufficiently scalded. Remove at once from heat and store in a cold place for 12 hours. Then skim the thick, clotted cream and serve it very cold, as a garnish for berries.

CRÈME FRAÎCHE

This is served in France with fruits. It is actually a crème aigre, a naturally matured,

slightly sour-flavored raw cream.
♦ To substitute 1 cup crème fraîche for 1 cup whipped cream, stir into:

1 cup raw 30% cream
1 teaspoon commercial buttermilk

Heat to 85°. Let stand at a temperature between 60° to 85° until it has thickened. Stir gently and refrigerate until ready to use.

SOUR CREAM SUBSTITUTE

A low-calorie substitute to be used only in uncooked dressings or for garnish.

I. ⅃ Mix for 2 or 3 seconds in a blender:

1 tablespoon lime or lemon juice
⅓ cup buttermilk
1 cup smooth cottage cheese

II. Mix:

1 cup 70° evaporated milk

with:

1 tablespoon vinegar

Allow it to stand until it clabbers and thickens.

SCALDING MILK

In this day of pasteurized milk, scalding is employed more often to hasten or improve a food process than to destroy bacteria. If, as a cook, you happen to talk to a food chemist about "scalding" milk, you may find yourself in an argument. To him, scalding will be that point at which milk begins to come up into a light froth, just as it boils, around 212°. To cooks, as high a temperature as this means scorched pots and frazzled tempers. In practice, we rely on the age-old visual test for scalding and, in this book, milk is scalded ♦ when tiny bubbles form around the edge of the pan and the milk reaches about 180°. Heating may be either over direct heat or in the top of a double boiler ♦ over—not in—hot water. Before heating milk for scalding, it is a help to rinse out the pan with cold water. To scald milk for bread, see page 240; for custards, page 436.

VEGETABLE MILKS

These are all valuable nutritionally, but not comparable to animal milks, as their protein is of lower biologic value (I, 2).

SOY BEAN MILK

This milk—which can be substituted cup for cup in any recipe calling for regular milk—also gives a taste and cooking reaction very similar to cow's milk in finished recipes. Though very different nutritionally from cow's milk and with a basic lack of iodine, it is, however, commonly used for feeding babies in the Orient.

I. Soak, well covered in water for 12 hours:

1½ lbs. dried soy beans

Drain the beans. Put them through a food grinder, pouring on them while grinding a slow, steady stream of:

Water

Continue pouring the water until the entire mixture reaches 1 gallon. Heat this mixture until it is disagreeable to hold a finger in it, 131°. Put the mixture in a cloth bag and allow it to drip. Heat the drippings in a double boiler for 45 minutes, stirring frequently. Sweeten with dextrose or honey to taste. Add enough water to make in all 5 quarts.

II. Mix gradually, so as to avoid lumping:

1 quart soy bean flour
4 cups water

Strain this mixture in a cloth bag. Heat the drippings for 15 minutes in a double boiler, stirring frequently. Cool and keep the milk under refrigeration.

NUT AND COCONUT MILKS

Almond and walnut milks have long been known to Europe's peasants and our own Indians used hickory nuts and pecans. These rather fragilely-flavored milks, as well as coconut milk, are a great delicacy in sauces and puddings. ♦ They are as perishable as cow's milk and should be stored the same way, page 129. To use them, see About Coconut Milk and Cream, page 193, a staple wherever these beautiful palms grow.

As nuts vary in weight, look up the measurement equivalent to almonds and blanch the nuts, if necessary. Then substitute accordingly in the following recipe. These milks are often used to substitute for milk in desserts, with sugar added. If using for sauces other than dessert sauces, you may use stock as your liquid base.

ALMOND MILK

I. Blanch:
    ⅔ cup almonds
    (2 or 3 bitter almonds)
Drain and discard the liquid. Cool the nuts. Pound them in a mortar with:
    ¼ cup sugar
    (1 tablespoon orange water)
If necessary, add from time to time a tablespoon or so ice water to keep the nuts from becoming oily. When this mixture is quite smooth, stir in:
    2 cups cold water
Stir well. Cover and refrigerate about 2 hours. Strain the liquid through a cloth-lined sieve and refrigerate until ready to use.

II. ⅄ For an American hurry-up version that will shock the painstaking French, use the above ingredients, but blend with:
    2 tablespoons water
    (2 tablespoons orange water)

Add the water gradually. Strain through a cloth-lined sieve. Refrigerate.

ABOUT STOCKS AND STOCK SUBSTITUTES

Antique dealers may respond hopefully to dusty bits in attics, but true cooks palpitate over even more curious oddments: mushroom and tomato skins, fowl carcasses, tender celery leaves, knucklebones, fish heads and chicken feet. These are just a few of the treasures for the stock pot—that magic source from which comes the telling character of the cuisine. The juices made and saved from meat and vegetable cookery are so important that in France they are called bases or "fonds." You will note in the recipes for gravies, aspics, soups or sauces the insistent call for stocks. While these need not always be heavily reduced ones ♦ do experiment by tasting the wonderful differences when these liquids replace water. ♦ When stocks are specified in long-cooking recipes, they are always meat stocks, as vegetable and fish stocks deteriorate in flavor under prolonged cooking.

You will want to store separately and use very sparingly certain strongly flavored waters, like cabbage, carrot, turnip and bean or those from starchy vegetables, if the stock is to be a clear one. You may look askance at the liquids in which modern hams and tongues have been cooked because of the many chemicals now used in curing. You will, of course, never want to use the cooking water from an "old" ham. And you will certainly reserve any light-fleshed fish and shell-fish residues for use in fish dishes exclusively. Fish and vegetable stocks with vegetable oils are important in "au maigre" cooking, as contrasted with "au gras" or meat and meat-fat based cooking. But, whether you are a purist who uses only beef-based stock with beef, or chicken with chicken or whether you experiment with less classic combinations, for both nutrient values and taste dividends ♦ do save and make stocks.

STOCK-MAKING

While we beg you to utilize the kitchen oddments described under Household Stock, page 142, we become daily more aware that the neat packaged meats and vegetables most of us get at the supermarket give us an increasing minimum of trimmings. The rabbits, old pheasants and hens that make for such picturesque reading in ancient stock recipes—fairly thrusting the hunter and farmer laden with earthy bounty straight into the kitchen—have given way to a well-picked-over turkey carcass and a specially purchased soup bunch. But even these are worthwhile. ♦ Stock-making is an exception to almost every other kind of cooking. Instead of calling for things young and tender ♦ remember that meat from aged animals and mature vegetables will be most flavorsome. Remember, too, that instead of making every effort to keep juices within the materials you are cooking, you want to extract and trap every vestige of flavor from them—in liquid form. So ♦ soaking in cold water and starting to cook in cold water—both of which methods draw juices—are the first steps to your goal; but have the ingredients to be cooked and the water at the same temperature at the onset of cooking. ♦ Bones are disjointed or crushed; meat is trimmed of excess fat and cut up; and veg-

etables, after cleaning, may even be ⅄ blended.

♦ In making dark stocks, browning a portion of the meat or roasting it until brown, but not scorched, will add flavor.
♦ For a strong meat stock, allow only 2 cups of water to every cup of lean meat and bone. They may be used in about equal weights. When this much meat is used, only a very few vegetables are needed to give flavor to the soup.

Bones, especially marrow bones and ones with gelatinous extractives, play a very important role in stock. But, if a too large proportion of them is used, the stock becomes gluey and is reserved for use in gravies and sauces. Raw and cooked bones should not be mixed if a clear stock is desired. Nor, for clear stock, should any starchy or very greasy foods be added to the stock pot. Starchy foods also tend to make the stock sour rapidly.

Before you put the browned meat and the cooking herbs in the pot, discard any fat that may have been extracted. The factor that retains the flavor of the extracted juices most is ♦ to have a steady low heat for the simmering of the brew. You may laugh at the following primitive suggestion. But it is

our answer to the thinness of modern pots and the passing of that precious source of household heat, "the back of the stove," now seldom found in modern equipment. ◗ If you do not have an asbestos pad to produce an evenly transmitted heat, get two or three bricks—depending on the size of your pot. Put them on your burner, set at low heat and place your soup pot on them, as shown on page 139. You need then have no worries about boiling over or about disturbing the steady, long, simmering rhythm. Or, for a similar effect, use a double boiler. When choosing a heavy stock pot, avoid aluminum, as it will affect the clarity of the stock.

As the stock heats, quite a heavy scum rises to the surface. ◗ If a clear soup is wanted, it is imperative to skim this foamy albuminous material before the first half hour of cooking. After the last skimming, wipe the edge of the stock pot at the level of the soup. Some nutritionists advise against skimming stocks to be used for brown sauces.

◗ Simmer the stock ◗ partially covered, with the lid at an angle, until you are sure you have extracted all the goodness from the ingredients—over 2 hours and at least 12 if bones are used. To keep the stock clear, drain it, not by pouring, but by ladling. Or use a stock pot with a spigot. Then strain it through 2 layers of cheesecloth that have been wrung out in water. Cool it ◗ uncovered. Store it ◗ tightly covered and refrigerate. The grease will rise in a solid mass which is also a protective coating. Do not remove this until you are ready to reheat the stock for serving or use. For more about this coating, see About Drippings, page 174.

Stocks keep 3 to 4 days refrigerated. The best practice is to bring them to a boil at the end of this period and cool before re-storing. It is also good practice to boil them if adding other pot liquors to them.

SEASONINGS FOR STOCKS AND SOUPS

These all-important ingredients should be ◗ added sparingly in the initial cooking of soups and stocks and the seasoning should be corrected just before the soup is served.

◗ Never salt heavily at the beginning of stock-making. The great reduction both in original cooking and in subsequent cooking—if the stock is used as an ingredient—makes it almost impossible to judge the amount you will need. And a little extra salt can so easily ruin your results. ◗ If stocks are stored, the salt and seasoning are apt to intensify and ◗ if any wine is used in dishes made from stock, the salt flavor will be increased.

◗ The discreet use of either fresh or dried herbs and spices is imperative. Use whole spices like peppercorns, allspice, coriander and celery seeds and bay leaf—but not too many. Add mace, paprika and cayenne in the stingiest pinches. Be sure to use a Bouquet Garni, page 220, and for a quick soup, try a Chiffonade (I, 151). An onion stuck with two or three cloves is de rigueur and, if available, add one or two leeks. Monosodium glutamate is a great help when the flavor of the stock is thin. For further details, see Seasonings, page 216.

CLARIFYING STOCK

If you have followed the directions in Stock-making carefully, your product should be clear enough for most uses. But for extra-sparkling aspic, jellied consommé, or chaud-froid you may wish to clarify stock in one of 2 ways. Both are designed to remove cloudiness; but the second method also strengthens flavor. ◆ Be sure the stock to be clarified has been well degreased; and never let it boil.

For the first method, allow to each quart of broth 1 slightly beaten egg white and 1 crumpled shell. If the stock to be clarified has not been fully cooled and is still lukewarm, also add a few ice cubes for each quart. Stir the eggs and ice into the soup well. Bring the soup very, very slowly ◆ without stirring, just to a simmer. As the soup heats, the egg brings to the top a heavy, crusty foam, over an inch thick. Do not skim this, but push it very gently away from one side of the pan. Through this small opening, you can watch the movement of the simmering—to make sure no true boiling takes place. Continue simmering 10 to 15 minutes. Move the pot carefully from the heat source and let it stand 10 minutes to 1 hour. Wring out a cloth in hot water and suspend it, like a jelly bag, above a large pan. Again push the scummy crust to one side and ladle the soup carefully so it drains through the cloth. Cool it ◆ uncovered. Store it ◆ covered tightly and refrigerate.

The second method of clarification produces a double-strength stock for consommé. Add to each quart of degreased stock ⅛ to ¼ lb. of lean ground beef, 1 egg white and crumpled shell and to the pot several uncooked fowl carcasses; and, if the stock is beef, fresh tomato skins. Some cooks also use a few vegetables. Beat these additions into the stock. Then ◆ very slowly, bring the pot just to a simmer.

Should the stock have boiled at any time during the process just described, the clarification is ruined. It will be necessary to start over again, proceeding as follows. After what should have been the simmering period in the second method, remove the pot from the heat and skim it. Allow the stock to cool to about 70°. Again add an egg white and a crumpled eggshell for each quart of stock. Then continue as for the first method above. Allow the simmer to last up to 2 hours. Then remove the pot from the heat source and let it rest an hour or more. Ladle and strain it, as previously described. Cool it ◆ uncovered. Store it ◆ tightly covered and refrigerated.

BROWN STOCK

I. [About 2 Quarts]
◆ Please read About Stocks, page 138.
Cut in pieces and brown in a 350° oven:

    6 lbs. shin and marrow bones

Place them in a large stock pot with:

    4 quarts water
    8 black peppercorns
    6 whole cloves
    1 bay leaf
    1 teaspoon thyme
    3 sprigs parsley
    1 large diced carrot
    3 diced stalks celery
    1 cup drained canned or fresh tomatoes
    1 medium diced onion
    1 small, white, diced turnip

Bring to boil. ◆ Reduce heat and simmer, uncovered, for 2½ to 3 hours or until reduced by half. Strain stock. Cool uncovered and refrigerate.

II. [About 3½ Cups]
While Brown Stock I is more strongly flavored and clearer, do not scorn stocks made from cooked meats and bones.

◗ Please read About Stocks, page 138.

Cut the meat from the bone. To:
   2 cups cooked meat and
      bones

Add, in a heavy stock pot:
   4 or 5 cups water
   ¼ teaspoon salt
   1 cup chopped vegetables:
      carrots, turnips, celery,
      parsley, etc.
   1 small onion
   1 cup tomatoes
   ½ teaspoon sugar
   2 peppercorns
   ¼ teaspoon celery salt

Bring the soup just to the boiling point, turn down the heat and ◗ simmer, uncovered, for 1½ hours. Strain the soup, chill it. For quick chilling, place it in a tall, narrow container set in cold water. Remove the fat and reheat the soup.

Correct the seasoning

VEAL OR LIGHT STOCK

[About 2 Quarts]

◗ Please read About Stocks, page 138.

Blanch II (I, 88):
   4 lbs. veal knuckles or
   3 lbs. veal knuckles and
      1 lb. beef

Drain and discard water and add meat and bones to:
   4 quarts cold water
   8 white peppercorns
   1 bay leaf
   1 teaspoon thyme
   6 whole cloves
   6 parsley stems
   1 medium diced onion
   3 stalks diced celery
   1 medium diced carrot

Bring to a boil. ◗ Reduce heat at once to a simmer and cook 2½ to 3 hours or until reduced by half. Strain stock and ◗ cool uncovered.

✪ QUICK STOCK   [4 to 6]

Wash and cut into 1-inch cubes:
   2 lbs. lean beef; soup meat

Brown it slowly in the pressure cooker in:
   2 tablespoons melted fat

Drain off the fat. Add:
   1 quart boiling water
   A cracked soup bone
   1 medium sliced onion
   1 diced carrot
   4 diced stalks celery with
      tender leaves
   ½ bay leaf
   2 peppercorns
   ½ teaspoon salt

◗ Do not have the pressure cooker more than ½ full. Adjust the cover and cook at 15 pounds pressure for 30 minutes. Reduce pressure instantly. Strain. Cool ◗ uncovered.

Correct the seasoning

✪ QUICK HOUSEHOLD STOCK

A careful selection of refrigerator oddments can often produce enough valid ingredients to make up a flavorful stock to use as a reinforcer for soups—canned, dried and frozen—and in gravies and sauces. If cooked and uncooked meats are combined, a darker, cloudier stock results. Put in a pressure cooker:
   1 cup nonfat meat, bone
      and vegetables, cooked
      and uncooked
   1 to 1½ cups water

Use the smaller amount of water if you are short on meat. For vegetables to include, see Vegetables for Soup, page 144. Do not fill the pressure cooker more than ½ full. If raw meat and bone are included, add:
   (2 tablespoons vinegar)

Cook them first 10 minutes at 15 lbs. pressure. Add the other food and cook 10 to 15 minutes longer.

Correct the seasoning

CHICKEN OR LIGHT STOCK

I. [About 2 Quarts]

◗ Please read About Stocks, page 138.

Blanch II (I, 88):

    4 lbs. chicken backs, necks, wings and feet

Drain, discard water and bring the chicken slowly to a boil in:

    4 quarts cold water

with:

    8 white peppercorns
    1 bay leaf
    1 teaspoon thyme
    6 whole cloves
    6 parsley stems
    1 medium diced onion
    3 diced stalks celery
    1 medium diced carrot

◗ Reduce the heat at once and simmer 2½ to 3 hours or until reduced by half. Strain stock. ◗ Cool uncovered and refrigerate until ready to use.

II. [From Chicken Feet]

This stock gives a jellied, not too flavorful, but economical base. Cover with boiling water:

    Chicken feet

Blanch them for about 3 minutes. Drain. Strip away the skin and discard. Chop off the nails. Place the feet in a pan and cover with:

    Cold water

Add:

    Vegetables

as suggested under Fowl Stock I. Simmer for about 1½ hours or use a ✪ pressure cooker. Strain and cool.

FOWL, RABBIT OR GAME STOCK

I. [About 9 or 10 Cups]

Put in a heavy pot:

    4 or 5 lbs. fowl or rabbit
    3 quarts cold water
    5 celery ribs with leaves
    ½ bay leaf
    ½ cup chopped onion
    ½ cup chopped carrots
    6 sprigs parsley

Simmer the stock for 2½ hours, uncovered. Strain it. Chill it. It will solidify and make a good aspic or jellied soup. Degrease it before serving.

II. [1½ to 2½ Pints]

The housewife frequently meets up with the leavings of a party bird from which a good stock can be made. Try this simpler soup when you have leftover cooked chicken, duck or turkey. Break into small pieces:

    1 cooked chicken, duck or turkey carcass

Add and simmer ◗ partially covered, for about 1½ hours in:

    4 to 6 cups water

The amount of liquid will depend on the size or number of carcasses you use. Add also to the pot:

    1 cup chopped celery with tender leaves
    1 large sliced onion
    ½ cup chopped carrot
    Lettuce leaves
    ½ bay leaf
    3 or 4 peppercorns
    Parsley
    A Bouquet Garni, page 220

Strain and chill it. Degrease before serving.

FUMET OR FISH STOCK

This is most useful for cooking "au maigre," on those days when religious observance calls for meatless meals. Combine the fumet with vegetables and cream as a base for soup or use it in sauces or aspics. It will keep for several days, covered, in the refrigerator, or for several weeks frozen.

Melt in a pan:

    3 tablespoons butter

Add and cook gently about 5 minutes:

    ½ cup chopped onions or shallots
    ¼ cup chopped carrot
    ½ cup chopped celery

Then add:

    6 white peppercorns
    3 or 4 cloves

½ cup white wine or 2
   tablespoons vinegar
2 cups cold water
   A Bouquet Garni, page
   220
   A twist of lemon rind
1 to 1½ lbs. washed fish
   bones, heads, tails, skins
   and trimmings

The fish heads are particularly flavorful, but ◗ avoid strong-flavored fish trimmings like mackerel, skate or mullet. Use salmon only for salmon sauce. Shells from crab, shrimp and lobster are delicious additions, but these are usually cooked with bay leaf, thyme and wine rather than with vinegar. Heat until the liquid begins to ◗ simmer and continue cooking, uncovered, over rather brisk heat, not longer than 20 to 30 minutes—or a bitter flavor may develop. Add, at the last minute:

   Any extra oyster or clam
   juices

Strain the stock and use in soups or sauces. To clarify fish fumet for aspic, proceed as for the quick method of beef stock clarification, page 140.

VEGETABLES FOR STOCK
AND SOUP

In vegetable stock for soup, your goal is to draw all the flavor out of the vegetable, see Vegetable Stock, page 145. To prepare, use about 1½ to 2 times as much water as vegetable. Prepare vegetables for soup as you would for eating—wash, scrape or pare, as needed, and remove bruised or bad portions. Onions are the exception, as the skins may be left on to give color to the soup.

◗ For quicker cooking and greater extraction, you may ↲ blend the vegetables before cooking. If the cooking liquid tastes palatable, keep it for judicious use with other full-bodied sauces or gravies.

It is very important to taste the vegetable liquors you reserve. They vary tremendously, depending on the age of the vegetable and whether the leaves are dark outer ones or light inner ones. Green celery tops, for instance, can become bitter through long cooking in a stock, while the tender yellowish leaves do not. Often, too, celery is so heavily sprayed with chemicals that the outer leaves and tops taste strongly enough of these absorbed flavors to carry over into foods. Nutritionists recommend the outer leaves of vegetables because of their greater vitamin content. Eat these raw in salads, where the bitterness is not accented as it is in soups.

Also balance the amounts and kinds of vegetables to other stock flavors. The cooking liquors from white turnips, cabbage, cauliflower, broccoli and potatoes, used with discretion, may be a real asset to a borsch and a real calamity in chicken broth. We find pea pods and water from peas, except in pea soups, a deadening influence. Carrots and parsnips tend to sweeten the pot too much. Tomatoes, unless just the skins are used, can make a consommé too acid and yet be just the touch you want in a vegetable soup or a sauce. Some vegetable juices like those from leeks, water cress and asparagus seem ever welcome. ◗ Use any of these liquids, whether from fresh, canned or frozen vegetables, if they taste good.

You may also purée leftover cooked vegetables as thickeners for soup.

There are several ways to bring up the flavor of soup vegetables. One is to sauté them gently in butter, see Brunoise (I, 109). The other is to cook them in meat stocks.

Unlike the above ♦ when you add vegetables to soup as a garnish, the trick is not to soften them to the point where their cells break down and they release their juices, but to keep them full of flavor. However, if the vegetables you are using as a garnish are strong like peppers or onions, blanch them first.

VEGETABLE STOCK

[About 1 Quart]
To add color to this stock made from raw vegetables, begin by caramelizing, page 169.

1 teaspoon sugar
in a heavy pot or sauté:
½ cup finely chopped onion
in:
2 tablespoons fat
Add:
A dash of white pepper
A dash of cayenne
½ teaspoon salt
A Bouquet Garni,
page 220
¼ cup each carrots, turnips,
parsnips
2 cups diced celery ribs
and yellow leaves
(1 cup shrededd lettuce)
(Mushroom or tomato
skins)
Add enough to cover:
Cold water
Bring to a boil ♦ cover partially and simmer about 1½ hours or until the vegetables are very tender. Strain and chill. Degrease before using, if necessary.

✪ PRESSURE COOKED STOCKS AND SOUPS

While these are not as delicate in flavor as stocks cooked at lower temperatures, they are not to be scorned.
♦ Allow one quart of liquid to about 2 lbs. of meat in a 4-quart pressure cooker. ♦ Season very lightly. You may prefer to almost finish cooking the meat,

about 30 minutes at 15 lbs. pressure. Then reduce the pressure and add the vegetables. If there is a mixture, you will have to judge the time it will take to release their juices. Add about 3 minutes to the time given in individual recipes for pressure cooked vegetables. Strain the stock.

If you want to make a vegetable soup, strain and degrease the stock before adding the vegetables. Then cook them in the soup for the same length of time you would normally cook them as indicated in individual recipes.

ABOUT GLAZES

Glazes are meat stocks cooked down very slowly until they solidify. These overpoweringly strong stocks from meat and fowl are our first choice when we have the patience to make them. Ideally, properly cooked food should produce its own glaze, but these results have all but vanished in most kitchens, as they prove both expensive and time consuming. Even meat glazes made by reducing stocks to a glutinous consistency are now the exception in home kitchens—but what a convenience and delight they are when skillfully used. They ✳ freeze very well, too.
♦ To make a glaze, or glace, reduce brown stock to the point where it evenly coats a spoon when inserted into it. ♦ Use glazes discreetly, as their strength can easily over-balance a sauce or gravy.

STOCK REINFORCERS

I. BEEF JUICE
This is another rich stock item. To make this, see Beef Tea (I, 111).

II. CANNED BOUILLON AND CONSOMMÉ

These are both a great help. You may prefer the bouillon—which is less sweet than the consommé.

III. CANNED, FROZEN AND DRIED SOUPS

Alone or when combined with household stocks, these can produce very sophisticated results. Suggestions for their use appear in detail under Soups, Sauces, Aspics and Gravies. Bouillon cubes and beef extracts, each diluted in ½ cup boiling liquid, are also useful.

IV. MILK AND CREAM

When diluted with stock and even the following seasoned water, milk and cream precede the use of plain water every time.

V. SEASONED WATER

Boil briskly for about 10 minutes:

    2 cups water

to which you have added:

    1 teaspoon monosodium
        glutamate
    1 peppercorn
    ½ teaspoon soy sauce or salt

ABOUT COURT BOUILLON

Court bouillons are seasoned liquids which, as their name implies, are cooked only a short time. Their composition varies. They may simply be Acidulated Water, page 148, acidulated water reinforced with braised or fresh vegetables, or even a hot marinade with oil.

They are not actual broths or stocks in themselves but, rather, prototypes that may develop into them. Sometimes they are used only as a blanching or cooking medium. Then they are discarded, as in the cooking of vegetables where their purpose is to retain color or leach out undesirable flavors. Sometimes they are used as a liquid in which to store the food processed in them, as in Vegetables à la Grecque (I, 257). Or they may be used as a hot marinade in which fish is soaked before cooking. And, sometimes, as in the cooking of delicately flavored fish, they become—after the fish is drained from them— a Fumet or Fish Stock, page 143.

COURT BOUILLON FOR FISH

Use this for any fish which is to be poached or "boiled." See also Truite au Bleu or Blue Trout (I, 419).
Trim and clean:

    3 lbs. fish

and rub with:

    Lemon juice

Meanwhile, in a large pan, bring to a boil:

    2 quarts water

Add:

    ½ bay leaf
    ¼ cup chopped carrot
    ½ cup chopped celery
    1 small onion stuck with
        2 cloves
    ½ cup vinegar or 1 cup
        dry white wine
    1 teaspoon salt
        (Parsley or a Bouquet
        Garni, page 220)

When the mixture is boiling, plunge the fish in and ♦ at once, reduce the heat so the court bouillon simmers. Simmer the fish ♦ uncovered, until tender. Drain and serve. You may keep and use this court bouillon for several days for poaching other fish, but it is not used in soups, sauces and gravies, as is a fumet or fish stock, see above.

COURT BOUILLON BLANC

For use in retaining good color in variety meats and vegetables.
I. Allow to every:

1 quart boiling water
2 tablespoons lemon juice

Blend until smooth and add to the above:

2 tablespoons water
1 tablespoon flour
(3 tablespoons chopped suet)

Add:

(An onion stuck with cloves, celery, carrot or leek)

II. Or add the vegetables to a mixture of boiling:

½ seasoned water
½ milk

Reduce to a simmer at once. The milk may curdle slightly, but this will not affect the food adversely.

ABOUT WATER

One of our family jokes involved an 1890 debutante cousin from Indianapolis who, when asked where her home town got its water, replied: "Out of a faucet." Many of us have come to assume that there is a kind of nationwide standardization in tap water. As long as it runs pure, plentiful, hot and cold and reasonably pleasant to the taste, we no more bother our heads with its further analysis than did our pretty Victorian cousin. Yet both its purity and its composition are of considerable importance in the kitchen.

In this book, when the word ♦ water appears in the recipes, we assume it has a 60°–80° temperature. ♦ If hotter or colder water is needed, it is specified.

♦ Soft water is best for most cooking processes, although very soft water will make yeast doughs soggy and sticky. ♦ Hard water and some artificially softened waters affect flavor. They may toughen legumes and fruits and shrivel pickles. They

markedly alter the color of vegetables in the cabbage family and turn onions, cauliflower, potatoes and rice yellow. If your water is hard, cooking these vegetables à blanc is a superior method of preparation. Hard water retards fermentation of yeast, although it strengthens the gluten in flour. Alkaline waters, however, have a solvent effect on gluten, as well as diminishing its gas-retaining properties—and the size of the loaf.

Water hardness is due to various combinations of salts and there are a number of ways by which it may be reduced. Passing hard water through a tank containing counteractive chemicals may be helpful, but most of these systems principally exchange sodium for calcium compounds and are more effective for water used in dish washing than in cooking. If the salts happen to consist of bicarbonates of calcium and magnesium, simply boiling the water for 20 or 30 minutes will cause them to precipitate. But if the water originally held in solution large amounts of sulphates, boiling it will increase hardness, rather than reduce it—because the sulphates are concentrated by evaporation. Certain types of hard water must be avoided by people who are on low sodium-free or salt-free diets.

Sodium chloride, or common salt, often occurs in inland, as well as ocean waters. Should you be interested in finding out what type of water you have, call your local waterworks or health department, if you live in a town, or your county agent, if you live in the country.

Most old recipes recommend long soaking of food in water. But we know that fruits, salad greens and vegetables should be washed as quickly and briefly as possible. Soaking leaches out

their water soluble vitamins.
♦ And, because of this leaching
action, it is a good plan to utilize all soaking and cooking
waters, unless they have bitter
or off-flavors.

Occasionally recipes indicate
♦ water by weight, in which
case use 1 tablespoon for ½
oz., 2 cups for 1 lb.

▲ The boiling temperature
of water at sea level—212°—
is increased in direct proportion
to the number of particles dissolved in it. The amount of salt
added in cooking is not enough
to change the normal sea level
boiling point. With the addition
of sugar, however, the boiling
point is lowered appreciably, see
Jellies, page 573. For boiling at
high altitudes, see (I, 72).

ACIDULATED WATER

I. To 1 quart water, add 1 tablespoon vinegar.

II. To 1 quart water, add 2
tablespoons vinegar or 3 tablespoons lemon juice (1 teaspoon
salt).

III. To 1 quart water, add ½
cup wine. Sometimes brines,
page 196, are stipulated.

WATER PURIFICATION

In using or storing water, be
sure of two things: that the
source from which you get it is
uncontaminated and that the
vessels you store it in are sterile.
The color of water has nothing
to do with its purity. As disease
germs are more often derived
from animal than from vegetable matter, a brown swamp
water may be purer than a blue
lake water. ♦ Should water have
been exposed to radioactive fall-
out, do not use it. Water from
wells and springs, if protected
from surface contamination,
should be safe from this hazard.
For water storage in shelters,

use nonbreakable glass or plastic
bottles that are surrounded by
and separated from each other
by excelsior or packing. Inspect
the stored water periodically
and replace any that is cloudy.
Allow for each person, for drinking, a minimum of 7 gallons
for each 2 week period and for
personal cleanliness, another 7
gallons.

If you are in doubt as to the
purity of water, treat it in one
of the following ways:
I. Boil water vigorously 3 minutes. Boiled water tastes flat,
but can be improved in flavor
if aerated by pouring it a number of times from one clean vessel to another.

II. Use water purification tablets in the dosage recommended
on the label.

III. Add to ♦ clear water, allowing 8 drops per gallon, any
household bleach solution that
contains hypochlorite in 5.25%
solution. The label should give
you this information. ♦ If the
water is cloudy, increase to 16
drops per gallon. ♦ In either
case, stir and allow the water to
stand 30 minutes after adding
the hypochlorite. ♦ The water
should have a distinct chlorine
taste and odor. This is a sign of
safety and, if you do not detect
it by smell, add another dose of
the hypochlorite and wait 15
minutes. If the odor is still not
present, the hypochlorite may
have weakened through age and
the water is not safe for storage.

IV. ♦ Add to clear water, allowing 12 drops per gallon, 2%
tincture of iodine. Stir thoroughly before storing. ♦ To
cloudy water, allow 24 drops
for each gallon. Stir thoroughly
before storing. This method is
not recommended for persons
with thyroid disturbances.

ABOUT WINE AND SPIRITS FOR COOKING

There is no doubt that the occasional addition of wine—or of spirits and cordials—gives food a welcome new dimension. If yours is a wine-drinking household, you have probably always enjoyed cooking with "the butts." If wine is a stranger to your table, you may be hesitant about breaking open a new bottle for experimentation. When you do decide to take the plunge ♦ remember that the wine you choose need not be a very old or expensive one, but that it should be good enough, at least, to be drunk with relish for its own sake.

What kind of wine to use? The specific answer depends on the kind of food used with it, as listed later. Start your purchasing with a dry white and a full-bodied red. Try Bonne Femme Sauce for fish (I, 402), a wine pot roast, an orange fruit soup; and before you know it you will have developed a palate and a palette, and be well on your way to some strikingly colorful effects in a new medium.

In general, however, keep wine away from very tart or very piquantly seasoned foods, unless you are using it as a Marinade (I, 380), or to mask an off-flavor. Incidentally, ♦ be sure that the dish in which you marinate is glazed or made of glass, stainless steel or enamel.

How much wine to use? ♦ Never add so much as to overbalance or drown out the characteristic flavor of the food itself. ♦ Count the wine as a part of any given sum total of liquid ingredients, not as an extra. A recipe for pot roast with wine may call for the addition of as much as a cup per pound. When you use it here,

be sure it is warmed before adding. In meat or fowl recipes calling for both wine and salt pork, watch for too great saltiness. Correct the seasoning at the end of cooking.

Brandy, sherry and whiskey combat graininess and fishiness of flavor. In general, 2 tablespoons of heavy wine—such as sherry, Madeira or port—will equal in flavoring strength about ½ cup of dry red or white wine. In aspics, replace part of every cup of other liquid indicated with 1 to 1½ tablespoons fortified wine or 2 to 2½ tablespoons ordinary wine. You may wish to reduce wine as a means of increasing its flavoring power and to avoid overdilution in saucemaking. If so, remember that 1 cup of wine will reduce to about ¼ cup in 10 minutes of cooking.

When to add wine? This question is a hotly disputed one. If a wine sauce is heated, it not only loses its alcoholic content but, if cooked too long, its flavor. Add wine to a sauce only during those periods when the dish can be covered, whether marinating, cooking, storing or chilling. While you may boil wine to reduce it ♦ never raise the heat to above a simmer when cooking food in wine. We feel that if you aim at mellow penetration or at tenderizing, the time to add wine is at the onset of cooking. ♦ To avoid curdling or separation, wine should always be added beforehand in any recipes which include milk, cream, eggs or butter. It should then be reduced slightly and the other ingredients mentioned added in turn, off the heat. If the dish cannot be served at once, it may be kept warm in a double boiler ♦ over—not in—hot water. To achieve a pronounced wine flavor, swirl reduced wine into the food at the very end of the cooking process, after it has been removed from the heat. In aspics, wine should be added after the gelatin is dissolved. One of our favorite practices is to add wine to a pan in which meat has been cooking, deglazing (I, 358), the pan juices and so building up a pleasant substitute for roux-based gravy.

Spirits, liqueurs and cordials are most frequently used in flavoring desserts. Whiskey is becoming increasingly popular but, except for desserts, do not use bourbon, as it is too sweet. One of the more spectacular wine-cooking techniques is flambéeing —sometimes at midpoint in preparation and sometimes as a final flourish in the dining room. To flambée fruits and other foods, see (I, 80). ◗ Flambéeing is sure-fire only if the liquor to be ignited is previously warmed as well as the food.

Exceptions not only prove the rule—they sometimes improve it. We list below certain time-tested combinations in wine-cookery; but we encourage defiance and initiative.

For Soups: Cream sherry or semisweet white wines.

For Fish, Poultry and Eggs: Dry white wines.

For Red Meat: Dry red wine or rosé.

For Pork, Veal, Lamb or Game: Red or white wine or rosé.

For Aspics and Wine Jellies: Any type—but red wines tend to lose their color. Brandy complements an aspic of game.

For Sauces: Dry or semisweet Bordeaux or Burgundy, champagne, riesling, vermouth, see individual sauce recipes.

For Desserts: Sweet sherry, port, Madeira, Tokay, muscatel, rum, liqueurs, cordials.

Beer and cider, as well as wine, have virtues in cooking,

especially if the beer is flat and the cider hard, as their fermentative qualities help tenderize meats, doughs and batters. You will find them indicated where their use is appropriate in a number of the recipes.

ABOUT VINEGAR

Whether a vinegar is sharp, rich or mellow makes a tremendous difference in cooking. ◗ All vinegars are corrosive—so be sure to mix pickled, vinaigretted or marinated foods in glass, enamel or stainless vessels. Keep away from copper, zinc, galvanized or iron ware.

Vinegars divide roughly into the following types:

DISTILLED WHITE VINEGAR

This is based on chemicals usually with a 40% acetic acid count or grain. It is used in pickling when the pickle must remain light in color.

CIDER AND MALT-BASED
WINE VINEGARS

These are full-bodied and usually run between 50% to 60% acetic acid.

WINE VINEGARS

Made from both red and white wines, these are the blandest. They have about a 50% acetic acid content.

We have often admired the lovely light quality of dressings based on Italian wine vinegar. A friend told us his secret lies in fermenting a homemade, unpasteurized red wine, but not allowing it to reach the point of bitterness. If you don't want to bother with this process, a substitute is to dilute sharp vinegars with red or white wine. Wine vinegars "mother," forming a strange, wispy residue at the base of the bottle. As they are of uncertain strengths, they are not recommended for pickling. Should you plan making spiced vinegars in quantity for gifts, please profit by our experience and mix in small batches.

HERB VINEGARS

These can be made with any of the above vinegars. Use individual herbs like tarragon or burnet or develop your favorite herb combinations—allowing not more than 3 tablespoons fresh herb leaves per quart of vinegar. If garlic is used, crush it and leave it in the jar only 24 hours. The reason for not overloading the vinegar is that its preservative strength may not be great enough to hold more vegetable matter. After 4 weeks of steeping, filter the vingar, rebottle it in sterilized containers and keep tightly corked.

FRESH HERB VINEGAR

Combine:
1 gallon cider or white wine vinegar
2 dozen peppercorns
1 dozen sliced shallots
¾ cup tarragon
8 sprigs rosemary
8 sprigs thyme
4 branches winter savory
1 sprig chervil
1 well-cleaned, unpeeled, sliced celeriac root
½ cup parsley
1 sliced parsley root
Bottle these ingredients. After 2 weeks, strain the vinegar through cheesecloth. Place in sterile bottles and cork tightly.

SPICED VINEGAR

An excellent, if deceptive, mixture. It tastes like a delicious blend of herbs, but it is flavored with spices whole or ground. If ground spices are used, filter the vinegar before using it. Combine, stir and heat slowly until just under the boiling point:
¼ cup whole cloves
¼ cup allspice
2 tablespoons mace
3 tablespoons celery seed
¼ cup mustard seed
6 tablespoons whole black pepper
3 tablespoons turmeric
¼ cup white ginger root
1½ gallons cider vinegar
2 cups sugar
Place these ingredients in jugs or fruit jars. Slice and add for 24 hours:
4 or more cloves garlic
Cork the jugs or screw down the jar lids tightly. The vinegar is ready for use in 3 weeks. Combine it with oil for French Dressing (I, 341).

GARLIC VINEGAR

Heat to the boiling point:
1 cup vinegar
Cut into halves and add for 24 hours:
4 cloves garlic
When the vinegar is cold, place it in a closed jar. After 2 weeks, strain it. Use it in dressings or sauces.

QUICK HERB VINEGAR

[About 1 Cup]
Combine:
1 cup well-flavored vinegar: wine or cider
1 teaspoon dried crushed herbs: basil, tarragon, etc.
You may use this at once with salad oil. You may add ½ clove of garlic and fish it out later. Shortly before serving, add:
2 tablespoons chopped parsley
1 tablespoon chopped chives

TARRAGON OR BURNET VINEGAR

[About 2 Cups]

Wash, then dry well:

1½ tablespoons fresh
tarragon or burnet
leaves

Crush them to bruise them slightly. Add them to:

2 cups warmed vinegar
2 whole cloves
1 skinned halved clove
garlic

Place these ingredients in a covered jar. After 24 hours, remove the garlic. After 2 weeks, strain and bottle the vinegar. This makes a strong infusion that may be diluted later with more vinegar.

RED RASPBERRY VINEGAR

Put in a large glazed or stainless steel bowl:

6 quarts red raspberries

Cover them with:

1 quart wine vinegar

Let stand in a cool place for about 20 hours. Then strain. Measure the liquid into an enamel or stainless steel pan and add an equal quantity of:

Sugar

Bring to a boil and ♦ simmer 10 minutes. Cool and store in tightly lidded sterile jars.

CHILI VINEGAR

You can make a really hot French dressing with this. See also Chilis Preserved in Sherry, page 590.

Steep:

1 oz. chilis

in:

1 pint vinegar

for 10 days. Shake daily. Then strain and bottle.

ABOUT WHEAT FLOURS
AND GRAINS

In our miraculously mechanical but standardized economy, the average housewife, oddly enough, finds at hand only two kinds of white flour, both the result of highly milled or "patent" processing. They must meet rigid government specifications and, when manufactured, contain not more than 15% moisture. But they often acquire more in careless storage. Or they dry out in high altitudes or during the winter months. These varying moistures affect the way flours "handle." So some recipes for breads and pastries may read "2½ to 2¾ cups flour." If they do ♦ add the smaller amount of flour first and enough of, or even more than, the remaining flour until the dough begins to clean the sides of the bowl. Don't add more than is needed for good handling. These two easily available flours, called "all-purpose" and "cake" are used as their names imply. ♦ The single word "flour" in our recipes always means wheat flour.

ALL-PURPOSE FLOUR

This is a blend of hard and soft wheat flours. The presence of more and tougher gluten in the hard wheat constituent results in a rather elastic and porous product. Some of the flours sold in our South as all-purpose are closer to cake flour in texture. If using them with yeast, give them only one rising period—to not quite double the volume —and then let the dough rise to normal, using the finger test sketched on page 242. ♦ You may substitute for 1 cup of all-purpose flour 1⅛ cups of cake flour.

CAKE FLOUR

This is made of soft wheats and their delicate, less expansive gluten bakes to a crumblier texture. Although you will not get the same result—you may, in emergencies ♦ substitute ⅞ cup of all-purpose flour for 1 cup cake flour.

BREAD FLOUR

Although not easily come by, this type is highly desirable, as its high gluten content allows the absorption of more moisture than either of the above. The elasticity from its higher gluten content also allows it to expand and still hold the gas liberated by the yeast. This flour feels almost granular or gritty when rubbed between the fingers.

PRESIFTED FLOURS

These are ground to a point of pulverization and whether resifted or not give a different texture to baking. Some of them also have a larger percentage of hard durum wheat and, although the manufacturers may suggest them to replace cake flour, the greater gluten content may tend to toughen cakes. If you use them, be sure to use 1 tablespoon less per cup than our recipes call for. ◗ We suggest resifting.

BROWNED FLOUR

This has many uses. It adds both color and flavor to sauces, but browning it destroys part of its thickening power. Heat all-purpose flour in a very slow oven 200° to 250° in a very heavy pan. Shake the pan periodically so the flour browns evenly. To substitute, use 1½ tablespoons brown flour for every tablespoon all-purpose flour.

PASTRY FLOUR

Finely milled, soft, low-gluten flour—often available in the South, where it is used for quick breads and pastries.

SELF-RISING FLOUR AND PHOSPHATED FLOURS

These contain the right amounts of leavens and salt for baking.

Many people do not like to use them because during delays in merchandising or storing the leavens are apt to lose their potency. If used in pastry, these flours give a spongy texture and are advised only for crusts where a low fat content is the objective and the fat in the recipe has been reduced. They are not recommended for making bread.

SEMOLINA

This is a creamy-colored, granular, protein-rich durum wheat flour used commercially for all types of pasta. It is not your fault if homemade pastas and noodles fail to hold their shape no matter how carefully you have prepared and cooked them. The trouble lies in the lower gluten content of all-purpose flour on which housewives usually have to depend.

FARINA

This is also a creamy-colored, granular, protein-rich meal made from hard—but not durum—wheat.

ENRICHED FLOUR

We have become so accustomed to our highly bleached white flours that we forget that earlier cooks knew only whole-kernel flours. These were not the so-called whole wheat of our commercial world, but the whole grain, which includes the germ. Even the fine manchet flour of tradition contained some germ. But flours in general use today completely lack it. As Dr. A. J. Carlson, a leading investigator on foods and nutrition, says so graphically, "When rats and gray squirrels are given corn in abundance, they eat the germ and leave the rest. People leave the germ and eat the rest." This nutritious and tasty entity, the germ, is removed in modern milling because flours made with it are both harder to mill and to keep. After the removal of the outer coats and germ, our flours may be "enriched," but the term is misleading. ◗ Enriched flour contains only four of the many ingredients known to have been removed from it in milling.

WHOLE-GRAIN OR GRAHAM FLOUR

These, and some commercial whole wheats, retain their original vitamins, mineral salts, fats and other still unknown components—whether coarsely or finely milled. Scientists are aware of about twenty of these substances, even if they have so far failed to isolate them all or to produce them synthetically.

Most grains are similar, in their structure, to the wheat kernel sketched in cross-section.

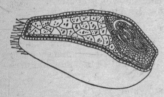

The outer bran layers contain, with the germ—indicated by the darker swirl on the right—most vitamins and minerals. The germ, which is only 2% of the entire kernel, contains the highest grade protein and all of the fat. The endosperm indicated on the left is largely starch with some protein—different from, but complementary to, the protein of the germ. But the outer coating and the germ—small compared with the whole kernel in this enlarged drawing—are of unchallenged importance in content and irreplaceable in flavor.

◗ You may substitute 1 cup of very finely milled whole-grain flour, sometimes called whole-kernel or graham flour, for 1 cup of all-purpose flour. For coarsely ground whole-grain flour, substitute 1 cup for ⅞ cup of all-purpose flour. This is stirred lightly rather than sifted before measuring.

Yeast breads from whole wheat flours do not have to be kneaded. They can be mixed and allowed to rise just once in the pan. If kneading is omitted, the texture will be coarse.

BRAN FLOUR

This flour often gives a dry result unless you soften the bran by allowing the wet bread mixture, minus the yeast or baking powder, to stand for eight hours or so. Bran flours are usually mixed with some all-purpose flour.

CRACKED WHEAT

This is cut rather than ground. It gives up little of its starch as a binder. Therefore, it must be mixed with some all-purpose flour in baking.

GLUTEN FLOUR

This is a starch-free flour made by washing the starch from high protein wheat flour. The residue is then dried and ground. See Gluten Bread, page 252. ◗ For 1 cup all-purpose flour, substitute 13 tablespoons gluten flour.

Gluten is found in its most complete form in wheat. Scientists think—but they do not know—that 2 substances, glutenin and gliadin, occurring separately in the wheat, interact to form gluten. Gluten can never develop except in the presence of moisture or when the grain is agitated—as in kneading. ◗ To prepare gluten from gluten flour, knead into a stiff dough:

4 cups whole-grain or
unbleached flour
1½ to 3 cups lukewarm water
Roll it into a ball and submerge

it in water for 2 hours. Then, still keeping the dough ball under water, work the starch out of it by kneading. At intervals, pour off the starchy water. Replace the water you pour off and continue to knead, repeating this operation until the water is almost clear. The gluten is then ready to cook. ◖ Form the starch-free dough into a loaf and cut it into ½-inch slices. Put in a 3-quart pan for which you have a tight lid:

¼ cup vegetable oil

You may flavor the gluten at this point by sautéeing until clear and golden:

1 medium-sized finely sliced onion

Put the gluten slices in the pan; cover with:

Boiling water

Simmer, closely covered, for 1 hour and drain. Store refrigerated and closely covered. Gluten can then be further cooked by dipping in egg and potato or rice flour and browning it slowly in an oiled pan. Or cover with undiluted tomato, mushroom or celery soup and heat in a preheated 350° oven for about 20 minutes or until it is hot all the way through.

WHEAT-GERM FLOUR

This may be ◖ substituted by using ⅛ cup of powdered wheat germ and ⅔ cup of all-purpose flour for 1 cup of all-purpose flour. Be sure that the wheat germ, either powdered or whole, is very slightly toasted before combining it with the dough.

ABOUT NON-WHEAT FLOURS

Some of the following non-wheat flours can be used alone. But in any bread recipe that fails to call for wheat flour—at least in part—you must expect a marked difference in texture,

as wheat gluten has an elastic quality which is unique. This protein gluten factor in wheat is activated when the flour is both moistened and handled, at which time the gluten is said to "develop." The flour is then able to absorb as much as 200 times its weight in moisture. In describing non-wheat flours, some of which are richer in over-all protein content than wheat, we give the closest substitutions we have been able to find but, if possible ◖ we advise using at least 1 cup wheat flour for every 2 cups other flour, or a very heavy dough results. For increased protein content, we suggest the use of Cornell Triple Rich Formula, page 243. ◖ Coarse flours need not be sifted before measuring. They do need more leavening than wheat types. ◖ Allow 2½ teaspoons baking powder for every cup of flour.

CORN FLOUR OR CORNSTARCH

Corn flour in its starchy, rather than its granular, form is a very valuable thickener. The new waxy starches made from certain varieties of corn are revolutionizing frozen sauces and fillings by their great stabilizing powers, but ◖ are not to be used in baking. For thickening ◖ substitute 1 tablespoon waxy corn flour for 2 tablespoons all-purpose flour. For non-waxy cornstarch ◖ substitute 1½ teaspoons cornstarch for 1 tablespoon all-purpose flour.

There is nothing more discouraging than the lumps any cornstarch can form or the raw taste it produces if it is badly handled or insufficiently cooked. Here are the things we have learned that help us to handle it more easily.

◖ Use a double boiler.

Avoid lumping, in recipes calling for sugar, by mixing

cornstarch, sugar and salt together just before adding it gradually to the ◆ cold liquid.

In recipes without sugar, make a paste of 1 tablespoon of cornstarch to 1 cup of the liquid called for in the recipe. Introduce this paste gradually into the ◆ hot, but not boiling, liquid.

Cornstarch, along with tapioca and arrowroot, is recommended for thickening very acid fruits because it does not lose its thickening power ◆ as quickly as does flour in the presence of acid. But if it is ◆ overcooked, it loses its thickening power very quickly, regardless of the presence of acid. These facts account for the endless letters we get on pie fillings. In the extra special care cooks lavish on fillings, they are apt to overcook or ◆ overbeat them after cooking. Be very careful to check the cooking stages described later on.

Other causes for breakdown of thickening may come from too high a percentage of sugar in the recipe and, strangely, even from using too much cornstarch.

Also, tests have shown that ◆ the material from which the double boiler is made has a direct effect on the thickening quality and the success of unmolding cornstarch puddings. Aluminum, stainless steel and enamel are superior—in that order—to heatproof glass or heavy crockery.

But to get on with the cooking. Once the cornstarch is properly added to the liquid, either dispersed in sugar or in a cold paste, it goes through 2 main cooking periods, 3 if eggs are added. To keep the temperature right for the timing given here, use an aluminum, enamel or stainless steel pan. Fill the base of the double boiler so that the water just dampens the bottom of the liner. ◆ Bring the water to a bubbling boil before starting the timing. During the first period of about 8 to 12 minutes ◆ constant, gentle stirring is necessary to blend the mixture free from lumps and to hold the starch particles in suspension until gelatinization takes place and the mixture thickens. In this time, it should have reached at least 185°, a temperature which is essential for proper unmolding.

Then follows the second period of about 10 minutes when the mixture is ◆ covered and cooked undisturbed to complete gelatinization. Maintain the 185° temperature.

A third period, of about 2 minutes, follows the addition of the eggs. This adding procedure is just like any other when eggs or egg yolks meet hot liquid. The eggs are well beaten first. A portion of the hot mixture is added to the eggs very gradually. This is returned to the original mass, which has temporarily ◆ been removed from the heat. ◆ The stirring is less constant and extremely gentle during the next 2 minutes. The pudding should thicken much more in cooling. Have ready molds, rinsed out in cold water. Stir the mixture very gently into them—releasing heat which would condense and thin the mixture. Cool for about 30 minutes at room temperature and 1 to 2 hours refrigerated—for successful unmolding of individual molds. Larger molds will take 6 to 12 hours.

Cornstarch can be used in combination as a wheat flour allergy substitute, see page 159.

CORN MEAL

When water-ground, corn meal not only retains the germ but has a superior flavor. Yellow corn meal has more vitamin A potential than white corn meal, but there is little difference in their nutritional or baking properties. Corn breads vary from all-corn Dodgers made without a riser, see page 278, to moist and tender corn and wheat bread prepared with yeast, see page 251. To avoid graininess in corn breads, mix corn meal and the liquid in the recipe, bring to a boil and cool before mixing with the other ingredients.

RICE FLOUR

This makes a close but delicately textured cake in recipes heavy in egg. To avoid graininess, see Corn Meal, above. ◆ Substitute ⅞ cup rice flour for 1 cup all-purpose flour. But be sure, in baking, not to choose a waxy type of rice flour, also known as "sweet flour." Instead, use these waxy rice flours in making sauces. They have remarkable stabilizing powers which prevent the separation of frozen gravies and sauces when reheated. They are also much less apt to lump.

RYE FLOUR

When used in most of the rye breads we buy, this flour is usually combined with a large proportion of wheat flour. This is because the rye flour gluten factor provides stickiness, but lacks elasticity. Breads made largely with rye flour are moist and compact and usually call for a Sour Dough Leavener, see page 163. ◆ Substitute 1¼ cups rye flour for 1 cup all-purpose flour.

RYE MEAL

This is simply coarsely ground whole-rye flour. ◆ Substitute 1 cup rye meal for 1 cup all-purpose flour. See Rye Flour, above.

SOY FLOUR

This flour has both a high protein and a high fat content. However, some soy flour is made from beans from which the fat has been largely expressed. It may be made from either raw or very lightly toasted beans. Because of the fat, it is not mixed with the dry ingredients but is creamed with the shortening or blended with the liquids. It is usually substituted ◆ 2 tablespoons of soy flour plus ⅞ cup of all-purpose flour for 1 cup of all-purpose flour. But it may constitute, if you like the flavor, up to 20% of the weight of the flour in the recipe. Soy flour causes heavy browning of the crust, so reduce baking temperatures about 25°.

POTATO FLOUR

Chiefly used in soups, gravies, breads and cakes, in combination with other flours or alone in Sponge Cakes, page 342. To avoid lumping, blend it with sugar before mixing—or cream it with the shortening before adding a liquid. In bread recipes, it gives a moist slow-staling loaf. ◆ To substitute as a thickener, use 1½ teaspoons potato flour for 1 tablespoon all-purpose flour or, in baking, ⅝ cup potato flour for 1 cup all-purpose flour.

TAPIOCA AND SAGO

These are similar in their uses. Tapioca is processed from the Brazilian cassava root and sago from certain Indian palms. Sago and the so-called pearl tapioca must both be soaked for at least 1 hour before using. Soak ¼ cup of the pearls in ½ cup water which should be completely absorbed. If it isn't, the pearls are too old to use. Should you have already embarked on mixing the recipe, you can substitute rice in equal parts for pearl tapioca. ◆ To substitute so-called minute or granular for pearl tapioca, allow 1½ tablespoons of this finer form for 4 tablespoons of the soaked pearl.

TAPIOCA FLOUR

Like the Waxy Rice and Corn Flours, page 155, these are popular for sauces and fruit fillings that are to be frozen. These sauces reconstitute without breaking down and becoming watery, as flour-thickened sauces may do during frozen storage.

◆ To use in freezing, substitute 1 tablespoon tapioca flour for 2½ tablespoons all-purpose flour to 1 cup liquid. ◆ In non-frozen sauces, substitute 1½ teaspoons tapioca flour for 1 tablespoon all-purpose flour.

Tapioca flour is popular for making very clear glazes. Cook the tapioca and fruit juice or water only to the boiling point. ◆ Beware of overcooking, as it will become stringy.

◆ Never boil. When the first bubbles begin to break through the surface, remove the pan from the heat at once. The mixture will still look thin and milky. After standing 2 or 3 minutes, stir. Wait 2 or 3 minutes longer and stir again. If the recipe calls for butter, stir it in at this time. After 10 minutes more of undisturbed cooling, the glaze should be thick enough to apply to the food you are glazing.

ARROWROOT FLOUR OR STARCH

This is another popular base for cream sauces and clear and delicate glazes. It cooks by the same method as cornstarch but ◆ substitutes in the amount of 1 tablespoon arrowroot to 2½ tablespoons flour for every cup of liquid. If arrowroot glaze is to be used on cold acid fruits—to ensure an attractive consistency—dissolve 1½ teaspoons gelatin in 1 tablespoon cold

water and add it to the hot glaze. Spoon the cooled, thickened glaze over the chilled fruit and keep cold until you serve it.

BARLEY FLOUR

◆ To substitute, use ½ cup barley flour for each cup of all-purpose flour.

COTTONSEED FLOUR

This flour is high in protein and may be used in baking to increase protein content. ◆ Substitute 2 tablespoons cottonseed flour plus ⅞ cup all-purpose flour for 1 cup all-purpose flour.

PEANUT FLOUR

High in protein, this flour may be ◆ substituted up to 2 tablespoons plus ⅞ cup all-purpose flour for 1 cup all-purpose flour.

OAT FLOUR AND OATMEAL

These are ground to different consistencies to combine with wheat flours up to ⅓. Oatmeal is better in baking if soaked in boiling water with the shortening and cooled before the yeast or other leaven is added.

ROLLED OATS

These are separate flakes that respond to steaming. They are popular for adding flavor to cookies. ◆ Substitute 1⅛ cups rolled oats flakes for 1 cup all-purpose flour—combining, in breads, with wheat flours, only up to ½ the total.

BEAN FLOUR

◆ Substitute 4 to 5 cups bean flour for 1 cup all-purpose flour.

NUT MEAL

These finely ground dry nuts are used as a flour substitute in many Torten, see page 366.

CAROB FLOUR

This is milled into a powder

from the pod of tamarind or St. John's bread. In sponge cakes, it can be used just like all-purpose wheat flour—provided the baking heat does not exceed 300°. It is more frequently used in baking to add flavor. ◗ To substitute, allow ⅛ to ¼ cup carob powder plus ⅞ to ¾ cup flour for every cup of flour. Do not bake in an oven higher than 300°, as carob powder scorches easily.

WHEAT FLOUR ALLERGY SUBSTITUTE

This can be kept on hand for use in gravies and some quick breads, pancakes and biscuits. Sift together, 6 times, ½ cup cornstarch with any of the following: ½ cup rye flour, potato flour or rice flour. If you use this combination for baking, you will need 2 teaspoons baking powder for each cup of the flour mixture. If using cornstarch or rice flour, be sure to avoid the waxy types in baking.

COOKED CEREAL

This may be ◗ substituted 1 cup cooked cereal for ¼ cup flour. But you must also cut the fluid in the recipe by 1 cup for each cup of cooked cereal used. To mix, stir the cooked cereal into the remaining fluid before combining with the other ingredients.

ABOUT CRUMBS

Be sure, in reading recipes, to note what kind of bread crumbs are called for. The results are very different, depending on whether they are dry, browned or fresh.

Finely crushed cracker crumbs, cornflakes or corn or potato chips are sometimes used in place of bread crumbs.

DRY CRUMBS

These are made from dry bread,

zwieback or cake. If these materials are not sufficiently dry, crisp them, on a baking sheet in a 250° oven, before making the crumbs. Do not let the crumbs color. If only a few are being made, grind them in a rotary hand grater, or as sketched on page 190, or in a ⅃ blender. If making them in large quantities, put them through a meat grinder with a medium chopping blade. Tie a bag tightly over the mouth of the grinder to catch them all.

◗ Measure dry bread crumbs as you would sugar, page 224. Store dry bread crumbs in a cool, dry place, not too tightly lidded, or they may mold.

BROWNED BREAD CRUMBS

◗ To prepare these, use dry bread crumbs, as described. Allow for each cup dry bread crumbs ½ teaspoon salt and brown them slowly in ⅓ cup butter. Use at once.

SOFT BREAD CRUMBS

◗ To prepare these, use two- to four-day-old bread. You may crumb it ◗ very lightly with your fingers. But a safer way to retain the light texture desired in such crumbs is to pull the bread apart with a fork—using a gingerly motion, as sketched. Do not crush the

bread with the hand that is holding it.

▶ To measure soft bread crumbs, pile them lightly into a cup. Do not pack them down. Use at once. Sometimes the recipe calls for soaking these fresh crumbs in water, milk or stock and pressing the moisture out before using.

ABOUT FLOURING, BREADING AND CRUMBING FOODS

When dredging food with flour or crumbs or with a more elaborately bound coating, the main thing to remember is this: you want a thin, even and unbroken covering that will adhere. The food should be about 75° and should be ▶ dry. If the food is floury to begin with or has a thickened sauce—like croquettes—the flouring may be omitted. But for fish fillets, shrimp, meat, anything with a moist surface, first a wiping and then a flouring is essential.

▶ To prepare a simple breading, have ready finely sifted crumbs, flour or cornmeal. Cornmeal gives the firmest coating. If the food is not fragile, simply put a small quantity of the seasoned coating material in a paper or plastic bag with the object you want to cover. Shake vigorously. You will find this

method gives a very even, quick and economical coating. Or prepare:

SEASONED FLOURING OR BREADING

I. Mix:

    1 cup all-purpose flour, finely sifted dry bread crumbs or finely crushed corn flakes

    1 teaspoon salt

    ¼ teaspoon pepper or ½ teaspoon paprika

    (⅛ teaspoon ginger or nutmeg)

II. Mix:

    1 cup finely sifted dry bread crumbs or crushed corn flakes or crackers

    3 tablespoons grated Parmesan cheese

    ½ teaspoon dried herbs: savory, chervil, chives, basil or tarragon or ¹⁄₁₆ teaspoon rosemary

III. To prepare a more adhesive bound breading—or coating à l'anglaise—requiring egg or milk, begin by wiping the food dry. Then dip the dry food into a shallow bowl of seasoned flour. Have ready, aside from the flour, two other bowls. In the first bowl, put a mixture of slightly beaten egg, diluted with 2 teaspoons to a tablespoon of water or milk for each egg used. You may also add 2 teaspoons oil for each egg. Stir these ingredients together with 10 or 12 mild strokes. Do not let the egg get bubbly, as this makes the coating uneven.

In the other bowl, have ready sifted, seasoned dry bread crumbs. Allow about ¾ cup crumbs for every diluted egg. This amount will coat about 8 croquettes.

As each piece of food is floured, toss it lightly from one palm to the other, patting it gently all over and encouraging any excess flour to fall off, as sketched on the left, below. Then slide the flour-coated food

through the egg mixture, making sure the entire surface is contacted, as shown at center. Allow any excess moisture to drip off. Then place the food in the crumb-lined bowl. See that the crumbs adhere evenly to the shallow sides of the food as well as to its larger surfaces. If you see any vacant places sprinkle a few crumbs on them. Again discourage by patting any excess crumbs which might fall off and brown too rapidly—thus discoloring the frying fat. Handle the food very gently, so that the coating will not be cracked.

◗ Place it on a rack to dry for about 20 minutes before frying.
◗ Do not chill this food before frying, as this will tend to make it absorb an undue amount of fat.

ABOUT LEAVENS

We are all so accustomed to light breads and cakes that we seldom question the part that leavens play in the results.

Where does this rising power lie? First, the steam converted from the moisture, in any baking, may account for ⅓ to ⅘ of the expansion of the dough. The greater amount is characteristic of popovers and cakes which are rich in egg white. So, to encourage the generation of this easily lost asset ◗ preheat your oven.

We usually think of leavens resulting from Baking Powders,

page 164, sour milk and soda, page 165, and yeast—all of which expand with the steam to form a gas as a major force. But we tend to forget the importance of the mechanical incorporation of air from which the rest of the rising power comes. To give a boost to the chemical reactions, be sure you know how to cream fat and sugar, page 335; how to fold and mix batters, page 335; how to beat eggs, page 180; and, especially, be sure to know how to beat the whites to that state called "stiff, but not dry," page 182.

ABOUT YEAST

Yeasts are living organisms with 3,200 billion cells to the pound —and not one is exactly alike. They feed on sugars and produce alcohol and carbon dioxide —the "riser" we are after. But you may prefer, as we do, to accept a Mexican attitude toward yeast doughs. They call them almas, or souls, because they seem so spirited.

When flour is mixed with water to form a dough which is kept covered—and in a warm place—the wild yeast coming from the air and in the flour will start working and form a sour dough. There are enzymes in the flour to convert the wheat starch into sugar, on which the yeast feeds, making alcohol and carbon dioxide. Organic acids and other fragrant compounds are also created to give the sour effect. Sour doughs, discussed later, are examples of this primitive bacterial method. They are so primitive that they are recorded in Egyptian history of 4000 B.C. This leavened bread has been called the first "convenience" food—as its yeast content gives it excellent keeping quality.

But with fine strains of yeasts available, it seems foolish to try so chancy a method. In case of necessity, this sour dough can still be made. ♦ Two cups of this foamy mixture are substituted for 1 cake of compressed yeast. A really well-developed sour dough may give bread an appealing tasty flavor. But the kind of uncontrolled starter you get from wild yeast in the air may well give you both poor rising power and disagreeable off-flavors—unless some commercial yeast is also used. For the more sophisticated taste that a sour dough gives, see page 250 —and for a modern version of this method.

Yeast, just because it is a living organism, is dependent on definite temperature ranges. It begins to activate at about 50° ♦ and is at its best between 78° and 82°. It begins to die around 120° and is useless for baking after 143°. These temperatures and the amount of food available limit its life span. Therefore, its force can be easily computed. One-half an ounce raises 4 cups of flour in about 1½ to 2 hours. One ounce raises 28 cups of flour in about 7 hours. For speedier raising, an excess of yeast is often added. But this is not necessary and often affects flavor and gives a porous texture. Small quantities of sugar also speed yeast activity, but too much will inhibit it. You may have noticed that it takes very sweet doughs longer

to rise. As salt also inhibits yeast, never use salted water for dissolving yeast. In very hot weather, after the yeast is dissolved and added to the flour, salt may be added in small quantities to control too rapid fermentation.

Yeast dough is allowed to rise and fall a number of times during dough-making to improve the texture, but if allowed to over-expand it can use up its energy. In this case, there is little rising power left for the baking period when it is most needed.

For different methods to incorporate yeast in doughs, read about sponge doughs and the direct method, page 239. The liquids added to yeast, either alone or in combination, are: water, which brings out the wheat flavor and makes a crisp crust, or skim milk which not only adds to the nutritive value but also gives a softer crumb. The fat in whole and homogenized milk tends to coat the yeast and prevent its proper softening. Potato water may also be used, but it hastens the action of the yeast and gives a somewhat coarser, moister texture to dough. Both milk and potato water increase the keeping quality of bread somewhat.

To produce the best yeast bread, the dough must be given time to rise slowly—the entire process taking about 4 to 5 hours before baking. If you use 1 cake of yeast to 1½ cups of liquid and if the temperature is right, you can count about 2 hours or more for the first rising; 1 hour or more for the second; and 1 hour in the pans. You may increase the yeast content in any recipe and reduce your rising time considerably. Some successful quick recipes are given, but if you are going to the effort of using yeast, you might as well work for the superlative result which comes from the slower process.

COMPRESSED YEAST

We like to use this moist cake weighing ⅔ oz. But it must be kept refrigerated. Although compressed yeast comes in larger sizes, when 1 cake is specified in this book it means the ⅔ oz. size. If bought fresh, it will keep about 2 weeks. In a freezer, it will keep for 2 months. When at its best it is a light grayish tan in color. It crumbles readily, breaks with a clean edge and smells pleasantly aromatic. When old, it becomes brownish in color. To test for freshness, cream a small quantity of yeast with an equal amount of sugar. It should become liquid at once. You may let crumbled, compressed yeast dissolve in warm water or warm pasteurized skim milk at about 80° for about 5 minutes before combining with other ingredients, as called for in the recipes.

DRY YEAST

This comes in granular form and is liked by many persons for its better keeping qualities. It comes dated and, if kept in a cool place, will hold for several months—and somewhat longer in a refrigerator. It needs greater heat and more moisture to activate it than compressed yeast. ♦ Use more water to dissolve it but ♦ decrease by that amount the liquid called for in the recipe and ♦ heat the dissolving water to between 105° and 115°. To dissolve it best, sprinkle the powdered yeast on the surface of the water.

♦ To substitute dry granular yeast for compressed yeast, use 2 teaspoons dry yeast granules to a ⅔ oz. cake of compressed yeast.

DEBITTERED BREWERS' YEAST

Another form of dry yeast—but one without leavening power—which adds nutritive value to foods. It may be added to breads in the proposition of 1 to 3 teaspoons to 1 cup of flour, without affecting flavor or texture adversely. See Cornell Triple-Rich Formula, page 243.

ABOUT SOUR DOUGH

This term brings to mind at once the hard-bitten pioneer whose sharing of the bread "starter" was a true act of friendship. Of course, the best French breads and many other famous doughs are also based on flour and water mixtures fermented in various ways to trap natural yeast. In kitchens where yeast baking has been going on for centuries, these organisms are plentiful and success is quickly assured. But in an uninitiated streamlined kitchen, we recommend beginning a sour dough with a commercial yeast, especially in winter.

Remember, the sour dough starter is just as fragile as the yeast and must be cosseted along. After you have made your starter, you can continue to use it for about 3 days at room temperature without reworking it and for about a week if it is refrigerated. But never allow it to freeze. And never add more at one time for each cup of sour dough than 1 cup 85° water and 1 cup sifted flour, then beat them until smooth. Let this rise for 3 hours. In about 2 days, but no sooner, you can increase the sour dough in the same way if you like. If possible, refrigerate until ready to use again. When reusing a refrigerated sour dough, let it stand for about 1 hour before mixing the bread. Expect the sour dough to have an odor very like salt rising bread. Should it develop any abnormal coloration discard it. To avoid spoilage, wash the starter crock about once a week with a detergent and warm water. Rinse and dry carefully before returning the starter to the crock. Try these suggestions if you are adventurous, persistent and leisurely. To use a sour dough, see page 250 and opposite column.

SOUR DOUGH

To make a sour dough more or less from scratch, sift into a ♦ large crockery jar—as the mixture will bubble up:

    4 cups flour
    2 teaspoons salt
    2 tablespoons sugar

Add:

    3 to 4 cups potato water

See Salt Rising Bread II for a good method of fermenting or let stand loosely covered at from 89° to 100° for about 2 days.

ABOUT BAKING POWDERS AND BAKING SODAS

When confronted with the questions growing out of the use of various baking powders now on the market, the puzzled layman is apt to sigh for the good old days, when this product was rather haphazardly mixed at home. ♦ Just in case you run out of baking powder, mix—for every cup of flour in the recipe —2 teaspoons of cream of tartar, 1 teaspoon of bicarbonate of soda and add ½ teaspoon salt. But don't try to store this mixture. ♦ Its keeping qualities will be poor. Commercial baking powders contain small amounts of such materials as starch, to prevent absorption of moisture from the air—a cause of loss of leavening power. Today's products are packed in airtight cans

which also keep your powder dry. If you doubt its effectiveness ♦ test any baking powder by mixing 1 teaspoon of baking powder with ⅓ cup of hot water. Use the baking powder only if it bubbles enthusiastically.

There are three major kinds of baking powders and you will find the ♦ type carefully specified on the label. In all of them there must be an acid and an alkaline material reacting with one another in the presence of moisture to form a gas—carbon dioxide—which takes the form of tiny bubbles in the dough or batter. In baking, these quickly expand the batter which is set by the heat to make a light textured crumb.

TARTRATE BAKING POWDERS

In these, the soda is combined with tartaric acid or a combination of cream of tartar and tartaric acid. They are the quickest in reaction time, giving off carbon dioxide the moment they are combined with liquid. Therefore, if you are using this kind, be sure ♦ to mix the batter quickly and ♦ have the oven preheated so too much gas does not escape from the dough before the cells can become heat-hardened in their expanded form. Especially ♦ avoid using tartrate powder for doughs and batters that are to be stored in the refrigerator or frozen before baking.

▲ Because of the decrease in barometric pressure at high altitudes, the carbon dioxide gas expands more quickly and thus has greater leavening action. For this reason, the amount of baking powder should be decreased if you are using a recipe designed for low altitudes. You may select recipes designed especially for high altitudes, if you wish; see pages 382 to 385.

PHOSPHATE BAKING POWDERS

These use calcium acid phosphate or sodium acid phosphate as the acid ingredient. They are somewhat slower in reaction but give up the greater part of their carbon dioxide in the cold dough, the remainder being released when the mixture is baked.

S.A.S. BAKING POWDERS

These use sodium aluminum sulfate and calcium acid phosphate as the acid ingredients. They, too, start work in the cold dough but the great rising impact does not begin until the dough contacts the heat from the hot oven. They are often referred to as ♦ combination, or double-acting, baking powders and are the baking powders we specify consistently in this book.

BICARBONATE OF SODA, OR BAKING SODA

This is often used in place of baking powder in recipes involving sour milk or some acid factor like molasses, honey or spice. This combination gives one of the very tenderest crumbs. For more details about soda and sour milk and cream reactions, see page 133. The reaction of the soda with the acid is essentially the same as that which takes place when the two ingredients in baking powder meet moisture. Some recipes with these acid ingredients may call for both baking powder and baking soda. If they do, use about ½ teaspoon baking soda and ½ teaspoon baking powder for each 2 cups flour. The small amount of soda is desirable for neutralizing the acid ingredients in the recipe, while the main leavening action is left to the baking powder.

The amounts of baking powder per cup of flour suggested above are for low altitudes.

▲ In high altitudes baking soda is decreased as for baking power where the symbol appears above; but, in recipes using sour milk where its neutralizing power is needed, never beyond ½ teaspoon for every cup of sour milk or cream called for in the recipe.

ABOUT SOLID SUGARS

Most of our cooking is done with sugars made from beets or from cane. Both are so similar in their cooking reactions and their taste that only the label gives us the clue to their sauce. But the various grinds of solid sugars affect not only their comparative volumes but their sweetening powers as well. Liquid sweeteners, again, according to type, react very differently in cooking combinations. Whichever type you use—more is needed to sweeten iced dishes or drinks.

For a quick survey of relative volumes and weights, see page 226. ♦ In substituting liquid for dry sweeteners, a moisture adjustment must be made, especially in baking, as described later. Sugar sirups are easily made and have many uses. See Sirups for Canning, page 535; Sirups for Beverages (I, 25); Sirups for Freezing, page 554; Sirups for Fruits, page 87; and Caramel for flavoring and coloring, page 169.

Among other things, sugars, like fats, give tenderness to doughs. In small amounts, with yeast, they hasten its working. However, too much sugar at this early juncture will inhibit yeast activity. Sugar in bread, rolls and muffins will also yield a golden brown crust. Small pinches added to some vegetables bring up their flavor.

Like flours, sugars are not always interchangeable—measure for measure—as their weights and sweetening powers vary greatly. For a quick comparison of sugar weights and volumes, see page 226. Many baking recipes call for the sifting of sugar before measuring. In America, where we are spoiled in having free-flowing, unlumpy granulated and powdered sugars, this initial sifting before measuring is usually ignored. But it is important to measure these and other sugars by filling the measuring cup with a scoop or spoon to overflowing. Be careful not to shake down the contents to even it. Then level off the top with a knife, as shown on page 224.

GRANULATED SUGAR

◗ In this book when the word sugar appears, the recipe calls for granulated sugar—beet or cane. As we buy it in America, it can be used for almost every purpose, even for meringues. The English granulated is too coarse for this and their castor sugar, closer to our powdered, is used instead. ◗ One pound of granulated sugar equals approximately 2 cups.

POWDERED SUGAR

This is a finer grind of granulated. It is sometimes called superfine or berry sugar, as it dissolves rapidly when put over fruits. It is also used in cold drinks. The term "powdered" is actually a misnomer, this grind being still coarse enough so that the individual crystals are easily discernible. Do not confuse it with confectioners' sugar, which is actually powdery in texture. ◗ It substitutes cup for cup with granulated sugar.

CONFECTIONERS' SUGAR

In its finest form—10X—this sugar might, at a quick glance, be mistaken for cake flour. Confectioners' sugar is approxi-

mately the European or English icing sugar. In order to lessen lumping, it comes with a small quantity of cornstarch added. Should it lump, sieve it. Measure confectioners' sugar as you would flour, page 225. Since the cornstarch tends to give so-called "uncooked" icings a raw flavor, it is wise, before spreading this kind of mixture, to let it heat for about 10 minutes ◗ over hot water, see page 426. The dense texture of confectioners' sugar also gives a different crumb to cakes in which it is used. ◗ Do not try to substitute it for granulated sugar in baking. However, in other uses, substitute 1¾ cups confectioners' for 1 cup granulated.

BROWN OR BARBADOS SUGAR

This is a less refined and moister beet or cane sugar which comes light or dark—the latter more strongly flavored. As both types harden and lump easily, keep them in tightly covered containers. Should the sugar have become lumpy, sprinkle it very lightly with a few drops of water and heat in a low oven for a few moments. ◗ In this book the term brown sugar means the light form. If a stronger flavor is wanted, the term dark brown sugar appears. ◗ To substitute either of the brown sugars for granulated sugar, use 1 cup firmly packed brown sugar for each cup granulated sugar. To measure brown sugar, see page 225.

RAW SUGAR

This unrefined residue after removal of molasses from cane juice has a coarse, squarish, beige-toned crystal. It is closest in character to yellow or brownish Demerara sugar—often called for in English recipes.

LUMP SUGARS

These are granulated sugars molded or cut into convenient rectangular sizes for use in hot drinks. Rock Candy Crystals, page 513, make an interesting stand-in for lump sugar and, when separated, a sparkling garnish for iced cakes.

CRYSTALLIZED SUGAR

See Rock Candy, page 513.

MAPLE SUGAR

This is treasured for its distinctively strong, sweet taste but, because of its high cost, is often reserved just for flavoring. As it dissolves slowly, grate or sliver it before combining it with other ingredients. ♦ In substituting, allow about ½ cup for each cup of granulated sugar.

ABOUT LIQUID SUGARS

There are a number of factors to contend with in substituting liquid for solid sweeteners. For one thing, their sweetening powers vary greatly. For another, their greater moisture content has to be taken into account and those that have an acid factor need neutralizing by the addition of baking soda. So if you plan substituting, read further to see just how to proceed. To measure liquid sugars, you may want to grease your measuring container first. Then pour these sticky substances into the measure, or spoon just to the level mark. Scrape out all the contents. ♦ Never dip the spoon into the honey or molasses container, for the added amount clinging to the bottom and sides may make your dough too sweet or too liquid.

CORN SIRUP

This comes in a light and dark form. ♦ In this book the term corn sirup applies to the light type. The stronger-tasting dark is specified, if needed. ♦ For the same amount of sweetening power, you have to substitute 2 cups corn sirup for 1 cup sugar. However, for best results ♦ never use corn sirup in cooking to replace more than ½ the amount of sugar called for in a recipe. In baking, you are taking a chance in substituting corn sirup in this proportion. But, if you have to, for each 2 cups of sugar in the recipe reduce the liquid called for—other than sirup—by ¼ cup. For example: suppose you are baking a cake that calls for 2 cups of sugar. "Maximum sirup tolerance" here would be 1 cup sugar, 2 cups sirup. And for each 2 cups of sugar originally called for, you would reduce the other liquid ingredients by ¼ cup.

HONEY

This is an extremely variable ingredient. Old German cooks often refused to use it until it had aged for about a year. Variations in honey today are due in part to adulterants, usually the physically harmless addition of glucose—a type of sugar sirup sweeter than sugar itself. Explore the many wonderful flavors in comb and liquid form: thyme from Hymettus, tupelo from Florida or orange blossom from California—all as memorable as good vintages. Honey is often stored covered at room temperature and, if it becomes crystallized, it can easily be reliquefied by setting the jar in a pan of very hot water. Do not heat it over 160°, as this affects the flavor adversely.

In puddings, custards and pie fillings ♦ it is often suggested that honey replace sugar, cup for cup. As honey has almost twice the sweetness of sugar, this will greatly alter flavor. Honey added to cake, cookies and bread doughs gives them remarkable keeping qualities as well as a chewy texture and a browner color. Also, in guarding flavor, see that the honey is not a very dark variety, as dark honey is often disagreeably strong.

Warm the honey or add it to the other liquids called for to make mixing more uniform. ♦ In baking breads and rolls, substitute 1 cup honey for 1 cup sugar. ♦ In baking cakes and cookies, use ⅞ cup honey for 1 cup sugar—but reduce the liquid called for in the recipe by 3 tablespoons for each cup of honey substituted.

Unless sour milk or cream is called for in the recipe, add a mere pinch—from 1/12 to 1/8 teaspoon—baking soda to neutralize the acidity of the honey. Usually, because of its acid content, too great browning results if honey is substituted for more than 1/8 the sugar called for in the recipe. But if it is extremely acid, add 1/4 to 1/2 teaspoon baking soda for every cup of honey substituted. If honey is substituted in jams, jellies or candies, a higher degree of heat is used in cooking. In candies, more persistent beating is needed and careful storage against absorption of atmospheric moisture.

MAPLE SIRUP

If so labeled, maple sirup must contain a minimum of 35% maple sap by government regulation. When properly processed so as neither to ferment or crystallize, one quart should weigh 2¾ pounds. The best grades are light in color. It is often stored covered at room temperature. But mold growth is inhibited if, after opening the sirup container, it is stored in the refrigerator. Should the sirup crystallize, set the jar in hot water

and the sirup will quickly become liquid and smooth again. Products labeled "maple flavored"—while not as rich in flavor—may be used just as you use maple sirup.

♦ To substitute for sugar in cooking, generally use only ¾ cup maple sirup to each cup of sugar. ♦ To substitute maple sirup for sugar in baking, use the same proportions, but reduce the other liquid called for in the recipe by about 3 tablespoons for every cup of sirup substituted. One pint maple sirup has the same sweetening power as 1 pound maple sugar.

MOLASSES

There are 3 major types of molasses.

1. Unsulphured molasses is made from the juice of sunripened cane which has grown from 12 to 15 months. It is a deliberately manufactured product. 2. Sulphured molasses is a by-product of sugar making. Sulphur fumes are used in the making of sugar—hence the presence of sulphur in the molasses. 3. Blackstrap molasses is a waste product. It is the result of a third boiling—with more sugar crystals extracted; and is unpalatable.

Molasses is best in sweetening power if it replaces no more than ½ the amount of sugar called for in the recipe. But in baking it is sometimes ♦ substituted—1 cup molasses for every cup of sugar. Add ½ teaspoon soda for each cup added, and omit the baking powder called for in the recipe, or only use a small amount. Make sure also to reduce the other liquid in the recipe by ¼ cup for each cup of molasses used.

CANE SIRUP

This is substituted like Molasses, above.

TREACLE OR GOLDEN SIRUP

This is milder in flavor and used only where specified as it does not substitute properly for molasses.

SORGHUM

This has a thinner, sourer flavor than cane molasses. Use the same substitutions as called for under Molasses.

I. CARAMELIZED SUGAR FOR GLAZES

A marvelous flavoring which can be made in several ways. While its caramel flavor is strong, its sweetening power is reduced by about one-half.

For hard glazes, heat in any ◗ very heavy, nonferrous pan, over ◗ very low heat, 1 cup granulated sugar. For a Croquant, or brown nougat, add 1 tablespoon water. Stir constantly with a long handled spoon for 8 to 10 minutes until the sugar is melted and straw-colored. Remove the pan from the heat. ◗ Add ¼ cup very hot water—very slowly and carefully—for a quick addition might cause explosive action. This safeguard against the spurting of the hot liquid will also help make the sirup smooth. To make the sirup heavier, return the pan to low heat for another 8 to 10 minutes, continuing to stir, until the sugar mixture is the color of maple sirup. Toward the end of this process, to avoid cooking it too dark, you may remove the pan from the heat and let the caramelization reach a bubbling state from the stored heat of the pan. Store the sirup covered on a shelf for future use. The sirup hardens on standing but, if stored in a heat-proof jar, is easily remelted by heating the jar gently in hot water. Should it burn, use it for coloring, see below.

II. CARAMELIZED SUGAR FOR COLORING

Melt in a ◗ very heavy nonferrous pan, over low heat, 1 cup sugar. Stir constantly until it is burned black to smoky. ◗ Remove from the heat and be sure to let it cool. Then, as in caramelizing above, ◗ add, almost drop by drop, 1 cup hot water. ◗ Quick addition of water to intensely hot sugar which is well over 300° can be explosive in effect and very dangerous. After the water is added, stir over low heat until the burnt sugar becomes a thin dark liquid.

If stored covered on a shelf, it will keep indefinitely. This can be used to replace the more highly seasoned commercial gravy colorings. The intense heat under which it is processed destroys all sweetening power.

SYNTHETIC SWEETENERS

There is some reason to question the systemic effect of all non-caloric sweeteners. Any substitutes should be used on doctor's orders only and, when cooked or used in baking, should follow manufacturer's directions. The saccharin types should not be cooked, as they produce a bitter flavor. Cyclamates are more suitable for cooking and baking, as they retain their sweetness when heated and, with some cooked foods, their sweetening power actually increases. Cyclamate substitutes do not give the same texture in baking as do true sugars and therefore should be used only in recipes specifically developed for them. For amounts to be used in substitutions, please see pages 236 and 237.

ABOUT SEASONED SUGARS

Keep these on hand for quick flavoring.

CINNAMON SUGAR

Mix 1 cup sugar with every 2 tablespoons cinnamon. Use for toast, coffee cake and yogurt toppings.

CITRUS FRUIT FLAVORED SUGARS

Extremely useful in custards and desserts. Prepare Citrus Zest, page 219. Allow 1 to 2 tablespoons zest for every cup of sugar. Store covered in a cool place.

VANILLA SUGAR

Make this by keeping a whole vanilla bean closed up in a canister of sugar. Or you can crush it with a few tablespoons of sugar before adding it to the sugar you are storing. Then, you may strain the sugar before using and replace it with new sugar until the bean loses its flavoring power.

ABOUT FATS IN COOKING

Nothing reveals the quality of a cuisine as unmistakably as the fat on which it is based. Bacon arouses memories of our South, olive oil evokes Mediterranean cooking and sweet butter will bring forth memories of fine meals in many places. Not only flavors but food textures change with the use of different fats whose materials are as individual as their tastes. ◗ Most of the recipes in this book call for sweet butter. Sometimes amounts vary in a single recipe. In such instances, the lesser amount will give you a palatable result, while the larger quantity may produce a superlative one.

Authorities grant that 20% to 30% of our dietary intake should come from fats. But our present per capita consumption is closer to 40%, representing 8% to 18% of all household money spent! Few of us realize that, like an iceberg, the larger part of the fat we eat is invisible. Who would guess that ripe olives and avocado are about ¼ fat, that egg yolk, cheese, peanut butter, chocolate and the average hamburger contain about ⅓ fat and that Bologna sausage and pecans can be almost ¾ fat! For more about the dietary and calorie role of fats, see (I, 1, 2, 3).

Let's take a bird's eye view of fat versatility in cooking. Fats, when used with discretion and skill, have the power to force flavor in foods, to envelop gluten strands and "shorten" them into more tender structure. Fats also form the emulsifying agent in gravies and mayonnaise and can act as a preservative in coating some foods like Stocks, page 138, and Terrines (I, 528). And butter gives the most beautiful browning in breads and pastries.

Fats for cooking, of course, include both solid fats and liquid oils. ◗ Fats are solid at about 70°. ◗ Oils remain liquid at these temperatures although they may become solidified when refrigerated. It is fashionable today to scorn fats for their weight-inducing power and to fear certain "saturated" fats for their alleged cholesterol-inducing tendencies (I, 3). ◗ Examples of highly saturated fats are butter and the hydrogenated fats. ◗ Other fats, like

¾   ⅓   ⅓   ⅓   ⅓   ¾   ⅓

vegetable and nut oils, are poly-unsaturated.

MEASURING FATS

Bulk butter and solid shortenings are most easily measured by the displacement method. ♦ To measure fats, see illustration, page 226.

ABOUT BUTTER

All butter is made from fresh or soured cream and by law must have a fat content of 80%. The remaining 20% is largely water with some milk solids. Small amounts of salt are sometimes added for flavor or for preservative action. Without the addition of color, most butter would be very pale rather than the warm "butter yellow" to which we are accustomed.

The word "creamery" which sometimes appears on both sweet and salt butter packages is a hangover from the days when cream went to a place called a creamery to be processed. The word now carries no standard or type significance —it's just meant to be reassuring!

♦ All butter should be stored in the refrigerator and kept covered to prevent absorption of other food flavors. Two weeks is considered the maximum storage time for refrigerated butter. For longer storage, it may be frozen, see page 563.

♦ One pound of butter equals 2 cups. ♦ To substitute butter for other fats, see page 232; for seasoned butters, see (I, 383); for nut butters, see pages 57 and 190.

SWEET BUTTER

The word butter, as used in this book, means first grade butter made from sweet cream with no added salt. Without this preservative factor, its keeping

qualities are less than those of salt butter. Its delicate flavor is especially treasured for table use and for preparing certain baked foods, see About Cakes, page 343.

SALT BUTTER

This may be made from sweet or soured cream. It too is very desirable and keeps longer than the sweet.

PROCESSED BUTTER

Often sold in bulk, this is made by rechurning less desirable butter with fresh milk to remove unwanted odors or flavors.

EXPANDED BUTTER

For dieters and frugal housewives, this is a favorite spread. Soak ¼ cup gelatin in 1 pint milk until dissolved and heat over hot water. Put 1 pound butter cut in pieces in a dish over hot water. Whip the gelatin mixture into the butter gradually. Add salt to taste. Should milk bubbles appear, continue beating until they go away. Pour the butter into molds and chill well before serving.

For Clarified or Drawn Butter, see (I, 383).

HOW TO MAKE SWEET BUTTER

Butter is just as good as the cream from which it is made. Clean whole milk is kept cool and covered during separation, which takes about 24 hours by gravity. Skim the cream, pasteurize it, page 130, stirring frequently to deter "skin" formation. Cool the cream at once to 50° or less and keep about 55° all during the butter-making period. Start to churn after 3 to 24 hours of chilling. Most of us have inadvertently turned small quantities of cream into butter in an electric beater or ⅄ blender. We may even have imitated churning by flipping a jar of cream rhythmically in a figure 8 motion. For larger quantities, use a churn and keep the cream between 55° and 60°. A higher temperature will produce a greasy consistency—a lower one, a brittle, tallowy one. A gallon of cream should yield about 3 lbs. of butter.

Using at least 30% cream, fill a sterile churn ⅓ to ½ full. Depending upon the quantity you are churning, the butter should "make" within 15 to 40 minutes. We used to visit a neighbor while she churned and were amazed at how much slower the process was in threatening or stormy weather. The cream usually stays foamy during the first half of churning. Afterwhile it will look like cornmeal mush. At this point, proceed cautiously. It then grows to corn kernel size. Now, stop churning. Drain off and measure the buttermilk. Wash the butter twice, with as much 50° to 70° pure water as you have buttermilk.

If you salt the butter, use ⅔ to 1 tablespoon salt to 1 pound butter, folding the salt into the butter with a wet paddle. Mold it in a form or fashion it into rolls, using a damp cloth. Wrap it in parchment or foil.

If you wonder why the lovely, pale, delicately fragrant, waxy curl on your Paris breakfast tray is so good, here is one reason. The Brittany cows are fed and milked so the butter-making can be coordinated with the first possible transportation to Paris, where it is served at once. So use butter promptly. ✻ Freeze butter not more than 6 months at 0° temperature. If no refrigeration is available, butter is best wrapped and kept in brine, page 196, in a cool place.

KNOW YOUR INGREDIENTS

ABOUT VEGETABLE SHORTENINGS

These have an oil base like soybean, corn, cottonseed or peanut, which is refined and deodorized. Frequently they are ◗ hydrogenated. This process of hydrogenation changes the form of the free fatty acids of oil, although it improves their keeping qualities—as the hydrogen binds the oxygen. It also makes them more acceptable for baking, as during the processing air is incorporated and plasticity is given to the solid fat. These solid fats and the shortenings based on them are bland and practically indistinguishable one from the other in taste or in use.

Some oil-based shortenings may further have animal or dairy fats blended with them during the processing. If color is added to any of these products, it is so stated on the label. They may also have minute additions of emulsifiers, mono- and diglyceride fats, which give to cakes and other baked foods greater volume and a softer, spongier texture.

◗ Vegetable shortening may be stored covered in a tin at 70° over long periods.

◗ To substitute solid shortening for butter, replace measure for measure as the water in the butter compensates for the air in the shortening. ◗ But, if substituting weight for weight, use 15% to 20% less shortening than butter.

ABOUT MARGARINES

Margarines, like butter, must, by law, contain 80% fat—the rest being water, milk solids and salt. Almost all margarines are enriched also with added vitamins and color, to try to make them equate butter. Margarines today are usually emulsions of milk and refined vegetable oils, although some have added animal or dairy fats. Read the label for this information.

♦ Margarines, because of their similar moisture content, may be substituted for butter, weight for weight or measure for measure. They produce textures somewhat different from butter in both cooking and baking and lack the desirable butter flavor. They are perishable and must be kept under refrigeration.

ABOUT OILS

Vegetable oils are pressed from various common seeds and fruits. Among these are corn, cottonseed, olive, soybean, sesame, safflower, sunflower. There are also such nut oils as peanut, walnut, hickory and beechnut, which are best for salads, as they break down under high heat.

After pressing, the oils are refined, bleached and deodorized so thoroughly that, except for olive, the end products are rarely distinguishable one from the other by flavor or odor, or in use.

Most oils for salad are further treated to remove cloudiness at refrigerator temperatures. Oils should not be held too long at 70° even if tightly closed and in dark bottles. Most of them remain in a liquid state under refrigeration. Olive oil, which becomes semisolid when refrigerated, should be allowed to stand at 70° to return to a liquid condition before using.

Olive oils are like wines in the way their flavors are affected by the soils in which they are grown. Greek, Spanish, Italian—try them all to find your favorite. It is so much cheaper to buy by the gallon but, as olive oil is susceptible to rancidity—especially the cold press type—when exposed to light and air, decant it into smaller containers. Use one and keep the other resealed bottles in a cool, dark place. For further discussion of their value in the diet, see (I, 3).

As oils are 100% fat, they ♦ must be reduced by about 20% when substituted for butter, either by weight or by measure. However, there are additional complications when substituting them for solid fats, especially in baking, see page 360. So in this book ♦ when oil is used in recipes, it is specifically indicated and the proper amounts are given.

ABOUT LARD

Lard, which is fat rendered from pork, is a softer, oilier fat than butter, margarine or the other solid shortenings. Due to its more crystalline structure, it cuts into flour to create flakier textures in biscuits and crusts, although this same crystalline character handicaps it for cake baking. This is less true for those lards which have been hydrogenated, refined and emulsified. Ordinary lards are offered in bulk or package form.

♦ All lards should be stored in covered containers in a cool place, preferably the refrigerator. ♦ To substitute lard for butter in cooking, use about 20% to 25% less lard.

LEAF LARD

Whether bought or home-rendered, this is a definitely superior type. It comes from the layered fat around the kidneys, rather than from trimmings and incidental fatty areas.

ABOUT POULTRY FATS

Fats from chicken, turkeys, ducks and geese, whether home or commercially rendered, are highly regarded for dietary reasons. When rendered from the leaf or cavity fat, they are firm, bland and light in color. From sources such as skimmed broth and other cooking, they are likely to be soft, grainy and darker in color. ♦ Store them covered in the refrigerator.

♦ To substitute, use ¾ cup clarified poultry fat to 1 cup butter.

ABOUT PORK FAT

This is used both in its fresh and salted form. Salt pork, which comes from the flank, is used to line Pâtés (I, 525), for Lardoons (I, 453), and for Larding (I, 453). It may also be sautéed in butter to use as a garnish for sweetbreads.

♦ To remove excess salt from salt pork Blanch II (I, 88), for about 2 minutes. Fresh pork fat, especially the kidney fat, is used as an ingredient in farces, sausages and in pâté mixtures.

ABOUT DRIPPINGS

These are fats which are rendered in the process of cooking fat meats. They are all desirable in reinforcing the flavors of the meats from which they come when making gravies, although lamb and mutton should be used with great discretion. Bacon and pork fats are often stored separately for use in corn breads and meat pie crusts and for flavoring other dishes where salt pork may be called for. Other fats may be mixed together for storage.

♦ To substitute drippings for butter, use 15% to 20% less drippings.

♦ All these fats should be clarified before storage in the refrigerator, to improve their keeping qualities. The natural desire to keep a container handy at the back of the stove to receive and reuse these drippings needs to be curbed. Exposed to varying degrees of warmth, these are subject to quick spoilage.

ABOUT RENDERING FATS

Trying out solid fats such as chicken, duck, suet tallow and lard improves the keeping quality by removing all connective tissue, possible impurities and moisture. Dice the fat and heat it slowly in a heavy pan with a small quantity of water. You may speed up this process by pressing the fat with the back of a slotted spoon or a potato masher. When the fat is liquid and still fairly warm, strain it through cheesecloth and store it ♦ refrigerated. The browned connective tissues in the strainer—known as "cracklings" —may be kept for flavoring.

ABOUT CLARIFYING FATS

To clarify fats that have been used in frying and to rid them of burned food particles and other impurities ♦ heat them slowly. You may add to the fat during this heating 4 to 5 slices of potato per cup of fat to help absorb unwanted flavors. When the potato is quite brown, strain the fat while still warm through cheesecloth. ♦ Store refrigerated.

ABOUT REMOVING EXCESS SALTS FROM FATS

To remove excess salt from bacon or salt pork, parblanch it before use for larding (I, 88), or in delicate braises and ragouts. Put it in a heavy pan. Cover it with ♦ cold water. Bring the water slowly to a boil and ♦ simmer uncovered for 3 to 10 minutes. Allow the longer time if the dice are as big as 1 x 1 x ½ inches.

To remove salt from cooking

butter, heat it slowly and avoid coloring it. Skim it. Allow it to cool in the pan and remove the fat cake. Any sediment and moisture should be in the bottom of the pan. Butter so treated is used in a number of ways, especially to seal off potted meats and in cooking where a slower browning is wanted, as in boned chicken.

ABOUT CHEESES

The ways of cheese-making are ancient and the results are not only chancy but extraordinarily varied—so varied that even to list their names is a geographical impossibility. Man makes cheese from many milks—goat, ass, ewe, camel and water buffalo, as well as the more reassuring cow. Natural cheese can substitute nutritionally for meat, milk or eggs, see (I, 2), since they retain large amounts of the protein and casein. Soft cheeses, described later, are richer in water-soluble vitamins than hard cheeses—although they are poorer in calcium. Except for pot and cottage types, all cheeses are heavy in fat, from at least 20 to 30 per cent.

Someone has said that while you cannot make a good cheese from poor milk, you can very easily make a poor cheese from good milk. The high fat and protein content demands gentle heats—usually not over 110°—during the making of cheese and always below boiling point when cooking with it later. Moreover any cooking period —even the heating of a cheese sauce under a broiler—should be as brief as possible to avoid separation or toughening, see (I, 3).

Some cheeses originate when milk comes in contact with the curdling enzymes from the stomachs of unweaned animals or from certain plants. This enzymatic material is rennet, often used in making puddings, although ◆ as compounded for this latter purpose it does not always have enough strength to act as a cheese-starter. Acid-curd cheeses form when bacteria in the lactic acid turn milk into curds and whey. ◆ Only raw, unheated milk will respond to the acid-curd method.

Originally, if the cheese bore a place name, that was its source. Now many molds and starters have been transplanted and you may find your Roquefort coming from South America instead of France, your Emmenthaler from Austria rather than Switzerland. Some of these transplants are delicious, some doubtful. Reserve judgment on "named" cheeses until you have tasted them as produced at their point of origin.

Let us stress again the marked individuality of cheeses within the same type and of the same provenance. In the first place ◆ natural cheeses are seasonal. Often the best milk is available in April or August. The flavor will depend not only on the soils of the fields on which the cattle are fed but also on the season and the aging.

If cheese is your hobby and it's "named" cheeses you are after, rather than give you elaborate charts which may prove meaningless, we suggest you find a good cheese broker who has the latest market knowledge. The other thing to do— which is rewarding—is to find sources of good cheese native to your region. Many cheese makers take great pride in their products and you may be pleasantly surprised as to what your locale may produce.

For Dessert Cheeses, see page 470, for cheese combinations for hors d'oeuvre, see Index, and for cheese entrées, see Luncheon Dishes (I, 237).

For Processed Cheese, see below.

All natural cheeses, no matter how they may vary in individual character, are divided into three basic types: soft, semihard and hard.

SOFT CHEESES

This type is the most easily made in the home and a few recipes are given later. They retain from 45% to 85% moisture and are highly perishable, lasting only 3 or 4 days. They must ♦ be kept under refrigeration and, for complete safety, should derive from pasteurized milk. The curds can be frozen before washing and stored for a month or two. Soft cheeses may be unripened, mold-ripened or bacteria-ripened.

Typical unripened soft cheeses are cottage, farmer's, pot, Neufchâtel, Primost, Petit Gervais, ricotta and bakers' cheese, which is high in rennet and very dry. Some unripened soft cheeses may be enriched with cream after forming, like creamed cottage cheeses, or may be brine-held, like the Greek variety called feta.

Mold-ripened soft cheeses are such types as Camembert, Brie, Pont L'Évêque and Livarot.

Soft cheeses may also be bacteria-ripened, such as Limburger, Liederkranz and hand cheese; and those we might designate as "near-cheeses," like Cultured Sour Cream, page 136, and Yogurt, page 135. Except for these last two and for cottage cheese and ricotta, soft cheeses are not generally used in cooking. When they are, the heat must be of a very mild character. They cook best in Cheese Cakes, page 326, Lasagne (I, 176), and Blini, page 116.

SEMI-HARD CHEESES

These are also ♦ poor for cooking, as they become gummy. If aged, they retain about 45% moisture. Their aging is as tricky as their manufacture. If aged 60 to 90 days, the milk need not be pasteurized. We feel that these so-called natural cheeses from raw milk are far superior in flavor to the processed cheeses which are made of pasteurized milk. Semi-hard types include mold-ripened crumbly cheeses like Gorgonzola, bleu, Stilton; and bacteria-ripened cheeses like Muenster, brick, Port du Salut, Bel Paese, Fontina, Gammelost, Gouda and Jack.

HARD CHEESES

After aging, these cheeses retain about 30% moisture. They are ♦ superlative for cooking. And they are made from raw milk and are all bacteria-ripened —for a longer or shorter period. Appitost, nokkelost and Kuminnost need 2 to 3 months; American, apple, asiago, cheddar, Edam, gjetost, Gruyère, provolone, sapsago, Sbrinz and Swiss need 3 to 12 months; and Cheshire, Parmesan, Reggiano, Romano and Sardo need 12 to 16.

In cooking with cheeses that are very hard ♦ grate just before using. Try combinations in cooking like grated Parmesan with Romano or Gruyère, cantal or caccio cavallo with cheddar.

TO STORE HARD CHEESES

To store a wheel or a large piece of cheese after cutting, butter the cut edges before wrapping in foil and refrigerating the rest.

ABOUT PROCESSED CHEESES

We can only echo Clifton Fadiman when he declares that processed cheeses represent the triumph of technology over conscience.

Processed cheeses are pasteurized blends of green new cheese, one or more aged cheeses, emulsifiers and water —which may run from 1% to 40% higher than in natural cheeses. If sold as so-called "cheese-food," they may legally contain up to 44% water or milk; if labelled "cheese-spread," up to 60% water, gums and gelatins. In fact, some "cheese-spreads" have no cheese in them at all, but are based on cheese-curds.

Processed cheeses are a convenience to a desensitized housewife—to say nothing of a profit-minded manufacturer. They have remarkable keeping qualities as they stand up sturdily to almost indefinite refrigeration. But here their interest ends. If you are willing to condone the gummy texture and the insipid taste of processed cheeses, you are still advised to read the list of ingredients on the package. Otherwise, you may find yourself paying an exorbitant price for some highly synthetic and commonplace materials.

ABOUT MAKING UNRIPENED SOFT CHEESES

Time was when milk was allowed to rest in a warm place until clabbered, when the curds and whey were separated by draining until the curds were firm to the touch. They were then refrigerated for several hours, after which they could be beaten with additional cream until smooth to make a cottage or Schmierkaese.

Commercial creamed cottage cheeses must by law have a 4% fat content.

For safety reasons, the recipes which follow are given for ◗ pasteurized milk. But, because the milk is pasteurized, ◗ Cultured Buttermilk, page 134, or Rennet, page 452, must be added to all the recipes to activate the curd. In making these cheeses use stainless steel, enamel or crockery vessels. Have ready: a dairy thermometer, a long wooden spoon, a large pan, a rack and a muslin sack or Chinese cap strainer (I, 145), for dripping the cheese.

Also useful, if you make these soft cheeses often, is a curd cutter made of a stainless wire looped into an elongated "U" with the arms about 2 inches apart, and deep enough to fit the pan in which you develop the curd. Make up the recipes as described. When the curd is ready, cut through it with your curd cutter, lengthwise and crosswise of the pan. Then cut through in depth at 2-inch intervals to form cheese curd cubes. Process as described in the recipe. When the curds are ready, you may add additional cream. ◗ Store these cheeses refrigerated. Do not keep more than 4 or 5 days. To serve these unripened cheeses, see:

> Cottage Dessert Cheese, page 472
> Coeur à la Crème, page 471

or serve with:

> Chopped chives, burnet, basil or tarragon, chopped olives

or use as a base for hors d'oeuvre and dips and to fill tomato cases.

COTTAGE CHEESE

[About 1½ Pounds]
This cheese goes by many other names: clabber, pot, Dutch, farmer's, Schmierkaese and bakers'. The latter is very, very dry. ◗ Please read About Making Un-

ripened Soft Cheeses, page 177.
Have at 70° to 72°:

 1 gallon pasteurized fresh
   skim milk

If whole milk is used, the cream
is lost in the whey. Stir in:

 ½ cup fresh cultured
   Buttermilk, page 134

Leave this mixture in an oven
70° to 75° temperature until
clabbered, about 12 to 14 hours.
Cube the curd, as described previously. Let rest for 10 minutes.
Add:

 2 quarts 98° to 100° water

Set the pan on a rack in a larger
pan of water and heat until the
curd reaches 98° to 100°. Hold
at this temperature ♦ not higher
or the curd will toughen, for
about 30 minutes to 1 hour, stirring gently every 5 minutes. Do
not break the curd. As the whey
is forced out, the curds will
settle. ♦ To test for doneness,
squeeze them. They should
break clean between the fingers
and, when pressed, should not
leave a semifluid milky residue.
Pour the curds and whey ♦
gently into a scalded sack or
Chinese cap strainer. Rough
handling can cause as much as
a 20% loss in bulk. Rinse the
curds with:

 (Cold water)

to minimize the acid flavor. Let
drain in a cool place until whey
ceases to drip; but the surface
of the cheese should not become
dry-looking. The cheese may
then be combined with:

 (Whipping cream)

To serve or store, see About
Making Unripened Soft Cheeses,
page 177.

NEUFCHÂTEL

[About 1½ Pounds]
♦ Please read About Unripened
Soft Cheeses, page 177.
Combine:

 1 gal. fresh pasteurized
   whole milk

 ½ cup fresh cultured
   Buttermilk, page 134

Dissolve in:

 ¼ cup cold water
 ¼ to ½ household rennet
   tablet

and mix with the milk, which
should be at 85°. ♦ Stir gently
for 10 minutes and begin to
watch for any thickening. ♦ Stop
stirring the moment you sense
the thickening. Put the filled
bowl you are using in a larger
one of warm water and maintain
the milk at 80° to 85° until
whey covers the surface and the
curds break clean from the sides
of the bowl when it is tipped.
Cut into 1-inch curds, as described previously. Now put the
curds and whey into a colander
and, when nearly drained, press
out any remaining whey. Reserve
and chill the whey until you can
skim off the butter, like cream,
and work the cream back into
the curds. When the cheese is
firm, add:

 1½ teaspoons salt
   (Additional seasoning)
   (Cream)

To serve or store, see About Unripened Soft Cheeses, page 177.

RICH CREAM CHEESE

[About 1½ Pounds]
♦ Please read About Making Un-
ripened Soft Cheeses, page 177.
Proceed as for:

 Neufchâtel, above

using:

 3½ quarts fresh pasteurized
   milk
 1 to 1½ pints whipping
   cream
 ½ cup cultured buttermilk
 ¼ to ½ rennet tablet

dissolved in:

 ¼ cup cold water

Save and chill the whey until
you can skim off the butter and
work the butter back into the
cheese.

 Correct the seasoning

ABOUT EGGS

Nothing stimulates the practiced cook's imagination like an egg.

Eggs can transform cake doughs by providing a structural framework for leaven, thicken custards and make them smooth, tenderize timbales and produce fine-grained ice creams. They bind gravies and mayonnaise; clarify or enrich soups; glaze rolls; insulate pie doughs against sogginess; create glorious meringues and soufflés; and make ideal luncheon and emergency fare.

Because fresh eggs do all these things better than old eggs and because there is no comparison in taste and texture between the two ◗ always buy the very best quality you can find. It doesn't matter if their yolks are light or dark or if their shells are white or brown—as long as the shells are not shiny. While there is no test, except tasting, for good flavor ◗ the relative freshness of eggs may be determined by placing them in a large bowl of cold water. The ones that float are not usable. Unshelled onto a plate ◗ a truly fresh egg has a yolk that domes up and stays up, and a thick and translucent white.

Strange as it may seem, after stressing the purchase of fresh eggs, we now tack on an amendment. ◗ Do not use eggs fresher than three days for hard-cooking, beating and baking. If you do, hard-cooked eggs will turn greenish and become difficult to peel and cakes may fail to rise properly because the eggs will not have been beaten to the proper volume.
◗ Never use a doubtful egg, one that is cracked or one that has any odor or discoloration. Fertile eggs have a small dark fleck which is easily removed with the tip of a knife if the egg is to be used in a light-colored sauce or confection.

Eggs should really be bought and measured by weight, but tradition is against this sensible approach. ◗ We assume in this book that you are using 2-ounce eggs. These are known in the trade as "large." They should carry a Grade A stamp as well as the date of grading. If in doubt about size, weigh or measure them. The yolk of a 2-ounce egg is just about 1 tablespoon plus a teaspoon; the white, about 2 tablespoons. For more equivalents, see pages 233 and 234. To realize how great a difference egg-size has on volume, notice below that two large eggs give you about half a cup, but it takes three medium eggs to fill that same half-cup. If you substitute the same number of larger or smaller eggs for the 2-ounce variety, you may be disappointed in the results—especially in baking. When you decrease a recipe and want to use only part of an egg, beat the egg slightly and measure about 1½ tablespoons for half an egg and about 1 tablespoon for one-third.

To substitute eggs of other fowl, from lark to ostrich—which, by the way, will serve 18 for brunch—allow 2 ounces for each hen's egg called for in the recipe. Don't expect the same texture or flavor. Be very sure of freshness in using offbeat eggs. This is especially important in duck eggs. When aging, they often carry dangerous bacteria, which can be destroyed by boiling the eggs for 10 minutes or by baking them in a cake for not less than 1 hour.

ABOUT COOKING EGGS

It is possible, on a hot summer day, "they" say, to fry an egg

on the sidewalk. We do not recommend this particular extravagance; we mention it to remind you that eggs cook quickly over any kind of heat—beginning to thicken at 144°.

Sometimes, even when their cooking has been carried on over hot water, the stored heat of the pan will cause eggs to curdle. Be doubly careful then ◗ with all egg dishes, not to use excessive heat and not to prolong the cooking period. Should you suspect you have done either of these things, dump the egg mixture at once into a cold dish and beat vigorously or add a tablespoon of chilled cream. You may in this way save the dish from curdling.

Only prior precautions, however, will produce smooth baked custard dishes. For, once the protein of the egg has shrunk, it can no longer hold moisture in suspension and the results are bound to be watery. If you are combining eggs with a hot mixture, add a small quantity of it to the beaten eggs first. This conditions eggs before their addition to the remaining mixture. Often, at this point in egg cookery—if you are preparing a soufflé base or thickening soup or sauces with yolks—there is enough stored heat in the pan to do the necessary cooking.

If you are going to cook an egg yolk and sugar mixture, beat the eggs, add the sugar and continue to beat until the mixture runs in a broad ribbon from the side of the spoon. When this condition is reached, the eggs will cook without graining.

Now, armed with 2 more se-

crets, you can expect real magic from the rich, complete and tasty protein that is so tidily packed inside an egg shell. For more details about the nutritive value of eggs, see (I, 2). In baking and in making omelets or scrambled eggs, remember that eggs will give better texture and volume if they are at about 75° when you start to use them. Also remember that egg yolk is almost ⅓ fat and that, as eggs cool in a pudding or sauce, you can count on some slight thickening action.

ABOUT BEATING EGGS

◗ To beat whole eggs to their greatest volume, have them at about 75°. Beat whole eggs and yolks vigorously—unless otherwise directed in the recipe—until they are light in color and texture, before adding them to batters and doughs.

For some recipes, whole eggs and yolks profit by as much as 5 minutes or more of beating in the electric mixer and will increase up to six times their original volume.

To describe the beating of egg whites is almost as cheeky as advising how to lead a happy life. But, because the success of a dish may rest entirely on this operation, we go into it in some detail. To get the greatest volume ◗ see that the egg whites are at about 75° and properly separated. We have already referred to the bride who couldn't boil an egg. But there are plenty of housewives who can't even break one. Here's how. Have 3 bowls ready, as sketched. Holding an egg in one hand, tap the center of the side of the egg lightly, yet sharply, on the edge of one of the bowls—making an even, crosswise break. Then take the egg in both hands with the break on the upper side. Hold it over the center of a small bowl and tip it so that the wider end is down. Hold the edges of the break with the thumbs. Widen the break by pulling the edges apart until the egg shell is broken into halves. As you do this, some of the egg white flows into the bowl underneath. The yolk and the rest of the egg white will remain in the lower half of the shell. Now pour the remaining egg back and forth from one half-shell to the other, letting some more of the white flow into the bowl each time until you have only the yolk left. During this shifting process, you will be able to tell quickly, with each egg in turn, if there is any discoloration or off-odor. This way you can discard it before it is put with the yolks on the left or with the whites in the large bowl on the right.

Should the yolk shatter during breaking, you can try to remove particles from the white by inserting the corner of a paper towel moistened in cold water and making the yolk adhere to it. Should you fail to clear the yolk entirely from the white, keep that egg for another use, because the slightest

fat from the yolk will lessen the volume of the beaten whites and perceptibly change the texture.

◗ Choose a large deep bowl in which to beat, shaped as sketched on the right, below. Be sure it is not aluminum, which will grey the eggs, or plastic, which frequently has a chemical that deters volume-development. The French dote on copper. But if cream of tartar is used—as it so frequently is —to give a more stable and tender foam, the acid which is present will turn the eggs greenish. Not to mention what the eggs in turn may do to you.

In recipes for meringues and in some cakes, a portion of the sugar, about 1 teaspoon per egg, is beaten into the egg whites when they are foamy. Although this reduces volume slightly and means a longer beating period, it does give a much more up-standing foam.

The lightness of the beating stroke, plus the thinness of the wire whisk used, also makes an appreciable difference in building up the air capacity of egg-white cells. ◗ Choose as a beater a many thin-wired long whisk, as shown. ◗ Be sure that both the bowl and the beater are absolutely free from grease. To clean them, use a detergent or a combination of lemon juice and vinegar. Rinse and dry carefully.

If you are going to use the

whites in baking, have the oven preheated. Start beating only when all other ingredients are mixed and ready. Be prepared to give about 300 strokes in 2 minutes to beat 2 egg whites. You can expect 2½ to 4 times the volume you start with. Begin slowly and lightly with a very relaxed wrist motion and beat steadily until the egg whites lose their yellowish translucency. They will become foamy. Then increase the beating tempo gradually. Beat without stopping ♦ until the whites are both airy and glossy and stand in peaks that are firm, but still soft and elastic, see page 180.

From start to finish, there should be no stopping until that state is reached that is best described as ♦ stiff, but not dry. Another test for readiness is the rate of flow when the bowl is tipped. Some cooks use the inverted bowl test in which the whites cling dramatically to the bottom of the upside-down bowl. Usually, when this is possible, the eggs have been beaten a trifle too long and are as a consequence too dry. Although they may have greater volume, their cells will not stretch to capacity, when baked, without breaking down.

Folding in egg whites should always be a manual operation rather than a mechanical one, since it is essential again to retain as much air in the whites as possible.
♦ Work both quickly and gently. Add the lighter mixture to the heavier one. Then combine the two substances with two separate movements. Various special tools, like wire "incorporators" and spatulas, have been suggested for this process, but nothing can compare for efficiency with the human hand. First use a sharp, clean action, as though cutting a cake. Then,

with a lifting motion, envelop the whites by bringing the heavier substance up from the bottom of the bowl. Repeat these slicing and lifting motions alternately, turning the bowl as you work.

ABOUT STORING EGGS

The storage of eggs is not difficult if you follow a few simple rules. ♦ To store eggs in the shell, wipe but do not wash them until ready to use. When taken from the nest, eggs are covered with a soluble film which protects the porous shell against bacterial entry. ♦ If there is no special storage area for them, place eggs still in their carton in the refrigerator. ♦ Raw eggs in the shell and foods containing raw eggs—like mayonnaise and custards in which the eggs are only slightly cooked—should be kept under refrigeration, 33° to 37°, and away from strong-smelling foods, as they absorb odors easily.

To store egg whites in the refrigerator, cover them closely and do not keep them longer than 4 days. ♦ Use them only in recipes that call for cooking. To store unbroken egg yolks, cover them first with water, which you then drain off before using. Cover the storage dish before refrigerating. Yolks may be stored uncooked up to 4 days or for a few days longer if poached in water until firm. They should only be used in recipes that call for cooking. Sieve the poached eggs with a pinch of salt. Use in sauces or as a garnish for vegetables. To use extra whites or yolks, see page 238.

Before we leave this subject, we pull out of our hat a conjurer's trick. Should you have any doubts about which eggs in your refrigerator are hard-boiled and which are not, a quick test is to twirl them on their pointed ends. The hard-boiled eggs will spin like a top; the others will simply topple over.

Dried eggs are a convenience when fresh eggs are not available, but they are not an economy. Because of bacterial dangers, they must always be used in recipes that call for cooking, unless a large percentage of acid is indicated. Packaged dried eggs should be stored at 70° and, if opened, should be refrigerated at about 45°. To reconstitute the equivalent of 12 fresh eggs, sift 6 oz. dried egg powder over 1⅞ cups water. Whip until smooth. To substitute for 1 egg, use 2½ tablespoons water. Beat until smooth. Use either of these mixtures within five minutes after combining. You may prefer to add the egg powder to the dry ingredients and the water to the rest of the liquid called for in the recipe.

✳ To use frozen eggs, see page 563.

Preserve eggs at home only if you have no alternative. The commonest method is immersion in waterglass or sodium silicate. If possible, use nonfertile eggs that are at least 12 hours old. Do not pack too many layers on top of each other, as the weight might crack those below. Eggs so kept are not good for boiling, as the shells become too fragile—nor do the whites beat well for meringues, soufflés, etc.

To preserve 10 dozen eggs, pour 9 quarts of boiling water into a 5 gallon sterile crock. Add 1 quart waterglass, stir thoroughly and add the eggs. The waterglass should cover the eggs 2 inches above the top egg. Cover crock and store in a cool place no longer than 6 months.

And a hint about washing egg-soiled dishes. Start with cold water, which releases rather than glues on the protein. Rub sulphur off stained silver with salt if polish is not handy.

ABOUT GELATIN

Gelatin is sympathetic to almost all foods ♦ except fresh or frozen pineapple which contains a substance that inhibits jelling. Cooked pineapple presents no problem.

Gelatin is full of tricks. It can turn liquids into solids to produce gala dessert and salad molds. It makes sophisticated chaud-froid and ingenuous marshmallows. It also makes a show case for leftovers and keeps delicate meats and fish in prime condition for buffet service. Chopped and used as a garnish or cut into fancy shapes, clear gelatins add sparkle to a dish that is dull in color.

♦ Gelatin dishes must, of course, be refrigerated until ready to use. And, in buffets, they are best presented on chilled trays or platters set over crushed ice.

While gelatin must be kept cold, it should ♦ never be frozen unless the fat content is very high—as in certain ice creams. Gelatin also gives a smoother texture to frozen desserts, jellies and cold soups. It thickens cold sauces and glazes (I, 387), and in sponge and whipped desserts it doubles the volume.

Gelatin's power to displace moisture is due to its "bloom," or strength. In household gelatins, this is rated at 150 and means that 1 tablespoon can turn about 2 cups of liquid into a solid. Gelatin often comes ready to use in granules, but the most delicate fish and meat aspics are made with stocks reduced from bones, skin and fish heads. It also comes in sheets. For equivalents, see page 234.

To get the most nourishment out of gelatin, which is not a complete protein, see (I, 2). To get the most allure ♦ never use too much. The result is rubbery and unpleasant.The finished gelatin should be quivery—not rigid—when jostled.

Unless a recipe is exceedingly acid, 1 tablespoon of gelatin to 2 cups of liquid should produce a consistency firm enough to unmold after 2 hours of chilling—if the gelatin is a clear one. But it must get 4 hours of chilling if the gelatin has fruits, vegetables or nuts added to it. Also allow proportionately more jelling time for large, as opposed to individual, molds. If you prefer a less firm texture, use 1 tablespoon of gelatin to 2¼ to 2½ cups liquid. These gelatins will not mold but are delightful when served in cups or in coupes.

In our high-speed age, we are told how quickly gelatins can be made by soaking them and then dissolving them in a small quantity of hot liquid, replacing the rest of the required liquid with the proper amount of ice. If you are in a hurry and are making a gelatin which calls for 1 cup water and 1 cup stock or fruit juice, you can prepare it by dissolving the gelatin as usual—boiling your cup of stock or fruit juice and then stirring about 8 large or 10 small ice cubes into the hot liquid to cool it. Stir the cubes constantly 2 to 3 minutes. Remove the unmelted ones. Let the mixture stand 3 to 5 minutes. Incorporate the fruit or other solids called for; and mold.

For an even faster gelatin with frozen fruit, see Blender Fruit Whip, page 456.

In recent years, various other gelatin-mixing methods have

been advocated, but we still get the best results using either one of the following.

I. Sprinkle 1 tablespoon of gelatin granules over the surface of ¼ cup cold water and let it soak for about 3 minutes until it has absorbed the moisture and is translucent. ♦ Do not disturb it during this period. Have ready just at the boiling point 1¾ to 2 cups stock, fruit juice, milk, wine or water. Combine it with the soaked gelatin and stir until dissolved.

II. If you do not want to subject the liquid in the recipe to high heat or reduce its flavor and vitamin content, use a double boiler and sprinkle 1 tablespoon gelatin over ¼ cup cold water. Dissolve this mixture ♦ over—not in—hot water. Add to the dissolved gelatin 1¾ to 2 cups 75° liquid and stir well. If you are making up your own sweet gelatin recipe, dissolve the sugar in the liquid before measuring and adjust the amount of gelatin needed because the liquefaction of the sugar must be counteracted. If you are ♦ doubling a gelatin recipe that originally called for 2 cups of liquid, use only ¾ cups in the doubled recipe. For further discussion of th' precaution, see page 228.

You may allow the dissolved gelatin to cool at room temperature, over a bowl of cracked ice or in the refrigerator—but not in the freezer, as a gummy look is apt to develop and the surface cracks miserably. It is interesting that gelatins which are slow to jell are also slow to break down when they are removed from the refrigerator, but any gelatin will begin to weep if exposed too long to high temperatures.

♦ For basic gelatin aspic recipes, see (I, 57) through (I, 71). For Gelatin Desserts, see pages 449–457.

▶ To make an aspic glaze for hors d'oeuvre or sandwiches ▶ be sure you have the food to be glazed and the tools you are working with well chilled. Apply a thin, even coat of aspic which has begun to jell. Chill. Repeat, if needed, with a second layer and chill again.

ABOUT MAKING FANCY GELATIN MOLDS

Have ready well-drained and chilled foods before starting to make fancy designs in gelatin. Allow about 1¼ cups of solids for each cup of aspic. Just as the aspic thickens to about the consistency of uncooked egg white, put a small amount in a chilled mold or dish with sloping sides, which has been rinsed in cold water. Sometimes oiling a mold is recommended, but with clear gelatins a blurred surface results. Roll and tip the mold in such a way that a thin layer of gelatin coats its inside surface. Refrigerate the mold to set the gelatin.

Now impale bits of food on a skewer or toothpick. Dip them one by one into the gelatin and place them just where you want them on the hardened layer in the mold, to form the design. When the decorations for one layer are in place, fill the spaces between with more aspic. Return the mold to the refrigerator until this has set and proceed with this method until it is filled.

When using a fish-shaped or other fancy mold, accent the lines of the design with slivers of egg white, cucumber or peppers, if for a salad; with citron, cherries, crystallized rinds or fruits, if for a dessert.

An easier way to make layered molds is to choose nuts, fruits and vegetables of different weights and porosity. Put them in a very slightly jelled mixture and let them find their own levels. The floaters are apple cubes, banana slices, fresh grapefruit sections or pear slices, fresh strawberry halves, broken nut meats and marshmallows. The sinkers are fresh orange slices, fresh grapes, cooked prunes and the following canned fruits: apricots, Royal Ann cherries, peaches, pears, pineapple, plums and raspberries. If you are making gelatins to serve in champagne coupes, you can decorate the tops with grape halves. Even though they are technically sinkers, you can wait until the gelatin is almost set and hold each grape for just a second until it makes enough contact not to turn wrong side up.

Another way to make fancy molds is to combine layers of clear and whipped or sponge gelatins, as described next. To make gelatin whips, it is essential ▶ to use a cold bowl or put a bowl over ice and be sure the gelatin has been chilled to a consistency slightly thicker than unbeaten egg white.

▶ If the gelatin is not firm enough when you start to beat it, it will revert to a clear gelatin in setting.

Use an electric mixer, a rotary beater or a ⅄ blender. To make sponges, follow these directions, but before beginning to beat ▶ add to the chilled gelatin the cold unbeaten egg whites. Beat until the mixture is very stiff.

Mousses and Bavarians are based on gelatinized custards and frequently have both beaten egg white and cream folded in before final chilling. In these desserts, the additions of egg and cream are made when the gelatin mixture mounds slightly if dropped from a spoon. They are then chilled until firm.

▶ To prepare molds for clear gelatins, rinse them well in cold water, as shown at the left below. After filling an undecorated mold, run a knife through the mixture to release any air bubbles that might be trapped in it. Then refrigerate until ready to unmold.

▶ To unmold aspics or gelatin puddings, have ready a chilled plate large enough to allow for a garnish. You may moisten the dish slightly. This will prevent the gelatin from sticking, and enable you to center the mold more easily. You may first use a thin knife at several points on the edge to release the vacuum. Then reverse the mold onto the plate. If necessary, place a warm damp cloth over the mold for a few seconds, as shown. If the food is still not released, shake the mold lightly, bracing it against the serving dish. Some people dip the mold into hot water for just a second. We find this risky with delicate gelatins, as the water must not go above 115°.

ABOUT NUTS

Whether they are seeds—like pecans and walnuts; fruits—like lichees; or tubers—like peanuts, nuts have concentrated protein and fats. Except for Chestnuts, page 188, they contain very little starch. But it is for their essential oils, which carry the flavor, that we treasure them so much. And the textural

contrast they bring always makes them welcome. The reason they are so often listed as an optional ingredient in our recipes is merely because the recipes will carry without them—and with so much less cost and calorie value. Except for green almonds and pickled green walnuts, nuts are nearly all eaten when ripe.

ENGLISH AND AMERICAN WALNUTS AND PECANS

These are perhaps the most familiar and most easily available types. The latter are probably the heaviest in fat of all our natives, sometimes as much as ¾ of their bulk.

HICKORIES AND BUTTERNUTS

Rich natives, like pecans, and they never need blanching.

FILBERTS OR HAZELNUTS

Varieties less rich than the above and almost identical in their sophisticated flavor. Filberts are the more subtle European versions of our native hazelnuts.

ALMONDS

These have comparatively little fat and come in two varieties, sweet and bitter. ▶ When mentioned in this book, they are the dry sweet form, which you find not only ground in Torten, page 366, Marzipan, page 505, and Almond Paste, page 504,

but slivered in Amandine (I, 401). The dry sweet almond may also be eaten, while green and soft, with cheese and wine.

ALMOND PASTE

This must be kept cool when you work with it—so the oil does not separate out. Should you buy, rather than make, almond paste—see that it is marked "genuine." If it has a slightly bitter taste, it may be crushed apricot, peach or plum seed.

ORGEAT SIRUP

An almond emulsion used to flavor drinks and sweets. Blanch and pound into a paste:

    1 lb. almonds
    10 bitter almonds

Squeeze out the oil. Mix the remaining powder with enough:

    Water

to make a paste. Let it rest for 24 hours in a cool place. Dissolve in:

    1½ cups water
    2 teaspoons tartaric acid

and add this mixture to the paste. Filter and add to the resulting liquid:

    2½ cups sugar
    (2 tablespoons orange
    water)

Stir until dissolved and store refrigerated.

BITTER ALMONDS

An altogether different type with a strangely bitter taste—an accent desirable in ▶ very small quantities for flavoring. Use as in Almond Milk, page 138, and Orgeat, above.

ALMOND OIL

An extract made from bitter almonds is often called for in European recipes. But it is dangerous to use it to excess and in America it is available only on prescription.

BRAZIL NUTS

The more delicate types do not ship well and we must rely on a rather coarse, tough variety that does. To slice these large kernels, cover the shelled nuts with cold water and bring slowly to a boil. Simmer 5 minutes. Drain. Slice lengthwise or make curls with a vegetable slicer. You may toast the slices at 350° for about 12 minutes.

MACADAMIA NUTS AND CASHEWS

These are also popular. Cashews have an edible, fleshy fruit covering which can be eaten raw, but ▶ the nuts must always be roasted carefully to destroy a poison they contain. Make cashew butter as for Peanut Butter, described later.

PISTACHIO NUTS

Although maddeningly small, these are delicious, loved for their color and often used in farces or pâtés.

PINE OR INDIAN NUTS

Known also as Piñon in Spain or Pignola in Italy—where the variety is richer. These are good in Dolmas (I, 522), and in Pesto, page 216.

BEECHNUTS

A real treat—but just try to beat the squirrels to this harvest.

PUMPKIN, SQUASH, MELON AND SUNFLOWER SEEDS

All of these are flavorful and nutritionally valuable. ▶ To roast the tiny nutlike seeds, see page 189.

PEANUTS

If you enjoy the flavor, peanuts are nutritionally valuable and are used in Nut Loaves, Nutburgers, Peanut Brittle, page 515, Cookies, page 397, and of course, Peanut Butter, see the recipe on page 190. These underground legumes—also called groundnuts or in their larger form, goobers—are high in valuable proteins. If the heart is left in, they make a real and economical contribution to the diet. The small Spanish types will grow in the northern states. All peanuts are best eaten right after roasting, before they get limp. If roasting them in the shell at home, keep the oven at 300° and roast 30 to 45 minutes—or 20 to 30 minutes if shelled. Turn them constantly to avoid scorching. Check for doneness by removing skins. The inner skins, heavy in thiamin, are pleasantly flavored. But little is gained by home roasting, as a steam process used commercially for peanuts in the shell gives superior results.

CHESTNUTS: MARRONS AND OTHER VARIETIES

These need long and loving care—just like navy beans, which are often substituted for them in frugal European kitchens. One of our more knowing friends insists you cannot tell the difference when a strong lacing of coffee, chocolate or almond paste is used in the dessert. Chestnuts are frequently used as stuffing for fowl and traditionally combined with Brussels sprouts and red cabbage. Do not confuse the chestnuts in these recipes with the ones you find under ornamental allées or with those crisp Chinese water chestnuts we usually know only in canned form.

▶ To shell chestnuts, make two crosscut gashes on their flat side with a sharp pointed knife. Sometimes the shell will come off when you do this, but the inner skin will protect the kernel. Place the nuts in a pan over a quick heat, dropping oil or

butter over them—1 teaspoon to 1 pound of nuts. Shake them until they are coated, then place them in a moderate oven until the shells and inner brown skins can be removed easily.

Or cover chestnuts with boiling water and simmer them 15 to 25 minutes. Drain them and remove the shells and skins. The meats should be sufficiently tender to be put through a purée strainer. If not, cover them with boiling water and cook them until tender.

For use as a vegetable, see (I, 283); as Marrons Glacés, page 525; or in desserts, page 450. Chestnuts are available fresh, canned in sirup and dried.

▶ To reconstitute dried chestnuts, soak in water to cover overnight. Rinse and pick over. Simmer in a deep pan covered with about 5 inches of water until they are tender and puffed up. Substitute them for cooked fresh chestnuts, cup for cup.

The Portuguese and Chinese are not as sweet as the Italian. The American chestnut is represented, since the blight, only by smaller types like the chinquapin.

Allow about 1½ lbs. in the shell for 1 lb. shelled. 35 to 40 whole large-type chestnuts make about 2½ cups peeled. The brown skin is bitter and must be peeled off while still warm.

ROASTED CHESTNUTS

Preheat oven to 425°.
Prick the skins of:
       Chestnuts
with a fork before putting them in the oven for 15 to 20 minutes or they may explode. More hazardous, but more fun, is to roast the chestnuts on a cold winter's evening, at the edge of an open fire. A childhood game was for each of us to cheer our own chestnut on to pop first.

SKEWERED CHESTNUTS

Prepare by boiling in:

> Milk
> Boiled Chestnuts I,
> (I, 283)

Omit the vinegar. When the chestnuts are cooked until soft enough to penetrate with a fork, roll them in a mixture of:

> Au Gratin III, (I, 389)

Place on a greased baking dish and run under the hot broiler for a few moments. Dust with:

> Chopped parsley

Serve at once on picks.

WATER CHESTNUTS

There are 2 types—both of which are crispy and delicious. In one type, the shell grows together into a horn at one end. The other is bulbous. Use water chestnuts in Hors D'oeuvre, page 79, Vegetables (I, 339), and Salads (I, 38).

LICHEE NUTS

Really, these are a soft, firm, sweet, spicy fruit, protected by a most exquisite fragile shell, as shown on page 93. Serve 3 to 5 nuts on green leaves or as a garnish on a fruit bowl for dessert. They are also available canned in sirup, but the flavor is not as hauntingly aromatic.

ABOUT STORING AND PREPARING NUTS

The best way to store nuts is to keep them in their shells. This protects them from light, heat, moisture and exposure to air—factors which tend to cause rancidity in the shelled product. The difference in the keeping time for shelled pecans, for instance, may range from 2 months at about 70° to as long as 2 years in a freezer. So, if nuts are already shelled, store them tightly covered in a cool, dark, dry place or in a freezer.

Some nuts, like pecans and Brazil nuts, are more easily shelled if boiling water is poured over them and they are allowed to stand for 15 to 20 minutes.

To open coconuts, see page 193.

▶ For yield of kernels from nuts in the shell, see page 236. Be sure to discard any kernels that are shrivelled or dry, as they may prove bitter or rancid.

TO BLANCH NUTS

In addition to the tough outer shell, nuts have a thin inner lining or skin. Just before using, try one of the following methods:

I. Pour boiling water over the shelled nuts. For large quantities, you may have to let them stand for about 1 minute at the most ▶ the briefer the length of time the better. Drain. You may pour cold water over them to arrest further heating. Redrain. Pinch or rub off the skins.

II. For peanuts, filberts and pistachio nuts, you may prefer to roast at 350° for 10 to 20 minutes and then rub off the skins.

TO ROAST AND TOAST NUTS

This both crisps them and brings up the flavor. Unless otherwise specified, place them blanched or unblanched in a 300° oven and turn frequently to avoid scorching. ▶ To avoid loss of flavor and toughening, do not overtoast.

Recipes for deep fat, roasting shelled, roasting in the shell, oven-roasted, spiced and seasoned nuts: see pages 70, 71, 514, and 515.

TO PREPARE NUTS FOR SALTING

▶ Coat a bowl with egg white, butter or olive oil, add the nuts and shake them until they are coated. Spread the nuts on

cookie tins and heat in a 250°
oven. If you salt before cooking, allow not more than ½ teaspoon salt to one cup of nuts.
Roast about 10 to 15 minutes,
stirring frequently to achieve
even browning. A more rapid
way is to heat in a heavy iron
skillet 2 tablespoons oil for
every cup of nuts. Stir constantly for about 3 minutes.
Drain on absorbent paper. Salt
and serve.

TO CHOP NUTS

If rather large pieces are
needed, simply break nuts like
pecans and walnuts with the
fingers. For finer pieces, use a
knife or a chopping bowl and
chopper. ◗ It is easier if the
nuts are moist and warm and if
the knife is a sharp French one
(I, 250). Group the nuts in a
circle with a diameter of about
the length of the blade. Grasp
the knife on top in both hands
as you would a bar at both
hilt and blade ends. Chop
briskly with a rocking motion
beginning at the knife point,
rocking from point to hilt and
gradually working the knife
back in a semi-circle from the
pointed end.

Almonds may be chopped in
a ⅄ blender. Process only ½
cup at a time for 30 seconds at
highest speed.

TO GRIND NUTS

◗ Use a special type of grinder
—one that shreds or grates them
sharply to keep them dry,
rather than a type that will
crush them and release their oils.
Do small quantities in a rotary
grinder, as sketched. Light, dry,
fluffy particles result, which can
be substituted for flour in Nut
Torten, page 366.

Sometimes, however, for butters and pastes, a meat grinder
or a ⅄ blender is used. We do
not otherwise recommend a

blender for grinding nuts, as it
tends to make the nuts too oily
—except for almonds.

Peanut butter is so popular
that it has overshadowed the
use of other nut butters. Try
grinding almonds, pecans or
walnuts into butter. These are
so rich they need no additional
oil. Use for every cup of nuts
⅛ teaspoon salt.

⅄ PEANUT BUTTER

Smooth and delicious as commercial peanut butters may be,
they are often made without the
germ of the nut. This valuable
portion—as in grains—contains
minerals, vitamins and proteins
and is literally fed to the birds.
The commercial objection to the
germ is twofold: 1. That the
flavor of the butter is made
somewhat bitter, 2. that, as with
whole grains, the heat of processing and the heat in storage
may cause the finished product
to grow rancid. If you are smart,
make your own full-bodied peanut butter in an electric blender.
Use:

> Fresh roasted or salted
> peanuts

It is wise to start with a bland
oil:

> Safflower or vegetable oil

Allow 1½ to 3 tablespoons to 1
cup peanuts. If nuts are unsalted, add salt to taste:

> About ½ teaspoon salt
> per cup

ABOUT DRIED FRUITS

The high caloric and nutritive values of dried fruits can be readily grasped if you realize that it takes 5½ lbs. of fresh apricots to yield 1 lb. when dried. A few dried fruits as a garnish or as a dessert go a long way. When fruits are dried without cooking, their subsequent contact with the air—as well as the enzymatic activity which takes place within them—tends to darken the pulp. A sulphur dioxide solution is often used to lessen darkening.

Dates, figs, apples, peaches, prunes, plums, apricots, currants and raisins are among the most used dried fruits. They must all be ◗ stored tightly covered in a cool, dark place. Under most household shelf conditions, they are likely to deteriorate in a matter of months. This is especially true of raisins. All varieties must be watched for insect infestation that develops in them with age.

Raisins divide into two major types: seedless, those which grow without seeds; and seeded, which have had the seeds removed. As their flavors are quite different, it is wise to use the types called for in the recipes—without interchanging. White raisins, often called muscats, are specially treated to retain their lovely color. Currants and raisins both profit, unless they are very fresh, by plumping, especially when used in short-cooking recipes. This can be done by soaking them in the liquid in which they are to be cooked—such as the liquid called for in cakes—for 10 to 15 minutes before use. Raisins and currants may also be plumped by washing briefly, draining, spreading on a flat pan and then heating, closely covered, in a 350° oven until they puff up and are no longer much wrinkled.

Small fruits are often messy to cut or chop. Flour them, if they are very sticky ◗ using for this purpose, when baking, a portion of the flour called for in the batter. Don't use additional flour, as it will make the dough too heavy. They may also be more easily cut if the scissors or knifeblade is heated. Handle the knife as for chopping nuts. But, if you are chopping in quantity, you may want to use a meat grinder instead. ◗ Heat the grinder very thoroughly in boiling water before feeding in the fruit.

Candied and preserved fruits are sometimes substituted for dried fruits. If candied fruits are used, allow for their extra sugar content. With preserved fruits, compensate for both sugar and liquid.

ABOUT CHOCOLATE AND COCOA

Both these delights come from the evergreen trees of the genus Theobroma, "Food of the Gods." Up to the moment when the chocolate liquor is extracted from the nibs, or hulled beans, and molded into solid cakes, the manufacture of chocolate and cocoa is identical. At this point, part of the "butter" is removed from some of the cakes, which become cocoa, and added to others which, in turn, become the bitter chocolate we know as cooking chocolate.

Cocoa butter is remarkable for the fact that, under normal storage conditions, it will keep for years without becoming rancid. There are many pharmaceutical demands for it and, in inferior chocolate, it is sometimes replaced by other fat.

Ideal storage temperature for chocolate is 78°. The bloom that turns chocolate greyish after it has been stored at high temperatures is harmless—merely the fat content coming to the surface.

The best sweet chocolate is made by combining the melted bitter cake with 35% cocoa butter, finely milled sugar and such additions as vanilla and milk—depending on the type of chocolate desired. In this book, when the magic word ♦ chocolate appears all alone in recipes, it means bitter cooking chocolate. An entire square equals 1 ounce. Two-thirds cup of semi-sweet chocolate is 6 ounces by weight—or 10⅔ tablespoons by volume. But in any semi-sweet chocolate, you have about 60% bitter chocolate and 40% sugar. German's chocolate, which is conditioned against heat, refers not to the country but to a very canny person of that name, who early realized there was a greater profit if the sugar was already added to the chocolate when it was sold.

Should you want to substitute semi-sweet for bitter, make the adjustment in the recipe using less sugar, more chocolate and a dash of vanilla.

♦ For exact substitution and equivalents of chocolate and cocoa, see page 232–233. In some quick-cooking recipes, this substitution may not be successful, as the sugar doesn't crystallize properly with the chocolate. If semi-sweet chocolate stiffens when melted—in sauces, for instance—add a small amount of butter and stir well until smooth. ♦ Substituting cocoa for chocolate in sauces can be adjusted more easily than in baking. Just add 1 tablespoon butter to 3 tablespoons cocoa for each ounce of chocolate. But ♦ in baking it is wiser to use recipes written either for cocoa or for chocolate, as the cocoa

has a flourlike quality that must be compensated for—or the cake will become too doughy.

♦ All chocolate scorches easily, so melt it over hot water. If you don't like to clean the pot, float the chocolate on a small foil "boat" and discard the foil after use. Place wrapped squares, folded edges up, in the top of a double boiler ♦ over, not in, hot water for 10 to 12 minutes. Cool chocolate to about 80° before adding it to cake, cookie or pudding mixtures.

♦ To grate chocolate, chill it and try shaving it or grating it in a rotary grinder, see page 190. If you grate it, have a big bowl ready to receive it—or you may be annoyed by its flighty dynamism. In cakes and cookies, soda is often used to give chocolate a ruddy tone. A few drops of vinegar serve the same purpose.

♦ To make chocolate curls for decorating parfaits or cream pies, hold a wrapped square of unsweetened chocolate in the hand to warm it slightly. Unwrap and shave chocolate with long thin strokes, using a vegetable peeler or a small, sharp knife.

♦ For chocolate as a seasoning, see Mole (I, 586).

Cocoa is pulverized from the dry cocoa cakes which, after processing, still contain from 10% fat for regular cocoa up to 22% to 24% fat for breakfast cocoa. The so-called Dutch type maintains the heavier fat content and the small quantity of alkali introduced during the processing produces a slightly different flavor. Instant cocoa, which contains usually 80% sugar, is precooked and has an emulsifier added—to make it dissolve well in either a hot or cold liquid. For details about cocoa and chocolate as beverages, see (I, 20). For Dipping Chocolate, see page 507.

If you live in coconut country, you know the delight of using the flower sap as well as the green and the mature fruit of this graceful palm. In cooking, you may substitute its "milk," "cream" and "butter" for dairy products. However, be aware that this exchange is not an equal one nutritionally—because the coconut is much lower in protein. ▶ Coconut milk and cream are very sensitive to high heat. For this reason, they are added to hot sauces at the last minute or are cooked over hot water. They are especially treasured in preparing curries and delicate fish and fruit dishes.

The first thing to do with a coconut, of course, is to get at it. Lacking power tools, you drop the large fruit onto a rock-like substance. If it doesn't crack open enough so that the husk pulls away, use your trusty axe. Out comes a fiber-covered nut. Shake it. A sloshing noise means that the nut is fresh and that you can count on some milk. If the husked coconut is green, the top can be lopped off with a large, heavy knife or a machete. The liquid within is clear and the greenish jellylike pulp makes ideal food for small children and invalids. To open the harder shell of the mature nut, you may pierce the three shiny black dots which form a monkey face at the peak. Use a skewer or sharp, sturdy knifepoint. Allow the liquid to drain. Reserve it. More about this milky substance, which is quite different from the coconut milk and cream extracted from coconut meat, follows. Tap the nut briskly over with a hammer. It usually splits lengthwise, and these halves can be used as containers for serving hot or cold food. See illustrations, page 194.

You may also open the shell with heat, but then the shell is useless for serving hot food. To do so, place the undrained husked coconut in a preheated 325° oven for 15 to 20 minutes. ▶ Do not overcook, as this destroys the flavor. Remove from the oven and cool until the nut can be handled. Wrap it in a heavy cloth to prevent any pieces from flying off. Then crack it with hammer taps. ▶ Have a bowl ready to catch the milky liquid—remembering that this liquid should be constantly under refrigeration and used within 24 hours. Coconut cream, very rich in fat, is made from the grated, mature, white stiff meat of the nut. The grating is sometimes done while the meat is still in the shell, see illustration. Or you may leave the thin brown skin on and use it to

protect the fingers as you handgrate. If the skin is removed, cut the meat into small chunks and chop in the ⚙ blender.

In the East Indies, they heat the grated coconut meat in its own natural milk ▶ just to the boiling point, then remove it from the heat and cool. In the West Indies, they pour boiling water over grated coconut and add the natural "milk"—allowing in all about 1 pint liquid for a medium coconut. In either case, when the mixture has

cooled, the coconut is drained through two thicknesses of cheesecloth and the meat, retained in the cloth, is squeezed and kneaded until dry. The drained liquid is allowed to set. When the "cream" rises, it is skimmed off and refrigerated.

Another way to extract milk from the coconut meat is to crack the outer casing and shell, but not to remove the brown rind that adheres to the white meat—unless the recipe so states. Wash, drain, grate or ⅄ blend the pulp. Add ¼ cup hot water. Then strain and measure. If more milk is needed than results, add more hot water, reblend and strain again.

Coconut "butter"—though vegetable in origin—contains completely saturated fatty acids. It is made from chilled coconut "cream"—also very rich in fat —by churning with a rotary beater or in a ⅄ blender. When the solid mass rises, force any excess water out of it with the back of a spoon. To utilize the coconut that remains, make polvo de amor, a garnish for breakfast foods and desserts, by simply browning it slowly in a heavy pan over low heat. Use about 2 tablespoons of sugar to 1 cup of coconut and cook until golden brown. To toast grated coconut, spread it thinly on a baking sheet and heat for about 10 minutes in a preheated 325° oven. Stir frequently. For a dessert or a spread made from grated coconut, see Coconut Dulcie, page 480.

The meat of the coconut is grated for many uses. You may grate it fresh, see sketch, page 193. You may buy it dry-shredded and use it as it comes. Or you may soak it for 6 hours refrigerated in milk to cover, and drain it before use. This gives it about the same moisture content as the canned, shredded or flaked types—for which it may be substituted.

▶ To substitute coconut, pack the measures and use 1⅛ cups flaked to 1 cup grated. Shown on page 193 is a grater given us by an Indian friend, which simplifies the preparation of coconut for cakes and garnishes.

Coconut shells can make interesting food and drink containers. For a bowl, saw the upper third off the shell. For a rack to hold this round-bottomed shell upright, cut about ½ off the smaller piece as sketched on the left, above. For serving salads, cut the shell lengthwise. The shells can also be used to heat and serve sauced foods. Cut off the top ⅓ to serve as a lid. The food may be heated in a 350° oven by placing the lidded nutshell in a small custard cup or on an inverted canning jar lid in a pan of hot water. Baste the shell about every 10 minutes. Then you may simply fill the shell with very hot food. The cup may form a base when you serve; or you may fold a napkin or ti leaf for support, as sketched, center and right.

ABOUT SALTS

Salt has many powers. The interplay of salt and water is essential to life itself. The maintenance of a proper salt balance is vital to the system and no attempts to cut down on or delete salt from the diet should be made without advice from a physician. ▶ Salt's powers of preservation made possible our ancestors' survival in the waters, wastes and wilderness through which they forged the world's great trade routes. While its use in preserving food has become much less important with the advance of refrigeration, it is surprising how much we still depend on it: in food processing of various kinds; in the curing of meats; in the brining and pickling of vegetables; in freezing ice cream; even, now and then, for heating oysters and baking potatoes.

In food preservation, the action of salt is twofold. It draws out moisture by osmosis, thus discouraging the microorganisms which are always more active in moist than in dry food. Afterwards, the brine formed by the salt and moisture in combination further prevents or retards the growth of surface microorganisms. In Sauerkraut, page 594, and Salt-Rising Bread, page 247, the more salt-tolerant friendly bacteria survive to give the food its characteristic quality, while the ones that cause spoilage are destroyed.

▶ Salting of present day meats is, in most cases—except for "old hams"—too mild to allow them to be held safely without refrigeration. To cook salted meats, see (I, 488); to remove excess salt from bacon and salt pork, see page 174, from anchovies, page 218.
▶ The power of salt to heighten the flavor of other foods is its greatest culinary asset. This is true even in candy-making, when a pinch of salt often brings out a confection's characteristic best, and with uncooked food, as when sprinkled on citrus fruits.

Its reaction on cooked foods is, otherwise, several-sided. It tends to dehydrate when added to water in which vegetables are cooked, and firms them. It draws the moisture from meats and fish in cooking processes. And it tends to deter the absorption of water by cereals, although it helps retain the shape of the grain. It toughens eggs. And it must be used cautiously in bread-making, as too much inhibits the growth of yeast and adversely affects gluten formation. For the effects of salt water on cooking, see page 147.

These diverse properties of salt have provoked arguments, from time to time, as to just when this very important ingredient should be added when cooking food. It must, of course, be used very sparingly, if at all, at the start of any cooking in which liquids will be greatly evaporated—such as the making of soups, stocks and sauces. But small quantities of salt, added early to soups and stews, will help in clarification. It is obviously good practice to sear grilled, broiled or roasted meat before adding salt, to retain juices and flavor—unless the meat is floured or breaded, page 160. And since it is almost impossible to get rid of salt in cooked foods—although occasionally a touch of sugar will make them more palatable—the amount must be calculated with care.

We know, from long experience, that the flavor-enhancing power of salt is most effective if it is added during, not after, cooking. Our best judgment is, in general, to add it judiciously toward the end of the process and to correct the seasoning just before serving. Don't taste with the tip of the tongue only, but with the middle and sides as well, where the greatest response to salt-stimulus lies.

Salt occurs within foods in varying amounts, animal sources having a higher salt content than vegetable. Sea fish, especially shellfish, are heavier in salt than fresh water types. Of course, pickled, cured or corned meats and sausages, broths, catsups and extracts, brine-processed frozen fish, sardines, herrings and anchovies, as well as canned soups, fish and meats —all are high in salt. Do watch your salting arm when dealing with any of the foods mentioned above, and in cooking beets, carrots, celery, chard, kale, spinach, dandelion greens, endive and corn—all of which are twice as naturally salty as most vegetables. And be cautious with dates, coconut and molasses.

Various kinds of salt are mentioned in this book. When the word salt is used without qualification, it means ◗ cooking or table salt.

◗ For amount of salt to use in seasoning, see page 216.

COOKING OR TABLE SALT

This is a finely ground free-flowing type, about 40% sodium chloride—to which dehydrators are frequently added.

IODIZED SALT

This is recommended for certain areas where the water and soils are lacking in this essential trace element (I, 4). ◗ To keep these fine-crystal salts free-flowing, put a few grains of rice in the salt cellars.

COARSE OR KOSHER SALT

This is squarish-grained sea salt, with a natural iodine and other minerals, very flavorful when used in cooking. It is often served sprinkled over meats, after carving and just before serving, so that it does not have time to melt completely. It is also sprinkled over rolls, pretzels and bread before baking, as a sparkling garnish.

BRINE

Brine is a solution of salt and water—preferably soft water. Its purpose is to draw the natural sugars and moisture from foods and form lactic acids which protect them against spoilage bacteria. A 10% brine, about the strongest used in food processing, is made by dissolving 1½ cups salt in 1 gallon of liquid or allowing 6 tablespoons salt to a quart of liquid. A 10% brine is usually strong enough to discourage even such destructive bacteria as botulinus. But after brining, as more liquid continues to be drawn from fruits and vegetables, the brine may be weakened. ◗ A rule of thumb to test for 10% brine is that it will float a 2 oz. egg. Allow about 2 gallons of 10% brine plus enough food to fill a 4 gallon jar.

PICKLING OR DAIRY SALT

A pure salt that is free from additives which might cloud the pickle liquid. Granulated and flake forms of salt may be substituted pound for pound. But, if measuring by volume, use for every cup granulated salt about 1½ cups flake salt.

ROCK SALT

A nonedible, unrefined variety which is used in the freezing of ice cream—also as a base for baking potatoes or heating oysters.

VEGETABLE SALTS

These are sodium chloride with added vegetable extracts—such as celery and onion. If you use them cut down on the amount of salt called for in the recipes.

SEASONED SALTS

These are usually a compound of vegetable salts, spices and monosodium glutamate. In using flavoring salts, be sure not to add regular cooking salt before tasting.

I.
- 10 tablespoons salt
- 3 tablespoons pepper
- 5 tablespoons white pepper
- 2 tablespoons red pepper
- 1 teaspoon each nutmeg, cloves, cinnamon, bay, sage, marjoram, rosemary

II.
- 4 tablespoons salt
- 1 tablespoon sugar
- 1 tablespoon monosodium glutamate
- 1 tablespoon paprika
- 1 teaspoon mace, celery salt, nutmeg, curry, garlic powder, onion powder, mustard

HERB SALTS

I. Blend in a mortar for 3 or 4 minutes:
- 1 cup non-iodized salt
- 1½ cups pounded fresh herbs

Spread the mixture on a heat-proof tray to dry.

II. You may also preserve some herbs by salting them down green in a covered crock, alternating ½-inch layers of salt with ½-inch layers of herbs. Begin and end with slightly heavier salt layers. After a few weeks, the salt will take on the flavor of the herbs you have chosen to combine and will be ready for use. The herbs which remain green may also be used.

MONOSODIUM GLUTAMATE

A concentrated form of sodium which is usually extracted from grains or beets. It is also present in bean curd and soy sauce. Long known as the magic powder of the East, where tons and tons of it are consumed annually, it is being used increasingly in this country—especially in commercially processed foods —because of its power to intensify some flavors. It seems to have no effect on eggs or sweets. It may modify the acidity of tomatoes, the earthiness of potatoes and the rawness of onions and eggplant. It acts as a blender for mixed spices used in meat and fish cookery. Monosodium glutamate is the ingredient that causes for some devotees of Chinese food the allergic reaction known as Chinese restaurant syndrome.

While it accentuates the saltiness of some foods, just as wine does, it lessens the saltiness of others. ♦ We, personally, detect a certain deadening similarity in foods when we use monosodium glutamate. And we prefer, if a meat or vegetable is prime, to let its own choice character shine through unassisted.

SOUR SALT

A citric acid which is sometimes used to replace a lemon flavoring or to avoid discoloration in fruits or canned goods.

SMOKED SALTS

Hickory or other scented smokes have been purified of tars and are chemically bound to these salts by an electrical charge.

SMOKY SALT MIXTURE

- 1 teaspoon smoked salt
- ½ cup catsup
- ¼ cup olive oil
- 2 tablespoons mustard

SALT SUBSTITUTES

These are chlorides in which sodium is replaced by calcium, potassium or ammonium. They should be used only on the advice of a physician.

ABOUT SPICES

Long before the first New England farm wife bought a wooden nutmeg, spice traders have known ways to camouflage their wares. We are lucky today that both government agencies and trade associations work hard to develop and maintain high standards in these relatively costly and still most important condiments.

Pepper, like salt, because of its preservative qualities, has been at times worth its weight in gold. And we are acquainted with a treasured bay leaf that on festive occasions—all during the last war—made the rounds of ten or fifteen beleaguered English households.

Perhaps our interest in spices is the greater because of our descent from a sailing family, not in New England but in the old Hansa town of Lübeck, where ships with their cargoes of Kolonialwaren anchored at the wharves on the Trave. And the spices were stored in the mowlike corbie-stepped warehouses hard by—above the merchants' living quarters.

Spices, indeed, bring all the world together. Like wines and cheeses, their individuality is intense and their identification with places a vivid one. We associate the best bay leaves with Turkey; the best real cinnamon with Ceylon; the best red hot peppers with Louisiana. And there have been lively controversies over the relative merits of Spanish and Hungarian paprika; of Mexican and Malagasy vanilla bean.

Since spices are used in such small quantities, we recommend that you purchase from impeccable sources. We also suggest that ◗ if you are using ground spices, they be replenished at least within the year, as they tend in this form to lose strength rapidly. Be sure to date your jars when you clean and fill them. Store spices in tightly covered nonabsorbent containers and in as dark and cool an area as your kitchen provides. But have them handy! Their discriminating use will pique many a dish from obscurity to memorableness.

In cooking, put whole spices in a cloth or a stainless metal tea ball—so you can remove them more readily when the dish is done. ◗ Do not overboil spices, in particular caraway, as they become bitter. And do not use high heat for paprika or curry, for they scorch easily. Some spices are available as distilled essences, and these clear additives are valuable in light Fruit Butters, page 578, or Pickles, page 584. Their flavor does not last long as that of whole spices cooked with the food. ✻ Frozen spiced foods do not hold up well when stored for any length of time. And in ◗ quantity cooking, if you are enlarging household recipes, spice to taste rather than to measure.

We have tried throughout this book to vary our recipes with appropriate seasoning which combines spices and herbs. We have suggested amounts which are pleasurable for the average person. Spice tolerances vary tremendously with individuals and you may wish to use more or less of the quantities we have indicated. For a further discussion of spice combinations, see Seasonings, page 216. The following comments describe various spices and their uses.

ALLSPICE

In this book, pimiento, the name for true peppers of the Capsicum family, see page 213, is reserved for them. And pimento, a probably perverted spelling, is kept for allspice only. Within its single small reddish-brown berry lies a mixture of cinnamon, clove, nutmeg and juniper berry flavors. And this is why the French sometimes call allspice "quatre épices." They also use this term for a blend of spices. Use allspice from soup to nuts, alone or in a combination with other spices.

THE CARDAMONS

Powder the plump seeds of Elettaria cardamomum only as needed, for otherwise the aromatic loss is great. Use as for cinnamon and cloves, alone or in combination. Delicious in coffee. The smaller type—amamum cardamomum—is used whole in barbecue, basting sauces and pickles.

THE CINNAMONS

True cinnamon—Cinnamomum zeylanicum—is the bark of a tree that flourishes in Ceylon and along the Malabar Coast. It is extremely mild whether rolled in a tight quill or stick or in powdered form. Most of the so-called cinnamon on the market is really cassia—Cinnamomum cassia. This is a similar bark that is not quilled, but formed as though a short scroll were rolled from both ends and left with its center portion flat. It has slightly bitter overtones compared to the warm, sweet, aromatic true cinnamon. The best forms of cassia come from Saigon. Use the stick form of either of these spices in hot chocolate, mulled wine, fruit compotes and pickles. We need hardly suggest trying cinnamon on toast, dustings on cookie tops

or incorporating it into desserts and baked items. But maybe its use, in small quantities, in meats and seafoods is new to you.

THE CLOVES

This spicy, dried, rich red, unopened bud of the clove tree—Caryophyllus aromaticus—contains so much oil that you can squeeze it out with a fingernail. Because its flavor is so strong, the heads of the cloves are sometimes removed so the seasoning will be milder. These milder portions are often used in the powdered form. Always remove any whole cloves used in cooking before serving. Oil of clove is available for use in light-colored foods, but watch out for its terrific pungency. The best cloves come from Madagascar and Zanzibar. Use in curries, stewed fruits, marmalades and chutneys, pickles, marinades and, in small quantities, with onions and meats; also of course, with ham, as well as in spiced baked stews. An onion stuck with 3 or 4 cloves is a classic addition to stocks and stews.

CURRY

We think of curry, which is really a highly seasoned sauce, mainly as a powder sitting on the shelf ready to be added when foods need a lift. But curry powders are best when the spices are freshly ground or incorporated into a paste with onion, garlic, fruits and vegetables as commonplace as apples and carrots and as exotic as tamarind and pomegranate.

The curry, either in powder or paste form, has its flavor developed in olive oil, or ghee, a clarified butter. The paste is then cooked in a low oven over a period of several hours before the final stage of preparation with the main food. Curries should be specially blended for each kind of dish: a dry one for coating meat; a sour one for marinated meats; and other mixtures in between for chicken or mutton, rice, beans, vegetables and fish. They range in strength from the fiercely hot curries of Madras to the mild ones of Indonesia. The mixtures below give you an idea of the variety and extent of curry bases. Amounts to use per portion are a matter of tolerance. Choose beer or a tart limeade as a beverage with curried foods. While making up the dish, use plenty of fresh garlic and onion and, if possible, fresh coconut milk, page 193.

I.

1 oz. each ginger, coriander and cardamon
¼ oz. cayenne
3 oz. turmeric

II.

2 oz. each of the seeds of coriander, turmeric, fenugreek, black pepper
2½ oz. cumin seed
1½ oz. each poppy and cardamon seeds
½ oz. mustard seed
½ oz. dry ginger
2 oz. dry chilis
1 oz. cinnamon

III.

1 oz. each turmeric, coriander and cumin
½ oz. dry ginger and peppercorns
¼ oz. dried hot peppers and fennel seed
⅛ oz. each mustard, poppy seeds, cloves and mace

GINGER

The root of a bold perennial, Zingiber officinale—with the most heavenly scented lily—must be harvested at just the right moment to avoid being fibrous and having a bitter after-taste. Whole fresh or green ginger should be smooth-skinned and even in color and must be kept dry or it will sprout and be useless for flavoring. It tastes best sliced thin, unpeeled and sautéed in oil to extract the flavor. When fresh it can also be mashed. When dry it may be cut into ½-inch cubes and steeped for several hours in marinades or in cold water, after which the liquid can be used as seasoning. Peeled or thinly sliced ginger can be added to stews or rubbed over duck or fish, as you would garlic. It will do much to remove "fishy" flavors. Boiled and then preserved in sirup, it is known, in this milder form, as Canton ginger. This is delicious in desserts, chopped fine and used with or without its sauce. And it is worth trying with bananas and even tomatoes, squash, onions and sweet potatoes. Ginger is also candied and, in a pinch, can in this form be washed of its sugar and substituted for fresh ginger. When ground, we all know the value of ginger for flavoring baked items. Equivalent flavoring strengths of the above forms are: ½ teaspoon ground equals 1 to 2 thinly sliced preserved, equals 2 tablespoons sirup.

NUTMEG AND MACE

These flavors are so closely allied because they come from the same tough-husked fruit of Myristica fragrans. It is sun- or charcoal-dried and, when opened, has a lacy integument which is used whole in cooking fruits or desserts or ground into mace for seasoning. The hard, inner kernel is the nutmeg. Use it sparingly but often and, for its full flavor, grind it fresh from a handy nutmeg grinder that merely needs a twist—like a pepper mill. Try it not only in baked items but in spinach, with veal, on French toast—and always with eggnog.

THE WHITE AND BLACK PEPPERS

Both these peppers come from the berry of Piper nigrum. There is some difference in flavor, the white being slightly more aromatic, but their use is almost interchangeable.

The white is made from the fully ripe berry from which the dark outer shell is buffed before the berry is ground. White pepper flavor holds up better in sausages and canned meats. This form is also used in all light-colored foods or sauces.

Black pepper is processed from the green, underripe, whole dried berries, and then cured. They are used in poivrade dishes, crushed—rather than ground—so the oils are not dispersed. And they are added the last few minutes before the sauce is strained. But pepper, which can be used in any food except sweets—and even here there is the further exception of Pfeffernuesse, page 395—is best freshly ground. It is not only a remarkable preservative but manages to strengthen food flavors without masking them as much as other spices do.

Unless otherwise specified, the word pepper in this book means black pepper.

POPPY SEED

This seed comes from Papaver phoeas, different from the opium poppy. The most desirable is grown in Holland and colored a slate blue. The seed is best when roasted or steamed and crushed before use in cooking—so its full flavor is released. If it is one of your favorite flavors, it is worth getting a special hand-mill for grinding it. Use it in baked items and try it on noodles.

TURMERIC

This Indian rhizome—Curcuma longa—is bitterish, and its rather acrid fugitive fragrance warms the mouth, so it must be used with discretion. Its golden color gives the underlying tone to curry powders and to certain pickles. In small quantities, it is used as a food coloring, often replacing saffron for this purpose.

VANILLA BEAN AND EXTRACT

Vanilla bean, before being marketed, is fermented and cured for 6 months. Vanilla extract is prepared by macerating the beans in a 35% alcohol solution. To retain its greatest flavor, add it only when food is cooling. Try 2 parts vanilla to 1 part almond flavoring—a great Viennese favorite. Or try keeping vanilla beans in brandy and using the flavored brandy as a seasoning. ▶ Beware of synthetic vanillas whose cheap flavor is instantly detected and which ruin any dish that is frozen. This tawdry quality is characteristic also of nonalcoholic liqueur seasonings.

MOCHA

This name is given to dishes flavored with a lightly roasted coffee bean. We include it here, for coffee can often be used profitably as a spice, especially when combined with chocolate.

OTHER SWEET EXTRACTS AND FLAVORINGS

There are a number of other extracts, all of which should be used sparingly, such as lemon and almond. Derivatives of almond are: orgeat, page 187, and falernum, a sirup of lime, almond and spices dominated by ginger; grenadine, made from the juice of pomegranates, and rose and orange waters which are both sweetened distillations.

We do not recommend nonalcoholic liqueur flavorings.

ABOUT HERBS

Confucius, a wise man, refused to eat anything not in season. Everyone who has tasted the difference between food served with fresh rather than dried herbs knows how wise he was. Few herbs can be bought in a fresh state at market, but the most important ones can be easily grown in a small sunny plot. We know, for we have grown and used all the culinaries in this section. Therefore, we beg you to exercise your green thumb at least on those whose evanescent oils deteriorate or almost disappear in drying. Chervil, borage, burnet and summer savory suffer the greatest losses. And those mainstays —chives, tarragon, parsley and basil—can never in their dry form begin to approach the quality of their fresh counterparts. Even the flavor of sage when fresh can be so delicate as to be almost unrecognizable.

ABOUT GROWING AND DRYING HERBS

As long ago as the 17th century, the herbalist Parkinson in his "Paradisi in Sole," stressed the importance of proper drainage in herb-growing. We, too, have discovered that good drainage, whether secured by boxing or simply by the selection of terraced ground, is the very first consideration in beginning an herb garden. We know, also, that some of the most pungent and aromatic herbs flourish in the seemingly impoverished soil of the Mediterranean area.

We do find that we can grow the various thymes, pot marjoram and winter savories in a dry rock garden, treat them with neglect and reap them for twenty years. But we also find, with our hot summers and variable winters, that sage and perennial culinaries, at least, are more apt to hold over a well-enriched garden soil.

A third factor, in raising practically all herbs well, is sun. Most varieties, including those which are most popular, require plenty of it. Exceptions are specifically mentioned later. In designing an herb garden, we like to define its pattern with some precision. The plants themselves, with their contrasting shapes and their tendency to sprawl, seem to need regimentation. To maintain year-round attractiveness we plant evergreen perennials alternating with deciduous types.

A 15-inch to 2-foot unit area for each of most culinaries is more than enough to supply household demands. Sometimes, if we want only a single specimen—for instance, a sage or a lavender—we keep it pruned to a central shrub and use the edges around it for small plants. Sometimes we repeat a color accent—like the gray of sage or lavender—to unify the whole complex of squares.

If you haven't room for a more extended layout, try setting out a few pots of annuals on your patio. Some of the evergreen perennials will weather the winter in a strawberry jar. To prepare the jar for herbs, fill it with a mixture of ⅓ rich friable soil and ⅔ sand. Try the thymes, sweet marjoram, burnet and chervil on the shady side. You can dwarf fennel, borage and sage by root confinement. Replace the coarse marjorams with dittany of Crete, coarse mints with Requienii.

Pots can be used, too, for growing herbs indoors in sunny windows. We have had moderate success with rosemary, sweet marjoram, the basils, dittany of Crete, lemon verbena and scented geranium. All of these were from late summer cuttings, and dill and bronze fennel from seed. Tarragon dug after cold weather dormancy and potted up indoors showed six inches of green within ten days. A small potted sweet bay is both decorative and useful. ❧ But most house plant herbs deteriorate in flavor, just as do hothouse tomatoes.

Many herbs are characterized by quite inconspicuous bloom; so if you clip constantly for fresh or dried culinary use you may never allow the plants to reach the blossoming stage. For ❧ most herbs are harvested—unless noted in the individual descriptions—just before their flowers form. At this time, when they are budding up, the leaves are at their most aromatic. Pick early in the day, as soon as the dew has dried off the leaves. Wash if necessary and dry the leaves without bruising.

It should not be necessary to note that herbs, which are remarkably free from insect pests, should be grown where they are not subject to sprays or the attention of dogs. You may tie them together and hang them, when dry, in small bunches. The location always traditionally recommended is a cool, airy attic. Since such spaces are becoming scarce, a shady breezeway will do. And lacking a breezeway, room-drying is preferable to oven-drying, for even when the oven is preheated as low as 200° and shut off the moment the herbs are inserted, their flavor is weakened. For thick-leaved varieties, the oven process may have to be repeated several times until the herbs are bone-dry.

❧ To test for dryness before packaging, put a few sprigs or leaves in a tightly stoppered glass jar and watch for condensation, mold development or discoloration. This is important, especially with basil. However you dry herbs ❧ store them in tightly covered, preferably light-proof, jars—in a dark, cool place. Should they show insect activity, discard them. You may want to strip leaves from the stems before drying or freezing herbs. ❧ Dried herbs retain their flavor best if pulverized just before using.

❧ To substitute dried herbs for fresh use ⅛ teaspoon powdered or ½ teaspoon crushed for every tablespoon fresh chopped herbs. ❧ To reconstitute dried herbs and develop their flavors, soak them in some liquid you can incorporate in the recipe—water, stock, milk, lemon juice, wine, olive oil or vinegar—for ten minutes to one hour before using. Or, simmer them in hot butter. For cooking, place non-powdered dry herbs in a cloth bag, or a stainless metal tea ball for easy removal. For blends, see pages 219–221.

You may freeze herbs. If so,

use them before defrosting. They are too limp for garnishes, but have much the same seasoning strength as fresh herbs. We find that some herbs, like chives, get slimy when frozen. ▶ To freeze, parblanch (I, 88), for ten seconds, plunge into ice water for one minute, dry between towels. Put them up individually in recipe-sized packets for seasoning a salad dressing or a batch of stew or freeze with mixed bouquets garnis for soups and sauces. You may also preserve herbs by salting them down in covered crocks, alternating ½-inch layers of salt and ½-inch layers of herbs. Herbs and savory salt will have stabilized within two weeks.

ABOUT USING HERBS

Handy as it might seem, we have refrained from giving an herb chart, because some herbs are overpowering and it is so difficult to indicate in a general way the amounts to use. Suitable quantities of herbs are listed in the individual recipes. Below we set down detailed characteristics of culinary herbs. Let us add that the delicately flavored types should be placed in sauces and soups only toward the end of preparation and left just long enough to lose their volatile oils. And once again, while we advocate a constant use of herbs, don't use too many kinds at once or too much of any one kind.

To familiarize yourself with herb flavors, some "lazy day," when you feel experimental, blend ½ pound mild cheddar cheese with 2 tablespoons sour cream and 2 tablespoons vodka. Divide the mixture into small portions and add herbs and herb combinations. Label the cheese samples as you mix them. Let them rest for about an hour to develop flavor. Then have a testing party with your husband, your wife or a friend.

ANGELICA

This slightly licorice-flavored plant can be candied, page 526, for use in desserts, as a decorative garnish. Its seeds are used in pastry.

THE ANISES

These have strangely subtle licorice overtones. Try the seeds for your family in Anise Cookies, page 394; the oil as a flavoring in sponge cake; or the Chinese star anise in watermelon-rind pickle. To release the full flavor of the seeds, crush them between towels with a rolling pin.

BEE BALM

Use the lemony leaves for tisane or as a garnish in fruit punch or fruit soup.

THE BASILS

Not without reason called l'herbe royale, these versatile herbs have a great affinity for tomatoes, fish and egg dishes, but are good in almost all savory dishes. They darken quickly after cutting. Serve them as they do in Italy—where basil is very popular—in a bouquet of sprigs set in a small vase of water. Be sure to try Pesto, page 218, with spaghetti.

THE BAYS

Always use these leaves, fresh or dry, with discretion—only ⅓ of a fresh leaf or ⅙ of a dry leaf in a quart of stew—and only a pinch if in powdered form. But do use them, not only in stuffings but in stocks, sauces, marinades, in the cooking of vegetables and meats and in a Bouquet Garni, page 220. Do not confuse the edible bay, Laurus nobilis, with the cherry laurel, Prunus laurocerasus, of our gardens—as the cherry laurel leaf is poisonous.

BORAGE

This herb is only good fresh—as its flavor vanishes as it dies. Use the leaves wherever you want a cucumber flavor in fish sauces or white aspics. It is traditional in some fruit punches and the choice blue starlike blooms are beautiful floated in punches and lemonades or used in food garnishes. Young borage can be cooked like spinach (I, 325).

BURNET

Sometimes called salad burnet, this herb has a haunting cucumberish flavor. It does not dry well but, as it keeps green all winter long, it can be picked at any time. Pick the center leaves, as the older ones are bitter. Use the leaves or soak the seeds in vinegar and use in salads.

Poterium sanguisorba, a hardy perennial growing to 2 feet, is almost fernlike in habit. It comes very quickly and easily from seed in any well-drained soil, in sun.

CAMOMILE

This is famous as a Tisane (I, 20), and a small quantity is occasionally put into beef stock. Sometimes the fresh leaves are used, but it is the center of the flower only that is most prized. The petals of this tiny daisy are removed after the flower is dried.

THE CAPERS AND CAPERLIKE BUDS AND SEEDS

When picked, these bulletlike buds of the caper bush taste like tiny sharp gherkins. Use them in Tartare Sauce (I, 349), with fish and wherever you wish a piquant note.

Also used as inadequate substitutes for true capers are the so-called English caper, a more loosely budded, less pungent blossom; also, pickled immature or mature nasturtium seeds and buds of marsh marigold. Similar in use are: Chinese fermented black beans, or toushi, which are available in cans; and the pickled green seeds of martynia —an annual growing to 2½ feet—easy and a pleasure to grow, with dramatic flowers, leaves and a horned pod.

CARAWAY

Use the leaves of this herb sparingly in soups and stews. The seeds, similar to cumin in flavor, are classic additions to rye breads, cheeses, stews, marinades, cabbage, sauerkraut, turnips. And they are the basic flavoring of kümmel. If added to borsch or other soups, put them in a bag for the last 30 minutes of cooking only, as protracted heating makes them bitter. Crush them before adding to vegetables or salads, to release their flavor.

THE CELERIES

The tender leaves of Apium graveolens, the celery you grow or buy, can be used fresh or dried in almost all foods. Celery salt is a powdered form of it combined with salt. But the seeds sold for flavoring are not those of the plant we grow, but those of a wild celery. These seeds, either whole or ground, have a powerful flavor and must be used sparingly: whole in stocks, and court bouillon, in pickles and salads; or in ground form in salad dressing, seafoods or vegetables.

CHERVIL

One of the famous "fines herbes," this is more delicate and ferny than parsley. The leaf is used with chicken, veal, omelets, green salad and spinach—as a garnish, of course—and always in the making of a Béarnaise (I, 370), or Vinaigrette Sauce (I, 341). It is one of the herbs it pays to grow—for when dried it is practically without flavor.

Pluches de cerfeuille are sprigs of fresh or fresh blanched chervil often specified in stocks and stews.

CORIANDER

Many of us know this flavor from childhood as the seed in the heart of a "jaw breaker," in gingerbread, apple pie or as an ingredient of curry. But few of us know the fresh leaves of this plant as Chinese parsley, as the Cilantro of the Caribbean, the Kothamille of Mexico or the Dhuma of India where its somewhat foetid odor and taste are much treasured. Use leaves only—no stems—and do not chop. Float the leaves in pea or chicken soups and in stews, place them on top of roasts or use them in a court bouillon for clams.

CUMIN

This flavor is classic in cheese, sauerkraut and unleavened bread. It is also used whole in marinades, chilis and tomato sauces. One of the principal ingredients of curry, it is even incorporated in baked items and eggs as well as in beans, rice dishes and Enchiladas (I, 214).

DILL

Both seed and leaf of this feathery, pungent and slightly bitter plant are used in sour cream, fish, bean, cucumber and cabbage dishes as well as in potato salad—or on new potatoes. If using dill butter sauce, do not brown the butter. The seed is also good in vinegar.

THE FENNELS

The leaves of both common and

Florence fennel can be used interchangeably where a slightly vigorous flavor is wanted. But it is only the white, bulbous-stalked finocchio that is used as a vegetable (I, 292)—either raw or cooked as for celery.

In flavoring, both the leaves and seeds are used—as for dill —especially for fat fish and in lentils, rice and potatoes. The seeds are often used in apple pies. Fish is sometimes cooked over fennel twigs. But in sauces —as with dill—do not let the leaves cook long enough to wilt, unless they have been previously blanched. The leaves do not retain flavor in drying.

FENUGREEK

This has the same odor as celery but a bitterer flavor. Popular as a Tisane (I, 20). It is also used in many African dishes and constitutes one of the main ingredients of curries and the base for artificial maple flavor.

FILÉ

Filé powder is a necessary ingredient of creole gumbos.

Any concoction of sassafras needs very careful handling and should be added to a hot dish ▶ off the heat, and never be allowed to boil—as then it strings most miserably. It leaves a pleasantly lasting astringent quality in the mouth.

To make filé, gather the very young leaves of Sassafras variifolium. Dry and powder in a mortar—adding dried okra, allspice, coriander and sage, if you wish. Store tightly lidded. The bark is used for Tisane (I, 20).

GERANIUM

The many-flavored geranium leaves—rose, nutmeg, lemon, apple—are used in pound cake, jellies, compotes or merely as floaters in fingerbowls.

Try a lemon-scented leaf in

custard or an apple-flavored one in baked apples.

HOREHOUND

The woolly leaves of this plant are made into an extract which is combined with sugar into confections.

HORSERADISH

Along with coriander, nettle, horehound and lettuce, horseradish is one of the five bitter herbs of the Passover. It is overpowering and it does get bitter if held more than 3 months. If you do not have fresh roots to grate into lemon juice or vinegar, it is best to reconstitute the ground dried root about 30 minutes before serving. Just soak 1 tablespoon of dried horseradish in 2 tablespoons of water and add ½ cup of heavy cream. The flavor of the dried reconstituted root, however, is strong and not nearly as desirable as the fresh.

It is also prized for use in fatty meat or cocktail sauces, in potato salad and for use with cold meats and fish.

HYSSOP

The leaves of this minty, spicy, somewhat bitter herb are used with salads and fruits; the dried flowers in soups.

JUNIPER BERRIES

Three to 6 per serving are prized for seasoning game, bean dishes and certain alcoholic drinks like gin. In fact, ½ teaspoon of these berries soaked for a long time in a marinade—or cooked long in a stew—gives a seasoning equivalent of ¼ cup gin.

LAVENDER

The leaves and flowers of this highly aromatic plant give a bitter pungency to salads. We prefer to use it as a sachet rather than as a seasoner. But its gray-ness lends a lovely accent to the herb garden.

LEMON VERBENA

This, like lavender, in our opinion is better reserved for sachets or closets than for food; although it is often used as a lemon substitute for drinks.

LOVAGE

The leaves of this bold herb whose stems can be candied like Angelica, page 526, or blanched and eaten like celery, are often used as a celery substitute with stews or tongue. The seeds are sometimes pickled like capers.

THE MARJORAMS

These, whether called sweet, pot, orégano, orégano dulce or wild, are all very pungent. While similar in their uses, they are not quite the same in their growth habits. Use them in sausages, stews, tomato dishes; with lamb, pork, chicken and goose; with omelets, eggs, pizzas, and cream cheeses; with all of the cabbage family and with other vegetables such as green beans; in minestrone and mock turtle soups; and, of course, don't fail to try them fresh and finely chopped for salads.

There is great horticultural confusion in regard to the oréganos of commerce and seeds ordered under the name oreganum vary enormously.

THE MINTS

We all know peppermint and spearmint. But there are many other mints worth trying, like the curly varieties and apple, orange and pineapple. These are less penetrating but equally refreshing. Use any of them in fruit cups, cole slaw, peas, zucchini, lamb, veal, cream cheeses; in chocolate combinations, teas and of course in jellies and juleps. These leaves, fresh or candied, see page 526, make attractive garnishes. If using fresh leaves, ¼ to ½ teaspoon—crushed just before using—is enough per serving. But, if using this flavoring in the form of oil, a drop is often too much—so go easy.

All of the following grow rampant in any soil, sun or partial shade, dry or moist: Mentha viridis, perhaps the most peppery of all; Mentha piperita, the peppermint we know best; Mentha spicata or spearmint; and the woolly apple mint—frosted in appearance and fine for a drink garnish.

All the mints are perennial and easily raised from root divisions. They should be in areas confined by metal or rock edgings to keep them from invading less sturdy neighbors in the herb garden. Keep them pruned to have bushy tops for beverage garnishes. If your growing area is confined, try Mentha Requienii or Corsican mint—a tiny-leaved plant, as discreet as a moss.

And, incidentally, field mice hate mint odor and will stay away from any food near which it is scattered.

MARIGOLD

The dried centers of this garden flower are sometimes used as a color substitute for saffron and the young leaves can be used in salads. The petals are used only when the recipe calls for cooking, as in stews.

THE MUSTARDS

Mustard fanciers will argue the merits of a mild champagne-based, or poupon Dijon, or a Louisiana mix—against the sharp English or the fiery Jamaican or Chinese. There are many ways to prepare mustards from mustard powder, which is the dry residue left after the oil

is expressed from the seed. But the freshness of the mix is an important factor. For the flavor changes rapidly once moisture is added and, especially, once a bottle is opened after mixing. Try keeping it fresh by putting a slice of lemon on top of it before closing the lid. The lemon needs renewal about once a week. The ground seed varies from white to yellow to brown. The white or English seed is very scarce and superb; the brown, the next best. Commercial mustards with their blends of flour and spices—often heavy in turmeric to color them—may be based on water, wine or vinegar. If you want to mix your own, allow 2 to 3 tablespoons liquid to ¼ cup dry mustard. More details about preparing mustard follow.

Mustard can be added advantageously in small quantities to cheese, seasoned flour, chicken or pot roasts and to sauces, hot or cold. It is classic served with cold meats and for use in pickles —both ground and as seed. Prepared mustard has about ⅛ to ½ the strength of dry mustard.

There are two basic ways to prepare mustards. ◗ Hot mustards are based on cold liquids —water, vinegar or flat beer. Add 2 to 3 tablespoons liquid to about ¼ cup dry mustard. If it is too hot, tone it with a little olive or cooking oil, garlic, tarragon leaves and a pinch of sugar. ◗ Suave mustards can be made in one of the following ways by using boiling water or herb-vinegar. The heat inhibits the reaction of two of the more violently pungent mustard elements, myrosin and sinigrin. But the vapors in processing the following formula are a secret weapon against the common ailment—sinus. We have tried valiantly throughout the spice and herb sections to refrain from mentioning herbal remedies. Allow us this one Dioscoridian lapse in **Double-Purpose Mustard.**

I. This recipe involves bringing water to a rolling boil. It is then poured 3 times over about 2 ounces of dry mustard and worked as follows. Use a heatproof glass or enamel dish. Pour enough boiling water over the mustard to make a paste. Cover the paste completely with boiling water. Let it stand until it no longer steams—15 to 30 minutes. While it is cooling, use a rubber scraper to churn the mustard around, down from the sides and across the top. All of this under water. Let settle slightly and drain off water. Cover the mustard with boiling water. Let stand 10 minutes. Drain. Cover the mustard again with boiling water. Let stand 5 minutes. Drain. Add 2 teaspoons sugar and ¼ to ½ teaspoon salt. If you want a bright mustard, add ¼ teaspoon turmeric, vinegar and other spices to your taste. Put mustard in a jar. Let cool uncovered 1 to 2 hours. Then cap tightly. Keep at room temperature. Do not refrigerate.

II. This is much easier to do, but without as great "curative" effects. Put in a heatproof glass double boiler top about 2 ounces of dry mustard. Pour water which has been brought to a rolling boil over it to cover. Place over ▶ not in, rapidly boiling water for 15 minutes. Before covering see that the mustard has been stirred into a paste but is still covered with the hot liquid. Drain any excess water. Cool and store as described above.

NASTURTIUM

Flowers, seeds and leaves are all used as flavorings. The leaves and lovely orange and yellow flowers are fine in salads and the pickled pods often replace capers. These pods are best picked just as soon as the blossom drops, and prepared at once. To preserve nasturtium pods, see page 590.

ABOUT ONIONS IN SEASONING

Never since our first encounter with the host of alliums in a bulb catalogue have these lilies lost their allure for us as food or flowers—from the tiniest chive to the enormous Schuberti with its choicest florets held captive within a flowered cage. This is a plea not only to use a variety of onions in your cooking, but to grow the perennial ones so you will always have them on hand. We have tried to indicate their use in individual recipes. To cook onions as vegetables, see (I, 301). Nothing can add such subtlety to a dish, yet none is more abused in the cooking than onions. And when we say onions, we mean any of these culinaries we list later.

Use onion bulbs fresh or dry; the green tops of onions or leeks in making soups and court bouillon; and don't forget that ▶ a touch of onion freshly added to canned vegetables and soups often disguises the "canned" taste and varies the expected one.

▶ High heat and a too long cooking period bring out the worst features. ▶ If you scorch onions, they will be bitter. ▶ Yet onions must be cooked long enough to get rid of any rawness. If you want them to taste mild in soups, like Potage St. Germain (I, 121), or in delicate stews, the flavor of the dish can be improved with less onion odor during the cooking if you follow this procedure. ▶ Parblanch the onions for 15 minutes, if they are 1 inch in size, before adding them to the soup or stew. If you want them ♦ mild in sautéing, cook them only until translucent—tender, but not flabby. If you want them ♦ penetrating, sauté until golden. If you want them ♦ all-pervasive, brown them very slowly, as for an onion soup, see (I, 113), or a Lyonnaise. To give color and flavor to a Petite Marmite, see (I, 110).

To shorten cooking time, onions are frequently chopped and minced fine. There are a number of ways to make this process less tearful. Pare them while holding them under running water, or use a special onion chopper that is enclosed in glass. Mincing is easier and safer if you first slice a flat base for your operations and use a sharp French knife, see (I, 250). Or when you haven't time to sauté an onion properly, but do not want a raw taste in cold dishes, hot sauces or dressings, use ♦ onion juice. Ream a cut onion on a lemon juicer or scrape the cut center of the onion with the edge of a spoon.

♦ To get rid of onion traces, rub your hands with salt, vinegar or lemon juice. Eat raw parsley, or see page 61 for the most perfect raw onion canapé. Or moisten pots, sprinkle them generously with salt, let stand and rinse with very hot water to rid them of onion taste.

We jokingly refer to onions in health (I, 301), but the use of onions for the bacteria-destroying power of their vapor was demonstrated on a large scale in World War II. However, this antibacterial action was present only when the onion was freshly cut. This power disappeared within 10 minutes. Onions deteriorate rapidly once the outer skin is removed and ♦ should not be stored for reuse after cutting.

♦ All onions are of easy cul-

ture. They prefer sandy, moist, rich earth, sun and shallow planting. The dry ones should all be sun dried a few days after being dug up. You may braid the tops so the bulbs can be hung in clusters for even airing during storage. If the tops are cut, do not cut too close to the neck of the bulb. Store all onions in a cool, dark, dry, well-ventilated place. Below are descriptions of onion types most used in cooking.

CHIVES—ALLIUM
SCHOENOPRASUM

An 8- to 10-inch variety and a slightly larger one called Sibericum are hardy. They are shown blooming in the center sketch, page 213 and are used widely in white cheeses, green sauces and with eggs. Cut and add them to hot and cold food just before serving. ♦ Do not put chives in a cottage cheese or any uncooked dish you plan storing even as long as overnight, as they get unpleasantly strong. To keep the plants looking well, cut a few of the thin tubular leaves low rather than bobbing the top which will brown where cut. Remember that, like all bulbs, chives rely for plant renewal strength on the leaves—so don't cut any one plant too often, 3 or 4 times a season. The leaves are tenderer after each cutting. Also keep the blooms picked low so the tougher stem does not get mixed with the leaves when you use them and so you are not bothered with seeding. About 3 to 6 small bulbs set in the fall will make a good cluster by the following summer.

GARLIC CHIVES—ALLIUM
TUBEROSUM

This coarser, flat-leaved, 14-inch-high perennial has a charming starry white bloom cluster which can be used sparingly as a garnish. Only the leaves are eaten—also sparingly. Use and cultivate as for chives.

GARLIC, AIL OR ORIENTAL GARLIC—ALLIUM SATIVUM

This is perhaps the most controversial addition to food. We couldn't live without it and we think we have learned to use it discreetly. For our guests have sometimes been obviously relishing and unawarely eating food with garlic in it—while inveighing loudly against it. If you are fond of it ▶ you have to keep a check on the amounts used—for tolerance to it may grow apace to the discomfort of your friends. Use the very young leaves, but the bulb second on the left, page 213, is the treasure. Note the "cloves" that make up the bulb sketched with it to the right in the lower left hand corner. ▶ In this book, when we say 1 clove garlic, it is assumed that the clove is peeled of its husk. Learn to rest slivers of garlic clove on meat before cooking it; to put a clove of garlic on a skewer, cook it in a sauce or stew and remove it before serving; to rub a salad bowl lightly with a cut clove; or to make Chapons (I, 33). Drop a peeled clove into French Dressing 24 hours before serving or put a small squeeze in a sauce. This is easy to do with a garlic press, a handy kitchen utensil. Should you not own a press, you may use the back of a spoon against a small bowl or a mortar and pestle to crush garlic with salt. The salt softens the bulb almost at once, but if you drop a whole clove into a liquid for seasoning ▶ be sure to strain it out before serving. ▶ Never allow garlic to brown. Always use fresh garlic. Powdered and salt forms tend to have rancid overtones. ▶ To blanch garlic,

drop the unpeeled cloves into boiling water. Cook for 2 minutes. Drain, peel and simmer slowly in butter for about 15 minutes. Add this, minced, to the dish for flavoring sauces. True garlic bulbs are not hardy. Bulbs planted in March should be ready for lifting in late July or in August, if the season is a wet one. Be sure to sun-dry the cloves until they are white.

TOPPING GARLIC, GIANT GARLIC, OR ROCHAMBOLE—ALLIUM SORODOPRASUM ·

This hardy plant has a beautiful glaucous leaf and an entrancing pointed bud—sketched—first, upper left, page 213—carried on a furled stem. Its unwinding is a source of great pleasure to watch. The edible bulbs that bunch at the top are indistinguishable in taste and form from the tender Oriental garlic shown below it.

SHALLOTS—ALLIUM ASCALONICUM

This bulb, queen of the sauce onions, is not hardy but well worth growing. It is shown fourth on the left, below the chives. Shallot flavor is perhaps closer to garlic than to onions, and although it has a much greater delicacy, it must still be used with discretion. Shallots are indispensable in Bercy Butter (I, 384), where they should be minced simultaneously with the herbs; and they taste especially good in wine cookery. In sautéing them, mince fine so as not to subject them to too much heat. ▶ Never let them brown, as they become bitter. ▶ Substitute 3 to 4 shallots for 1 medium-sized onion.

Shallot sets should be put in, barely covered, in the early spring. They should be harvested by late June when the leaves are no longer upright—

caving in at the neck—but not yet turning in color. Allow them to dry off on the ground for several days and then braid the leaves so the shallots can be hung in strands in a dry place for use as wanted.

BUNCHING, TOPPING OR TREE ONIONS—ALLIUM CATAWISSA

These are a good substitute for a medium-sharp onion and, unlike dry onions purchased in markets, are perennial. They have a fibrous root system, and the onions develop early in the season at the top of the blooming stock. In fact, some even begin to sprout there too, see second sketch on top row, page 213—and, in turn, produce more onions at the top of the second sprout, the same season. The nonsprouting bulblets can be kept for planting the following August or the next spring. The original plants may also be separated. There is really no excuse for not trying anything that easy. These are the American version of the Egyptian topping onion—Cepa viviparum—which, being tender, is more troublesome, even if it has an additional usable bulb at the base.

LEEKS, THE BELOVED FRENCH POIREAU—ALLIUM PORRUM

King of the soup onions. These biennials grow their first year—as sketched, second from the right, page 213, with an elongated root and with closely interlaced foliage. They are often hilled to keep them white. This practice traps grit unless the leeks are grown with a paper collar. Be sure to rid them of this grit by washing well. They are choice the first year. When you buy leeks, if they show a tough, hollow stem—from which the glorious silver-green bloom was cut from the center of the

foliage—and a more bulbous form at the base as sketched, upper right, the leek is in its second year and will prove too tough to eat. However, the green portion can be utilized in soups and seasonings. Leeks lend themselves to braising.

DRY ONIONS—ALLIUM CEPA

Shown in a group on the lower right, page 213. These are biennials, the major onions of commerce. They vary greatly in flavor, skin color and shape. On the whole, American cepa varieties are smaller, have stronger flavors and keep better than foreign cepa types. Mild in cooking are the big, yellow or white Bermudas. Even more so are the flat Spanish reds, which are a favorite raw garnish on hamburgers and salads. They mush somewhat in cooking, so if you want a mild red cooker, try the rounder, more elongated Italian redskins. Pearl onions, including the kind you find in the bottom of your Gibson cocktail, are cluster sowings of cepa varieties. Cepa types, if planted in sets in February, are harvested in July when the browning leaves have died down.

SCALLIONS—ALLIUM CEPA OR ALLIUM FISTULUM

These are either the thinnings of Allium cepa plantings or special onions like fistulum which do not form a bulb. They are shown illustrated in the center, above, to the right of the chives. The leaf is good as a soup flavoring, the white flesh with about 4 inches of leaf is often braised as for Celery or Leeks (I, 282), and they are eaten raw by self-assertive people.

WILD LEEKS, RAMPS OR THE BROAD-LEAVED WOOD ALLIUM—ALLIUM TRICOCCUM

Around these bulbs many folk

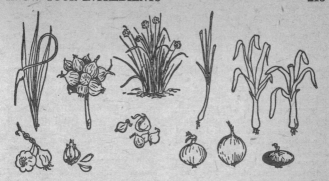

festivals revolve. These and the strong field garlic—Allium vineale—in your lawn are not recommended by us although we frequently see them praised by others.

This is true also of ◗ onion substitutes, which we scorn, but if you care to try them, use ¼ teaspoon garlic powder for 1 small clove of garlic or ¾ teaspoon onion powder for 1 small onion. Cut down on the salt in the recipe, though.

THE PARSLEYS

These plants—root, stem and leaves—have a high protein-carrying factor. They are flavorful in themselves but also valuable as an agent for blending the flavors of other herbs, and have the power to destroy the scent of garlic and onion, see page 210. There is practically no salad, meat, or soup in which they cannot be used. But they should be handled with discretion, particularly the root of the soup, or Hamburg-type, parsley. These roots are sometimes cooked as for Parsnip, see (I, 305).

There are at least 37 varieties of curly parsley, varying in strength. In mincing or deep-fat frying, remove the florets from the more strongly scented stems.

The stems are used in white stocks and sauces for their strength of flavor and because they do not color them as does the leaf. Petroselinum hortense and its curled varieties—crispum —are the parsleys seen most frequently in the markets. This biennial grows to about 1 foot in rich loamy soil and sun.

To grow from seed, soak in water to cover about 24 hours. The uncurled type or Italian is better for fall use, as its leaves shed the snow and stay green longer. Carum petroselinum, the coarser-growing, heavier-rooted biennial, grows to 3 feet. Soak seeds as above.

THE RED AND GREEN PEPPERS

These plants of the Capsicum family are heavy in vitamin A and C values and also are said to have a bacteria-deterrent quality. Native to the Americas, they are widely grown in Europe and very different from the white and black peppers which come from the Orient, see page 201. The capsicums all have this in common: that the ◗ seeds and membranes are irritating and should always be removed if you use them fresh. The condiments from these dried peppers are made both with and without the seeds. ◗ To skin fresh peppers, place them in a 350° oven until the skin is slightly scorched, when it is easily removed, or blanch them for a moment in deep fat at 375°.

The sweet or broad bell peppers, variety C. grossum, are the ones frequently misnamed "mangoes" in the market. These 4- to 5-inch peppers, both green and, in their more ripened state, red, are used for stuffing and diced for flavoring. Also to this general type belong the bonnet or C. tetragonna peppers from which paprikas are ground. The mild Hungarian types are seeded and deprived of their stalks before grinding. Paprika is sensitive to heat and should be added toward the end of the cooking period. When added to broiled food to color, it browns when scorched. Buy in small quantities, as paprika develops insect life in storage.

The longer peppers, variety C. longum, which include most of the chili peppers and cayenne, come in many colors, from chartreuse green to yellow to red. There are hundreds of crosses and in the endless regional recipes for chili or mole powder, as many as 6 or 8 varieties of capsicum will be indicated with names like anchos, pasillo, chipotle.

Cayenne, which comes from C. annuum L., is often adulterated or replaced in commerce by C. fructescens, a small, red, dried tree berry, or C. croton annuum, known also as bird peppers. ♦ Cayenne is so very hot, it should be used only in the smallest pinches. Very hot too are the red clustered C. fasciculatum varieties, with fruit over 6 inches long, for which the seeds are supposed to have come from Tabasco in Mexico. Grown in Southern Louisiana, they constitute the base for hot pepper sauces which are often

matured 2 to 3 years. Red pepper, not as hot as cayenne, is ground from this type.

♦ To prepare dried chili peppers for use in sauces, soak 6 dry chilis in 1 cup water and simmer until tender for about 20 minutes. Drain and reserve the water. When chilis are cool, split them, remove and discard seeds. Scrape the pulp from the skin and add it to the reserved water. For other Capsicum recipes see Chili Powder, page 219, Chili Vinegar, page 152, and Sherry Peppers, page 590. ♦ For decorating with pimientos, see Truffle Garnish (I, 300).

ROSEMARY

The stiff resinous leaves of this sub-shrub are extremely pungent and must be handled with caution. In marinades, for which this flavoring is popular, allow about ⅛ to ¼ teaspoon fresh for 4 servings. Use the lightly crushed leaves sparsely with lamb, duck, partridge, rabbit, capon and veal; and on peas, spinach and pizza.

RUE

This perennial herb is sometimes suggested as a flavoring for fruit cups. As many people are allergic to its irritant qualities which produce symptoms comparable to poison ivy ♦ we do not recommend its use.

SAFFRON

The golden orange stigmas of the autumn crocus are used to both color and flavor cakes, breads, and dressings and are classic in Risottos (I, 165), and Bouillabaisse (I, 136). Even a ♦ small amount of saffron has an overpoweringly medicinal quality, so use only as directed in the recipes. If using mainly for color, just ¼ teaspoon to 2 tablespoons hot water will suffice for 5 to 6 cups of flour. Use only about ¼ to ⅓ teaspoon in 2 tablespoons hot water or white wine to season 6 to 8 servings of a sauce.

THE SAGES

Sage and Clary Sage leaves should both be used sparingly for seasoning. Sage is perhaps the best known and loved of all American seasonings for fatty meat like pork and sausages; and for duck, goose and rabbit. It is also used in cheeses and chowders. There is no comparison between the flavor of the freshly chopped tender leaves and the dried ones which lose much of their volatile oil. Dry carefully, as the leaves are thick and mould easily. Fresh clary sage is used in omelets and fritters.

THE SAVORIES

Winter savory is a rather resinous perennial evergreen subshrub whose leaves are useful in stews, stuffings and meat loaves. The leaves of the annual summer savory are much more delicately flavored and have many more uses. It is classic in green beans and green bean salad; in horseradish sauce and lentil soup; and even in deviled eggs. It is also used with fat fish, roast pork, potatoes, tomatoes and French dressing.

SESAME SEED OR BENNE

This is a favorite topping for breads, cookies and vegetables. Its nutty flavor tastes strongest when the seeds are lightly toasted for about 20 minutes in a 350° oven and stirred frequently. Crushed, it is made into an oily paste, called tehina when mixed with chick peas. Crushed sesame and peas also form the base for Halvah. Sesame oil from the seeds is desirable in salads.

THE SORRELS

The elongated leaves of these plants are rather high in oxalic acid and are used to flavor soups or sauces or to combine with other vegetables, rather than to serve alone. The somewhat acid purée is good as a garnish for goose or pork. The leaves may be pounded in a mortar with sugar and vinegar to make a tart sauce.

SWEET WOODRUFF OR WALDMEISTER

The beautiful dark green starlike whorled fresh leaves of this plant are floated in Maibowle, page 45, or other cold punches, but should not be left in longer than about ½ hour.

SWEET CICELY

The green seeds and fresh leaves of this soft, ferny plant may be used as a garnish in salads and cold vegetables. Use dry seeds in cakes, candies and liqueurs.

TARRAGON

Called "estragon" by the French, this herb when fresh is one of the luxuries of cooking. The flavor, chemically identical to anise, is pretty well lost in drying. Also in drying, the leaf vein stiffens and does not resoften when cooked. So, if the dry leaf is used, it must be carefully strained out before the food is served. To avoid straining and to retain flavor better than by drying, we hold tarragon in vinegar and remove the leaves as needed. Do not crowd the vinegar bottle, allowing about 3 tablespoons of leaves to 1 quart mild vinegar. This gives enough acid to keep the leaves from spoilage. Always keep them well immersed. If you do dry and store tarragon, watch it for insect activity. The fresh leaves are often blanched for decorations, see (I, 88). Although tarragon is too pungent to be cooked in soups it is good added to practically everything else: eggs, mushrooms, tomatoes, sweetbreads, tartar and mustard sauces, fish or chicken. And in a Béarnaise sauce it is essential. True tarragon can be propagated only by division.

THE THYMES

There are so many of these charming plants and their flavors are so varied that a collection of them makes a garden in itself. The narrow-leaved French with its upright habit and grey-green balsamic leaves and the glistening, small-bushed, strongly-scented lemon variety are the thymes most commonly found in commerce. Caraway-scented thyme or Herba Barona is traditional with a baron of beef. Thymes may also be used sparingly on mutton, veal, pork and rabbit; in creole and gumbo dishes; in brown sauces; with pickled beets and tomatoes; with tomatoes; with fat fish, stews, stuffings and most vegetables; and are always found in stocks.

ABOUT SEASONINGS

"Correct the seasoning"—how that time-tested direction stimulates the born cook! We have spoken of herbs and spices and of how they can complement and compliment food. Now we would like to discuss herb and spice blends. By the traditional combinations of both we may give to a dish its finishing touch.

Because the sense of taste reacts most frankly to seasonings, it may be well to reveal for a moment just how it does so. The anatomy of taste is the tongue; and it acknowledges and differentiates between only four basic sensations. The top of the tongue detects sweet and sour; the sides

salt and acid; the back bitter. When we taste things, they pass so quickly over these areas that usually a quick sequence of tastes results, like an arpeggio or a chord. When we were young, lollipops were their sweetest. This not without reason, because senses dull with age and our taste buds were more impressionable to sweets when we too were unopened blossoms. When we were young, we were told not only to gulp our medicines fast—to get them over that bitter-sensitive back band—but were often given them iced to reduce their impact. By the same token, as adults, we hold chilled wine in our mouths until it has had a chance to warm up and release its flavor. Similarly, also, the ice cream we freeze, to taste normally sweet, must be sugared more than warm foods.

Sweet, sour, bitter and salt are only the foundations of taste. Upon them we build a far more complex and subtle structure and its charm is due rather to the olfactory organs than to those which lie in the mouth. If you don't believe us, try tasting food while holding your breath and notice that flavor at its fullest and most characteristic is only realized when the breath is expelled through the nostrils. Prolonged drinking before and smoking during a meal tend to desensitize the passages along which food is appreciated. The prudent hostess will do her tactful best to discourage both but, failing, will season her dishes a little more.

There is an interplay between types of seasoning. Salt, for example, can make sugar less cloying and tone down acidity. Sugar, as a corollary, or vinegar, sometimes modifies saltiness; and monosodium glutamate—though it loses its magic over starches and eggs—heightens the taste of commonplace foods. The use of ginger, brandy or sherry lessens "gaminess" in fish and wild fowl; while salt, pepper and parsley seem to act as catalysts for other flavors.

The history of seasonings is an ironical one. Back in medieval days the spice routes to the Orient were fiercely contended for so that the poorly preserved food of Europe could be rendered palatable enough to eat. Today many foods in our Western world are so successfully and uniformly preserved that seasonings must be used to make them interesting enough to eat.

First and best, of course, even before seasoning, are the built-in flavors—from food grown in rich soils or from animals which have been nourished on flavor-inducing vegetation. Examples are: the famous sea-marsh-grazed lamb of France, the heather-dieted grouse of Scotland, our own southern peach-fed pigs or northern game birds —after they have taken their fill of juniper and lingonberries.

Next come the flavors accentuated by heat: the glazes on browned meats; the essential roasting of coffee and cocoa beans; the toasting of nuts, seeds and breads; the highly treasured "ozmazome"—as the gourmet calls it—which results from rich broths, as well as the blending of flavors achieved generally through slow cooking.

Then there are the flavors induced by fermentation and bacterial activity, as in wines and cheeses; those created by distillation in extracts and liqueurs; and those brought about by smoking, see page 543. Intensification of flavor in foods can be purely mechanical, too. The cracking and softening of seeds —like those of poppy, anise, coriander and caraway—releases

their essential oils. This is also true of the mincing of herbs, the crushing of spices in a mortar, the puréeing of pods to remove their more fibrous portions. And include marinating, also, as an integral flavoring process in which the acids of wine, milk, lemon or vinegar react chemically with food.

◗ When adding seasoning, the greatest care must be used to enhance the natural or previously acquired flavor of the food at hand. The role of the seasoner is the role of the impresario, not the actor: to bring out the best in his material, not to stifle it with florid, strident off-key delivery or to smother it with heavy trappings.

A good many of our adult preferences in seasoning go back to family tradition. Some, more imperatively, may stem from oversensitivity to certain types of condiment. Today we are becoming increasingly appreciative of a broader range—the more exotic seasonings like Indian curry, Mexican chili, Italian pesto—some of which are distinctly an acquired taste.

An observation to seasoners on bland diets—it is worth asking your doctor if he agrees with some recent research which tends to show that while cloves, mustard seed and peppers— black, white and chili—should be avoided, the following condiments are nonirritating to the intestinal mucosa: mustard in powdered form, cinnamon, allspice, mace, thyme, sage, paprika, caraway, bay, onion, nutmeg, curry powder, garlic, peppermint, vanilla bean, vanilla and almond extract.

What quantities of seasoning to use, of course, is a question which can only be resolved by sound judgment and successive sampling. Good taste, like charity, began at home—more specifically in the kitchen. And while it was spread about to things like furniture, music and etiquette, it still applies with all its original pertinency to the flavoring of food.

Here are, for what they are worth, a few rules of thumb. Allow 1 teaspoon salt to each of the following: 1 quart soup, 4 cups flour, 1 lb. meat, 2 cups of the liquid in which cereals are cooked. Substitute ⅓ to ½ dried herbs or ¼ teaspoon powdered herbs for 1 tablespoon fresh herbs. Allow ½ teaspoon dried herbs to 2 cups flour.

▶ In using wine, soy sauce or vegetable-flavored salts for seasoning, be sure to taste before adding regular salt. And, in seasoning sauces to which unseasoned or mildly seasoned solids are added, be sure to retaste after adding the food. Above all, perhaps ▶ heat seasoned food with great care, since certain spices like cayenne, paprika and curry blends scorch easily, and others, if overheated, become bitter.

Keep scissors handy to add bits of flavorful foods, see below.

ANCHOVIES AS SEASONING

The uses of anchovies for seasoning are really a trick to know about. For, if discreetly added to food, they can bring a piquancy the source of which is most difficult to trace. About ⅛ of an anchovy to a cup of sauce will turn the trick, or ⅛ of a

teaspoon of anchovy paste. The paste is both less strong in flavor and apt to be saltier than the whole anchovies, which may be treated in several ways:

I. For a salad, soak anchovies in cold water or milk for about ½ to 1 hour. Drain and dry on paper towels before using.

II. For a sauce, soak them in warm water 5 to 10 minutes. Drain before using. Anchovies are sometimes used to season meats as lardoons, see (I, 453).

ANCHOVY PESTO

Crush together:
    1 anchovy fillet
    2 tablespoons grated
        Parmesan cheese
Combine with:
    Equal parts of butter

BASIL PESTO

This uncooked seasoning can be used on pasta, about 2 tablespoons to a portion, with equal parts of butter; or 1 tablespoon to a dish of minestrone or on a baked potato. It can be made in advance and stored in a cool place. Run a film of olive oil over the top before covering, and store refrigerated.
Pound in a mortar about:
    1½ cups fresh basil leaves
Parsley may be substituted but, of course, the flavor is very different.
    2 cloves garlic
    ¼ cup pine nuts
Add, until it forms a thick purée:
        About ¾ cup thinly
        grated Sardinia or
        Parmesan cheese
When the mixture is really thick, add very slowly, stirring constantly:
        About ¾ cup olive oil
until of the consistency of creamed butter.

CHIFFONADE OF FRESH HERBS

One of our very favorite ways to disguise canned soup combinations is to gather a bouquet of tender fresh herbs. These we mince or blend, if we are in a hurry, right in with the soup; except for chives, which we mince separately to keep them from being too pervasive.

CHILI

Chili blends may be based on a combination as varied as cumin, coriander, orégano, black pepper, clove seeds and sweet and hot peppers, or may be made up quickly from a combination of:

   3 tablespoons paprika
   ⅛ teaspoon cayenne
   1 tablespoon turmeric

But, no matter how simple or how complex the mix, use with it plenty of:

   Garlic

CITRUS ZESTS AND JUICES

What better name than "zest" could be found for the gratings of the colorful outer coatings of lemons, oranges, tangerines and limes—those always available, valuable, yet somewhat not fully appreciated ingredients! Zest is the very quality they add to baked items, stuffings, sauces, soups, meats and desserts. Laziness—or perhaps unawareness—may be the only reason that deprives the cook of this magic wand for transforming commonplace or heavy combinations. Zests must, however, be used with a light touch. If you keep an easily cleaned hand grater hanging near the stove, you will be amazed at the subtlety you can add quickly to your seasoning.

Use only the colored portions of the skin, as the white beneath is bitter. These rinds are more intense in flavor than juice because of their heavy oil concentration. Fold them into icings, for instance, when the major beating is over, so as not to disturb the texture. Another way to get this oily residue for flavor is to grate the rinds coarsely, place them in a piece of cheesecloth and wring the oils onto sugar. Let stand about 15 minutes before using.

And enough can never be said in favor of the frequent use of small quantities of citrus juices—especially in salt-free diets where these flavors serve as cover up for lack of salt. Use them as a substitute for vinegar wherever delicacy is wanted. Lemons and limes can be juiced quickly by holding the cut side against the palm and allowing a tablespoon or so of juice to run into a sauce. If properly held, the seeds will be trapped. Although we give equivalents for dried zest and extracts ◗ it is only the fresh rind and juice of these citrus fruits that we feel hold the really magic seasoning power. Approximate substitutions are: 1 teaspoon dried zest = 1 teaspoon freshly grated zest = ½ teaspoon extract = 2 tablespoons fresh juice = 2 teaspoons grated candied peel. ◗ To get the greatest amount of juice out of citrus fruit, roll the whole fruit—gently but firmly pressing it with the palm while rolling—before cutting for juicing.

In buying citrus, choose yellow-colored lemons. If tinged with green, they are not properly "cured." In choosing limes, the dark green ones are usually stronger in acid and preferable to the yellow types. And, if they are available, don't neglect the use of Seville or bitter oranges. These give their name to such famously flavored dishes as Duck Bigarade (I, 588), and are very distinctive as beverage flavoring. ♦ Keep on hand seasoned sugars, page 170. ♦ To make citrus peels for fruit sauces, take off just the colored portion of the peel with a potato peeler. Blanch for 3 minutes to a limp stage. Wash in cold water. Shred and resimmer with the sauce.

DUXELLES

A delicious seasoning, used in meat and fish cookery or added to sauces and gravies. It is sometimes strained out before serving. Use also in stuffings. Whenever a mushroom flavor is wanted, duxelles can be added. Allow 2 tablespoons added to 1 cup chicken sauce. A convenient way of using up mushroom stems and storing or preserving them.

Chop very fine:
    ½ lb. mushrooms
Squeeze in a cloth, twisting to extract as much moisture as possible. Cook until golden:
    ¼ cup chopped onion or 2
        tablespoons chopped
        shallots
in:
    2 tablespoons butter
    3 tablespoons olive oil
Add the mushrooms and:
    ¼ teaspoon grated nutmeg
    Correct the seasoning
Sauté on high heat until the mushroom moisture is absorbed. Keep duxelles in a covered jar, refrigerated, until ready to use.

FINES HERBES

This classic phrase connotes a delicate blend of fresh herbs suitable for savory sauces and soups, and all cheese and non-sweet egg dishes. Fines herbes are usually equal parts of parsley, tarragon, chives and chervil —although some other milder herbs may creep in. Their charm

lies in their freshness and the quality they achieve when minced together with a sharp knife and added the last minute to the food being cooked, so their essential oils are not lost.

BOUQUETS GARNIS OR FAGGOTS

Nothing helps a soup or stock as much as one of the combinations below. They are best made of fresh materials. To make removal easier, the smaller ingredients can be bound inside an informal tube made from the overlapping celery stalks and tightly tied with white string.
I. Bunch together:
    3 or 4 sprigs parsley or
        chervil
    ⅓ to ½ bay leaf
    2 sprigs fresh thyme
    (1 leek, white portion only)
    (2 cloves)
Place them inside:
    Several celery stalks
and bind tightly with a white string.

II. Tie in a bunch:
    3 sprigs chervil
    3 sprigs parsley
    ½ bay leaf
    2 sprigs fresh thyme

III. If you cannot get fresh materials, wrap your freshly dried herbs still on the stem or coarsely crumbled but not powdered in 4-inch squares of cheesecloth. Tie them into bags and store them in a tightly covered container, see sketch, page 202. ♦ Cook them not longer than 25 to 30 minutes, during the last part of the cooking period.
Allow for 12 bags:
    2 tablespoons dried parsley
    1 tablespoon each thyme
        and marjoram
    2 bay leaves
    2 tablespoons dried celery

FOUR SPICES OR SPICE PARISIENNE

Also called Quatre Épices. This is a mixture which is such a favorite for sweets and meats. Mix:

    1 teaspoon each clove,
      nutmeg and ginger
    1 tablespoon cinnamon

MIREPOIX AND MATIGNON

[About ⅔ Cup]

These vegetable blends, made just before using, are alike in ingredients and use—but differ in size. They can cover or be used as a base for cooking roasts of meat and fowl or shellfish and are essential to Sauce Espagnole (I, 365). If minced, the term is **Matignon**. For mirepoix, dice the ingredients. For Lenten dishes, omit the ham or salt pork. Dice:

    1 carrot
    1 onion
    1 celery heart: the inner
      ribs

Add:

    ½ crushed bay leaf
    1 sprig thyme
    (1 tablespoon minced raw
      ham or bacon)

These may be used raw as a base under meat or, if for a seasoning, on top of it. Simmer the above in:

    1 tablespoon butter

until the vegetables are soft. Deglaze the pan with:

    Madeira

MUSHROOMS AS SEASONING

This family, as seasoning, contributes some of the most coveted of all flavors. ▶ Never discard stems nor, particularly, the skins—for it is here that the greatest amount of seasoning lies. Even the scrapings of their rarefied cousins, truffles, are sold at a good price and can be cooked with gelatin to form

pungent garnishes for cold foods, see (I, 300). To bring more flavor into canned mushrooms, sauté them in butter. Consider also for seasoning—powdered mushrooms. And for a classic mushroom seasoning, see Duxelles, page 220.

Agaricus campestris, the variety most commonly in our markets, is strengthened in flavor as it withers but must be kept free of moisture in drying, so as not to mold.

▶ To dry mushrooms for storage, select fresh, firm specimens. You may wash them and dry them on paper towels or simply place them on a screen or thread them on a string to sun-dry them. When thoroughly dry, put them in sterile, tightly sealed glass jars. Keep from all moisture until ready to reconstitute for use. Wash briefly in 3 waters then soak them 1 to 3 hours in 70° water. The soaking-water may be used in stocks.

For mushroom types and a discussion of the dangers of collecting, see (I, 294). Mushroom spores are often sold in brick form for basement culture, but unless conditions are ideal and temperatures constantly between 50° and 60° experience has shown it is cheaper and safer to buy your mushrooms at market.

DRIED MUSHROOMS

Wash in 3 waters and then soak in boiling water 15 minutes:

    ½ lb. dried mushrooms

Drain, bring them quickly to a boil and cook over high heat for 10 minutes in:

    3 cups cold water
    3 teaspoons soya sauce
    1 teaspoon salt
    (2 teaspoons sugar)

Reduce heat and simmer 50 minutes. Keep these refrigerated to use in Chinese recipes.

GREMOLATA

A mixture of seasonings for sauces and pan gravies.
Mix:

2 tablespoons parsley
1 clove minced garlic
½ teaspoon lemon rind

Sprinkle this mixture on hot dishes. Continue to process the food over very low heat, covered, for 5 minutes, so it can absorb the flavor.

SALT PORK, BACON AND HAM AS SEASONING

These give an interesting fillip to many bland foods. Bacon and salt pork are often blanched (I, 88), to remove excess salt. Although they may be used interchangeably, the flavors are quite distinct.

SEASONED LARD

This yellow lard is called Soffrito in the Caribbean, but this same term in Italy is applied to Mirepoix, page 221. It gets its color from the annatto seed—a coloring often used here to accentuate the yellow in pale butter. It is made in advance of use and stored refrigerated. Wash, drain and melt ▶ uncovered over slow heat in a heavy pan, stirring occasionally:

1 lb. salt pork

Remove from heat and strain into another heavy pan.
Wash and drain:

¼ lb. annatto seeds

Add them to the strained melted lard and heat slowly for about 5 minutes. Strain the colored lard into a large heavy kettle. Grind and add:

1 lb. cured ham
1 lb. cored and seeded green peppers
¼ lb. seeded sweet chili peppers
1 lb. peeled onions
6 peeled cloves garlic

Mash in a mortar and add:

15 coriander leaves
1 tablespoon fresh orégano

Cook these ingredients over low heat, stirring frequently, for about 30 minutes more. After the mixture has cooled, store ▶ covered and refrigerated.

TOMATOES AS SEASONING

The tomato weaves its way into innumerable dishes—whether fresh, canned, cooked puréed; as paste or catsup, and even as soup. To get the flavor without too much moisture, fresh tomatoes should be cut at the stem end and squeezed to release extra moisture and seeds and then be peeled before using. Canned and cooked ones are best drained, then strained so thoroughly that the tasty pulpy part is forced through the sieve leaving only the skin to discard. In substituting purées, pastes and catsups, be sure to compensate for moisture differences and allow for the variations in strength of flavor.

ABOUT COMMERCIAL SAUCES

Ali Bab—in his great "Gastronomie Pratique"—refers to soy, Worcestershire, catsups, tabascos and other such commercial condiments as "sauces violentes" which mask out all other flavors. We find them useful as occasional accents, much too powerful to use unmodified; and we indicate suitable quantities as components in various sauces.

SOY SAUCE

This is made from fermenting soybeans, roasted wheat and salt. It contains glutamic acid, see monosodium glutamate, page 197. Never add it to a light-colored dish which needs more cooking, as the soy will darken the dish. Add after removing from heat or serve separately.

WORCESTERSHIRE SAUCE

This sauce is claimed as original by the English. Its roots are said to be Roman and, unlike their Garum, has a base of anchovy.

TABASCO SAUCE

This is made from hot tabasco peppers. ▸ Go easy—a few drops may be too much. Use in soups, cocktail sauce, piquant sauces.

ABOUT COLOR IN FOOD

Don't, we urge you, be a culinary lily-gilder! Resist the impulse to add color to food from little bottles or by the use of chemicals like soda. Instead, determine, in general, to maintain whatever color is inherent in the food itself and to heighten it by skillful cooking and effective contrast.

First steps begin with the selection of fresh, well-grown foods, properly washed, dried and trimmed, then prepared according to the "pointers" in our individual recipes. ▸ Choose utensils made of materials suitable to the foods cooked in them (I, 101). If you have done so and are still unhappy with the results, check the kind of water you are using, page 147. ▸ Never overcook foods: nothing so irrevocably dulls the kitchen palette.

Here are some further ways to keep foods colorful. While the color of soups and sauces is built into them by the way their stocks are made, see page 141, it will be least affected if they are scummed while heating and cooked uncovered. Meats, if light, maintain better color if scummed. If dark, their color will be improved by browning; by greasing during roasting or broiling; by glazing or flambéing. Fish and light meat grills profit in color by a prior dusting of paprika.

Cook variety meats—or vegetables and fruits that discolor on exposure to air—in slightly acidulated water, or à blanc, page 148. But first sprinkle the cut surfaces of such foods with a little lemon juice. Vent stews by the use of poaching paper (I, 183). And keep in mind that color in all foods is enhanced if they are not held hot and covered after cooking.

Breads and pastries develop beautiful crust color not only through the use of fat in their doughs, but by the discreet addition of saffron or safflower. And color may also be improved just before baking by butter-brushing, page 433, egg-glazing, page 433, or sugar-coating. Foods served in light sauces may be gratinéed (I, 389), or glazed (I, 386). And sauces may be glamorized with herb chiffonades; tomato or red pepper; lobster coral (I, 436); Lobster Butter (I, 385); egg yolks, saffron, meat glaze, mushrooms and browned flour.

If you are faced with really listless-looking vegetables, a green coloring additive may be very quickly made up in a blender—use spinach, parsley or watercress mixed with a small quantity of stock. And if you are tempted to disregard our earlier advice and go in for artificial color—watch out for greens and reds. Dilute yellows and just plain avoid blue.

As to color combinations and color contrasts, no one can lay down hard and fast rules, except to say that they need not be spectacular. Even so simple a combination as light and dark lettuces in a salad—or an accent of cress—will make for substantially greater interest. The occasional use of edible garnishes—suggestions for which are scattered throughout this book, see pages 74, (I, 39), (I, 144)—will be helpful. Do consider, too, the total background: dishes and colorful tableware, table surface, linens and decor are all part and parcel of satisfactory and colorful food presentation.

ABOUT WEATHER

Weather—moist, dry, hot or cold—plays an important part in cooking. When its role is decisive, it is so noted in individual recipes. Let's review just a few instances. Since flour and cereals tend to dry out in winter, our indications for rice and flour amounts, pages 152–153 and (I, 158), are more variable than we would like to have them. Damp weather will greatly affect sugars after food is cooked—as in meringues and during candy-making, page 499. Cold and heat have a tremendous effect on the creaming of butter and sugars and on success with Puff Paste, page 300, Anise Wafers, page 394, or the rising of bread, page 241. Threatening weather will even delay the "making" of butter, page 171, and Mayonnaise (I, 346). In storing foods, note if they are to be kept tightly lidded. It is evident that Mark Twain was wrong when he complained that nobody did anything about the weather. The circumspect cook takes account of its vagaries and acts accordingly.

ABOUT MEASURING

◗ All recipes in this book are based on standard U.S. containers: the 8 oz. cup and a tablespoon that takes exactly 16 level fillings to fill that cup level. We suggest that you test for size the tablespoon you select for this purpose—because those on sale do not invariably meet standard requirements.

All our recipes, in turn, are based on level measurements, hedgers like "heaping" or "scant" having been weeded out of our instructions years ago. Until you are experienced, we strongly urge you to make a fetish of the level standard measure.

To prove how very much careful measurement affects quantity, conduct this simple experiment. Dip the standard spoon into flour or baking powder and then level its contents. Don't shake. But, as recommended, use a knife, as shown second on the left below. Then scoop up a heaping spoonful of the same ingredients without leveling. You will find that lighter materials, if casually taken, often triple or quadruple the amounts indicated in the recipes. Ten to one the cook who prides herself on using nothing but her intuition as a guide to

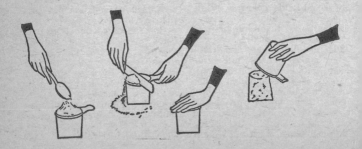

quantity is the same "old hand" who, for years, has used the same bowls, cups and spoons, the same stove, even the same brands of staples and who, in addition, gets more than her share of lucky breaks. Like as not, too, she doesn't mind variations in her product.

▶ Accuracy in measuring basic ingredients is especially necessary when making bread, pie and cake and in using recipes which include gelatin.

Most cake recipes call for sugar to be sifted before measuring. We confess that, instead, we sometimes short-cut by spooning our granulated sugar lightly into a measuring cup and then level it off, as sketched second on the left, page 224.

▶ For dry ingredients, use a cup which measures 1 cup even —with a flush rim for leveling. Put brown or powdered sugar, if lumpy, through a sieve, using a spoon. ▶ But, in measuring, brown sugar is always packed firmly into a measuring cup. See the sketch second from the right on page 224. And then unmold it as shown next, sandcastle-wise.

▶ No short-cuts should be adopted if the recipe requires the sifting of flour. If they are, the outcome is chancy, to say the least. In fact, frequent sift-

ing after measurement will improve the texture of all cakes. ▶ Sifting salt, leavens and spices with the flour insures even distribution.

It is particularly important that flour is not packed in measuring. ▶ In baking, sifting-before-measuring is essential. There is a very easy way to do this neatly and quickly. Keep two 12-inch squares of stiff paper, foil or plastic on hand. Sift the flour on to the first square, as shown bottom left. Rest your sifter on the second. Pick up the first sheet and curve it into a slide from which the flour can funnel itself into the measuring cup, which should be a dry measure shape, center. For very accurate measuring, cups designed for ¼, ⅓ and ½, as

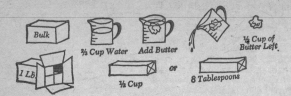

Bulk   ⅔ Cup Water   Add Butter   ¼ Cup of Butter Left

1 LB.   or   ½ Cup   8 Tablespoons

shown underneath are also desirable. When the measure is filled, take a knife and level the flour by running it across the top of the cup; see sugar, sketched, page 224. ◗ Never try to level the flour contents by shaking the cup, as this just repacks the sifted flour. Now you are ready to resift the flour with the other dry ingredients. Between siftings, move the sifter to the empty sheet and funnel the dry ingredients of the other sheet into the sifter top, the same way you did in measuring the flour in the center illustration.

Forgive us if we have said this repeatedly before, but always remember the important fact that ◗ flour can vary over 20% in its ability to absorb moisture, depending on the type of wheat from which it is milled, its processing and the amount of moisture absorbed during storage. For this reason, even the most accurate measurement may sometimes not produce unqualified success and adjustments must be made, on a purely experimental basis. See details on flour and flour substitutes, page 152.

◗ We suggest measuring bulk fats by this displacement method. If you want ⅓ cup fat, fill the measuring cup ⅔ full of water. Put in fat until the water reaches the 1 cup calibration mark. Drain the cup of water. The amount of fat remaining in the container will then, of course, equal ⅓ cup. One pound of but-

ter or butter substitute equals 2 cups and, when the pound is wrapped in quarters, each stick equals 8 tablespoons or ½ cup. See sketch above.

Some people prefer to use the sets of measuring cups especially for oils. These held respectively ¼, ⅓, ½ and 1 whole cup. ◗ But, if you use them, push the solid shortening down well into the bottom of these measures or a considerable space may be left, which will make your measurement inaccurate.

The measurement of what we might call side-ingredients, such as flavorings and spices, is important too, but here much depends on individual taste, to say nothing of the age of the spices, and amounts may vary considerably without risking failure.

ABOUT SUBSTITUTIONS AND EQUIVALENTS

You're a new cook and you run out of granulated sugar. Don't think that this doesn't happen to old cooks too! So you just substitute confectioners' sugar. And then when the cake is not as sweet as it should be and the texture is horrid you wonder what happened.

Good recipes and the reasonable use of standard measures allow you to cook well without knowing that it takes about 2 cups of sugar or butter to make a pound, but that you will need about 4 cups of flour for that same pound. This you discover fast enough if you leave the United States, for almost everyone else cooks by weight, not volume.

Let's look at a few lucky volume-weight relationships that for the moment protect you, as a new cook, from the menace of that old dragon Mathematics—and his allies, Physics, Chemistry and Semantics. Here are some of our victorious, if homely, weapons, tested in many a battle with these old tricksters.

By weight, if not quite by volume, 2 tablespoons butter equal 2 tablespoons butter, melted. But try to incorporate this positive knowledge in a cake and utter failure results. See About Butter and Shortening Cakes, page 343, and About Cakes with Melted Butter or Oil, page 360.

By weight, if not by volume, 1 cup 32% whipping cream equals 1 cup 32% cream, whipped. By volume, 1 cup 32% whipping cream equals about 2 cups 32% cream, whipped.

◆ If the recipe calls for whipped cream rather than for whipping cream, you need the solider, drier texture that results from whipping.

Let's take a closer look at sugars.

1 cup granulated = 8 oz.
1 cup confectioners' = 4½ oz.
1 cup brown = 6 oz.
1 cup molasses, honey or corn sirup = 12 oz.

These are only differences in weight. But you have to reckon with changes in sweetening power, in texture and—in the case of molasses and honey—with liquids that also have an acid factor. And don't forget about taste, that most important element of all.

If any of the foregoing ingredients are called for in a recipe, it is written to take care of inequalities. But if you are substituting in emergencies, say, sugar for molasses, please read About Molasses first. Some substitutions work fairly well, others only under special circumstances. ◆ But never expect to get the same results from a friend's recipe if she uses one kind of shortening and you use another. Your product may be better or worse than hers, but it won't be the same.

Before leaving you to delve in the tables which follow, like English standard measures versus those of the United States or the complexities of the metric system, we would like to introduce our ◆ multiply-and-conquer principle for fractions.

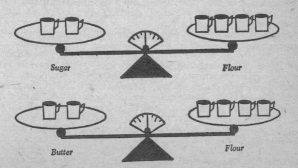

Sugar   Flour

Butter   Flour

You are preparing only ⅓ of a given recipe. The recipe calls for ⅓ cup of flour. Well, ⅓ cup of flour equals 5⅓ tablespoons. 1 tablespoon equals 3 teaspoons. So 5⅓ tablespoons equals 16 teaspoons, and, finally, 16 teaspoons divided by 3—to give you working for ⅓ of the recipe, remember?—give you 5⅓ teaspoons. Now maybe you can get this result by leaving out some of these steps, but we can't.

Here is another tried and true kitchen formula—one for proportions. You want to make your grandmother's fruit cake that has a yield of 11 pounds. You'd like only 3 pounds. The recipes calls for 10 cups of flour. How much flour should you use for 3 pounds of cake? Make yourself a formula in simple proportion: 11 lbs. of cake is to 3 lbs. of cake as 10 cups of flour is to ? or X cups of flour: i.e. 11:3 = 10:X. Multiply the end factors—11 x X—and the inside factors—3 x 10—to get 11X = 30. Divide 30 by 11 to find that X = 2⁸⁄₁₁ or approximately 2¾ cups. If you are in any doubt that ⁸⁄₁₁ is close to ¾, divide 8 by 11, finding the decimal closest to the standard measure. It is worth going through the same reducing process for the other basic ingredients such as egg, liquid and fruit—so the cake will hold together. Approximate the spices. But one more caution in changing recipes. ◗ Don't increase or enlarge recipes by dividing or multiplying by any number larger than 4—purists recommend 2. This sounds and is mysterious. But the fact remains that recipes are just not indefinitely expandable or shrinkable.

TABLES OF EQUIVALENTS AND CONVERSIONS

It is most unfortunate that in United States' measuring systems the same word may have two meanings. For instance, an ounce may mean ¹⁄₁₆ of a pound or ¹⁄₁₃ of a pint; but the former is strictly a weight measure and the latter a volume measure. Except in the case of water, milk or other ingredients of the same "density," a fluid ounce and an ounce of weight are two completely different quantities. A little thought will make clear that a "fluid ounce"—volume measure—of gold, for instance, will be much, much heavier—in terms of weight—than a "fluid ounce"—volume measure—of feathers! ◗ So always read recipes carefully to determine which kind of ounce you are dealing with.

UNITED STATES MEASUREMENTS

All these equivalents are based on United States "fluid" measure. In this book, this measure is used not only for liquids such as water and milk, but also for materials such as flour, sugar and shortening, since the volume measure for these is customary in the United States.

LIQUID MEASURE VOLUME EQUIVALENTS

A few grains	= Less than ⅛ teaspoon
60 drops	= 1 teaspoon
1 teaspoon	= ⅓ tablespoon
1 tablespoon	= 3 teaspoons
2 tablespoons	= 1 fluid ounce
4 tablespoons	= ¼ cup
5⅓ tablespoons	= ⅓ cup
8 tablespoons	= ½ cup
16 tablespoons	= 1 cup or 8 ounces
8 tablespoons	= 1 tea cup or 4 ounces

LIQUID MEASURE VOLUME
EQUIVALENTS Cont'd

¼ cup	= 4 tablespoons
⅜ cup	= ¼ cup plus 2 tablespoons
⅝ cup	= ½ cup plus 2 tablespoons
⅞ cup	= ¾ cup plus 2 tablespoons
1 cup	= ½ pint or 8 fluid ounces
2 cups	= 1 pint
1 gill, liquid	= ½ cup or 4 fluid ounces
1 pint, liquid	= 4 gills or 16 fluid ounces
1 quart, liquid	= 2 pints
1 gallon, liquid	= 4 quarts

DRY MEASURE VOLUME
EQUIVALENTS

Be careful not to confuse dry measure pints and quarts with liquid measure pints and quarts. The former are about ⅙ larger than the latter. Dry measure is used for raw fruits and vegetables, when dealing with fairly large quantities.

1 quart	= 2 pints
8 quarts	= 1 peck
4 pecks	= 1 bushel

WEIGHT OR AVOIRDUPOIS
EQUIVALENTS

1 ounce	= 16 drams
1 pound	= 16 ounces
1 kilo	= 2.20 pounds

COMPARATIVE U.S. AND BRITISH MEASUREMENTS

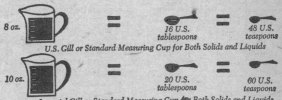

8 oz. = 16 U.S. tablespoons = 48 U.S. teaspoons

U.S. Gill or Standard Measuring Cup for Both Solids and Liquids

10 oz. = 20 U.S. tablespoons = 60 U.S. teaspoons

Imperial Gill or Standard Measuring Cup for Both Solids and Liquids

◗ Although many British or "Imperial" units of measurement have the same names as United States units, not all are identical. In general ◗ weights are equivalent, but volumes are not. The most important difference for the cook, and one we were slow to realize until we had had consistent failures using English recipes with American measures is shown graphically above, and in chart form below.

LIQUID MEASURE VOLUME EQUIVALENTS

1¼ U.S. teaspoons	= 1 English teaspoon
1¼ U.S. tablespoons	= 1 English tablespoon
1 U.S. gill	= ⅚ English teacup
2 U.S. gills	= ⅚ English breakfast-cup
1 U.S. cup	= ⅚ English breakfast-cup
1 U.S. gill	= ⅚ English—Imperial—gill
1 U.S. pint	= ⅚ English—Imperial—pint
1 U.S. quart	= ⅚ English—Imperial—quart
1 U.S. gallon	= ⅚ English—Imperial—gallon

DRY MEASURE VOLUME EQUIVALENTS

1 U.S. pint	=	1 English pint
1 U.S. quart	=	1 English quart
1 U.S. peck	=	1 English peck
1 U.S. bushel	=	1 English bushel

WEIGHT EQUIVALENTS

1 U.S. ounce	=	1 English ounce
1 U.S. pound	=	1 English pound

METRIC DRY MEASURE VOLUME EQUIVALENTS

1 U.S. pint	=	.551 liters
1 U.S. quart	=	1.101 liters
1 U.S. peck	=	8.81 liters
1 U.S. bushel	=	35.24 liters

LIQUID MEASURE VOLUME EQUIVALENTS

1 U.S. teaspoon	=	5 milliliters
1 U.S. tablespoon	=	15 milliliters
1 U.S. cup	=	¼ liter, approx.
1 U.S. gill	=	.118 liters
1 U.S. pint	=	.4732 liters
1 U.S. quart	=	.9463 liters
1 U.S. gallon	=	3.785 liters

WEIGHT EQUIVALENTS IN GRAMS

1 U.S. ounce	=	approximately 30 grams
1 U.S. pound	=	approximately 454 grams
1 teaspoon cornstarch	=	3 grams
½ cup, less 1 tablespoon butter— 7 tablespoons	=	approximately 100 grams
¾ cup, less 1 tablespoon of all-purpose flour—11 tablespoons	=	approximately 100 grams
½ cup, less 1 tablespoon sugar— 7 tablespoons or 21 teaspoons	=	approximately 100 grams
2 oz. egg	=	approximately 60 grams
1 microgram	=	0.001 milligram
1 milligram	=	1000 micrograms
1 gram	=	1000 milligrams

LINEAR MEASURES

1 centimeter	=	0.394 inches
1 inch	=	2.54 centimeters
1 meter	=	39.37 inches

APPROXIMATE TEMPERATURE CONVERSIONS

	FAHRENHEIT	CENTIGRADE
Coldest area of freezer	−10°	−23°
Freezer	0°	−17°
Water freezes	32°	0°
Water simmers	115°	46°
Water scalds	130°	54°
Water boils—at sea level	212°	100°
Soft Ball	234°–238°	112°–114°
Firm Ball	240°–242°	115°–116°
Hard Ball	248°–250°	120°–121°
Slow Oven	268°	131°
Moderate Oven	350°	177°
Deep Fat	375°–400°	190°–204°
Hot Oven	450°–500°	232°–260°
Broil	550°	288°

▶ To convert Fahrenheit into Centigrade, subtract 32, multiply by 5, divide by 9.
To convert Centigrade into Fahrenheit go into reverse. Multiply by 9, divide by 5, add 32.

$$100°C \times 9 = 900°$$
$$900° \div 5 = 180°$$
$$180° + 32 = 212°$$

CAN SIZES	WEIGHT	APPROXIMATE CUPS
8 oz.	8 oz.	1
Picnic	10½ to 12 oz.	1¼
12 oz. vacuum	12 oz.	1½
No. 300	14 to 16 oz.	1¾
No. 303	16 to 17 oz.	2
No. 2	1 lb. 4 oz. or 1 pint 2 fl. oz.	2½
No. 2½	1 lb. 13 oz.	3½
Baby Foods	3½ to 8 oz.	
Condensed Milk	15 oz.	1⅓
Evaporated Milk	6 and 14½ oz.	⅔–1⅔

AVERAGE FROZEN FOOD PACKAGES

Vegetables	9 to 16 oz.
Fruits	10 to 16 oz.
Canned Frozen Fruits	13½ to 16 oz.
Frozen Juice Concentrates	6 oz.

EQUIVALENTS AND SUBSTITUTIONS FOR COMMON FOODS

Almonds		
Unblanched, Whole	1 cup	6 oz.
Unblanched, Ground	2⅔ cups	1 lb.
Unblanched, Slivered	5⅔ cups	1 lb.
Blanched, Whole	1 cup	5⅓ oz.
Ammonium Carbonate	1 teaspoon ground	1 teaspoon Baking Powder
Apples—see approximate yield fruits, page 534	3½ to 4 lbs. raw	1 lb. dried
Apples	3 cups pared, sliced	1 lb. unpared
Apples	1 cup pared, sliced	4 oz.
Apricots, dried	3 cups	1 lb.
Apricots, cooked, drained	3 cups	1 lb.
Arrowroot—see Flour		
Baking Powder Rising Equivalent	1 teaspoon	⅓ teaspoon baking soda plus ½ tsp. cream of tartar

	1 teaspoon	¼ teaspoon baking soda plus ½ cup buttermilk or yogurt
Double Acting, SAS	1 teaspoon	1½ tsps. phosphate or tartrate
Bacon	1 lb. rendered ...	1 to 1½ cups grease
Bananas	3 to 4 medium-sized	1 lb. 2 cups mashed
Beans, Kidney, dry.	1½ cups = 1 lb. ...	9 cups cooked
Beans, Lima, dry...	2⅓ cups = 1 lb. ...	6 cups cooked
Beans, navy, dry ...	2⅓ cups = 1 lb. ...	6 cups cooked
Bread Crumbs, dry.	⅓ cup	1 slice
soft	¾ cup	1 slice
Butter		
1 stick	8 tablespoons	½ cup
4 sticks	2 cups	1 lb.
Butter	1 cup	1 cup margarine
Butter	1 cup	⅘ cup bacon fat, clarified
Butter	1 cup	¾ cup chicken fat, clarified
Butter	1 cup	⅞ cup cottonseed, corn, nut oil, solid or liquid
Butter	1 cup	⅞ cup lard
Butter	1 cup	⅘ to ⅞ cup drippings
Butter	8 oz.	7.3 oz. hydrogenated fats

You may note there is a weight difference between butter and hydrogenated fats, but in cooking use cup for cup.

Buttermilk	1 cup	1 cup yogurt
Cabbage	½ lb. minced	3 cups packed
Can Sirup, see About Liquid Sugars, page 167		
Castor or fine granulated	1 cup	1 cup granulated
Cheese, dry	4 cups	1 lb.
Cheese, freshly grated	5 cups	1 lb.
Cheese, cottage ...	1 cup	½ lb.
Cheese, cream	6 tablespoons	3 oz.
Cherries, candied ..	3 cups	1 lb.
Chestnuts	1 lb. shelled	1½ lbs. in shell
Chicken	2 cups cooked, diced	3½ lb. drawn chicken
Chocolate	1 square	3 tablespoons cocoa, plus 1 tablespoon fat
Chocolate	1 square	1 oz.
Chocolate	1 square	4 tablespoons, grated

Chocolate	1 oz., plus 4 tea-spoons sugar	1⅔ oz. semi-sweet chocolate
Cocoa	4 cups	1 lb.
Cocoa	3 tablespoons cocoa, 1 table-spoon fat	1 oz. chocolate
Coconut, fine grated	3½ oz.	1 cup
Coconut, flaked	3½ oz.	1⅓ cups
Coconut	1 tablespoon dried, chopped	1½ tablespoons fresh
Coconut	5 cups shredded	1 lb.
Coconut Milk	1 cup	1 cup milk
Coconut Cream	1 cup	1 cup cream, see page 193
Coffee	40 cups	1 lb.
Coffee, Instant	25 servings	2 oz. jar
Cornmeal	3 cups	1 lb.
Cornmeal	1 cup uncooked	4 cups cooked
Cornstarch, see Flour		
Cracker Crumbs	¾ cup	1 cup bread crumbs
Cream, Sour—see About Cream, page 134	1 cup	3 tablespoons butter, plus ⅞ cup sour milk
Cream, Sour, Cul-tured—see About Cream, page 134.	1 cup	⅓ cup butter, plus ¾ cup sour milk
Cream, Coffee, at least 20%	1 cup	3 tablespoons butter, plus ¾ cup milk
Cream, 40%	1 cup	⅓ cup butter, plus ¾ cup milk
Cream, Whipping, at least 32%	1 cup	2 to 2½ cups whipped
Dates	2½ cups pitted	1 lb.
Eggs, Hen, large, whole	5—2 oz.	About 1 cup
medium	6	About 1 cup
small	7	About 1 cup
Eggs, Whites, large.	8—2 oz.	About 1 cup
medium	10–11	About 1 cup
small	11–12	About 1 cup
Eggs, Yolks large	12—2 oz.	About 1 cup
medium	13–14	About 1 cup
small	15–16	About 1 cup
Eggs, dried	2½ tablespoons sifted and beaten with 2½ table-spoons water	1 whole egg
Eggs, Bantam	1	⅔ oz.
Eggs, Duck	1	3 oz.

Eggs, Goose	1	8 to 10 oz.
Figs	2⅔ cups chopped	1 lb.
Flour, All-Purpose	1 cup sifted	1 cup, plus 2 tablespoons cake flour
Cake	1 cup sifted	⅞ cup sifted all-purpose—1 cup less 2 tablespoons
Bread	4 cups	1 lb.
Cake	4¾ cups	1 lb.
White	4 cups or 1 lb.	3½ cups cracked wheat
White	1 cup	2 tablespoons farina
		½ cup barley flour
		1 cup corn meal
		½ to ⅝ cup potato flour
		⅞ cup rice flour
		1½ cups rye flour
		1½ cups ground rolled oats—bake more slowly
		13/16 cup gluten flour
Graham, Whole Grain or Whole Wheat	3¾ to 4 cups finely milled	1 lb.

➧ Be sure to read About Flours, page 152.

Flours For Thickening	1 tablespoon flour.	1½ teaspoons corn-starch, potato starch, rice starch, arrow-starch or 2 tea-spoons quick-cooking tapioca
	1 tablespoon flour.	1 tablespoon waxy rice flour
	1 tablespoon flour.	1 tablespoon waxy corn flour
	½ tablespoon flour.	1 tablespoon browned flour
Garlic	⅛ teaspoon powder	1 small clove
Gelatin	¼ oz. envelope	1 tablespoon
Gelatin for 1 qt. liquid	1 oz.	6 medium sheets—4½ x 6
Ginger	1 tablespoon candied, washed of sugar or 1 tablespoon raw	⅛ teaspoon powdered ginger
Gum Tragacanth	¼ oz.	1 tablespoon
Herbs	⅓ to ½ teaspoon dried	1 tablespoon fresh

Honey, see About Liquid Sugars, page 167		
Horseradish	1 tablespoon fresh	2 tablespoons bottled
Horseradish	6 tablespoons dried	6 oz. bottled
Lemon	1	2 to 3 tablespoons juice, 2 teaspoons rind
Lemon	1 teaspoon juice ..	½ teaspoon vinegar
Lime	1	1½ to 2 tablespoons juice
Macaroni	4 cups dry	1 lb.
Macaroni	1 cup uncooked ..	2 to 2¼ cups cooked
Maple Sirup, see About Liquid Sugars, page 167		
Maple Sugar, grated and packed	1 tablespoon	1 tablespoon white granulated
Maple Sugar	1 gallon	11 lbs.
Maple Sugar	½ cup	1 cup maple sirup

♦ For sweetening power, and use in recipes, see page 168.

Meat		
Beef, cooked	3 cups minced ...	1 lb.
Beef, uncooked ..	2 cups ground ...	1 lb.
Milk	1 cup	½ cup evaporated, plus ½ cup water
Milk	1 cup	4 tablespoons powdered milk, plus 1 cup water
Milk	1 cup	1 cup soy or almond milk
Milk	1 cup	1 cup fruit juice or 1 cup potato water in baking
Milk	1 cup	1 cup water, plus 1½ teaspoons butter
Milk .... To Sour	1 cup sweet	Add 1 tablespoon vinegar or lemon juice to 1 cup minus 1 tablespoon lukewarm milk. Let stand 5 minutes
Milk, whole	1 qt.	1 qt. skim milk, plus 3 tablespoons cream
Milk, whole dry solids	1 lb.	3½ cups

Milk, dry, nonfat solids	1 lb.	4 cups
Milk, whole	1 cup	3 to 4 tablespoons dry whole milk solids, plus 1 cup water
Milk, skim	1 cup	3 to 4 tablespoons dry nonfat milk solids
Molasses, see About Liquid Sugars, page 167		
Mushrooms	3 oz. dried	1 lb. fresh
Mushrooms	6 oz. canned	1 lb. fresh
Mushrooms	½ lb. sliced raw	2½ cups raw
Noodles	1 cup uncooked	1¾ cups cooked
Nuts	½ lb. kernels, a little less for heavier nuts and a little more for lighter ones	1 lb. in shell
Oatmeal	2⅔ cups	1 lb.
Oil	2 cups	1 lb. fat
Onions, see About Onions, page 209		
Orange	1 medium	6 to 8 tablespoons juice
Orange Rind	1 medium	2 to 3 tablespoons rind
Peanuts	1 lb. in the shell	2¼ quarts
	1 lb. shelled	2¼ cups
Peas, dry	2½ cups	1 lb.
Peas, cooked	5½ cups	1 lb.
Peas, split	2 cups—1 lb.	5 cups cooked
Pecans	3½ cups	1 lb.
	2½ lbs. in the shell	1 lb. shelled
Pomegranate	1 average	½ cup pulpy seeds
Potatoes	1 lb. raw unpeeled	2 cups mashed
Prunes, raw	2¼ cups pitted	1 lb.
Prunes, cooked, drained	2 cups	1 lb.
Raisins		
Seeded Whole	3¼ cups	1 lb.
Seedless Whole	2¾ cups	1 lb.
Rennet	1 tablet	1 tablespoon liquid rennet
Rice		
Long Grain	2½ cups uncooked	1 lb.
Cooked	2½ cups uncooked	8 cups
Rolled Oats	4¾ cups	1 lb.
Saccharin	¼ grain	1 teaspoon sugar
Salt	1 cup	12 ounces
Sorghum Molasses, see About Liquid Sugars page 167		

Sugar Sirups, see pages 25, 87, 167, 535 and 554

Sugar, in baking ...	1 cup	1 cup molasses, plus ¼ to ½ teaspoon soda. Omit baking powder
Sugar, in baking ...	1 cup	½ cup maple sirup and ¼ cup corn sirup. Lessen liquid by 2 tablespoons
Sugar, granulated ..	2 cups	1 lb.
Sugar, brown, packed	2¼ cups	1 lb.
Sugar, brown, packed	1 cup	1 cup granulated sugar
Sugar, powdered ...	1 cup	1 cup granulated sugar
Sugar, confectioners, packed	3½ cups	1 lb.
Sugar, confectioners, packed	1¾ cups	1 cup granulated sugar
Sweetener—non-caloric solution ..	⅛ teaspoon	1 teaspoon sugar
Tapioca	1½ to 2 tablespoons quick-cooking ..	4 tablespoons pearl, soaked
Tapioca	2 teaspoons	1 tablespoon flour
Tea	125 cups	1 lb.
Water	2 cups	1 lb.
Walnuts	3½ cups	1 lb.
Yeast, fresh	1 package	⅗ oz. or 2 tablespoons
Yeast, dry	1 package	Reconstitute in 2 tablespoons water 1¾ tablespoons dry yeast. Decrease liquid in recipe by 2 tablespoons
Yogurt	1 cup	1 cup buttermilk

ABOUT LEFT-OVERS

The minister's bride set her luncheon casserole down with a flourish, and waited for grace. "It seems to me," murmured her husband, "that I have blessed a good deal of this material before."

Left-overs can, of course, stand for simple repetition; but they can also stimulate a cook's ingenuity. For our part, we feel positively blessed when we have a tidy store of them garnered away in the refrigerator. So often they give a needed fillip to a dish we are making from scratch. Sometimes they combine to make a vegetable soufflé or to dress up an omelet. And how often they turn a can of soup into a real delicacy!

One secret we have learned is to limit the number of left-over ingredients we are working with so that they retain some semblance of identity. If there is too much of a mish-mash, the flavors simply cancel out—as well as the appetite.

Another secret is to watch left-overs for color. Freshen them up by presenting them with the more positive accents of tomatoes or bright greens; or with a color-contrasting sauce.

Still another secret is to be careful that you create some contrast in texture. When left-over mixtures are soft, contrast can be achieved by adding minced celery or peppers, nuts, water chestnuts, crisp bacon or freshly minced herbs.

Consult the Index under the category you wish to utilize or try one of the following suggestions:

See About Uses for Ready-Baked and Left-over Breads, Cakes and Crackers, page 288; also About Crumbs, page 159 and Bread Dressing (I, 560).

For uses of cooked cereals and pastas, see Cooked Cereal Muffins, page 282, or Garnishes for Soups (I, 148) and (I, 149). Also see Croquettes, page 122, and Griddle Cakes, page 117, or Calas, page 470.

See About Stocks, page 138, and About Soups (I, 106), for uses of bones, and for meat, fowl, fish and vegetable trimmings.

For cooked meat, fish and vegetable left-overs, see Brunch, Lunch and Supper Dishes (I, 208), mousses, soufflés, timbales, meat pies, About Cases for Food (I, 208), and Stuffed Vegetables (I, 256). See also About Economical Use of Large Cuts of Meat (I, 461) and (I, 463).

For cooked potatoes, see the Index; use in Shepherd's Pie (I, 225).

Use left-over gravies and savory sauces with vegetables, pastas, meats, and hot sandwiches.

For cheese, see Soufflés, Timbales, Sauces and Au Gratin (I, 389).

For uses for egg yolks, see Sponge Cakes, page 341, Yolk Cookies, page 404, yolk cakes, salad dressings, custards; and use poached yolks in sauces or riced as a garnish.

For uses for egg whites, see Angel and White Cakes, pages 339 and 344, meringues of all kinds, fruit whips hot and cold, page 455, dessert soufflés, page 443, Icings, page 419, insulation for pie crusts; and for breading, page 294, and Eggs in a Nest (I, 193).

For citrus peels, see Candies, page 524, and Zests, page 219.

For uses for sour or buttermilk, see About Sour and Fermented Milks, page 134.

For fruit juices, see fruit drinks or gelatins. Use as the liquid in cakes and custards, for meat basting, for sauces or fruit salad dressings.

For uses for left-over coffee, see coffee and mocha desserts and dessert sauces.

YEAST AND QUICK BREADS AND COFFEE CAKES

There was a time when the word from which "lady" sprang meant a "loaf-kneader." To our own and our families' distinct profit—and with little effort—we housewives can become "ladies" again. Begin, if you like, with a loaf of whole wheat, which requires neither sifting nor kneading, and go on from there to more cunning triumphs. Brioche, biscuit, corn pone, scones—the very names conjure up cultures that produced breads as characteristic as their makers. Will our culture be judged by the pallid commercial bread loaf in general use today? What a heritage for our children!

ABOUT YEAST BREAD MAKING

If you have never made real bread, behold one of the great dramas of the kitchen. Every ingredient is a character. As a producer-director assemble your cast. Yeast is the prima donna. Her volatile temperament is capable of exploitation only within given limits of heat—and does she resent a drafty dressing room! For more intimate details, see page 161. Wheat flour is the hero. He has a certain secret something that makes his personality elastic and gives convincing body to his performance. Rice, rye, corn —no other flour can touch him for texture; but he is willing to share the stage with others—if

they give him the limelight. For differences, in flours, see page 152. Water, milk or other liquid ingredients are the intriguers. Any one of them lends steam to the show, see page 161. As for salt and sugar, they make essential but brief entrances. Too much of either inhibits the range of the other actors. Fat you can enlist or leave. Use him to endow your performance with more tender and more lasting appeal. There are quite a few extras too, which you can ring in to give depth and variety, see page 243.

As director you also control the pace. Be quick and casual in batter bread. But the more emphatic your rhythm in kneaded dough, the finer your crumb. Success depends greatly on the relation of temperature to timing. Watch your prima donna, yeast. She has just so much energy to give. Don't keep her dangling in her big moments. If you are new at producing, give her her head in a simple part like Whole Grain Bread or No-Knead Light Rolls, that call for neither working nor shaping. Gain her confidence before you plunge her into the longer, more classic role of White Bread. Now, knowing our actors and their quality, "the play's the thing." Let's look into the types, the mixing and the baking of bread.

Batters are the simplest of all doughs. For baking powder batters, see page 271. Yeast, if

used, is dissolved first and added to the other liquids. Batter yeast breads call for stirring and beating. They are usually allowed to rise only once, so put them to rise in the pan in which you intend to bake them. Small unbroken bubbles will appear all over the surface when the dough has risen sufficiently.

Sponge breads were favorites in days when yeast strains were poorly controlled. Today they are often made with dry yeast. To mix sponge breads, dissolve the yeast in a larger than usual amount of water, to which a portion of the flour is added. When this batter has fermented —and it takes sometimes as long as one hour—it becomes foamy and spongy, as the name of the product implies. The sponge is then added to the rest of the ingredients. Sponge doughs make a lighter textured, coarser grained loaf or roll than straight dough, the complete mixing of which is described next. In all bread types, butter and eggs, if called for, additional salt and sugar and the remaining flour are then mixed into the dough with the yeast mixture.

ABOUT MIXING BREAD DOUGH

♦ To prepare the yeast for the straight dough method, dissolve it, if compressed, in liquid at 85°. If the yeast is in dry powdered form, it will need liquid between 110° and 115°. For-

merly milk was always scalded to kill bacteria. Now, with pasteurized milk, air-dried milk solids and canned milk, this operation is no longer needed. However, scalding does save time in dissolving the sugar and melting the fat.

Small quantities of sugar and salt help activate the yeast. But ♦ do not use more of either than called for. If the yeast is active, you should be conscious of its working within a few minutes, and it should dissolve in about 10 minutes without stirring. ♦ To mix a kneaded bread, start stirring the flour into the dissolved yeast mixture with a spoon. Mix in half the required flour, gradually, and beat about one minute. Then, as the rest of the flour is added, mix by hand. When the dough begins to leave the sides of the bowl, turn it out onto a lightly floured board or pastry cloth.

♦ To flour a board lightly, allow about 1 tablespoon flour for each cup of flour in the recipe. Use even less if you want a very light dough.

ABOUT KNEADING, PROOFING, SHAPING AND BAKING BREAD

Flours vary in moisture content, see page 152, and only experience can tell you exactly how much to add at this point. Hence, some variations in flour amounts are indicated in the recipes. ♦ Cover the dough with a cloth and let it rest 10 to 15 minutes. Now the kneading begins. When the dough is first turned out on the board it is slightly sticky, as can be seen on the left, page 240. Then, as the gluten develops in the wheat flour through continued kneading, the dough becomes smooth and elastic. The first kneading of about 10 minutes must be thorough, but ◆ the pressure exerted on the dough should be neither heavy nor rough.

◆ To knead, fold the dough over toward you. Then press it with the heel of the hand, as shown on page 240, give it a slight turn, fold it and press it again. Repeat this process rhythmically until the dough becomes smooth, elastic and satiny. Air blisters will appear just under the surface coating. The dough at this point should no longer stick to the board or cloth. Next, grease a large bowl evenly, put the dough in it and then turn it over ◆ so that the entire surface will be lightly greased. ◆ Cover the bowl with a damp cloth that has been well wrung out. Set the dough to rise. This process and the covering step after separating the bread into loaf sizes are shown graphically to emphasize the importance of these so-called "proofing" periods. During this resting time, a smooth film develops over the surface of the dough and makes it much easier to handle.

Yeast dough should rise at a temperature of about 75° to 80°. If the room is cold, you may place the dough in the bowl on a rack ◆ over a pan of warm water. The first time it rises it should double in bulk, if the loaf is to have a moist crumb. Should the dough rise to more than double its bulk, it will fall back in the bowl. Do not permit this to happen unless the recipe calls for it, as it may result in a coarse, dry bread. To make sure that dough has risen sufficiently press it well with the fingertips. When it has doubled in bulk, usually in about 2 hours ◆ the imprint of the fingertips will remain in the dough, as shown in the center below. ◆ Now punch down the dough with a balled hand, as illustrated on the right. Work the edges to the center and turn the bottom to the top.

▲ Yeast bread dough rises more rapidly at high altitudes and may become overproofed if it is not watched carefully and allowed to rise only until doubled in bulk.

Now you will be ready for the second kneading. ◆ Note that it is not called for if soft flour is used. Its purpose is to give a finer grain. It lasts only a few minutes and may be done in the bowl. Then permit the covered dough to rise again, if indicated, until it has a second time ◆ almost, but not quite, doubled in bulk.

Now you are ready to prepare for shaping the loaves. Pinch the dough into the number of pieces called for in the recipe. Shape

them lightly into mounds. Place the pieces on a board ▶ cover them with a cloth and allow them to rest for 10 minutes.

Meanwhile get your pans ready. Glass and enamel pans require a lower temperature than darkened tin or dull aluminum ones. Any of these will give you a well-browned crust. To form the loaf, throw down onto the board one of the pieces of dough which have been resting. You may use a rolling pin or your palm to press it evenly before forming. Professional bakers form it first into a circle and fold the curved segments toward the center to make their rectangle before shaping the loaf. You may be content to roll yours as shown, using the heel of your hand to fasten one loop to the next as you roll. Then with your stiffened hands at either end of the roll, compress the short ends and seal the loaf as shown below on the left, folding under any excess as you slide the dough into the pan. Practice first by baking some small loaves. But no matter

what the size ▶ it is important that the finished dough contact the short ends of the pan to help support the dough as it rises. When the loaf is in the pan, you may grease its top lightly.

Cover the pan with a damp cloth. The dough will eventually fill out to the corners of the pan. While it is rising—to almost, but not quite, double in bulk—preheat your oven. When ready to bake, the loaf will be symmetrical and ▶ will allow a slight impression to remain when you press it lightly with your fingers. To bake, see directions in the recipes.

ABOUT TESTING, COOLING AND STORING BREAD

▶ To test for doneness, notice if the loaf has shrunk from the sides of the pan. Another test is to tap the bottom of the pan to release the loaf. Then tap the bottom of the loaf and if a hollow sound emerges, the bread is done. Otherwise, return the loaf to the pan and bake a few min-

utes longer. When the bread has finished baking, remove it at once from the pan and place it on a wire rack to cool. ◗ Keep it away from drafts which cause shrinkage.

People have passions for different kinds of crust. ◗ The choice of pan will affect the crust. Glass, darkened tin and dull aluminum will all give a thick one. Vienna breads, hard rolls and rye breads sometimes are baked on a greased sheet sprinkled with corn meal, which prevents these low-fat breads from sticking. Milk, either used in the recipe or brushed on at the end of the baking period, gives a good all-over brown color. Cream or butter may also be brushed on for color, then the bread is returned to the oven for about 5 to 10 minutes. Setting a pan of warm water in the bottom of the oven during baking will harden crusts—also brushing them, when partially baked, with salted water. Allow 1 teaspoon salt to ½ cup water.

For a glazed crust, you may brush the top toward the end of baking with an egg glaze, page 434. To keep the crust soft, brush the crust with butter after the bread is out of the pan, then cover it with a damp cloth. ◗ Permit the bread to cool completely before wrapping, storing or freezing. Bread is best stored in covered tins in which there are a few pinhole-size openings for ventilation. It is sterile as it comes from the oven, but if not cooled sufficiently before wrapping, condensation may cause rapid molding. Most breads can be ✳ frozen, page 567, but dry out rapidly after thawing.

ADDITIONS TO YEAST DOUGHS

Raisins, dates, prunes, citron, nuts, slightly sautéed onions,

wheat germ, milk solids and brewers' yeast, page 163, often called improvers, are added to yeast doughs for flavor and increased nutritional values. With the exception of milk solids and yeast, they are not added to the dough until it is ready to set for the last rising. See Cornell Triple-Rich Flour Formula, below. Unless gluten flour is substituted for some of the regular flour, improvers are never used in greater quantity than up to about ¼ the weight of the flour called for in the recipe. Some of the flour called for can be used to dust the fruits, which tend to stick together. Dusting helps disperse them more evenly throughout the dough.

CORNELL TRIPLE-RICH FLOUR FORMULA

Especially among low-income and institutionalized groups, commercial bread is still the staff of life. How weak a staff in most instances can be seen on page 153. Work accomplished under Dr. Clive McCay at Cornell has done much to raise this standard for large segments of the population by the addition of supplements in their natural forms to unbleached, synthetically enriched bread flours.

Use this Cornell Triple-Rich Formula, which follows, in your favorite bread, cookie, muffin or cake recipe, as described. When you measure the flour in the directions, put in the bottom of each cup of flour called for:

1 tablespoon soya flour
1 tablespoon dry milk solids
1 teaspoon wheat germ

Then fill the cup with sifted unbleached enriched flour.

WHITE BREAD

[Two 5 x 9-Inch Loaves]

This is an even-grained, all-purpose bread which stales slowly and cuts well for sandwiches.

◗ Have all ingredients at about 75°. Scald:

    1 cup milk

Add:

    1 cup hot water
    1 to 1½ tablespoons
        shortening or lard
    1 to 1½ tablespoons butter
    2 tablespoons sugar
    2½ teaspoons salt

In a separate large bowl, crumble:

    1 cake compressed yeast

and soak about 10 minutes or until dissolved, in:

    ¼ cup 85° water

When the milk mixture has cooled to 85°, add it to the dissolved yeast. Sift before measuring:

    6½ cups all-purpose flour

◗ To mix, beat, knead, shape and proof, follow the arrow symbols and illustrations on pages 240, 241, 242, allowing the bread to rise once in the bowl and once in the pan.
Preheat oven to 450°.
To achieve the kind of crust you like, see page 243. Bake the bread in greased tins for 10 minutes. Reduce heat to 350° and bake for about 30 minutes longer. Test for doneness, page 242. Remove loaves at once from pans and cool on a rack before storing.

WHITE BREAD PLUS

[Three 5 x 9-Inch Loaves]
"Plus" for flavor, keeping quality and nutrition.
◗ Have ingredients at about 75°. Dissolve:

    1 cake compressed yeast
    1 tablespoon sugar

in:

    ½ cup 85° water

Permit to stand in a warm place for about 10 minutes. Beat in:

    1 beaten egg
    ½ cup melted lard or
        shortening
    2 cups lukewarm water
    1½ teaspoons salt
    ½ cup sugar

Sift:

    8 cups all-purpose flour

◗ To mix, beat, knead, shape and proof, follow the arrow symbols and the illustrations on pages 240, 241, 242, allowing the bread to rise once in the mixing bowl and once in the baking pan. To bake, place loaves in a cold oven. Turn the heat to 400°. After 15 minutes, reduce heat to 375° and bake 25 minutes longer. Test for doneness, page 242. Remove the loaves at once from the pans and cool on a rack before storing.

RAISIN, PRUNE OR NUT BREAD

Add to any unflavored bread doughs:

    1 cup drained, cooked,
        chopped prunes or 1 cup
        washed, well-drained,
        seeded raisins or 1 cup
        nuts

Sprinkle the above with:

    1 tablespoon flour

Add them to the dough just before the last rising.

CHEESE BREAD

[Two 5 x 9-Inch Loaves]
◗ Have all ingredients at about 75°. Scald:

    1½ cups milk

Add to it and cool to about 85°:

    ⅓ cup sugar
    ¼ cup butter
    1 tablespoon salt

In a large bowl, dissolve for 10 minutes:

    2 cakes compressed yeast

in:

    ½ cup 85° water

Stir in the cooled milk mixture. Add and beat until smooth:

    1 well-beaten egg

1½ cups grated sharp
    cheddar cheese
Beat in well:
    3 cups sifted all-purpose
        flour
Add, and then continue beating
and stirring until the dough begins to leave the sides of the
bowl, another, more or less:
    3 cups sifted all-purpose
        flour
◗ To knead the dough and shape
the loaves, follow the illustrations and arrow symbols on
pages 240, 241, 242. Brush the
loaves with:
        (Melted butter)
Allow to rise in the pans, covered, until doubled in bulk. Bake
in a preheated 375° oven about
30 minutes. To test for doneness, to cool and to store, see
page 242.

BRIOCHE LOAF
COCKAIGNE

This light egg loaf has a feathery, tender crumb. While very
similar to a true brioche, page
258, it is very much easier to
make. Serve it right out of the
oven, if possible. Use an angel
cake server, page 340, or 2 forks
held back to back, leaving a
pulled surface rather than a cut
surface. ◗ Have all ingredients
at about 75°. Dissolve and let
stand for 10 minutes:
    2 cakes compressed yeast
in:
    3 tablespoons warm milk:
        80° to 85°
Beat well:
    3 tablespoons sugar
    3 eggs
Add:
    ½ cup soft butter
    2 cups sifted all-purpose
        flour
    ½ teaspoon salt
Add the yeast mixture to the
batter. Beat well for 3 minutes.
Place in a greased bread pan or
a 9-inch tube pan. Permit to rise

in a warm place, until doubled
in bulk, about 2 to 2½ hours.
Bake in a preheated 450° oven
for about 15 to 20 minutes. Test
for doneness as for cake, page
242.

FRENCH BREAD

To an American who travels in
France, the commonest of tour-
ist sights at the noon hour is
what looks like "tout le monde"
coming from the baker, afoot
or a-cycle, with a couple or
three long loaves of French
bread, naked and gloriously un-
ashamed, strapped on behind.
French cookbooks ignore French
bread, and French housewives
leave the making of this characteristic loaf to the commercial
baker. Why? Because he alone
has the traditional wood-fired
stone hearth with its evenly reflected heat, and the skilled
hand with sour dough—both of
which are necessary to produce
it. We regard French bread as
uniquely delicious and consider
the closely approximate substitute recipe given below as rather
more than well worth following.
It was contributed some years
ago by Mr. Julian Street.

[2 Long Loaves]
Scald:
    ½ cup milk
Add to it:
    1 cup boiling water
While this liquid cools to 85°,
dissolve:
    1 cake compressed yeast
in:
    ¼ cup 85° water
After the yeast rests 10 minutes,
add it to the milk mixture with:
    1½ tablespoons melted
        shortening
    1 tablespoon sugar
Measure into a large mixing
bowl:
    4 cups sifted all-purpose
        flour

2 teaspoons salt
2 teaspoons sugar

Make a hole in the center of these ingredients. Pour in the liquid mixture. Stir thoroughly, but do not knead. The dough will be soft. Cover with a damp cloth and set in a warm place to rise, allowing about 2 hours for it. Break down the dough. Place on a lightly floured board and pat into 2 equal oblongs. Form each into a French loaf by rolling the dough toward you, as sketched below. Continue rolling, pressing outward with the hands and tapering the dough toward the ends until a

long, thin form is achieved. Place the 2 loaves on a greased baking sheet, cut diagonal, ¼-inch deep slits across the tops with sharp-pointed scissors to form customary indentations. Set in warm place to rise to ♭ somewhat less than double in bulk. Preheat oven to 400°.
On bottom of oven, place a pie tin filled with ½ inch boiling water. Bake the bread for 15 minutes, then reduce the heat to 350° and bake about 30 minutes longer. About 5 minutes before the bread is finished,

brush the loaves with a glazing mixture of:

1 beaten egg white
1 tablespoon cold water

We once received a letter from a gentleman in Junction City, Kansas, which began: "My wife is too old to cook and I am too old to do anything else." It seems that he was an enthusiastic baker of French bread, but he complained that his loaves turned out too flat. We suggested that he try shaping them in the following manner: Make a long oblong of the dough, fold over one edge to the center, repeat the operation for the second edge and taper the ends slightly. The bottom of the loaf may be pressed on a board which has been dusted with corn meal and the loaf then placed on a large greased sheet for baking. This correspondent

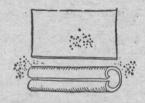

made several batches of bread and then wrote again: "Your plan works fine in shaping the loaves and I am also using ¼ cup less water. This makes the loaves come up a better shape, although it makes the dough harder to mix thoroughly. I think, however, the bread is just as good, and my French son-in-law says it is the best French bread he has eaten outside of France."

BREAD STICKS OR GRISSINI

Prepare:

French Bread, page 245

Roll into an oblong about ¼ inch thick, one dimension of which is about 8 inches. Cut into strips 2 inches wide and 8 inches long. Roll them to form sticks. Place on a greased baking sheet and brush with:

Egg Wash, page 433

Sprinkle with:

Coarse salt
(Caraway, sesame or dill seeds)

Allow to rise until not quite doubled in bulk. Bake in a preheated 400° oven for about 15 minutes. Try serving the sticks warm.

SALT-RISING BREAD

This unusually good formula, which has provoked the most dramatic correspondence, relies for its riser on the fermentation of a bacterium in corn meal or potato which is salt-tolerant.
◗ The corn meal must be water-ground. Since water-ground corn meal is not always available, we give also a potato-based recipe.
◗ Do not attempt this bread in damp, cold weather unless the house is heated, and protect the batter well from drafts.
◗ Have all ingredients at about 75°.

I. Corn Meal Salt-Rising Bread
[Three 5 x 9-Inch Loaves]
Measure:

½ cup coarse, white
◗ water-ground corn meal

Scald and pour over the corn meal:

1 cup milk

Permit it to stand in a warm place until it ferments, about 24 hours. By then it should be light and have a number of small cracks over the surface. If it isn't light in texture, it is useless to proceed, as the bread will not rise properly. Scald:

3 cups milk

Pour it over:

1 tablespoon salt
1 tablespoon sugar
5 tablespoons lard

Stir in:

3½ cups sifted all-purpose flour

Stir in the corn mixture. Place the bowl containing these ingredients in a pan of lukewarm water for about 2 hours, until bubbles work up from the bottom. Keep water warm this length of time. Stir in:

5 cups sifted all-purpose flour

Knead in until smooth, but not stiff:

2½ cups sifted all-purpose flour

Place dough in 3 greased 5 x 9-inch pans, cover and let rise until it has doubled in bulk.
◗ Watch it, for if it gets too high, it may sour. Preheat the oven to 400° and bake the bread for 10 minutes. Reduce the heat to 350° and bake 25 to 30 minutes more. To test for doneness, to cool and to store, see page 242.

II. Potato Salt-Rising Bread
[Three 5 x 9-Inch Loaves]
A fan, trapped by her grandchild's measles, sent us a treatise on lessening the fantastic odors of "salt-rising." She says, "Use non-mealy, 2½-inch-diameter, new red-skinned potatoes for the starter. Place them in a stainless steel bowl. Set bowl in water in an electric dutch oven with heat maintained at about 115° to 120°. Perfect results are produced in 15 hours with only a mild odor—like that of good Italian cheese." As we lived for some years in an apartment with a salt-rising bread addict and shared the endless variety of smells she produced, we would settle any day for a mild cheese aroma. If you do not own the electric equipment suggested, use the same principle as described above in a reliable contraption we devised for making yogurt, described on page 135. Pare, then cut into thin slices:

2½ cups new non-mealy
    potatoes
Sprinkle over them:
    1 tablespoon salt
    2 tablespoons water-ground
        corn meal
Add and stir until salt is dissolved:
    4 cups boiling water
Permit the potato mixture to stand, covered with a cloth for 15 hours. Now squeeze out the potatoes. Discard them. Drain the liquid into a bowl and add, stirring until very well blended:
    1 teaspoon soda
    1½ teaspoons salt
    5 cups sifted all-purpose
        flour
Beat and beat "until the arm rebels." Set the sponge in a warm place to rise until light. Bubbles should come to the surface and the sponge should increase its volume by about ⅓. This will take about 1½ hours. Scald:
    1 cup milk
    1 teaspoon sugar
When lukewarm, add:
    1½ tablespoons butter
Add this mixture to the potato sponge with:
    6 cups all-purpose flour
Knead dough for about 10 minutes before shaping into 3 loaves. Place in greased pans. Permit to rise, covered, until ◗ light and not quite double in bulk. Bake in a preheated 350° oven for about 1 hour.

WHOLE-GRAIN BREAD

[Two 5 x 9-Inch Loaves]
◗ Please read About Whole-Grain Flour, page 154.
Sift before measuring:
    2¼ cups all-purpose flour
Crumble:
    1 to 2 cakes compressed
        yeast
into:
    ¼ to ½ cup 85° water
Stir in:
    1 tablespoon sugar

Let stand about 10 minutes until foamy. Combine in mixing bowl:
    2 cups scalded milk
    2 tablespoons melted
        shortening
    2 tablespoons sugar
    1 tablespoon salt
When lukewarm, stir in the yeast mixture. Stir in and beat well:
    3¾ cups whole-grain flour
Stir in enough of the all-purpose flour to make a soft dough. Knead while working in more flour until dough is pliable but not sticky.
Allow the dough to rise once in the mixing bowl and once in the baking pans.
Preheat oven to 400°.
Bake at 400° for 10 minutes, then in a 375° oven for about 25 to 30 minutes longer.

WHOLE GRAIN
BREAD PLUS

[Three 5 x 9-Inch Loaves]
One of the best breads we know. Prepare the yeast as for White Bread Plus, page 244. Then use the following ingredients. You will note there is less fat and more liquid adjustment required with the use of the whole-grain flour.
◗ Have all ingredients at about 75°.
Beat together:
    1 beaten egg
    ¼ cup melted butter
    2½ cups lukewarm water
    1½ teaspoons salt
    ½ cup sugar
Add, without sifting, a mixture of:
    4 cups whole-grain flour
    4 cups all-purpose flour
◗ To mix, beat, knead, shape and proof, follow the arrow symbols and illustrations, pages 240, 241, 242, allowing the dough to rise once in the mixing bowl and once in the baking pan. Bake as for White Bread Plus, page 244.

WHOLE-GRAIN BREAD COCKAIGNE

[Two 4 x 8-Inch Loaves]
♦ Have ingredients at about 75°.
Dissolve and soak for about 10 minutes:

    ½ to 1 cake compressed
        yeast
    1 tablespoon brown sugar

in:

    ¼ cup 85° water

The larger quantity of yeast makes the rising more rapid and is not enough extra to taste in the finished product. Measure and combine:

    6 cups whole-grain flour
    ½ cup dry milk solids

Combine:

    2 cups 85° water
    1 tablespoon salt
    1 to 3 tablespoons melted
        bacon fat
    4 to 6 tablespoons dark
        molasses or honey

Combine the yeast and water mixtures gradually. Beat in the flour. Knead briefly, adding flour if necessary. Allow the dough to rise once in the mixing bowl and once in the baking pans. Bake in a 350° oven for 45 minutes. To test for doneness, to cool and to store, see page 242.

CRACKED-WHEAT BREAD

[Two 5 x 9-Inch Loaves]
This quick recipe contributed by a fan makes a coarse, heavy bread which is delicious with cheese.
♦ Have all ingredients at about 75°.
Dissolve:

    2 cakes compressed yeast

in:

    ¾ cup 85° water

Permit to stand about 10 minutes. Mix with:

    3 tablespoons melted
        shortening
    3 tablespoons sugar
    6 cups sifted all-purpose
        flour

    3 cups cooked, lukewarm
        cracked wheat
    1 tablespoon salt

Knead and allow to rise once in bowl and once in greased pans. Bake in a preheated 400° oven for about 1 hour. To test for doneness, to cool and to store, see page 242.

SWEDISH RYE BREAD

[2 Loaves]
A moist aromatic loaf that keeps well.
♦ Have all ingredients at about 75°.
In a large bowl, crumble:

    2 cakes compressed yeast

into:

    1½ cups 85° water

Let rest 10 minutes and stir until dissolved. Add:

    ¼ cup molasses
    ⅓ cup sugar
    1 tablespoon salt
    2 tablespoons grated
        orange rind
    1 tablespoon fennel seed
    1 tablespoon anise seed

Stir in:

    2½ cups sifted, finely milled
        rye flour
    2 tablespoons softened
        butter

Beat all these ingredients together until smooth. Add:

    2½ to 3 cups sifted all-purpose
        flour

If the dough is soft to handle, use the larger amount of flour.
♦ To knead, follow the arrows and illustrations, pages 240, 241, 242. Allow the dough to rise once in the bowl and once on the baking sheet. To shape, form into two slightly flattened ovals on a greased baking sheet dusted with corn meal. Cover with a damp cloth and let rise until almost double in bulk, about 1 hour. Make four ¼-inch-deep diagonal slashes in the top of the loaves. Bake in a preheated 375° oven for 30 to

35 minutes. To test for doneness, to cool and to store, see page 242.

ALL-RYE FLOUR BREAD

[2 Rather Flat Loaves]
Rye flour lacks the gluten of wheat, so a loaf made of all rye has a dense, heavy texture, similar to that of pumpernickel.
◗ Have all ingredients at about 75°.
Dissolve and soak for about 10 minutes:

    1 cake compressed yeast

in:

    ½ cup 85° water

Scald:

    2 cups milk

As it cools, add:

    2 tablespoons butter
    1 tablespoon sugar
    2 teaspoons salt

When it reaches about 85°, add the yeast mixture and stir in:

    2 cups rye flour

Let this sponge rise for about 1 hour. Then add slowly, while stirring:

    3 cups rye flour

Let rise for about 2 hours. Sprinkle a board with:

    1 cup rye flour

Knead the dough into it for 10 minutes. Divide into 2 parts. Put on a well-greased baking sheet, grease the tops of the loaves, cover and allow to rise for about 2 hours more. Bake in a preheated 350° oven for about 1 hour. To test for doneness, to cool and to store, see page 242.

SOUR DOUGH RYE BREAD

[2 Round or 2 Long Loaves]
The best-flavored rye breads call for sour doughs, page 163. In this recipe, the sour dough is used more for its flavor than for its rising power. Today, when controlled strains of yeast are easily available, we suggest, in households where baking is not done daily, that the sour dough

be remade for each baking. We love this recipe which comes from Merna Lazier who has, among many other successful projects, run a bakery of her own. She says: "You may object to the number of stages in this process, but I must say that old-time bakers who were proud of their rye bread really nursed it along—so there must be a reason." For this recipe, on one day you make a sour dough, using ½ cake of yeast. The following day, you make two sponges, using the other ½ cake of yeast. The first day, prepare the sour dough. Mix in a bowl and work together lightly:

    ½ cup rye flour
    ¼ cup water
    ½ cake compressed yeast

Cover this sour dough tightly so it will not dry out and keep it in a warm place at about 80° for 24 hours. Then work into it:

    ¾ cup water
    1 cup rye flour

The sour dough should be ready to use after it has fermented, covered, 4 hours longer.
I. To prepare Sponge I, mix with the sour dough until a smooth but firm dough is obtained:

    1¾ cups rye flour
    ⅔ of ½ cake compressed yeast

Allow this sponge to ferment, covered with a damp cloth at an 80° temperature until it drops. This means it will expand to its fullest and fall back on itself.

II. To prepare Sponge II, add to Sponge I:

    1¾ cups rye flour
    1¾ cups all-purpose flour
        Remaining ⅓ of ½ cake compressed yeast
    1 cup water

The sponge should be of a consistency similar to that of Sponge I. Allow to ferment until it drops. Then add:

1 cup water
1 tablespoon salt
1¾ cups all-purpose flour
1 tablespoon caraway seed

Let the mixture rest, covered, for about 15 to 20 minutes. Turn the dough out onto a floured board and knead with:

1¾ to 2 cups all-purpose flour

until you have a stiff dough—one that will not flatten or spread. Divide it, shape it into 2 long or 2 round loaves. ♦ Place them on a greased pan and allow to rise, but not double in bulk. Too much rising will result in a flat loaf.

Preheat oven to 425°.

Place a flat pan, filled about ¼ full of water, in the oven. Bake the loaves for about 1 hour. You may have to replenish the water, but remove the pan after 20 minutes. As soon as the bread is done, spread it with:

Melted butter

or, if you wish a glazed crust, spread it with:

Salted water—1 teaspoon salt to ½ cup water

Cool loaves on a rack, away from drafts.

CORN-MEAL OR ANADAMA BREAD

[One 5 x 9-Inch Loaf]

♦ Have all ingredients at about 75°.

Scald:

1¼ cups milk

Combine 1 cup of this hot milk in a large bowl with:

½ cup yellow corn meal
2 tablespoons sugar or ¼ cup molasses
2½ teaspoons salt
2 tablespoons shortening

When the remaining ¼ cup of milk cools to about 85°, dissolve in it for 10 minutes:

1 cake compressed yeast

Meanwhile sift, then measure:

3½ to 4 cups all-purpose flour

Combine yeast and milk mixtures. Stir in enough of the sifted flour to make a dough that will knead well. Knead for 10 minutes. Place dough in a greased bowl, covered, in a warm place, about 80°, until it has ♦ almost doubled in bulk, about 1 hour. Punch down and shape in greased pan. Allow to rise until almost doubled in bulk. Bake in a preheated 375° oven for about 40 minutes. To test for doneness, to cool and to store, see page 242.

STEEL-CUT OAT BREAD

[One 5 x 9-Inch Loaf]

♦ Have all ingredients at about 75°.

Measure into a mixing bowl:

1 cup steel-cut oats
¼ cup dark molasses
1 tablespoon softened shortening
¾ teaspoon salt

Pour over these:

2 cups ♦ boiling water

Stir in:

2 cups sifted all-purpose flour

While this is cooling, crumble and dissolve:

1 cake yeast

in:

¼ cup 85° water

After soaking for 10 minutes add the yeast mixture to the oats mixture. Work in:

2 cups sifted all-purpose flour

You may incorporate:

(1 cup broken pecan meats)

♦ To knead, shape and proof, follow the arrow symbols and the illustrations on pages 240, 241, 242, allowing the dough to rise once in the greased mixing bowl and once in the greased baking pan. Bake in a preheated 375° oven for about 40 minutes. To test for doneness, to cool and to store, see page 242.

GLUTEN BREAD

[Two 5 x 9-Inch Loaves]
◗ Have all ingredients at about 75°.
Combine:

    3 cups 85° water
    1 crumbled cake
       compressed yeast

After 10 minutes, when the yeast is dissolved, beat in:

    2 cups gluten flour

Permit this sponge to rise in a warm place until light and foamy. Combine, beat and then stir into the sponge:

    1 beaten egg
    2 tablespoons melted
       shortening
    ½ teaspoon salt
    (2 tablespoons sugar)

Stir in:

    About 4 cups gluten flour

Use only enough flour to make a dough that will knead well. Knead and then shape into 2 loaves. Allow to rise until double in bulk. Bake in a preheated 350° oven for about 1 hour. To test for doneness, to cool and to store, see page 242.

HEALTH BREAD

[Two 5 x 9-Inch Loaves]
For nutritious additions to use in your other baking, see Cornell Triple-Rich Flour Formula, page 243.
◗ Have all ingredients at about 75°.
Crumble and dissolve for about 10 minutes:

    2 cakes compressed yeast

in:

    ¼ cup 85° water

Scald:

    2 cups milk

And pour it over:

    1 cup rolled oats

Add:

    2 teaspoons salt
    ¼ cup cooking oil

    ½ cup brown sugar

Cool this mixture to 85° and add the dissolved yeast, plus:

    1 or 2 slightly beaten eggs
    ¼ to ½ cup wheat germ
    1 cup soy flour
    2 cups whole-wheat or
       rye flour
    3 to 4 cups sifted,
       unbleached, all-purpose
       flour

◗ To knead, shape and proof, follow the arrow symbols and illustrations on pages 240, 241, 242, allowing the dough to rise once in the mixing bowl and once in the baking pan. Bake in a preheated 350° oven for about 1 hour. To test for doneness, to cool and to store, see page 242.

BREAD PRETZELS

[4 Dozen 6-Inch Sticks or Twelve 6-Inch Pretzels]
Let stand for 1 hour:

    1¼ cups 85° water
    1 cake compressed yeast
    ½ teaspoon sugar

Mix with:

    4½ cups flour

Knead for about 7 or 8 minutes. Let the dough rise ◗ covered, in a greased bowl until double in bulk. Form into sticks or pretzels. Place on a greased sheet. Apply a thin:

    Egg Wash, page 433

Sprinkle lavishly with:

    Coarse salt

Allow the pretzels to rise until not quite double in bulk. Bake in a preheated oven at 475° for about 10 minutes. To cool and store, see page 242.

ABOUT YEAST ROLLS

There is little difference in bread and roll making, so if you are a novice ◗ please read About Yeast Bread Making, page 239. The visual appeal of delicately formed, crusty or glazed rolls is a stimulant to the appetite. For varied shaping suggestions, see the illustrations in this chapter.

Professional cooks weigh the dough to keep the rolls uniform in size for good appearance and even baking. If you do not use muffin pans, place the dough at regular intervals over the entire baking sheet.

You may use additions to bread dough and coffee cake, page 243, to vary the flavor. Sprinkle the tops with poppy, celery, fennel, caraway, or lightly toasted sesame seeds, depending on the rest of your menu.

To bake, follow the individual recipes. ♦ Remove the rolls at once from the pan to a cooling rack. ♦ To reheat, sprinkle them lightly with water and heat, covered, in a 400° oven or in the top of a double boiler. Sometimes, the suggestion is made that the rolls be put in a dampened paper bag and heated until the bag dries. We find, however, that some types of bags can transmit a disagreeable flavor.

NO-KNEAD LIGHT ROLLS

[Eighteen 2-Inch Rolls]
These are the rolls we remember as light as a feather and served in a special, soft linen napkin. Although they require no kneading, they are best chilled from 2 to 12 hours. They are not true refrigerator rolls since this recipe is not heavy enough in sugar to retard the rising action, and all the dough should be baked after the 2- to 12-hour period.
♦ Have all ingredients at about 75°.
Dissolve for 10 minutes:
  1 cake compressed yeast
in:
  ¼ cup 85° water
Place in a separate bowl:
  ¼ cup butter or shortening
  1¼ teaspoons salt
  2 tablespoons sugar

Pour over these ingredients and stir until they are dissolved:
  1 cup boiling water
When they reach 85°, add the yeast. Beat in:
  1 egg
Stir in and beat until blended:
  About 2¾ cups sifted
    all-purpose flour, to make
    a soft dough
Place the dough in a large greased bowl, then turn it over, so it is lightly greased on top. Cover with foil and chill from 2 to 12 hours—or, you may place it in a greased bowl, covered with a damp cloth, until it doubles in bulk. Punch it down. Shape the rolls to fill about ⅓ of greased muffin tins. Permit them to rise until about double in bulk. Bake in a preheated 425° oven for about 15 to 18 minutes. Cool at once.

CLOVER LEAF ROLLS

[Twenty-Four 2-Inch Rolls]
♦ Have all ingredients at about 75°.
Cream:
  1 tablespoon lard
  1 tablespoon butter
  1½ tablespoons sugar
Add and beat well:
  1 cup scalded milk
Dissolve for about 10 minutes:
  1 cake compressed yeast
in:
  ¼ cup 85° water
Add these ingredients to the milk mixture. Sift before measuring and add:
  1½ cups all-purpose flour
Beat well. Cover with a cloth and permit to rise until double in bulk. Sift before measuring:
  1½ cups all-purpose flour
Add it to the batter with:
  1¼ teaspoons salt
Beat well. Place the dough in a greased bowl and turn it, so that it is lightly greased all over. Cover with a cloth and permit to rise until about double in

bulk. Now, fill greased muffin tins about ⅓ full with 3 small balls, as sketched below. Brush the tops with:

Melted butter

Permit the rolls to rise, covered, in a warm place until about double in bulk. Bake in a preheated 425° oven for about 15 to 18 minutes. Remove at once from pans.

PARKER HOUSE ROLLS

[About Thirty 2-Inch Rolls]
♦ Have all ingredients at about 75°.
Scald:
   1 cup milk
Add and stir until dissolved:
   1 tablespoon sugar
   2 tablespoons butter
   ¾ teaspoon salt
When these ingredients are at 85°, add:
   ½ cake compressed yeast
dissolved for 10 minutes in:
   2 tablespoons 85° water
Beat in:
   (1 egg)
Sift before measuring and add:
   2⅔ cups all-purpose flour
Stir in part of the flour, knead in the rest. Use only enough flour to form a dough that can be handled easily. Place in a greased bowl. Brush the top with:

Melted butter

Cover and let rise in a warm place until doubled in bulk. Roll the dough and cut into rounds with a floured biscuit cutter. Dip the handle of a knife in flour and use it to make a deep crease

across the middle of each roll. Fold the rolls over and press the edges together lightly. Place rolls in rows on a greased pan. Permit to rise in a warm place until light, only about 35 minutes. Bake in a preheated 425° oven for about 20 minutes. Remove at once from pans.

PALM LEAF ROLLS

[About 4 Dozen Leaves]
Sweet enough for a dessert. Serve with coffee and fruit.
♦ Have all ingredients at about 75°.
Crumble and dissolve for 10 minutes:
   1 cake compressed yeast
in:
   ¼ cup 85° water
Sift:
   3 cups all-purpose flour
   1½ teaspoons salt
Cut in, until reduced to the size of peas:
   ½ cup butter
Blend and add:
   2 beaten eggs
   1 cup cultured sour cream
   1 teaspoon vanilla
and the dissolved yeast. Cover and chill for about 2 hours or more. When ready to bake, sprinkle a board with:
   ½ cup vanilla sugar, see page 170
or a mixture of:
   ½ cup sugar
   1 teaspoon cinnamon
Roll ½ the dough into a 6 x 18 x ¼-inch strip. Fold as sketched on page 255, top left, bringing the short ends to within about ¾ inch of each other. Repeat this folding as shown in the right foreground and again as shown in the rear. Slice into ¼-inch-thick "palms." Repeat this process with the other half of the dough, first sprinkling the board with the sugar mixture. Fold and cut as directed above. Put palms on an ungreased baking

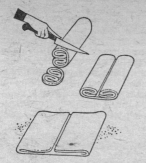

thick. Brush the dough with melted butter. Cut into strips 1½ inches wide. Stack them. There should be from 6 to 8 layers of strips stacked. Cut off pieces about 1½ inches wide, with a string, as shown below. Place them in buttered muffin tins, with the cut edges up. Permit to rise in a warm place until doubled in size. Bake in a preheated 425° oven from 15 to 20 minutes until well browned.

sheet. Allow to rise about 20 minutes. Bake in a preheated 375° oven until golden brown, about 15 minutes.

BUTTERMILK ROLLS OR FAN TANS

[About 24 Rolls]

Rolls prepared in this way need not be buttered. Fine for a serve-yourself party.

▶ Have all ingredients at about 75°.

Sift before measuring:

>   4 cups all-purpose flour

Heat:

>   2 cups buttermilk

Cool to about 85°. Dissolve for 10 minutes:

>   1 cake compressed yeast

in ⅛ cup of the lukewarm buttermilk. Add to the remaining buttermilk, with:

>   ¼ teaspoon soda
>   2 teaspoons salt
>   ¼ cup sugar

Beat well, then stir in gradually half the flour. Add:

>   2 tablespoons melted butter

and the rest of the flour. Place dough in a greased bowl and turn it, so it is lightly greased all over. Cover with a moist cloth and permit to rise until more than double in bulk. Knead lightly for 1 minute. Separate into 2 parts. Roll each part into a square, about ⅛ inch

SOUR CREAM ROLLS OR KOLATCHEN

[About Thirty-Six 2-Inch Rolls]

▶ Have all ingredients at about 75°.

Beat until creamy:

>   6 tablespoons butter
>   Grated rind of 1 lemon
>   2 tablespoons sugar

Beat in well:

>   4 beaten eggs
>   1 cup cultured sour cream

Dissolve for 10 minutes:

>   1 cake compressed yeast

in:

>   2 tablespoons 85° water

Beat this into the egg mixture.

Measure:

>   3 cups sifted all-purpose flour

Resift with:

>   ½ teaspoon salt
>   1 teaspoon soda

Beat these ingredients into the egg mixture. Fill greased muffin tins ½ full. Cover the dough and let it rise in a warm place 85° until doubled in bulk. Brush the tops with:

>   1 slightly beaten egg white

Decorate them with:

Chopped nut meats

Bake the rolls in a preheated 375° oven for about 15 to 20 minutes.

Dust before serving with:

Confectioners' sugar

OVERNIGHT ROLLS

[About 48 Rolls]

◗ Have all ingredients at about 75°.

Combine:

1 crumbled cake
    compressed yeast
2 teaspoons sugar

Permit these ingredients to stand until dissolved, about 10 minutes. Scald:

1 cup milk

Add and stir until melted:

7 tablespoons lard

Cool. Combine and beat well:

7 tablespoons sugar
3 beaten eggs
1 teaspoon salt

Stir in the milk mixture and cool to 85°.

Stir in the yeast mixture and:

4½ cups sifted all-purpose
    flour

Beat the dough about 5 minutes. Place in a foil-covered bowl in the refrigerator overnight. Take out just before baking. Divide dough into 3 parts. Roll each part into a circle about 9 inches in diameter.

Cut each circle into 16 wedge-shaped pieces. Before they are rolled further, brush with:

Melted butter

and dust with:

Sugar and cinnamon

or fill with:

Coffee Cake Filling,
    page 268

Roll each piece by beginning at the wide end. Stretch the end a bit as you start to roll it. Brush with:

Egg Wash, page 433

Permit rolls to rise until double in bulk. Bake for 15 to 18 minutes on a greased sheet in a preheated 425° oven. Take care. They burn easily.

FILLED PINWHEEL ROLLS

Follow the recipe for:

Overnight Rolls, above

Prepare the dough and let rise until doubled in bulk. Roll to ¼-inch thickness. Cut into 4-inch squares. Spread the squares generously with:

Butter
Sugar and cinnamon

Place in the center of each square:

6 or more raisins or 2
    teaspoons apricot jam

Cut diagonally into the dough from each corner to within ½ inch of the center. Fold the points toward the center. Place pinwheels on a greased pan. Let

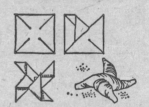

them rise slightly. Bake in a preheated 425° oven for about 18 minutes.

CHEESE ROLLS

Prepare:

Cheese Bread, page 244

Shape and bake as for:

Overnight Rolls, page
    256

✳ VERSATILE ROLLS

[About 5 Dozen Rolls]

You may make these excellent rolls in advance and reheat them before serving. Wrap and keep them in a refrigerator 2 weeks or in a freezer 3 months. As they call for neither eggs nor shortening, they appeal to the allergic and the dieter.

◗ Have all ingredients at about 75°.

Scald:

    2 cups milk

Add:

    5 teaspoons salt
    ¼ cup sugar

Cool this mixture to 85°. Dissolve for 10 minutes:

    2 cakes compressed yeast

in:

    1 cup 85° water

Combine above ingredients and mix until smooth. Add gradually:

    8 to 10 cups all-purpose
        flour

Knead the dough well and let it rise, covered, until almost double in bulk. Shape the dough as you prefer. Permit rolls to rise in covered pans until almost double in bulk. Bake for about 40 minutes in a preheated 275° oven. If storing, leave them in the pans to cool for 20 minutes. When they reach room temperature, wrap them well. To serve, reheat until brown on a greased baking sheet about 10 minutes in a 400° oven.

BUTTERMILK POTATO ROLLS

[About 46 Clover Leaf Rolls]

◗ Have all ingredients at about 75°.

Prepare:

    ¾ cup freshly cooked, riced
        potatoes

While still hot, mix with:

    ½ cup butter

Heat:

    2 cups buttermilk

Cool to about 85°. Crumble into about ½ cup of the buttermilk:

    1 cake compressed yeast
    2 tablespoons sugar
    1 teaspoon salt

and rest it for 10 minutes. Add the remaining buttermilk and mix with the potatoes. Beat until light and add:

    2 eggs

Sift before measuring:

    7½ cups all-purpose flour

Stir in 6 cups of the flour. Knead in the rest. Place the dough in a greased bowl and turn it, so that it is greased lightly on all sides. Cover with a damp cloth and let rise until double in bulk. Punch down. Shape as for Clover Leaf Rolls, page 253. Glaze tops with:

    (Egg Wash, page 433)

Sprinkle with:

    (Poppy seeds)

Bake in a preheated 425° oven for 15 to 18 minutes. Remove at once from pans.

CINNAMON BUNS OR SNAILS

Prepare:

    Stollen, page 265, or
    Scandinavian
    Pastry, page 267, or
    Overnight
    Rolls, page 256

When the dough has doubled in bulk, roll it on a floured board to the thickness of ¼ inch. Spread generously with:

    Melted butter

Sprinkle with:

    Cinnamon
    Brown sugar

Add, if desired:
>   Chopped nut meats
>   Seedless raisins
>   Chopped citron
>   Grated lemon rind

Roll the dough like a jelly roll, page 373. Cut into 1-inch slices. Rub muffin tins generously with:
>   Butter

Sprinkle well with:
>   Brown sugar
>   (Chopped nut meats)

Place each slice of roll firmly on bottom of a muffin tin. Permit to rise in a warm place for ½ hour. Bake in a preheated 350° oven for about ½ hour.

CARAMEL BUNS OR SCHNECKEN

Prepare one of the doughs in:
>   Cinnamon Snails, above

▶ Be sure to use in the filling:
>   Grated lemon rind
>   Raisins
>   Pecans

Roll as for Jelly Roll, page 373. Cut into 1½-inch slices, as shown on page 257. Fill bottom of each muffin tin with a mixture of:
>   1 teaspoon melted butter
>   1 teaspoon warmed honey

Cover with:
>   2 teaspoons brown sugar
>   A few chopped or whole pecans

Lay the slices of dough over sugar mixture. Bake in a preheated 350° oven for about 20 minutes. Watch closely for signs of scorching.

WHOLE-GRAIN ROLLS

[About 40 Rolls]
Prepare:
>   Whole-Grain Bread Plus, page 248

Shape dough into rolls after the second rising. Butter the tops. Sprinkle with:
>   (Coarse salt, chopped nuts or sesame seeds)

Bake in a preheated 400° oven for 15 to 20 minutes.

RYE ROLLS

[About 36 Rolls]
Prepare:
>   Swedish Rye Bread, page 249

Shape rolls after the first rising. Sprinkle tops with:
>   Coarse salt

For the crust of your choice, see About Cooling Bread, page 242. Bake in a preheated 375° oven about 20 minutes. Remove from pans at once and cool on a rack.

OAT-MOLASSES ROLLS

Prepare:
>   Steel-Cut Oats Bread, page 251

After the first rising, butter your fingers and pinch off pieces large enough to fill greased muffin tins about ⅓ full. Permit the dough to rise until about double in bulk. Bake in a preheated 375° oven for about 18 minutes.

BRIOCHE

[About 15 Brioches]
Our recipes for French bread, due to a number of special circumstances, are close approximations. So, for similar reasons, is our recipe for another superb French specialty—the brioche. But we are proud of them all. The method for making brioche is more complicated to describe than to carry out. It involves good timing between the rising of a small amount of floating yeast paste, or starter, and the working of the rest of the dough. Please read about this process before plunging in.
Have ready:
>   6 tablespoons butter, creamed at 85°

Sift and then measure:
>   2 cups all-purpose flour

Make a well, see page 301, with

about ¼ of this flour and crumble into it:

1 cake compressed yeast at 75°

◗ Be sure to use this much. A high yeast and butter content distinguishes this dough. Mix the flour and crumbled yeast with:

2 tablespoons 85° water

Gradually work the flour into a paste. When it becomes a small soft ball, snip a cross in the top with scissors and then drop it into a 2-quart pan, filled with water at 85°. ◗ The ball will sink to the bottom of the pan, so be sure it is not over a burner, where additional heat might kill the yeast. As the yeast develops, the ball of dough, or starter, rises to the surface and doubles in size in about 7 to 8 minutes—if the water temperature is right. If the water chills too much, add hotter water to bring the temperature back to 85°. ◗ When the starter has doubled in bulk, it must be removed from the water. Should this state be reached before you are ready to use it, drain and cover it. Meanwhile, once you have dropped the starter in the water, shape into another well the remaining flour, mixed with:

1 tablespoon sugar
1 teaspoon salt

Break into the center of it:

2 eggs, room temperature

Mix them in by drawing the flour from the sides of the well gradually. Also work in:

2 to 3 tablespoons milk

until the ingredients form a sticky but cohesive mass which you continue to work as follows. Use only one hand. Do not try to release it from the dough. Just keep picking up as much as will adhere and throw it back hard onto the board with a turn of the wrist, gathering more from the board each time. ◗ This rough throwing process develops the gluten and is repeated about fifty times. By then the dough should be glistening and smooth and your fingers will have become free. At this point, work the butter into the paste. When it is all absorbed, scoop the floating starter out of the water by spreading wide the fingers of one hand and ◗ drain the starter for a moment on a dry towel. Work the starter into the smooth paste, which will remain shining and of about the consistency of whipped cream. ◗ Now, get the paste ready to chill for at least 1 hour. Gather up as much as you can, releasing the rest of the dough from the board with a spatula. Put it into a greased or floured bowl and chill, covered. Have ready the classic, fluted and flaring brioche forms —or muffin tins. When the dough has chilled, knead it with floured hands. It should be firm enough not to require a floured board. Now for each brioche, make 2 balls—about 2 tablespoons of dough for one, 1 tablespoon for the other. The first ball is placed in the base of a tin. The smaller ball will form the characteristic topknot of this bread. Mold it into a

pear-shaped form. Cut a small gash in center of the large ball, then 3 more shallow gashes radiating out from the center. Now, insert the point of the "pear," so it is seated firmly. The brioches are then permitted to rise until

almost doubled in bulk—under
good conditions for about 15 to
20 minutes. Glaze them with
Egg Wash, see page 433 ▶ but
be sure it does not slip into the
crack and bind the topknot to
the base, as it would keep the
topknot from rising properly.
Preheat oven to 450°.
Bake the brioches about 10 minutes or until the egg-washed
portions are a lovely brown.
Should the topknots brown too
rapidly, cover them loosely with
a piece of foil. They should have
puffed when baked to the pro-
portionate size shown in the
illustration. Serve at once or release from the tins and cool on
a rack. Reheat before serving.

BRIOCHE AU CHOCOLAT

A favorite French after-school
treat.
Prepare:
   **Brioche, above, or
   Scandinavian Pastry,
   page 267**
Cut in 2-inch squares. Roll in
each square a pencil-shaped
piece of:
   **Semi-sweet chocolate:
   about ¼ oz.**
Bake as directed for Scandinavian Pastries, page 267.

FRENCH CRESCENTS
OR CROISSANTS

[About 18 Crescents]
Rich, somewhat troublesome,
but unequaled by any other form
of roll.
Have all ingredients at about
75°.
Scald:
   ⅞ cup milk
Stir into it, until melted and dissolved:
   1 tablespoon lard
   1½ tablespoons sugar
   ¾ teaspoon salt
Cool until lukewarm. Add:
   1 cake yeast
dissolved in:

⅓ cup 85° water
Stir in or knead in to make a
soft dough about:
   2½ cups sifted all-purpose
   flour
Knead the dough on a lightly
floured surface until smooth and
elastic. Place it in a greased
bowl and turn it so all sides are
lightly greased. Cover with a
damp cloth. Permit to rise until
doubled in bulk, about 1½
hours. Cover the dough with a
lid and place in the refrigerator
until thoroughly chilled, at least
20 minutes. Then roll it out into
an oblong ¼ inch thick. Now
beat until creamy:
   1 cup butter
Dot ⅔ of the surface of the
dough with ¼ cup of the butter.
Fold the undotted third over the
center third. Then, fold the doubled portion over the remaining
third of the butter-dotted portion. The dough is now in 3
layers, see Puff Paste, page 300.
Swing the layered dough a ¼
turn—or, as in bridge, bring East
to South. Roll it again into an
oblong ¼ inch thick. Again, dot
⅔ of the surface with ¼ of the
butter. Fold the undotted third
over the center dotted third.
Then fold the doubled portion
over the remaining dotted third
as before. Swing the dough a
quarter turn. Roll and fold it
twice more, dotting each time
with ¼ cup butter. Cover and
chill the dough for at least 2
hours. Then, roll it again on a
slightly floured surface to the
thickness of ¼ inch. Cut off any
folded edges which might keep
the dough from expanding. Cut
the dough into 3-inch squares.
Cut the squares on the bias. Roll
the triangular pieces beginning
with the wide side and stretching it slightly as you roll. Shape
the rolls into crescents, as
sketched on page 261. Place
them on a baking sheet. Chill
them at once for ½ hour. Never

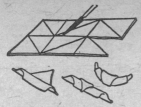

allow them a final rising, as they will not be crisp if you do. Preheat oven to 400°. Bake the crescents for 10 minutes, then reduce the heat to 350° and bake them until they are done—about 10 to 15 minutes longer.

ENGLISH OR RAISED MUFFINS

[About Twenty 3-Inch Muffins]

These are heavenly when eaten fresh and do not taste at all like "store-bought" ones, but begin to resemble them the second day. They may be baked with or without muffin rings. The classic size is about 4 inches. We make our own rings from small unlacquered fish cans and deviled meat cans. The tops and bottoms are removed and the rims are thoroughly scrubbed. English muffins are always baked on a greased griddle.

◗ Have all ingredients at about 75°.

Combine in a mixing bowl:

    1 cup hot water
    ½ cup scalded milk
    2 teaspoons sugar
    1 teaspoon salt

Dissolve for 10 minutes:

    1 cake compressed yeast

in:

    2 tablespoons 85° water

Combine the two mixtures. Sift before measuring:

    4 cups all-purpose flour

Beat 2 cups flour gradually into the milk mixture. Cover the bowl with a damp cloth. Permit the sponge to rise in a warm place,

85°, for about 1½ hours or ◗ until it collapses back into the bowl. Beat in:

    3 tablespoons softened
      butter

Beat or knead in the remaining flour. Let the dough rise again until doubled in bulk. You may put it in greased rings for the final rising, filling them ½ full. If not using rings, place the dough on a lightly floured board. Pat or press it until about ¾ inch thick. Cut it into rounds about 3 inches in diameter. Let

them stand until the dough has doubled in bulk. Cook until light brown on a fairly hot, well-buttered griddle. Turn them once while cooking, using a pancake turner. Cool them slightly on a rack. To separate the muffins before the traditional toasting, take 2 forks back to back and pry them open horizontally. Butter generously and toast. The uneven browning gives them great charm. Serve with:

    Marmalade or
    (Poached egg)

CRUMPETS

Crumpets are essentially similar to English muffins, except that muffin rings must be used when preparing them, see illustration on this page, as the batter is more liquid. Follow the recipe for English Muffins, using in all:

    2⅔ cups milk

FILLED SWEET CRESCENTS

[About 28 Crescents]

Prepare the dough for:

> Refrigerator Potato Rolls, page 263, or
> Scandinavian Pastry, page 267

Use for each crescent:

> 2 teaspoons nut or fruit filling, page 269

If using the refrigerator dough, roll out to ¼-inch thickness before chilling and cut into 3-inch squares. If using the Scandinavian dough, shape it after chilling. Cut the squares diagonally. Shape as shown, page 261. Begin the roll with the wide edge of the triangle. Curve the rolls into crescents. Place on a greased sheet. Let them rise until double in bulk. Brush lightly with:

> Egg Wash, page 433

Bake in a preheated 375° oven for about 18 to 20 minutes. Cool on a rack or serve hot.

ORANGE TEA ROLLS

These must be served the same day they are baked.
Prepare:

> Refrigerator Potato Rolls, page 263

Shape them into bite-size rolls. In the center of each roll, embed:

> A section of fresh orange

which has been rolled in:

> Brown sugar

Bake in a preheated 400° oven 8 to 10 minutes. Before reheating, glaze with a mixture of equal parts of:

> Sugar, water and Cointreau

HARD OR VIENNA ROLLS

[Twelve 3-Inch Rolls]
♦ Have all ingredients at about 75°.
Sift:

> 4 cups all-purpose flour

Crumble and dissolve for 10 minutes:

> 1 cake compressed yeast

in:

> ¼ cup 85° water

Combine:

> 1 cup water
> 1 tablespoon sugar
> 1 teaspoon salt
> 2 tablespoons melted shortening

and the dissolved yeast mixture. Fold in thoroughly, but lightly:

> 2 stiffly beaten egg whites

Add enough of the sifted flour to make a soft dough. To knead and proof, see page 240. Allow the dough to rise twice. After the second rising, punch down and knead for about 1 minute, then let rest, covered, for about 10 minutes before shaping into 12 oblong pieces. Place them about 3 inches apart on a greased baking sheet. ♦ To insure a hard crust, have in the oven a 9 x 13-inch pan, filled with ½ inch boiling water. Bake at once in a preheated 450° oven for about 20 minutes or until golden brown.

ABOUT REFRIGERATOR DOUGHS

By "refrigerator," we mean just that—these are not freezer doughs. If it's a freezer product you're after, by all means ♦ bake before freezing for the best results. We find the following recipes somewhat limited in use as ♦ the milk-based ones can be kept chilled only three days and the water-based ones five days. Yeast action is slowed by the cold, but it does continue, so both more fat and more sugar are needed in refrigerator doughs than in other kinds to keep the yeast potent during the storage period. We find that kneading before storage helps to retain rising power.

The advantage of this type of dough, of course, is that you can bake some at once and keep the rest for later. To store for chilling, you must ♦ keep the dough from drying out. Store in a greased plastic bag large enough to allow for expansion, or place the balled dough in a greased bowl, turn it so the entire surface is evenly coated, cover it closely with wax paper or foil and weigh it down with a plate.

After removal from refrigeration, always ♦ rest the dough, covered, for 30 minutes before shaping it. Then ♦ punch it down to let the gases escape before further handling. After shaping or filling, see About Yeast Rolls, page 252. Be sure the dough at least doubles in bulk. Allow ample time for rising because of the chilled condition of the dough. To bake, see individual recipes.

NO-KNEAD REFRIGERATOR ROLLS

[Eighteen 2½-Inch Rolls]
♦ Have all ingredients at about 75°.
Sift before measuring:
    3½ cups all-purpose flour
Scald:
    1 cup milk
Stir in, until dissolved:
    6 tablespoons shortening
        or butter
    6 tablespoons sugar
    1 to 1½ teaspoons salt
Cool to 85°. Place in a measuring cup:
    1 cake compressed yeast
Dissolve it in:
    ½ cup 85° water
Allow it to rest for 10 minutes, then beat in:
    1 egg
Add these ingredients to the milk mixture. Beat in ½ the flour. Beat the dough for 2 minutes. Add the remaining flour and beat the dough until it blisters. To store for chilling, to shape and to prepare for baking, see About Refrigerator Doughs,

page 262. Bake in a preheated 425° oven for about 15 minutes.

REFRIGERATOR POTATO ROLLS

[About Forty 2-Inch Rolls]
♦ Have all ingredients at about 75°.
Prepare:
    1 cup freshly cooked and
        riced potatoes
Dissolve for about 10 minutes:
    1 cake compressed yeast
in:
    ½ cup 85° water
Place in a separate bowl:
    ½ cup lard or shortening
Scald and pour over it:
    1 cup milk
Stir until the lard is melted. When the mixture reaches about 85°, add the dissolved yeast and the riced potatoes. Add:
    3 beaten eggs
    ¾ cup sugar
    2 teaspoons salt
Beat well. Sift before measuring:
    5 cups all-purpose flour
Add 4 cups of the flour and beat the batter thoroughly. Stir in the remaining flour or toss the dough on a board and knead the flour in. To store for chilling, to shape and to prepare for baking, see About Refrigerator Doughs, page 262. Bake the rolls in a preheated 425° oven for about 15 minutes.

REFRIGERATOR WHOLE-GRAIN ROLLS

[About Twenty 2-Inch Rolls]
♦ Have all ingredients at about 75°.
Dissolve for about 10 minutes:
    ½ to 1 cake compressed
        yeast
in:
    1 cup 85° water
Beat until creamy:
    ¼ cup shortening
    6 tablespoons sugar
Stir in the yeast mixture. Sift before measuring:

1¾ cups all-purpose flour
Mix in:
    1¼ teaspoons salt
    1½ cups whole-grain flour
Stir the flour mixture gradually into the yeast mixture. Beat until well blended. To store for chilling, to shape and to prepare for baking, see About Refrigerator Doughs, page 262. Bake in a preheated 425° oven for about 15 minutes.

REFRIGERATOR BRAN ROLLS

[About Forty-Eight 2-Inch Rolls]
◗ Have all ingredients at about 75°.
Combine:
    1 cup shortening
    ¾ cup sugar
    1½ to 2 teaspoons salt
Pour over these ingredients and stir until the shortening is melted:
    1 cup boiling water
Add:
    1 cup bran or bran cereal
In a separate bowl, dissolve for about 10 minutes:
    2 cakes compressed yeast
in:
    1 cup 85° water
When the first mixture reaches about 85°, add to it:
    2 well-beaten eggs
and the dissolved yeast. Sift before measuring and add:
    6 cups all-purpose flour
Beat the batter well. To store for chilling, to shape and to prepare for baking, see About Refrigerator Doughs, page 262. Bake in a preheated 425° oven for about 15 minutes.

WHITE, WHOLE-GRAIN, GRAHAM OR RYE BREAD STICKS

Pinch off small pieces of:
    Bread Dough, page 240,
    or Refrigerator Roll
    Dough, page 262
that has risen once. This may be done with buttered hands. Roll into sticks. Brush with:
    Melted butter or 1 beaten
    egg
Place the sticks on a buttered sheet. Sprinkle them with a choice of:
    (Coarse salt)
    (Poppy seed)
    (Fresh celery seed)
    (Chopped nut meats)
    (Caraway seed)
Permit to rise until doubled in bulk. Bake in a 425° oven until brown and crisp.

ABOUT YEAST COFFEE CAKES

Remember when you are baking bread and rolls that many of these doughs can be made into very acceptable coffee cake and sweet rolls. Try some with the special fillings suggested at the end of this section. For a comparatively effortless but delicious result, bake the No-Knead Coffee Cake, below. If you have a little time on your hands, don't fail to try the Scandinavian varieties.

NO-KNEAD YEAST COFFEE CAKE OR PANETTONE

[Two 9-Inch Tube Pans]
Baked in 1 lb. greased coffee cans and attractively packaged, this cake makes wonderful gifts.
◗ Have all ingredients at about 75°.
Dissolve for about 10 minutes:
    2 cakes compressed yeast
in:
    1 cup 85° water
Sift and stir in:
    1 cup all-purpose flour
Cover this sponge and permit it to rise in a warm place until it has doubled in bulk. Sift:
    ½ cup sugar
Beat until soft:
    ½ cup butter
Add the sugar gradually. Blend these ingredients until they are

light and creamy. Beat in, one at a time:

  2 to 3 eggs

Add:

  1 teaspoon salt
  2 teaspoons grated lemon rind

Beat in the sponge. Sift and beat in gradually:

  3½ cups all-purpose flour

Beat the dough for 5 minutes more. Add:

  (⅛ cup chopped citron)
  (¼ cup white raisins or chopped candied pineapple)
  (1 cup broken nut meats)

Cover the bowl with a cloth and permit the dough to rise for about 2 hours or until it has almost doubled in bulk. Place it in greased tube pans and let it rise for about ½ hour. Brush the tops with:

  Melted butter

If you have added no fruit or nut meats to the batter, you may combine:

  ½ cup blanched, shredded almonds
  ¼ cup sugar

Sprinkle this mixture on the dough.

Preheat oven to 350°.

Bake in either the tubes or the greased pans for about ½ hour. If you have omitted the top dressing of almonds and sugar, you may, after the cake has baked and cooled, spread on it:

  Milk or Lemon Glaze, page 434

★ KNEADED COFFEE CAKE FOR FILLED BRAIDS, RINGS OR VANOCKA

Prepare:

  Buttermilk Potato Roll Dough, page 257 or White Bread Plus, page 244

adding an additional:

  ¼ cup sugar

To give these breads an interesting color, use the tiniest smidgen of:

  Saffron, page 214

Consider beforehand whether to make a wreath, to roll like a jelly roll, to shape a filled roll as shown under Scandinavian Coffee Cake, page 268, or to braid. One of the most famous Christmas breads is Vanocka—the finished loaf is supposed to resemble the Christ Child in swaddling clothes. To shape Vanocka or the filled cake sketched above, see the following.

To make Vanocka, divide the dough into 9 parts. First, braid a 4 plait strip, then a 3 plait, last, a 2 plait. Use the widest for a base and center the 3 plaits on it. Then top with the centered 2 plait. A way to braid a filled coffee cake so the filling is well protected is shown above. Make a rectangle about 9 x 12 inches and ¼ inch thick. Put the filling down the center lengthwise, cut the outer thirds diagonally into 2 inch strips and lace them as shown, folding the ends inside.

★ STOLLEN OR CHRISTMAS LOAF

[2 Loaves]

◗ Have all ingredients at about 75°.

Sift before measuring:

  6 to 8 cups all-purpose flour

Crumble:

    1½ to 2 cakes compressed yeast

in:

    1½ cups 85° water or scalded, cooled milk

for about 10 minutes, until dissolved. Add 1 cup of the sifted flour. Permit this sponge to rise in a warm place until doubled in bulk. Sprinkle a little of the sifted flour over:

    ½ lb. raisins
    ½ lb. blanched chopped almonds
    (½ cup chopped candied fruits)

Sift:

    ¾ cup sugar

Beat until soft:

    1½ cups butter

Add the sifted sugar gradually. Blend until light and creamy. Beat in, one at a time:

    3 eggs

Add:

    ¾ teaspoon salt
    ¾ teaspoon grated lemon rind
    (2 tablespoons brandy or rum)

Add the fruit and nuts. Add the sponge and the remaining flour and knead the dough until smooth and elastic. Permit it to rise until it almost doubles in bulk. Toss it onto a floured board. Divide it into 2 loaves and place them in greased pans. Brush the tops with:

    Melted butter

Let the loaves rise, covered, until they again almost double in bulk.

Preheat oven to 350°.

Bake the loaves for about 45 minutes. When cool, brush them with:

    Milk or Lemon Glaze, page 434

BUNDKUCHEN OR KUGELHOPF

A true Kugelhopf is baked in a fluted tube pan. It is the traditional Name Day cake—not your birthday, but the birthday of the saint for whom you were named. This recipe also makes a good Baba or Savarin, page 371

▶ Have all ingredients at about 75°.

Sift before measuring:

    4 cups all-purpose flour

Scald:

    1 cup milk

When cooled to about 85°, pour it over:

    3 cakes crumbled compressed yeast

After the yeast has dissolved, beat in 1 cup of the sifted flour and set the sponge to rise in a warm place until about double in bulk. Sift:

    ¾ cup sugar

Beat until soft:

    1 cup butter

Add the sifted sugar gradually. Blend these ingredients until very light and creamy. Beat in, one at a time:

    5 eggs

Beat in:

    1 teaspoon salt

Add the sponge, the remaining flour and:

    ½ teaspoon grated lemon rind
    1 cup seedless raisins

Beat the batter well until smooth and elastic. Spread in the bottom of a greased 9-inch tube pan:

    ⅓ cup blanched almonds

Place the dough on top of them and permit it to rise until almost double in bulk.

Preheat oven to 350°.

Bake the cake from 50 to 60 minutes. When cool, sprinkle the top with:

    Confectioners' sugar

FRUIT-TOPPED YEAST COFFEE CAKE

[Four 8-Inch Cakes]

For other versions of Galette, see page 297.
Prepare:

> White Bread Plus Dough, page 244

adding an additional:

> ¼ cup sugar

After the last rising, pat the dough out thin in the greased pans, perforate it and allow it to relax. Then make a rim by pinching the top edges all around. Brush the surface with:

> Melted butter

or apply an:

> Egg Wash, page 433

Although the egg wash always tends to toughen, it does prevent sogginess. Now cover the entire surface of the cake closely with rows of:

> Fruit—cored, sliced apples, peaches, seeded cherries or plums

Cover the fruit with:

> Streusel, page 433, or cinnamon and sugar

◗ Allow the fruit-covered dough to rise only half as high as usual for bread.
Preheat oven to 385°.
Bake for about 25 minutes. ◗ If using an electric oven, see (I, 100). When the cake cools somewhat, you may cover it with:

> Apricot Glaze, page 434

For a simpler, quicker and, we think, quite delicious solution, simply bake:

> Fresh Fruit Cake Cockaigne, page 319

SCANDINAVIAN COFFEE CAKE OR PASTRY

[Two 9-Inch Rings]
Call them Danish, Swedish or Norwegian, these light confections fall between rich coffee cakes and rich pastries. The method of folding and rolling the dough, similar to that used in Croissants, page 260, accounts for the characteristic flakiness of the superbly light crumb. The basic dough can be used for the ring shown below. Fillings and toppings are usually rich in nuts, with cardamon and saffron frequent in the flavoring.
◗ Have all ingredients at about 75°.
Beat well:

> 2 eggs

Add:

> ¾ cup 85° water

Dissolve in this mixture:

> 1 cake compressed yeast

Let all these ingredients rest refrigerated for about 15 minutes. Meanwhile blend with a pastry blender or by hand, until smooth:

> 4 cups sifted all-purpose flour
> 1 teaspoon salt
> 2 tablespoons sugar
> ½ cup butter
> 10 crushed cardamon seeds or 1½ teaspoons powdered cardamon

Make a ring of the blended flour prepared in the step above. Now pour the chilled yeast mixture into the center and work it gradually into the dry ingredients. Knead until smooth for about 2 minutes. Form the dough into a ball and rest it, covered, for about 20 minutes in the refrigerator. Roll out the dough ◗ lightly into an oblong about ⅜ inch thick. Beat until creamy:

> 1⅓ to 1½ cups butter

Dot the dough over ⅔ of its surface with ¼ of the butter. Fold the undotted third over the center third. Then fold the doubled portion over the remaining third of the butter-dotted portion. The dough is now in 3 layers, see Puff Paste, page 300. Swing the layered dough a ¼ turn or, as in bridge, bring East to South. Roll it ◗ lightly again into an oblong about ⅜ inch thick. Again dot ⅔ of the surface with ¼ of the butter. Fold the undotted third over the center dotted third.

Then fold the doubled portion over the remaining butter-dotted third as before. Swing the dough a quarter turn. Roll and fold it twice more, dotting each time with ¼ of the butter. Cover and chill the dough for at least 2 hours. Then roll it again on a slightly floured surface, to the thickness of ⅜ inch. Cut off any folded edges that might keep the dough from expanding. To shape the ring as shown above, roll it first into an oblong, about 29 x 11 inches. Fill it with any rich filling for coffee cake, below. It is not necessary to shape the roll on a cloth but you may need to use a spatula or pancake turner to help lift it if the dough should stick to the lightly floured board. Bring the two ends of the roll together using a little water for glue to make them hold. Place the ring on a greased baking sheet. With floured scissors held perpendicularly to the roll, cut bias gashes about 1 to 2 inches apart into the outer edges of the ring, to within one inch of the inner circle. As you cut, you may turn each partially cut slice flat onto the tin. Sometimes the slices are cut very narrow and one slice is turned toward the outer rim, the other twisted and turned toward the inner rim, as shown on the right. Wash the top areas with:

Egg Wash, page 433

being careful not to cover the cut portions as the glaze may harden later too rapidly in baking and inhibit further rising of the dough. Cover the cut ring with a damp cloth and allow to rise for about 25 minutes, until the mass has doubled in bulk. Preheat the oven to 400° for a ring, to 375° for filled rolls or croissants.

Bake a ring about 25 minutes. Bake rolls for about 15 minutes. If a Fruit Glaze, page 434, is to be applied, allow the pastry to cool and apply the glaze warm. For other glazes, see page 433.

ABOUT SEASONINGS, FILLINGS AND TOPPINGS FOR COFFEE CAKE

Housewives often wonder why their coffee cakes and fillings seem insipid in flavor and in color when compared with some of the more sophisticated commercial products. First of all, a slight touch of yellow coloring often used in commercial coffee cakes lends them a more convincing "eggy" look. Often too, for gusto, bakers add to their crumb mixtures crushed macaroons, almond paste, rolled cake crumbs, and finely ground nuts —especially hazelnuts. Sometimes they use pecans, walnuts, almonds and, occasionally, brazil nuts. Considerably less effective

—and not usually recommended —are finely chopped peanuts, coconut and cashews.

Home bakers may also add distinction to pastry fillings with a small quantity of lemon juice, grated lemon rind, dried currants, a bit of finely chopped citron; or, for piquancy, they can avoid more solid fillings altogether and substitute a thin layer of jam or marmalade. Fillings are added to doughs during the final shaping and last rising. A 9-inch ring needs a cup or a little more of filling, individual rolls about 2 teaspoons. For various toppings and glazes, see pages 431–435.

NUT FILLINGS FOR COFFEE CAKES

I. [For One 9-Inch Ring]
If made with almonds, this is known as **Edelweiss**.
Cream:
>½ cup confectioners' sugar
>¼ to ½ cup butter

Stir in:
>½ teaspoon vanilla or 1 teaspoon grated lemon rind
>½ cup blanched shredded or ground almonds or other nuts
>(1 egg)

II. [For One 9-Inch Ring]
Combine:
>½ cup ground hazelnuts or other nuts
>½ cup sugar
>2 teaspoons cinnamon
>½ teaspoon vanilla
>2 tablespoons finely chopped citron or orange peel

Beat well and add:
>1 egg

Thin these ingredients with:
>Milk

until they are of the right consistency to spread over the dough.

III. [For One 9-Inch Ring]
Chop:
>¼ cup each blanched almonds, citron and raisins

Melt:
>¼ cup butter or ⅛ cup butter and ⅛ cup cultured sour cream

After rolling the dough, spread it with the melted butter and the chopped ingredients. Sprinkle with:
>(Sugar)
>(Cinnamon)

IV. [For Three 9-Inch Rings]
If you buy canned almond paste to use in coffee cake fillings, mix:
>10 oz. almond paste
>1 cup sugar
>2 egg whites

Work it in a bowl placed over ice to keep it cool, so the oil in the almonds is not released.

CRUMB FRUIT FILLING

[For One 9-Inch Ring]
Mix well:
>¾ cup crushed macaroons
>3 tablespoons melted butter
>2 tablespoons sugar
>½ cup raisins or chopped dates, cooked prunes or grated coconut
>(¼ cup chopped nuts)

APPLE COFFEE CAKE FILLING

[For Two 9-Inch Rings]
Combine and boil for 4 minutes:
>2½ cups pared and chopped apples
>1 cup brown sugar
>⅓ cup butter
>1 cup raisins
>½ teaspoon cinnamon
>½ teaspoon salt

Cool slightly and spread over dough.

PRUNE OR APRICOT FILLING FOR COFFEE CAKE AND ROLLS

[For One 9-Inch Ring]
Combine:
- ½ cup sweetened puréed prunes or apricots
- 2 to 4 tablespoons butter
- 2 teaspoons orange or lemon rind
- (¼ cup nuts or coconut)

DATE OR FIG FILLING FOR COFFEE CAKE

[For One 9-Inch Ring]
Melt and simmer about 2 minutes:
- ¼ cup butter
- ⅓ cup brown sugar

Remove from heat and stir in:
- ¾ cup chopped dates or figs
- ¼ cup almond paste
- ½ teaspoon cinnamon
- A grating of fresh nutmeg

Cool slightly before using.

POPPY SEED FILLING COCKAIGNE

[For One 9-Inch Ring]
This filling is for that special occasion.
Grind or crush in a mortar:
- ½ cup poppy seeds

Put the poppy seeds in the top of a double boiler and bring to a boil with:
- ¼ cup milk

Remove pan from the heat and add:
- ⅓ cup brown sugar
- 2 tablespoons butter

Put the pan ♦ over—not in—hot water and add:
- 2 egg yolks

Heat until the mixture thickens, stirring constantly. When it has cooled slightly, add:
- ⅓ cup almond paste or ½ cup ground almonds
- (3 tablespoons citron)
- (2 teaspoons lemon juice)
- (1 teaspoon vanilla)

Cool and have ready to add to strudel or use for coffee cake.

POPPY SEED OR MOHN FILLING

I. [For Two 9-Inch Rings]
Mix together well:
- ¾ cup ground poppy seeds
- ¼ cup sugar
- ¼ cup raisins
- ½ cup sour cream
- ⅛ teaspoon cinnamon
- 1 teaspoon grated lemon rind

II. [For Four 9-Inch Rings]
Grind or mash between towels with a wooden mallet:
- 2 cups poppy seeds

Mix in:
- 1 egg
- ⅓ cup honey
- 1 tablespoon lemon juice
- ¼ cup chopped nuts

III. [For One 9-Inch Ring]
Grind or mash between towels with a wooden mallet:
- ¼ cup poppy seeds

Place in a bowl and add:
- About 2 tablespoons milk

just enough to make this mixture feel buttery between your fingers. Then add:
- 2 tablespoons melted butter
- 2 tablespoons dry cake crumbs
- 1 teaspoon cinnamon
- 1 teaspoon grated lemon rind

POT-CHEESE OR RICOTTA FILLING

[For One 9-Inch Coffee Cake Ring]
Put through a ricer or a strainer:
- 1½ cups pot or Ricotta cheese

Mix well with:
- ¼ cup sugar
- 1 slightly beaten egg yolk
- ¼ to ½ cup raisins
- 2 teaspoons lemon rind

Beat until ♦ stiff, but not dry, and fold in:
- 1 egg white

ABOUT QUICK TEA BREADS AND COFFEE CAKES

These sweet breads are delightful but, with the exception of nut and fruit breads, should be served immediately after baking as they wither young. If you want breads that keep and reheat well, see recipes for yeast breads and yeast coffee cakes.

Nut and fruit breads are attractive baked in 6 oz. fruit juice cans so that they slice prettily for tea. If you use cans, do not fill them more than ¾ full to allow for expansion of the dough. Quick nut and fruit breads slice better if, after baking, they are wrapped in foil and refrigerated for about 12 hours.

▲ When baking quick breads at high altitudes, reduce the baking powder or soda in the recipe by ¼. ◗ But do not decrease the soda beyond ½ teaspoon for each cup of sour milk or cream used.

QUICK NUT OR DATE BREAD

[A 9 x 5-Inch Loaf]
Preheat oven to 350°.
◗ Have all ingredients at about 75°.
Sift into a bowl:
    2 cups all-purpose flour
    ⅓ cup white or ½ cup brown sugar
    2 teaspoons double-acting baking powder
    1 teaspoon salt
Melt and cool slightly:
    2 tablespoons butter
Beat until light:
    1 egg
Beat with the egg:
    1 cup milk
Add the melted butter. Beat the liquid ingredients into the sifted ones until well mixed. Fold in:
    ¾ cup broken nut meats or part dates and part nut meats
Place the dough in a greased

bread pan and bake for about 40 minutes.

QUICK SALLY LUNN

[A 9 x 13-Inch Pan]
A light bread. For an even lighter one, try Brioche Loaf Cockaigne, page 245, cr Brioche, page 258.
Preheat oven to 425°.
◗ Have all ingredients at about 75°.
Sift before measuring:
    2 cups all-purpose flour
Resift with:
    2¼ teaspoons double-acting baking powder
    ¾ teaspoon salt
Combine and cream well:
    ½ cup shortening
    ½ cup sugar
Beat in, one at a time:
    3 eggs
Add the sifted ingredients to the batter in about 3 parts, alternately with:
    1 cup milk
Stir the batter lightly ◗ until the ingredients are just blended. Bake in a greased pan for about 30 minutes. Break the bread into squares. Serve hot.

QUICK PRUNE, APRICOT OR CRANBERRY BREAD

[A 9 x 5-Inch Loaf]
Preheat oven to 350°.
◗ Have all ingredients at about 75°.
Sift before measuring:
    1½ cups all-purpose flour
Resift with:
    ½ teaspoon salt
    1 teaspoon soda
Add:
    1½ cups whole-grain flour
Cream:
    ¼ cup shortening
with:
    ½ cup sugar
Beat in:
    1 egg
Add:
    ¾ cup unsweetened,

cooked, mashed prune,
apricot or cranberry
pulp
¼ cup prune, apricot or
cranberry juice
Add the sifted ingredients
alternately to the butter mixture
with:
1 cup buttermilk
Stir the batter ▶ with a few
swift strokes, until just blended.
Fold in:
1 cup broken nut meats
Grated rind of 1 orange
Place the dough in a greased
loaf pan. Bake the bread for
about 1¼ hours. Let it cool in
the pan.

QUICK ORANGE BREAD

[Two 8½ x 4½-Inch Loaves]
This is an economical, easily
made tea bread. If you want a
quick treat, break it apart and
eat it while hot, with or without
lots of good butter. If you intend it for sandwiches, bake it
in cans, see About Quick Tea
Breads, page 271. You'll find it
easier to slice on the second
day.
Preheat oven to 350°.
▶ Have all ingredients at about
75°.
I. Sift, then measure:
3 cups all-purpose flour
Resift it into a large bowl with:
3 teaspoons double-acting
baking powder
Combine and add:
1 tablespoon grated orange
rind
½ to ¾ cup sugar
For a more cakelike result, use
the larger amount of sugar. ▶
Combine and beat:
1 egg
¼ cup orange juice
1¼ cups milk
2 tablespoons melted
shortening
You may add:
1 cup chopped or broken
nut meats

Pour the liquid mixture into the
bowl. Combine all ingredients
with a few swift strokes. Stir
lightly until barely blended.
Bake the bread in two greased
loaf pans for about 50 minutes
or until done.

II. [Two 8½ x 4½-Inch Loaves
or 3 Round Cans That Hold 1¾
Cups]
Fill the cans only ¾ full. Parboil 3 times, for 10 minutes each
time:
Rind of 3 navel oranges
Then cut them into strips, as for
marmalade, and cook them
with:
1 cup water
½ cup sugar
until almost dry. Cool.
Preheat oven to 350°.
Cream:
1 cup sugar
3 tablespoons butter
Add:
1 beaten egg
Sift together:
3 cups sifted all-purpose
flour
3 teaspoons double-acting
baking powder
1 teaspoon salt
and add it alternately to the
creamed ingredients with:
1 cup milk
until the mixture is smooth.
Fold in the orange rinds and
bake for about 1 hour in
greased pans or cans.

QUICK BANANA BREAD

[An 8½ x 4½-Inch Loaf]
Preheat oven to 350°.
▶ Have all ingredients at about
75°. Sift before measuring:
1¾ cups all-purpose flour
Resift with:
2¼ teaspoons double-acting
baking powder
½ teaspoon salt
Blend until creamy:
⅓ cup shortening
⅔ cup sugar

¾ teaspoon grated lemon
rind

Beat in:

1 to 2 beaten eggs
1–1¼ cups ripe banana
pulp

Add the sifted ingredients in about 3 parts to the sugar mixture. Beat the batter after each addition until smooth. Fold in:

(½ cup broken nut meats)
(¼ cup finely chopped
apricots)

Place the batter in a greased bread pan. Bake the bread for about 1 hour or until done. Cool before slicing.

QUICK BANANA
WHEAT-GERM BREAD

Prepare:

Banana Bread, above

Use in all:

1½ cups all-purpose flour

Add:

¼ cup wheat germ

QUICK IRISH SODA BREAD

[A 9 x 5-Inch Loaf]
Preheat oven to 375°.
◗ Have all ingredients at about 75°.
Sift together in a large bowl:

2 cups sifted all-purpose
flour
¾ teaspoon baking soda
½ teaspoon salt
1 tablespoon sugar

Cut into the flour mixture with a pastry blender, until of the consistency of coarse corn meal:

6 tablespoons chilled
shortening

Stir in:

½ to 1 cups raisins
1 tablespoon caraway
seeds

Add gradually:

½ to ⅔ cup buttermilk

The mixture should not be dry. Knead briefly and shape into a round loaf or a 9 x 5-inch one. Put the dough in a greased bread pan. Cut a bold cross on

top, letting it go over the sides so the bread will not crack in baking. Brush the top with:

Milk

Bake for 40 to 50 minutes. To test for doneness, see page 242. To bake ▤ outdoors, see Skillet Bread, page 277.

QUICK SWEET
WHOLE-WHEAT BREAD

[A 9 x 5-Inch Loaf]
A "homely" coarse sweet bread, good served with fruit salads and cottage cheese.
Preheat oven to 375°.
◗ Have all ingredients at about 75°.
Mix:

2½ cups whole-wheat flour
½ teaspoon cinnamon
¼ teaspoon salt
1 teaspoon soda

Combine:

1 beaten egg
½ cup molasses
¼ cup brown sugar
¼ cup sesame, peanut or
safflower oil
1 teaspoon grated lemon
or orange peel

Add the egg mixture, alternately with:

⅔ cup yogurt

to the dry ingredients. Pour into a buttered pan and bake for about 50 minutes.

QUICK BRAN BREAD
WITH MOLASSES

[Two 8½ x 4½-Inch Loaves]
Preheat oven to 375°.
◗ Have all ingredients at about 75°.
Combine:

2 cups bran
2 cups whole-grain flour
2 teaspoons double-acting
baking powder
1 teaspoon salt
1 teaspoon soda

Combine and beat:

1 egg

1¾ cups sour milk or
   buttermilk
½ cup molasses or ¾ cup
   packed brown sugar
Beat in the dry ingredients. You
may add:
   1 cup raisins, figs or nut
      meats
Place the batter in 2 greased
pans. Bake for 1 hour or more.

QUICK BRAN DATE BREAD OR MUFFINS

[Two 8½ x 4½-Inch Loaves]
Preheat oven to 350°.
▶ Have all ingredients at about
75°.
Prepare:
   2 cups chopped dates
Pour over them:
   2 cups boiling water
In a separate bowl, beat until
light:
   2 eggs
Add slowly, beating constantly:
   ¾ cup brown sugar or
      ½ cup molasses
When these ingredients are
creamy, sift in:
   1 cup whole-grain flour
   2 teaspoons double-acting
      baking powder
   1 teaspoon soda
Add ½ the date mixture and:
   1 cup whole-grain flour
   2 cups bran
   1 teaspoon vanilla
Add the remaining date mixture
and:
   1 cup or less chopped nut
      meats
Place the dough in a lightly
greased loaf pan or greased
muffin tins. Bake for about 1
hour.

ALMOND BRAN BREAD

[A 9 x 5-Inch Loaf]
This makes a one-inch-high loaf.
Preheat oven to 325°.
▶ Have all ingredients at about
75°.
Beat until light:
   2 egg yolks

Cream with:
   2 tablespoons butter
Grind in a nut grinder and mix
in:
   1 cup finely ground
      blanched almonds
   1 teaspoon double-acting
      baking powder
Fold in:
   2 tablespoons bran
   2 stiffly beaten egg whites
Pour batter into greased bread
loaf pan and bake for about 25
minutes.

BAKED BROWN BREAD

[Two 8½ x 4½-Inch Loaves]
Preheat oven to 350°.
▶ Have all ingredients at about
75°.
Sift before measuring:
   2 cups graham flour
   1 cup all-purpose flour
Resift with:
   2 tablespoons sugar
   ¾ teaspoon salt
   1 teaspoon soda
Stir in:
   1 cup buttermilk
   1 cup dark molasses
You may add:
   1 cup broken nut meats
      and/or raisins
Combine all ingredients well
and bake in two greased pans
or fill buttered cans ¾ full and
bake about 1 hour.

BOSTON STEAMED BROWN BREAD

[Two 1-Pound Loaves or Two
1-Quart Pudding Molds]
▶ Have all ingredients at about
75°.
Combine:
   1 cup yellow water-ground
      corn meal
   1 cup rye flour
   1 cup graham flour
   2 teaspoons soda
   1 teaspoon salt
Combine in a separate bowl:
   2 cups buttermilk
   ¾ cup molasses

1 cup chopped raisins

Add the liquid to the dry ingredients. Pour the batter into 2 buttered one-quart pudding molds or fill buttered cans about ¾ full. Butter the lids before closing molds and tie the lids or tape them on, so rising bread does not break the seal. ♦ Steam 3 hours in one inch water if not using a pressure cooker. ✪ Otherwise, add 2 cups hot water to the pressure cooker. Adjust cover. Steam over low heat for 15 minutes without pressure, that is, with the valve open. Then cook for 30 minutes at 15 pounds pressure. Reduce heat instantly. To cut without crumbling, use a tough string and slice with a sawing motion.

QUICK COFFEE CAKE

[A 9 x 9-Inch Pan]
Preheat oven to 375°.
♦ Have all ingredients at about 75°.
Sift before measuring:
    1½ cups all-purpose flour
Resift with:
    ¼ teaspoon salt
    2 teaspoons double-acting
        baking powder
Sift:
    ¼ to ½ cup sugar
Cream until soft:
    ¼ cup butter
Add the sugar gradually and cream these ingredients until light. Beat in:
    1 egg
    ⅔ cup milk
Add the sifted ingredients to the butter mixture. Add:
    (¾ teaspoon grated lemon
        rind or ½ teaspoon
        vanilla)
Stir the batter until smooth. Spread in a greased pan and bake for about 25 minutes. Cover with a Streusel, page 432.

QUICK KUGELHOPF

[A 7-inch Tube Pan]

Preheat oven to 350°.
♦ Have all ingredients at about 75°.
Sift before measuring:
    3½ cups all-purpose flour
Resift with:
    3 teaspoons double-acting
        baking powder
    ½ teaspoon salt
Cream until soft:
    1 cup butter
Add gradually:
    1 cup sifted sugar
Cream until very light. Beat in, one at a time:
    5 eggs
Add the sifted ingredients to the butter mixture in 3 parts, alternately with thirds of:
    1 cup milk
Stir the batter until smooth after each addition. Add:
    1 cup seedless raisins
    1 teaspoon grated lemon
        rind
    1 teaspoon vanilla
Bake the cake in a greased tube pan for about 45 to 50 minutes. When cool, sprinkle with:
    Confectioners' sugar

QUICK SOUR CREAM COFFEE CAKE

[A 9 x 9-Inch Pan]
Made on a muffin principle, this cake is wonderfully good and easy.
Preheat oven to 350°.
♦ Have all ingredients at about 75°.
Sift before measuring:
    1½ cups all-purpose flour
Resift with:
    1 cup sugar
    2 teaspoons double-acting
        baking powder
    ½ teaspoon soda
    ¼ teaspoon salt
Combine and beat well:
    1 cup cultured sour cream
    2 eggs
Add the sifted ingredients to the cream mixture. Beat until smooth. Spread in a lightly

greased pan. Sprinkle with:
> Streusel, page 432

Bake for about 20 minutes.

QUICK, RICH, MOIST COFFEE CAKE

[A 9 x 13-Inch Pan]
Preheat oven to 350°.
◗ Have all ingredients at about 75°.
Sift together:

> 2 cups all-purpose flour
> ¾ cup sugar
> 2 teaspoons double-acting baking powder
> ½ teaspoon salt

Cut in:

> ½ cup butter

Break into a measuring cup:

> 1 egg

Fill with:

> Milk

enough to make 1 cup. Beat and add to the dry ingredients with:

> 1 teaspoon vanilla

Pour batter into a greased pan and cover with:

> Honey Bee Glaze, page 433

Bake about 25 minutes.

QUICK SPICE COFFEE CAKE WITH OIL

[An 8 x 8 x 2½-Inch Pan]
Preheat oven to 350°.
◗ Have all ingredients at about 75°.
Combine in a mixing bowl:

> 2 cups sifted all-purpose flour
> ⅔ cup sugar
> ¾ teaspoon each baking powder and soda
> ½ teaspoon salt
> ½ teaspoon freshly grated nutmeg
> 1 teaspoon cinnamon

Combine in another bowl and mix well:

> ½ cup vegetable oil
> 1 beaten egg
> ½ cup buttermilk or yogurt

> ⅓ cup corn sirup: light or dark
> ¾ cup raisins

Pour this into the flour mixture, stirring rapidly until blended. All the lumps need not have vanished. Pour into a greased pan and cover the top with:

> Topping for Coffee Cake I, page 268

Bake the cake about 35 minutes or until done.

EGGLESS, ALL RYE, HONEY CAKE COCKAIGNE

[One 4½ x 8-Inch Loaf]
Like a soft, deliciously spiced **Lebkuchen,** this confection keeps for weeks. It also toasts well for tea. Age it three days or more in a plastic bag or tin box before eating.
Preheat oven to 350°.
◗ Have all ingredients at about 75°.
Heat in the top of a double boiler until small bubbles appear through the mixture:

> ⅓ cup honey
> ¾ cup water
> ½ cup sugar

Remove from the heat and beat into the following mixture:

> 2 cups very finely milled rye flour
> ½ teaspoon soda
> 2 teaspoons double-acting baking powder
> 1 tablespoon cinnamon
> ½ teaspoon each cloves and allspice
> ⅛ teaspoon cardamon

Beat 10 minutes in an electric beater. When thoroughly amalgamated, beat in:

> ¼ cup pecans or blanched shredded almonds
> 1 tablespoon grated orange rind
> ¼ to ½ cup finely chopped citron

Place a pan of water on the bottom shelf of the oven. Bake the cake for about 1 hour.

SKILLET OR GRIDDLE BREADS

Prepare:

Irish Soda Bread, page 273, or Skillet Corn Bread, below

Either one of these simple doughs will make acceptable, even good skillet bread on an open fire ▤ especially over charcoal. But our results on these heats did not compare in quality with those obtained when the same recipes were oven-baked. Bake them covered. If you prefer **Irish Farls**, cut the bread in triangular wedges, about 1 inch thick and bake them on a griddle heated to about 370° and lightly rubbed with oil. Allow about 10 minutes for one side, turn and allow 10 minutes more.

ABOUT CORN BREADS

Anyone who grew up on Southern corn breads hankers for a rich brown crust and a light but slightly gritty bite. We can assure you that without waterground corn meal and a heavy, hot pan, your end product will be pale and lifeless. For a very crisp crust, grease the pan well and heat it by itself first in a 425° oven. Whether you bake as muffins, sticks or bread, you may vary the corn and wheat proportion within a 2 cup limit to your own taste. We like 1¼ cups corn meal to ¾ cup all-purpose flour.

▲ When baking corn breads at high altitudes, reduce the baking powder or soda by ¼.
♦ But do not reduce soda beyond ½ teaspoon for each cup of sour milk or cream used.

CORN BREAD, MUFFINS OR STICKS

[A 9 x 9-Inch Pan, or About Fifteen 2-Inch Muffins]
Preheat oven to 425°.

♦ Have all ingredients at about 75°.

Grease the pan with butter, oil or bacon drippings. Place it in the oven until sizzling hot. Sift together:

¾ cup sifted all-purpose flour
2½ teaspoons double-acting baking powder
1 to 2 tablespoons sugar
¾ teaspoon salt

Add:

1¼ cups yellow or white water-ground corn meal

Beat in a separate bowl:

1 egg

Beat into it:

2 to 3 tablespoons melted butter or drippings
1 cup milk

Pour the liquid into the dry ingredients. Combine with a few rapid strokes. Place the batter in the hot pan. Bake for about 25 minutes.

SKILLET CORN BREAD

Follow the rule for:

Corn Bread above

▤ Cook it in a 10-inch covered skillet for about ½ hour or until done. You may add to the dough about:

¼ to ½ cup cooked ham or bacon bits

BUTTERMILK CRACKLING CORN BREAD

[A 9 x 9-Inch Pan or Twenty 2-Inch Muffins]
Preheat oven to 425°.
♦ Have all ingredients at about 75°.
Sift, then measure:

1 cup all-purpose flour

Resift with:

½ teaspoon soda
1½ teaspoons double-acting baking powder
1 tablespoon sugar
1 teaspoon salt

Add:

¾ cup yellow water-ground
    corn meal
Combine and beat:
    1 cup buttermilk
    2 eggs
    3 to 4 tablespoons melted
        butter or bacon fat
Stir the liquid into the dry ingredients with a few swift
strokes. You may add:
    ¼ cup salt pork cracklings
Pour the batter into a preheated
greased pan and bake the bread
for about ½ hour.

CORN ZEPHYRS
COCKAIGNE

[About Twenty 2-Inch Puffs]
In our endless search for the
best recipe of its type, we
welcomed the offer of a Southern acquaintance to send us the
Zephyr recipe she was raving
about. It arrived, and was word
for word our own favorite
Zephyr recipe in "The Joy." We
consider this the highest of com-
pliments. These puffs are delicate and delicious with a salad
course or luncheon dish.
▶ Have all ingredients at about
75°.
Combine:
    1 cup white water-ground
        corn meal
    1 tablespoon lard
Scald these ingredients by pouring over them:
    4 cups boiling water
Add:
    1 teaspoon salt
Cook the corn meal in a double
boiler for 30 minutes, stirring
frequently. Before cooling it,
butter the top slightly to keep
it from crusting. Cool. Preheat
oven to 350°. Whip until stiff:
    4 egg whites
Fold them lightly into the corn
meal mixture. Drop the batter
from a teaspoon onto a greased
baking sheet. Bake for about
½ hour.

GOLDEN CORN PUFFS

[About Twenty 2-Inch Puffs]
Preheat oven to 425°.
▶ Have all ingredients at about
75°.
Pour:
    2¼ cups boiling water
over:
    1 cup yellow water-ground
        corn meal
Add:
    1 tablespoon sugar
    1 teaspoon salt
    2 tablespoons butter
Cook and stir over low heat
until you obtain a thick mush.
Cool. Beat in:
    2 beaten egg yolks
Beat until stiff, then fold in:
    2 egg whites
Drop the batter from a teaspoon
onto a hot buttered pan. Bake
the puffs for about 20 minutes.

CORN MEAL CRACKLES

[About 20]
Preheat oven to 350°.
Combine and stir well:
    1 cup yellow corn meal
    ½ cup sifted all-purpose
        flour
    ¼ teaspoon salt
    ¼ teaspoon soda
    ⅛ teaspoon paprika
    2 tablespoons bacon fat,
        oil or other shortening
    ⅓ cup milk
Knead the dough for about 10
minutes. Roll it into 1-inch balls,
flatten them well by rolling
them or slapping them between
the palms of your hands, Mexi-
can-tortilla fashion. They should
be paper thin. Bake on an ungreased sheet for about 15 minutes. While hot, brush with:
    1 tablespoon butter
Sprinkle with:
    Salt
Cool on a rack.

CORN DODGERS

[About 24]
Preheat oven to 400°.

Combine:

> 1 cup water-ground corn
> meal
> 1 teaspoon salt
> 1½ teaspoons sugar
> 1 to 2 tablespoons butter or
> bacon drippings

Pour over the dry ingredients and stir:

> 1 cup boiling water

Beat in:

> (1 beaten egg)

Beat until blended. Drop the batter from a spoon onto a greased sheet or dip your hand in cold water, fill it with batter and reverse the hand, releasing the batter "splat" on the sheet. The hand method was learned from our Sarah, who, as a child, helped her father make dodgers at the Kentucky Derby. Bake for about 20 minutes.

CRUSTY OR   [4]
SOFT-CENTER SPOON
BREAD

Preheat oven to 375°.
Combine, then sift:

> ½ cup yellow corn meal
> ¼ cup all-purpose flour
> 1 tablespoon sugar
> ¾ teaspoon salt
> 1 teaspoon double-acting
> baking powder

Stir in:

> 1 beaten egg
> 1 cup milk

Beat until well blended. Melt in an 8 x 8-inch baking dish:

> 2 tablespoons butter

Pour in the batter. Pour over the top:

> ½ cup milk

Place in the oven. Bake for 45 minutes or more, until good and crusty.

CORN OR RICE   [6]
SPOON BREAD

In Italy, bits of cooked ham and cooked seafood are added to the batter, which is baked until very crisp.

Preheat oven to 325°.
Combine in the order given, then stir until blended:

> 1 cup boiled rice or boiled
> corn meal
> ¼ cup corn meal
> 2 cups buttermilk
> ½ teaspoon soda
> 1 teaspoon salt
> 2 beaten eggs
> 2 tablespoons melted fat or
> butter

Place the batter in a greased ovenproof dish. Bake for about 1 hour. This is good with a meat course or served as a main dish with:

> Mushroom Sauce
> (I, 367), or Tomatoes
> Provençale (I, 333)

HUSH PUPPIES

[About Twelve 2½-Inch Puppies]

Fishermen cooked these finger-shaped concoctions at their fish fries. Rumor has it that they threw the fatty bits as a sop to the dogs with the exclamation, "Hush, puppy!" Maybe this is still the best use for them.
Mix together:

> 1 cup water-ground corn
> meal
> ½ teaspoon double-acting
> baking powder
> ½ teaspoon salt
> 2 tablespoons minced onion

Beat together:

> 1 egg
> ¼ cup milk

Combine with dry ingredients and form finger-shaped patties. Deep fry, see (I, 75), at 370° until golden brown. Drain on absorbent paper and serve at once.

ABOUT MUFFINS

Muffin batters are easily made. ◗ To mix, add the beaten liquid ingredients to the sifted, combined dry ones in a few swift strokes. ◗ The mixing is held to an absolute minimum, a light stirring of from 10 to 20 seconds, which will leave some lumps. Ignore them. The dough should not be mixed to the point of pouring, ribbonlike, from the spoon, but should break in coarse globs. If the batter has been beaten too long, the gluten in the flour will develop and toughen the dough. The grain of the muffin will be coarse and full of tunnels, as shown in the drawing on the right.

Good muffins should be straight-sided and slightly rounded on top, as shown on the left. The grain of the muffin is not fine but uniform and the crumb is moist. The center drawings show, first, the weary muffin peak caused by oven heat that is too slow. The next drawing shows the cracked, wobbly-peaked, unsymmetrical form caused by oven heat that is too high.

To bake, fill well-greased tins about ⅔ full. Should the dough not fill every muffin cup, put a few tablespoons of water in the empty forms, both to protect the pans and to keep the rest of the muffins moist. Unless a different indication is given in the individual recipe ♦ bake at once in a preheated 400° oven for 20 to 25 minutes. ♦ If muffins remain in the tins a few moments after leaving the oven, they will be easier to remove. They are really best eaten at once. If you must reheat them, enclose them loosely in foil and heat about 5 minutes in a preheated 450° oven.

ADDITIONS TO MUFFINS

Muffins may be enriched by these additions, but have them all ready and beat them in so that the total beating time agrees exactly with the one described above.

I.
¼ to ½ cup nuts, riced apricots, prunes, dates, figs, alone or in combination
½ cup mashed ripe bananas or chopped apples
½ cup very well drained crushed pineapple
6 to 8 slices cooked, crumbled bacon

II.
2 tablespoons milk solids, replacing 2 tablespoons flour

III.
2 teaspoons brewer's yeast

MUFFINS

[About 2 Dozen 2-Inch Muffins]
Preheat oven to 400°.
♦ Have all ingredients at about 75°.
Sift before measuring:
2 cups cake flour or 1¾ cups all-purpose flour
Resift with:
¾ teaspoon salt
¼ cup sugar
2 teaspoons double-acting baking powder
Beat in a separate bowl:
2 eggs
Combine and add:
2 to 4 tablespoons melted butter
¾ cup milk
♦ To mix and bake, see About Muffins, page 279.

SOUR CREAM MUFFINS

[About 2 Dozen 2-Inch Muffins]

Preheat oven to 400°.
▶ Have all ingredients at about 75°.
Sift before measuring:

> 2 cups cake flour or 1¾ cups all-purpose flour

Resift with:

> 1 teaspoon double-acting baking powder
> ½ teaspoon salt
> 2 tablespoons sugar
> ½ teaspoon soda

Measure:

> 1 cup cultured sour cream

Combine with:

> 1 beaten egg

▶ To mix and bake, see About Muffins, page 279.

BUTTERMILK MUFFINS

Prepare:

> Sour Cream Muffins, above

Substitute for the sour cream:

> 1 cup buttermilk

Add to the milk:

> 3 tablespoons melted butter

WHOLE-GRAIN MUFFINS

[Twenty 2-Inch Muffins]
Preheat oven to 400°.
▶ Have all ingredients at about 75°.
Combine:

> ⅔ cup sifted all-purpose flour
> 1⅓ cups whole-grain flour
> 2 tablespoons molasses
> 1 teaspoon salt
> 2 teapoons double-acting baking powder
> (¼ cup chopped dates or raisins)

You may omit the all-purpose flour and use instead 1½ cups whole-grain flour. Beat in a separate bowl:

> (1 egg)

Beat in:

> 1 cup milk
> 2 to 3 teaspoons melted butter

▶ To mix and bake, see About Muffins, page 279.

EGGLESS GRAHAM MUFFINS

[Twenty 2-Inch Muffins]
Preheat oven to 400°.
▶ Have all ingredients at about 75°.
Sift before measuring:

> 1 cup all-purpose flour

Resift with:

> ¼ cup sugar
> ½ teaspoon salt
> 1 teaspoon soda
> ¾ teaspoon double-acting baking powder

Add:

> 1½ cups graham flour

In a separate bowl beat:

> (2 eggs)

The eggs are optional. They add richness and flavor, but the muffins are crisp and good without them. Add and beat in:

> 3 tablespoons melted butter
> 1½ cups buttermilk or yogurt

Combine the liquid and the dry ingredients with a few swift strokes. ▶ To mix and bake, see About Muffins, page 279.

BRAN MUFFINS

[About Twenty-Two 2-Inch Muffins]
These muffins are rather hefty. Served with cheese, they make excellent picnic companions.
Preheat oven to 350°.
▶ Have all ingredients at about 75°.
Combine and stir well:

> 2 cups all-purpose or whole-grain flour
> 1½ cups bran
> 2 tablespoons sugar
> ¼ teaspoon salt
> 1¼ teaspoons soda
> (1 to 2 tablespoons grated orange rind)

Beat:

> 2 cups buttermilk
> 1 beaten egg
> ½ cup molasses
> 2 to 4 tablespoons melted butter

Combine the dry and the liquid ingredients with a few swift strokes. Fold in, before the dry ingredients are entirely moist:

> 1 cup nut meats or nut meats and raisins combined
>
> (½ cup mashed bananas)

Bake about 25 minutes.

RICE FLOUR MUFFINS

[About Two Dozen 2-Inch Muffins]

As these muffins need special handling, please read ♦ About Rice Flour, page 157, and About Muffins, page 279.

Preheat oven to 450°.

♦ Have all ingredients at about 75°.

Measure into a bowl:

> 1 cup rice flour
> ½ teaspoon salt
> 2 teaspoons double-acting baking powder
> (1 to 2 tablespoons sugar)

Melt:

> 2 tablespoons shortening

and, when slightly cooled, add it to:

> 1 well-beaten egg
> 1 cup milk

Mix the dry ingredients well and then with a few light strokes combine with the liquid mixture. About 10 strokes are all that is necessary. The muffins are less crumbly if you add to them, before the dry ingredients are completely moistened:

> ⅛ cup raisins or 2 table-spoons orange or pineapple marmalade

If you add the marmalade, omit the sugar. Bake 12 to 15 minutes and serve at once.

COOKED-CEREAL MUFFINS

[About Thirty 2-Inch Muffins]

A good way of utilizing leftover cereals or rice.

Preheat oven to 400°.

Beat:

> 2 egg yolks

Add:

> 1 cup cooked rice, oatmeal or cornmeal
> 1¼ cups milk
> 2 tablespoons melted butter

Sift before measuring:

> 1½ cups all-purpose flour

Resift with:

> 1 tablespoon sugar
> ½ teaspoon salt
> 2 teaspoons double-acting baking powder

Beat until stiff:

> 2 egg whites

Combine the liquid and the dry ingredients with a few swift strokes, then fold in the egg whites. To bake, see About Muffins, page 279.

CHEESE MUFFINS

[About Thirty-Two 2-Inch Muffins]

Preheat oven to 350°.

♦ Have all ingredients at about 75°.

Sift before measuring:

> 2 cups cake flour or 1¾ cups all-purpose flour

Resift with:

> 3 teaspoons double-acting baking powder
> 1 tablespoon sugar
> ½ teaspoon salt

Stir into the sifted ingredients, until all the particles of cheese have been separated:

> ¼ to ½ cup grated American cheese

Combine and beat well:

> 1 egg
> 1 cup milk
> 3 tablespoons melted butter

♦ To mix and bake, see About Muffins, page 279.

BLUEBERRY OR CRANBERRY MUFFINS

[About Thirty 2-Inch Muffins]

Preheat oven to 400°.

♦ Have all ingredients at about 75°.

Prepare:

Muffins, page 280

Use in all:

⅓ cup sugar

¼ cup melted butter

Fold into the batter, before the dry ingredients are completely moist:

1 cup fresh blueberries, 1 cup canned, well-drained blueberries, lightly floured or 1 cup chopped cranberries

(1 teaspoon grated orange or lemon rind)

▶ To mix and bake, see About Muffins, page 279.

POPOVERS

[About 9 Popovers]

Everyone enthusiastically gives us a favorite popover recipe and is equally enthusiastic, but contradictory, about baking advice. We prefer a preheated 450° oven. Popovers, like soufflés, need bottom heat only, so be sure ▶ if your oven is the type that supplies top heat when set on Bake, to remove the upper heating element. Have ready buttered deep muffin or popover tins. If you use highly glazed deep custard cups, grease them lightly and—depending on what you are serving with the popovers—dust the cups with sugar, flour or grated Parmesan cheese. This will give the egg something to cling to. ▶ Have all ingredients at about 75°.

Beat just until smooth:

1 cup milk

1 tablespoon melted butter

1 cup all-purpose flour

¼ teaspoon salt

Add, one at a time, but ▶ do not overbeat:

2 eggs

The batter should be no heavier than whipping cream. Fill the buttered deep bakers ¾ full. Don't overload—too much batter in the pans will give a muffinlike texture. ▶ Bake at once. After 15 minutes, lower the heat ▶ without peeping, to 350° and bake about 20 minutes longer. To test for doneness, remove a popover to be sure the side walls are firm. If not cooked long enough, the popovers will collapse. You may want to insert a sharp paring knife gently into the other popovers to allow the steam to escape, after baking.

WHOLE-GRAIN POPOVERS

Prepare:

Popovers, above

Substitute for the flour:

⅔ cup fine whole-grain flour

⅓ cup all-purpose flour

CHEESE POPOVERS

Preheat oven to 450°.

Prepare:

Popovers, above

Grate into a separate bowl:

½ cup sharp cheddar or Parmesan cheese

Add:

⅛ teaspoon paprika

A few grains cayenne

Pour 1 scant tablespoon of batter into each cup and cover it with a few teaspoons of cheese and another tablespoon of batter. To bake, see Popovers, page 283.

ABOUT HOT BISCUITS

Now, as in pioneer times, biscuits are popular for the speed with which they can be made. A light hand in kneading gives the treasured flaky result. The amount of liquid called for in the recipe determines if the biscuit is a rolled or dropped type. ▶ Use shortening and liquids at a temperature of about 70°. The solid shortening, preferably part lard, is ▶ cut into the dry ingredients with a pastry blender or 2 knives, until the mixture is of the consistency of coarse corn meal. Make a well in the center of these ingredients. ◗ Pour all the milk or milk and water in, at once. Stir cautiously until there is no danger of spilling, then stir vigorously until the dough is fairly free from the sides of the bowl. The time for stirring should be a scant ½ minute. Turn the dough onto a lightly floured board. ◗ Knead the dough gently and quickly for another scant ½ minute—just long enough so the dough is neither knobby nor sticky and until the riser is well distributed. If it isn't, or if soda is used in excess, tiny brown spots will show on the surface of the baked biscuits. Roll the dough with a lightly floured rolling pin or pat it gently with the palm of the hand until it has the desired thickness—about ¼ inch is right for a plain biscuit, ½ inch or less for a tea biscuit and 1 inch or more for shortcake. Cut the dough in typical rounds, with a biscuit cutter that has been lightly dipped in flour. Do not twist the cutter.

There are many ways to shape biscuit dough. For easy filled biscuits, pat 2 thin squares of dough. Put a filling on the first. Cover with the second. Glaze the top with milk. Cut into smaller squares. For a breakfast ring, see Quick Drop Biscuits, page 285. Make for the children Biscuit Easter Bunnies, page 286. You may also place small rounds of dough on top of a casserole, cut dough in sticks for hors d'oeuvre or fill as for Pin Wheels, page 256. Use a spatula to place these on an ungreased baking sheet.

For a brown finish, brush the tops of the biscuits with milk or butter. Place biscuits 1 inch apart if you like them crusty all over, close together if not. Bake in a ◗ 450° preheated oven for about 12 to 15 minutes, depend-

ing on their thickness. To reheat, see page 253.

▲ At high altitude, baking powder biscuits should require no adjustment in leavening.

ADDITIONS TO BISCUITS

Biscuit flavors are easily varied to suit the menu. Dust them, before baking, with:

> Cinnamon and sugar

or, just before they are finished, with:

> Grated Parmesan and
> paprika

Or, press into the top center:

> 1 lump sugar

soaked in:

> Orange juice

Or incorporate into the dough:

> 2 tablespoons finely
> chopped parsley or chives
> or 2 teaspoons finely
> chopped fresh sage or ⅓
> cup Roquefort or cheddar
> cheese
> 3 to 6 slices cooked,
> crumbled bacon or 3
> tablespoons chopped
> cooked ham or 4
> tablespoons sautéed
> chopped onions

Prepare them like rissoles, placing between the layers either of the following:

> 1 cup fresh, sugared straw-
> berries, raspberries or
> blueberries
> ¼ cup nuts, dates or figs
> ½ cup raisins or currants
> 1 cup cooked, ground and
> seasoned meat, poultry,
> sausage or ham

ROLLED BISCUITS

[About Twenty-Four 1½-Inch Biscuits]
◗ Please read About Hot Biscuits, page 283.
Preheat oven to 450°.
Sift before measuring:

> 2 cups cake flour or 1¾
> cups all-purpose or
> whole-wheat flour

Resift the cake flour, or mix the whole-wheat flour in a bowl with:

> 1 teaspoon salt
> 2½ teaspoons double-acting baking powder

Add:

> 2 to 6 tablespoons chilled butter or shortening or a combination of both

Cut solid shortening into dry ingredients with a pastry blender until the mixture is of the consistency of coarse corn meal. Make a well in the center of these ingredients. Add, all at once:

> ⅔ to ¾ cup milk

Stir until the dough is fairly free from the sides of the bowl. The time for stirring should be a scant ½ minute. Turn the dough onto a lightly floured board. Knead gently and quickly for a scant ½ minute, making about 8 to 10 folds. Roll with a lightly floured rolling pin until the dough has the desired thickness. Cut with a biscuit cutter dipped in a very little flour. ♦ Cut straight down with the cutter and be careful not to twist it. Brush the tops of the biscuits with:

> (Milk or melted butter)

Place on an ungreased baking sheet. Bake until done—12 to 15 minutes.

QUICK DROP BISCUITS

No kneading or rolling is necessary in these recipes. The biscuits are very palatable but less shapely, unless you drop them into muffin tins. For a good breakfast ring, bake the Drop Biscuit I, below, at 400° for about 25 minutes. Form the dough into 12 balls, roll them in melted butter. Bake them in a 7-inch ring mold, into the bottom of which you have poured Caramel Roll Topping, page 433.

I. Preheat oven to 450°.
Prepare:

> Rolled Biscuits, page 284

using in all:

> 1 cup milk

♦ Stir the dough for 1 scant minute. Drop onto an ungreased sheet and bake 12 to 15 minutes or until lightly browned.

II. [About Twenty-Four 1½-Inch Biscuits]

If, for some reason, you must use oil, it is preferable to flavor the biscuit highly. See Additions to Biscuits, page 284.
Preheat oven to 475°.
Sift into a bowl:

> 2 cups sifted all-purpose flour
> 3 teaspoons double-acting baking powder
> 1 teaspoon salt

Pour over the top, all at once, without mixing:

> ⅓ cup cooking oil
> ⅔ cup milk

Stir with a fork until the mixture leaves the sides of the bowl readily and can be formed into a ball. It may now be dropped from a spoon onto an ungreased sheet. Bake for about 10 to 12 minutes.

BISCUIT STICKS

Prepare any recipe for:

> Rolled biscuit dough

Cut it into sticks ½ inch thick, ½ inch wide, 3 inches long. Brush the sticks with:

> Melted butter

Bake them and stack them log-cabin fashion.

BUTTERMILK BISCUITS

[About Twenty-Four 1½-Inch Biscuits]

This recipe, because of the sour milk and soda, has a very tender dough. ♦ To mix, please read About Hot Biscuits, page 283.
Preheat oven to 450°
Sift before measuring:

2 cups cake flour or 1¾
cups all-purpose flour
1 teaspoon salt
2 teaspoons double-acting
baking powder
1 teaspoon sugar
½ teaspoon soda
Cut in:
¼ cup lard or 5 tablespoons
butter
Add, as directed:
⅔ to ¾ cup buttermilk
After lightly mixing, turn the
dough onto a floured board.
Knead it lightly for ½ minute.
Pat the dough to the thickness
of ¼ inch. Cut with a biscuit
cutter. Bake from 10 to 12
minutes.

WHIPPED CREAM
BISCUITS

[About Eighteen 2-Inch
Biscuits]
Preheat oven to 450°.
Sift before measuring:
2 cups all-purpose flour
Resift with:
2¼ teaspoons double-acting
baking powder
¾ teaspoon salt
Whip until stiff:
1 cup whipping cream
Fold lightly into the flour mix-
ture, using a fork. Turn the
dough onto a floured board.
Knead it lightly for ½ minute.
Pat to the thickness of ¼ inch.
Cut with a biscuit cutter. Bake
from 10 to 12 minutes.

FLUFFY BISCUITS OR
SHORTCAKE DOUGH

[About Twenty-Four 1½-Inch
Biscuits]
For other shortcakes, see Index.
▶ To mix, see About Hot Bis-
cuits, page 283.
Preheat oven to 450°.
Sift before measuring:
2 cups cake flour or 1¾
cups all-purpose flour
Resift with:

2½ teaspoons double-acting
baking powder
1¼ teaspoons salt
1 tablespoon sugar
Cut in, as directed:
⅛ to ¼ cup butter
Add:
¼ cup milk or cream
Stir lightly into the flour mixture, using a fork. Turn dough
onto a floured board. Knead
lightly for ½ minutes. Pat to the
thickness of ¼ inch. Cut with a
biscuit cutter. Bake for 10 to
12 minutes.

PINEAPPLE BISCUITS

Preheat oven to 450°.
Prepare:
Fluffy Biscuits, above
Use part rich milk and part:
Canned pineapple juice
Dent the top of each biscuit.
Fill the depression with:
Drained, canned, crushed
pineapple
Sprinkle lightly with:
Confectioners' sugar
Bake for 15 or 20 minutes.

PINWHEEL BISCUITS

Use this same form also for
other fillings such as meat or
cheese.
Preheat oven to 450°.
Prepare any:
Rolled biscuit dough
Roll it to the thickness of ½
inch. Spread the surface with:
¼ cup soft butter
¾ cup brown sugar
(Chopped nuts)
(Chopped raisins)
Roll the dough like a jelly roll,
but rather loosely. Cut into
1-inch slices. Lift them carefully
with a pancake turner onto a
lightly greased cookie sheet.
Bake about 12 minutes.

BISCUIT EASTER BUNNIES

Preheat oven to 425°.
Prepare:

Fluffy Biscuits, page 584

Pat or roll out the dough to the thickness of ½ inch. Cut it out with 3 sizes of cutters: 1—large, about 3 inches; 2—½ as large, and 3—¼ as large. Assemble your bunnies as sketched below. Use the large biscuit for the body, the second one for the head and roll the third one into a ball for the tail. Flatten some of the second-size biscuits slightly and shape them into ovals for the ears. Place the bunnies on a greased sheet. Bake for about 15 minutes or until done.

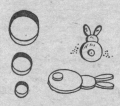

▤ GRIDDLE BISCUITS

Prepare:

Biscuit Dough, page 284

Bake the biscuits on a hot, lightly greased griddle, 1 inch apart. Brown them on one side for about 5 to 7 minutes, turn and brown them on the other side for the same amount of time.

BEATEN BISCUITS

[About Forty-Four 1½-Inch Biscuits]

Preheat oven to 325°.

To win interminable gratitude, serve this classic accompaniment to Virginia hams to any home-sick Southerner. The following lines by Howard Weeden in "Bandanna Ballads" sum up in a nutshell the art of making biscuits:

"Of course I'll gladly give de rule
    I meks beat biscuit by,
Dough I ain't sure dat you will mek
    Dat bread de same as I.

"'Case cookin's like religion is—
Some's 'lected an' some ain't,
An' rules don't no more mek a cook
    Den sermons mek a saint."

Sift 3 times:
    1 tablespoon sugar
    4 cups all-purpose flour
    1 teaspoon salt
    (1 teaspoon double-acting baking powder)
Cut into the flour, with a pastry blender or 2 knives:
    ¼ cup chilled leaf lard
When ingredients are of the consistency of corn meal, add to make a stiff dough:
    Equal parts of chilled milk and ice water approximately 1 cup in all
Beat the dough with a mallet until it is well blistered or put it 10 times through the coarse chopper of a meat grinder. Fold it over frequently. This is a long process, requiring ½ hour or more.

Miss Weeden's verse goes on to say:

"Two hundred licks is what I gives
    For home-folks, never fewer,
An' if I'm 'specting company in,
    I gives five hundred sure!"

If you make these often, it might be worth investing in a biscuit machine, available from a bakers' supply company. When the dough is smooth and glossy, roll it to the thickness of ½ inch and cut it with a floured biscuit cutter. Spread the tops with:

Melted butter

Pierce through the biscuits with a fork. Bake for about 30 minutes.

SHIP'S BISCUITS

[About Twenty-Four 1½-Inch Biscuits]

These are really a simpler version of Beaten Biscuits, above. The longer they are folded and beaten, the better the results, so let the children have a fling with these.

Preheat oven to 325°.

Mix:

2 cups all-purpose flour
½ teaspoon salt

Work in, with the finger tips:

1 teaspoon shortening

Stir in to make a very stiff dough:

About ½ cup water

Beat this dough to a ½ inch thinness with a mallet. Fold it into 6 layers. Beat it thin again and refold 5 or 6 times until the dough is very elastic. Before cutting with a floured biscuit cutter, roll to ½ inch again. Bake for about 30 minutes and store tightly covered.

SWEET POTATO BISCUIT

[About Twenty-Four 1½-Inch Biscuits]

Preheat oven to 450°.

Into:

¾ cup cooked mashed sweet potatoes

beat:

¼ cup melted butter

Stir in:

⅔ cup milk

Sift, then measure:

1¼ cups all-purpose flour

Resift with:

4 teaspoons double-acting baking powder
1 tablespoon sugar
1 teaspoon salt

Stir the sifted ingredients into the sweet potato mixture. Turn the dough out on a floured board and toss it lightly until smooth on the outside. Roll or pat it to the thickness of ½ inch and cut with a floured biscuit cutter. Bake on a greased pan for about 15 minutes.

SCONES

[About 12 Scones]

These are richer than ordinary biscuit because of the addition of cream and eggs. Fine with a light luncheon.

Preheat oven to 450°.

Sift:

2 cups sifted cake flour or 1¾ cups sifted all-purpose flour
2¼ teaspoons double-acting baking powder
1 tablespoon sugar
½ teaspoon salt

Cut into these ingredients, until the butter is of the size of a small pea, using a pastry blender or 2 knives:

¼ cup butter

Beat in a separate bowl:

2 eggs

Reserve 2 tablespoons of this mixture. Add to the remainder and beat:

⅓ cup cream

Make a well in the dry ingredients. Pour the liquid into it. Combine with a few swift strokes. Handle the dough as little as possible. Place it on a lightly floured board. Pat until ¾ inch thick. Cut with a knife into diamond shapes or Biscuit Sticks, page 285. Brush with the reserved egg and sprinkle with:

Salt or sugar

Bake for about 15 minutes.

ABOUT USES FOR READY-BAKED AND LEFTOVER BREADS, CAKES AND CRACKERS

An involuntary feeling of guilt sweeps over everyone who

wastes food, especially the bread that so often accumulates. There are many ways to convert these bits and pieces into attractive assets.

A bread surplus can be put to many good uses—so don't throw a piece away! It can be used for Melba Toast, page 290, Bread Pudding, page 460, Bread Sauce (I, 364); and it can become a thickener for soups and gravies—see Panada, below.

Many recipes in "The Joy" call for dry bread, cracker or cake crumbs. In fact, dry cake crumbs are so prized that commercial bakeries make sheets of cake solely for this purpose.

In recipes, we always specify ♦ dry, page 159, or ♦ soft, page 159, bread crumbs. Even the way they are measured is different. So, in puddings, timbales, stuffings and au gratin foods, be sure to use what is called for ♦ because the kind of bread crumbs added makes a tremendous difference in the texture of the finished product.

ABOUT PANADAS

These are thickeners made of leftover breads or based on flour, potato and rice. If used as thickeners, see Quenelles (I, 180), and Farces (I, 560), or Thickeners for Soups (I, 108); as a soup, see (I, 123); as a sauce, see (I, 364).

TOASTED BUTTERED BREAD LOAF OR GARLIC BREAD

Preheat oven to 350°.
Cut into very thin slices:
      A medium-size loaf of
         bread or French bread
Do not slice it all the way through; leave the bottom crust undisturbed. Spread the bread with:
      ½ cup melted butter
The butter may be flavored with

garlic and/or your favorite herb. You may also crush 2 cloves of garlic with a little salt, until smooth. Spread a little on each slice. Follow up with a melted butter, as shown below. Separate the slices slightly, so that the butter will be evenly distributed. Cover the loaf with a piece of foil. Place it in the

oven until the bread is light brown, for about 20 minutes. Remove from the oven, place on a platter and permit the guests to serve themselves.

CINNAMON LOAF

Slice a loaf of:
      French or Vienna bread
and spread it, as illustrated above, with the following mixture, baking 8 minutes:
      ⅓ cup melted butter
      ⅓ cup sugar
      2 teaspoons cinnamon
         A grating of nutmeg
      ¼ teaspoon grated lemon
         peel

CINNAMON TOAST OR STICKS

Remove the crusts from bread. Spread the tops of:
      Thin bread slices
or spread all 4 sides of:
      ¾-inch bread sticks
with a mixture of:
      3 tablespoons softened
         butter
      5 tablespoons
         confectioners' or light
         brown sugar

1 to 1½ teaspoons
   cinnamon or a
   combination of 1
   teaspoon cinnamon and
   freshly grated nutmeg

You may sprinkle the bread sticks with:

   (Rum)

Place the slices or strips in a 400° oven for about 8 minutes. Be sure to toast the sticks on all sides. You may also place them under a broiler to crisp them. Applesauce is a good complement to this dish.

FRENCH TOAST

Beat slightly:
   4 eggs
Add:
   ½ teaspoon salt
   1 cup milk
Flavor with:
   (½ teaspoon vanilla or
   1 tablespoon rum)
Dip into this mixture:
   8 slices bread
The bread may be cut in rounds with a doughnut cutter. Brown the bread on each side on a well-buttered hot griddle. Serve hot, sprinkled with:
   Sugar
   Cinnamon
Garnish the cooked rounds with:
   Bright red jelly
or serve with pie cherries, sweetened, slightly thickened and flavored with lemon, with applesauce flavored with cinnamon and cloves or with maple sirup.

MELBA TOAST

Cut into the thinnest possible slices:
   White or other bread
Remove crusts. Place bread in an oven that is at about 250°. Leave it in until it becomes crisp and a light golden brown and until all the moisture is withdrawn.

HONEY BUTTER TOAST

Prepare:
   Honey Butter, page 480
Spread it on a slice of bread. Cover it with another slice. Cut the bread into 1-inch strips. Toast the strips on both sides under a broiler. Serve sprinkled with:
   Cinnamon

ORANGE TOAST

Good with tea.
Combine:
   Grated rind of 1 orange
   ¼ cup orange juice
   ½ cup sugar
Cut:
   6 slices of bread
Remove the crusts and toast the bread. Spread it, while hot, with:
   Butter
Cover it with the orange mixture. Put the toast in the oven or under a broiler, just long enough to brown the tops lightly.

ZWIEBACK OR
TWICE-BAKED BREAD

Bake:
   White Bread Plus, page
   244
using in all 2 eggs. Replace the 2 cups of water with 2 cups of milk. The finished loaf should be just half as high as a normal slice of bread, so bake in six, rather than in three, pans. Maybe this shape was evolved to suit baby mouths, for no one enjoys this confection more than the very, very young. When the bread is cool, cut it in ½-inch slices and toast as for Melba Toast. You may want to glaze it before toasting with:
   Lemon Topping for
   Cookies or Bars, page
   434
In the slow heat of the oven, this turns a golden brown.

BIRTHDAY BREAD HORSE

As our children have always demanded a piece of their birthday cake for breakfast, we concocted a bread horse to be supplemented later in the day by the candle-lighted birthday cake of richer content. This also makes a good Christmas or Fourth of July breakfast decoration.

You will need a well-rounded loaf of bread—a log-shaped cinnamon roll is fine—an oval bun or roll, about 2½ x 3½ inches, 2 braided rolls about 1 x 3½ inches, 5 peppermint candy sticks 1 x 8 inches, 2 raisins, 2 almonds and a piece of cherry or a redhot. Use the loaf for the body. Mount it on 4 of the candy sticks. Break off about ⅓ or less of the fifth candy stick. Use it for the neck. Stick it into one end of the loaf at an angle. Put the oval roll on the other end for the head. Use the braided rolls for the mane and tail, the raisins for eyes, the almonds for ears and the piece of cherry for the lips. Bed the horse on leaves or grass. Add ribbon bridle, if you care to.

PIES, PASTES AND FILLED PASTRIES

At home and abroad, Americans boast about pie. It has apparently always been so. Way back in the clipper era, sailors brought home, not only heart-shaped boxes crusted over with tiny rare shells, but the pie-jaggers they had carved to while away the doldrum days in outre-mer. These implements of bone, often furnished with as many as three wheels, but marvelously precise all the same, sped the fancy cutting of lattice in many a New England cottage. Whatever the nation, skill in pastry making has been regarded as a worldwide passport to matrimony. In Hungarian villages, for example, no girl was considered eligible until her strudel dough had become so translucent that her beloved could read the newspaper through it.

Let's consider what makes for success, whether your objective be pie, strudel, puff paste, Muerbeteig or poppadums:

♦ Have all ingredients, to begin with, at about 70°.

♦ Handle your dough lightly, for two reasons: to incorporate as much air as possible and to inhibit the development of gluten. The aim here is a flaky and tender crust.

♦ Avoid too much flour, which toughens pastry.

♦ Avoid too much liquid, which makes it soggy.

▲ In making pies at high altitudes, you may find the greater evaporation will mean that you have better results if you add a trifle more liquid.

♦ Avoid too much shortening, which makes doughs greasy and crumbly.

♦ Chilling pastry dough after mixing tenderizes it, keeps it from shrinking during baking and makes it easier to handle. We recommend refrigerating it, covered, for 12 hours or more. Be sure to remove the dough from the refrigerator at least one hour before shaping, otherwise you will be obliged to over handle it. Pinch off just enough dough for one pie shell. Press it into the approximate shape needed. Roll as lightly and as little as possible, using the directions in the illustration below. Pie dough will hold for a week or more in the refrigerator.

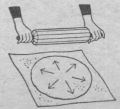

▶ Choose non-shiny pie pans for good browning.

▶ Always start the baking in a very hot oven, preheated to the temperature indicated. The contrast between the coolness of the dough and the heat of the oven causes rapid air expansion and contributes to the desired lightness of texture. Everyone has a favorite recipe for pie dough. But our own basic one made with lard we find especially satisfactory. Many pie doughs ✻ freeze well. ▶ It is better to shape them before freezing. See Frozen Baked Pie, page 568, Frozen Unbaked Pie, page 568.

ABOUT BASIC PIE DOUGH

For a one-crust, 9-inch pie, use ½ the recipe below. For a double-crust, 9-inch, or a single-crust pie with a generous lattice, use the following:
Sift, then measure:
      2 cups all-purpose flour
Resift it with:
      1 teaspoon salt
Measure and combine:
      ⅓ cup 70° leaf lard or
         shortening
      ⅓ cup chilled butter
or use in all ⅔ cup shortening. Cut ½ of the shortening into the flour mixture with a pastry blender, see page 292, or work it in lightly with the tips of your fingers until it has the grain of cornmeal. Cut the remaining half coarsely into the dough until it is pea size. Sprinkle the dough with:
      5 tablespoons water
▶ Blend the water lightly into the dough. You may lift the ingredients with a fork, allowing the moisture to spread. If needed, add ▶ just enough water to hold ingredients together. When you can gather the dough up into a tidy ball, as shown on page 292, stop handling it.

ABOUT ROLLING PIE DOUGH

▶ To make 2 pie shells, divide the dough evenly before rolling it. To make a double crust pie, divide the dough into 2 slightly uneven parts, keeping the smaller one for the top. ▶ A pastry cloth and roller stocking are highly recommended. They practically do away with sticking and require the use of very little additional flour. Rolling the dough between 2 sheets of foil or wax paper, although more difficult, also avoids adding unwanted flour. When ready, remove the top paper, reverse the crust into pan and then remove the other paper.

If you use neither of the above methods, flour the rolling surface and the rolling pin lightly. As to the roller, whether it's a French broomstick-type or a bottle, the important thing is how you use it. ▶ Roll the dough from the center out. Lift the roller. Do not push it to and fro, stretching the dough. Roll the dough to at least a ⅛-inch thickness or less. Should it have a few tears, patch them carefully rather than trying to reroll.

ABOUT CUTTING AND FORMING PIE DOUGH

▶ To cut pie dough, allow a piece about 2 inches larger than the pan dimensions, as shown on page 293, to take care of inevitable shrinkage. It is fun to cut fancy edges with a pastry wheel.

▶ To form the crust, have ready a 9-inch pie pan. It's a poor pie crust that requires a greased pan, but buttering will help brown the bottom of the crust. Loosen the pastry from the board, fold it in half, lift it, lay the fold across the center of the pan and unfold it; or, after rolling it around the rolling pin, unroll it onto the pan. See page 293, where this method is being used to form a top crust.

Ease the dough into the pan loosely, but firm it in place so that no air will be left between dough and pan to form blisters in baking. You may cut a small square of dough, form it into a ball, dip it in flour and use it to press the dough down and shape it against the pan. Trim off the excess with a knife, using an easy slashing motion against the edge of the pan; or use scissors. Trimmings can be given to the children for play dough or baked up into bits for hors d'oeuvre or small pastries.

ABOUT FILLED PIES

▶ For filled pies, use a deep pie pan with a wide channeled rim to catch any juices. For a one-crust pie, make a fluted edge with the dough that laps over, or build up a rim with a strip of pastry. Full it on. Use a fork to press it down or pinch it with the thumb and forefinger, as shown below on the left. This edge is important, as it will help to hold the juices in the pie. Do not prick the lower crust. If the filling for the pie is to be juicy, first brush the bottom crust lightly with the white of an egg, melted butter or a solution of gum arabic. Any of these will keep the crust from becoming soggy. Putting the filling in very hot helps, too.

There are many attractive ways to make the lattice. You may cut plain ½-inch strips with a knife or pink them with a jagger. Or you may roll, then twist ½-inch rope-like pieces and weave any of these together or place them crisscross.

To weave, place ½ the strips from left to right over the pie about ¾ inch apart. Fold back every other strip half-way, as shown below, at right. Place a strip across the unfolded strips from front to back. Unfold the strips. Fold back the alternates. Place the next strip ¾ inch from the last. Continue until ½ the pie is latticed. Then, repeat the process, beginning on the other side of the center line.

When the whole pie is latticed, attach the strips to the

pie edge loosely to allow for shrinkage. Moisten the ends slightly to make them stick. Cut them off before crimping the pie.

For a solid top crust, cut the rolled ⅛-inch-thick dough 1 inch larger than the pan. To allow the steam to escape, prick it with a fork in several places, double it over and gash it along the fold or make fancy patterns with whatever cutting tool you like. Place the top crust on the pie. Full in the surplus dough and press it down around the edges with a fork. Or you may tuck it under the lower crust and press it around the edge with a fork, or cut the lower crust ½ inch larger than the upper crust and fold it over like a hem. ◗ Allow 4 cups of filling for a 9-inch pie and 3 cups for a 7-inch pie. If you prefer, after sealing the edges by pressing with a fork, you may make a vent with a one-inch hollow tube of dough—3 inches high— only partially sunk into a hole in the center of the upper crust. Support it with a round border of fulled on dough which will hide any discoloration from juices bubbling over when you cut the vent down to the decorative support after the baking. Should any juice spill over onto the oven, sprinkle it with salt to prevent smoke and smell.

Be sure to thicken acid fruits with tapioca, cornstarch or arrowroot as suggested in the recipes, because the acidity of the fruit may neutralize the thickening power of the flour.

ABOUT UNFILLED PIE SHELLS

◗ If the pie shell is to be baked unfilled, ◗ prick the dough generously with a fork after you have placed it in the pie pan, or weight the bottom of the shell

with dry rice, beans, or, as they do in France, with small clean round pebbles. This keeps it from heaving and baking unevenly. Remove the beans or pebbles a few minutes before the oven period is over. To cut a round for a prebaked top crust, prick it and bake it on a baking sheet.

When making individual pies, use an inverted muffin tin or, for deeper shells, inverted custard cups. Cut the rounds of dough 4½ or 5½ inches in diameter and fit them over the cups or, with the help of foil as a support, create your own fancy shapes—fluted cups, simple tricornes, long barquettes. You may even make your tarts into baskets by forming handles with strips of dough molded over inverted custard cups. When baked, sink the handles into the filling just before serving. ◗ Prick shells before baking. When you fill baked shells, spoon the filling in carefully.

To protect a baked crust from overbrowning when heating a filling in it, put the pie, still in its pan, into an extra pan to keep it from too much heat.

◗ To glaze pie crust, choose one of the many glazes which add either flavor or color to your pie, see pages 432–435—but they also tend to toughen crusts.

◗ Baking time will vary according to the material of which the pan is made. If it is ovenproof glass or enamelware, cut the baking time indicated by ⅛ to ¼. When tins are used, those that are perforated, have lost their shininess or have a base of screen material are helpful for producing a well-browned crust.

◗ It is essential that the oven be preheated to the temperatures indicated in the recipes. For meringue pies, please turn to pages 309, 431. For baking filled pies, note directions in each recipe. Unbaked shells, whether for individual or big pies, are baked in a preheated oven 450° for about 12 minutes or until lightly browned.

FLOUR PASTE PIE CRUST

[A 9-Inch Double-Crust]
Preheat oven to 450°.
Sift, then measure:
    2 cups all-purpose flour
Resift it into a bowl with:
    1 teaspoon salt
Measure ⅓ cupful of this mixture and place it in a small bowl or cup. Stir into it, to form a smooth paste:
    ¼ cup water
Cut into the flour mixture in the first bowl, with a pastry blender, until the grain in it is the size of small peas:
    ⅔ cup 70° shortening
Stir the flour paste into the dough. Work it with your hand until it is well incorporated and the dough forms a ball.

QUICK AND EASY PIE CRUST

I. [A 9-Inch Single Crust]
Preheat oven to 425°.
Sift, then measure:
    1½ cups all-purpose flour
Resift into a bowl with:
    ½ teaspoon salt
With a pastry blender, work in:
    ½ cup 70° shortening
until the grain in the mixture is pea size. Stir in, 1 tablespoon at a time:
    3 tablespoons water
until the mixture holds together when you gather it into a ball. Pat it evenly into the pie pan. For details on lining a pan, see page 294. Bake 12 to 15 minutes. Cool before filling.

II. [Two 9-Inch Pie Shells or 8 Tarts]
Preheat oven to 425°.
The oil gives this a somewhat mealy rather than a flaky texture.
Sift into a pie pan:
    2 cups sifted all-purpose flour
    1¼ teaspoons salt
Mix in a cup until creamy:
    ⅔ cup cooking oil
    3 tablespoons cold milk
Pour the mixture over the flour all at once. Stir these ingredients lightly with a fork until blended. Form them into a crust, right in the pan, by patting out the dough with your fingers. Bake 12 to 15 minutes. Cool before filling.

HOT-WATER PIE CRUST

[A 9-Inch Double-Crust]
Hot water crust is apt to be mealy rather than flaky.
Preheat oven to 450°.
Place in a bowl:
    ¾ cup 70° lard
Pour over it:
    6 tablespoons boiling water
Beat these ingredients until they are cold and creamy. If there is time, chill them. Sift before measuring:
    2 cups cake flour
Resift with:
    ½ teaspoon any baking powder
    1 teaspoon salt
Combine the liquid and the sifted ingredients and stir until they form a smooth ball. Cover the dough and chill until firm. Roll or form and bake 8 to 10 minutes.

WHEATLESS PIE CRUST

[A 9-Inch Single-Crust]
▶ Sift 6 times:
    ½ cup cornstarch
    ½ cup finely milled rye flour
The repeated sifting is very important. Work as for pastry and add:
    ½ cup fine dry cottage cheese

½ cup 70° butter
½ teaspoon salt

Chill the dough from 2 to 12 hours. To roll, form and bake, see the illustrations on page 589.

PÂTE BRISÉE

[A 9-Inch Pie Shell]

This short French pie dough has a remarkable way of withstanding a moist filling. The recipe can be doubled or tripled and stored refrigerated for a week or more before baking. Allow:

½ cup butter plus 2 tablespoons lard

to reach 70°. ♦ Rub it very lightly into:

2 cups sifted all-purpose flour
½ teaspoon salt

This can be done best by working the flour and butter first with the fingers and then between the palms of the hands. Make a well, page 301, of the rubbed flour and butter. Pour in gradually:

5 to 6 tablespoons water

The index finger is used to stir the liquid ♦ quickly into the flour, in a spiral fashion, beginning at the inside of the well and gradually moving to the outer edge. The dough should be soft enough to gather up into a ball but should not stick to the fingers. ♦ Allow the dough to rest refrigerated from 2 to 36 hours. Cover it with a damp, wrung-out cloth for the shorter period or a piece of foil for the longer one. The resting of the dough breaks any rubbery reactions it might develop when rolled and handled. To roll, shape and bake, see page 293.

ABOUT PASTRY FOR MEATS

For meat pies, rissoles or turnovers, use any unsweetened crust. For Meat en Croûte, see (I, 458); for Pâté en Croûte (I, 525).

RICH EGG PIE CRUST, MUERBETEIG OR PÂTE SUCRÉE

[Six 3-Inch Tart Shells]

There are many versions of this paste, varying in richness and sweetness. This one makes a very tender paste for fresh fruit fillings. For a sweeter dough, use Rolled or Rich Rolled Cookie Dough, page 401. See illustration, page 301, to combine and make a well with:

1 cup flour
2 tablespoons sugar
½ teaspoon salt

Add and work with your fingers until light and creamy:

1 egg yolk
½ teaspoon vanilla
1 tablespoon lemon juice

Work into it as you would for pastry, using a pastry blender or the tips of your fingers:

6 tablespoons softened 70° butter

until the mixture forms one blended ball and no longer adheres to your fingers. Cover it and refrigerate for at least ½ hour. Roll to ⅛-inch thickness, as for pie dough, see page 293. Line the greased tart pans with this dough. Weight down with beans or pebbles, see page 295. Bake in a 400° oven 7 to 10 minutes or until lightly browned. Unmold the pastry shells and cool on a rack. Fill with fresh fruit. Glaze with:

Melted, cooled Currant or Apricot Glaze, page 434

Garnish with:
(Whipped cream)

ABOUT GALETTE DOUGH

Fifty million Frenchmen can't be wrong; but it is hard to get two of them to agree on the exact formula for this classic pastry. In some regions, galette is almost like a Kuchen dough. Perhaps the most famous is Galette des Rois, served on Twelfth Night. Regardless of the type of dough used for the "King's Galette," it has a dried bean baked in it, which is expected to bring good fortune to the guest who gets the lucky slice.

Our version of galette which, we hope, will merit majority approval, is a well-pricked Rough Puff Paste, see page 303, rolled to 1-inch thickness and coated with a heavy French Egg Wash glaze, page 433. ♦ Keep the glaze on the top surface only, for if it runs over the edge it will solidify early in the baking and prevent the dough from puffing as it should.

Another version is to use a yeast coffee cake dough. After the last rising, pat it out thin and make a rim by pinching the dough edges all around. Put the fruit in the depression and cover it with a Streusel, page 433. Bake as directed for bread. You may, as the cake cools, cover it with Apricot Glaze, page 434. A simpler and, we think, delicious solution is simply to bake Apple, Peach or Plum Cake Cockaigne, page 319.

VIENNA PASTRY

[Eight 3-Inch Tarts]
Delicious as tart shells, turnovers or thin wafers served with soup or salad. Sift before measuring:
    1 cup all-purpose flour
Resift with:
    (¼ teaspoon salt)
Cut into these ingredients with a pastry blender:
    ½ cup 70° butter
    4½ oz. soft cream cheese
When the ingredients are well blended, wrap the dough in foil

and refrigerate for at least 12 hours. When ready to use, roll to ⅛-inch thickness, using as little additional flour as possible.
I. To use as tarts, form pastry over inverted muffin tins and bake at 450° for about 12 minutes.

II. To use as turnovers, see page 54.

III. To use as wafers, roll and cut the dough into rounds or put it directly into a cookie press without rolling. Before baking, dot with sesame or poppy seed. Bake 8 to 10 minutes at 450°.

ABOUT COOKIE AND KUCHEN CRUSTS

If a sweet or spicy crust is desired, try Rolled Cookie Doughs, page 401. For a pie-like Kuchen dough, see the very good German Cherry Pie, page 313. There are many, many forms of fruit Kuchen, see Apple, Plum or Peach Cake Cockaigne, page 319, French Apple Cake, page 320, Quick Sour Cream Coffee Cake, page 275. For less sweet versions, try fruit toppings on raised coffee cake doughs, page 264 to 268.

CHEESE-CAKE CRUST

[To Line a 10-Inch Pan]
This crust works well if filled before baking with dry cheese-cake fillings such as Ricotta, page 329.
Have at about 70°:
    ½ cup butter
Work this into a crust with:
    ¼ teaspoon salt
    2 cups flour
to mix pie dough, see page 293.
Gradually add:
    1½ to 2 tablespoons cognac
Chill about half an hour before rolling to line the pan. Roll about ⅛ inch thick.

SUGGESTED ADDITIONS TO CRUSTS

Vary your favorite basic pie crust by adding, before rolling, for a double crust, one of the following:

1 tablespoon poppy or caraway seed

3 tablespoons toasted sesame seed

¼ to ½ cup chopped nuts

¼ to ⅓ cup grated aged cheese

2 tablespoons confectioners' sugar

⅛ teaspoon cinnamon or nutmeg

1 teaspoon grated citrus rind

1 tablespoon sugar

ABOUT CRUMB CRUSTS

These crusts, mixed and patted into the pan, are a shortcut to pie making. To avoid over-browning, use ▶ a shiny metal or enamel pan which will reflect heat. An easy way to form crumb crusts is to place the crumb mixture in a pie pan, distributing the crumbs fairly evenly. Now press another pie pan of the same diameter firmly into the crumbs. When the top pan is removed, presto!—a crust of even thickness underneath. Trim any excess which is forced to the top edge.

Crumb crusts need not be baked before filling ▶ but, if used unbaked, must be first chilled thoroughly or the filling will immediately disintegrate the crust. If baked before filling, they require a 300° oven for about 15 minutes. ▶ It is best to cool the empty baked shell before filling.

Fill a prebaked shell with:

A gelatin pie filling or sweetened fresh fruit

Top with:

Whipped cream

For a meringue pie, chill the unbaked shell and fill with a previously cooked and cooled:

Custard, cream or fruit filling

Cover with a Meringue, see page 309. Bake in a 300° oven for about 15 minutes.

GRAHAM CRACKER, ZWIEBACK OR GINGER SNAP CRUST

[A 9-Inch Crust and Topping]
Preheat oven to 350°.
Crush or grind fine, or put in a ⅄ blender until very fine:

1½ cups crumbs of graham crackers, zwieback, or Ginger Snaps, page 159

Stir into them until well blended:

¼ cup sifted confectioners' sugar

6 tablespoons melted butter

(1 teaspoon cinnamon)

Reserve ¼ to ½ of the crust. Pat the rest into the pan to the desired thickness. When the pie is filled, use the reserved crumbs as topping. To form the shell and bake, see About Crumb Crusts, opposite.

LUXURY CRUMB CRUST

[For a 10-Inch Torte]
Preheat oven to 350°.
Crush, blend or grind until very fine:

1½ cups crumbs of graham crackers or zwieback

Stir into them:

6 tablespoons ground unblanched almonds

6 tablespoons sugar

¼ cup light cream

½ cup melted butter

(⅓ teaspoon cinnamon)

Pat the dough into the pan. To form the shell and bake, see About Crumb Crusts, opposite.

BREAD OR CAKE CRUMB CRUST

Preheat oven to 350°.
A good way of utilizing stale

bread or cake. To be successful, this crust must be fully baked before filling. Follow the rule for Graham Cracker Crust, above. Substitute for the graham cracker or zwieback crumbs:

1½ cups toasted, sifted bread or cake crumbs

If you use cake crumbs, omit sugar. To form the shell and bake, see About Crumb Crusts, page 299.

CEREAL PIE CRUST

[A 9-Inch Crust]
Preheat oven to 350°.
Roll or grind:

6 cups flaked or puffed type breakfast cereal

There should be 1½ cups after crushing. Combine with:

½ cup melted butter
¼ cup sugar—if the cereal is not presweetened
(½ teaspoon cinnamon)

To form the shell and bake, see About Crumb Crusts, page 299.

COOKIE CRUMB CRUST

Follow the rule for Graham Cracker or Luxury Crusts, page 299. Omit sugar. Substitute for graham cracker, etc., crumbs in whole or in part:

Ginger Snaps
Vanilla Wafers
Chocolate Wafers

The flavor of your filling should determine which of the above cookies you use. Form the shell and bake as directed in About Crumb Crusts, page 299.

PUFF PASTE OR PÂTE FEUILLETÉE

Puff paste recipes usually start "Choose a bright, windy, chilly day . . ." We stand off unfavorable weather with an electric fan, but are careful not to train it on the work surface. If you ask, "What does a commercial bakery do about puff paste and the weather?"—the answer is: they use a highly emulsified, very impervious margarine. To become an amateur champion, keep in mind first and foremost that this most delicate and challenging of pastries must be made the way porcupines make love—that is, very, very carefully. Then shut off the telephone for an hour or two, cut yourself some paper patterns as shown on page 302 and set to work.

◗ It is best to use flour that has a high gluten content, to develop real elasticity—and this is hard to come by. We do succeed however with all-purpose flour by using the procedure we describe. To be "puffy" ◗ the paste must be chilled, well-kneaded and handled in such a way as to trap air and finally ◗ baked in a high, thoroughly preheated oven. Then the air inside the dough expands with almost explosive effect. ◗ The surface on which you work—preferably marble—the tools, the ingredients and your fingers should be chilled throughout the operation, as it is necessary to hold the fat, which is in very high proportion to the flour, in constant suspension.

◗ The paste must not absorb undue moisture, but it must never dry out. ◗ It must entirely envelop the butter. Try not to let any cracks or tears develop, as they release the air which is your only riser. If they do appear, mend them at once to keep the butter encased. With these ideas firmly in mind, try making this small quantity first. As you become experienced, double or triple the recipe. Knead:

¼ lb. sweet butter

in ice water or under very cold running water. The butter should become soft through kneading, but in no sense soft through melting. Quite on the contrary—it must stay soft and chilled at the same time throughout the operation. The final kneading of the butter is best done on a marble slab; or the butter may be patted briskly in the hands until no water flies. Shape it into an oblong, about 4 x 6 x ¾ inches. Wrap in foil and chill for about 15 minutes. Mix:

¼ lb. all-purpose flour

which must be weighed, not measured. Make a ring, as shown below, on a chilled smooth surface with the flour, allowing about a 6-inch hollow center.

Pour into the ring gradually—meanwhile forming the flour into a ball with it—a mixture of:

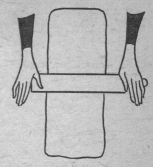

2 to 2½ oz. ice water
(1 teaspoon lemon juice)
¼ teaspoon salt

Knead the dough lightly until smooth. The whole process should not take more than about 2 minutes if you are experienced. Cover the dough carefully and refrigerate it for 15 minutes or so. When you remove the butter and dough from the refrigerator, they should be of about the same consistency—chilled but not hard. Roll the dough into a very neat oblong measuring about 6 x 16 inches and less than ⅛ inch thick, as in the following sketch. At this

point, the dough is somewhat elastic and may have to be cajoled into the rectangle. Make the edges as even and thickness as constant as possible. Quickly place the chilled butter pad about 1 inch from a short end

and sides of the dough oblong, as shown above.

Fold the rest of the dough over the butter to make a pouch with one side folded and the three others sealed. Seal the two layers firmly together on all three sides pressing with the fingers, as shown on page 301, top left, or with the sides of your hands.

With the narrow dimension always toward you as you work, roll the dough evenly, being careful not to break the layers nor force the roller in such a way that the edges of the dough

envelope become cracked. Should any opening develop, be sure to patch it at once with a small piece of dough taken from the long sides. Keep the pastry 6 inches in width while rolling and extend it to about 16 inches in length, as shown, page 301.

The use of 2 paper patterns makes this measuring very quick

to judge. Fold the pastry into three exact parts, see above. Make sure that the corners match neatly. Compress it slightly with the roller. At this point, the dough should have a transparent quality. The yellow of the butter should show through, but not break through anywhere. Wrap the dough, now approximately 4 x 6 x 1 inch, in foil and chill for 30 minutes. You have now made your first "turn" and, if you need a reminder, you can professionally make one shallow finger tip imprint in one

corner, as shown above, before refrigerating. You can keep track of your turns by increasing the finger prints after each rolling.

After the dough has chilled, remove it from the refrigerator and repeat the rolling. ♦ Always roll with the narrow dimension of the dough toward you as you work. Roll as before, until the dough again measures about 6 x 16 inches. Fold once more in three equal parts. This time, make two finger tip impressions before refrigerating, covered, for 30 minutes. Repeat the turns until you have six prints in the dough. You may store the dough for 24 hours before baking. Wrap it first in foil and then in a dry towel. Refrigerate it.

If you prefer to bake the same day, rest the dough after the 6th turn for 30 minutes to 1½ hours. Then roll it to about ³⁄₁₆ of an inch. This paste can be cut in many shapes. ♦ Whichever you choose, be sure to cut off a narrow slice along the folded edges. The folds have the inhibiting character of a selvage on cloth and do not allow the dough to expand evenly and freely.

♦ Always cut puff paste with a very sharp and thin hot knife, a hot cutter or a sharp, hot pastry wheel. Do not let the knife drag, as this will distort the layering.

Since making puff paste is

time-consuming, you will want to use every scrap. But never, after cutting, reroll the dough for the same purpose. Get your patty shells and Vol-au-vent and other classic shapes, see below, from the first cutting. Make out of rerolled scraps only those related types of pastry—such as flan, barquettes, croissants—for which the puff requirement is less exacting.

To prepare the pan for baking any of the classic shapes, sprinkle it lightly with cold water, but ▶ be sure to see that the side that was up when cut is now down against the wet baking surface. Puff paste, if properly made and cut, should rise six to eight times the height of the rolled dough.

Before baking an unsweetened paste, you may give it a lovely color by brushing the top with a combination of egg, salt and milk, see page 433. ▶ Do not let this glaze spill over the edge, as the quick setting of the egg will have a deterrent effect on the rising. For a paste to be used with sweetened food, brush with a combination of sugar and milk. For a real crispy finish, glaze also with a light sugar and water sirup just as the finished product comes from the oven.

To bake ▶ have ready an oven that has been thoroughly preheated to 500° for at least 20 minutes. Bake at this temperature for 5 minutes, reduce the heat to 375° and bake for 25 to 30 minutes more, depending on the size of the pastry. If it colors too rapidly, place a piece of baker's paper or bond over it during the last stages of baking. The pastry is done when very light when lifted. Should it rise unevenly, the fault may lie with uneven rolling or with the uneven heat of the oven. In hot weather, it may tend to slide to

one side. Nothing can be done about this.

All puff paste recipes are best used fresh, but will keep closely covered and stored in a refrigerator for several days or frozen for a few weeks. For shapes to make with puff paste, see the illustration below and some of the following recipes.

Top left shows the cutting of a Vol-au-vent, page 304. It is really a larger version of the bouchée or patty shell illustrated in its dough and baked form in the three drawings on the left.

At the top right is a Napoleon, page 305. The remaining three forms are the successive development of Cream Rolls, page 304. To cut Palm Leaves, see page 254. Do not try to make these shapes with the Rough Puff Paste below, which is placed here because it is folded and baked just like puff paste.

ROUGH OR HALF-PUFF PASTE OR PÂTE DEMI-FEUILLETÉE

Do not expect this crust to rise even half as high as does Puff Paste. It is made from the ingredients described below, but given fewer turns; or is formed from the rerolled parings of true Puff Paste, when additional handling has driven off some of the trapped air. Use this paste for barquettes or croissants. Prepare:

Puff Paste, page 300

using in all:

6 oz. butter
2 oz. water

Give it only 3 to 4 turns. To cut, shape and bake, see Puff Paste, page 300.

PALM LEAVES

[About 20 Palm Leaves]
Roll:

Puff Paste, page 300

into a 6 x 18-inch strip, ¼ inch thick. To sugar, fold and cut, see pages 301 and 302.

✳ PATTY SHELLS OR BOUCHÉES

[Ten 4-Inch Shells]
Prepare:

Puff Paste, see above
and note ◗ pointers

Roll the chilled paste into an oblong, 7 x 16 inches. Use a 3¼-inch hot cutter on the dough ten times. ◗ Be sure that the cutter is well within the rounded edge of the dough. Using a 2½-inch cutter and centering it in turn on each of the 3¼-inch rounds, make incisions, as shown on page 303, about ⅔ through the dough. To chill, place and bake the dough, see Puff Paste, page 300. As soon as the patty shells come from the oven, release the inner circles that were cut ⅔ into the shell. The first ⅓ will act as the lid when the shell is filled. The second is usually damp and is discarded. The third uncut portion forms the base of the shell. These shells are suitable for luncheon entrées. They can be made into much smaller sizes for hors d'oeuvre, and are then called Petites Bouchées, or "little mouthfuls."

✳ VOL-AU-VENT

[One 9-Inch Shell]
Prepare:

Puff Paste, page 300, and
note ◗ pointers

Roll the chilled paste into an oblong 9 x 17 inches. Use the removable bottom of an 8-inch round cake pan or make an 8-inch cardboard circle as a cutting guide. Cut two circles with a sharp, hot knife. Leave one whole. Place the cut-side down on a baking sheet sprinkled with water. Cut a 5-inch round out of the center of the other circle. Place the 1½-inch rim which this cut forms also cut-side down over the whole circle and gash it diagonally along the edge, as shown on page 303. You may bake the 5-inch circle separately as a lid or cut it into petites bouchées, see above. To chill and bake, see Puff Paste, page 300. Fill at once with creamed food and serve, or cool to serve filled with fruits.

CREAM ROLLS

[Eight Rolls]
If you visit a Konditorei in Weimar, you will find Schillerlocken or cream rolls, named after the long curls worn by the romantic German poet. To make them, you need a special cone-shaped form known as a cornet.
Prepare:

Puff Paste, see page 300
and note ◗ pointers

Roll the chilled paste into an oblong, 12½ x 9 inches. Remove the rolled edges of the paste with a very sharp hot knife or pastry wheel. Cut the dough into eight 12-inch strips. Roll the strips around the cones, as shown on page 303. Chill the cornets, covered, for at least ½ hour. Glaze the top of the strips with:

Milk Glaze, page 434

Stand the cornets on a baking

tin. To bake, see Puff Paste, page 300.

NAPOLEONS

[About Forty 2 x 3 Inch Bars]
Could the Emperor have had these in mind when he contended that "an army marches on its stomach"?
Preheat oven to 450°.
Prepare:

Puff Paste, page 300

Roll the chilled paste into an oblong, 24 x 33 inches to a thickness of ⅛ inch or less. ▶ Trim all folded edges carefully to a depth of ½ inch. Divide the paste into three 11 x 24-inch oblongs. Place the 3 thin equal oblongs upside down on baking sheets that have been sprinkled with cold water. Prick them uniformly with a fork. Bake them about 25 to 30 minutes in all, see Puff Paste, page 300. When cool, you may glaze the layer reserved for the top with 2 successive coats of:

Quick Icing I, page 426

Let the first coat dry before applying the second or dust the top layer with:

Powdered sugar

Stack the 3 layers and cut into 2 x 3-inch oblongs. Put between the layers:

Sweetened Whipped Cream, page 377 or
Crème Patissière, page 378

The finished pastry is shown at the top right of the illustration on page 303.

ABOUT CREAM PUFF SHELLS, PÂTE À CHOUX OR POUF PASTE

Please cease to think of this basic, quite easy paste as something for adventurous moments only. Use it unsweetened as a base for Gnocchi (I, 156); for Dauphine Potatoes (I, 320); as a bland foil for fillings; as soup

garnishes or as hors d'oeuvre cases. Pâte à choux, when sweetened, imparts great individuality to the presentation of food, as you can see in the sketches below. With a pastry tube you may make elegant Éclairs, page 306, Beignets, page 468, characteristic cabbagy or choux shapes for cream puffs, Swans, page 306, dainty choux paste cases or the towering pyramid, Croquembouche, page 307. If you serve éclair cases filled with ice cream or cream and covered with a sauce, they are called Profiteroles, page 307.

CREAM PUFF SHELLS

[Two Dozen 3-Inch Shells]
Preheat oven to 400°.
Have the eggs at room temperature. It is best to use a high-gluten flour. Sift before measuring:

1 cup high-gluten or all-purpose flour
⅛ teaspoon salt
1 tablespoon sugar, if the puffs are to be used with a sweet filling

Place in a heavy pan:

1 cup water or milk
⅓ cup butter

When the mixture boils, add the flour in one fell swoop and stir quickly with a wooden spoon. It looks rough at first, but suddenly becomes smooth, at which point you stir faster. In a few minutes the paste becomes dry, does not cling to the spoon or the sides of the pan and when the spoon is pressed on it lightly, it leaves a smooth imprint. ◗ Do not overcook, for then the dough will fail to puff. ◗ Remove pan from heat for about 2 minutes. It never returns to the heat and this is why, to cook properly, ◗ the eggs must be at room temperature. Add ◗ one at a time, beating vigorously after each addition:

4 to 5 eggs

Continue to beat each time until the dough no longer looks slippery. The paste is ready to bake when the last egg has been incorporated, and it has reached proper consistency when a small quantity of the dough will stand erect if scooped up on the end of the spoon. It is best to use the dough at once.

Use a spoon or a pastry bag to form the different shapes. Be sure to press the filled bag until you are rid of all the air in the tube. Allow space for expansion around shapes, as you squeeze them onto the greased pan. To form the puff or characteristic cabbagy, choux shape ◗ hold the tube close to the baking sheet. ◗ Do not move the tube. Simply let the paste bubble up around it until the desired size is reached. To form éclairs, draw the tube along for about 3 to 4 inches while pressing and always ◗ finish with a lifting reverse motion. To form small pastry cups, make one-inch globules. The small point left when you lift the bag can be pressed down with a moistened finger. Before baking, sprinkle a few drops of water over the shapes on the pan —lightly—as you would sprinkle laundry. Bake cream puff shells and éclairs in a preheated 400° oven for 10 minutes. Reduce the heat to 350° and bake for about

25 minutes longer. Do not remove them from the oven until they are quite firm to the touch. Cool the shells away from any draft before filling. For filling, cut them horizontally with a sharp knife. If there are any damp dough filaments inside, be sure to remove them. For suggested cream puff fillings, see next page.

CHOUX PASTE SWAN

Use a simple cut-off round tube, see Decorative Icings, page 423, to form the head and neck all in one piece. Squeeze hard at the inception of the movement to force a greater quantity of paste for the head and swing the tube in an arc for the neck, as shown on the tray, page 305. Head and neck sections are baked on a greased sheet for only 10 minutes in a 400° oven. For the rest of the swan's anatomy, use a serrated tube to form 3-inch éclairs. Cut them lengthwise. Just before serving, fill the bottom piece with cream. Divide the top piece lengthwise for the wings. Imbed them and the neck in the fluffy cream filling. The wings are braced somewhat diagonally to steady the neck. Dust the whole swan lightly with confectioners' sugar. Perfect for a little girl's party!

CHOCOLATE ÉCLAIRS

To form and bake the shells, see Cream Puff Shells, page 305. Gash the shell sufficiently to get the filling in or squirt it in with a pastry tube. Fill the shells as close to serving time as possible with:

Whipped cream or
Custard Chocolate or
Coffee Fillings, see
page 378

Cover them with:
A chocolate icing, page

428, or Caramel Icing,
page 425
Garnish with:
Slivered toasted almonds

PROFITEROLES

To form and bake the shells, see
Cream Puff Shells, page 305. Divide the shells horizontally and
fill as close to serving time as
possible with:
Crème Chantilly, page
377, or ice cream
Cover with:
Chocolate Sauce,
page 477
or fill with:
Whipped Cream,
page 132
and serve with a strawberry
sauce.

CROQUENBOUCHE

[Serves 10 to 12]
This spectacular dessert is a
mechanical marvel. It needs considerable organization, for it is
best when assembled as close to
serving time as possible. See illustration on preceding page.
Caramelize:
2 cups sugar, page 169
Form on the base of a 9-inch
greased pie pan or directly on a
footed cake tray a thin caramelized layer. Keep the rest of the
caramelized sugar soft in a 250°
oven. When the thin layer has
hardened, put it on the platter
on which you intend to serve the
dessert. Have ready:
Cream puffs under 2
inches in size, made
from Pâte à Choux,
page 305
filled with:
Whipped or flavored
cream, page 377
Remove the caramel from the
oven and work quickly. Reheat
the sirup slowly if it tends to
harden. ◗ Dip a portion of each
filled puff in turn, as you place
it in decreasing circular layers

on the caramel disc. Arrange the
puffs on the outer layers so their
tops form the exposed surface.
Serve by pulling apart with 2
forks.

ABOUT FILLINGS FOR
CREAM PUFF SHELLS
AND ÉCLAIRS

Use Sweetened Whipped
Creams, page 377, Custards,
page 436, Crème Patissière,
page 378, or almost any of the
fillings in Complete Dessert
Cakes, page 376. ◗ Fill as close
to serving time as possible to
avoid sogginess. In any case, remember ◗ that cream-based and
particularly egg-based fillings
must be kept cool or refrigerated.
Egg fillings, if carelessly stored,
are subject to bacterial activity
which may be highly toxic although they give no evidence of
spoilage. For unsweetened puff
shells, see Canapés, page 54.
With a sweetened dough try one
of the following:
I. For a marvelous tea-teaser,
put in the base of a puff shell a
layer of:
Whipped cream
Lightly insert with the pointed
end up:
A flawless ripe strawberry

II. Or fill the puffs with:
Soft cream cheese
A dab of bright jelly

STRUDEL

When the last princess slip was
freshly beribboned, our beloved
Hungarian laundress sometimes
gave us a treat. She would make
strudel. Draping the round dining room table with a fresh
cloth, she patiently worked flour
into it. Neighborhood small fry
gathered on the fringes of the
light cast by the Tiffany dome,
and their eyes would pop as she
rolled the dough, no larger than
a soft ball, into a big thin circle.

Then, hands lightly clenched, palms down, working under the sheet of dough and from the center out, she stretched it with the flat plane of the knuckles, as shown below. She would play it out, so to speak, not so much pulling it as coaxing it with long, even friction, moving round and round the table as she worked.

In our house hold, the filling was invariably apple. But whether you make strudel dough yourself or buy it—for it now comes ready to use—there are endless possibilities for "interior decoration": poppy seed, ground meat mixtures, cheese, cherries or just pepper worked originally into the dough. This last makes an excellent hors d'oeuvre pastry.

Our Janka had organized her filling well in advance. Browned bread crumbs, lemon rind grated into sugar, raisins, currants, very finely sliced apples, almonds and a small pitcher of melted butter were all set out on a tray. These were strewn alternately over the

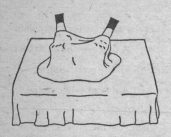

surface of the dough. Then came the forming of the roll. Using both hands, Janka picked up one side of the cloth and, while never actually touching the dough itself, tilted and nudged the cloth and the sheet this way and that until the dough rolled over on itself —jelly-roll fashion—and com-completely enclosed the filling.

Finally, she slid the long cylinder onto a greased baking sheet and curved it into a horseshoe. From beginning to end the process had masterly craftsmanship. Would that we could give you her skill as easily as we give you her recipe. Now are you ready? Prepare the filling ingredients. Do not feel limited by these proportions or materials. See other fillings, page 268.

Mix:

    1 tablespoon cinnamon

with:

    4 to 6 tablespoons browned bread crumbs
    1 tablespoon lemon rind

grated into:

    1 cup sugar
    ¾ cup raisins or currants
    (½ cup shredded blanched almonds)
    6 to 8 cups finely chopped tart apples

Have ready:

    5 tablespoons melted butter

Preheat oven to 400°.

Have a cloth ready on a large table-height surface, around which you will be able to walk. Work lightly into the cloth:

    Flour

Sift onto a board:

    1½ cups all-purpose flour
    ¼ teaspoon salt

In testing, we have tried as many as 3 different commercially available flours during the same morning with amazingly different results. Part of the fame of this age-old pastry rests on fine flours formerly available in Hungary. Add gradually, as you work the dough with your fingers:

    1 egg

beaten with:

    ⅓ to ½ cup tepid water or milk
    (2 teaspoons vinegar)

Depending on your flour, you may have to add a few tablespoons more of tepid water. Combine the ingredients quickly with your fingers and knead them on a board until the dough no longer sticks to it. You may brush the surface with melted butter. Cover the ball of dough with a warm bowl and let it rest for 20 to 30 minutes. Roll it out on the board as thin as possible. Move to the table. Begin to stretch the dough gently from the center out, trying not to tear it, as patching is difficult. If you are skillful, this should stretch to about a 2-yd. square. A heavier edge of dough or a border will develop as you work and whatever remains of this must be cut off with a knife before the filling is spread or the pastry rolled up. Use this excess dough for making patches. Before filling, brush the dough with some of the melted butter. Sprinkle over the surface the bread crumbs, sugar and lemon rind, currants, raisins, almonds and apples. Dust with:

Cinnamon

Form the roll as described above ▶ not too tightly, as the dough will expand. Slide it onto the greased baking sheet. Brush the surface of the roll with some of the melted butter and sprinkle it lightly with water. Bake for 20 minutes at 400°, then lower the heat to 350°, brush the strudel again with the remaining butter, and bake about 10 minutes longer, until brown. Remove from oven and dust with:

Confectioners' sugar

Cut in wide diagonal slices and serve.

ABOUT MERINGUE PASTE

There are many variations of meringue—all based on egg white and sugar. They include glamorous glacées and vacherins, served with ices or creams; including ice cream; Christmas meringue cookies, of which cinnamon stars are, perhaps deserv-edly, the best beloved; mountainous, fluffy pie toppings; more discreet Italian types of meringue, used over puddings and tarts; insulating meringues like those prepared for Omelette Soufflé Surprise and Baked Alaska; Swiss Meringue or Royal Glaze. Each calls for special treatment.

In this day of the electric mixer, showy meringue desserts have become effortless to make. There are several ways of confecting and baking meringues, and they have attracted vociferous partisans. You will find them described below.

Ingredients and proportions do not vary. For every 4 egg whites (from 2-oz. eggs) use ½ lb. sugar. As you know, sugars of the same weight differ tremendously in volume, see About Solid Sugars, page 165. Eggs should be at about 70° and you should open, separate and whip them when you are ready to mix the meringue. The baking is more a drying than a heating process. ▶ Use bottom heat only. A preheated 225° oven will give you a soft, crunchy meringue; a preheated 275° oven, a chewy one. A third, highly recommended baking method, if you have a very well-insulated oven, is to preheat it to 475°. Have your meringues ready to bake; pop them quickly into the 475° oven; turn off the heat immediately and forget about them for 8 hours.

If you wonder about the indestructible meringues served in public places, they are based on confectioners' sugar; the egg whites are heated over hot water as for Génoise, page 370; and the meringues dried overnight in a warming oven, not over 175°. Whichever baking procedure is chosen, the classic confectioner does not allow his meringues to color. ▶ Store meringues tightly covered, as they absorb moisture and disintegrate easily.

To form meringue paste, use a spoon and spatula or a pastry bag. Make individual kisses or rings to fill with ices, ice creams or frozen desserts for meringue glacées. Shape the paste into a large nest on a heat-resistant platter and fill it with fruits and cream for **Pinch Pie.** Bake it in spring form layers and fill them for **Schaumtorten,** or swirl the paste into flat coils, one plain and one decorated at the edges with large contiguous baroque dots, to place as a crown on the cream filling for **Vacherin Rings.** For filling suggestions and an all-in-one meringue baked with cake, see Cake Fillings, page 376, and Meringue Cream Tart, page 372.

I. [Twelve 3-Inch Meringues or a 9-Inch Pie]
Preheat oven to 225°.
◗ Have egg whites at about 75°. Beat until foamy in an electric mixer:
      4 egg whites
Add:
      1 teaspoon vanilla
      (⅛ teaspoon cream of tartar)
Add, while continuing to beat, 1 teaspoon at a time:
      1 cup sifted finely
         powdered sugar or
      1 cup minus 1 tablespoon
         sifted sugar
When the mixture stands in stiff peaks on the beater, it is ready to be baked. ◗ Do not overbeat. To shape, see above. For a glaze, you may dust the meringues lightly with:
      Granulated sugar
Cook on baking sheets covered with parchment paper for about 1 hour or longer, depending on the size. The reason for the use of paper is not to prevent sticking but to diffuse the heat. In some famous kitchens the meringues are baked on a thick board. ◗ Do not remove from

the oven at once, but turn off the oven, open the door and leave them for at least 5 minutes. Cool them gradually, away from a draft. Remove them from the sheet when cool. If kisses are to be filled, crush the smooth side lightly with the thumb while the meringues are still warm. Shortly before serving, fill the hollows with:
      Sweetened and flavored
         whipped cream or a
         frozen mixture
Place 2 filled meringues together. Serve them with:
      Ice cream or whipped
         cream
covered with:
      Sweetened crushed fruit,
         or a chocolate sauce,
         page 477

II. [Twelve 3-Inch Meringues or a 9-Inch Pie]
Preheat oven to 225°.
◗ Have egg whites at about 75°.
Sift:
      1 cup very finely powdered
         sugar or 1 cup minus
      1 tablespoon sugar
Beat until foamy:
      4 egg whites
Add:
      1 teaspoon vanilla
      (⅛ teaspoon cream of tartar)
Add, while continuing to beat, 1 teaspoon at a time:
      1 tablespoon sifted sugar
Beat this mixture until ◗ stiff but not dry, see To Beat Egg Whites, page 180. ◗ Fold in by hand, quickly and lightly, the rest of the sugar. If this is not done quickly the meringues will be soft. To bake, see Method I.

ABOUT FRUIT PIES

If you don't find the fruit combination you are looking for in our fruit pie recipes, perhaps you would like to experiment with fillings for yourself. A 9-inch fruit pie needs about 4 cups of fresh fruit or 3 cups of cooked fruit. Use about 2⅔ tablespoons quick-cooking tapioca to thicken the fruit juice. Let the fruit and tapioca stand for 15 minutes before filling the shells and baking. Correct the sweetening, then proceed as directed in berry pies. Some suggested proportions are:

½ apple and ½ pear
½ rhubarb and ½ strawberry
⅓ gooseberry and ⅔ strawberry
½ cherry and ½ rhubarb
⅓ cranberry and ⅔ apple
½ mincemeat, ¼ apple sauce and ¼ crushed pineapple
½ fresh strawberries and ½ bananas, plus sugar and whipped cream
⅔ raspberries and ⅓ currants

Fruit pies ❋ freeze well, but ▶ do not freeze those with a custard base.

APPLE PIE

[A 9-Inch Pie]
Call it "à la mode" if you garnish your pie with ice cream.
Preheat oven to 450°.
Line a 9-inch pie pan with:
        Pie Crust, page 296, or
        Cheese Pie Crust,
        page 298
Peel, core and cut into very thin pieces:
        5 to 6 cups apples
Have you ever tried half apples and half green tomatoes? The result is amazingly like a very tart apple pie—with an interesting difference. If you are using dried apples, allow 1 lb. apples to 1 quart water and cook 35 to 45 minutes. Combine and sift over the apples:
        ½ to ⅔ cup white or brown
        sugar
        ⅛ teaspoon salt

1 tablespoon to 1½ tablespoons cornstarch
(¼ teaspoon cinnamon)
(⅛ teaspoon nutmeg)
Only very tart apples require the larger amount of sugar. Only very juicy apples require the larger amount of cornstarch. Stir the apples gently until they are well coated. Place them in layers in the pie shell. Dot them with:
        1½ tablespoons butter
If the apples lack flavor, sprinkle them with:
        1 tablespoon lemon juice
        ½ teaspoon grated lemon
        rind
        (1 teaspoon vanilla)
If you are serving the pie with cheese, omit the above flavors and use:
        (1 teaspoon fennel or anise
        seed)
If the apples are very dry, add:
        2 tablespoons water or
        cream
Cover the pie with a pricked upper crust, see Pie Crust, page 293. Bake the pie in a 450° oven for 10 minutes. Reduce the heat to 350°. Bake the pie until done, from 45 minutes to 1 hour in all. For a delicious touch, sprinkle the top crust lightly with sugar and cinnamon as you put it into the oven. Some cooks brush it first with milk. The pie may be made without an upper crust. Bake in a 450° oven for 20 minutes, then sprinkle over the top:
        (1 cup grated cheese)
Run under a broiler to melt the cheese.

APPLE TARTS

[8 Tarts]
Preheat oven to 375°.
Line eight shallow 3-inch muffin cups or individual pie pans with:
        Any Pie Crust, page 296
Fill them with:

4 cups peeled, thinly sliced
apples
Combine and pour over the
fruit:
½ cup sugar
2 slightly beaten eggs
2 tablespoons melted
butter
1 tablespoon lemon juice
1 cup cream or ½ cup
evaporated milk and ½
cup water
(½ teaspoon cinnamon)
(⅛ teaspoon nutmeg)
Place on cookie sheet. Bake
about 40 minutes.

PEACH PIE

I. [A 9-Inch Pie]
Preheat oven to 400°.
Line a pie pan with:
Any Pie Crust, page 296
Combine and blend well:
1 egg or 2 egg yolks
2 tablespoons flour
⅔ to 1 cup granulated sugar
(⅓ cup melted butter)
Pour this mixture over:
Halves of canned or
fresh peaches
that have been placed cut side
up in the pie shell. Bake for 15
minutes at 400°, then reduce
the heat to 300° and bake it
about 50 minutes longer. Serve
hot or, if cold, garnish with:
(Whipped Cream)

II. [A 9-Inch Pie]
Follow the recipe for:
Apple Pie, page 311
Substitute for the apples:
5 cups peeled, sliced
peaches
Use the smaller amount of
sugar.

BERRY PIE WITH
FRESH FRUIT

[A 9-Inch Pie]
Use:
Gooseberry, Currant,
Blackberry, Raspberry,
Strawberry, Blueberry,
Huckleberry or
Loganberry
Preheat oven to 450°.
Line a pie pan with:
Any Pie Crust, page 296
Prepare by picking over and
hulling:
4 cups fresh berries
At this point we should like to
raise the question of thickening
for berries. Technically, each
batch would require a different
amount of thickener, depending
on the variety of fruit, degree
of ripeness, etc. For practical
purposes, an often suggested
formula is 4 tablespoons of flour
for 4 cups of fruit. But we much
prefer either of the following
substitutions, the first dry, the
second moist. Either add and
mix:
2⅔ tablespoons
quick-cooking tapioca
to:
⅔ to 1 cup sugar
or mix:
2 tablespoons cornstarch
with:
¼ cup water or fruit juice
until very smooth and then
blend with:
⅔ to 1 cup sugar
Whether you use tapioca or
cornstarch, let the mixture stand
for 15 minutes after blending it
gently into the fresh berries and
before putting it into the pie
shell. Season the fruit with:
1½ tablespoons lemon juice
or ½ teaspoon cinnamon
Dot the fruit with:
1 to 2 tablespoons butter
Cover the pie with a top crust
or with a lattice, page 294. Bake
the pie in a 450° oven for 10
minutes. Reduce the heat to
350° and bake about 40 to 45
minutes.

FRESH CHERRY PIE

[A 9-Inch Pie]
Follow the recipe for Berry Pie
with Fresh Fruit, page 312. Use

fresh, pitted, sour cherries and thicken with tapioca or cornstarch. Omit the cinnamon. Add:

  2 drops almond flavoring
    or 2 tablespoons kirsch

This pie may call for as much as 1⅓ cups of sugar in all. Fine made with a lattice top. Bake as for Berry Pie with Fresh Fruit, page 312.

BERRY OR CHERRY PIE WITH COOKED FRUIT

[A 9-Inch Pie]
Allow approximately:

  2½ cups sweetened canned
    or cooked berries or
    cherries
  1 cup fruit juice

Proceed as directed in the above recipe for Berry Pie with Fresh Fruit, but for thickening use only:

  1½ tablespoons quick-
    cooking tapioca or
    1 tablespoon cornstarch

mixed with:

  2 tablespoons water

and ▶ be sure to combine as described above. You may bake the filling in the unbaked pie shell as in Berry Pie with Fresh Fruit or you may thicken the fruit juice by heating it separately with the thickener, then mix it with the fruit and put it in a baked shell to serve.

BERRY OR CHERRY PIE WITH FROZEN FRUIT

[A 9-Inch Pie]
Preheat oven to 450°.
Line a pie pan with:

  Any Pie Crust, page 296

Mix and let stand for 15 minutes:

  2 pkgs. frozen berries or
    cherries—20 oz.—
    defrosted enough so that
    the fruit separates easily
  3 tablespoons quick-
    cooking tapioca
  ½ cup sugar

  ⅛ teaspoon salt
  2 tablespoons melted
    butter

Fill the pie shell. Cover with crust or lattice and bake in a 450° oven for 10 minutes. Reduce the heat and bake at 350° for 45 minutes to 1 hour.

GERMAN CHERRY PIE

[About 5 Servings—A 9-Inch Pie]
The Germans who became political refugees in 1830 and 1848 brought with them to their new American home this treasured recipe for their Cherry Cake or Pie. There are, of course, different versions of the same pie. Ours is a fairly modern one, which may call the displeasure of old-timers down on our heads. However, even a German Cherry Cake or Pie recipe must bow to the Zeitgeist.
Drain and keep the juice from:

  2½ cups solid pitted cherries,
    fresh or canned

Pour over the cherries:

  6 tablespoons sugar

Very acid cherries may require more sugar. Permit to stand for about ½ hour, until the sugar is dissolved. Stir gently several times. Drain and reserve juice. Prepare:

  1½ cups sifted flour

Resift it with:

  1½ teaspoons cinnamon
  6 tablespoons sugar
  ⅛ teaspoon salt

Cut into these ingredients with a pastry blender or 2 knives, until blended:

  ½ cup butter

Add to the above:

  1 beaten egg

Now, wade in with your hands and work the dough until it holds together, but no longer. Chill it. Pat it into a 9-inch oven-proof glass pie pan. Let it come to the upper edge of the pan. See that it is spread evenly.

Crimp the dough around the edge with the tines of a fork.
◗ Preheat oven to 350°.
Measure the sirup drained from the cherries. There should be ¾ cup. Taste it. Add sugar if it seems to be too sour. Reserve ¼ cup. Place the rest over low heat. Stir into the ¼ cup, until smooth:

　　4 teaspoons cornstarch

When the rest of the juice is boiling, stir in the cornstarch mixture. Stir and cook over low heat for 2 or 3 minutes until the mixture is no longer cloudy. Add:

　　(¼ teaspoon almond extract)

Place the cherries in the pie shell, pour the hot juice over them and bake from 50 to 60 minutes.

SOUR CREAM CHERRY PIE

[A 9-Inch Pie or 6 Tarts]
Preheat oven to 325°.
Follow the rule for a 9-inch pie shell of:

　　Zwieback or Ginger Snap
　　　Pie Crust, page 299

Fill the chilled shell with the following cherry custard. Beat:

　　3 eggs

Add:

　　¾ cup sugar
　　¾ cup cultured sour cream
　　2 cups fresh or canned
　　　drained cherries

Bake the pie until the custard is firm, about 1 hour. Serve it very hot or very cold.

STRAWBERRY OR RASPBERRY CREAM PIE

[A 9-Inch Pie]
Prepare any:

　　Any Baked Pie Shell,
　　　page 296

When cool, fill with:

　　Bavarian Berry Cream,
　　　page 451

GLAZED FRUIT PIE

[A 9-Inch Pie]
Prepare with a generous high rim:

　　Any Baked Pie Shell,
　　　page 296

Clean and hull:

　　1 quart strawberries or red
　　　or black raspberries

Reserve and ⅄ blend or sieve 1 cup of the fruit. Combine and cook, stirring until thickened over low heat for about 10 to 15 minutes:

　　¾ cup sugar
　　2½ tablespoons cornstarch
　　¼ teaspoon salt
　　1 cup water

Add the blended fruit to give color. Put the whole berries into the pie shell, evenly distributed. Pour the sirup over the berries, coating them thoroughly by turning but not displacing them. Chill the pie in the refrigerator at least 4 hours. Serve it garnished with:

　　(Whipped cream)

BLUEBERRY OR HUCKLEBERRY TART

[A 9-Inch Pie]
If seeds are small, it's blueberries you have; if many and large —huckleberries. The flavor is almost identical.
Prepare:

　　Galette, page 297, or Pie
　　　Dough, page 293

Place it in a pan and chill as directed. Bake in a 450° oven for about 15 minutes. Cover with:

　　1 quart blueberries
　　½ cup sugar
　　(3 tablespoons lemon juice)

Bake the tart in a 375° oven for about 10 minutes. Cook and stir over—not in—boiling water until thick:

　　½ cup cream
　　2 or 3 beaten egg yolks
　　½ cup sugar
　　⅛ teaspoon salt

Cool the custard and pour it

over the slightly cooled tart. Cool it well. Cover with a:
    (Meringue, page 431)

RHUBARB PIE

[A 9-Inch Pie]
Use:
    4 cups young, unpeeled, diced rhubarb stalks
    ¼ cup flour
    1¼ to 2 cups sugar
    1 tablespoon butter
    (1 teaspoon grated orange rind)

Follow the rule for baking Berry Pie with Fresh Fruit, page 312.

GRAPE PIE

[A 9-Inch Pie]
Preheat oven to 450°.
Stem:
    4 cups blue grapes

Slip the pulp out of the skins. Reserve the skins. Cook the pulp until the seeds loosen. Press through a colander to remove seeds. Combine the pulp, the skins and:
    ¾ cup sugar
    1½ tablespoons lemon juice
    1 tablespoon grated orange rind
    1 tablespoon quick-cooking tapioca

Permit these ingredients to stand for 15 minutes. Prepare:
    Any Pie Crust, page 296

To form the shell, see page 294. Fill the shell with the grape mixture and form a lattice of pastry over the top, see page 294. Bake the pie for 10 minutes at 450°, then lower the heat to 350° and bake for about 20 minutes more.

★ MINCEMEAT

This is enough filling for about 20 pies. Some of our fans make this recipe for Christmas gifts. It is best if prepared at least 2 weeks before using.
Prepare:

    9 quarts sliced, peeled apples
Combine with:
    4 lbs. lean, chopped beef or ox heart
    2 lbs. chopped beef suet
    3 lbs. sugar
    2 quarts cider
    4 lbs. seeded raisins
    3 lbs. currants
    1½ lbs. chopped citron
    ½ lb. dried, chopped, candied orange peel
    ½ lb. dried, chopped, candied lemon peel
    Juice and rind of 1 lemon
    1 tablespoon each cinnamon, mace, cloves
    1 teaspoon each salt and pepper
    2 whole grated nutmegs
    1 gallon sour cherries with juice
    2 lbs. broken nut meats
    (1 teaspoon powdered coriander seed)

Cook these ingredients slowly for 2 hours. Stir frequently. Seal in sterile jars. Before serving, season with:
    Brandy

★ MINCE PIE

[A 9-Inch Pie]
Preheat oven to 450°.
Line a pie pan with:
    Any Pie Crust, page 296
Fill it with:
    Mincemeat, above
Add to the mincemeat:
    (2 to 4 tablespoons brandy)
Cover the pie with an upper crust. Bake at 450° for 10 minutes, then bake at 350° for about 30 minutes.

MINCE PIE FLAMBÉ

A quickly assembled gala dessert.
Bake:
    Cookies or pie crust rounds
Heap:
    Hot mincemeat
in the center of an ovenproof

dish. Surround it just before serving with:

> Baked rounds of pie crusts or cookies

Have ready to pour over the mincemeat:

> ⅓ cup warmed brandy

To flambé, see (I, 80).

★ MOCK MINCE PIE

[A 9-Inch Pie]
Cut into pieces:

> 1½ cups seeded raisins

Pare, core and slice:

> 4 medium-size tart apples or a combination of apples and green tomatoes

Combine the raisins and apples. Add:

> Grated rind of 1 orange
> Juice of 1 orange
> ½ cup cider or other fruit juice

Cover these ingredients and simmer until the apples are very soft. Stir in until well blended:

> ¾ cup sugar
> ½ teaspoon each cinnamon and cloves
> 2 or 3 tablespoons finely crushed soda crackers

If the apples are dry, use the smaller amount. This mixture will keep for several days. Shortly before using it, add:

> (1 or 2 tablespoons brandy)

Line a pie pan with:

> Any Pie Crust, page 296

Fill it with mock mincemeat. Cover with an upper crust or with a lattice of pastry. Bake in a 450° oven for 10 minutes and about 20 minutes longer at 350°.

PRUNE OR APRICOT PIE

[A 9-Inch Pie]
Preheat oven to 325°.
Prepare by any recipe:

> Any baked Pie Shell, page 296

Put stewed, unsweetened prunes or apricots through a ricer. Combine:

> ¾ cup prune or apricot pulp
> 1 teaspoon grated lemon rind
> 1 tablespoon lemon juice
> ½ cup sugar

Beat until stiff but not dry:

> 3 egg whites

Beat in very slowly:

> ½ cup sugar

Fold the egg whites into the fruit mixture. Fill the pie shell. Bake for about 20 minutes or until set.

RAISIN PIE

[A 9-Inch Pie]
Prepare by any recipe:

> Any baked Pie Shell, page 296

Cook to the boiling point:

> 1 cup seedless or seeded white raisins
> 1 cup water

Add:

> ½ cup white or brown sugar

Cool ½ cup of this mixture. Stir into it gently:

> 2 tablespoons butter
> 2 tablespoons all-purpose flour

Return it to the saucepan. Cook and stir these ingredients over low heat until the flour has thickened. Remove the pan from the heat. Beat in:

> 2 egg yolks
> 1 teaspoon grated lemon rind
> 3 tablespoons lemon juice

Cool the filling. Fill the pie shell. Cover with Meringue I, page 432, and bake as directed.

✳ LINZERTORTE

[A 9-Inch Pie or Cake]
The following is a delicious German "company" cake or pie. It looks like an open jam pie and, being rich, is usually served in thin wedges. It should serve 16. Preheat oven to 400°.
Sift:

> 1 cup sugar

Beat until soft:
>   ½ to ⅞ cup butter

Add the sugar gradually. Blend these ingredients until very light and creamy.
Add:
>   1 teaspoon grated lemon rind

Beat in, one at a time:
>   2 eggs

Stir in gradually:
>   1¼ cups sifted all-purpose flour
>   1 cup unblanched almonds, ground in a nut grinder or a ⅄ blender
>   ½ teaspoon cinnamon
>   ¼ teaspoon cloves
>   1 tablespoon cocoa
>   ¼ teaspoon salt

The old recipe reads, "Stir for one hour," but of course no high-geared American has time for that. If the dough is very soft, chill it. Pat it into an oven-proof dish to the thickness of ⅛ inch. Rechill it for 2 hours. Cover the bottom of the cake generously with a good quality of:
>   Raspberry jam, preserves or apple butter

Place the remaining dough in a pastry tube and give the pie a good edge and lattice by forcing the dough through the bag. Bake the cake in a 400° oven about 25 minutes. Before serving, fill the hollows with additional preserves. You may also dust the top with:
>   Confectioners' sugar

BANBURY TARTS

[About Six 4-Inch Tarts]
Have ready:
>   Individual baked Pie Shells, page 296

Combine:
>   1 cup seeded raisins
>   1 cup sugar
>   2 tablespoons cracker crumbs
>   1 well-beaten egg
>   Grated rind of 1 lemon
>   1½ tablespoons lemon juice
>   2 tablespoons butter
>   ¼ cup chopped candied fruits

Cook and stir these ingredients over low heat until they begin to thicken. Remove from the heat. Cool. Partly fill the tart shells. Top with:
>   (Whipped cream)

You may use this filling in Turnovers, page 321.

CRUMB OR GRAVEL PIE

[A 9-Inch Pie]
Preheat oven to 325°.
Use a:
>   Baked Pie Shell, page 296

for this Pennsylvania Dutch specialty. Sprinkle the bottom of shell with:
>   (½ cup raisins)

Combine and cook in a double boiler until thick:
>   1 cup brown sugar, mild molasses or honey
>   ½ cup hot water
>   3 beaten eggs

Cool and pour these ingredients into the pie shell. Combine and work like pastry:
>   1 cup cake or cookie crumbs
>   ⅓ cup flour
>   ½ to 1 teaspoon cinnamon
>   ¼ teaspoon nutmeg
>   ⅛ teaspoon ginger
>   ⅓ cup soft butter

Sprinkle this mixture over the filling. To make **Gravel Pie** don't combine the above ingredients. Instead, sprinkle them alternately over the pie—with the crumbs on top. Bake for 20 to 30 minutes.

JEFFERSON DAVIS PIE

[A 9-Inch Pie]
Preheat oven to 325°.
Prepare:
>   A baked Pie Shell, page 296

Cream:
  ½ cup butter
  2 cups packed light brown
    sugar
Beat in:
  4 egg yolks
Mix, then add:
  2 tablespoons all-purpose
    flour
  1 teaspoon cinnamon
  ½ teaspoon allspice
  1 teaspoon freshly grated
    nutmeg
Stir in:
  1 cup cream
  ½ cup chopped dates
  ½ cup raisins
  ½ cup broken pecan meats
Fill the shell. Bake the pie until
set, about 30 minutes. When
cool, top with:
  Meringue I, page 432
Bake as directed.

CHESS TARTS

Fill:
  Baked Tart Shells, page
    296
with filling for:
  Jefferson Davis Pie,
    above
omitting the dates and spices.
When cool, cover with:
  Whipped cream

PECAN PIE

[A 9-Inch Pie]
This pie may also be made with
walnuts. Preheat oven to 450°.
Prepare:
  An unfilled Pie Shell,
    page 295
and bake it only partially, from
5 to 7 minutes. Allow it to cool.
Reduce oven heat to 375°.
Cream:
  ¼ cup butter
  1 cup firmly packed brown
    sugar
Beat in, one at a time:
  3 eggs
Stir in:
  ½ cup light corn sirup or
    molasses

  1 to 1½ cups broken
    pecans or walnuts
  1 teaspoon vanilla or 1
    tablespoon rum
  ½ teaspoon salt
Fill the shell. Bake the pie about
40 minutes or until a knife inserted in the filling comes out
clean. Serve warm or cold.

TRANSPARENT PIE

We have encountered this great
Southern favorite at all sorts of
gatherings, from fiestas to fu-
nerals. There are many variations, but we like to use our
recipe for Pecan Pie, above,
omitting the pecans and replacing the vanilla with:
  A grating of nutmeg or
  1 tablespoon lemon juice
You might try adding some tart
jelly for flavor.

ABOUT PUMPKINS

When Halloween comes 'round,
we welcome pumpkins as symbols of harvest and sources of
shivery fun. For holiday decorations, why not have each of the
children carve his own small
pumpkin? ▶ Then stack them
into a totem pole. Use the topmost cutout as a lid, the remainder for ears and noses.
Stems make good features, too.
Choose pumpkins of varied
shapes, as shown on page 319,
and encourage the sculptors to
vary their expressions.

Abroad, we find almost ev-
erywhere that a great diversity
of puddings, soups and vegetable dishes are prepared from
these members of the squash
family. Here in America we re-
strict their use mostly to pie.

▶ To cook pumpkin, wash and
cut it in half, crosswise. Remove
seeds and strings. Place it in a
pan, shell side up, and bake it
in a 325° oven for 1 hour or
more, depending on size, until
it is tender and begins to fall
apart. Scrape the pulp from the

shell and put it through a ricer or strainer.

PUMPKIN OR SQUASH PIE

[A 9-Inch Pie]

Prepare:

A baked Pie Shell, page 296

Mix in the top of a double boiler and cook over, not in, hot water until thick:

1½ cups cooked pumpkin or squash

1½ cups undiluted evaporated milk or rich cream
½ cup brown sugar
¼ cup white sugar
½ teaspoon salt
1 teaspoon cinnamon
½ teaspoon ginger
⅛ teaspoon cloves
4 slightly beaten eggs

Cool slightly and add:

(1 teaspoon vanilla or 2 tablespoons brandy or rum)

(¾ cup black walnut meats)

Pour the mixture into the baked pie shell. Serve with:

Whipped cream

ABOUT FRUIT PASTRIES

Here we include cobblers, deep-dish pies, fresh fruit cakes, shortcakes, upside-down cakes, crisps and crunches. Remember that large shortcakes, fresh fruit cakes and crunches lend themselves well to baking for individual servings.

COBBLERS AND DEEP-DISH PIES

A cobbler, first cousin to a deep-dish pie, involves a rich biscuit dough, page 286, and fruit. It is baked with the fruit either under or over it. It is usually served with Hard Sauce, Sweetened Butters, or Dessert Sauces, page 473; but try a fresh hot blackberry cobbler with vanilla ice cream.

Preheat oven to 425°.

Prepare the fruit as for any fruit pie filling. ▶ Have the fruit boiling hot. Have ready:

Fluffy Biscuit Dough, page 286

Use ½ the amount given. Place the dough in a greased 8 x 8-inch pan and cover it closely with the hot fruit or place the hot fruit in the bottom of an 8-inch baking dish and cover it with the dough. Dot the fruit with:

2 tablespoons butter

Sprinkle it with:

(¾ teaspoon cinnamon)

Bake the cobbler for about ½ hour.

APPLE, PEACH OR PLUM CAKE COCKAIGNE

[A 9 x 9 x 2½-Inch Pan]

Our friend Jane Nickerson, formerly Food Editor of the New York Times, suggests using fresh guavas in this dish.
Preheat oven to 425°.
If the fruit used is very juicy, reduce the liquid in the dough by at least 1 tablespoon. Sift before measuring:

   1 cup all-purpose flour

Resift with:

   1 teaspoon double-acting
    baking powder
   ¼ teaspoon salt
   2 tablespoons sugar

Add:

   1½ to 3 tablespoons butter

Work these ingredients like pastry, page 292. Beat well in a measuring cup:

   1 egg
   ½ teaspoon vanilla

Add:

   Enough milk to make a
   ½-cup mixture

Combine with the flour and butter to make a stiff dough. You may pat the dough into the pan with a floured palm or spread it in part with a spoon and then distribute it evenly by pushing it with the fruit sections when you place them closely in overlapping rows. Use about:

   3 to 4 cups sliced, pared
    apples or peaches or
    sliced, unpared plums

Sprinkle with a mixture of:

   About 1 cup sugar
   2 teaspoons cinnamon
   3 tablespoons melted
    butter

Bake about 25 minutes.

FRENCH APPLE OR PEACH CAKE

[A Deep 8-Inch Pie Pan]
Sweet and rich.
Preheat oven to 425°.
Grease the pan or ovenproof dish and cover the bottom well with:

   2 cups or more sliced
    apples, peaches or other
    fruit

Sprinkle the fruit with:

   ⅔ cup sugar
   Cinnamon or nutmeg
   Grated rind and juice of
   1 lemon

Dredge with:

   1 tablespoon flour

Pour over surface:

   2 to 4 tablespoons melted
    butter

Prepare the following batter. Sift before measuring:

   1 cup all-purpose flour

Resift with:

   ½ cup sugar
   1 teaspoon any baking
    powder
   ¼ teaspoon salt

Beat and add:

   2 egg yolks
   1 tablespoon melted butter
   ¼ cup milk

Beat these ingredients with swift strokes until blended. Cover the fruit with the batter. Bake the cake for about 30 minutes. Reverse it on a platter. Cool slightly. Use the egg whites for:

   (Meringue II, page 432)

SKILLET OR UPSIDE-DOWN CAKE

[A 9- or 10-Inch Heavy Skillet]
Vary this recipe, which conventionally calls for canned pineapple, by using canned peaches or apricots. The last two require only ½ cup sugar. Fresh fruit, peaches, cherries, apples, etc., may require more than 1 cup, according to the acidity of the fruit.
Preheat oven to 325°.
Melt in a skillet:

   ¼ or ½ cup butter

Add, cook gently and stir until dissolved:

   1 cup packed brown sugar

Remove the pan from the heat and add:

   (1 cup pecan meats)

Drain and place on the bottom of the skillet:

   Slices or halves of

drained canned fruit
Cover the fruit with the following batter:
Sift:

    1 cup cake flour

Resift with:

    1 teaspoon double-acting baking powder

Beat in a separate bowl:

    4 egg yolks

Add:

    1 tablespoon melted butter
    1 teaspoon vanilla

Sift in a separate bowl:

    1 cup sugar

Whip until ♦ stiff but not dry:

    4 egg whites

Fold in the sugar, 1 tablespoon at a time, then the yolk mixture and finally the sifted flour, ¼ cup at a time. Bake the cake for about ½ hour. Serve upside down, after sprinkling the fruit with:

    (Brandy or rum)

The cake may be garnished with:

    Whipped cream or a
    dessert sauce, page 473

For individual servings, try this method: Put butter, sugar and fruit in base of custard cups, run batter given above on top of the fruit and bake until done in a 350° oven.

FRESH FRUIT CRISP
OR PARADISE   [6]

This dessert may be baked in an ovenproof dish from which you can serve at table. Its success, when made with apples, depends upon their flavor. See About Apples, page 93.
Preheat oven to 375°.
Peel, core and slice into pie pan or dish:

    4 cups tart apples

or use the same amount of:

    Peaches, slightly sugared
    rhubarb or pitted cherries

Season with:

    (2 tablespoons lemon juice
    or kirsch)

Work like pastry with a pastry

blender or with the finger tips:

    ½ cup all-purpose flour
    ½ cup packed brown sugar
    ¼ cup butter
    ½ teaspoon salt, if butter is
    unsalted
    (1 teaspoon cinnamon)

The mixture must be lightly worked so that it does not become oily. Spread these crumbly ingredients over the apples. Bake in a 9-inch pie pan or dish for about 30 minutes. Serve hot or cold with:

    (Sweet or cultured sour
    cream)

QUICK CHERRY CRUNCH

[A 9 x 9 x 2-Inch Pan]
A well-flavored, easy cherry pastry.
Preheat oven to 350°.
Mix and let stand 15 minutes:

    ½ cup cherry juice
    1½ tablespoons quick-
    cooking tapioca

Melt in a large pan:

    ½ cup butter

Mix with it:

    1 to 1½ cups packed
    brown sugar
    1 cup flour
    1 cup quick-cooking
    oatmeal
    ¼ teaspoon each baking
    powder, salt and soda

Put half of this mixture in the baking pan. Scatter over it:

    2 cups drained canned red
    cherries

and the juice and tapioca mixture. Cover the fruit with the other half of the pastry mixture. Bake about 30 to 35 minutes or until brown.

SWEET TURNOVERS OR
RISSOLES

To shape these tea pastries, see Filled Cookies, page 406.
Prepare:

    Any Pie Crust, page 296

Use for filling:

    Well-flavored apple sauce

Preserves or jam
Mincemeat, page 315
Banbury Tart Filling
Filled Cookie Filling

To cook, see Rissoles, page 54. While still warm, dust pastries with:

Powdered sugar

FRUIT DUMPLINGS

[4 Dumplings]

Prepare:

Pie Crust, page 296, Cheese Pie Crust, page 298, or Biscuit Dough, page 284.

Chill it. Pare and core:

4 medium-size apples or 4 peeled, pitted and halved peaches or apricots

If using canned fruit, drain well and sprinkle with:

Lemon juice or rum

and use less sugar. Combine until blended:

¾ cup packed brown sugar
¼ cup soft butter
½ teaspoon salt
½ teaspoon cinnamon
(Grated lemon rind or citron)

Fill the core hollows with this mixture or with:

Raspberry jam

and spread the remainder over the fruit. Preheat oven to 450°. Roll out the dough in a thin sheet, ⅛ inch for pastry, ¼ inch for biscuit dough. Cut it into 4 squares. Brush squares with the white of an egg, to keep the dough from becoming soggy. Place an apple on each square. Enclose the apple entirely within the dough. Press the edges together, using a little water, if necessary, to make them stick. Prick the tops of the dumplings in several places. They may be chilled for several hours or baked at once. Brush the tops with milk. Bake for about 10 minutes at 450°, reduce the heat to 350° and bake for about 45 minutes, until the

apples are tender. Test them with a toothpick. Serve with:

Brown Sugar Butter Sauce, page 479

If you wish to bake the dumplings in sauce, combine and simmer for 5 minutes:

1 cup water
½ cup sugar
2 tablespoons butter
½ teaspoon cinnamon

For enhanced flavor, if you are using apples, you may simmer the cores and peelings in 1½ cups water for 15 minutes. Drain and use the fruit liquid in place of the water. Pour it boiling hot over the dumplings when they begin to color. Dumplings that are not baked in sauce may be served hot or cold with:

Fluffy Hard Sauce with Rum, page 481, Foamy Sauce, page 481, Lemon Sauce, page 473, or cream

RAISED DUMPLINGS OR DAMPFNUDELN

[About 16 Dumplings]

It has been fun to dig in old cookbooks for this recipe, if only because it made us realize that the modern method of writing for cooks is an immense improvement over the old. Our grandmothers had to hack through a labyrinth, undoubtedly armed with a ball of string, plus a rabbit's foot, in order to arrive at their goal. This homely old-time favorite is worth resurrecting. Try it in its modern form. A well-known Cincinnati hostess serves it as a dessert at formal dinners with much success.

Dissolve:

½ cake compressed yeast

in:

½ cup scalded milk, cooled to 85°

Work in:

1 tablespoon sugar

1¼ cups sifted all-purpose
   flour

Permit this heavy sponge to rise, covered with a cloth in a warm place, until light, for about 1 hour. Cream:

1 tablespoon butter
2 tablespoons sugar
½ teaspoon salt

Beat in and stir until light:

1 whole egg

Add this to the sponge and work in about:

½ cup sifted all-purpose
   flour

or enough to stiffen, as for yeast cake. Cover the bowl with a cloth. Permit the dough to rise until doubled in bulk. Shape it into about 16 biscuits. They may be rolled out and cut. If you have time, permit them to rise again. From here on there is a great divergence in treatment. The old method required the use of a Dutch oven, but a covered, deep, 10-inch oven-proof glass baking dish is preferable, as it enables you to watch the cooking process. Place in it one of the hot liquids indicated below and then the dumplings. If they are to be served with a meat course with lots of gravy, use ½ cup butter and ½ cup scalded milk. If they are to constitute a dessert, use 1½ cups sirup, fruit juice, preserves or stewed fruit. ♦ Cover the pot closely, place it in a 275° oven and cook the dumplings for about 1½ hours. If you have not used a glass baker, do not lift the lid, even to peek. Old recipes add that your sense of smell must be your guide as to when to uncover. Do it when the dumplings begin to give off a tempting fragrance of finality, telling you that the liquid has been absorbed. Test the dumplings with a straw. Remove them from the pot and serve at once. An outstanding accompaniment for this dessert is stewed blue plums or prunes.

Use part of the sirup in the pot. Serve the dumplings with the remaining fruit. The plums or prunes may be stewed with part white wine and part water. In addition, it is customary to serve:

Custard Sauce, page 475,
   or Rich Custard, page
   438

ABOUT CUSTARD PIES

How many puzzled inquiries we have answered about "Custard, my family's favorite pie"! In a recent one, our correspondent gloomily points out: "My mother thinks it's lumpy because I cook it too long. My husband thinks it gets watery because I put it in the icebox." How right, unfortunately, are both of this bride's critics! ♦ Custard and cream pies, unless eaten almost at once, must be kept well chilled. The lightly cooked eggs are especially subject to adverse bacterial activity, even though they may give no evidence of spoilage. It is Hobson's choice here: eat within 3 hours if the pie is left unrefrigerated or risk wateriness under refrigeration.

Again, pie dough needs a high heat, while the custard itself demands a low one. How to reconcile these contradictions? We find that the easiest way to satisfaction is to prebake crust and filling separately; then, just before serving, to slip the cooled filling into the cooled shell. To prebake the filling, select a pie pan of the same size as the crust. Grease well. Bake a custard in the pie pan, until just firm. Cool quickly. Before serving, slide the filling into the crust, see page 324. This method takes a bit of dexterity but, after you get used to it, you will prefer it. The filling need not even be preformed but, if precooked, can be spooned carefully into the prebaked shell. If

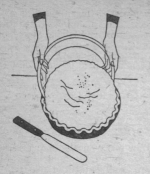

you use a topping, see page 433, no one will be the wiser. Two more important comments about fillings which are precooked, but not preformed. ◗ Always cook them over—not in—hot water. ◗ When they are thickened, beat them until they are cool to allow all steam to escape. The steam will otherwise condense and thin the filling too much. Mark Twain inelegantly wrote of a frustrated crow that it was "sweating like an ice pitcher," and this is exactly what custard filling will do, unless beaten until cool. When it is 70° or cooler, place the filling in the prebaked shell and the pie is ready to serve.

CUSTARD OR CREAM PIE

[A 9-Inch Pie]
Preheat oven to 450°.
The partial baking of this pie shell before filling insures a crisper undercrust. Line a pie pan with any:

    Pie Crust, page 296

Build up a fluted rim. Prick the crust and bake it in a 450° oven for about 10 minutes. Reduce heat to 325°. Fill the shell with the following custard which should be ready and cool. Pull the oven rack part way out and pour the filling into the crust or remove the crust from the oven only long enough to fill it. Beat slightly:

    3 eggs or 6 egg yolks

Add and stir well:

    ½ cup sugar
    ¼ teaspoon salt
    2 cups milk or milk and
        light cream
    1 teaspoon vanilla or
    1 tablespoon rum

Pour these ingredients into the partly baked pie shell. Sprinkle the top with:

    (¼ teaspoon nutmeg)

Bake the pie in the already reduced 325° oven for about 30 minutes or until done. See About Custard Pies, page 323.

CUSTARD TARTS OR FLAN WITH FRUIT

To be assembled just before serving.
Fill:

    Prebaked Tart Shells,
        page 296

with:

    ½-inch layer of Baked
        Custard

Top the custard with:

    Strawberries or other
        berries, cooked drained
        apples, drained cherries,
        peaches, bananas,
        pineapple or coconut

Coat the fruit with Glaze for Tarts, page 434, to which you may add:

    (1 tablespoon or more of
        brandy or rum)

Garnish with:

    (Whipped cream)

CHOCOLATE-TOPPED CUSTARD PIE

Follow the recipe for:

    Custard Pie, this page

Omit the nutmeg. Stir and cook in a double boiler ◗ over—not in—hot water:

    1½ oz. chocolate
    5 tablespoons sugar
    2 beaten eggs
    ⅛ teaspoon salt

Cook these ingredients until

slightly thickened, about 4 minutes. ◗ Beat until slightly cooled. Add:

>1 tablespoon rum or ½
>teaspoon vanilla

Pour the mixture over the baked custard.

CARAMEL CUSTARD PIE

[A 9-Inch Pie]
Prepare:

>A baked Pie Shell, page
>296

and:

>Caramel Custard
>Pudding, page 438

Cool the pudding and fill the slightly cooled pie shell. Garnish with:

>Sweetened Whipped
>Cream II, page 377

CHOCOLATE PIE

[A 9-Inch Pie]
Prepare by any rule:

>A baked Pie Shell,
>page 296

Scald in a double boiler or over very low heat with constant stirring:

>2½ cups milk

Cut up and add:

>2 oz. chocolate

In a separate bowl, mix until smooth:

>⅓ cup flour

in:

>¼ cup milk

Add:

>¼ teaspoon salt
>1 cup sugar
>(⅛ teaspoon cinnamon)

Add to the mixture in double boiler. Cook and stir ◗ over, not in, hot water, for 15 minutes. Pour a small quantity over:

>3 to 4 beaten egg yolks

Beat and add to mixture in double boiler. Stir and cook the custard for 3 minutes. Add:

>2 tablespoons butter

Remove from heat. Beat gently until very smooth. Add:

>1 teaspoon vanilla

>(½ cup chopped nut meats)

Cool this mixture. Pour it into the pie shell. Cover with:

>Meringue I, page 432

and bake as directed.

CHOCOLATE CREAM PIE

[A 9-Inch Pie]
Here are some of the many good ways to make this pie. Prepare:

>A baked Pie Shell,
>page 293

Fill it with ½ the recipe for:

>Pots de Crème,
>page 441

Garnish with:

>Whipped cream or
>French Chocolate
>Mousse, page 441 or
>Rum Chocolate Mousse,
>page 441, or Mocha
>Filling, page 379

and keep chilled until ready to serve, or, follow the recipe for:

>Custard Pie, page 324

Melt in the scalded milk:

>2 oz. chocolate
>⅔ cup sugar

◗ Cool slightly and proceed with the recipe. Cover with:

>¼-inch layer whipped
>cream

or top with:

>Meringue II, page 432

and bake as directed.

COFFEE TARTS OR PIE

Prepare:

>6 baked Tart Shells or
>baked Pie Crust,
>page 293

I. Prepare:

>2 cups hot strong coffee

Combine and stir until smooth:

>1 cup cream or evaporated
>milk
>6 tablespoons sifted
>all-purpose flour
>⅔ cup sugar
>¼ teaspoon salt

Stir these ingredients into the hot coffee. Cook and stir the mixture over low heat in a double boiler over, not in, hot

water, until it thickens, about
20 minutes. Pour part of it over:
>   2 beaten eggs or 5 egg
>   yolks

Return this to the pan, stir and
cook for 2 or 3 minutes over
low heat to permit the eggs to
thicken slightly. Add:
>   2 tablespoons butter

◗ Cool, then add:
>   1 teaspoon vanilla or
>   2 teaspoons rum

Fill tart shells or pie crust. Chill
and serve topped with:
>   Whipped cream
>   Crushed Nut Brittle,
>   page 515

II. Or use:
>   Coffee Marshmallow
>   Cream, page 457

BUTTERSCOTCH PIE

[A 9-Inch Pie]
Prepare by any recipe:
>   A baked Pie Shell,
>   page 293

Combine in a double boiler
◗ over—not in—hot water:
>   1 cup brown sugar
>   ¼ cup all-purpose flour
>   3 tablespoons butter
>   ¼ teaspoon salt

Stir and cook these ingredients
until blended. Add:
>   2¼ cups scalded milk

Beat until light:
>   4 egg yolks

Pour a little of the milk mixture
over them. Beat well and return
it to the double boiler. Stir and
cook until the yolks thicken
slightly. ◗ Beat custard until
cool and add:
>   ½ teaspoon vanilla
>   (½ cup nut meats or crushed
>   Peanut Brittle, page
>   515)

Pour the custard into the baked
pie shell.
Cover with:
>   Meringue, page 432

and bake as directed or cover
with:
>   Whipped cream

ORANGE CREAM PIE

[A 9-Inch Pie]
Prepare:
>   A baked Pie Shell, page
>   296

Mix thoroughly in a double
boiler over, not in, hot water:
>   ½ cup sugar or more if the
>   orange juice is very tart
>   ¼ cup all-purpose flour
>   ⅛ teaspoon salt

Add:
>   1 cup scalded milk

Cook and stir these ingredients
over very low heat until thick.
Pour part of this mixture over:
>   3 well-beaten egg yolks

Return to pan. Add:
>   ⅔ cup orange juice
>   2 teaspoons grated orange
>   rind
>   1 teaspoon butter

Stir and cook the custard over
very low heat until the eggs
thicken slightly. Add:
>   (½ cup pecan meats)

◗ Cool the custard and pour it
into the baked pie shell. Cover
with:
>   Meringue I, page 432

and bake as directed.

ABOUT CHEESECAKE

No wonder pictures of starlets
are called cheesecake! We think
the six following recipes are
starlets. Take your pick, but remember to ◗ watch temperatures. If the recipe calls for
baker's cheese, or curd, procure
this very dry, lean cottage
cheese or use farmer's cheese.
Put it through a sieve, as shown
on page 225, or a food-mill, or
grind it. Cheesecakes are egg-
based. They need low heat and
are usually left in the turned-off
oven with the door open, after
baking. Expect a slight shrinkage, as they cool. If there is
great shrinkage, you have baked
them with too high a heat. They
all profit by ◗ thorough chilling

before serving, preferably 12 hours. For storing safely, see About Custards, page 436.

A few wine-soaked currants, finely shaved almonds, tiny pieces of angelica or citron are sometimes mixed with the filling or used as topping. Shaved curled chocolate may be added as a surface garnish. To glaze cheesecakes, see Strawberry Glaze and Apricot Glaze, page 434 and 435.

BAKER'S CHEESE PIE [12] OR CAKE

This cheese pie or cake is luscious. It should be 1½ inches or more in depth. Bake it in a pan with a removable rim or in an ovenproof baking dish, 9 inches wide, 2⅝ inches high.
Prepare:
    Zwieback Crust or
    Crumb Crust, page
    299
Reserve ½ cup of the mixture. Line a deep baking dish and press the crust lightly on the bottom and against the sides. Chill thoroughly. Fill with:
    Cheese Filling
To make filling, dissolve:
    1 cup sugar
in:
    ⅓ cup whipping cream
Add:
    2 lbs. baker's cheese: about
        2 pints
    4 beaten egg yolks
    3 tablespoons flour
    1 teaspoon vanilla or 2½
        tablespoons lemon juice
        and 1 teaspoon grated
        lemon rind
Whip until stiff, but not dry:
    4 egg whites
Fold them into the cheese mixture. Fill the shell and sprinkle the reserved crumbs over the top. Bake the pie in a 350° oven for about 1 hour.

WHIPPED CREAM [16] CHEESECAKE

Double the recipe for:
    Graham Cracker Crust,
    page 299
Reserve 1 cup of this mixture. Press the remainder with a spoon or the palm of the hand on the bottom and sides of a 12-inch spring form pan. Chill this shell thoroughly. Or you may line a spring mold with galette dough, page 297.
To make the filling, sift:
    1½ cups sugar
Beat until light:
    6 eggs
Add the sugar gradually. Beat these ingredients until very light.
Add:
    ⅛ teaspoon salt
    2 teaspoons grated lemon
        rind
    3 tablespoons lemon juice
    1 teaspoon vanilla
Whip and fold in:
    1 cup whipping cream
Blend well:
    ½ cup all-purpose flour
    3½ pints smooth cottage
        cheese: 2¼ lbs.
Put these ingredients through a sieve. Fold into the egg and cream mixture. Fill the pie shell. Sprinkle the reserved crumb mixture over the filling. Bake in a 350° oven for about 1 hour. Turn off the heat and permit the pie to stand in the oven for 1 hour longer with the door open or until cooled.

SOUR CREAM [12] CHEESECAKE

Line a 9-inch, 2½-inch-deep spring mold with:
    Zwieback Crust, page
    299
Chill the crust well.
Preheat oven to 375°.
Mix well, then pour into the shell:
    2 well-beaten eggs

4 packages soft cream
  cheese: ¾ lb.
½ cup sugar
1 teaspoon lemon juice or
  ½ teaspoon vanilla
½ teaspoon salt

Bake for about 20 minutes. Remove from oven. Dust the top with:

Cinnamon

Let cool to room temperature. Heat oven to 425°. Mix well and pour over the cake:

1½ cups thick cultured sour
  cream
2 tablespoons sugar
½ teaspoon vanilla
⅛ teaspoon salt

Bake in the oven for about 5 minutes to glaze it. Permit it to cool, then refrigerate from 6 to 12 hours before serving. You may garnish with a crumb lattice topping.

GELATIN CHEESECAKE

[A 10-Inch Cake]

This sumptuous Torte will serve 18 persons. It is handsome and delectable and may be made a day in advance.

Prepare:

Zwieback Crust, page
  299

Reserve ¼ of the crumbs. Spread or pat the rest in a thin layer over the bottom and sides of a 3-inch-deep, 10-inch spring mold. Bake the crust for about 15 minutes. Cool it. Scald in the top of a double boiler:

⅓ cup milk

with:

A vanilla bean

Beat:

4 egg yolks
¾ cup sugar
¼ teaspoon salt

Remove the vanilla bean. Add the milk gradually to the beaten egg mixture. Heat and stir this custard over, not in, hot water until it thickens. Soak:

2 tablespoons gelatin

in:

½ cup water

Stir this mixture into the hot custard until dissolved. Cool the custard. Add:

(⅓ cup lemon juice)

Work with a fork until smooth:

1½ lbs. soft cream cheese

Stir into the custard until well blended. Whip until stiff ◗ but not dry:

4 egg whites

Whip in gradually:

½ cup sugar

Fold this into the custard. Beat until stiff, then fold in:

1 cup whipping cream

Fill the zwieback crust with the custard. Sprinkle the reserved crumbs over the top. Chill the Torte well in the refrigerator until ready to serve.

FRUIT GELATIN   [8]
CHEESECAKE

Prepare:

Zwieback Crust, page
  299

Line a deep 10-inch dish with it. Drain and reserve the juice of:

2½ cups canned cubed
  pineapple or apricots

Soak:

2 tablespoons gelatin

in:

½ cup fruit juice

Beat until light:

3 egg yolks

Beat in gradually:

½ cup sugar
½ cup pineapple or
  apricot juice

Cook and stir these ingredients in a double boiler ◗ over, not in, hot water, until they thicken. Add the soaked gelatin. Stir until it is dissolved. Cool the custard. Stir in:

1 lb. smooth cottage cheese
1 teaspoon grated lemon
  rind
3 tablespoons lemon juice
¼ teaspoon salt

Fold in ¾ of the pineapple cubes and:

   2 cups whipped cream

Fold in:

   3 stiffly beaten egg whites

Fill the pie shell. Garnish the top with the remaining pineapple cubes. Sprinkle with:

   Cinnamon

Chill the pie for at least 3 hours.

RICOTTA CHEESE PIE OR CAKE

[A 10-Inch Pie]

This North Italian delight is a favorite of our friend, Jim Beard, who has generously allowed us to include it. Cheesecake Crust with cognac should accompany it. To prepare it, see page 298. Preheat oven to 375°. Have all ingredients at 75°. Combine:

   1½ pounds ricotta cheese
   3 tablespoons toasted
      pine nuts
   2 tablespoons chopped
      blanched almonds
   2 tablespoons chopped
      citron

and dust with:

   1 tablespoon flour

Beat until light and lemony in color:

   4 eggs

Gradually add:

   1 cup sugar
   1½ teaspoons vanilla

Add the cheese mixture to the eggs until well blended. Pour the filling into the unbaked crust and bake about 40 minutes or until done.

LEMON MERINGUE PIE

[A 9-Inch Pie]

Prepare:

   A baked Pie Shell,
      page 296

Combine in the top of a double boiler:

   1 cup sugar
   5 to 6 tablespoons
      cornstarch

   ⅛ teaspoon salt

Add very gradually:

   2 cups water or milk

Stir and cook these ingredients ♦ over—not in—hot water for about 8 to 12 minutes or until the mixture thickens. See About Cornstarch, page 155. Cover and cook for 10 minutes more. Stir occasionally. Remove the mixture from the heat. Pour a little of it over:

   3 beaten egg yolks

Beat this and return to mixture in double boiler. Cook and stir gently, still over boiling water, about 5 minutes more. Remove from heat. Beat in:

   3 tablespoons butter
   ⅓ cup lemon juice
   2 teaspoons grated lemon
      rind

Some people prefer the rind coarsely grated. ♦ If you want a very lemony flavor add more rind—rather than more juice. Additional acid liquid may thin the filling too much. Cool the custard by stirring very, very gently to release any steam which might condense to thin the filling. Pour it cool into the cold pie shell. Cover with:

   Meringue I, page 432

and bake as directed.

LEMON OR LIME PIE COCKAIGNE

[A 9-Inch Pie]

Prepare:

   A baked Pie Shell,
      page 296

Preheat oven to 325°.

Beat until very light:

   4 egg yolks

Beat until soft:

   ½ cup butter

Add very slowly:

   1 cup white or packed
      brown sugar

Blend these ingredients until creamy. Beat in the egg yolks and:

   3 tablespoons lemon juice

and 1½ teaspoons grated
lemon rind

Fill the pie shell with this mixture. Bake the pie until firm,
about 30 minutes. It may be
cooled and:

Meringue II, page 432

may be placed on it. Bake as
directed.

EGGLESS LEMON OR
LIME CREAM PIE

[A 9-Inch Pie]
Prepare:

A baked Pie Shell,
page 296

Combine:

1 can sweetened condensed
milk: 15 oz.
⅓ cup lime or lemon juice
1 tablespoon grated lemon
or lime rind
¼ teaspoon salt

♦ Stir until thickened. The thickening results from the reaction
of the milk and citrus juice.
Blend in gently:

(⅔ cup well-drained canned
pineapple)

Turn the filling into the baked
shell. Chill about 3 hours. Serve
garnished with:

(Whipped cream)
(Shaved sweet chocolate)

✳ FROZEN LEMON [5 to 6]
OR LIME CREAM PIE

[A 4½ x 11 x 1¼-Inch
Refrigerator Tray]
If fresh cream is not available,
try this recipe using:

1 cup evaporated milk

chilled for 12 hours. Otherwise
use:

1 cup whipping cream

Butter the refrigerator tray well.
Line it with ¾ recipe for:

Crumb Crust, page 299

reserving ¼ for a topping. Combine in the top of a double boiler
♦ over—not in—hot water and
cook until it forms a custard:

6 tablespoons sugar
2 slightly beaten egg yolks

Grated rind of ½ lemon
⅓ cup lemon juice

Cool the custard. Whip until
stiff, but not dry:

2 to 3 egg whites

Gradually beat in:

2 tablespoons sugar

Fold the egg whites into the
custard. Whip the cream or the
chilled evaporated milk and fold
into it:

2 tablespoons confectioners'
sugar

Fold into the custard. Place the
filling lightly into the crumb-
lined refrigerator tray. Top it
with a sprinkling of the reserved
crumb crust. Freeze until firm.

ANGEL PIE

[A 10-Inch Pie]
Prepare a shell of:

Meringue Paste, page 309

Butter the bottom of a deep 10-
inch ovenproof dish, and cover
with the meringue. Bake as directed. Let cool in the oven
with the door open. Prepare the
following filling in a double
boiler ♦ over—not in—hot water.
Beat well:

4 egg yolks

Add:

½ cup sugar

Cook until thickened, beating
constantly. Add:

Juice and rind of 1 lemon

Whip:

1 cup whipping cream

Put ½ of the cream in the meringue shell, then the cooked
lemon filling. Cover with the remaining cream. Chill for 24
hours.

ABOUT CHIFFON PIES

Many chiffon pies call for egg
white that is not cooked—a state
of affairs that is not approved by
some health authorities, see page
453. Only in Frozen Lemon or
Lime Cream Pie, and when the
word gelatin appears in the title

do our pie fillings call for uncooked egg white.

LEMON OR LIME CHIFFON PIE

[A 9-Inch Pie]
One version of this pie is made
with Key limes. If you are a
Floridian or can otherwise avail
yourself of this pungent fruit, by
all means try it in any of our
recipes that call for lemon.
Prepare:

    A baked Pie Shell,
      page 296

Combine in a double boiler:

    ⅓ to ½ cup sugar
    2 tablespoons water
    4 to 5 egg yolks

Cook and stir these ingredients
◗ over—not in—hot water, until
thick. Add:

    Grated rind of 1 lemon
    3 tablespoons lemon juice

Cool the mixture.
Preheat oven to 400°.
Whip:

    3 egg whites

until stiff, but not dry. Fold in:

    ¼ cup sugar

Fold this mixture lightly into the
custard. Fill the pie shell. Brown
the pie in the oven for about 10
minutes or place it under a
broiler until lightly browned.

ORANGE CHIFFON PIE

[A 9-Inch Pie]
Use well-flavored orange juice
for this pie. Indifferently flavored orange juice may be improved by the addition of 2
teaspoons of vanilla.
Prepare:

    A baked Pie Shell,
      page 296

Cook and stir in a double boiler
◗ over—not in—hot water, until
thick:

    3 tablespoons all-purpose
      flour
    3 egg yolks
    2 tablespoons lemon juice
    1 cup orange juice

    ½ teaspoon grated orange
      rind
    ¼ cup sugar

Use more sugar if the orange
juice is acid. Cool these ingredients. Whip until stiff, but not
dry:

    3 egg whites

Fold them into the orange custard. Fill the pie shell. Brown
the pie in a preheated 400° oven
for about 10 minutes.

CHOCOLATE GELATIN CHIFFON PIE

[A 9-Inch Pie]
Prepare:

    A baked Pie Shell,
      page 296

Soak:

    1 tablespoon gelatin

in:

    ¼ cup cold water or strong
      coffee

Combine and stir until smooth:

    6 tablespoons cocoa or
      2 oz. melted chocolate
    ½ cup boiling water or
      strong coffee

Stir in the soaked gelatin until
it is dissolved. Combine gently:

    4 lightly beaten egg yolks
    ½ cup sugar

Combine both mixtures and chill
until about to set. Add:

    1 teaspoon vanilla

Beat with a wire whisk until
light. Whip until ◗ stiff, but not
dry:

    4 egg whites

Fold them into the chocolate
mixture with:

    ½ cup sugar

Fill the pie shell. Chill the pie
to set it. Shortly before serving,
cover the top with thinly sliced
ripe:

    (Bananas)

Spread with:

    Whipped cream

RUM GELATIN CREAM PIE

[A 9-Inch Pie]

The headiest of them all.
Prepare:

A baked Crumb Crust,
page 299, or Pie Shell,
page 296

Beat until light:

6 egg yolks

Beat in gradually:

⅞ cup sugar

Soak:

1 tablespoon gelatin

in:

½ cup cold water

Place this mixture in the top of a double boiler ▶ over—not in— hot water and stir until the gelatin is dissolved. Pour it over the egg and sugar combination in a slow stream, beating constantly. Cool. Stir in:

½ cup Jamaica rum

Whip until stiff:

1 pint whipping cream:
2 cups

Fold into the egg mixture. Cool the filling, but before it begins to set pour it into the pie shell. When set, sprinkle the top with:

Grated bittersweet
chocolate or toasted,
grated coconut or finely
shaved pistachio nuts

Chill pie to set.

BLACK BOTTOM GELATIN PIE

[A Deep 9-Inch Pie]
Prepare:

Baked Crumb Crust,
page 299, or
Pie Crust, page 296

Soak:

1 tablespoon gelatin

in:

¼ cup cold water

Scald:

2 cups rich milk

Combine:

½ cup sugar
4 teaspoons cornstarch

Beat until light:

4 egg yolks

Slowly stir the scalded milk into the eggs. Stir in the sugar mix-

ture. Cook these ingredients over, not in, hot water, stirring occasionally, about 20 minutes —or until the custard coats a spoon heavily. Take out 1 cup of the custard. Add to it:

1½ oz. melted chocolate

Beat these ingredients until well blended and cool. Add:

½ teaspoon vanilla

Pour this custard into the pie shell. Dissolve the soaked gelatin in the remaining custard. Be sure it is hot. Let it cool, but do not permit it to stiffen. Stir in:

1 tablespoon or more rum

Beat until well blended:

3 egg whites

Add:

¼ teaspoon cream of tartar

Beat the egg whites until they are stiff, but not dry. Beat in gradually, a teaspoon at a time:

¼ cup sugar

Fold the egg whites into the custard. Cover the chocolate custard with the rum-flavored custard. Chill to set. Whip until stiff:

1 cup whipping cream

Add gradually:

2 tablespoons confectioners'
sugar

Cover custard with the cream. Top with:

½ oz. shaved chocolate

MOCHA GELATIN CHIFFON CREAM PIE

[A 9-Inch Pie]
Prepare:

A baked Pie Shell,
page 296

Soak:

2 tablespoons gelatin

in:

½ cup cold water

Dissolve:

2 tablespoons cocoa

in:

2 cups hot strong coffee

and bring to a boil. Dissolve the soaked gelatin in this mixture. Stir in:

⅓ cup sugar

Cool slightly and pour these ingredients slowly onto:

2 to 3 well-beaten egg yolks

Cook and stir these ingredients in a double boiler ▶ over, not in, hot water, until they thicken. Cool the filling until about to set. Beat with a wire whisk until fluffy. Add:

1 teaspoon vanilla
(1 tablespoon brandy)

Whip until stiff:

1 cup whipping cream

Fold in:

1 tablespoon sugar

Whip until stiff but not dry:

2 to 3 egg whites

Fold the whipped cream and beaten egg whites into the coffee mixture. Pour filling into pie shell. Chill pie thoroughly.

MAPLE GELATIN CHIFFON PIE

[A 9-Inch Pie]

Prepare:

A baked Pie Shell,
page 296

Soak:

1 tablespoon gelatin

in:

2 tablespoons cold water

Heat and stir in a double boiler:

½ cup milk
½ cup maple sirup
⅛ teaspoon salt

Pour part of this over:

2 beaten egg yolks

Return to double boiler. Stir and cook the custard ▶ over, not in, hot water, until thickened. Add the soaked gelatin and stir until dissolved. Chill these ingredients until they begin to thicken.

Whip until stiff:

1 cup whipping cream

Fold into ¾ of it:

⅓ cup chopped hickory nuts
1 teaspoon vanilla

Whip until stiff but not dry:

2 egg whites

Fold these and the cream and nuts into the custard. Fill the pie shell. Garnish with the remaining cream. Chill to set.

PUMPKIN GELATIN CHIFFON PIE

[A 9-Inch Pie]

Prepare:

A baked Pie Shell,
page 296

Soak:

1 tablespoon gelatin

in:

¼ cup cold water

Beat slightly:

3 egg yolks

Add:

½ cup sugar
1¼ cups canned or cooked pumpkin
½ cup milk
¼ teaspoon salt
½ teaspoon each cinnamon and nutmeg

Cook and stir these ingredients over, not in, hot water until thick. Stir in the soaked gelatin until dissolved. Chill. Whip until stiff but not dry:

3 egg whites

When the pumpkin mixture begins to set, stir in:

½ cup sugar

and fold in the egg whites. Fill the pie shell. Chill to set. Serve garnished with:

Whipped cream

CAKES, CUP CAKES, TORTEN, AND FILLED CAKES

At weddings and birthdays, a cake can become the center of interest; and this interest, happily, has been known to extend to the cook. Thirty years of fan mail prove to us that almost every woman wants to bake a perfect cake. If you are a born baker, skip our advice to the "cakelorn." Otherwise, it will be more than worth your while to learn a few simple but highly significant mixing and baking techniques.

♦ Start, of course, with high-quality materials. Never jeopardize your results with damp flour, old milk or eggs or doubtful fats. Pay attention to the ♦ measurements and proportions you use ♦ the temperature of the ingredients and ♦ the heat of your oven, page 99. Most recipes call for ingredients at room temperature. As kitchen temperatures vary, we suggest ♦ ingredients be about 75°, the ideal recommended by professional bakers. Pay attention also to ♦ the physical states you induce by stirring, creaming and folding. Our drawings and descriptions can only get you off to a flying start. The proper "look" of well-creamed butter and eggs, of batter ready for the oven—these and other critical stages in cake making you will learn to recognize most effectively through practice.

ABOUT CAKE TYPES

We divide cakes according to their leavens. If you know what makes them rise or fall, it will help you to preserve their lifting action during mixing. Angel and sponge cakes are sometimes called ♦ foam cakes, because they depend for their leavening exclusively on the expansion of the vapor trapped in their light egg-rich doughs. Egg white contains no fat, but egg yolk does. As a consequence, angel cakes are fat-free; but ♦ sponge cakes, though light in texture, contain appreciable fat by reason of their yolk-content, see page 170.

♦ Butter and shortening cakes need baking powder for proper leavening. We feel that all cakes in this category are more delicious if butter alone is used as the fatty ingredient. If you care to use, instead, one of the bland white vegetable shortenings now on the market, you will trade distinctive flavor for a measure of economy, a spongier texture and a somewhat greater volume. Whatever the fat used, "butter" cakes gain lightness if the butter ingredient, at about 70°, is creamed with the sugar as a first step. To this mixture the beaten egg yolk is added and the combination, in turn, well beaten. Dry and liquid ingredients are then added alternately and the beaten egg whites folded in last. For quicker, but not better, results the entire egg may be beaten into the creamed mixture. See About Quick Cakes, page 362.

In commercial baking and

mixes, the use of emulsifying agents not available to the housewife gives extremely fine spongy textures. In cakes made with ♦ melted butter, such as the classic Génoise, page 370, the butter is put in last. In cakes made with oils, special mixing procedures are used to allow the incorporation of air into the batter. Our cake recipes are all adjusted in method to the specific demands of the ingredients. So, for success, please follow directions as given.

All these cake types may be ✶ frozen, see page 567, but dry out rapidly after thawing.

▲ In high altitudes, reduce the baking powder or soda by ½. ♦ But do not reduce soda beyond ½ teaspoon for each cup of sour milk or cream used.

ABOUT CAKE MIXING

After reading About Leavens, page 161, look at the bottom of this page. At the left, you see how to stir batter. Begin at the center of the bowl, using a circular motion and widening the circle as the ingredients become blended. ♦ To cream, work fat at about 70° lightly with the finger tips—or use the back of a wooden spoon. Press the mixture in a gently gliding motion between the back of the spoon and the side of the bowl, in short rocking strokes, over a rather

limited area shown between the arrows in the sketch. The sugar mixture should become light in color, even, smooth and creamy in texture. If it looks curdled and frothy, you have worked it too long and the oil in the butter has separated and will result in a coarsely grained cake. To beat or whip, use a long, free-swinging, lifting motion, which brings the bottom mass constantly to the top, trapping as much air as possible in the mixture, as shown on the right. A slotted spoon makes the work quicker; a wooden, rather than a metal, spoon keeps the ingredients in the best condition. Whipping is done rapidly with an increasing tempo. If you use a longer, thinner whip, such as the one shown immediately next to the bowl, you will get the best results in handling egg white. For beating cream, use a wider whisk like the one shown to its left. In choosing a mechanical mixer, see that the beaters have many wires that are as thin as is consistent with durability.

Folding in is one of the most tactful of cake making operations: the objective is to blend thoroughly, yet not lose any of the air you have previously worked into your materials.

♦ To fold, first of all have a large enough bowl. A flat whip as shown on page 336 is usually recommended, but this tool can

be maddening because it cuts through the whites and its too widely spaced wires allow the heavier substances to fall through. We commonly dispense with tools for this step and use the flat of the hand. You may begin by folding into the dough a small quantity of the whites. When thoroughly mixed, fold in the rest of the whites by scooping up some of the more solid material and covering the whites. Then, cut it in with a determined, gentle slicing motion to the base of the mixing bowl. Turn the bowl slightly with the other hand each time you repeat the folding motions. It is surprising how well and quickly blending is achieved by this simple procedure.

▶ Baking directions are given with each recipe. If you use an electric oven ▶ be sure to remove the upper heating element before heating the oven.

▶ To test for doneness, insert a wire cake tester or a toothpick, and if it emerges perfectly clean the cake is done. It should be lightly browned and beginning to shrink from the sides of the pan. If pressed with a finger, it should at once come back into shape, except in very rich cakes and chocolate cakes which may dent slightly and still be done. When removed from the oven, the cake is cooled in the pan on a rack, for about 5 minutes, and

then cooled out of the pan, on a rack, until all heat has left. For exceptions, see About Angel, page 339, Sponge, page 341, Génoise, page 370, and Fruit Cakes, page 355. For an obstinate cake, set the pan on a cloth rung out in hot water. This often helps in removing the cake from the pan.

ABOUT CAKE PANS

If you want a thin, evenly browned crust, try using ▶ medium weight metal pans, shiny on the upper surfaces and slightly dulled beneath. If you prefer heavier, browner crusts, use glass or enamel pans or those that are dark in color—all of which absorb and hold more heat. Should you choose from the second group, reduce the oven heat by 25°. In baking layer cakes, use pans with straight sides. Note also that too-high sides will prevent good browning. But even more important to the crumb and volume of your cake is the relation of dough to the size of the pan. All our cake recipes indicate the proper pan sizes. Cake pans are measured across the top.

The dough, for a velvety texture, should be at least 1 inch deep in the pan. If the pan is too big, the cake will not rise properly and may brown unevenly. If the pan is too small,

the texture will be coarse and the batter may overflow before it sets. If it doesn't overflow, it will probably sink in cooling. Most pans are filled at least half full, but not more than ⅔. Loaf and tube pans can be filled higher. If you have no pan corresponding to the size called for in the recipe, see the chart below to find out what area is called for. Then substitute a pan size you own that has the approximate area. For instance, a recipe calls for a 9-inch round pan which has an area of approximately 64 square inches. From other tables you see that you could equally well use an 8 x 8-square inch pan, which offers also an area of 64 square inches. Should your pan be too large, you can reduce the baking area of a rectangular pan by folding a piece of foil as shown in the drawing on the right below. The dough will help to hold the divider in place on one side. Place dry beans or rice on the other, see center sketch.

♦ Note that a round 9-inch-diameter pan equals only about ¾ the area of a square 9-inch pan. This ¾ proportion holds for any round pan, the diameter of which equals the side of the square pan, as you can see illustrated below by comparing the square pan surface, left, with the area of the dotted circle.

♦ To know how much batter to mix for oddly shaped pans or molds, first measure their contents with water. Then make up ⅔ as much dough as the amount of the water measured.

COMPARATIVE PAN SIZES

ROUND CAKE PANS

8 x 1½	50 sq. inches
9 x 1½	64 sq. inches
10 x 1½	79 sq. inches

RECTANGULAR CAKE PANS

7¾ x 3⅝ x 2¼	28 sq. inches
8 x 8 x 1½	64 sq. inches
9 x 5 x 2¾	45 sq. inches
9 x 9 x 1½	81 sq. inches
11 x 4½ x 2¾	50 sq. inches
11 x 7 x 1½	77 sq. inches
13 x 9 x 2	117 sq. inches
15 x 10 x 2	150 sq. inches
15½ x 10½ x 1	160 sq. inches
16 x 5 x 4	80 sq. inches

ABOUT CAKES IN A MIXER

Electric mixers are the greatest boon to cake bakers but, as models vary in speed and efficiency ♦ be sure to read the manual which comes with your particular appliance. The following comments can give only approximate speeds and times. So-called one-bowl cakes can be mixed in as little as 3 minutes. Butter cakes may take as long as 8 to 10 minutes. Basically, you apply the same principles that you use in hand mixing. ♦ Have all ingredients assembled. If chocolate, honey or molasses mixtures are called for,

melt or heat them ♦ and cool, before using, to about 75°, which should be the approximate temperature of all your ingredients. Sift and measure the flour, sift it once again with the baking powder, the soda, the spices and the cocoa, if called for. You may then mix just as though you were working by hand or use the one-bowl method described below. ♦ The main things to observe are the beating speed and the timing of each process. We find it wise to stop the beating during the addition of most ingredients. During these breaks is the time, too, when the sides of the bowl should be scraped down with a rubber or plastic scraper, unless you have a heavy duty mixer which revolves with an off-center motion, covering every bit of the mixing area.

To mix a typical butter cake, cream the ♦ butter conditioned to 75°, until light, at low speed. Then cream it with the sugar at medium speed until the mix is of the consistency of whipped cream. If the recipe calls for whole eggs, they may be creamed from the beginning with the sugar and butter. If the eggs are separated, add the yolks at the end of about a 3 to 5 minute creaming period of the butter and sugar. The whites are added later. For descriptions of the textures that these ingredients should have, read About Butter Cakes, page 343. Then ♦ using low speed and ♦ stopping the mixing between additions, add the flour mixture in 3 parts and the milk in 2 parts. Begin and end with the flour. Mix until just smooth after each addition. The whole operation should not take more than about 2 minutes or you will have a too finely grained cake. If nuts and other lumpy substances are to be added, fold

them in lightly with a fork at the end of the mixing period or briefly use the low speed on the beater. If the recipe calls for separated whites, beat them at this time in a grease-free bowl. Having an extra mixer bowl and beater is a great convenience if you bake often.

Be sure ♦ before you begin beating the egg whites that your oven has reached the right temperature and that your pans are greased. Beat the whites at medium speed for about ½ minute—until foamy. Now, the cream of tartar, if called for, is added. Then beat at high speed for another ½ minute until the whites are ♦ stiff, but not dry, see page 180. For the best results from this point on, the beater is no longer used and the beaten whites are folded in by hand, see page 335.

To mix so-called one-bowl cakes with unseparated eggs and solid fats, conditioned to 75° ♦ assemble and sift all dry ingredients needed. ♦ Have pans greased and oven preheated. Put sifted flour, baking powder, spices and cocoa, if called for, the fat and ⅔ of the liquid into the mixer bowl at once. Beat on medium speed about 2 minutes. Add the rest of the liquid. Add, unbeaten, the whole eggs, the yolks or the whites, as called for in the recipe, and beat for 2 minutes more. ♦ Scrape the bowl several times during this beating period. ♦ Overbeating will reduce the volume and give a too densely grained cake.

ABOUT PACKAGED BAKING MIXES

"Mother!" cried a little girl, "it says here in this book that you take milk and eggs and mix—but it doesn't say what kind of mix." We say it could be almost any kind of packaged mix, because those added expensive ingredients which make results taste something like the homemade article are left to the initiative of the housewife. We know that people think they save time by using mixes—just how much time is a sobering consideration—but we also know they do not save money, nor are they assured of good ingredients and best results. Use mixes if you must, in emergencies. But consider that, under present distribution methods, the mix you buy may be as old as 2 years—if the store has a slow turnover. Remember that, in contriving the mix originally, everything has been done to use ingredients that will keep. Egg whites are used in preference to whole eggs, as the fat from the yolks may turn rancid. For the same reason, non-fat dry milk solids are preferred. Even when the natural moisture content of flour has been greatly lowered, what remains in the packaged mix can still deteriorate baking powders, flavorings and spices. Furthermore, even the most elaborate packaging is not proof, over a protracted storage period, against spoilage by moisture from without. So why not become expert at a few quick cakes and hot breads? Build up your own baking speed, control your ingredients, create really topnotch flavor and save money.

ABOUT ANGEL CAKES

Laboratory research in some types of recipes—and no cake has a larger bibliography than angel cake—has become so elaborate as to intimidate the housewife, who can rarely know the exact age of the eggs she uses or the precise blend of flour. Yet, working innocently as she must, she can still con-

trive a glamorous result with a little care. The main risers in angel cake are air and steam, so the egg white volume is important. See About Eggs, page 179.

♦ Have egg whites ready. They should be at least 3 days old, at about 60° to 70° and separated just before use. These are preferable to leftover egg white. Divide the beating time into 4 quarters. During the first quarter, beat whites gently ♦ until foamy. Add salt, cream of tartar and liquid flavoring. Be sure the cream of tartar has been in a closely covered container. It is added midway during the first quarter of the beating and controls both the stabilizing of the foam and the whiteness of the cake. End the first quarter of the beating with an increasing speed and gradually add, while continuing to beat at high speed, ¾ of the sugar called for in the recipe. Finely granulated fruit or berry sugar is best.

If you are using an electric mixer, this sugar addition begins in the second quarter because it guards against overbeating the whites. If you are beating by hand with a flat whip—and this gives the best results—or a rotary one, the gradual addition of sugar is made in the last half of the beating time. In either case, the remaining ¼ of the sugar is sifted with the cake flour to keep the flour well dispersed when it is folded into the egg and sugar mixture. ♦ The folding should never be done mechanically. As in all ♦ hand folding, the movement is both gentle and firm, but rapid. Avoid breaking down the cellular structure of the egg whites which have trapped air.

The pan and its preparation are integral with good results. Choose a tube pan with a removable rim. Since the dough is light, it helps to have a central tube to give it additional support while it rises. If the pan has been used for other purposes and any grease remains, the batter will not rise. Wash a suspect pan with detergent, scrubbing well to remove every trace of grease. After putting the batter in the pan, draw a thin spatula gently through the dough to destroy any large air pockets.

Endless experiments have been performed for baking angel cakes—starting with a cold oven and ending with a very hot one. But ▶ the best oven is one that is not so slow that it will dry and toughen the cake and not so hot that it will set the protein of the whites before they can expand to the fullest volume. In other words, the ideal is a moderate, preheated oven. We use 350° for about 45 minutes for the recipes given here. Place the pan on a rack, adjusted in the lower third of the oven. When the cake is done ▶ reverse the pan when you remove it from the oven, as shown in the illustration. Use an inverted funnel to rest the pan on, if the tube is not high enough to keep the cake above the surface of the table. Let the cake hang for about 1½ hours until it is thoroughly set. Be sure to remove it

from the pan before storing. Do not cut a fresh angel or sponge cake with a knife, but use a divider such as the one shown on

the left or 2 forks inserted back to back to pry the cake gently apart. To make an angel cake for a roll, use ½ the recipe for a 10½ x 15½-inch pan. Grease the pan-bottom.

ANGEL CAKE

I. [A 9-Inch Tube Pan]
Preheat oven to 350°.
Sift twice:
 1¼ to 1½ cups sugar
Sift separately before measuring:
 1 cup cake flour
Resift the flour 3 times with ½ cupful of the sifted sugar and:
 ½ teaspoon salt
Whip until foamy:
 1¼ cups egg whites: 10 to 12 egg whites
 (2 tablespoons water or 1 tablespoon water and 1 tablespoon lemon juice)
Add:
 1 teaspoon cream of tartar
Whip the egg whites ▶ until stiff, but not dry. Gradually whip in, about 1 tablespoon at a time, 1 cup of the sifted sugar.
Fold in:
 ½ teaspoon vanilla
 ½ teaspoon almond extract
Sift about ¼ cup of the sugar and flour mixture over the batter. Fold it in gently and briefly with a rubber scraper. Continue, until all the mixture is used. Pour the batter into an ungreased tube pan. Bake about 45 minutes. To cool, see About Angel Cakes, page 339.

II. [A 10-Inch Tube Pan]
Preheat oven to 350°.
Sift, then measure:
 1 cup cake flour
Add and resift 6 times:
 ½ cup sugar or confectioners' sugar
Combine:
 1½ cups egg whites
 2½ tablespoons cold water
 1½ teaspoons cream of tartar
 1 scant teaspoon vanilla

1 teaspoon almond extract
or (1 or 2 drops anise
flavoring)
½ teaspoon salt

Beat ▶ until stiff, but not dry.
Stop while the mixture is still
glossy. Fold in, about 2 tablespoons at a time:

1 cup sifted sugar

Fold in the dry ingredients
lightly—a little at a time—with
a rubber scraper. Fold in:

(1 cup chopped black
walnut meats or ¾ cup
blanched, thinly sliced,
toasted almonds)

Bake the batter in an ungreased
tube pan for about 45 minutes.
To cool, see About Angel Cake,
page 339.

COCOA ANGEL CAKE

[A 9-Inch Tube Pan]
This is incredibly delicate.
Preheat oven to 350°.
Sift before measuring:

¾ cup cake flour

Resift 5 times with:

¼ cup cocoa
¼ cup sugar

Sift separately:

1 cup sugar

Place on a large platter and
whip until foamy:

1¼ cups egg whites: 10 to
12 egg whites

Add:

1 teaspoon cream of tartar

Whip until stiff, but not dry.
Fold in the sifted sugar, 1 tablespoon at a time. Add:

1 teaspoon vanilla
½ teaspoon lemon extract

Sift a small amount of the flour
mixture over the batter and fold
it in. Repeat this process until
the flour is used up. Bake the
cake in an ungreased tube pan
for about 45 minutes. When
cool, cover the cake with:

White Icing, page 419,
and Chocolate Coating,
page 423, or with
Coffee Icing, page 429

FLAVORED ANGEL CAKE

These are choice as cup cakes.
See About Cup Cakes, page 358.
Add to the flour for Angel Cake:

1 teaspoon cinnamon
½ teaspoon nutmeg
¼ teaspoon cloves

or, crush with a rolling pin:

⅓ cup soft peppermint
sticks

Fold into the egg and flour mixture. This is good iced with
Boiled White Icing, page 419,
to which you may add more
crushed candy for color or:

(1 to 2 teaspoons instant
coffee)

MARBLE ANGEL CAKE

Prepare:

Angel Cake I, page 620

Prepare:

Cocoa Angel Cake

Alternate the batters in 2 ungreased 9-inch tube pans. Bake
the cake by any rule for Angel
Cake.

ANGEL ALMOND CAKE

[A 7-Inch Tube Pan]
Preheat oven to 350°.
A fairly fat-free cake. Blanch,
then grind in a nut grinder, page
190:

1½ cups almonds

Sift:

1½ cups confectioners' sugar

Beat until stiff:

7 egg whites

Fold in the sugar and almonds.
Bake for about 45 minutes or
until done. To cool, see About
Angel Cakes, page 339.

ABOUT SPONGE CAKES

In true sponge cakes, as in angel
cakes, the main riser is air, plus
steam, so all the suggestions for
trapping air given in About
Angel Cakes apply here—with
this added admonition: egg
yolks beat to a greater volume
if they are at about 75°. Beat

the yolks until light and foamy;
add the sugar gradually, while
continuing to beat, until the
mixture is pale in color and thick
in texture. It has reached proper
consistency when a sample
dropped from a spoon remains
raised for a moment above the
rest of the batter and then rather
reluctantly settles down to the
level in the bowl.

◗ In sponge cakes, an electric
or rotary beater gives a better
result than a hand whip. You
can beat the egg and sugar mixture mechanically as long as 7
minutes, with good results for
the amounts given in the recipes
here. Then stir the dry ingredients carefully in, by hand. When
they are blended, use the folding technique illustrated, page
335. For pan preparation and
baking, see About Angel Cakes,
page 339.

True-blue sponge cake en-
thusiasts scorn baking powder,
but it does give added volume
in the basic recipe just below.
Sponges may be flavored by
adding one teaspoon grated
lemon or orange rind. Or these
citrus rinds may be omitted in
favor of 4 drops of anise oil, 1½
teaspoons vanilla, or additions
as for Flavored Angel Cakes,
page 341.

SPONGE CAKE

Economical, if you use the minimum number of eggs. Especially delightful, if you vary the
flavors.
[A 9-Inch Tube Pan]
Preheat oven to 350°.
Grate, then stir:
　　1 teaspoon lemon or
　　　　orange rind
into:
　　1 cup sifted sugar
Beat until very light:
　　3 to 6 egg yolks
Beat in the sugar gradually. Beat
in:

　　¼ cup boiling water or
　　　　coffee
When cool, beat in:
　　1 tablespoon lemon juice
　　　　or 1 teaspoon vanilla
　　　　or 3 drops anise oil
Sift before measuring:
　　1 cup cake flour
Resift with:
　　1½ teaspoons double-acting
　　　　baking powder
　　¼ teaspoon salt
Add the sifted ingredients gradually to the yolk mixture. Stir
the batter until blended. Whip
◗ until stiff, but not dry:
　　3 to 6 egg whites
Fold them lightly into the batter. Bake the cake about 45
minutes. To prepare the pan,
bake and cool, see About Angel
Cakes, page 339.

RICE OR POTATO FLOUR
SPONGE CAKE

[A 9-Inch Tube Pan]
Because rice and potato flours
have different glutens from
wheat, do not expect the same
cake texture.
Preheat oven to 350°.
Sift 3 times or more:
　　¾ cup potato or rice flour
　　½ cup sugar
Beat until light and creamy:
　　8 egg yolks
Stir them into the flour mixture.
Beat ◗ until stiff, but not dry:
　　9 egg whites
Fold the egg whites into the
yolks gently but rapidly. Bake
the cake for about 45 minutes.
To prepare pan, bake and cool,
see About Angel Cakes, page
339.

SUNSHINE CAKE

[A 9-Inch Tube Pan]
Preheat oven to 350°.
Sift before measuring:
　　1 cup cake flour
Resift with:
　　½ teaspoon cream of tartar

Boil to the soft-ball stage at 240°, see page 500:

    ⅓ cup water
    1¼ cups sugar

Whip ♦ until stiff, but not dry:

    5 to 7 egg whites

Pour the sirup over them in a fine stream. Beat constantly until the mixture is cool. Add:

    1 teaspoon vanilla

Beat well and fold in:

    5 to 7 eggs

Fold in the sifted flour, 1 tablespoon at a time. Bake the cake about 45 minutes. To prepare pan, bake and cool, see About Angel Cakes, page 339.

CHOCOLATE SPONGE CAKE

[A 7-Inch Tube Pan]
Butterless but rich in taste.
Preheat oven to 350°.
Melt:

    4 oz. chocolate

in a pan with:

    1 cup milk

Sift before measuring:

    1¼ cups cake flour

Resift with:

    ½ teaspoon salt
    2½ teaspoons double-acting
      baking powder

Cool the chocolate mixture and add it to:

    4 beaten egg yolks

creamed with:

    2 cups sifted confectioners'
      sugar
    1 teaspoon vanilla

Stir in the sifted flour. Beat ♦ until stiff, but not dry:

    4 egg whites

Fold the beaten whites into the chocolate mixture. Bake about 50 minutes. To prepare pan, bake and cool, see About Angel Cakes, page 339.

DAFFODIL CAKE

[A 9-Inch Tube Pan]
A yellow and white marble cake.
Preheat oven to 350°.
Sift before measuring:

    1⅛ cups cake flour

Resift it twice. Sift separately:

    1¼ cups sugar

Whip on a platter until frothy:

    10 egg whites

Add:

    ½ teaspoon salt
    1 teaspoon cream of tartar

Whip until they hold a point. Fold the sifted sugar in gradually. Separate the mixture into halves. Fold into one half, a little at a time, ¾ cups of the sifted flour and:

    6 beaten egg yolks
    Grated rind of 1 orange

Fold into the other half, a little at a time, ½ cup of the sifted flour and:

    1 teaspoon vanilla

Place the batters, a cupful or more at a time, in the ungreased tube pan, alternating the colors. Bake about 45 minutes or until done. To prepare pan, bake and cool, see About Angel Cakes, page 339.

ABOUT BUTTER OR SHORTENING CAKES

For flavor and texture, butter is our strong preference. It is not a very novel one, for way back when the cathedrals were white, one of the spires at Rouen was nicknamed The Butter Tower, having been built, reputedly, with money paid for indulgences permitting the use of butter during Lent.

The butter, margarine or shortening—but not lard, as it is best reserved for pastries, see page 292—♦ should be at about 70° when ready to cream. If much cooler, it fails to disperse into the other ingredients to best advantage. If melted, it prevents the proper incorporation of air into the batter. ♦ So don't try to hasten the conditioning of shortenings with heat.

Creaming softens and lightens cake ingredients. If the weather is very hot, cream butter and sugar in a bowl immersed in a pan of 60° water. Add the sugar ♦ gradually, continuing to cream with a light touch.

♦ Add beaten egg yolk gradually, or add egg yolks unbeaten, one at a time, beating well after each addition. ♦ The sifted dry ingredients and the 75° liquids are added in 3 or more alternating periods, usually beginning with the dry ingredients. ♦ After the addition of flour the blending should be gentle, so as not to develop the gluten and then continued until the flour is no longer dry. ♦ Overblending will cause too fine a crumb. We suggest, for a cake made with double-acting baking powder, about 200 strokes by hand or 2 minutes at medium speed with an electric mixer. If you use other baking powders, they may require about ⅓ less beating. The whites are beaten ♦ just before incorporating them in the batter to a state described as "stiff, but not dry." ♦ The whites are then simultaneously folded and cut in gently but quickly, as shown in the illustrations, page 336. For a more stable foam, reserve ¼ of the sugar called for in the recipe and beat it in as described in Fudge Meringue Cake, page 351. ♦ Bake the cake in a preheated oven. Grease the bottoms of pans—not the sides. ♦ Use the pan sizes indicated for each recipe or adjust by consulting the Pan Size Chart, page 337.

WHITE CAKE

This recipe is amazing in that it can be multiplied by 8 and still give as good a result as when made in the smaller quantity below. See formula for Enlarging Recipes, page 228. We once saw a wedding cake made from this recipe which contained 130 eggs and was big enough to serve 400 guests. This formula is also the classic base for Lady Baltimore Cake, page 346, for which, in the Good Old Days, 5 layers were considered none too many.

I. [Three 8-Inch Round Pans]
Preheat oven to 375°.
♦ Have all ingredients at about 75°.
♦ Sift before measuring:
  3½ cups cake flour
Resift it twice with:
  4 teaspoons double-acting
    baking powder
  ½ teaspoon salt
Sift:
  2 cups sugar
Cream well:
  1 cup butter
Add the sifted sugar gradually and continue creaming until very light. Add the flour mixture to the butter mixture in 3 parts, alternately with thirds of:
  1 cup milk
Stir the batter until smooth after each addition. Beat in:
  1 teaspoon vanilla
  (¼ teaspoon almond extract)
Whip ♦ until stiff, but not dry:
  7 or 8 egg whites
Fold them lightly into the cake batter. Bake in greased pans for about 25 minutes. Spread the cake when cool with:
  A choice of Icings,
    page 418

II. Children love this cake. When baked, the recipe will fill a mold of 7-cup capacity, see below, or use two 9-inch round pans.
Preheat oven to 350°.
♦ Have all ingredients at about 75°.
Sift before measuring:
  2¼ cups cake flour
Resift with:
  2½ teaspoons double-acting
    baking powder
  ½ teaspoon salt
Cream until fluffy:

1¼ cups sugar
½ cup butter
Combine:
1 cup milk
1 teaspoon vanilla
Add the sifted ingredients to the butter mixture in 3 parts, alternating with thirds of the liquid combination. Stir the batter until smooth after each addition. Whip ◗ until stiff, but not dry:
4 large egg whites
Fold them lightly into the batter and bake in layers, about 25 minutes. When cool, ice with:
Luscious Orange, page 424, or Quick Chocolate Icing, page 429

ABOUT TWO-PIECE CAKE MOLDS

Lambs, bunnies and Santas need firm, compact doughs. Prepare:
White Cake II, above, or One Egg Cake, page 364
Keep nuts, raisins, etc., for decorations, rather than using them in the dough itself, because these solid ingredients, while they make the cake more interesting, tend to break down the tensile strength of the dough. Ground spices, however, are a good addition. Grease the mold with unsalted fat or oil. Use a pastry brush and be rather lavish. Then dust the greased surface with flour, reversing the mold to get rid of any excess. If the mold has steam vents, fill the solid section with the dough, to just below the joint. We have baked successfully in cake molds, even when they had no steam vents, using the following directions. Move a wooden spoon gently through the dough to release any air bubbles. ◗ Be careful not to disturb the greased and floured surface of the mold. Insert wooden toothpicks upright in the snout or lengthwise into the ears where they join the head. ◗ Watch for the toothpicks, though, when you cut the cake. Put the lid on the mold, making sure it locks, and tie or wire together so the steam of the rising dough will not force the two sections apart.

To bake, put the filled mold on a cookie sheet in a 370° preheated oven for about 1 hour. Test as you would for any cake, inserting a thin metal skewer or toothpick through a steam vent. Put the cake, still in the mold, on a rack for about 15 minutes. Carefully remove the top of the mold. Before you separate the cake from the bottom, let it continue to cool for about 5 minutes more to let all steam escape and to allow the dough to firm up a little. After removing, continue to cool on a rack. ◗ Do not try to let it sit upright until it is cold. If the cake has constitutional weaknesses, reinforce it with a wooden or metal skewer before icing. Ice with:
Boiled White Icing, page 419, or Seven Minute Icing, page 424, or Caramel Icing, page 425
If you ✳ freeze the cake before frosting it, the job is somewhat easier. Or if you are in a hurry, try a:
French Icing, page 427
Caramel icing is a good variation for a bunny mold. Increase the recipes by ½ for a heavy coat. For woolly or angora effects, press into the icing:
½ to 1 cup shredded coconut

To accentuate the features use:
    **Raisins, nuts, cherries
        and citron**
Surround your animals with seasonal flowers and ferns. If bunnies or lambs are made for Easter, you may want to confect cake eggs and decorate them with icings of different colors. See Angel Cake Balls, page 359.

ABOUT WEDDING OR LARGE CAKES

Be sure for any big cake to ▶ choose a recipe that enlarges successfully, see comment under White Cake I, or use a large fruit-cake recipe. We find that, when rather shallow pans are used—not more than 2 inches deep for each layer—the cake bakes more evenly and cuts more attractively. For any large cake, lower the oven temperature indicated by 25°. For more even baking, swing it around in the oven frequently during the necessarily longer baking period. Test for doneness as you would with any cake, see page 336. To ice, see Decorative Boiled Icing, page 423, or Royal Glaze, page 426.

After the bride's first slice, whether the wedding cake is round or rectangular, the cutting begins at the lowest tier. To make the cuts even in depth, run

a knife perpendicularly through the bottom layer, where it abuts the second layer. Continue this process at each tier. Cut successive slices until a single cylindrical center core remains, crested by the ornate top, as shown on the left. Remove and save this, see page 567, or freeze it for the first anniversary party. Then finish slicing the central core beginning at the top.

LADY BALTIMORE CAKE

Prepare the batter for:
    White Cake I, page 344
Bake it in 3 layers. When cool, place the following filling between the layers. Chop:
    **6 figs
    ½ cup seeded raisins
    1 cup nut meats**
Prepare:
    **Boiled White Icing or
    Seven Minute White
    Icing, page 424**
Reserve a generous third of this. To the rest, add the nuts, figs and raisins. Spread the filling between the layers and the reserved icing over the top.

COCONUT MILK CAKE

[Two 9-Inch Round Cakes]
Some years ago we gave a pet recipe to a friend who later presented us with the one which follows—best made with fresh coconut milk. She said that, in her family, whenever a treasured recipe was received, they gave an equally treasured one of their own in return. We love this festive adopted child.
Preheat oven to 350°.
▶ Have all ingredients at about 75°. Have ready:
    **1½ cups freshly grated
        coconut**
▶ Sift before measuring:
    3 cups cake flour
Resift it with:
    **3 teaspoons double-acting
        baking powder**

½ teaspoon salt
Sift:
1½ cups sugar
Cream well:
¾ cup butter
Add the sifted sugar gradually and continue creaming until these ingredients are very light. Beat in:
3 beaten egg yolks
Add the sifted flour mixture in 3 parts to the butter mixture, alternately with:
¾ cup coconut milk or milk
½ teaspoon vanilla
Stir the batter until smooth after each addition. Then add ¾ of a cup of the grated coconut. Whip
◗ until stiff, but not dry:
3 egg whites
Fold the egg whites gently into the batter. Bake in greased layer pans for about 25 minutes. To serve, fill between the layers with:
Currant, strawberry or raspberry jelly
Cover the cake with:
Sea Foam Icing, page 424
Coat it with the remaining ¾ cup grated coconut.

MARBLE CAKE

[A 9-Inch Tube Pan]
This old-fashioned cake is still a great favorite.
Preheat oven to 350°.
Prepare:
White Cake II, pag 344
Before whipping the egg whites separate the batter into 2 parts. Add to ½ the batter:
1½ oz. melted, cooled chocolate
1 teaspoon cinnamon
¼ teaspoon cloves
⅛ teaspoon soda
Whip the egg whites as directed and fold ½ into the dark batter. Grease a tube pan. Place large spoonfuls of batter in it, alternating light and dark dough.

Bake for about 1 hour. Spread when cool with:
Boiled White Icing, page 419, or Banana Icing, page 430

WHIPPED CREAM CAKE

[Two 9-Inch Layers]
Preheat oven to 350°.
◗ Have all ingredients except the whipping cream at about 75°. Sift before measuring:
2 cups cake flour
Resift twice with:
2¾ teaspoons double-acting baking powder
¾ teaspoon salt
Whip until stiff:
1 cup whipping cream
Fold into the cream:
1⅓ cups powdered sugar
and add gradually, stirring gently until smooth:
½ cup water
1½ teaspoons vanilla or almond flavoring
Whip ◗ until stiff, but not dry:
3 egg whites
Combine the cream and the egg whites. Fold the sifted ingredients into the cream mixture, about ⅓ at a time. Bake in layer pans for about 25 to 30 minutes. Fill with:
Ginger Fruit Filling, page 380

SOUR CREAM CAKE

[Two 8-Inch Round Pans]
Preheat oven to 375°.
◗ Have all ingredients at about 75°. Sift before measuring:
1¾ cups cake flour
Resift with:
¼ teaspoon soda
1¾ teaspoons double-acting baking powder
¼ teaspoon salt
Sift:
1 cup sugar
Cream until soft:
⅓ cup butter

Add the sugar gradually. When these ingredients are creamy, beat in:

2 beaten egg yolks
1 teaspoon vanilla

Add the sifted flour mixture to the butter mixture in 3 parts, alternating with thirds of:

⅔ cup yogurt or 1 cup cultured sour cream

Stir the batter after each addition until smooth. Whip until
▶ stiff, but not dry:

2 egg whites
¼ teaspoon salt

Fold them lightly into the batter. Bake in greased pans for about 25 minutes. When cool, spread with:

Almond, Fig or Raisin Filling, page 381

Cover with:

Boiled White Icing, page 419

GOLD LAYER CAKE

[Two 8-Inch Round Layers]
Preheat oven to 375°.
▶ Have all ingredients at about 75°. Sift before measuring:

2 cups cake flour

Resift with:

2 teaspoons double-acting baking powder
¼ teaspoon salt

Sift:

1 cup sugar

Cream until soft:

½ cup butter

Add the sugar ▶ gradually, creaming these ingredients until light. Beat in:

3 well-beaten egg yolks

Add:

1 teaspoon vanilla or
1 teaspoon grated lemon rind

Add the flour mixture to the butter mixture in 3 parts, with thirds of:

¾ cup milk

Stir the batter until smooth after each addition. Bake in layer

pans for about 25 minutes. Spread layers, when cool, with:

A lemon icing, page 427, or other icing

or spread between the layers:

Lemon Filling, page 379

This cake is delicious filled with a layer of good raspberry jam. Dust the top with:

Powdered sugar

FOUR-EGG CAKE

[Three 9-Inch Round Pans]
This is the old-time One-Two-Three-Four Cake, slightly modernized.
Preheat oven to 350°.
Have all ingredients about 75°. Sift before measuring:

2⅔ cups cake flour

Resift with:

2¼ teaspoons double-acting baking powder
½ teaspoon salt

Sift:

2 cups sugar

Cream until soft:

1 cup butter

Add the sugar gradually. Cream these ingredients until very light. Beat in, one at a time:

4 egg yolks

Add:

1½ teaspoons vanilla or
1 teaspoon vanilla and
½ teaspoon almond extract

Add the flour mixture to the butter mixture in about 3 parts, alternating with thirds of:

1 cup milk

Stir the batter until smooth after each addition. Whip ▶ until stiff, but not dry:

4 egg whites

Fold them lightly into the batter. Bake in greased layer pans from 30 to 35 minutes. Spread the layers, when cool, with:

Pineapple or Ginger Fruit Filling, pages 377 and 380

Cover with:

Whipped cream

COCONUT LOAF OR LAYER CAKE

Follow the recipe for:
> Four-Egg Cake, above

Add to the batter, before folding in the egg whites:
- ¾ cup shredded coconut
- 1½ teaspoons grated lemon rind
- ¼ teaspoon salt

Bake in a greased 8-inch tube pan for about 1 hour.

EIGHT-YOLK CAKE

[Three 9-Inch Layers]

Bake it as a second cake after making Angel Food Cake with the whites.

Preheat oven to 375°.

Have all ingredients about 75°.

Sift before measuring:
- 2½ cups cake flour

Resift 3 times with:
- 2⅓ teaspoons double-acting baking powder
- ¼ teaspoon salt

Sift:
- 1¼ cups sugar

Cream until soft:
- ¾ cup butter

Add the sugar gradually. Cream these ingredients until very light. In a separate bowl, beat until light and lemon colored:
- 8 egg yolks

Beat them into the butter mixture. Add the flour mixture in 3 parts, alternating with thirds of:
- ¾ cup milk

Stir the batter after each addition. Add and beat for 2 minutes:
- 1 teaspoon vanilla
- 1 teaspoon lemon juice or grated lemon rind

Bake in greased layer pans for about 20 minutes. Sprinkle with:
> Powdered sugar

or, when cool, spread with:
> Quick Orange Icing, page 428, or with one of the Seven-Minute Icings, page 424

POUND CAKE

[Two 9 x 9-Inch Pans or Two 4½ x 8-Inch Loaf Pans]

We have tried traditional pound cakes: 1 lb. butter, 1 lb. sugar, 1 lb. flour, 1 lb. eggs—about 8 to 10—and any number of variations. But we like this one best. It differs from a true pound cake in that milk is one of the components.

Preheat oven to 325°.

Have all ingredients about 75°.

Sift before measuring:
- 4 cups cake flour

Resift with:
- 1 teaspoon salt
- 4 teaspoons double-acting baking powder
- (½ teaspoon mace)

Cream very well:
- 1½ cups butter

Add and continue creaming until light:
- 3 cups sugar

Add, one at a time, and continue beating well after each addition:
- 8 eggs

Add the flour mixture alternately with:
- 1 cup milk
- 2 teaspoons vanilla
- (2 tablespoons brandy or 8 drops rose wtaer)

▸ Stir only until thoroughly blended. Bake in greased pans for 15 to 20 minutes, if in layers. If baked in loaf pans, prepare them by lining each one with parchment paper.

Let the paper project for easy removal of the loaves and bake for 1 hour.

▲ In baking pound cakes at high altitudes, omit any leavening called for.

Powdered sugar
or spread, when cool, with:
    Quick Lemon Icing, page 427

SEED CAKE

A cake that reminds us of antimacassars and aspidistras.
Prepare:
    Pound Cake, preceding page
Add:
    2 teaspoons caraway seed
    ⅓ cup shaved citron
    1 teaspoon grated lemon rind

LADY CAKE

[A 9-Inch Tube Pan]
This makes a tube or loaf cake or an excellent base for Petits Fours, see page 360. It tastes and looks a great deal like a conventional white wedding cake.
Preheat oven to 350°.
Have all ingredients about 75°.
Sift before measuring:
    1¾ cups cake flour
Resift twice with:
    2 teaspoons any baking powder
Sift:
    1 cup sugar
Cream until soft:
    ¾ cup butter
Add the sugar gradually, creaming these ingredients until very light. Add the flour mixture in 3 parts to the butter mixture, alternating with thirds of:
    ½ cup milk
Stir the batter for a few minutes after each addition. Add:
    1 teaspoon almond extract
    Grated rind of 1 lemon
Whip ♦ until stiff, but not dry:
    3 egg whites
Fold them lightly into the cake batter. Bake in a greased tube pan for about 45 minutes. Sprinkle with:

CHOCOLATE CAKE

[A 9 x 13-Inch Pan]
Known as "Rombauer Special."
A delicious light chocolate cake, always in demand.
Preheat oven to 350°.
Have ingredients at about 75°.
Sift before measuring:
    1¾ cups cake flour
Resift with:
    3 teaspoons double-acting baking powder
    ¼ teaspoon salt
    (1 teaspoon cinnamon)
    (¼ teaspoon cloves)
    (1 cup coarsely chopped nuts)
Melt over hot water:
    2 oz. chocolate
Add:
    5 tablespoons boiling water
Sift:
    1½ cups sugar
Beat until soft:
    ½ cup butter
Add the sugar gradually. Blend until very light and creamy.
Beat in, one at a time:
    4 egg yolks
Add the cooled chocolate mixture. Add the flour mixture in 3 parts to the butter mixture, alternating with thirds of:
    ½ cup milk
Stir the batter until smooth after each addition. Add:
    1 teaspoon vanilla
Whip ♦ until stiff, but not dry:
    4 egg whites
Fold them lightly into the cake batter. Bake in a greased pan for about ½ hour. Spread with thick:
    White Icing, page 419, and Chocolate Coating, page 423, or Quick Chocolate or Peppermint Cream Filling, page 378

FUDGE LAYER CAKE

[Two 8-Inch Round Layer Pans]
Preheat oven to 350°.
Prepare:

> Brownies, page 389

Separate eggs and fold in the stiffly beaten whites after the batter is mixed. Bake as directed. Garnish with:

> Whipped cream

FUDGE MERINGUE CAKE

[A 9 x 13-Inch Pan]
Preheat oven to 350°.
Have all ingredients at about 75°. Sift:

> 2 cups cake flour

Resift with:

> 1 tablespoon double-acting
>   baking powder
> ¼ teaspoon salt

Melt ♦ over—not in—hot water:

> 4 oz. chocolate

Cream:

> ¼ cup butter

Add gradually; continue to cream and mix:

> 1½ cups sugar

Add:

> 3 well-beaten egg yolks
> 1 teaspoon vanilla

and the cooled chocolate. Then add, alternating in 3 parts with:

> 1 cup milk

the sifted flour. Stir well after each addition. Beat ♦ until stiff, but not dry:

> 3 egg whites

Fold in:

> ½ cup sugar

Beat to a meringue consistency before adding to batter. Bake about 35 minutes in a greased pan. When cool, ice with:

> French Butter Icing, page
>   427

DEVIL'S FOOD CAKE COCKAIGNE

[Two 9-Inch Round Layers]
The best chocolate cake we know. Whether made with 2 or 4 oz. chocolate, it is wonderfully light, but rich and moist.
Preheat oven to 350°.
Prepare the following custard:
Cook and stir in a double boiler
♦ over—not in—hot water:

> 2 to 4 oz. chocolate
> ½ cup milk
> 1 cup light brown sugar,
>   firmly packed
> 1 egg yolk

Remove from the heat when thickened. Have other ingredients at about 75°. Sift before measuring:

> 2 cups cake flour

Resift with:

> 1 teaspoon soda
> ½ teaspoon salt

Sift:

> 1 cup white sugar

Beat until soft:

> ½ cup butter

Add the sugar gradually. Blend until very light and creamy. Beat in, one at a time:

> 2 egg yolks

Add the flour to the butter mixture in 3 parts, alternating with thirds of:

> ¼ cup water
> ½ cup milk
> 1 teaspoon vanilla

Stir the batter until smooth after each addition. Stir in the chocolate custard. Whip ♦ until stiff, but not dry:

> 2 egg whites

Fold them lightly into the cake batter. Bake in greased pans for about 25 minutes. Spread, when cool, with:

> Caramel Icing, page 425
>   or Chocolate Fudge
>   Icing, page 425

★ OLD-WORLD CHOCOLATE SPICE CAKE WITH CITRON

[A 9-Inch Tube Pan]
A tempting tube cake with a firm texture.
Preheat oven to 350°.
Have all ingredients about 75°.

Sift before measuring:
2⅓ cups cake flour
Resift with:
1½ teaspoons any baking
powder
½ teaspoon cloves
1 teaspoon cinnamon
½ teaspoon freshly grated
nutmeg
Cream until soft:
½ cup butter
Add gradually and cream until
light:
1½ cups sugar
Beat in, one at a time:
4 eggs
Stir in:
4 oz. grated sweet
chocolate
½ cup very finely shaved
citron, candied orange
or lemon peel
Stir the flour mixture into the
butter mixture in about 3 parts,
alternating with thirds of:
⅞ cup milk
Stir the batter after each addition until smooth. Most European cakes are stirred a long
time. This gives them a close,
sandy texture. Bake the cake in
a greased tube pan or in a loaf
pan for about 1 hour. Ice the
cake, when cool, with:
Chocolate Butter Icing,
page 428
or dust with:
Powdered sugar

SPICED CHOCOLATE PRUNE CAKE

[A 9 x 13-Inch Pan]
A delightful dessert when served
with whipped cream or pudding
sauce.
Preheat oven to 350°.
Have all ingredients about 75°.
Cook and cool:
1 cup lightly sweetened
puréed prunes
Sift before measuring:
1½ cups cake flour
Resift with:
1⅓ teaspoons double-acting
baking powder
¼ teaspoon soda
¼ teaspoon salt
(1 teaspoon cinnamon)
(½ teaspoon cloves)
Sift:
¾ cup sugar
Cream until soft:
⅓ cup butter
Add the sugar gradually. Cream
until light. Melt and add when
cool:
1 oz. chocolate
Beat well and add to the butter
mixture:
2 eggs
Add the flour mixture to the
butter mixture in 3 parts, alternating with thirds of:
½ cup milk
Stir the batter until smooth after
each addition. Add the prunes
and:
½ teaspoon vanilla
Bake in a greased pan for about
25 minutes. Spread, when cool,
with:
French Icing, page 427

CHOCOLATE APRICOT CAKE

Follow the recipe for:
Chocolate Prune Cake,
above
Substitute for the prunes:
1 cup cooked, lightly
sweetened, well-drained
apricots
Omit the spices. Ice, when cool,
with:
Whipped cream
or serve with:
Foamy Sauce, page 481

VELVET SPICE CAKE

[A 9-Inch Tube Pan]
This cake has a very delicate
consistency. Among spice cakes
its flavor is unequaled. ▶ Be
sure to bake it in a 9-inch tube
pan.
Preheat oven to 350°.
Have all ingredients about 75°.
Sift before measuring:

2⅓ cups cake flour
Resift twice with:
  1½ teaspoons double-acting
    baking powder
  ½ teaspoon soda
   1 teaspoon freshly grated
    nutmeg
   1 teaspoon cinnamon
  ½ teaspoon cloves
  ½ teaspoon salt
Sift:
  1½ cups sugar
Cream until soft:
  ¾ cup butter
Add the sifted sugar gradually.
Cream until very light. Beat in:
   3 egg yolks
Add the sifted ingredients to
the butter mixture in 3 parts, alternating with thirds of:
  ⅞ cup yogurt or buttermilk
Stir the batter after each addition until smooth. Whip ♦ until
stiff, but not dry:
   3 egg whites
Fold them lightly into the cake
batter. Bake in a greased tube
pan for 1 hour or more. Spread,
when cool, with:
     Chocolate Butter Icing,
     page 428, or Boiled
     White Icing, page 419

BURNT-SUGAR CAKE

[Two 9-Inch Round Pans]
A handsome creation.
Have all ingredients about 75°.
Caramelize:
  ½ cup sugar, page 169
and add ♦ very slowly:
  ½ cup boiling water
Boil the sirup until it is of the
consistency of molasses. Cool it.
Preheat oven to 375°.
Sift before measuring:
  2½ cups cake flour
Resift with:
  2½ teaspoons any baking
    powder
  ¼ teaspoon salt
Sift:
  1½ cups sugar
Cream until soft:
  ½ cup butter

Add the sugar gradually. Cream
until very light. Beat in, one at
a time:
   2 egg yolks
Add the flour mixture in 3 parts
to the butter mixture, alternating with thirds of:
   1 cup water
Stir the batter after each addition until smooth. Stir in:
   3 tablespoons of the
    caramelized sirup
   1 teaspoon vanilla
Whip ♦ until stiff, but not dry:
   2 egg whites
Fold them lightly into the cake
batter. Bake in greased pans for
about 25 minutes. Spread, when
cool, with:
    A white icing, page 419
In making the icing, flavor it in
addition to the vanilla with:
   4 teaspoons of the
    caramelized sirup
Place any remaining sirup in a
closed jar. It will keep indefinitely.

BROWN-SUGAR SPICE CAKE

[An 8½ x 4½-Inch Loaf Pan]
Preheat oven to 375°.
Have all ingredients at about
75°. Sift before measuring:
  2½ cups cake flour
Resift with:
   1 teaspoon salt
  ¼ teaspoon soda
  2½ teaspoons double-acting
    baking powder
   1 teaspoon cinnamon
  ½ teaspoon cloves
  ¼ teaspoon nutmeg
  (2 teaspoons grated orange
    rind)
Cream until light:
  1½ cups packed brown
    sugar
  ½ cup butter
Beat in:
   3 egg yolks
Stir the flour mixture into the
butter mixture in about 3 parts,
alternating with thirds of:

1 cup milk
Stir the batter after each addition until smooth. Have ready a greased loaf pan. Bake for about 40 minutes or until done. Cover the top of the cake with:
French Icing, page 427

APPLESAUCE CAKE

[A 9-Inch Tube Pan]
Preheat oven to 350°.
Have all ingredients at about 75°. Sift before measuring:
1¾ cups cake flour
Sift a little of the flour over:
1 cup raisins
1 cup currants, nut meats or dates
Resift the remainder with:
½ teaspoon salt
1 teaspoon soda
1 teaspoon cinnamon
½ teaspoon cloves
Sift:
1 cup white or packed brown sugar
Cream until soft:
½ cup butter
Add the sugar gradually. Cream until light. Beat in:
1 egg
Stir the flour mixture gradually into the butter mixture until the batter is smooth. Add the raisins, nut meats and:
1 cup thick, lightly sweetened applesauce
Stir it into the batter. Bake in a greased tube pan for about 50 to 60 minutes. Spread, when cool, with:
Caramel Icing, page 425

FIG SPICE CAKE

[A 9-Inch Tube Pan]
Have all ingredients at about 75°. Cool, drain, then cut into ¼-inch cubes and reserve the sirup:
1 lb. dried stewed figs
There should be 2 cups of figs.
Combine:
½ cup fig juice
½ cup buttermilk or yogurt

Preheat oven to 350°.
Sift before measuring:
1½ cups cake flour
Resift with:
1 teaspoon any baking powder
1 teaspoon salt
½ teaspoon cinnamon
¼ teaspoon cloves
½ teaspoon soda
Sift before measuring:
1 cup sugar
Cream until soft:
½ cup butter
Add the sugar gradually. Cream until very light. Beat in, one at a time:
2 eggs
Add the flour mixture to the butter mixture in about 3 parts, alternating with thirds of the milk and fig juice. Stir the batter after each addition until smooth. Add the figs and:
1 teaspoon vanilla
(1 cup broken nut meats or raisins)
Bake in a greased tube pan for about 50 minutes. Spread, when cool, with:
Coffee or Mocha Icing, page 429

DATE SPICE CAKE

[An 8½ x 4½-Inch Loaf]
Preheat oven to 325°.
Have all ingredients at about 75°. Cut into small pieces:
1 cup dates
Pour over them:
1 cup boiling water or coffee
Cool these ingredients. Sift before measuring:
1½ cups cake flour
Resift with:
1½ teaspoons double-acting baking powder
¾ teaspoon freshly grated nutmeg
¼ teaspoon salt
¼ teaspoon soda
Cream together:
3 tablespoons butter

1 cup sifted sugar
1 beaten egg

Add the flour mixture to the butter mixture in about 3 parts, alternating with thirds of the date mixture. Stir the batter well after each addition. Fold in:

1 cup raisins
1 cup broken pecan meats

Bake in a greased loaf pan for about 45 minutes. Dust with:

Powdered sugar

TUTTI FRUTTI CAKE

[A 9-Inch Tube Pan]
A well-flavored summer fruit cake.
Preheat oven to 350°.
Sift before measuring:

2 cups and 2 tablespoons cake flour

Resift with:

1 teaspoon each cloves, cinnamon, nutmeg
1 teaspoon soda
½ teaspoon salt

Sift:

1½ cups packed brown sugar

Cream until soft:

½ cup butter

Add the sugar gradually. Cream until light. Beat in, one at a time:

2 eggs

Stir the flour mixture into the batter mixture in about 3 parts, alternating with thirds of:

1 cup lightly drained crushed pineapple

Stir in:

½ cup each raisins and currants
1 cup broken nut meats

Bake in a greased tube pan for about 1 hour.

BANANA CAKE

[Two 9-Inch Round Pans]
Do try this, if you like a banana flavor.
Preheat oven to 350°.
Have all ingredients at about 75°. Sift before measuring:

2¼ cups cake flour

Resift with:

½ teaspoon any baking powder
¾ teaspoon soda
½ teaspoon salt

Sift:

1½ cups sugar

Cream:

½ cup butter

Add the sifted sugar gradually. Cream until very light. Beat in, one at a time:

2 eggs

Prepare:

1 cup lightly mashed ripe bananas

Add:

1 teaspoon vanilla
¼ cup yogurt or buttermilk

Add the flour mixture to the butter mixture in about 3 parts, alternating with thirds of the banana mixture. Stir the batter after each addition until smooth. Bake in greased pans for about ½ hour. When cool, place between the layers:

2 sliced ripe bananas

Spread the cake with:

A white icing, page 419

If served at once, this cake is good without icing—just sprinkled with powdered sugar or served with whipped cream.

ABOUT FRUIT CAKES

Many people feel that these cakes improve greatly with age. When they are well saturated with alcoholic liquors, which raise the spirits and keep down mold, and are buried in powdered sugar in tightly closed tins, they have been enjoyed as long as 25 years after baking.

Fruit cakes are fundamentally butter cakes with just enough dough to bind the fruit. Raisins, figs and dates can be more easily cut if the scissors or knife used is dipped periodically in water.

For a 2½ lb. cake, use an 8-inch ring mold or a 4½ x 8½-

inch loaf pan, either filled to about 2½ inches. To prepare loaf pans, see Pound Cake, page 349. To prepare a tube pan, line the bottom with a round of greased waxed paper or foil and cut a straight strip for sides. Bake as long as indicated in individual recipes.

Fruit cakes, still in the pan, are cooled from 20 to 30 minutes on a rack. Then the parchment or foil in which they are baked is carefully removed and the cake rack-cooled further until entirely free from heat. To decorate the cakes with candied fruit or nut meats, dip the undersides of the decorations into a light sugar sirup before applying them, or simply cover the cake with a sugar sirup glaze and arrange the trimming on it.

To store, wrap the loaves or tubes in brandy- or wine-soaked linens. If you prefer, you may make a few fine skewer punctures in the cake and pour over it very slowly, drop by drop, ¼ to 1 cup heated, but not boiling, brandy or wine. However you glaze or soak the cake, wrap it in liquor-soaked linen, then in foil. For very long storage, bury the liquor-soaked cake in powdered sugar. In any case, place it in a tightly covered tin in a cool place.

▲ In baking fruit cakes at high altitude, omit any leavening called for.

★ **FRUIT CAKE COCKAIGNE**

[Two 4 x 8½-Inch Loaves]
Not unlike a pound cake. The fruits stay light in color.
Preheat oven to 350°.
◗ Please review About Butter Cakes, page 343, and About Fruit Cakes, page 355.
◗ Have all ingredients at about 75°. Sift before measuring:
    4 cups all-purpose flour

Reserve ½ cup. Mix it with 4 cups nuts and fruits.
We particularly like:
    1⅓ cups pecans or hickory nuts
    1⅓ cups white raisins
    1⅓ cups seeded and chopped preserved kumquats
Resift the remainder of the flour with:
    1 teaspoon double-acting baking powder
    ½ teaspoon salt
Cream until light:
    ¾ cup butter
Then cream it with:
    2 cups sugar
Beat in, one at a time:
    5 eggs
Add:
    1 teaspoon vanilla
and continue to beat until light. Stir the flour mixture into the egg mixture and continue beating until thoroughly mixed. Fold in the reserved floured nuts and fruits. Bake for about 1 hour. To prepare pans, cool, remove and store, see About Fruit Cakes, above.

★ **CURRANT CAKE**

Prepare the dough for:
    Fruit Cake Cockaigne, above
Add, instead of the suggested fruit mixture:
    1 to 1½ cups currants
Bake, cool and store as for the above cake.

★ **WHITE FRUIT CAKE**

[Two 4 x 8½-Inch Loaves]
Preheat oven to 350°.
Prepare the batter for:
    Fruit Cake Cockaigne, above
Beat in:
    1 cup chopped nut meats, preferably blanched, slivered almonds
    ½ cup finely sliced citron, candied orange or lemon peel

1 cup white raisins
¼ cup chopped candied
   pineapple
¼ cup chopped candied
   cherries
(½ cup finely shredded
   coconut)
Bake about 1 hour. To prepare
pans, cool and store, see About
Fruit Cakes, above.

★ DARK FRUIT CAKE

I. [Two 4½ x 8-Inch Loaves,
plus Two 9-Inch Tube Pans—
About 12 Pounds]
▶ Please review About Butter
Cakes, page 343, and About
Fruit Cakes, page 355.
Preheat oven to 275°.
▶ Have all ingredients at about
75°. Sift before measuring:
   4 cups all-purpose flour
Reserve 1 cup. Resift the remainder with:
   1 tablespoon each of
      cinnamon, cloves, allspice
      and nutmeg
   ½ tablespoon mace
   1½ teaspoons salt
Wash:
   2½ lbs. currants
Cut up:
   2½ lbs. raisins
   1 lb. citron
Break coarsely:
   1 lb. pecan meats
Sprinkle these ingredients well
with the reserved flour. Sift:
   1 lb. brown sugar: 2⅔
      cups, packed
Cream until soft:
   1 lb. butter
Add the sugar gradually. Cream
until very light. Beat in:
   15 beaten egg yolks
Add the flour mixture to the
butter mixture, alternately with:
   ¼ cup bourbon whisky and
      ¼ cup wine or ½ cup
      thick fruit juice: prune,
      apricot or grape
Fold in the floured fruits and
nuts. Beat ▶ until stiff, but not
dry:

   15 egg whites
Fold them into the butter mixture. Bake a 2½ lb. cake in prepared pans, for 3 to 4 hours.
Over 5 lbs., allow at least 5
hours. Place a shallow pan filled
with water in the oven. Remove
it the last hour of baking. Cool
and store.

II. [Two 4½ x 8-Inch Loaves,
plus Two 8-Inch Tube Pans—
About 11 Pounds]
▶ Please review About Butter
Cakes, page 343, and About
Fruit Cakes, page 355.
Preheat oven to 275°.
▶ Have all ingredients at about
75°. Sift before measuring:
   4 cups all-purpose flour
Reserve 1 cup. Resift the remainder with:
   1 teaspoon cinnamon
   ½ teaspoon cloves
   ½ teaspoon nutmeg
   1 teaspoon salt, if butter is
      unsalted
Sprinkle the reserved flour over:
   2 lbs. seedless raisins
   1 lb. chopped citron
   ¼ lb. chopped candied
      orange peel and lemon
      peel
   1 lb. chopped figs or dates
   2 lbs. whole pecan meats
   12 candied cherries
Sift:
   2 cups sugar
Cream until soft:
   2 cups butter
Add the sugar gradually. Cream
until very light. Beat in:
   12 beaten egg yolks
Add the flour mixture to the butter mixture ½ cupful at a time,
alternately with:
   ½ cup grape jelly
   ½ cup grape juice
   ½ cup brandy or dry wine
Stir the floured fruits into the
batter. Whip ▶ until stiff, but
not dry and fold in gently:
   12 egg whites
   ¼ teaspoon salt

To bake, see Dark Fruit Cake, I, page 357. Cool and store.

III. [Two 4½ x 8 x 2½-Inch Loaves, plus Two 8-Inch Tube Pans—About 11 Pounds]

In this recipe the fruit is preconditioned, so it does not draw moisture from the cake during or after baking.

◖ Please review About Butter Cakes, page 343, and About Fruit Cakes, page 355.

◖ Have all ingredients at about 75°. Place and cook in a heavy pot for 5 minutes, stirring constantly:

    1½ cups apricot nectar
    2½ cups seedless white
        raisins
    2½ cups seedless raisins
      1 cup pitted, chopped dates
      1 cup diced candied
        pineapple
      2 cups diced candied
        cherries
      1 cup diced candied
        apricots

Remove from heat, cover and let stand 12 to 15 hours.
Preheat oven to 300°.
Sift before measuring:
      6 cups all-purpose flour
Resift with:
      2 teaspoons salt
      ½ teaspoon soda
      2 teaspoons cinnamon
      1 teaspoon each allspice
        and nutmeg
      ½ teaspoon cloves
      ¼ teaspoon cardamon
Cream until light:
      2 cups butter
      2 cups sugar
Add and beat in well:
    10 beaten eggs
Add:
      2 tablespoons vanilla
Stir in the sifted flour mixture. Combine the batter with the fruit sirup and fruit and:
      3 cups coarsely chopped
        pecans
until well mixed. Pour into the loaf and tube pans and bake for

3 to 3½ hours or until the tests indicate that the cake is done. To prepare pans, see About Fruit Cakes, page 355. Cool and store.

ABOUT CUP CAKES

Nearly all cake doughs lend themselves to baking in individual portions. Bake them in muffin, madeleine or ladyfinger molds. On informal occasions, like children's parties, bake and serve in fluted paper baking cups. If the papers are set in muffin tins, the cakes retain their shape better. ◖ Fill molds about ⅓ full and bake in a 375° preheated oven for 20 to 25 minutes. The baked cakes can be filled and iced. For suggested combinations, see Filled Cakes and Torten, page 366. For quick icing methods, see page 426, or garnish the cakes with nuts, diced dried fruits or a dusting of powdered sugar.

YELLOW CUP CAKES

[About Two Dozen 2-Inch Cakes]
Preheat oven to 375°.
See About Cup Cakes, above.
Prepare:
      Hurry-Up Cake, page
      362, or Lightning Cake,
      page 363

ONE-EGG CUP CAKES

◖ See About Cup Cakes, above.
Preheat oven to 375°.
Prepare:
      One-Egg Cake, page 364
Add to the batter:
      (1 cup raisins or washed,
        dried currants)
When cool, sprinkle the tops with:
      Confectioners' sugar

SPONGE CUP CAKES OR MARGUERITES

See About Cup Cakes, above.

Preheat oven to 375°.
Prepare:

Any sponge cake

Permit the cakes to cool in the pans, then sprinkle with:

Powdered sugar

MADELEINES

[About 15 Cakes]
These light-as-a-feather French tea cakes are usually baked in scalloped madeleine shells or muffin tins. Who could guess that their tender crumb results from an overdose of butter? The method of making them is just like that of Génoise.
Preheat oven to 450°.
Melt and allow to cool:

¾ cup butter

Heat in a double boiler until lukewarm:

2 eggs
1 cup sugar

Stir constantly. Remove from heat and beat until thick but light and creamy, incorporating as much air as possible. When cool, sift and add gradually:

1 cup sifted cake flour

Add the cool, melted butter and:

1 tablespoon rum
1 teaspoon vanilla or 1 teaspoon grated lemon rind

Bake for about 15 minutes.

LADYFINGERS

[About 30 Small Cakes]
Preheat oven to 375°.
◗ Have ingredients at about 75°.
Sift before measuring:

⅓ cup cake flour

Resift it 3 times. Sift:

⅓ cup confectioners' sugar

Beat until thick and lemon colored:

1 whole egg
2 egg yolks

Whip until stiff, but not dry:

2 egg whites

Fold the sugar gradually into the egg whites. Beat the mixture until it thickens again. Fold in the egg yolk mixture and:

¼ teaspoon vanilla

Fold in the flour. Shape the dough into oblongs with a paper tube, see page 337, on ungreased paper placed in a pan; or pour it into greased layfinger or small muffin tins. Or you may put it through a cookie press. Bake for about 12 minutes.

CORNSTARCH PUFF CAKES

[Fifteen Small Cupcakes]
Preheat oven to 350°.
Have ingredients at about 75°.
Cream:

½ cup butter
1 cup sifted powdered sugar

Add and beat until light:

4 well-beaten eggs
1 teaspoon vanilla

Sift before measuring:

1 cup cornstarch

Sift 3 times afterwards, with:

2 teaspoons double-acting baking powder

Combine the creamed and the sifted ingredients until blended. Fill muffin tins ½ full and bake about 15 minutes.

JAM CUP CAKES

Prepare the batter for:

Rombauer Jam Cake, page 365

Bake in greased muffin tins, at 375° for about 20 minutes.

ANGEL CUP CAKES OR BALLS

[About Sixteen 2½-Inch Cup Cakes]
Preheat oven to 375°.
Prepare the batter for:

Angel Cake, page 340, or Flavored
Angel Cake, page 341

Place it in ungreased, deep muffin tins. Bake for about 20 minutes. When cold, split the cup cakes horizontally and fill them.

See Filled Cakes and Torten, page 366. For a luxurious tea cake, ice with a rather soft icing and roll in chopped nuts or shredded chopped coconut.

LANGUE DE CHAT OR CAT'S TONGUE

[About 2 Dozen]
Preheat oven to 350°.
Cream:
    ¼ cup butter
    ¼ cup sugar
Beat in:
    4 eggs
Fold in:
    ½ cup all-purpose flour
    1 teaspoon vanilla
The pans for these wafers are similar in shape to ladyfinger pans. Bake about 15 minutes or until done. Serve frosted, or put a filling between two of the cakes of 3 parts chocolate icing and 1 part crushed nut brittle, to form Maquis.

CHOCOLATE CUP CAKES

♦ Read About Cup Cakes, page 358.
Preheat oven to 375°.
Prepare any recipe for:
    Chocolate Cake, page 350
Bake for 20 to 25 minutes or until done.

CARAMEL CUP CAKES

[About Twenty-Four 2-Inch Cakes]
♦ Read About Cup Cakes, page 358.
Preheat oven to 375°.
Prepare:
    Hurry-Up Caramel Cake, page 363
Bake in greased muffin tins for 20 to 25 minutes or until done.

SOUR MILK SPICE CUP CAKES

[About Twenty 2-Inch Cakes]

♦ Read About Cup Cakes, page 358.
Preheat oven to 375°.
Prepare:
    Sour Cream Layer Cake, page 347
substituting for the white sugar:
    Brown sugar
Add:
    ½ teaspoon cinnamon
    ¼ teaspoon cloves
Fold in:
    ¾ cup nut meats
Bake in greased muffin tins for about 20 minutes or until done.

COCONUT CUP CAKES

Prepare batter for:
    Coconut Loaf Cake, page 349
Bake in small greased muffin tins.

✳ PETITS FOURS

Prepare:
    Lady Cake, page 350, or Génoise, page 370
Pour the dough into pans, so that you may cut the cake into small cubes. You may cut the cubes in half horizontally and apply a filling, page 378. To apply Fondant, the traditional icing, see page 424, and the illustration below.

ABOUT CAKES WITH MELTED BUTTER OR OIL

If liquid fats are used in cake

making, they demand special mixing processes. Génoise, page 370, and Madeleines, page 359, are examples of melted butter batters. In this book, all cakes made with cooking oil carry the word "oil" in the title. They are included not for their excellence, for they have too fine a grain, but for those who use unsaturated fats.

▶ Olive oil should never be used because its flavor is too strong. To be light in texture, oil cake recipes need a disproportionate amount of sugar. ▶ Because of the difference in mixing and the greater demand for sugar ▶ do not try to substitute oil for solid fats in other cake recipes. You may vary the recipes given for oil cakes, however, by the addition of spices, flavorings, nuts and raisins.

CHIFFON OIL CAKE

[A 10-Inch Pan or a 9 x 13-Inch Oblong]

This cake has a very fine light texture, but requires a larger amount of sugar than a solid shortening cake. ▶ Mix it exactly as indicated.

Preheat oven to 325°.

Sift twice and put in a beater bowl:

2¼ cups sifted cake flour
1½ cups sugar
3 teaspoons double-acting baking powder
1 teaspoon salt

Beat until smooth and fold in all at once:

½ cup cooking oil
6 beaten egg yolks
¾ cup water
1 teaspoon grated lemon rind
2 teaspoons vanilla

Beat until foamy:

6 to 10 egg whites

Add:

½ teaspoon cream of tartar

Beat until ▶ stiff, but not dry.

Fold the flour, egg and oil mixture gently into the egg whites. Do this by hand, not in the mixer, see page 181. Bake the cake in an ungreased tube pan about 1 hour and 10 minutes or in an ungreased 9 x 13-inch flat pan for about 30 to 35 minutes. Place the pan on a rack adjusted in the lower third of the oven. Reverse the tube pan to cool the cake, as shown on page 340, or set the oblong pan reversed and supported at the edges by two other pans while the cake cools. Ice with:

Banana Icing, page 430

CHIFFON MOCHA OIL CAKE

[A 10-Inch Tube Pan or a 9 x 13-Inch Oblong]

Mix and bake as for preceding cake.

Preheat oven to 325°.

Melt over hot water:

3 oz. chocolate

Sift twice and put in a beater bowl:

2¼ cups sifted cake flour
1⅔ cups sugar
3 teaspoons double-acting baking powder
2 teaspoons instant coffee
1 teaspoon salt
¼ teaspoon cinnamon

Beat until smooth and fold in all at once:

½ cup cooking oil
6 beaten egg yolks
½ cup milk
2 teaspoons vanilla

and the cooled melted chocolate. Blend well. Beat until frothy:

6 to 8 egg whites

Add:

½ teaspoon cream of tartar

Continue to beat until the whites are ▶ stiff, but not dry. Gently fold the egg whites into the flour, egg and oil mixture. Place the batter in an ungreased tube pan or an ungreased oblong pan. Place the pan on a rack adjusted in the lower third of the oven. If in a tube pan, bake for about 1 hour and 10 minutes; if in the oblong pan, for about 35 minutes. To cool, reverse the tube pan or let the oblong pan rest reversed on two other pans. Ice with:

> Luscious Orange Icing, page 424

QUICK WHITE OIL CAKE

[Two 9-Inch Square Pans]
Preheat oven to 375°.
Have all ingredients at about 75°. Sift into a mixing bowl:

   2¾ cups sifted cake flour
   3½ teaspoons double-acting baking powder
   1 teaspoon salt

Mix and add:

   ⅔ cup cooking oil
   ¾ cup water
   ½ cup skimmed milk

Beat the two mixtures together until you have a smooth batter. Beat until foamy:

   4 egg whites

Add:

   ¼ teaspoon cream of tartar

Continue to beat until the whites are ♦ stiff, but not dry. Continue to beat, adding gradually:

   1½ cups sugar

until a meringue-like texture results. Fold the egg white mixture into the other ingredients. Bake in greased pans for 25 to 30 minutes.

QUICK SPICE OIL CAKE

Prepare:

> Quick White Oil Cake, above

using in all:

   2½ cups, plus 2 tablespoons cake flour
   2 teaspoons cinnamon
   ½ teaspoon each cloves and allspice
   2 teaspoons grated orange rind

Mix and bake exactly as directed in Quick White Oil Cake.

QUICK CHOCOLATE OIL CAKE

Prepare:

> Quick White Oil Cake, above

using in all:

   2¼ cups cake flour
   ⅓ cup cocoa

Beat in, at the last, in all:

   1¾ cups sugar

Mix and bake exactly as directed in Quick White Oil Cake.

ABOUT QUICK CAKES

We all want a good cake in a big hurry. But let's not delude ourselves that the shortcuts listed in the Index as Quick Cakes and made with unseparated eggs are as lovely in texture as those which require separation of the eggs. Lightning Cake, especially if made with a heavy duty mixer, is amazingly moist and tender. All quick cakes, especially those calling for oil or emulsified hydrogenated fats, demand a larger proportion of sugar than cakes baked with solid shortening, and have a closer grain. ♦ Mix oil cakes just exactly as described, page 360; and quick butter cakes as in the following recipes. Deviation spells disaster. ♦ Never try to mix just any recipe by the one-bowl method.

HURRY-UP CAKE

[A 9 x 13-Inch Pan]
This cake—and its variations which can be made in one bowl —speaks for itself. It can be mixed by hand or with a rotary or electric mixer. It is best as a flat cake, iced and cut into cubes. Be sure to have all ingredients at 75°.
Preheat oven to 350°.
Sift before measuring:

1¾ cups cake flour
Resift with:
    1 cup sugar
Add:
    ½ cup soft butter
    2 eggs
    ½ cup milk
    ½ teaspoon salt
    1¾ teaspoons double-acting
      baking powder
    1 teaspoon vanilla
Beat vigorously with a wire whisk or a rotary beater for 2 to 3 minutes. Bake in a greased pan for about ½ hour. Spread with:
    Chocolate Butter Icing,
    page 428, or
    Quick Lemon Icing,
    page 427

HURRY-UP CARAMEL CAKE

Prepare:
    Hurry-Up Cake, above
Substitute for the white sugar:
    1 cup packed brown sugar
You may add to the batter:
    ¾ cup nut meats
    ¾ cup chopped dates
Spread the cake, when cool, with:
    Caramel Icing, page 425

HURRY-UP COCOA CAKE

Prepare:
    Hurry-Up Cake, above
Deduct ¼ cup cake flour.
Add:
    ¼ cup Dutch process cocoa
Ice the cake, when cool, with:
    European Chocolate
    Icing, page 428

HURRY-UP SPICE CAKE

Prepare:
    Hurry-Up Cake, above
Add:
    1 teaspoon cinnamon
    ½ teaspoon cloves
When cool, dust the cake with:
    Confectioners' sugar

CARAMEL CORNFLAKE [8] RING

Stir, melt and cook to the soft-ball stage, at 238°:
    1 cup packed brown sugar
    1½ tablespoons light corn
      sirup
    ⅓ cup milk
    2½ tablespoons butter
Place in a large buttered mixing bowl:
    4 cups cornflakes
Stir in the hot sirup until blended. Pack the flakes in a buttered 8-inch ring mold. Cool. Invert and serve, filled with:
    Sugared or stewed fruit

LIGHTNING OR WHIPPED TEA CAKE

[Two 8-Inch Square or
Two 8-Inch Round Pans]
Prepare this cake as described, or vary it in flavor by making the substitutions as directed in any of the variations for Hurry-Up Cake, page 362.
Preheat oven to 375°.
◉ Have all ingredients at about 75°. Let soften to the consistency of mayonnaise:
    ½ cup butter
If you want a wonderful, thin tea cake, have ready a topping of:
    ½ cup powdered sugar
    1 tablespoon cinnamon
    ¼ cup chopped pecans
and prepare the 8-inch square pans. If you want a thicker layer cake to ice, use the 8-inch round pans and omit the topping. Sift into a beater bowl:
    1¾ cups cake flour
    ½ teaspoon salt
    1 cup sugar
Add:
    2 eggs
    ½ cup, plus 2½ teaspoons
      milk
and the softened butter. Using the ◉ whip attachment of your beater, whip for 1 minute at low speed. Scrape the bowl. Whip

for 1½ minutes at slightly higher speed. Scrape the bowl again and fold in:

1½ teaspoons baking powder

Whip for 30 seconds on first speed. Pour the batter into 2 pans, sprinkle with the topping and bake for 20 minutes.

ONE-EGG CAKE

[Two 8-Inch Round Pans]
Preheat oven to 375°.
Have all ingredients at about 75°. Sift into an electric mixer bowl and mix for about 2 minutes at medium speed:

1¾ cups sifted all-purpose flour
1¼ cups sugar
2½ teaspoons double-acting baking powder
1 teaspoon salt
⅓ cup soft butter
⅔ cup milk

Add and mix for ▶ 2 minutes more, scraping bowl constantly:

1 egg
⅓ cup milk
1 teaspoon vanilla

Pour the batter into greased pans and bake for about 25 minutes. See Quick Icings for a choice and apply when cake is cool.

GINGERBREAD

[A 9 x 9 x 2-Inch Pan]
Preheat oven to 350°.
Melt in a heavy pan and let cool:

½ cup butter

Beat together well:

½ cup sugar
1 beaten egg

Sift:

2½ cups sifted all-purpose flour
1½ teaspoons soda
1 teaspoon each cinnamon and ginger
½ teaspoon salt
(1 tablespoon grated orange rind)

Combine:

½ cup light molasses
½ cup honey
1 cup hot water

Add the sifted and liquid ingredients alternately to the butter mixture until blended. Bake in a greased pan about 1 hour.

WHEATLESS GINGERBREAD

[A 9 x 9 x 2-Inch Pan]
Unusual, yet perhaps the best of all.
Preheat oven to 325°.
Sift together 6 times:

1¼ cups rye or rice flour
1¼ cups cornstarch
2 teaspoons soda
1 teaspoon cinnamon
¼ teaspoon each cloves and ginger

Mix:

½ cup sugar
1 cup molasses
½ cup butter

with the flour mixture. Add:

1 cup boiling water

Add:

2 well-beaten eggs

Bake in a greased pan about 45 minutes.

PARKIN

[An 8 x 8-Inch Pan]
A not-too-sweet Guy Fawkes Day cake.
Preheat oven to 350°.
Heat ▶ over—not in—hot water, until the butter is melted:

½ cup butter
½ cup treacle

Mix in a bowl:

⅔ cup rolled oats
1 cup all-purpose flour
1 tablespoon sugar
½ teaspoon ginger
¼ teaspoon cloves
½ teaspoon salt
½ teaspoon soda
(1 teaspoon grated lemon rind)

Add alternately with the melted butter mixture:

⅔ cup milk

Combine until the dry ingredients are just moist. The batter will be thin. Bake in a greased pan for about 35 minutes or until the cake begins to pull from the sides of the pan.

ROMBAUER JAM CAKE

[A 7-Inch Tube Pan]
Preheat oven to 350°.
Have all ingredients at about 75°. Sift, then measure:
    1½ cups all-purpose flour
Resift with:
    1 teaspoon double-acting
        baking powder
    ½ teaspoon soda
    ½ teaspoon cloves
    1 teaspoon each cinnamon
        and nutmeg
Cream until light:
    6 tablespoons butter
    1 cup brown sugar
Beat in, one at a time:
    2 eggs
Beat in:
    3 tablespoons cultured sour
        cream
Stir the flour mixture into the butter mixture until barely blended. Stir in:
    1 cup rather firm raspberry
        or blackberry jam
    (½ cup broken nut meats)
Pour the batter into a greased tube pan. Bake it for about ½ hour or until done. When cool, ice the cake with:
    Quick Brown Sugar
        Icing, page 428

EGGLESS, MILKLESS SPICE CAKE

[A 7-Inch Tube Pan]
Preheat oven to 325°.
Boil for 3 minutes:
    1 cup water or beer
    2 cups seeded raisins
    1 cup brown sugar
    ⅓ cup butter or margarine
    ½ teaspoon each cinnamon
        and allspice
    ½ teaspoon salt
    ⅛ teaspoon nutmeg

Cool these ingredients. Sift before measuring:
    2 cups cake flour
Resift with:
    1 teaspoon double-acting
        baking powder
    1 teaspoon soda
Stir the flour gradually into the other ingredients. Stir the batter until smooth. Add:
    (1 cup chopped almonds)
By the addition of 1 cup chopped dates, figs and citron, this becomes an acceptable fruit cake. Bake in a greased tube pan for 1 hour or more. Spread with:
    Caramel Icing, page 425

MYSTERY CAKE

[A 9-Inch Tube Pan]
This curious combination of ingredients makes a surprisingly good cake. But why shouldn't it? The deep secret is tomato, which after all is a fruit.
Preheat oven to 350°.
Have all ingredients at about 75°. Sift before measuring:
    2 cups all-purpose flour
Resift with:
    ½ teaspoon salt
    1 teaspoon cinnamon
    ½ teaspoon each nutmeg
        and cloves
    1 teaspoon soda
Sift:
    1 cup sugar
Cream until soft:
    2 tablespoons butter
Add the sifted sugar gradually and cream these ingredients well. Stir the flour mixture in about 3 parts into the sugar mixture, alternating with thirds of the contents of:
    1 can condensed tomato
        soup: 10½ oz.
Stir the batter until smooth after each addition. Fold in:
    1 cup nut meats
    1 cup raisins
Bake in a greased tube pan for

about 45 minutes. Spread, when cool, with:

Boiled White Icing,
page 419

ABOUT TORTEN

So many people speak of Torten as unattainable, not realizing that mixing a Torte is just a matter of replacing the flour in certain recipes with crumbs not too finely ground, and nuts ground to a dry meal. There are 3 tricks in making Torten. 1. ♦ The nuts should never be ground in a meat grinder, which simply crushes them and brings up the oil. A small hand grinder with a sharp cutting edge like the one shown in About Nuts, page 186, will produce the light, dry, fluffy particles needed. 2. ♦ Never grease the pan sides. 3. ♦ Use a pan with a removable rim— either a spring form or a tube from which you can remove the bottom, see sketch below, because this kind of pastry is often too delicate in texture to stand much handling. Torten are good just as baked, with black coffee. But who can possibly object to a whipped cream or fruit sauce garnish?

✳ ALMOND TORTE COCKAIGNE

[An 8-Inch Removable-Rim Pan]
The following recipe is the well-known German Mandeltorte. It

may also be baked in a loaf or in layers. ♦ Please read About Torten, opposite.
Preheat oven to 350°.
Have all ingredients at about 75°. Sift:

1 cup sugar

Beat:

6 egg yolks

Add the sugar gradually and beat until very creamy. Add:

Grated rind and juice of
1 lemon or of 1 small
orange
1 teaspoon cinnamon
1 cup ground unblanched
almonds
½ cup toasted white bread
crumbs
(½ teaspoon almond extract)

Whip ♦ until stiff, but not dry:

6 egg whites

Fold them lightly into the batter. Bake for about 40 minutes in an ungreased pan. Permit to cool in the pan. Spread with:

Chocolate Butter Icing,
page 428

or bake it in two 8-inch ungreased removable-rim layer pans. Spread between the layers:

Lemon and Orange
Custard Filling, page 379

Spread the top with:

Sifted confectioners'
sugar

or with one of the fillings suggested on page 376. This cake is very light and consequently difficult to remove from the pan, so be careful.

✳ PECAN TORTE

For a richer, moister cake, prepare:

Almond Torte, above

substituting pecans for the almonds. ♦ Be sure to grind the nuts in a nut grinder.

✳ BREAD TORTE OR BROTTORTE

[A 9-Inch Removable-Rim Pan]

In the following recipe for a celebrated German confection, the ingredients differ only slightly from those in the preceding Mandeltorte, but the results, thanks to the wine bath, are amazingly different.
Preheat oven to 350°.
♦ Have all ingredients at about 75°. Sift:

1 cup sugar

Beat:

6 egg yolks

Add the sugar gradually. Beat until creamy. Combine and add:

1¼ cups dry bread crumbs
½ teaspoon double-acting baking powder
½ teaspoon cinnamon
2 oz. citron, cut fine
1 cup unblanched almonds, ground in a nut grinder
Rind and juice of 1 lemon

Whip ♦ until stiff, but not dry:

6 egg whites

Fold them lightly into the cake batter. Bake for 1 hour or more in an ungreased pan. Heat, but do not boil:

¾ cup dry sherry
2 tablespoons water
2 whole cloves
1 stick cinnamon
¼ cup sugar

Strain these ingredients and place the sirup in a small pitcher. Pour it very slowly onto the hot cake. When all the liquid has been absorbed, cool the cake and remove it from the pan. Spread with:

A flavored Crème Patissière, page 378

DOBOS OR DRUM TORTE

The many-tiered Hungarian chocolate-filled torte that looks rich, is rich and enriches everyone who eats it.
♦ Have all ingredients at 75°. Prepare:

Génoise, page 370

Using well-greased 8-inch cake pans, bake the cake in 9 layers, 5 to 9 minutes each. Work rapidly. If your oven will not hold so many layers, bake thicker ones and slice them in two, professionally, holding them as shown on page 377. Stack them so that you apply the icing to the baked rather than to the cut surfaces. When cool, spread between the layers the following filling. Place in a double boiler:

½ cup sugar
4 eggs
1 inch vanilla bean

or omit the vanilla bean and add 1 teaspoonful of vanilla extract after the filling has cooled. Beat until the eggs begin to thicken. Cool the filling slightly. Cut into pieces and dissolve:

4 oz. chocolate

in:

2 tablespoons boiling water

Keep this warm. Cream until light:

⅞ cup butter: 1¾ sticks

Add the chocolate mixture. Beat into the egg mixture. This filling may also be spread over the top and sides of the cake, but the true Hungarian will spread it between layers only, reserving the best looking layer for the top. Glaze this chef d'oeuvre with:

½ cup Clear Caramel Glaze, page 435

The hard topping gives the cake its name. Before the caramel sets, use a hot buttered knife to cut 12 to 18 radial lines into the top glaze, so the cake may be easily sliced. "Rest" the cake in a chilled place for 12 hours or more before serving.

✳ HAZELNUT TORTE

[A 10-Inch Removable-Rim Pan]
♦ Please read About Torten, page 366.
Preheat oven to 350°.
♦ Have all ingredients at about 75°. Sift:

1 cup sugar
Beat:
    12 egg yolks
Add the sugar gradually. Beat well until ingredients are very creamy. Grind in a nut grinder:
    ¼ lb. hazelnuts
    ¼ lb. pecans or walnuts
Add:
    (2 tablespoons bread
        crumbs)
Whip ◗ until stiff, but not dry:
    8 egg whites
Fold them lightly into the other ingredients. Bake the cake in an ungreased pan for about 40 minutes. When cool, spread between the layers:
    Whipped cream, flavored
        with vanilla or sweet
        sherry
Spread the cake with:
    (Coffee or Caramel Icing,
        page 425)

CHOCOLATE WALNUT TORTE

[A 9-Inch Removable-Rim Pan]
◗ Please read About Torten, page 366.
Preheat oven to 325°.
◗ Have all ingredients at 75°.
Sift:
    ⅞ cup sugar
Beat until light:
    6 egg yolks
Add the sugar gradually. Beat until well blended. Add:
    ½ cup finely crushed
        cracker crumbs
    ¼ cup grated chocolate
    ¾ cup chopped walnut
        meats
    2 tablespoons brandy or
        rum
    ½ teaspoon double-acting
        baking powder
    ½ teaspoon cinnamon
    ¼ teaspoon each cloves
        and nutmeg
Whip ◗ until stiff, but not dry:
    6 egg whites
Fold them lightly into the cake

batter. Bake in an ungreased pan for about 1 hour. Spread with:
    Chocolate Butter Icing,
        page 428
or serve with:
    Wine Custard, page 440

CHOCOLATE DATE TORTE

[A 9-Inch Tube Pan]
A richly flavored, exceedingly good cake.
Prepare:
    Chocolate Sponge Cake,
        page 343
Sprinkle:
    2 tablespoons sifted flour
over:
    ¾ cup chopped dates
    1 tablespoon grated
        orange rind
    (½ cup chopped nut meats)
Beat these ingredients into the cake batter before folding in the egg whites. Bake as directed.
Sprinkle with:
    Powdered sugar
We serve this to everybody's intense satisfaction with:
    Liqueur Cream Sauce,
        page 482, or Foamy
        Sauce, page 481

POPPY SEED CUSTARD TORTE

[Two 9-Inch Round Layer Pans]
Preheat oven to 375°.
◗ Have all ingredients at 75°.
Combine and soak for 2 hours:
    ⅔ cup poppy seed
    ¾ cup milk
Beat until soft:
    ⅔ cup butter
Add gradually:
    1½ cups sugar
Cream these ingredients until fluffy. Sift before measuring:
    2 cups cake flour
Resift with:
    2½ teaspoons double-acting
        baking powder
    ½ teaspoon salt
Combine the poppy seed milk mixture with:
    ¼ cup milk

1 teaspoon vanilla

Add the sifted ingredients to the butter mixture in about 3 parts, alternating with the liquid ingredients. Beat the batter after each addition until blended. Whip ▸ until stiff, but not dry, then fold in:

4 egg whites

Bake for about 20 minutes. Place between the layers:

Crème Patissière,
page 378

Serve with:

Chocolate Sauce
Cockaigne, page 474

or dust with:

Powdered sugar

SACHERTORTE

[A 9-Inch Removable-Rim Pan]

A recipe of the famous restaurant keeper Frau Sacher, who fed the impoverished Austrian nobility long after they had ceased to pay.

Preheat oven to 325°.

▸ Have all ingredients at about 75°.

Melt in a double boiler over, not in, hot water:

5 oz. semi-sweet chocolate,
not in chip form

Cream until fluffy:

¾ cup sugar
¾ cup butter

Beat in gradually until light in color:

5 egg yolks

and add the melted cooled chocolate. Sift and add gradually:

¾ cup all-purpose flour

Beat until stiff but not dry:

5 to 6 egg whites

Gently fold the whites into the chocolate mixture. Bake in an ungreased pan 50 minutes to 1 hour. When cool slice the Torte horizontally and insert a filling of:

Puréed Apricot Jam

Cover the torte with:

European Chocolate
Icing, page 428

using strong coffee instead of the cream.

If you are really Viennese you put on a great gob of "Schlag" or whipped cream.

ABOUT FILLED CAKES

In modern service, especially for buffets, a ready-to-serve, complete dessert often replaces the separate presentation of ice cream and cake, pudding and cake or fruit and cake. Such combinations may take varied forms—see illustrations in this section. They may also be as rich and substantial or as light in texture and calorie content as you choose.

We have assembled in the next pages some individual recipes that we enjoy serving as complete desserts. We also suggest a number of ways that basic cakes can be combined with fillings. Read about Pinch Pies, Roll Cakes, Charlottes, Torten, Trifles, Savarins and Filled Rolled Cookies. See illustrations for making a secret filling, page 377, lining pudding molds, page 448, or turning a simple Baked Alaska into an Omelette Surprise, page 448.

If you must, buy your basic angel and sponge cakes, ice cream and ice fillings. But when you combine them, make a delicious sauce of your very own with fresh eggs or fruit and—most important of all—real vanilla, fresh spices and quality spirits. The quantities you need for flavorings are small and should be of the best, see About Spices on page 198. And all the recipes for sponge, angel cakes, Génoise, Daffodil Cake, roll cakes, nut Torten, ladyfingers and rolled cookies are suitable for mold linings. For additional fillings and combinations, see page 376.

REFRIGERATOR CAKES

Line molds, page 449, or make a secret panel cake, page 377. Fill with:

> Bavarians or mousses
> Whipped gelatin
> puddings
> Pastry creams or
> charlotte mixtures
> Cream pie or chiffon pie
> fillings
> Sweetened whipped
> creams

Refrigerate at least 6 hours, covered, before serving. Garnish with:

> Fruits and nuts

or serve with:

> Sauce or whipped cream

Dust with:

> Toasted nuts
> Shredded coconut or
> Praliné, page 514

✳ GÉNOISE

[Two 9-Inch Layers]

This rich, moist Italian cake, which the French and we have borrowed, has no equal for versatility. It also keeps well and freezes well. It may be used for dessert rolls with cream fillings, see About Roll Cakes, page 372, or Baked Alaska, page 448; also with butter icings or as a foil for fruit. You may bake it as Ladyfingers, page 359, or in layers. For a very elaborate Génoise, sprinkle it after cooling with Cointreau or kirsch, fill it with Sauce Cockaigne, page 474, or cover it with whipped cream, or European Chocolate Icing, page 428. For a children's party, bake favors in the cake, see Galette des Rois, page 298.

Preheat oven to 350°.

Melt and put aside:

> ¼ cup butter

Do not let it get cooler than about 80°. Break into a double boiler ▶ over—not in—hot water until they are lukewarm:

> 6 eggs

Add:

> ⅔ cup sugar

Beat with a rotary or electric mixer at medium speed for 7 minutes. Add:

> ⅓ cup sugar

Increase speed and beat for 2 minutes longer or until the mixture is lemony in color and stands in soft peaks. Gently add:

> 1 teaspoon vanilla

Fold in:

> 1 cup sifted cake flour

Add the melted butter with a folding motion. Pour the batter into the pans and bake about 40 minutes or until done. ▶ Turn cakes out at once onto a rack to cool.

MOHRENKOEPFE OR MOORS' HEADS

These Moors' heads, along with Individual Nut Tarts, page 408, and Macaroon Jam Tarts, page 407, were specialties of a famous St. Louis bakery, now extinct, and graced a thousand Kaffeeklatsches. While the true Mohrenkopf is baked in a special half-round mold, the full taste effect can be gained by the following method:

Cut in rounds or squares:

> Thin Génoise, above

Make a "sandwich" filling of:

> Hazelnut flavored
> whipped cream

Cover with:

> European Chocolate
> Icing, page 428 or
> Chocolate Sauce
> Cockaigne, page 474

TRIFLE OR RASPBERRY RUM CAKE

A good use for dry cake. Combine it with raspberries, which are traditional. But apricot jam or other preserves, thickened pie cherries, fresh or cooked drained fruit, may be substituted.

Place in a deep dish:

Rounds of yellow, sponge
or layer cake, etc.
Sprinkle the cake with:
(2 tablespoons rum or
sherry)
Spread the pieces with:
½ cup jam or jelly or 1 to
2 cups sweetened fruit
(¼ cup blanched, slivered
almonds)
Prepare:
Rich Custard, page 438
Pour the custard over the cake.
Whip until stiff:
(1 cup whipping cream)
Garnish the dish with the cream.

BABA AU RHUM
OR SAVARIN

Beloved by the French, who frequently serve it with tea. This
is an American version. Savarin
is really a larger version of Baba
au Rhum. The same dough and
the same sirup are used, but the
dessert is baked in a ring mold
with a rounded base. When it is
turned out, the center is filled
with fruit. If you fill it with tart
red cherry compote, you need
hardly be told it will have become Savarin Montmorency!
Prepare:
Bundkuchen, page 266,
or Brioche dough,
page 258
Place it in a greased 8-inch tube
pan. Permit it to rise, and bake as
directed. Remove from the pan,
cool and return to the pan. Prepare a sirup by boiling for 10
minutes:
½ cup water
1 cup sugar
Cool it slightly. Flavor it generously with:
Rum or whisky: at least
¼ cup
Place the sirup in a small pitcher.
One hour before serving the
cake, pour slowly, drop by drop,
onto the baba. Use as much as
will be absorbed. Permit the
cake to stand until ready to

serve. Remove it from the pan.
If it is to be a dessert, top it
with:
Whipped cream
You may serve individual baba
cakes. Bake them in muffin tins.
Soak them as directed or cut a
slice from the top, hollow the
cakes slightly and fill the hollows with the raspberry or apricot jam. Serve with:
Lemon Sauce, page 473
or, slice the muffins in half, cover
each half with a slice of fresh
pineapple and currant jelly,
sprinkled with confectioners'
sugar and kirsch.

ORANGE-FILLED CAKE

[Three 9-Inch Round Pans]
Most recipes for orange cake
prove to be disappointing, for
upon reading them you find that
they are merely sponge or butter
cake with an orange filling. This
one calls for orange juice in the
batter plus orange filling and
icing. Earrings for an elephant
with no apologies!
Preheat oven to 375°.
Have all ingredients at about
75°. Sift before measuring:
3 cups cake flour
Resift with:
¾ teaspoon salt
3½ teaspoons double-acting
baking powder
Grate:
Rind of 1 orange
into:
1½ cups sugar
Cream this until light with:
¾ cup butter
Beat in, one at a time:
3 eggs
Measure:
½ cup orange juice
½ cup water
2 tablespoons lemon juice
Add the flour mixture in about 3
parts to the butter mixture, alternately with the liquid. Stir
the batter after each addition
until smooth. Bake the cake in

3 greased layer pans for about ½ hour. When the cake is cool, spread between the layers:

Orange Cream Filling, page 380

BOSTON CREAM PIE OR CAKE

Traditionally called a pie, this is really a 2-layer cake. There are many versions, but the most prevalent one today reads as follows.

Place between 2 layers of:

Gold Layer Cake, page 348

a thick coating of:

Crème Patissière, page 378

Leave the sides exposed, but cover the top with:

A chocolate icing, page 428

CREAM MERINGUE TART COCKAIGNE

[Two 8-Inch Layer Pans]
The following recipe is not at all difficult to make, yet it is an optical as well as a gastronomic treat. A cake batter and a meringue are baked at the same time.
Preheat oven to 325°.
Blanch and shred:

(⅓ cup almonds)

Sift:

1½ cups sugar

Beat until soft:

¼ cup butter

Add ½ cup of the sifted sugar gradually. Blend until light and creamy. Beat in, one at a time:

4 egg yolks

Add:

½ teaspoon vanilla

Sift before measuring:

1 cup cake flour

Resift with:

1 teaspoon double-acting baking powder
¼ teaspoon salt

Add the sifted ingredients to the butter mixture, alternately with:

5 tablespoons cream

Beat the batter until smooth. Spread it in 2 greased pans with 1½-inch sides. Cover it with the following meringue. Whip until stiff, but not dry:

4 egg whites

Add the remaining cup sifted sugar slowly, about 1 tablespoon at a time. Beat constantly. When all the sugar has been added, continue to beat for several minutes. Fold in:

1 teaspoon vanilla

Spread the meringue lightly over the cake batter in both pans. If using the almonds, stud one meringue with the blanched, shredded almonds, placing the shreds close together. Bake the layers for about 40 minutes. Remove them from the oven and permit them to cool in the pans. Shortly before serving the cake, place the unstudded layer, meringue side down, on a cake plate. Spread one of the following fillings over it, reserving ¼ cup for the top. Place the almond studded layer, meringue side up, on the cream filling and place the reserved filling in the center on top using:

A Cream Filling, page 377; Sauce Cockaigne, page 474, and whipped cream

ABOUT ROLL CAKES

Any number of doughs lend themselves to rolling, see Jelly Rolls, below, Angel Cake Roll, page 374, Chocolate Cream Roll, page 374, etc. They may be baked in sheets, 10½ x 15½ x 1 inch. Simply grease the baking sheet well, pour in the batter and bake in a 375° oven for about 12 minutes. ◗ To roll, loosen the edges as soon as the cake comes from the oven. Reverse the pan onto a clean towel that has been dusted with:

Sifted confectioners'
sugar

Trim off any crusty edges. There are 2 ways to roll the cake. If the filling is a perishable one, roll the cake while it is still hot, with the towel, as shown in the illustration below. Place the

cake, still wrapped in the towel, on a rack to cool. Later, when ready to fill, unroll the cake, fill it and use the towel to roll it again, as shown in the lower sketch.

 ½ cup jelly or tart jam or
 1 cup or more cream
 or custard filling

When the cake is rolled after filling ▶ place it on the serving plate with the seam side down.

JELLY ROLL

[A 10½ x 15½ x 1-Inch Pan]
This standard roll cake, or jelly roll, recipe also bakes well in two 8-inch round layer pans. To prepare pan, bake and roll, see About Roll Cakes, above.
Preheat oven to 375°.
Sift:
 ¾ cup sugar
Beat until light:

4 egg yolks

Add the sugar gradually. Beat until creamy. Add:
 1 teaspoon vanilla
Sift before measuring:
 ¾ cup cake flour
Resift with:
 ¾ teaspoon double-acting
  baking powder
 ½ teaspoon salt
Add the flour gradually to the egg mixture. Beat the batter until smooth. Whip ▶ until stiff, but not dry:
 4 egg whites
Fold them lightly into the cake batter with:
 ½ cup finely chopped nuts
Bake for about 13 minutes. When cold, spread with at least:
 ½ cup jelly

LEMON ROLL

Prepare:
 Jelly Roll, above
Substitute for the jelly:
 Lemon Filling, page 379
 Roll and fill.

BUTTERSCOTCH
SPICE ROLL

[A 10½ x 15½ x 1-Inch Pan]
▶ To prepare pan, see About Roll Cakes, page 372.
Preheat oven to 400°.
Place in a bowl over hot water:
 4 eggs
 ¼ teaspoon salt
Beat until the eggs are thick and lemon colored. Beat in gradually:
 ¾ cup sugar
Remove from the heat. Sift before measuring:
 ¾ cup cake flour
Resift with:
 ¾ teaspoon double-acting
  baking powder
 1 teaspoon cinnamon
 ½ teaspoon cloves
Fold in the sifted ingredients and:
 1 teaspoon vanilla
Bake the batter for about 13

minutes. To roll and fill, see About Roll Cakes, page 372. A good filling is:

> Butterscotch Filling, page 379

ALMOND SPONGE ROLL

◗ To prepare pan and bake, see About Roll Cakes, page 372. Preheat oven to 325°.
Beat until light:
    8 egg yolks
Beat in gradually:
    ½ cup sugar
Add:
    ½ cup blanched, ground almonds
Beat ◗ until stiff, but not dry:
    8 egg whites
Fold in:
    1 teaspoon vanilla
Fold the egg whites into the yolk mixture. Bake about 15 minutes, roll and, when cold, spread with any desired filling, see pages 377–381.

ANGEL CAKE ROLL

Preheat oven to 350°.
Sift twice:
    1¼ to 1½ cups sugar
Sift separately before measuring:
    1 cup cake flour
Resift the flour 3 times with ½ cupful of the sifted sugar and:
    ½ teaspoon salt
Whip until foamy:
    1¼ cups egg whites: 10 to 12 egg whites
    (2 tablespoons water or
    1 tablespoon water and
    1 tablespoon lemon juice)
Add:
    1 teaspoon cream of tartar
Whip the egg whites ◗ until stiff, but not dry. Gradually whip in, about 1 tablespoon at a time, 1 cup of the sifted sugar. Fold in:
    ½ teaspoon vanilla
    ½ teaspoon almond extract
Sift about ¼ cup of the sugar and flour mixture over the batter. Fold it in gently and briefly

with a rubber scraper. Continue until all the mixture is used. Pour the batter into an ungreased tube pan. Use the smaller amount of egg whites and sugar, as suggested at the end of the recipe. Make only ½ the amount if you wish to have 1 roll. Pour the batter in a shallow, 10½ x 15½-inch pan which has been greased with greased parchment paper and bake in a 300° oven for about 20 minutes. The pan is greased here in order to get the cake out intact for rolling. To roll and fill, see About Roll Cakes, page 372. Use any of the fillings suggested for the various Cake Rolls in this chapter. Raspberry or apricot jam and whipped cream are fine.

CHOCOLATE FILLED ROLL

Preheat oven to 375°.
Sift:
    ¾ cup sugar
Beat until light:
    4 egg yolks
Add the sugar gradually. Beat until creamy. Add:
    1 teaspoon vanilla
Sift before measuring:
    ¾ cup cake flour
Resift with:
    ¾ teaspoon double-acting baking powder
Add the flour gradually to the egg mixture. Beat the batter until smooth. Whip ◗ until stiff, but not dry:
    4 egg whites
Fold them lightly into the cake batter with:
    ½ cup finely chopped nuts
Bake for about 13 minutes. When cold, spread with:
    Chocolate Sauce Cockaigne, page 477
    Whipped Cream

★ CHOCOLATE CREAM ROLL OR BÛCHE DE NOËL

For Christmas this can be made

into a Yule Log by roughing up the icing and adding snowy cream details. Trim it the same way for Washington's Birthday. Preheat oven to 325°.

Sift:

    ½ cup powdered sugar

Beat until light:

    3 to 6 egg yolks

Add the sugar gradually and beat these ingredients until creamy. Add:

    1 teaspoon vanilla

Sift and add:

    2 to 6 tablespoons cocoa

If you use less than 4 tablespoons cocoa, add:

    (2 tablespoons all-purpose
        flour)
    ⅛ teaspoon salt

Whip ▶ until stiff, but not dry:

    3 to 6 egg whites
    ½ teaspoon cream of tartar

Fold lightly into the cake batter. Line a shallow 8 x 12-inch pan with heavy greased paper and spread the dough in it to the thickness of ¼ inch. Bake the cake for about 25 minutes. Let it cool in the pan for 5 minutes. To roll and fill, see About Roll Cakes, page 372. Cover with:

    Chocolate Sauce,
    page 477

ABOUT CHARLOTTES

How dull seem the charlottes of our youth, with only a cream and a cherry, when compared with those put together in the sophisticated society we now seem to frequent!

Today's fillings include all kinds of creams and Bavarians, nuts, angelica, citron, jams, chestnuts, fruits and ices. Whether the mold is lined with ladyfingers, sponge or Génoise, it may still be called a charlotte. For combinations, see below.

CHARLOTTE RUSSE   [6]

Soak:

    ¾ tablespoon gelatin

in:

    ¼ cup cold water

Dissolve it in:

    ⅓ cup scalded milk

Beat in:

    ⅓ cup powdered sugar

Cool. Flavor with:

    2 tablespoons strong coffee

Whip until stiff:

    1 cup whipping cream

Fold it lightly into the chilled ingredients. Line a mold with:

    Ladyfingers, page 359

Pour the pudding into it. Chill thoroughly. Unmold and serve with:

    Custard Sauce, page 475,
    flavored with rum

CHOCOLATE CHARLOTTE

Prepare:

    French Chocolate
    Mousse, page 441 or
    Rum Chocolate Mousse,
    page 441

adding:

    (¼ cup almond paste)

Line a mold as described in About Dessert Molds, page 449. Fill the ladyfinger-lined mold with the mousse.

MAPLE CHARLOTTE   [10]

Soak:

    1 tablespoon gelatin

in:

    ¼ cup cold water

Dissolve it in:

    ¾ cup hot maple sirup

Chill until it falls in heavy sheets from a spoon. Whip until the cream holds soft peaks:

    2 cups whipping cream

Fold in with a spoon:

    (½ cup blanched, chopped
        almonds)

Fold in the gelatin until well blended. Line a bowl with pieces of:

    Sponge Cake, page 342
    Ladyfingers, page 359

Pour the gelatin into it. Chill

until firm. Unmold and serve
garnished with:

> Whipped cream

INDIVIDUAL SHORTCAKES

Prepare:

> Fluffy Biscuit Dough,
> page 286

Cut the dough into 3-inch
rounds. Bake the biscuits, split
them while they are hot and
spread them with:

> Butter

Place between the biscuit halves
and pour over them:

> Sugared or cooked fruit

LARGE SHORTCAKE

Prepare:

> Fluffy Biscuit dough,
> page 286
> Scone dough, page 288,
> or any of the plain
> sponge cakes, page 342

Bake it in 2 layers. Place between the layers and over them:

> Sugared or cooked fruit

✷ QUICK MOCHA
FREEZER CAKE

[About 10 to 12 Servings]
Cut:

> Angel Cake, page 339

in 4 layers. Soften:

> ½ gallon Mocha Ice Cream,
> page 489

Stir in:

> 3 shaved sweet chocolate
> and almond bars

Put the ice cream between the
layers and cover the cake all over
with it. Put into the ✷ freezer
and allow to set for about an
hour. Should you have made this
the day before and kept it in the
freezer, be sure to unfreeze ½
hour before serving.

SEMISWEET   [6]
CHOCOLATE CASES

Melt in the top of a double
boiler:

> 6 squares semisweet
> chocolate
> 1 tablespoon butter

When melted, beat thoroughly.
Swirl the mixture into the insides of crinkled paper baking
cups. Place cups in muffin tins
and allow the chocolate to
harden. To serve, carefully remove the paper, and fill the
chocolate cases with:

> Ice Cream or Custard,
> page 436

ABOUT FILLINGS

If you happen to be pressed for
time or are just plain lazy, you
may prefer occasionally to buy
the "baked goods"—sponge,
angel cakes, macaroons, ladyfingers—which make the foundation for many and varied
fancy desserts. Such pastries
may be mixed or matched to
your preference and filled with
seasonally flavored creams, pastry creams, Bavarians, mousses,
zabagliones or layers of jam or
jelly. Garnish these desserts with
candied fruits and creams. Many
pie fillings, fruit, custard and
chiffon, as well as whipped gelatin puddings, also lend themselves to use with cake bases.
Try a cream base, flavored with
lemon, apricot, orange or pineapple, with nut Torten. Should
you choose flavored creams and
the less-stable fillings such as
gelatins or ice creams, add them
to your cake just before serving
to forestall sogginess. For the
same reason, be sure to choose
fillings heavy in cream for freezing.

Thickened fillings, such as
those having the word custard
in the title, or the heavier nut
and fruit fillings, can stand
somewhat longer storage before
serving; but do not hold them
over 24 hours—especially those
based on gelatin. Fillings seem
to adhere better if the cakes are

placed with the bottom crusts facing one another. For a charming but not rich finish, coat filled cakes with a dusting of confectioners' sugar, see page 418. Filling yields are given in cups. For approximate coverage, see Chart on page 418.

To prepare a tube cake for a secret filling, see the illustrations below. If your knife is sharp and you feel bold, you may hold a cake on the palm of your left hand and slice deftly across the cake, one inch from the top. If your knife is not sharp, we suggest you mark the cutting line with about six toothpicks as shown, then, with the cake firmly on the table and your left hand on top of it, you can easily feel if the knife is going up or down and so control an even cut. Reserve the top slice for the lid.

Then start to cut a smooth-rimmed channel in the remaining section, to receive the filling. Allow for 1-inch walls by making 2 circular, vertical incisions, to within 1 inch of the base. To remove the cake loosened by these incisions, insert your knife next diagonally, first from the top of the inside of the outer rim to the base cut of the inner rim, and continue to cut diagonally all around through the channel core. Then reverse the action and repeat the cut from the top of the inside of the inner rim to the base cut of the outer rim. These two X-like operations, performed with a saw-bladed knife, should give you 3 loose triangular sections which are easily removed. The fourth triangle protruding into the channel but still attached at the base is then cut free one inch from the base of the cake. A curved knife is a help here. The cake which formed the channel area can be used for Angel Balls, page 359, or be shredded and mixed with the filling. Ladle the filling of your choice into the channel as shown in the center. Replace the lid. Top this whole cake with whipped cream or icing. When you cut the cake, each slice will look like the cross-sections sketched on the cake-stand.

SWEETENED WHIPPED CREAM OR CRÈME CHANTILLY FILLINGS

[About 3 Cups]
Whip until stiff:
    1 cup whipping cream
I. Fold in:
    (1 to 3 tablespoons sifted
        confectioners' sugar)
    ½ teaspoon vanilla
You may use this way or add any one of the following:

II.
    ½ cup blanched, slivered,
        toasted almonds, walnuts,
        pecans or hazelnuts, or
    ¼ cup nut paste

III. or:
    ½ cup lightly toasted
        coconut
    1 tablespoon rum

IV. or:
  ½ cup jam or orange or
    ginger marmalade

V. or:
  ¾ cup fresh, canned or
    frozen fruit purée
  (2 tablespoons kirsch)

VI. or:
  ¾ cup fresh fruit
Reserve ¼ cup of perfect berries
or fruit slices for garnish.

VII. or:
  ½ cup crushed soft
    peppermint stick candy

VIII. or:
  ⅔ cup brown sugar or
    ½ cup maple sugar
  1 teaspoon vanilla or
    ¼ teaspoon nutmeg

IX. or:
  1 teaspoon instant coffee
  ¾ cup crushed nut brittle

X. or:
  ¼ cup almond or hazelnut
    paste, page 504

Here are two other variations:
I. Prepare an angel or sponge
cake shell. Shred the removed
cake. Combine it with the
whipped cream.
Then add:
  2 cups crushed drained
    pineapple
  1 cup shredded coconut
  12 or more maraschino
    cherries
  (20 diced marshmallows)
  2 teaspoons semi-sweet
    chocolate
  2 teaspoons rum or
    Cointreau
Chill the cake for 6 hours.

II. Heat in a double boiler 2
tablespoons of the whipped
cream and:
  ¼ cup sugar
  ⅛ teaspoon salt

  1 oz. chocolate, cut in
    pieces
When the sugar is dissolved and
the chocolate melted, beat the
filling with a wire whisk until
well blended. Cool. Blend in the
remainder of the whipped
cream.

CUSTARD CREAM PASTRY FILLING OR CRÈME PATISSIÈRE

[About 2 Cups]
The custardy pastry fillings below can all be varied. Enrich
them by the folding in ¼ to ¾
cups of whipped cream and/or
chopped nuts, candied fruits
and liqueur flavorings.
I. Vanilla custard
Scald:
  1½ cups milk
    A vanilla bean
Blend and mix in the top of a
double boiler ▶ over—not in—
hot water:
  ½ cup sugar
  ¼ cup flour
  3 to 4 well-beaten egg
    yolks or 2 eggs and 2
    yolks
Cream this mixture until light.
Now remove the vanilla bean
and add the scalded milk
gradually. Stir until all is well
blended. Cook, stirring constantly, until it just reaches the
boiling point. Remove from the
heat and continue to stir to release the steam and prevent
crusting. Do not fill the pastry
until the mixture is cool.

II. Chocolate
Add to the milk, when scalding:
  2 to 4 oz. semisweet
    chocolate

III. Coffee
Add to the milk, when scalded:
  1 to 2 teaspoons instant
    coffee
    (Ground hazelnuts)

IV. Banana

Before spreading the custard, add to it:

    2 or more thinly sliced
      bananas

FRANGIPANE CREAM

Prepare Crème Patissière opposite, but after removing from the heat, beat in:

    2 tablespoons butter
    ¼ cup crushed macaroons
      or chopped blanched
      almonds
    2 teaspoons chopped
      candied nuts

BUTTERSCOTCH FILLING

[About 1½ Cups]

Prepare:

      Butterscotch Pie Filling,
        page 326

using in all:

    1½ cups milk

MOCHA FILLING

[About 2½ Cups]

Combine, cook and stir in a double boiler ◗ over—not in— hot water, until smooth:

    2 oz. chocolate
    ⅔ cup cream
    1⅓ cups strong coffee

Then add and stir into this mixture a smooth paste of:

    2 teaspoons cornstarch
    2 tablespoons cold coffee

Stir and cook the filling for about 8 minutes. Cover and continue to cook for 10 minutes more. Meanwhile, combine and beat:

    4 egg yolks
    1 egg
    ¼ teaspoon salt

Beat in gradually:

    1¾ cups sugar

Pour some of the hot cornstarch mixture over the egg mixture and then gradually return it to the double boiler. Cook for 2 minutes longer, stirring gently and constantly. Remove the filling from the heat and stir gently until cool.

RICOTTA CHOCOLATE FILLING

[About 3½ Cups]

Combine and beat until light and fluffy:

    2¾ cups ricotta cheese:
      1¼ lbs.
    2 cups sugar
    1 teaspoon vanilla
    2 tablespoons crème de
      cacao

Fold in:

    2 tablespoons shaved
      semisweet chocolate
    2 tablespoons chopped
      candied fruit

LEMON FILLING

[About 1½ Cups]

Mix in the top of a double boiler:

    2½ tablespoons cornstarch
    ¾ cup sugar
    ¼ teaspoon salt

Gradually stir in:

    ½ cup water or orange
      juice
    3 tablespoons lemon juice
    ½ teaspoon grated lemon
      rind
    1 tablespoon butter

Cook ◗ over—not in—boiling water about 5 minutes, stirring constantly. Cover and cook gently 10 minutes longer without stirring. ◗ Remove from heat and stir in gently:

    3 slightly beaten egg yolks

Return to heat and cook for about 2 minutes longer. To cool, see About Cornstarch, page 155.

LEMON ORANGE CUSTARD FILLING

[About 1½ Cups]

Stir and cook in a double boiler ◗ over—not in—hot water, until thick:

    2½ tablespoons lemon juice
    6 tablespoons orange juice

⅓ cup water
½ cup sugar
2 tablespoons flour
⅛ teaspoon salt
3 egg yolks or
1 egg and 1 yolk
(½ teaspoon grated lemon
or orange rind)
Cool the filling.

ORANGE CUSTARD FILLING

[About 1½ Cups]
Stir in the top of a double
boiler ▶ over—not in—hot
water:
½ cup sugar
5 tablespoons all-purpose
flour
¼ teaspoon salt
Stir in until smooth:
1 cup milk
Then stir in:
½ cup orange juice
Cook for about 10 minutes, stirring frequently. Beat slightly:
1 egg
Beat about ⅓ of the sauce into
it. Return it to the pan. Continue to cook and stir for about
2 minutes or until it thickens.
Cool, then spread the filling.

CHOPPED FRUIT FILLING

[About 1¾ Cups]
Cook in a double boiler over—
not in—hot water:
¾ cup evaporated milk
¼ cup water
¾ cup sugar
⅛ teaspoon salt
When the sugar is dissolved,
add and cook until thick:
¼ cup each chopped dates,
figs
Cool these ingredients and add:
1 teaspoon vanilla
½ cup chopped nut-meats

APRICOT CUSTARD FILLING

[About 2 Cups]
Follow the rule for:

Lemon Orange Custard
Filling, page 379
Add:
½ to ⅔ cup sweetened
thick apricot pulp

ORANGE CREAM FILLING

[About 2½ Cups]
Soak for about 5 minutes:
1 teaspoon gelatin
in:
1 tablespoon water
Combine in a double boiler:
2 tablespoons each
cornstarch and flour
¾ cup sugar
Add:
¾ cup hot water
Stir and cook these ingredients,
over—not in—hot water for 8
to 12 minutes. Stir constantly.
▶ Cover and cook undisturbed
for 10 minutes more. Add:
1 tablespoon butter
Pour part of this mixture over:
2 egg yolks
Beat and pour back into the
double boiler. Cook and stir the
custard gently, about 2 minutes,
to permit the yolks to thicken.
Add the soaked gelatin. Stir
until dissolved. Remove custard
from heat. Add:
Grated rind of 1 orange
3 tablespoons each orange
and lemon juice
Cool the custard. Beat until
stiff:
½ cup whipping cream
Fold it into the custard. Chill
for 1 hour. Spread between the
layers of cake. Ice with:
Luscious Orange Icing,
page 424

GINGER FRUIT FILLING

[About 1½ Cups]
Mix well in the top of a double
boiler and cook, stirring constantly, over—not in—hot water
for about 8 to 10 minutes or
▶ unitl the mixture thickens, see
About Cornstarch, page 155:

¼ cup sifted confectioners'
   sugar
3 tablespoons cornstarch
½ teaspoon salt
1 cup canned pineapple
   juice
Cover and cook about 10 minutes longer. Remove from the
heat and add:
   ½ cup mashed banana
   ½ cup canned crushed
      pineapple
Return to the heat for 2 minutes
more, stirring gently. Add:
   3 tablespoons finely
      chopped drained
      candied ginger
   1 teaspoon vanilla
   (¼ cup slivered, blanched
      almonds)

ALMOND, FIG OR RAISIN FILLING

[About 1½ Cups]
Blanch, sliver, then toast:
   ¾ cup almonds
Combine:
   ½ cup sugar
   1 tablespoon grated orange
      rind
   ½ cup orange juice
   2 tablespoons flour
   ½ cup water
   1½ cups chopped or ground
      figs or seeded raisins
   ⅛ teaspoon salt
Simmer these ingredients for 5
minutes. Stir constantly. Add
the almonds and:
   ½ teaspoon vanilla

TOASTED WALNUT OR PECAN FILLING

[About ¾ Cup]
Combine, stir and heat in a
double boiler ♦ over—not in—
hot water, until sugar is dissolved:
   ½ cup packed brown sugar
   ¼ teaspoon salt
   2 tablespoons butter
   1 tablespoon water
Stir part of this into:
   1 slightly beaten egg yolk

Return it to the double boiler.
Stir and cook until the egg yolk
is slightly thickened. Cool. Add:
   ¾ cup toasted walnuts or
      pecans
   ½ teaspoon vanilla

ALMOND OR HAZELNUT CUSTARD FILLING

[About 1½ Cups]
Stir and heat in a double boiler
♦ over—not in—hot water:
   1 cup sugar
   1 cup cultured sour
      cream
   1 tablespoon flour
Pour ⅓ of this mixture over:
   1 beaten egg
Return it to the double boiler.
Stir and cook the custard until
thick. Add:
   1 cup blanched or
      unblanched shredded or
      ground almonds or
      ground hazelnuts, see
      page 190
When the custard is cool, add:
   ½ teaspoon vanilla or
   1 tablespoon liqueur

▲ ABOUT HIGH ALTITUDE BAKING

Cake doughs at high altitudes
are subject to a pixie-like variation that often defies general
rules. Read the comments and
then launch forth on your own,
keeping records at first until you
know what gives you the greatest success. On the whole,
♦ cup and layer cakes are better
textured than loaf cakes.

Up to 3000 feet, if you reduce the air in the cakes by
♦ not overbeating eggs, you will
probably need no adjustment of
the cake formula. ♦ Also raise
the baking temperature about
25°. In elevations higher than
3000 feet, continue to under-
beat the eggs as compared to

sea level consistency. Another way to reduce their volume is to keep the eggs refrigerated until almost ready to use.

At around 5000 feet, it will also help to reduce the double-acting baking powder by ⅛ to ¼ teaspoon for each teaspoon called for in the recipe. Decrease sugar 1 to 2 tablespoons for each cup called for and increase liquid 2 to 3 tablespoons for each cup indicated. Raise the baking temperature about 25°.

At 7000 feet, decrease double-acting baking powder by ¼ teaspoon for every teaspoon called for. Decrease sugar by 2 to 3 tablespoons for each cup indicated and increase liquid by 3 to 4 tablespoons for each cup in the recipe. Raise the baking temperature about 25°.

At 10,000 feet, decrease the double-acting baking powder by ¼ teaspoon for every teaspoon called for in the recipe and add an extra egg, but do not overbeat the eggs. Decrease the sugar 2 to 3 tablespoons for each cup in the recipe. Increase the liquid by 3 to 4 tablespoons for each cup liquid indicated. Increase the baking temperature about 25°.

Following are some basic high altitude recipes from Government sources. But should you hate to give up your own recipes from home, we also throw in as a talisman the homely formula of a friend who has for years had luck with it at 7000 to 8000 feet, using her old Chicago favorites. She merely uses ¾ the amount of double-acting baking powder called for, adds 1 additional tablespoon flour and 1 extra egg, decreases the butter by a few tablespoons if the recipe is very rich and increases the oven heat by about 25°.

But whatever formula you use

▶ grease your baking pans well and dust them with flour or line them with waxed paper. For, at high altitudes, cakes have a tendency to stick to the pan.

▲ HIGH ALTITUDE ANGEL CAKE

[10-Inch Tube Pan]
This recipe is for baking at 5000 feet. If baking at 7000 feet, add 1 tablespoon cake flour and decrease sugar by 2 tablespoons. If baking at 10,000 feet, add 2 tablespoons cake flour and decrease sugar by 4 tablespoons. ▶ Please read About Angel Cakes, page 339.
Preheat oven to 375.°
Mix and sift together 3 times:
    1 cup plus 2 tablespoons
        sifted cake flour
    ½ cup sugar
Keep refrigerated until ready to use:
    1½ cups egg whites
Beat the egg whites until foamy and add:
    1½ teaspoons cream of tartar
    ½ teaspoon salt
Continue beating until egg whites are glossy and ▶ form peaks which just barely fall over. Fold in, with about 25 strokes:
    1 cup sugar
Beat until mixture is fluffy and meringue-like. Beat briefly while adding:
    1½ teaspoons vanilla
Add the dry ingredients about ¼ at a time by sifting them over the egg mixture, using about 15 folding strokes after each addition. After last addition, use about 10 more strokes to blend completely. Pour into ungreased tube pan. Cut through batter with knife to release air bubbles. Bake for about 40 minutes. Invert pan, as shown on page 340, and allow cake to cool before removing it from the pan.

CAKES, CUP CAKES, TORTEN, AND FILLED CAKES · 383

▲ HIGH ALTITUDE CHOCOLATE ANGEL CAKE

Prepare:
High Altitude Angel
Cake, page 382
Use in all 1 cup cake flour and add:
¼ cup cocoa
¼ cup sugar

▲ HIGH ALTITUDE SPICE ANGEL CAKE

Prepare:
High Altitude Angel
Cake, page 382
Omit the vanilla and substitute by sifting with dry ingredients:
¼ teaspoon cloves
½ teaspoon nutmeg
1 teaspoon cinnamon

▲ HIGH ALTITUDE WHITE CAKE

[Two 8-Inch Round Pans]
This recipe is for baking at 5000 feet. If baking at 7500 feet, reduce baking powder by ½ teaspoon. If baking at 10,000 feet, reduce baking powder by 1 teaspoon.
◗ Please read About Butter or Shortening Cakes, page 343.
Preheat oven to 375°.
Place in a mixer:
½ cup soft butter
Mix, sift together twice and then sift into the beater bowl with the butter,
2 cups sifted cake flour
2 teaspoons double-acting baking powder
½ teaspoon salt
1 cup sugar
Add and mix 2 minutes:
¾ cup milk
1 teaspoon vanilla
Beat until foamy:
4 egg whites
Add and beat ◗ until stiff, but not dry:
¼ cup sugar

Add this meringue to batter with:
3 tablespoons milk
and beat 1 minute. Grease the pans and dust well with flour or line with waxed paper, pour in the batter and bake about 35 minutes or until done.

▲ HIGH ALTITUDE FUDGE CAKE

[Two 8-Inch Square Pans]
This recipe is for baking at 5000 feet. If baking at 7500 and 10,000 feet, decrease baking powder by 1 teaspoon and if baking at 10,000, decrease sugar by ¼ cup.
◗ Please read About Butter or Shortening Cakes, page 343.
Preheat oven to 350°.
Melt over hot water:
4 squares chocolate
Mix, sift together 3 times:
2 cups sifted cake flour
2 teaspoons double-acting baking powder
1 teaspoon salt
Soften:
½ cup butter
Add slowly to butter and cream longer than you would at sea level:
2¼ cups sugar
Remove from the refrigerator and separate:
3 eggs
Beat and add the yolks and the cooled melted chocolate. Add alternately by thirds the dry ingredients and:
1½ cups milk
2 teaspoons vanilla
After each addition of flour, beat about 25 strokes. After each addition of liquid, beat about 75 strokes. Whip the egg whites until ◗ stiff but not dry. Fold them into the batter. Grease pans and dust well with flour or line with waxed paper. Pour in the batter and bake for about 45 minutes or until done.

▲ HIGH ALTITUDE TWO-EGG CAKE

[Two 8-Inch Pans]

The following high altitude recipe is for a cake baked at 5000 feet. If baking at 7500 feet, decrease baking powder by ¼ teaspoon and add 2 tablespoons milk. If baking at 10,000 feet, decrease baking powder by ½ teaspoon and add 2 tablespoons milk. Preheat oven to 375°.

Mix and sift together 3 times:

    2 cups sifted cake flour
    1½ teaspoons double-acting
        baking powder
    ½ teaspoon salt

Have ready at 70°:

    ½ cup butter

Add gradually to the butter:

    1 cup sugar
    1 teaspoon vanilla

Cream until light and fluffy, somewhat longer than you would at sea level. Beat, add to creamed mixture and mix thoroughly:

    2 eggs

which were refrigerated until ready to use. Add alternately by thirds the sifted dry ingredients and:

    ¾ cup plus 1 tablespoon
        milk

using about fifty strokes each time the liquid is added. Grease the layer pans, dust them well with flour or line them with waxed paper. Bake for about 50 minutes or until done.

▲ HIGH ALTITUDE COCOA CAKE

Prepare:

    High Altitude Two-Egg
        Cake, above

observing the adjustments depending upon altitude at which you are baking. Add to the dry ingredients before the final sifting:

    ½ teaspoon nutmeg
    ¼ teaspoon cloves

    1 teaspoon cinnamon

Replace ½ cup cake flour with:

    ½ cup cocoa

▲HIGH ALTITUDE SPONGE CAKE

[An 8-Inch Tube Pan]

This recipe is for an altitude of 5000 and 7500 feet. If baking at 10,000 feet, add 5 tablespoons sifted cake flour and bake at 350°.

◗ Please read About Sponge Cakes, page 341.

Preheat oven to 350°.

Remove from the refrigerator and separate:

    6 eggs

Beat the yolks slightly. Add to them:

    1½ tablespoons water
    1 teaspoon vanilla
    ½ teaspoon salt

Continue to beat while adding gradually:

    ½ cup sugar

Beat until thick and lemon yellow in color. Beat the egg whites until foamy and add:

    ½ teaspoon cream of tartar

Then add gradually to egg whites:

    ½ cup sugar

◗ Beat just until peaks form and fall over slightly when beater is removed from mixture. Fold yolk mixture into the beaten whites. Add one-fourth at a time, using about 15 strokes after each addition:

    1¼ cups plus 1 tablespoon
        sifted cake flour

After last addition, mix for about 10 additional strokes. Fold in:

    1½ tablespoons lemon juice
    1 tablespoon grated lemon
        rind

Bake in an ungreased tube pan for about 50 minutes. Invert pan, as shown on page 340, and allow cake to cool completely before removing from pan.

▲ HIGH ALTITUDE GINGERBREAD

[A 9 x 2½-Inch Square Pan]
This recipe is for baking at 5000 feet. If baking at 7500 feet, decrease soda by ¼ teaspoon. If baking at 10,000 feet, reduce soda by ½ teaspoon sugar by 3 tablespoons and molasses by 2 teaspoons.
Preheat oven to 350°.
Mix, sift together 3 times:

    2⅓ cups sifted all-purpose
        flour
    ¾ teaspoon soda
    ½ teaspoon salt
    ¼ teaspoon cinnamon
    ¼ teaspoon nutmeg
    ¼ teaspoon allspice
    1 teaspoon ginger

Beat:

    ½ cup soft shortening

Add gradually to shortening and cream somewhat longer than you would at sea level until light and fluffy:

    ½ cup sugar

Add 1 at a time and beat well after each addition:

    2 eggs

Add and mix in thoroughly:

    ¾ cup molasses

Add the dry ingredients alternately by fourths with:

    ⅔ cup boiling water

Beat about 20 strokes after each addition of flour and 30 strokes after each addition of liquid. Grease the pans and flour them well or line with waxed paper, pour in the batter and bake about 50 minutes.

COOKIES AND BARS

★ ABOUT CHRISTMAS COOKIES

Christmas and cookies are inseparable. Stars, angels, bells, trees, Santas and even pretzels —the pilgrim's token—are memorialized in rich holiday confections. Why not make use of these charming cookie shapes to decorate a small table tree at Christmas? To cut molds, see Gingerbread Men, page 403. You can bake the strings for hanging right into the cookies. It irks us that such delightful sweets as Christmas cookies should be relegated to a period of a few weeks. In the hope that you will prolong the season, we have marked with this symbol ★ recipes which are generally recognized as traditional, as well as some which have become traditional with us, if for no other reason than that they can be baked in advance of a busy season.

We find that egg-white cookies, a natural by-product of Christmas baking, need special handling. Some of the meringues heavy in nuts, like Cinnamon Stars, page 415, keep well if tightly tinned. In packing mixed boxes, though, be sure to ▶ add meringue-based cookies at the last moment, for, unwrapped, they dry out quickly; and, if freshly made and stored with cookies rich in fruit, they may disintegrate. To soften hard dry cookies, put them with a piece of bread into a tightly closed container. Replace the bread every few days, for it molds easily. Another way to restore moisture is to use a dampened paper napkin, wrapped in punctured foil.

▶ Most cookie doughs freeze satisfactorily. If you have frozen baked cookies and are serving them for immediate consumption ▶ thaw them unwrapped, then heat them for a moment on a cookie sheet in a 300° oven to restore crispness. This is also a good plan for weary "bought" cookies. If you are sending cookies or cakes to out-of-towners, wrap them individually or put them into a polyethylene bag and bed them down in popcorn. Fill all the crannies of the box with the corn, until it just touches the lid.

ABOUT COOKIES

Having put the cart before the horse, we have told you how to

pack and store cookies. Now let's talk about making and baking them. If you are planning a number of kinds, see that they complement each other in texture and flavor and that they use up ingredients economically. Choose shapes which will look pleasant on serving dishes. Many of these recipes call for butter as the basic fat. ‣ If you feel that, for reasons of economy, you cannot afford all butter, do try to use at least ⅓ butter. You will notice a marked superiority in flavor.

The mixing of cookies is usually quick, because, with most types, overworking the dough tends to cause toughness. Some ingredients must be well stirred together; some are creamed like cakes and, abroad, are called biscuits; others are blended like pastry. Use whatever mixing process the recipe calls for.

Electric equipment has eased the beating of tough, tight, honey and molasses doughs, the kind that often include carbonate of ammonia—a favorite leaven of commercial bakers. Baking powder may be substituted for this leaven, see page 164, but the results are somewhat different.

You may want to combine different flours. If you do so ‣ be sure to see the note on flour substitutions, page 159. To avoid flat flavors, taste the dough before cooking and correct the seasoning. ‣ Chill cookie doughs well and keep them covered until ready to bake.

To decorate cookies, dip the garnish before baking either into a simple sirup or unbeaten egg white. Then press the garnish firmly onto the cookie surface. Or dust sugar onto the cookies after placing them on the sheet and press it in with a wide spatula. See also Icings and Glazes, page 418.

Would you like your cookies not only to taste better because of your choice of quality ingredients but to look as uniform in size and color as professionally made ones? Then preheat the oven to the degree indicated. Choose a flat baking sheet or use the bottom of a reversed baking pan. Treat the dough as shown illustrated on the left, page 401; or, if you prefer, cut the cookies on a board and transfer them to the reversed pan bottom. The heat can then circulate directly and evenly over the cookie tops. A pan with high sides will both deflect the heat and make the cookies hard to remove when baked. The very best aluminum sheets have permanently shiny baking surfaces and specially dulled bottoms to produce an even browning. ‣ Dark cookie sheets absorb heat and cookies may brown too much on the bottom.

Grease cookie sheets with unsalted fats, preferably sweet butter or beeswax. For delicate cookies, use a greased parchment paper or foil liner from which they peel off easily when slightly cooled. ‣ The baking sheet should always be cold when you put the cookie on it so it will not lose its shape. ‣ Always fill out a sheet, placing the cookies ‣ of even size and thickness about 1 inch apart, unless otherwise indicated. On a partially filled sheet the heat is drawn to the area where the cookies lie and the batch may burn on the bottom. If you haven't enough dough on your last baking to fill a whole baking sheet, reverse a pie pan or turn a small baking pan upside down, as shown on page 401.

‣ Always preheat the oven. The placement of the pans during baking is very important.

◗ Fill only one rack and be sure the pan or pans are disposed at least 2 inches from the oven walls. If using two smaller pans, see that they are spaced evenly one from the other.

Heat should circulate all around the pans. Should you use 2 large sheets on 2 racks, you will find that the heat circulates so that the bottoms of the cookies on the lower rack and the tops of the cookies on the upper rack brown too rapidly. Few ovens are so perfect that they will brown a large sheet evenly. During the baking process, do turn the sheet sometimes to compensate for uneven baking. Oven thermostats are also variable, so watch closely, especially when baking molasses and brown-sugar cookies, which burn easily. Even a few seconds matter. Should cookies bake too brown at the edges and still be soft in the middle, run them under a broiler—about 5 or 6 inches from the heat—until the desired color is achieved. When done ◗ take cookies from the baking sheet at once or they will continue to cook. ◗ Always cool cookies on a rack ◗ not overlapping, and store as suggested above.

Our recipes are completely tested, but the consistency of your dough may have to be modified, due to variations in the size of eggs and in the moisture content of honey, molasses and flour. To test for consistency, see About Rolled Cookies, page 401.

▲ In altitudes up to 5000 feet, simple cookies usually need no adjustment. But for cookies rich in chocolate, nuts, or dates a reduction of about ½ the baking powder or soda may be advisable. And, at very high altitudes, a slight reduction in sugar may help. ◗ But the soda should not be reduced beyond

½ teaspoon for each cup of sour milk or cream used.

If you wonder why commercial cookies are often large, the answer lies in handling and oven costs. A true sign of home baking is a small delicate cookie. However, you, too, want to save time and energy, so plan your cutting and baking patterns efficiently. To color cookies for special occasions, stir into 1 egg yolk ¼ teaspoon water. Divide the mixture into several custard cups and color each one with a few drops of different food coloring. This coloring applied with a soft brush before baking allows you to make elaborate patterns.

Successful baking depends on the preheating of the oven, as well as on the kind of baking sheet used, its size, the material of which it is made—even its temperature.

ABOUT SQUARES AND BARS

The quickest and easiest way to produce uniform small cakes is in squares and bars. Bake them in pans with at least a 1½-inch rim. ◗ Do observe pan sizes indicated in recipes, because the texture is much affected by thickness, etc. A pan smaller than indicated in the recipes will give a cakey result —not a chewy one. Too large a pan will give a dry, brittle result. If your pan is too large, divide it with a piece of foil folded as illustrated on page 337. The dough over the horizontal lap will help hold the divider in place. Most bars, unless meringue based, bake about 25 minutes in a preheated 350° oven. We suggest the use of muffin tins for individual servings with ice cream, or pie tins to make festive rounds. See

Chart of comparative pan sizes, page 337.

If for immediate use, store bar cookies in the pan in which they are baked. Cover with aluminum foil. However, to prolong freshness, be sure to wrap these bars individually in foil after cooling and cutting. They are then all ready for serving, freezing or for packing lunch boxes. Different flavors, wrapped in different colored foils, or one dull side up and one shiny side up in regular foil, make an attractive dessert to pass at an informal outdoor buffet.

BROWNIES COCKAIGNE

[About 30 Brownies]
Almost everyone wants to make this classic American confection. We guarantee good results if you follow the ▶ signals. Brownies may vary greatly in richness and contain anywhere from 1½ cups of butter and 5 ounces of chocolate to 2 tablespoons of butter and 2 ounces of chocolate for every cup of flour. If you want them chewy and moist, use a 9x13-inch pan; if cakey, use a 9 x 9-inch pan. We love the following. Preheat oven to 350°.
Melt in a double boiler:
    ½ cup butter
    4 oz. chocolate
▶ Cool this mixture. If you don't, your brownies will be heavy and dry. Beat until ▶ light in color and foamy in texture:
    4 eggs ▶ at room
        temperature
    ½ teaspoon salt
Add ▶ gradually and continue beating until well creamed:
    2 cups sugar
    1 teaspoon vanilla
With a few swift strokes, combine the cooled chocolate mixture into the eggs and sugar.
▶ Even if you normally use an electric mixer do this manually.

Before the mixture becomes uniformly colored, fold in, again by hand:
    1 cup sifted all-purpose
        flour
And before the flour is uniformly colored, stir in gently:
    1 cup pecan meats
Bake in a 9 x 13-inch pan for about 25 minutes. Cut when cool. Wrapped individually in foil, these keep well 3 or 4 days. A good way to serve Brownies is to garnish with whipped cream.

BUTTERSCOTCH BROWNIES

[About 16 Thin 2¼-Inch Squares]
An all-time favorite, easily made.
Preheat oven to 350°.
Melt in a saucepan:
    ¼ cup butter
Stir into it until dissolved:
    1 cup brown sugar
Cool these ingredients slightly.
Beat in well:
    1 egg
    1 teaspoon vanilla
Sift, then measure:
    ½ cup all-purpose flour
Resift it with:
    1 teaspoon double-acting
        baking powder
    ½ teaspoon salt
Stir these ingredients into the butter mixture. Add:
    ½ to 1 cup finely chopped
        nuts or ¾ cup grated
        coconut
Chopped dates and figs may be substituted entirely or in part. Use a little of the flour over them. Pour the batter into a greased 9 x 9-inch pan. Bake for about 20 to 25 minutes. Cut into bars when cool.

MOLASSES BARS

[About Sixteen 2-Inch Squares]
Preheat oven to 375°.
Sift:

½ cup powdered sugar
Beat until soft:
    6 tablespoons butter
Add the sugar gradually. Blend
these ingredients until they are
very light and creamy. Beat in:
    1 egg
    ⅓ cup molasses
    ⅛ teaspoon each salt and
      soda
Sift before measuring:
    ⅞ cup all-purpose flour
Add the flour in 3 parts to the
butter mixture. Stir in:
    1 teaspoon vanilla
Beat the batter after each addi-
tion until smooth. Fold in:
    1 cup broken nut meats
Bake in a greased 8 x 8-inch
pan, about 15 minutes. Cut the
cake into bars before it is cold.
Roll them in:
    Powdered sugar

★ CHRISTMAS
  CHOCOLATE BARS
  COCKAIGNE

[About 108 Bars, 1 x 2 Inches]
These bars differ very much
from the preceding cakes, for
they are opulently flavored with
chocolate. If you cannot choose
between them, better bake them
both and ice one with chocolate
icing, and the other with a
white glaze.
Preheat oven to 350°.
Sift:
    2¾ cups light brown sugar:
      1 lb.
Beat until light:
    6 eggs
Add the sugar gradually and
beat these ingredients until well
blended. Grate and add:
    4 oz. chocolate
Combine and sift:
    3 cups all-purpose flour
    1 tablespoon cinnamon
    1½ teaspoons cloves
    ½ teaspoon allspice
    1 teaspoon each soda and
      salt

Add the sifted ingredients to the
egg mixture, alternately with:
    ½ cup honey or molasses
Chop and add in all:
    2½ cups citron, candied
      lemon, orange,
      pineapple and nuts—
      preferably blanched
      almonds
Spread the dough with a spatula
in two 9 x 13-inch greased pans.
Bake about 20 minutes. When
cool, ice with:
    Chocolate Butter Icing,
      page 428
Cut into bars.

★ GERMAN HONEY BARS

[About Three 8 x 8-Inch Cakes,
Plus One 9 x 9-Inch Cake]
Honey, like molasses, may be
troublesome. Old German cooks
used to insist on its being over
a year old. Very good cakes are
made with fresh honey, but then
the amount of flour is a little
hard to gauge. Carbonate of
ammonia can be the leaven, if
a crisper bar is desired. Substitute it for the baking powder
and soda given below. Use 1
teaspoon carbonate of ammonia
dissolved in 2 tablespoons warm
water, rum or wine. These German Honey Bars will keep 6
months in a tightly closed tin.
Preheat oven to 350°.
Heat slightly in a large saucepan:
    1⅓ cups honey or molasses
    ¾ cup sugar
Add and melt:
    3 tablespoons butter
Sift and add:
    About 2 cups all-purpose
      flour, enough to make a
      semi-liquid dough
    1 teaspoon baking powder
    (½ teaspoon soda)
Add:
    ½ cup blanched almonds
    ¼ cup each chopped citron
      and chopped candied
      orange or lemon peel

¼ teaspoon ginger
½ teaspoon cardamon
2 teaspoons cinnamon
⅛ teaspoon cloves

Add:

1½ to 2 cups more flour

The dough should be sticky to the touch. You may age the dough or pat it out at once into a ¼-inch thickness in buttered pans. If you age it, you may find it necessary to heat it slightly before working it into the pans. Bake about 25 minutes. Cut into squares and ice with:

Lemon Glaze, page 434

★ DATE, FIG OR PRUNE BARS

[About Forty-Two 2½ x 1-Inch Bars]

Preheat oven to 325°.

Sift:

1 cup sugar

Beat until light:

3 eggs

Add the sugar gradually. Blend these ingredients until very light. Sift before measuring:

⅞ cup all-purpose flour

Resift with:

1 teaspoon double-acting baking powder
⅛ teaspoon salt

If spices are desired, add:

¼ teaspoon each cloves and cinnamon
(½ teaspoon allspice)

Add the sifted ingredients to the egg mixture with:

1 teaspoon vanilla

Beat until ingredients are well blended.

Add about:

2 cups chopped dates, figs or prunes
1 cup broken nut meats

Pour the batter into a greased and floured 9 x 13-inch pan. Bake for about 25 minutes. When cool, cut into bars, roll in:

Confectioners sugar

ABOUT CAKE AND COOKIE HOUSES

No matter how peculiar the medium or incongruous the scale, the instinct to build persists. We have tried and discarded many cake construction methods. Professionals use Pastillage, page 519, and Royal Glaze, thus achieving rather cold-looking but clean-cut and intricate models. We suggest two simple approaches. The first is the less nerve-racking.

I. Prepare any close-grained cake like:

Cake for a Lamb Mold
Chocolate Old World
Spice Cake
Eggless All Rye Honey Cake

Bake in deep loaf tins or in oblong angelcake pans. ◗ When the cake is thoroughly cool, lay it broad-side down. Cut off a slice for chimney material—about 1 inch. Then cut the remainder into 2 pieces, ⅓ and ⅔ of the length. To roof it, cut the shorter piece diagonally so that, by putting the two triangular pieces together you form a gable as long as the house portion. Ice the whole, and then apply, in icing of contrasting color, windows, door, shingle tiles and other details. See Decorative Icings, page 420.

II.

★ Prepare slabs of:

German Honey Cookies, page 395

Cut a paper pattern with 2 oblongs for the side walls, two gabled short walls, one of them ◗ carrying the outline of an end-wall chimney. This gives you a good solid element on which to affix later the other three chimney walls. ◗ Now, find an extra pair of hands. To assemble, mitre the edges where the walls meet and shamelessly drive

toothpick "nails." ◗ Watch for
these when the cake is eaten.
When the walls are in place, use
slabs for the roof, nailing them
again with toothpicks where
they touch the side walls, or
fold in half an oblong of:

> Light wire screening

that projects over the long side
walls and the gables to form
eaves. With the help of:

> Royal Glaze, page 426

build up overlapping roof tiles
and make doors and shutters of
thin:

> Molasses Crisps
> Cockaigne, page 400

Affix these with the glaze. This
icing, which dies hard and
colors easily, makes a perfect
cement for the various building
elements and whatever decorations you want to glue onto the
house.

ABOUT DROP COOKIES

Drop cookie doughs vary in texture. Some fall easily from the
spoon and flatten into wafers in
baking. Stiffer doughs need a
push with a finger or the use of
a second spoon to release them,
as shown at the top of page 393.
When chilled, some of these
doughs are formed into balls.
These can be baked round, as
shown on the left. You may, in
molding these want to dust
your hands with flour or powdered sugar; or, if the cookies
are a dark or chocolate dough,
use cocoa for dusting. If you
care to flatten the balls, as
shown on the right, use a glass
tumbler greased lightly on the
bottom or dusted with flour,
powdered sugar or cocoa, or a
spatula dipped in ice water. To
make uniform soft drops, use a
measuring teaspoon or half teaspoon.

TORTELETTES

[About Forty 1½-Inch Cookies]

Preheat oven to 375°.
Prepare recipe for:

> Butter Thins, page 402

Season them with:

> Grated rind of ½ lemon

Shape into 1-inch balls. Flatten
balls until dough is very thin.
Beat slightly:

> 1 egg white
> 1 tablespoon water

Brush the cakes with this mixture. Combine:

> 1 cup blanched, shredded
> almonds or other nut
> meats
> ½ cup sugar
> 1 tablespoon cinnamon
> ¼ teaspoon nutmeg
> ⅛ teaspoon salt

Sprinkle the cakes with this
mi ture. Bake until light brown.

BUTTERLESS DROP
COOKIES

Preheat oven to 325°.
Prepare:

> Anise Drop Cookies,
> page 394

If you prefer a different flavor,
omit the anise and use:

> 1 teaspoon grated lemon
> rind or 2 teaspoons
> grated orange rind
> 1 teaspoon vanilla

Do not let them stand for 12
hours—bake at once.

DROP BUTTER WAFERS

[About Forty-Eight
2¼-Inch Wafers]
These, when baked, automatically produce a lovely brown
paper-thin rim.
Preheat oven to 375°.
Cream until light:

> ½ cup butter
> ⅓ to ½ cup sugar

Beat in:

> 1 egg
> 1 teaspoon vanilla
> ¼ teaspoon grated lemon
> rind

Add:

> ¾ cup sifted cake flour

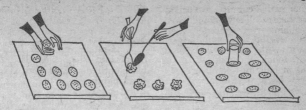

1½ tablespoons poppy seed or
1 teaspoon grated orange
rind)

Drop the cookies from a teaspoon, well apart, on a greased
sheet. Bake for about 7 minutes
or until the rims brown.

CHOCOLATE-CHIP DROP COOKIES

[About Forty-Five 2-Inch
Cookies]
Preheat oven to 375°.
Cream:
½ cup butter
Add gradually and beat until
creamy:
½ cup brown sugar
½ cup white sugar
Beat in:
1 egg
½ teaspoon vanilla
Sift and stir in:
1 cup and 2 tablespoons
sifted all-purpose flour
½ teaspoon salt
½ teaspoon soda
Stir in:
½ cup chopped nut meats
½ cup semi-sweet chocolate
chips
Drop the batter from a teaspoon, well apart, on a greased
cookie sheet. Bake for about 10
minutes.

SUGAR DROP COOKIES WITH OIL

[About 5 Dozen Cookies]
Preheat oven to 375°.
Sift together:
2½ cups all-purpose flour
1½ teaspoons double-acting
baking powder

¾ teaspoon salt
1 teaspoon cinnamon or
¼ teaspoon freshly
grated nutmeg
Combine:
1 cup sugar
¾ cup cooking oil
Add to this mixture and beat
well after each addition:
2 eggs
1 teaspoon vanilla
Add the flour mixture all at once
and beat well. Shape the dough
into ½-inch balls. Dip the balls
in:
Granulated sugar
or, flatten the balls as thin as
you can between very lightly
floured hands. To give a corru-
gated effect, score them in parallel lines, as shown below, with
a fork dipped in flour. Sprinkle
with:
Granulated sugar
Bake about 10 to 12 minutes on
a lightly greased baking sheet.

★ GINGER THINS

[About Three Hundred
¾-Inch Wafers]
Mme. Bu Wei, in her charming
book, "How to Cook and Eat in
Chinese," tells us that these little cakes, served between meals

in her native country, are called "dot hearts." They should have the diameter of a quarter when baked for, if they are larger, they toughen.

Preheat oven to 325°.

Cream:

    ¾ cup butter
    1 cup brown sugar
    1 beaten egg
    ¼ cup molasses

Sift before measuring:

    1½ cups all-purpose flour

Resift with:

    ¼ teaspoon salt
    ½ teaspoon soda
    ½ teaspoon each cloves,
        cinnamon and ginger

Combine the above ingredients and stir until smooth. Put dots of ⅛ teaspoon of dough 1 inch apart on a buttered pan and bake for 5 to 6 minutes. Cool cookie sheet on a rack. Cookies snap off if you twist the sheet slightly.

ANISE DROP COOKIE

[About Ninety-Six 1-Inch Cookies]

These professional-looking, self-glazing cookies with the charming puffed top are best made in cool weather. They do not turn out well if the humidity is over 50%.

Sift:

    1 cup sugar

Beat until light:

    3 eggs

Add the sugar gradually. Beat at least 3 to 5 minutes on medium speed with an electric beater, longer if beating by hand, then add:

    ½ teaspoon vanilla

Sift before measuring:

    2 cups all-purpose flour

Resift with:

    1 teaspoon double-acting
        baking powder

Add:

    1½ tablespoons crushed
        anise seed

Beat the batter another 5 minutes. Drop ½ teaspoon at a time, well apart, on a cookie sheet lined with foil. The ½ teaspoon of dough should flatten to 1-inch round, but should not spread more. If it does, add a little more flour. Permit the drops to dry at room temperature for 18 hours. Bake the cakes in a preheated 325° oven, until they begin to color, about 12 minutes. When done, they will have a puffed meringue-like top on a soft cookie base.

ROCKS OR FRUIT DROP COOKIES

[About Thirty 2-Inch Cookies]

Preheat oven to 375°.

Sift:

    ¾ cup brown sugar

Beat until soft:

    ½ cup butter

Add the sugar gradually. Blend these ingredients until very light and creamy. Beat in, one at a time:

    2 eggs

Sift before measuring:

    1½ cups all-purpose flour
        or whole grain flour

Resift with:

    ½ teaspoon soda
    1 teaspoon cinnamon
    ½ teaspoon cloves
    ¼ teaspoon allspice
    ⅛ teaspoon salt

Add the sifted ingredients in 3 parts to the butter mixture, alternately with thirds of:

    ¼ cup water or sherry

Beat the batter until it is smooth after each addition. Stir in:

    1 cup broken nut meats
    1 cup raisins, chopped
        dates, figs, apricots or
        citron

Drop the batter from a teaspoon onto a greased tin. Bake for about 12 minutes.

HERMITS

[About Thirty 2-Inch Cookies]

Preheat oven to 375°.
Sift:

> 1 cup brown sugar

Beat until soft:

> ½ cup butter

Add the sugar gradually. Blend these ingredients until very light and creamy.
Beat in:

> 1 egg
> ½ cup cultured sour cream, sour milk or strong coffee

Sift before measuring:

> 1⅓ cups all-purpose flour

Resift with:

> ¾ teaspoon cinnamon
> ½ teaspoon cloves
> ¼ teaspoon soda

If coffee has been used above, the spices are optional. Add the sifted ingredients to the butter mixture. Beat the batter until smooth. Stir in:

> ½ cup chopped raisins
> ¼ cup hickory or other nut meats
> ¼ cup coconut may be added, if desired

Drop batter from a teaspoon onto a greased sheet. Bake for about 15 minutes.

★ PFEFFERNÜSSE

[About 3 Dozen 2-Inch Cookies]
The classic recipe for these ball-like Peppernuts is made with a great deal of flour. In our judgment, it is both hard and uninteresting in texture. We have substituted a more subtle seasoning in a rather rich base. This version makes a flat cookie.
Preheat oven to 350°.
Cream together:

> ½ cup butter
> ½ cup sugar
> 2 well-beaten eggs

Sift together and add:

> 1 cup sifted all-purpose flour
> ¼ teaspoon each salt and soda
> ½ teaspoon each freshly

> ground black pepper, nutmeg, cloves and allspice
> 1 teaspoon cinnamon
> ⅓ teaspoon cardamon
> 1 to 3 drops of anise
> ¼ cup ground blanched almonds
> 1½ tablespoons grated lemon peel
> ¼ cup chopped citron

Drop the dough from a teaspoon onto a well-greased cookie sheet. Space cookies about 2 inches apart. Bake 10 to 12 minutes. Store tightly covered.

★ GERMAN HONEY COOKIES

[About Two Hundred 2½-Inch Cookies]
Cut into small pieces and combine:

> 3 oz. each of citron, candied orange peel and candied lemon peel

Add:

> 1 cup chopped blanched almonds
> 1 teaspoon grated lemon rind
> 3 tablespoons cinnamon
> 1 tablespoon cloves
> 3⅓ cups confectioners' sugar

Beat until light and add:

> 6 eggs
> ¼ cup orange juice

Bring to the boiling point and cool until lukewarm:

> 1 pint honey
> 2 tablespoons hot water

Stir this into the egg mixture with:

> 5 cups sifted all-purpose flour
> 1 tablespoon soda

Cover the dough and let it stand for 12 hours or more.
Preheat oven to 350°.
Drop the batter from a spoon, well apart, on a greased baking sheet. Bake the cakes until light

brown. When cool, decorate
with:

Lemon Glaze, page 434
or decorate before baking with:
Blanched almonds

CARROT DROP COOKIES

[About Thirty 2½-Inch
Cookies]
A sophisticatedly flavored soft
tea cookie with an oil base.
Preheat oven to 350°.
Beat:
1 egg
Add and beat well:
⅓ cup cooking oil
⅓ cup sugar
Measure:
¾ cup all-purpose flour
⅔ teaspoon double-acting
baking powder
¼ teaspoon salt
1 teaspoon grated orange
rind
⅓ cup cooked, mashed
carrots
(2 to 4 tablespoons white
raisins or citron)
(½ teaspoon ginger)
Drop from a teaspoon on a
greased tin. Space generously.
Bake 10 to 12 minutes or until
cookies are golden brown.

QUICK OATMEAL COOKIES

[About 3 Dozen 2-Inch
Cookies]
Preheat oven to 350°.
Measure:
½ cup brown sugar, firmly
packed
½ cup granulated sugar
Cream with:
½ cup butter
Combine and beat in until
smooth:
1 egg
1 teaspoon vanilla
1 tablespoon milk
Sift together and add to the
above ingredients:
1 cup all-purpose flour
½ teaspoon soda

½ teaspoon double-acting
baking powder
½ teaspoon salt
When beaten smooth, add:
1 cup uncooked quick
rolled oats
(¾ cup chocolate chips)
(1 teaspoon grated orange
rind)
Beat the mixture well. Drop
cookies 2 inches apart on well-
greased cookie sheet and bake
until light brown.

✳ OATMEAL GEMS

[About Fifty 2-Inch Cookies]
Preheat oven to 350°.
Cream:
½ cup butter
½ cup granulated sugar
½ cup light-brown sugar
Add:
1 unbeaten egg
¼ teaspoon salt
½ teaspoon double-acting
baking powder
1 teaspoon vanilla
1 cup uncooked quick
rolled oats
¾ cup flour
1 can flaked coconut
You may spice these with:
(½ teaspoon cinnamon)
(¼ teaspoon each cloves and
freshly grated nutmeg)
Bake 8 to 10 minutes or until
browned.

GLAZED OR FLOURLESS
OATMEAL WAFERS

[About Eight Dozen
2-Inch Wafers]
A pale yellow, crisp yet chewy
cookie with a shiny bottom.
Preheat oven to 350°.
Beat:
3 whole eggs
Add gradually, beating constantly:
2 cups sugar
Stir in:
2 tablespoons melted butter
¾ teaspoon vanilla
1 teaspoon salt

Remove beater. With a spoon, stir in:

1 cup shredded coconut
2 cups uncooked rolled oats

Line cookie sheet with foil. Drop by ½ teaspoons 1 inch apart into pan. Bake about 10 minutes or until the edges are lightly browned. Lift foil from pan, cool until wafers can be easily removed.

ORANGE-MARMALADE DROPS

[About Forty-Eight 2-Inch Cookies]

This cookie is chewy and also pleasantly tart in flavor.
Preheat oven to 375°.
Sift:

⅔ cup sugar

Beat until soft:

⅓ cup butter

Add the sugar gradually. Blend these ingredients until light and creamy. Beat in:

1 whole egg
6 tablespoons orange
    marmalade

Sift:

1½ cups all-purpose flour

Resift with:

1¼ teaspoons double-acting
    baking powder

Stir the sifted ingredients into the butter mixture. Drop the batter from a teaspoon, well apart, on a greased sheet. Bake the cookies for about 8 minutes. It is difficult to prescribe the right amount of flour, as marmalades differ a great deal in consistency. Follow the rule, then try out 1 or 2 cookies. If they are too dry, add a little more marmalade; if too moist, a little more flour and some grated lemon rind.

PEANUT BUTTER COOKIES

[About Sixty 1½-Inch Cookies]

For those who dote on peanut-butter cookies, try these rich and crumbly ones.

Preheat oven to 375°.
Sift:

½ cup brown sugar
½ cup granulated sugar

Beat until soft:

½ cup butter

Add the sugar gradually and blend these ingredients until creamy. Beat in:

1 egg
1 cup peanut butter
½ teaspoon salt
½ teaspoon soda

Sift before measuring:

1½ cups all-purpose flour

Add the flour to the batter and:

½ teaspoon vanilla

Roll the dough into small balls. Place them on a greased tin. Press them flat with a fork, as illustrated on page 393. Bake for about 15 minutes.

BUTTERSCOTCH NUT COOKIES

Preheat oven to 375°.
For flavor, chewiness and ease of making we prefer:

Butterscotch Brownies,
389

Should you prefer the look of a drop cookie to that of a bar, follow the recipe for the Brownies, but add:

2 tablespoons flour

Drop well apart on a greased cookie sheet and bake for about 6 minutes.

COCONUT MERINGUE COOKIES

[About Fifty 1½-Inch Kisses]
Preheat oven to 300°.
Sift:

1 cup sugar

Beat until stiff:

3 egg whites
⅛ teaspoon salt

Add the sugar very slowly, beating constantly. Fold in:

1 teaspoon vanilla
1¼ cups shredded coconut

Drop the batter from a teaspoon onto a greased and well-floured tin. Bake for about 30 minutes.

COCONUT MACAROONS

[About Twenty 1-Inch Cookies]
Preheat oven to 250°.
Use:
    ¼ lb. shredded coconut
Add:
    1 teaspoon vanilla
    ⅛ teaspoon salt
Combine these ingredients with sufficient:
      Sweetened condensed
      milk
to make a thick paste. Roll the paste into balls or drop it from a teaspoon onto greased tins, about 2 inches apart. These cookies are much improved by folding into the batter:
    1 to 3 stiffly beaten egg
    whites
Drop the batter from a spoon. Bake until lightly browned. Remove from the oven when the balls can be taken from the tin without breaking. They may be rolled in:
      Sifted confectioners'
      sugar

CHOCOLATE COCONUT MACAROONS

Prepare the preceding:
      Coconut Macaroons
Heat the milk and add:
    2 tablespoons cocoa or
    ¾ oz. chocolate
Cool the mixture before adding it to the coconut.

COCOA KISSES

[About Forty 1-Inch Meringues]
Preheat oven to 250°.
Sift:
    1 cup sugar
Whip until stiff but not dry:
    3 egg whites
    ⅛ teaspoon salt
Add gradually ½ of the sugar.
Combine:

    2 teaspoons water
    1 teaspoon vanilla
Add the liquid, a few drops at a time, alternately with the remaining sugar. Whip constantly.
Fold in:
    3 tablespoons cocoa
    ½-1 cup chopped pecans
Drop the batter from a spoon onto a lightly greased tin and shape into cones. Bake until the kisses are partly dry and retain their shape. Remove from the pan while hot.

CHOCOLATE CRACKER KISSES

[About Sixty 1-Inch Kisses]
The only people who will guess these ingredients are those who, in adolescence, happened to be devotees of thin chocolate candy bars between salted crackers.
Preheat oven to 350°.
Heat over hot water:
    ⅔ cup semi-sweet chocolate
    chips or 1 oz. chocolate,
    plus ¼ cup sugar
Cool for about 5 minutes. Beat until very stiff:
    2 egg whites
Add:
    ¼ teaspoon vanilla
    ¼ teaspoon cream of tartar
Beat in gradually:
    ⅔ cup sugar
Fold in gently:
    3 tablespoons crushed
    salted soda crackers
and the cooled chocolate mixture. Drop the meringue-like dough, a teaspoonful at a time, onto a well-greased cookie sheet. Bake about 10 to 12 minutes. Remove from the oven when a glazed cap has formed and puffed up over a ¼-inch platform of the dough—similar in looks, but more peaked than that of Anise Cookies, page 656. Store, when cool, in a tightly closed container.

ABOUT REFRIGERATOR COOKIES

Their production proves quicker than that of rolled cookies and they are usually more delicate because their chilling and quick-shaping characteristics permit a reduction in flour content. After mixing the dough, form it into a 2-inch-diameter roll on a piece of foil, in which you wrap it securely. Chill the roll for 12 to 24 hours, after which time it can be very thinly sliced for baking. You may hasten the chilling by placing the roll in the freezer.

An added advantage of these doughs is that they can all be dropped before chilling if you want to make up a batch immediately. Whole nut meats may be combined with the dough or they may be used to garnish the slices; or else, the entire roll of dough may be rolled in chopped nuts, so as to make a border when the cookie is cut, as shown on the left, below

Two sheets of differently colored dough may be rolled together, see below. These, when sliced, become pinwheel cookies. To bake drop cookies, see page 392. Bake the refrigerated cookies on a greased cookie sheet, in a 400° oven, for 8 to 10 minutes. Refrigerator cookies ✳ freeze well baked or unbaked.

VANILLA REFRIGERATOR COOKIES

[About Forty 2-Inch Cookies]
This cookie resembles a Sand Tart, but is less troublesome to prepare. It makes a good Filled Cookie, page 406, or rich Drop Cookie if the lesser amount of flour is used.
Sift:
    1 cup sugar
Beat until soft:
    ½ cup butter
Add the sugar gradually. Blend these ingredients until very light and creamy. Mix in:
    1 beaten egg
Add:
    1 teaspoon vanilla
    (½ teaspoon grated lemon
      rind or cinnamon)
Sift before measuring:
    1½ to 1¾ cups all-purpose
      flour
Resift with:
    ½ teaspoon salt
    1½ teaspoons double-acting
      baking powder
Stir the sifted ingredients into the butter mixture. Add:
    (½ cup nut meats)
To chill, form and bake, see About Refrigerator Cookies, opposite. Before baking, sprinkle the cookies with:
    (Sugar)
to make them sandy, or with:
    (Chopped or half nut
      meats)

BUTTERSCOTCH REFRIGERATOR COOKIES

Prepare:
    Vanilla Refrigerator
    Cookies, above
Substitute for the white sugar:
    1¼ cups firmly packed
      brown sugar

You may substitute for the nut
meats:
> (1 cup grated coconut or
> 1 teaspoon cinnamon)

CHOCOLATE
REFRIGERATOR COOKIES

Prepare:
> Vanilla Refrigerator
> Cookies, above

Melt, then cool and mix into the
dough:
> 2 oz. chocolate
> (1 tablespoon brandy or
> rum)

To chill, form and bake, see Refrigerator Cookies, page 399.

PINWHEEL
REFRIGERATOR COOKIES

Prepare:
> Vanilla Refrigerator
> Cookies, page 399

Divide the dough in half. Add
to ½ the dough:
> 1 oz. melted chocolate

If the dough is soft, chill until
easily rolled. Then roll the white
and brown dough separately into
oblongs to the thickness of ⅛
inch. Place the dark dough on
the light dough and roll the
layers like a jelly roll. To chill,
form and bake the rolled layers,
see About Refrigerator Cookies,
page 399.

★ MOLASSES CRISPS
COCKAIGNE

[About 6 Dozen 2 x 3-Inch
Cookies]
Heat to the boiling point over
hot water:
> ½ cup dark molasses

Remove from heat, add and beat
until blended:
> ¼ cup sugar
> 6 tablespoons butter
> 1 tablespoon milk
> 2 cups all-purpose flour
> ½ teaspoon salt
> ½ teaspoon double-acting
> baking powder

> ½ teaspoon each fresh
> ground nutmeg and
> cloves
> 2 teaspoons cinnamon

Wrap in foil and cool until firm.
To form, slice very thin and, if
necessary, pat thin on tin with
fingers until they are translucent. Press into the center of
each:
> ½ a pecan or blanched
> almond

Preheat oven to 325° and bake
for 10 to 12 minutes on greased
cookie sheets.

★ REFRIGERATOR
LACE COOKIES

[About Sixty 2-Inch Cookies]
Stir until well blended:
> ½ cup white sugar
> ½ cup brown sugar
> ¾ to 1 cup sifted all-
> purpose flour
> ½ teaspoon each soda and
> salt
> ½ cup soft butter
> 1 egg
> 1 tablespoon milk
> (1½ teaspoons grated orange
> or lemon rind)
> ½ teaspoon almond or
> vanilla extract

Work in with the hands:
> 1 cup rolled oats

To vary the flavor, you may use
1½ tablespoonfuls of molasses
and 2 additional tablespoonfuls
of flour. Chill, form and bake:
see About Refrigerator Cookies,
page 399.

★ JUBILEE WAFERS

[About Seventy 2-Inch Wafers]
Good for all those festive anni-
versaries, as they can be con-
fected long before the pressure
of events threatens to crowd
them off the calendar. Soften
and mix over hot water:
> ⅔ cup honey
> 1 cup sugar
> ¼ cup butter

Sift together and add:

2½ cups all-purpose flour
1 teaspoon double-acting
    baking powder
¼ teaspoon each mace and
    cardamon
½ teaspoon soda
2 teaspoons cinnamon
½ teaspoon cloves

Combine with all the above ingredients:

½ cup whisky

Add:

1 cup blanched, grated
    almonds
2 tablespoons each
    chopped citron, candied
    orange and lemon rind

Roll, chill, slice and bake as for Refrigerator Cookies, page 399.

ABOUT ROLLED AND MOLDED COOKIES

Aunties and grandmothers who roll cookies for and with children are scarce these days. But shaping cookies is such fun that children should be encouraged to learn to make them for themselves. Inexperienced bakers often ruin rolled cookies by using too much flour in the rolling process. To use as little extra flour as possible ♦ chill the dough at least 1 hour before rolling it and ♦ use a pastry cloth and rolling pin cover. These practically do away with sticking and require the use of very little additional flour. ♦ Remember never to use a pan with deep rims for cookie baking. Removal of the cookies from such a pan is very difficult.

♦ Use cutters that interlock, as shown above, so that dough need be handled as little as possible and baking time is economically employed. An even easier method to form fancy shapes which will not be distorted by handling is to grease the back of a baking pan. Spread dough on pan, as shown on left, above. Place cutters for maximum yield. Lift out the dough scraps between the shapes and reroll or reform them on another pan to make more cookies.

The roller cutter shown on the right speeds cookie-cutting. Two time-saving molds are an old French one of dove-tailed hearts and diamonds and a wheel cutter, also shown, which spins out the shapes with great rapidity. Amusing cutters lurk in antique shops. We wish a designer today would charm us with something contemporary. If you have a yen to do your own, take your designs to a tinsmith or make them from cardboard. See Gingerbread Men, page 403.

ROLL COOKIES

[About Forty 2-Inch Cookies]
This dough is remarkable for its handling quality. It can be shaped into crusts and dumpling covers, as well as cut into intricate patterns.

Cream:
> ½ cup white or brown sugar

with:
> ½ cup butter

Beat in:
> 2 eggs
> 2½ to 2¾ cups all-purpose
> flour
> 2 teaspoons double-acting
> baking powder
> 1 teaspoon vanilla

Chill the dough 3 to 4 hours
before rolling. Preheat oven to
375°.
To roll, cut and bake, see About
Rolled Cookies, page 401. Bake
7 to 12 minutes.

RICH ROLL COOKIES

[About Sixty 2-Inch Cookies]
Just what they are named, and
delicious! Cream:
> 1 cup butter
> ⅔ cup sugar

Beat in:
> 1 egg

Combine and add:
> 2½ cups sifted all-purpose
> flour
> ½ teaspoon salt
> 1 teaspoon vanilla

Chill dough 3 to 4 hours before
rolling.
Preheat oven to 350°.
Roll out and cut. See illustration
and read About Rolled Cookies,
page 401. Bake for 8 to 10 minutes or until slightly colored.

BUTTER THINS

[About Twenty-Eight 2-Inch
Cookies]
Blend until creamy:
> 6 tablespoons to ½ cup
> butter
> ⅓ cup sugar or ½ cup
> brown sugar

Beat in:
> 1 egg or 2 egg yolks
> ½ teaspoon vanilla or
> almond extract
> ¼ teaspoon grated lemon
> rind or 1 tablespoon
> cinnamon

> 1 cup sifted all-purpose
> flour
> ⅓ teaspoon salt
> (2 tablespoons poppy seed)

Chill the dough for several
hours.
Preheat oven to 375°.
Roll the dough on a board or
shape it into 1-inch balls. Flatten between lightly floured
hands or with the bottom of a
tumbler. Place on a greased
cookie sheet. You may decorate
them with:
> Sugar, sugar and cinna-
> mon or colored sugar
> ½ nut meat or a candied
> cherry

Bake from 10 to 12 minutes
until the edges are brown.

SAND TARTS

[About Eighty 1½-Inch
Cookies]
When touring in Normandy we
met up with a famous local specialty which, curiously enough,
proved to be our very own sand
tarts.
Sift:
> 1¼ cups sugar

Beat until soft:
> ¾ cup butter

Add the sugar gradually. Blend
these ingredients until very soft
and creamy. Beat in:
> 1 egg
> 1 egg yolk
> 1 teaspoon vanilla
> 1 teaspoon grated lemon
> rind

Sift before measuring:
> 3 cups all-purpose flour

Resift with:
> ¼ teaspoon salt

Stir the flour gradually into the
butter mixture until the ingredients are well blended. The last
of the flour may have to be
kneaded in by hand. Chill the
dough for several hours.
Preheat oven to 400°.
Roll the dough until very thin.
See page 401 for rolling cookies.

Cut into rounds. Brush the tops of the cookies with:

The white of an egg

Sprinkle generously with:

Sugar

Garnish with:

(Blanched, split almonds)

Bake on greased tins for about 8 minutes. A good sand tart with a slightly different flavor may be made by following this recipe, but substituting for white sugar 1⅓ cups brown sugar.

GINGER SNAPS

[About 10 Dozen 2-Inch Cookies]

Like "boughten" ones in texture, but with a dreamy flavor.

Preheat oven to 325°.

Cream:

¾ cup butter

with:

2 cups sugar

Stir in:

2 well-beaten eggs

½ cup molasses

2 teaspoons vinegar

Sift and add:

3¾ cups all-purpose flour

1½ teaspoons soda

2 to 3 teaspoons ginger

½ teaspoon cinnamon

¼ teaspoon cloves

Mix ingredients until blended. Form dough into ¾-inch balls. Bake on a greased cookie sheet for about 12 minutes. As the ball melts down during baking, the cookie develops the characteristic crinkled surface. A topping to delight the children is ½ a marshmallow, cut side down, on the almost baked cookies. Return to oven about 4 minutes. When cool, ice to taste.

★ GINGERBREAD MEN

[About Eight 5-Inch Long Fat Men or 16 Thinner Ones]

Even quite young children are good at making these, if the modeling method suggested below is followed.

Preheat oven to 350°.

Blend until creamy:

¼ cup butter

½ cup white or brown sugar

Beat in:

½ cup dark molasses

Sift:

3½ cups all-purpose flour

Resift with:

1 teaspoon soda

¼ teaspoon cloves

½ teaspoon cinnamon

1 teaspoon ginger

½ teaspoon salt

Add the sifted ingredients to the butter mixture in about 3 parts, alternately with:

¼ cup water, if you roll the dough or ⅓ cup, if you model it

You may have to work in the last of the flour mixture with your hands if you are not using an electric mixer. If you are satisfied with a crude approximation, roll a ball for a head, a larger one for the body and cylinders for the arms and legs. Stick them together on a greased pan to form a fat boy or girl. Be sure to overlap and press these dough elements together carefully, so they will stay in one piece after baking. If you want something looking less like Primitive Man, roll the dough first to any thickness you like. A good way to do this is to grease the bottom of a baking sheet and to roll the dough directly onto it. Now, cut out your figures, either by using a

floured cookie tin or by making a pattern of your own, as follows. Fold a square of stiff paper or light cardboard lengthwise and cut it. Unfold it and you have a symmetrical pattern. Grease or flour one side of the pattern and place it on the rolled dough. Cut around the outlines with a sharp knife. Remove the scraps of dough between the figures, using them to make more men. Decorate before baking with small raisins, bits of candied cherry, redhots, decorettes, citron, etc., indicating features, buttons, etc. The men may receive further decorations, as described later. Bake the cookies for about 8 minutes or longer, according to their thickness. Test them for doneness by pressing the dough with your finger. If it springs back after pressing, the gingerbread cookies are ready to be cooled on a rack. Stir in a small bowl, to make a paste:

> ¼ cup confectioners' sugar
> A few drops water

You may add:

> A drop or two of
> vegetable coloring

Apply the icing with a toothpick or a small knife for additional garnishes—caps, hair, mustaches, belts, shoes, etc.

★ ALMOND PRETZELS OR MANDELPLAETTCHEN

[About 3 Dozen 2-Inch Pretzels]

Sift:

> 1 cup sugar

Beat until soft:

> 1 cup butter

Add the sugar gradually. Blend these ingredients until very light and creamy. Beat in:

> 1 to 2 egg yolks
> 2 eggs
> ¼ cup cultured sour cream

Sift and stir in:

> 2½ cups all-purpose flour

You may add:

> 1 teaspoon double-acting baking powder
> 1 teaspoon cinnamon
> 1 teaspoon grated lemon rind

Chill the dough for several hours until easy to handle.
Preheat oven to 375°.
Shape the dough into long thin rolls and twist these into pretzel shape. Place the pretzels in a greased tin. Brush with:

> Yolk of an egg

Sprinkle the tops with:

> Blanched, chopped almonds
> Sugar

Bake them at once for 10 to 15 minutes. Do not let them color.

SCOTCH SHORTBREAD

Prepare:

> Almond Pretzels, this page.

You may omit the egg yolk and seasoning. Use the almonds blanched and sliced as a topping with added candied citrus peel.
Preheat oven to 325°.
Press dough into 4 8-inch rounds. Flute the edges with prick dough well. Bake about 20 minutes or until lightly colored. Cut into wedges while still warm.

YOLK COOKIES

[About 100 Initials or Thin 1½-Inch Cookies]

A great lexicographer said that an expression such as—"It's me"—was a sturdy indefensible. These cookies are our version of a sturdy indefensible. While not unusual, they use up leftover yolks. They have good tensile strength and make an excellent base for filled nut or jam tarts. We have used them as "initial" cookies for engagement parties.
Sift:

> 1 cup sugar

Beat until soft:

> 1 cup butter

½ teaspoon salt, if unsalted
butter is used
Add the sugar gradually. Blend
these ingredients until very light
and creamy. Add:
½ teaspoon grated lemon
rind
1½ tablespoons lemon juice
Beat in:
8 egg yolks
Stir in:
4 cups all-purpose flour
Chill the dough for 1 hour.
Preheat oven to 375°.
Roll the dough into sticks ¼
inch in diameter. Shape these
into letters. Brush them with:
Yolk of an egg
Sprinkle them with:
Colored or white sugar
Bake them on a greased tin, 6
to 8 minutes.

★ SPRINGERLE

[About 5 Dozen Cookies]
This recipe produces the well-
known German Anise Cakes,
which are stamped with a
wooden mold, shown at the
upper right, page 386, or roller,
into quaint little designs and
figures. If you have no mold,
cut the dough into ¾ x 2½-inch
bars. Sift:
2 cups sugar
Beat until light:
4 eggs
Add the sugar gradually. Beat
the ingredients until creamy.
Sift before measuring about:
3 to 3½ cups all-purpose
flour
½ teaspoon double-acting
baking powder
Sprinkle a half cup flour on a
pastry cloth. Turn the dough
onto the cloth and knead in
enough flour—about ½ cup
more—to stiffen dough. Roll to
the thickness of ⅛ inch and the
size of your mold. Use the
floured Springerle board and
press it hard upon the dough to
get a good imprint. If the dough

is too soft, pick it up and add
more flour. Separate the squares,
place them on a board and permit them to dry for 12 hours,
uncovered, in a cool dry place.
Preheat oven to 300°.
Grease cookie sheets and sprinkle
them with:
1 tablespoon crushed anise
seed
Place the cakes on them. Bake
about 15 minutes or until the
lower part is light yellow. To
store, see page 386.

★ CHOCOLATE ALMOND
SHELLS

[About Sixty 1½-Inch Cookies]
This batter is usually pressed
into little wooden molds in the
shape of a shell, but any attractive ones like individual butter
molds will do. If molded, the
batter must stand for 12 hours.
If not molded, it may be baked
after mixing.
Grind, in a nut grinder:
½ lb. unblanched almonds
Sift:
1 cup sugar
Whip until stiff:
4 egg whites
¼ teaspoon salt
Add the sugar gradually. Whip
constantly. Fold in the ground
almonds and:
1½ teaspoons cinnamon
⅛ teaspoon cloves
1 teaspoon grated lemon
rind
1 tablespoon lemon juice
2½ oz. grated chocolate
Permit this batter to stand uncovered in a dry cool place for
12 hours.
Preheat oven to 300°.
Shape the batter into balls. Prepare shell molds by dredging
them with a mixture of:
Sugar and flour
Press the balls into the molds.
Unmold them. Bake in a greased
sheet for about 30 minutes.

★ SPECULATUS

[About Twenty-Eight 2 x 4-Inch Thin Cookies]
A rich cookie of Danish origin, pressed with carved wooden molds into Santas and Christmas symbols.
Work as for pie dough, until the particles are like coarse corn meal:

⅔ cup butter
1 cup flour

Cream:

1 egg

with:

½ cup brown sugar

Add:

⅛ teaspoon cloves or
1/16 teaspoon cardamom
1 teaspoon cinnamon

Combine the egg and butter mixtures well. Spread the dough on a 14 x 17-inch baking sheet. Let it rest chilled for 12 hours. Preheat oven to 350°.
Stamp the figures with the floured molds. Bake about 10 minutes or until done.

COOKIE-PRESS OR SPRITZ COOKIES

[About 5 Dozen Cookies]
These may also be made in a pastry bag.
Sift together:

2¼ cups all-purpose flour
¾ cup sugar
¼ teaspoon double-acting baking powder
½ teaspoon salt

Blend in, until mixture resembles coarse crumbs:

1 cup butter

Break into a measuring cup:

1 egg

If it does not measures ¼ cup, add water up to ¼ cup line. Stir into the crumb mixture the egg and:

1 teaspoon vanilla

Beat well, then chill. Put dough through cookie press onto ▶ an ungreased cookie sheet. ▶ The dough should be pliable but, if it becomes too soft, re-chill it slightly. Bake for 10 to 12 minutes in a 350° oven.

ABOUT FILLED COOKIES AND FILLED BARS

The recipes which follow describe individual ways to shape and fill cookies and bars. But, first, here are simple and basic ways to shape and fill them as sketched below.
Prepare:

Rolled or Rich Rolled Cookies, page 401;
Butter thins, page 402;
Sand Tarts, page 402, or
Yolk Cookies, page 404

Form a ball and make an imprint with your thumb to hold a filling as shown on the left, below. Or roll the dough thin and cut into rounds. For a turnover, use a single round of dough and less than a tablespoon of filling. Fold over and seal edges firmly by pressing them with a floured fork. A closed tart takes 2 rounds of dough. Place a tablespoon of filling on one and cover with the other, then seal. For a see-

through tart, employ the same bottom round and filling, but cut the top with a doughnut cutter and seal outer edge in the same way.

To make bars, line a 9 x 13-inch pan with ⅔ of the dough, spread one of the fillings over it see below, and cover the filling with the remaining ⅓ of the dough. Bake at 350°, 20 to 25 minutes. Here are 3 basic fillings. For others, see Nut Bars, or Pecan Slices, page 408.

I. Raisin, Fig or Date Filling

Boil and stir until thick:

1 cup chopped raisins, figs or dates
6 tablespoons sugar
5 tablespoons boiling water
½ teaspoon grated lemon rind
2 teaspoons lemon juice
2 teaspoons butter
⅛ teaspoon salt

II. Coconut Filling

Combine:

1 slightly beaten egg
½ cup brown sugar
1 tablespoon flour
1½ cups flaked or chopped shredded coconut

III. ★ Drained Mincemeat, page 315

JELLY TOTS

[About Forty-Two 1¼-Inch Cookies]

You may call these Hussar Balls, Jam Cookies, Thumbprint Cookies, Deep-Well Cookies or Pits of Love—the latter borrowed from the French—but a rose by any other name, etc.
Preheat oven to 375°.
Prepare the dough for:

Butter Thins, page 402

Use the larger amount of butter. Roll the dough into a ball. You may chill it briefly for easier handling. Pinch off pieces, to roll into 1-inch balls.

I. Roll the balls in:

1 slightly beaten egg white

then in:

1 cup finely chopped nut meats

For baking, follow directions under II, below.

II. Roll the balls in:

Sugar

Place them on a lightly greased and floured sheet. Bake for 5 minutes. Depress the center of each cookie with a thimble or your thumb, as shown in sketch on page 406. Continue baking until done, for about 8 minutes. When cool, fill the pits with:

A preserved strawberry, a bit of jelly or jam, a candied cherry or pecan half, or a dab of icing

III. Before baking, make a depression in each ball. Fill with jam. Close over depression with dough. Bake, widely spaced, on a butter sheet.

MACAROON JAM TARTS

[About Fourteen 3-Inch Cakes]
The star of stars.
Blend until creamy:

2 tablespoons sugar
½ cup butter

Beat in:

1 egg yolk
½ teaspoon grated lemon rind

1½ tablespoons lemon juice

Stir in gradually, until well blended:

1½ cups sifted all-purpose flour

alternately with:

2 tablespoons cold water

Chill the dough for 12 hours.
Preheat oven to 325°.
Roll out dough to ⅛ inch. Cut into 3-inch rounds. Whip until stiff but not dry:

3 egg whites

Beat in gradually:

1⅓ cups sifted confectioners'
     sugar
1 teaspoon vanilla
Fold in:
     ½ lb. almonds, blanched
          and ground in a nut
          grinder
Place mixture around the edge
of each cookie, making a ¾-inch
border. Use a pastry bag, a
spatula or spoon, as sketched on
page 406. Bake 20 minutes
or until done. When cool, fill
centers with:
     Jam

INDIVIDUAL NUT TARTS

[About 10 to 12 Tarts]
Prepare and chill for 12 hours:
     Vanilla Refrigerator
          Cookie Dough, page 399
Preheat oven to 350°.
Pat or roll the dough until very
thin. Line shallow muffin pans
with it. Beat until light:
     3 egg yolks
Beat in gradually:
     1 cup sugar
     ¼ teaspoon salt
Grind in a nut grinder and add:
     1 cup blanched almonds
          or other nuts
Stir in:
     1½ tablespoons lemon juice
Fold in:
     3 stiffly beaten egg whites
Fill the lined shallow muffin tins
with this mixture and bake until
done, for about 20 minutes.

★ NUT BARS

[About Forty-Eight 1 x 2-Inch
Sticks]
Preheat oven to 350°.
These, like the following Pecan
Slices, are made on a rich, sweet
pastry base. They are equally
good and popular.
Cream until well blended:
     ½ cup butter
     (¼ cup sugar)
Beat in well:
     1 egg
Combine:

1¼ cups sifted all-purpose
     flour
⅛ teaspoon salt
Add these dry ingredients in
about 3 parts to the butter mixture, blending them well. Work
in:
     (½ teaspoon vanilla)
Use your hands to pat the dough
evenly in a 9 x 12-inch pan.
Bake for about 15 minutes. Beat,
in a heavy saucepan:
     2¼ cups finely chopped
          pecans
     1 cup sugar
     1½ teaspoons cinnamon
     4 egg whites
Cook and stir this mixture over
low heat. After the sugar has
dissolved, increase the heat
slightly. Stir and cook until the
mixture leaves the sides of the
pan, but remove it from the
heat before it is dry. Spread it
over the pastry base. Bake the
cake for about 15 minutes
longer. When cool, cut into
sticks.

★ PECAN OR ANGEL
   SLICES

[About Forty-Eight
1 x 2-Inch Bars]
Many a copy of the "Joy" has
been sold on the strength of this
recipe. One fan says her family
is sure these are the cakes St.
Peter gives little children at the
Gates of Heaven, to get them
over the first pangs of home-
sickness. Her family has dubbed
them Angel Cookies.
Preheat oven to 350°.
Line a pan with dough, as for
the preceding Nut Bars. Bake as
directed. Spread with the following mixture:
     2 beaten eggs
     1½ cups brown sugar
     ½ cup flaked coconut
     1 cup chopped pecan meats
     2 tablespoons flour
     ½ teaspoon any baking
          powder

½ teaspoon salt
1 teaspoon vanilla

If preferred, omit the coconut and use 1½ cups nut meats instead. Bake the cake for about 25 minutes. When cool, ice with:

1½ cups sifted confectioners' sugar

thinned to a good spreading consistency with:

Lemon juice

Cut the cake into oblongs.

PLUM BOMBS

[About 2 Dozen Bombs]

Prepare and chill well:

Rolled Cookie Dough, page 401

Preheat oven to 350°.

Drain thoroughly and remove pits from:

Canned plums

Stuff them with a combination of:

Pine nuts or chopped larger nuts
White raisins

Enclose the plums in thin wrappings of the rolled dough. Place well apart on a greased baking sheet and bake about 25 minutes or until slightly colored.

FRANKFURTER OBLATEN

Prepare:

Butter Krumkakes, page 410

Fill in, between two wafers, a thin layer of:

Soft flavored fondant or French Icing, page 427

ABOUT CURLED COOKIES

Some curled cookies are simply dropped on a baking sheet, others require a special iron. In either case they are very dressy looking—whether they make a tube or cornucopia or are just partially curled, after being shaped over a rolling pin while still warm. Filled ▶ just before serving, they make a complete dessert. Use flavored whipped cream fillings, page 377, a cake filling, page 378, or cream cheese. Serve them as tea cakes with a contrasting butter-cream filling. Dip the ends in:

Ground pistachio or chocolate shot "gimmies"

to lend a most festive look.

SCANDINAVIAN KRUMKAKES

To make these fabulously thin wafers, you will need the inexpensive iron shown above, left. It fits over a 7-inch surface burner, either gas or electric, and is ▶ always used over moderate heat. For each baking period the iron should be lightly rubbed at the beginning with unsalted butter; but after this initial greasing, nothing more is required. The dough needs a preliminary testing as it is quite variable, depending on the condition of the flour; so, do not add at once all the flour called for in the recipe. Test the dough for consistency by baking 1 teaspoonful first. The iron is geared to use 1 tablespoon for each wafer and the dough should spread easily over the whole surface, but should not run over when pressed down. If the batter is too thin, add more flour. Should any dough drip over, lift the iron off its frame and cut off the dough with a knife run along the edge of the iron. Cook each wafer about 2 minutes on each side or until barely colored. As soon as you remove it from the iron, roll it on a wooden spoon handle or cone form as illustrated and, when cool, fill it. You may prefer to use these cookies as round filled sandwich cookies. For suggestions for filling, see Curled Cookies, page 409.

I. Butter Krumkakes
[About Thirty 5-Inch Wafers]
A teenage neighbor recommends an ice cream filling. We like cultured sour cream with a spot of tart jelly or a flavored whipped cream, page 377.
Beat until light:

> 2 eggs

Add slowly and beat until pale yellow:

> ⅔ cup sugar

Melt and add slowly:

> ½ cup butter

Stir in, until well blended:

> 1¾ cups flour
> 1 teaspoon vanilla

To cook, roll and fill, see Krumkakes, above.

II. Lemon Krumkakes
[About Thirty 5-Inch Wafers]
Cream:

> 1 cup sugar
> ½ cup butter

Combine and add:

> 3 beaten eggs
> ½ cup cream, whipped
> ½ teaspoon grated lemon rind

Add enough flour to make a dough that spreads easily on the iron—not more than:

> 1½ cups flour

To bake, form and fill, see Krumkakes, above.

III. Almond Krumkakes
[About Twelve 5-Inch Wafers]
To make Fortune Cookies, see page 411.
Cream and beat well:

> ¼ cup butter
> ½ cup sifted confectioners' sugar

Add by degrees:

> 3 unbeaten egg whites
> 2 tablespoons ground almonds
> ½ cup sifted flour
> 1 teaspoon vanilla

To cook, roll and fill, see Krumkakes, above.

ICE CREAM CONES OR GAUFRETTES
[7 Large or 12 Small Cones]
If made on a krumkake iron, as illustrated, this dough can be rolled into delicious thin-walled cones. If made on an oblong waffled gaufrette iron, they become the typical French honeycombed wafer or gaufrette, so often served with wine or ices. Preheat the krumkake or gaufrette iron over a moderate surface burner. Melt and let cool:

> ¼ cup butter

Beat until very stiff:

> 2 egg whites

Fold in gradually:

> ¾ cup sifted confectioners' sugar
> ⅛ teaspoon salt
> ¼ teaspoon vanilla

Fold in:

> ½ cup sifted all-purpose flour

Add the cooled butter, folding it in gently. Put 1 tablespoon of this batter into the preheated iron. After about 1½ minutes, turn the iron and bake on the other side until a pale golden beige in color. Remove and use flat or curl the wafer into a cone. When cool, fill and serve.

ALMOND COOKIES OR FORTUNE COOKIES

[About 5 Dozen Cookies]
Preheat oven to 350°.
If you want to make these cookies, or Almond Krumkakes, into fortune favors for a party, have your remarks printed on thin papers, 3 x ¾ to 1 inch in size. After the cookies are curled, insert a slip in each, letting part of the paper project. Pinch the ends of the roll closed while the cookie is still warm. Combine and mix, until sugar is dissolved.

   ¾ cup unbeaten egg whites:
     5 to 6
   1⅔ cups sugar
   ¼ teaspoon salt
Stir in separately and beat until well blended:
   1 cup melted butter
   1 cup all-purpose flour
   ¾ cup finely chopped
     blanched almonds
   ½ teaspoon vanilla or
     1 tablespoon lemon juice
Drop the dough in tablespoonfuls, well apart, onto an ungreased baking sheet. Bake about 10 minutes or until the edges are a golden brown. Mold cookie over a wooden spoon handle. See illustration, page 409, and Curled Caramel Cookies, below.

BRANDY SNAPS

[About Twenty 3½-Inch Cookies]
Preheat oven to 300°.
Stir over low heat:
   ½ cup butter
   ½ cup sugar or ¼ cup
     sugar plus ¼ cup
     grated, packed maple
     sugar

   ⅓ cup dark molasses
   ¼ teaspoon ginger
   ½ teaspoon each cinnamon
     and grated lemon or
     orange rind
Remove from heat and add:
   1 cup all-purpose flour
   2 teaspoons brandy
Roll into ¾ inch balls.
Bake on an ungreased sheet, for about 12 minutes. Remove cookies from pan, after a minute or so, with a spatula. Roll over a spoon handle, see sketch, page 409. Store in a tightly covered tin.

MAPLE CURLS

[About Fifteen 3-Inch Curls]
Preheat oven to 350°.
Bring to a hard boil for about ½ minute:
   ½ cup maple sirup or maple
     blended sirup
   ¼ cup butter
Remove from heat and add:
   ½ cup sifted flour
   ¼ teaspoon salt
Stir this in well. When blended, drop the dough onto a greased cookie sheet, 1 tablespoonful at a time, 3 inches apart. Bake, from 9 to 12 minutes or until the cookie colors to the shade of maple sugar. Remove pan from oven. When slightly cool, remove cookies with a spatula, roll as shown on page 409, and cool on a rack.

CURLED CARAMEL COOKIES

[About 24 Cornucopias]
Preheat oven to 400°.
Cream well:
   ¼ cup butter
   ½ cup brown sugar
Beat in:
   1 egg
When well blended, beat in:
   ½ teaspoon vanilla
   ⅛ teaspoon salt
   3 tablespoons all-purpose
     flour

Stir in:

  ¼ cup ground or minced
    nut meats

Black walnuts or hazelnuts are excellent. Drop the batter from a teaspoon, well apart, on a greased sheet—about 6 to a sheet. Flatten the cookies with the back of a spoon. Bake for 8 or 9 minutes. Cool slightly and remove from pan with a small pancake turner. Then roll the cookies over a wooden spoon handle or a rolling pin, or roll them with your hands. If they cool too quickly to manipulate, return them ▶ for a minute to the oven.

CURLED NUT WAFERS

[About 20 Wafers]
Preheat oven to 375°.
Sift:

  ⅔ cup sugar

Beat until soft:

  2 tablespoons butter
  2 tablespoons shortening

Add the sugar gradually. Blend these ingredients until very light and creamy. Beat in:

  1 egg
  2 tablespoons milk
  ½ teaspoon vanilla
  ¼ teaspoon almond extract

Sift before measuring:

  1⅓ cups all-purpose flour

Resift with:

  1 teaspoon double-acting
    baking powder
  ½ teaspoon salt

Add the sifted ingredients to the butter mixture. Beat batter until smooth. Grease a cookie sheet. Spread the batter evenly, to the thickness of ⅛-inch, over the pan with a spatula. Sprinkle dough with:

  ½ cup chopped nut meats

Bake for about 12 minutes. Cut the cake into ¾ by 4-inch strips. Shape the strips while hot over a rolling pin. If the strips become too brittle before they are shaped, return them to the oven until they become pliable again.

ABOUT NUT COOKIES

The first six recipes, all delicious, may read as though they are much alike, yet they differ greatly when baked. They have in common a brown sugar and egg base ▶ so don't try to bake them in hot humid weather. In such weather, choose, instead, Pecan Puffs or Florentines. To prepare nuts, please read About Nuts, page 186.

Most of these cookies are fragile. But if made small and baked on a beeswaxed sheet or a foil pan liner they are easy to remove intact. ▶ Should they harden on the pan, return the baking sheet for a moment to the oven before trying to remove them.

PECAN DROP COOKIES

[About Fifty 1½-Inch Wafers]
Preheat oven to 325°.
See About Nut Cookies, above.
Grind in a nut grinder:

  1 cup pecan meats

Put through a sieve:

  1⅓ cups firmly packed brown
    sugar

Whip until stiff but not dry:

  3 egg whites

Add the sugar very slowly, beating constantly. Fold in the ground pecans and:

  1 teaspoon vanilla

Drop the batter from a teaspoon, well apart, onto a greased and floured tin. Bake for about 15 minutes.

NUT WAFERS

[About 30 Cookies]
At Williamsburg this cookie is served with Greengage Ice Cream.
Preheat oven to 325°.
See About Nut Cookies, page 412. Work:

(1 tablespoon flour)
into:
    1 cup brown sugar
Beat until stiff, then fold in:
    1 egg white
Fold in:
    ¾ teaspoon vanilla
    1⅛ cups coarsely chopped
        pecans or hickory nuts
Drop the batter from a teaspoon
onto a greased and floured
cookie sheet. Bake about 15 minutes or until done.

PECAN OR BENNÉ WAFERS

[About Fifty 2½-Inch Wafers]
Preheat oven to 375°.
See About Nut Cookies, page
412. Whip until light:
    2 eggs
Add gradually:
    1⅓ cups firmly packed
        brown sugar
Beat these ingredients until they
are well blended. Add:
    5 tablespoons all-purpose
        flour
    ⅛ teaspoon salt
    ⅛ teaspoon double-acting
        baking powder
    1 teaspoon vanilla
Beat the batter until smooth,
then add:
    1 cup broken nut meats or
    ½ cup toasted benné
        seeds
Grease and flour baking sheets.
Drop the batter on them, well
apart, from a teaspoon. Bake for
about 8 minutes. Remove from
sheets while still warm.

MOLASSES NUT WAFERS

[About Fifty 2½-Inch Wafers]
Preheat oven to 375°.
See About Nut Cookies, page
412.
Sift:
    1 cup dark brown sugar
Whip until light:
    2 eggs
Add the sugar gradually. Beat
these ingredients until well
blended. Add:

    1 tablespoon dark molasses
    ¼ teaspoon double-acting
        baking powder
    6 tablespoons all-purpose
        flour
    ⅛ teaspoon salt
Beat the batter until smooth.
Stir in:
    1 cup chopped black or
        English walnuts,
        hazelnuts or mixed
        nut meats
Drop the batter, well apart, from
a teaspoon onto a well greased
sheet. Bake for about 8 minutes.

★ HAZELNUT WAFERS

[About Sixty 1½-Inch Cookies]
Preheat oven to 325°.
This dough, when cut in 2½ x 4-
inch oblongs and baked on fish-
food-like wafers from bakers'
suppliers, is much like the one
used for Nürnberger Lebkuchen.
See About Nut Cookies, page
412.
Grind in a nut grinder:
    1 lb. hazelnut meats
Sift:
    2¾ cups brown sugar
Whip until stiff:
    6 egg whites
    ⅛ teaspoon salt
Add the sugar gradually. Whip
constantly. Add:
    1 teaspoon vanilla
Fold in the ground nuts. Shape
the batter lightly into 1-inch
balls. Roll them in:
    Granulated sugar
Bake on a greased tin until light
brown, about 15 minutes.

★ FLOURLESS NUT BALLS

[About Thirty-Six
1¼-Inch Balls]
Preheat oven to 325°.
See About Nut Cookies, page
412.
Grind in a nut grinder:
    1½ cups almonds or pecans
Combine in a pan with:
    1 cup brown sugar
    1 egg white

1½ teaspoons butter

Stir these ingredients over very low heat until well blended. Cool the mixture. Shape the dough into small balls or roll it out and cut it into shapes. If the dough is hard to handle, use a little confectioners' sugar. Place the cookies on a very well greased sheet. Bake for 30 to 40 minutes. Leave on the sheet until cool. Ice with:

> Lemon Glaze, page 434, or Chocolate Icing, page 429

PECAN PUFFS

[About Forty 1½-Inch Balls]
Rich and devastating.
Preheat oven to 300°.
Beat until soft:

½ cup butter

Add and blend until creamy:

2 tablespoons sugar

Add:

1 teaspoon vanilla

Measure, then grind in a nut grinder:

1 cup pecan meats

Sift before measuring:

1 cup cake flour

Stir the pecans and the flour into the butter mixture. Roll the dough into small balls. Place balls on a greased baking sheet and bake for about 30 minutes. Roll while hot in:

Confectioners' sugar

To glaze, put the sheet back into the oven for a minute. Cool and serve.

★ FLORENTINES

[30 Very Thin 3-Inch Cookies]
A great European favorite—really choice. Preheat oven to 350°.
Stir well:

½ cup whipping cream
3 tablespoons sugar

If you can get a heavier cream, use it. Stir in:

⅓ cup blanched, slivered almonds

¼ lb. preserved diced orange peel
¼ cup all-purpose flour

Spread a cookie sheet with unsalted shortening, flour it lightly. Drop the batter on it from a teaspoon, well apart. Bake the cookies until golden brown, from 10 to 15 minutes. They burn easily—so watch them. When cool, spread the bottoms of the cookies with:

4 oz. melted semi-sweet chocolate

Use a spatula or impale a cookie on a fork and dip it into the chocolate. Dry on wax paper, bottoms up. Used without the chocolate, the dough makes a delicious "lace" cookie.

LEAF WAFERS

These thin crisp wafers add distinction to a cookie tray when, like Florentines, they are dipped on one side in icing, chocolate or glaze. You may roll the dough very thin on a greased cookie sheet and cut the leaves around a pattern. Then remove the excess dough between the leaves. However, there are metal stencils which make all this easier. Put the stencil on the greased sheet. Spread dough over the leaf opening with a spatula. Remove excess dough and lift the stencil. Bake at 375° for about 10 minutes. Remove from the pan at once to prevent sticking.

I. Black Walnut Leaves
[About 60 Thin Leaves]
Preheat oven to 375°.
Cream together:

¼ cup butter
1 cup brown sugar

Add and mix well:

1 beaten egg
½ teaspoon each baking soda and cream of tartar
¼ teaspoon salt
1¾ cups cake flour

Stir in:

½ cup very finely chopped
   black walnuts
To form, bake and ice, see
above.

II. Almond Leaves
[About 50 Thin Leaves]
Preheat oven to 375°.
Cut into thin slices:
   ½ lb. almond paste: 1 cup
Knead in gradually and work
until the mixture is very smooth:
   2 egg whites
   1 tablespoon water
Stir in and beat well:
   ¾ cup sifted confectioners'
      sugar
   ¼ cup cake flour
To form, bake and ice, see
above.

RUM DROPS, UNCOOKED

[About Forty-Five 1-Inch Balls]
Fine served with tea or with
lemon ice.
Place in a mixing bowl:
   2 cups finely sifted crumbs
      of toasted sponge cake,
      zwieback or graham
      crackers
Add:
   2 tablespoons cocoa
   1 cup sifted powdered
      sugar
   ⅛ teaspoon salt
   1 cup finely chopped
      nut meats
Combine:
   1½ tablespoons honey or
      or sirup
   ¼ cup rum or brandy
Add the liquid ingredients
slowly to the crumb mixture.
Use your hands in order to tell
by the "feel" when the consistency is right. When the ingredients will hold together, stop
adding liquid. Roll the mixture
into 1-inch balls. Roll them in:
   Powdered or granulated
      sugar
Set the drops aside in a tin box
for at least 12 hours to ripen.

★ ALMOND MERINGUE RINGS

[About 36 Rings]
Decorative in Christmas boxes,
but add them at the last minute
as they do not keep well.
Preheat oven to 300°.
Blanch:
   ¼ lb. almonds
Cut them lengthwise into thin
shreds. Toast lightly. Whip until
stiff but not dry:
   2 egg whites
Add gradually, beating constantly:
   1 cup sifted confectioners'
      sugar
Our old recipe says "stir" for ½
hour, but of course you won't
do that, so whip until you are
tired or use an electric beater.
Fold in the almonds and:
   1 teaspoon vanilla
Shape the batter into rings on a
greased tin. Bake until the rings
just begin to color.

★ CINNAMON STARS

[About Forty-Five
1½-Inch Stars]
Deservedly one of the most popular Christmas cakes, also one of
the most decorative. See About
Nut Cookies, page 412.
Preheat oven to 300°.
Sift:
   2 cups confectioners' sugar
Whip until stiff but not dry:
   5 egg whites
   ⅛ teaspoon salt
Add the sugar gradually. Whip
these ingredients well. Add:
   2 teaspoons cinnamon
   1 teaspoon grated lemon
      rind
Whip constantly. Reserve ⅓ of
the mixture. Fold into the remainder:
   1 lb. ground unblanched
      almonds
Dust a board or pastry canvas
lightly with confectioners' sugar.
Pat the dough to the thickness
of ⅓ inch. It is too delicate to

roll. If it tends to stick, dust your palms with confectioners' sugar. Cut the cakes with a star or other cutter or simply mold them into small mounds. Glaze the tops with the reserved mixture. Bake on a greased sheet for about 20 minutes.

★ NUT AND DATE COOKIES

[Two 9 x 13-Inch Pans]
Not a German classic, but very like Basler Leckerle in flavor. See About Nut Cookies, page 412.
Preheat oven to 350°.
Grind in a nut grinder:
        1 cup nut meats
        1 cup seeded dates
Sift:
        1 cup sugar
Whip until stiff but not dry:
        2 egg whites
        ⅛ teaspoon salt
Add the sugar gradually. Whip constantly. Fold in:
        1 tablespoon cream
Sift before measuring:
        1 cup all-purpose flour
Resift with:
        1 teaspoon double-acting baking powder
Fold in the sifted ingredients, the nuts and the dates. It may be necessary to combine them with the hands. Grease and flour a baking sheet. Place the batter on it and pat it down to the thickness of ¼ inch. If the batter is sticky, dip the palms of the hands in confectioners' sugar. Bake for about 10 minutes. Spread while hot with:
        Lemon Glaze, page 434
Cut while hot into bars or squares.

MACAROONS

[About Thirty 2-Inch Macaroons]
Work with the hands, until well blended:

        1 cup Almond Paste, page 504: ½ lb.
        ⅞ cup sugar
Work in:
        3 egg whites
        ½ teaspoon vanilla
Sift, then add and blend in:
        ⅓ cup powdered sugar
        2 tablespoons cake flour
        ⅛ teaspoon salt
Force the dough through a pastry bag, well apart, onto parchment paper or the shiny surface of foil. Let cookies stand covered for 2 hours or more. Glaze with:
        (Gum Arabic solution, see Glazed Mint Leaves, page 523)
Preheat oven to 300°.
Bake for about 25 minutes. When cool, store tightly closed.

TEA WAFERS

[About 300 Paper-Thin Wafers]
Sometimes when a recipe looks as innocuous as this one, it's hard to believe the result can be so outstanding. These tender, crisp squares are literally paper thin.
▶ They must be placed, as soon as cool, in a tightly covered tin. They keep several weeks this way, but we have a hard time hiding them successfully enough to prove it.
Preheat oven to 325°.
Cream:
        ½ cup butter
Sift, then measure and beat in:
        1 cup confectioners' sugar
Beat until smooth. Add:
        1 teaspoon vanilla
Sift, then measure:
        1¾ cups all-purpose flour
Resift and add to the creamed mixture, alternately with:
        ½ cup milk
Beat until creamy. Butter a cookie sheet lightly. Chill the sheet. With a spatula, spread some of the mixture over it as

thinly and evenly as possible, no more than $\frac{1}{16}$ inch thick. You may sprinkle the batter with:

Chopped nut meats or cinnamon and sugar or grated lemon rind

It is well to press them down a bit so that they will stick. Take a sharp knife and mark off the batter in $1\frac{1}{2}$-inch squares. Bake about 8 to 10 minutes or until light brown. When done, take from oven and, while still hot, quickly cut through the marked squares. Slip a knife under to remove from sheet. The cakes grow crisp and break easily as soon as they cool, so you have to work fast.

ICINGS, TOPPINGS AND GLAZES

Icing some cakes is like gilding lilies. If a cake is sweet and rich enough by itself, there is no need to gold-plate or gold-fill it. But we always make sure that the filling adds contrast in texture and color—and subtlety in flavoring. Many cakes need no icing but are made more attractive with a mere dusting of con-

fectioners' sugar, as shown here and described in the variation on page 431. Try Old World Chocolate Spice, Sponge, Poppy Seed Custard and Pound Cakes this way.

For easy handling of an iced cake, try this method: lay several strips of sturdy paper on working area. Place cake on top so that ends of paper project on opposite sides. After cake has been iced, lift it by the strip ends onto the serving platter. Now, pull out strips or tear off ends.

ABOUT ICING YIELDS

Yields on icing and filling recipes are given in cups, so you can mix or match your choice in sizes. For Comparative Pan Sizes and Areas, see page 337. We consider the following list a sufficient coverage:

For the top and sides of one 9-inch round layer cake, use ¾ cup.

For the tops and sides of two 9-inch round layers, use 1½ cups.

For the tops and sides of three 9-inch round layers, use 2¼ cups.

For the top and sides of a 9½ x 5½ x 3-inch loaf pan, use 1 to 1½ cups.

For a 16 x 5 x 4-inch loaf pan, use 2 to 2½ cups.

For 16 large or 24 small cupcake tops, use 1 to 1¼ cups.

For glazing a 10 x 15-inch sheet, use 1⅓ cups.

For filling a 10 x 15-inch roll, use 2 cups.

ABOUT BOILED ICINGS

Just as in candy making, success with boiled icing depends on favorable weather and the recognition of certain stages in preparing sugar sirup. If the icing is too soft or too hard take the corrective steps suggested below. ◗ Never ruin a good cake with a doubtful icing. ◗ In high altitudes it helps to add to the sugar ⅛ teaspoon glycerin and to allow a longer cooking period.

For boiled icings ◗ the cake must be cooled before the icing is applied. If the cake is uneven, you may want to trim it slightly. In some cases, icing will adhere better and apply more evenly if you reverse the cake bottom-side up. Should the layers tend to slip, skewer them together until the icing starts to set. If you are doing a complicated decorative icing, a stand or turntable is a great help.

If you are at all disinclined to make a boiled icing, turn to the many good, foolproof, quick icings, page 426, and to the fillings which can double for soft icings, page 376.

Boiled white icings are based upon a principle known as Italian Meringue—the cooking of egg whites by beating into them ♦ gradually, a hot but not boiling sirup.

♦ Have all utensils absolutely free of grease, and eggs at room temperature. Separate the whites ♦ keeping them absolutely free of yolk and put them in a large bowl. You may start with unbeaten, frothy, or stiffly whipped whites. ♦ Have available a stabilizer: lemon juice, vinegar, cream of tartar or light corn sirup; and also a small quantity of boiling water—in case the icing tends to harden prematurely.

Cook the sirup to 238° to 240°. It will have gone through a coarse thread stage and, when dropped from the edge of a spoon, will pull out into thickish threads. When the thick thread develops a hairlike appendage that curls back on itself, remove the sirup from the heat. Hold the very hot, but not bubbling, sirup above the bowl and let it drop in a slow and gradual thin stream onto the whites as you beat them. In an electric mixer, this is no trick. If you are beating by hand, you may have to steady your bowl by placing it on a folded wet towel.

As the egg whites become cooked by the hot sirup, the beating increases the volume of the icing. By the time all the

sirup is poured, you should have a creamy mass, ready for spreading. At this point, add any of the stabilizers—a few drops of lemon juice or vinegar, a pinch of cream of tartar or a teaspoon or two of light corn sirup. These substances help to keep the icing from sugaring and becoming gritty. Then beat in the flavoring of your choice. When the icing begins to harden at the edges of the bowl it should be ready to put on the cake. ♦ Do not scrape the bowl.

If the sirup has not been boiled long enough and the icing is somewhat runny, beat it in strong sunlight. If this doesn't do the trick, place the icing in the top of a double boiler or in a heatproof bowl ♦ over—not in —hot water, until it reaches the right consistency for spreading. If the sirup has been overcooked and the icing tends to harden too soon, a teaspoon or two of boiling water or a few drops of lemon water will restore it. If raisins, nut meats, zest or other ingredients are to be added to the icing, wait until the last moment to incorporate them. They contain oil or acid which will thin the icing.

BOILED WHITE ICING

[About 2 Cups]
Stir until the sugar is dissolved and bring to a boil:

> 2 cups sugar
> 1 cup water

♦ Cover and cook for about 3 minutes, until the steam has washed down any crystals which may have formed on the sides of the pan. ♦ Uncover and cook to 238° to 240°. At that temperature the sirup will spin a very thin thread on the end of a coarser thread. This final thread will almost disappear, like a self-consuming spider web. Whip until frothy:

2 egg whites
⅛ teaspoon salt

Add the sirup in a thin stream, whipping eggs constantly. When these ingredients are all combined, add:

(⅛ teaspoon cream of tartar or a few drops lemon juice)
1 teaspoon vanilla

WHITE-MOUNTAIN ICING

[About 1¾ Cups]
You need an electric mixer for this recipe. Stir until the sugar is dissolved, then cook covered until the sirup boils rapidly:

1 tablespoon white corn sirup
1 cup sugar
⅓ cup water

Beat for about 2 minutes in a small bowl at high speed:

1 egg white

Add 3 tablespoons of the boiling sirup. Let the mixer continue to beat. Meanwhile ♦ cover the remaining sirup and cook covered about 3 minutes, until the steam has washed down from the sides of the pan any crystals which may have formed. ♦ Uncover and cook until the sirup reaches 238° to 240°. Pour the remaining sirup gradually into the egg mixture, while continuing to beat at high speed. While still beating, add:

1 teaspoon vanilla

Now, beat the icing until it is ready to be spread—4 to 6 minutes.

RAISIN OR NUT ICING

Chop:

1 cup seeded raisins or
½ cup raisins and
½ cup nuts

Add them at the last minute to:
Boiled White Icing, page 419

or, sprinkle raisins and nuts on the cake, and spread the icing over them.

COCONUT ICING

Coconut enthusiasts would tell you to add as much shredded or grated fresh or dried coconut as the icing will hold. One good way to do this is to press the coconut into the icing lightly. Or, as illustrated below, while

the icing is still soft you can hold the cake firmly on the palm of one hand, fill the palm of the other hand with grated coconut and cup it to the curve of the cake, to let it adhere to the icing. Have a bowl underneath to catch excess coconut, which can be re-used.

To prepare fresh coconut, see page 193.

ABOUT DECORATIVE ICINGS

There are several types of pastry bags available in stores. They are made of canvas or plastic. And there is also a rigid metal "bag" on the market. If you choose canvas, be sure to use it with the ragged fabric seam outside. Several metal tips, with cut outs for making different patterns, are included in pastry bag kits. The most useful tips have a rose, star or round cutout.

Here's how to make your own decorating bag: Using heavy bond or bakery paper, cut an oblong about 11 x 15 inches.

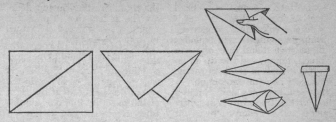

Fold the oblong diagonally as shown on the left, above. Keep the folded edge away from you. Make an imaginary line from the folded edge to the center of the left-hand point, as indicated in sketch. Roll the paper from right side into a cornucopia with a tight point, until you reach the imaginary line. If the point is tight at the bottom, the bag will not give way later when pressure is applied. Keeping the point firm, continue to roll the remaining paper to form a cornucopia. Turn it with the seam toward you. The seam should lie in a direct line with the point of one of the highest peaks of the bag, so that, by folding the peaks outward and toward you, you stabilize the shape of the cornucopia and the seam. This is shown by the two horizontal bags illustrated. If you could see through the lower one, you would find the hollow cone ready to receive the icing. The upright bag at the end shows the final fold at the top after the bag is filled and closed —with the peaks folded inward. However, before filling, the point must be cut. Press the tip of the paper bag flat and cut off the end. If you plan to use the metal tips from your pastry bag kit, be sure the opening is large enough for the tip to fit, but not so large that the tip will slip through under pressure. If you plan on using the paper point to make its own

designs, make three paper cornucopias. Cut one straight across to make a small round opening; clip the others with a single and a double notch, to achieve the star and rose cutouts. These three cuts will make all of the patterns shown in the drawings on page 423, depending upon the angle at which the bags are held and the amount of pressure you give them. You can control the scale of the decoration by the size of the cut.

Now, for the actual decorating. You have a choice of two fine icings—Royal Glaze, page 426, or Decorative Icing, page 420. The Decorative Icing is tastier to eat, but less versatile in handling and does not keep as well as the Glaze. Apply a smooth base coat of either icing to the cake. ◗ Use a spatula dipped in tepid water for a glossy finish. ◗ Allow the base coat to dry. If using several colors for decoration, divide the icing into small bowls and tint with: Vegetable Paste or Liquid Vegetable Coloring. ◗ Keep the bowls covered with a damp cloth. Fill the bag, but never more than to ½ or ⅔ of its capacity. For colors needed in small quantities, make the bags half size. Use a small spatula to push the icing well down into the bag.

Now, still holding the seam toward you, start to close the bag by pressing the top edges together and roll them inward

—until the seam is locked tightly by the roll.

Before beginning any trimming, press the bag to equalize the icing in it and force any unwanted air toward the tip so no bubbles will later destroy the evenness of your decorations. If the bag becomes soft through use or has been unsatisfactorily made, cut a generous piece off the point and press the icing directly into a new bag.

Practice making and filling bags. Then apply the icing on an inverted cake pan. The icing can be scraped off repeatedly and re-used. Make patterns like old-fashioned Spencerian-writing doodles until you have achieved some ease. ◗ Experiment with the feel of the bag, until you can sustain the pressure evenly for linear effects and with a varying force in the formation of borders, petals and leaves. With the bag in your right hand, you may work with as much freedom as in drawing.

Now you are ready to make the designs. It is a great help if the cake can be on a turntable or lazy susan. In any case, when working on the sides, try to have the cake just above elbow level as you work. The responsibility for pressure and movement, as we said before ◗ lies in the right hand. ◗ The left is used only for steadying, see picture below. As shown in the drawing, grasp the bag lightly but firmly in the palm of the hand ◗ with the thumb resting on top, leaving the fingers free to press the bag, as the hand and wrist turn to form the designs.

Sometimes, the bag rests in the scissorlike crotch of the first two fingers. At other times it acts as a mere guide, as shown in the second to last figure at the right of the page. As the icing diminishes, refold the bag at the top so that the icing is pushed down to the bottom.

First shown at the bottom, next page, are forms executed from a bag with simple crosscut at the tip—making a small round opening. The second group was achieved with a notch—like a "V"; and the elaborate composite-type flower needed a double notch—like a "W." The decoration on the cake involves the use of all three types of cuts.

As in any work of art, the concept must dominate the technique. Make a sketch first of what you would like to do, or have your goal clearly in mind. The patterns shown below are conventional ones; try them—and then develop your own style. We remember a cake that Alexander Calder did for a mutual friend—complete with mobile and showing a clarity of line so characteristic of his talent.

It is a great temptation when decorating cakes to overload them. Try out some asymmetrical compositions. Partially bind the top and sides of the cake with garlands, heavy in relief

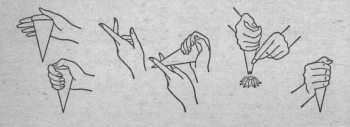

but light in values, and remember to leave plenty of undecorated space to set them off. At first, you may make some of the more complicated designs separately on a piece of wax paper and let them dry before applying them to the cake. Use Royal Glaze as an adhesive.

DECORATIVE ICING OR TWICE-COOKED ICING

[About 1¾ Cups]
This is a fine recipe for decorative icing. It will keep without hardening for a long time if closely covered with waxed paper. Stir until the sugar is dissolved, then boil without stirring:

    1 cup sugar
    ½ cup water
Meanwhile, whip until stiff but not dry:

    2 egg whites
    ⅛ teaspoon salt
Sift and add very slowly, whipping constantly:

    3 tablespoons sugar
When the sirup begins to fall in heavy drops from a spoon, add a small quantity of it to the eggs and sugar; continue beating. Repeat this process, adding the sirup to the eggs in 4 or 5 parts. If these additions are properly timed, the last of the sirup will have reached the thread stage. Beat the icing constantly. Have a pan ready, partly filled with water. Place it over heat. The bowl in which the icing is being made should fit closely into this pan, so that the bowl will be over—but not in—the water. When the water in the pan begins to boil, add to the icing:

    ¼ teaspoon icing powder:
        equal parts of baking
        powder and tartaric acid
Continue to beat the icing until it sticks to the sides and the bottom of the bowl and holds a point. Remove from heat. Place as much as is required for the decoration, usually about ⅓, in a small bowl. Cover it closely with waxed paper. To the remainder, add:

    1 teaspoon or more hot
        water
to thin it to the right consistency to be spread. Beat it well and spread it on the cake. To decorate, see About Decorative Icings, page 420.

CHOCOLATE COATING OVER BOILED WHITE ICING

[About 2¼ Cups]
The supreme touch to something that is already good in itself. Melt:

    2 oz. chocolate
Cool and spread with a broad knife or spatula over:

    Boiled White Icing, page
    419, or Seven-minute
    White Icing, page 424
This may be done as soon as the white icing is set. Allow several hours for the coating to harden. In summer or moist weather,

add to the chocolate before spreading it:

(¼ teaspoon melted paraffin)

This coating is always thin when applied, and hardens more rapidly if refrigerated. ◗ It is not recommended for use in damp hot weather. Transfer the cake to a fresh plate before serving.

SEVEN-MINUTE WHITE ICING

[About 2 Cups]

A very fluffy, delightful icing, that never fails. Place in the top of a double boiler and beat until thoroughly blended:

    2 unbeaten egg whites
1½ cups sugar
    5 tablespoons cold water
    ¼ teaspoon cream of tartar
(1½ teaspoons light corn sirup)

Place these ingredients ◗ over rapidly boiling water. Beat them constantly with a rotary beater or with a wire whisk for 7 minutes. Remove icing from heat. Add:

    1 teaspoon vanilla

Continue beating until the icing is the right consistency to be spread. You may add to it, at this point:

    ½ cup chopped nut meats or grated coconut or 1 stick crushed peppermint candy

SEVEN-MINUTE LEMON ICING

Prepare:

    Seven-Minute White Icing, above

Use only:

    3 tablespoons water

Add:

    2 tablespons lemon juice
    ¼ teaspoon grated lemon rind

SEVEN-MINUTE ORANGE ICING

[About 1½ Cups]

Place in the top of a double boiler and beat until thoroughly blended:

1½ cups sugar
    2 egg whites
    1 tablespoon lemon juice
    ½ teaspoon orange rind
    ¼ cup orange juice

Follow the rule for Seven-Minute White Icing, this page.

SEVEN-MINUTE SEA-FOAM ICING

Cook:

    Seven-minute White Icing, this page

for 8 minutes. Fold in:

    4 teaspoons caramelized sugar I, page 169

Don't forget the vanilla.

FONDANT ICING

[About 2 Cups]

This is the classic icing for Petits Fours and is tricky to apply evenly.

Prepare:

    Basic Fondant, page 501

Just before you are ready to use it, heat the fondant ◗ over—not in—boiling water, beating it constantly until it melts. Then add any desired flavoring or coloring. Spread at once, as this icing tends to glaze over rapidly and then needs reheating. Let the icing drip across, from one narrow edge of the cake to the other, as shown on page 360. Reheat and re-use any icing that falls onto the sheet below. If you have only a very few cakes to frost, place them one at a time on a slotted pancake turner or spoon held over the pot and ice them individually.

LUSCIOUS ORANGE ICING

[About 1½ Cups]

This icing becomes firm on the outside and remains soft inside. Stir over heat until dissolved:

1 cup granulated sugar
1 tablespoon white corn sirup
⅛ teaspoon cream of tartar
½ cup water

◆ Cover and cook for about 3 minutes or until the steam has washed down any crystals which may have formed on the sides of the pan. ◆ Uncover and cook to 238° to 240° without stirring. Pour the sirup in a slow stream, over:

2 beaten egg whites

Beat for 10 minutes. Add:

¼ cup powdered sugar
1 teaspoon grated orange rind
1 tablespoon orange juice or ¾ teaspoon vanilla

Beat the icing until it is of the right consistency to be spread.

CARAMEL ICING

[About 1½ Cups]

Stir until the sugar is dissolved:

2 cups brown sugar
1 cup cream or ½ cup butter plus ½ cup milk

◆ Cover and cook for about 3 minutes or until the steam has washed down any crystals which may have formed on the sides of the pan. ◆ Uncover and cook without stirring to 238° to 240°. Add:

3 tablespoons butter

Remove the icing from the heat and cool to 110°. Add:

1 teaspoon vanilla

Beat the icing until it is thick and creamy. If it becomes too heavy, thin it with a little:

Cream

until it is the right consistency to be spread. Top with:

(Chopped nuts)

MAPLE SUGAR ICING

[About 1½ Cups]

Combine and cook, stirring frequently until the mixture reaches a boil:

2 cups maple sugar
1 cup cream

Then ◆ cover and cook about 3 minutes or until the steam has washed down any crystals which may have formed on the sides of the pan. ◆ Uncover and cook to 234°. Remove the icing from the heat. Cool to 110°. Beat well until creamy.
Fold in:

½ cup chopped nut meats, preferably butternut meats or slivered toasted almonds

CHOCOLATE MARSHMALLOW ICING

[About 2 Cups]

Stir until the sugar is dissolved:

1½ cups sugar
1½ cups water

Then ◆ cover and cook for about 3 minutes or until the steam washes down any crystals which may have formed on the sides of the pan. ◆ Uncover and cook without stirring to 238° to 240°. Remove from the heat and add:

2 oz. grated chocolate
1 dozen large marshmallows, cut into eighth and steamed until soft

Permit these ingredients to stand until the mixture no longer bubbles. Add:

⅛ teaspoon cream of tartar

Whip until stiff but not dry:

2 egg whites
⅛ teaspoon salt

Pour the sirup over the egg whites in a thin stream. Whip constantly, until the icing is of the right consistency to be spread.

CHOCOLATE-FUDGE ICING

[About 2 Cups]

See:
> Fudge Cockaigne, page
> 506

Use in all:
> 1 cup milk

Beat until the icing is of the right consistency to be spread.

BROWN-SUGAR MARSHMALLOW ICING

[About 1½ Cups]

Cut into small cubes:
> 12 large marshmallows

Stir over low heat until dissolved:
> 2 cups brown sugar
> ½ cup milk

♦ Cover the sirup for about 3 minutes or until the steam has washed down any crystals which may have formed on the sides of the pan. ♦ Uncover and cook without stirring to 238°. Remove from the heat, add the marshmallows and:
> ¼ cup butter

When these ingredients are melted and the icing reaches 110°, beat until it is of a good consistency to be spread. If too heavy, thin with a little:
> Cream

Pour the cream a few drops at a time.

Add:
> (½ cup chopped nut meats)

ABOUT QUICK ICINGS

Most quick icings, unless heavy in butter, are best spread on warm cakes. ♦ Those which have eggs in them, if not consumed the day they are made, should be refrigerated. Recipes calling for confectioners' sugar are tastier when ♦ allowed to stand over—not in—hot water for 10 to 15 minutes, to cancel out the raw taste of the cornstarch filler. If you don't mind that taste, you can mix these icings more quickly in a ⅄ blender. ♦ Any delicate flavoring should be added after the icing leaves the heat. A glossy finish can be achieved by dipping your spatula frequently in hot water while icing the cake.

QUICK WHITE ICING

I. [About 1 Cup]

Sift:
> 2 cups confectioners' sugar

Beat until soft:
> 3 tablespoons butter or hot whipping cream

Add the sugar gradually. Blend these ingredients until creamy. Add:
> ¼ teaspoon salt
> 2 teaspoons vanilla or
> 2 tablespoons dry sherry, rum, coffee, etc.

If the icing is too thin, add:
> Confectioners sugar

If too thick, add:
> A little cream

See About Quick Icings, above.

II. [About ¾ Cup]

Melt and stir in a skillet until golden brown:
> 6 tablespoons butter

Blend in gradually:
> 1½ cups confectioners' sugar

Add 1 tablespoon at a time, until the icing is of a good consistency to be spread:
> Hot water

Flavor with:
> 1 teaspoon vanilla

ROYAL GLAZE, SWISS MERINGUE OR QUICK DECORATIVE ICING

[About 2 Cups]

This icing will become very hard. To avoid a naturally grayish tone that develops during preparation, add to portions that you want to keep white a slight amount of blue vegetable coloring. Do not use blue in any icing that you plan to color yellow, orange or any other pale warm tint.

Sift:
>   3½ cups confectioners' sugar

Beat until stiff, not dry:
>   2 egg whites

Gradually, add the sifted sugar and:
>   Juice of a lemon
>   1 to 2 drops glycerin

until it is of a good consistency to be spread. Cover with a damp cloth until ready to use.

To apply as piping or for decorative effects, see About Decorative Icing, page 423. Should you want the icing stiffer, add a little more sifted sugar. To make it softer, thin it ⬧ very, very gradually with lemon juice, more egg white or water.

LEMON TOPPING FOR COOKIES OR BARS

[About 1½ Cups]

Whip until stiff but not dry.
>   2 egg whites
>   ⅛ teaspoon salt

Sift and add gradually about:
>   2 to 2½ cups confectioners' sugar
>   Grated rind and juice of 1 lemon

QUICK LEMON ICING

[About 1 Cup]

A very subtle flavor may be obtained by grating the rind of an orange or lemon coarsely, wrapping it in a piece of cheesecloth and wringing the citrus oils onto the sugar before it is blended. Stir the oils into the sugar, and allow it to stand for 15 minutes or more.

Blend well:
>   2 cups confectioners' sugar
>   ¼ cup soft butter

Beat in:
>   1 or more teaspoons cream

If you have not treated the sugar as suggested above, add:
>   Grated rind and juice of 1 lemon or 3 tablespoons liqueur such as apricot or crème de cacao

THREE-MINUTE ICING

Use this soft icing as a substitute for whipped cream or meringue.

Beat until blended, then place in a double boiler over boiling water:
>   2 egg whites
>   ½ cup sugar
>   ⅛ teaspoon salt
>   2 tablespoons cold water

Beat these ingredients for 3 minutes, or until stiff, with a wire whisk. Remove the icing from the heat. Add:
>   1 teaspoon vanilla or almond extract

Beat the icing well. Spread it over jellied fruit, pies or tarts, cakes, etc., that have been cooled. Top it with:
>   Chopped nut meats or coconut

FRENCH ICING

[About 1½ Cups]

Sift:
>   2 cups confectioners' sugar

Beat until soft:
>   ¼ cup butter

Add the sugar gradually. Blend these ingredients until creamy. Beat in:
>   1 egg
>   1 teaspoon vanilla

See About Quick Icings, page 426.

CREAM CHEESE ICING

[About ¾ Cup]

Sift:
>   ¾ cup confectioners' sugar

Work until soft and fluffy:
>   3 oz. cream cheese
>   1½ tablespoons cream or milk

Beat in the sugar gradually. Add:
>   1½ teaspoons grated lemon or orange rind

or:
>   1 teaspoon vanilla and
>   ½ teaspoon cinnamon

or:

> A good dash liqueur,
> lemon or orange juice
> and grated rind

If you want a pink icing, blend in:

> 1 tablespoon chopped
> maraschino cherries

QUICK ORANGE ICING

[About 1 Cup]
Place in the top of a double boiler:

> 2 cups sifted confectioners'
> sugar
> 1 tablespoon melted butter
> 1 tablespoon grated orange
> rind
> ¼ cup orange juice or 3
> tablespoons orange juice
> and 1 tablespoon lemon
> juice

Place these ingredients ▶ over—not in—hot water for 10 minutes. Beat the icing until cool and of a good consistency to be spread. See About Quick Icings, page 426.

BUTTERSCOTCH ICING

[About 1¼ Cups]
Combine, stir and heat in a double boiler until smooth:

> ¼ cup butter
> ½ cup brown sugar
> ⅛ teaspoon salt
> ⅓ cup rich or evaporated
> milk

Cool this slightly. Beat in, to make of a good consistency to be spread:

> 2 cups, more or less, of
> confectioners' sugar

You may add:

> ½ teaspoon vanilla or
> 1 teaspoon rum
> ½ cup chopped nut meats

CHOCOLATE BUTTER ICING

[About 1½ Cups]
This icing can be used for decorating.

Melt over very low heat:

> 2 to 3 oz. chocolate

Melt in it:

> 2 teaspoons to 3
> tablespoons butter

Remove these ingredients from the heat and add:

> ¼ cup hot water, cream or
> coffee, or an egg
> ⅛ teaspoon salt

Add gradually about:

> 2 cups sifted confectioners'
> sugar
> 1 teaspoon vanilla

You may not need quite all the sugar.

QUICK BROWN-SUGAR ICING

[About ¾ Cup]
A quick, but rather coarse icing. Combine, stir and cook slowly to the boiling point:

> 1½ cups brown sugar
> 5 tablespoons cream
> 2 teaspoons butter
> ⅛ teaspoon salt

Remove from the heat. Cool slightly, add:

> ½ teaspoon vanilla

Beat the icing until it can be spread.
You may add:

> ½ cup chopped nut meats

CHOCOLATE CREAM CHEESE ICING

[About 2 Cups]
Melt:

> 3 oz. chocolate

Soften:

> 3 oz. cream cheese

in:

> ¼ cup milk

Add gradually:

> 4 cups confectioners' sugar
> ½ teaspoon salt

Combine this mixture with the melted chocolate and beat until smooth and ready to be spread.

EUROPEAN CHOCOLATE ICING

[About ⅔ Cup]

A homesick letter from an American bride made us realize that familiar tastes abroad have as foreign an accent as English words do when spoken by other nationals. Where to get bitter chocolate for icing, to make it taste as she thought it should? Chef James Gregory made her feel almost at home with this semi-sweet solution.
Melt in a double boiler ▶ over—not in—hot water:

    1 tablespoon butter
    4 oz. semi-sweet chocolate

When melted, add and beat well:

    6 tablespoons whipping cream

Sift and add, until the desired sweetness is reached and the icing is smooth, about

    1½ cups confectioners' sugar
    1 teaspoon vanilla

Spread while warm.

EASY CHOCOLATE ICING

[About 1¾ Cups]
Melt in a double boiler ▶ over—not in—hot water:

    3 oz. chocolate
    2 tablespoons butter

Combine in a blender or mixer with:

    2¾ cups sifted confectioners' sugar
    ½ teaspoon salt
    1 teaspoon vanilla
    6 tablespoons light cream

Combine with the butter and chocolate mixture in the double boiler and heat for 10 minutes to destroy the uncooked taste of the cornstarch in the confectioners' sugar. Add:

    1 teaspoon vanilla

If stiff, blend in:

    1 tablespoon cream

before spreading.

QUICK CHOCOLATE ICING

Melt over hot water:

    Sweet chocolate bars or chocolate peppermints

Cool slightly, then spread the icing. If the chocolate seems stiff, beat in a little:

    Cream

and to perfect the flavor, add:

    Vanilla

COFFEE OR MOCHA ICING

[About 1¼ Cups]
Sift:

    1⅔ cups confectioners' sugar
    1 to 2 tablespoons cocoa

Beat until soft:

    ¼ to ½ cup butter

Add the sugar gradually. Blend these ingredients until creamy. Add:

    ⅛ teaspoon salt
    3 tablespoons strong, hot coffee

Beat for 2 minutes.
When the icing is cool, add:

    1 teaspoon vanilla or rum

Permit it to stand for 5 minutes. Beat well and spread.

QUICK MAPLE ICING

[About 1 Cup]
Sift:

    2 cups confectioners' sugar

Add and blend:

    1 tablespoon butter
    ¼ teaspoon salt
    ½ teaspoon vanilla

Beat in, to make of a good consistency to be spread:

    Maple sirup
    (½ cup toasted coconut)

QUICK HONEY PEANUT-BUTTER ICING

This appeals mainly to the small fry.
Combine and bring to a boil:

    2 tablespoons shortening
    2 tablespoons butter
    ¼ cup honey

Remove from heat and add:

    ½ cup coarsely ground peanuts

Stir until well blended. Spread on a warm cake. Toast it very lightly under a broiler at medium heat. Watch it carefully.

APRICOT OR PINEAPPLE ICING

[About 1 Cup]
This is a soft icing. Stir until smooth:

>   ½ cup sweetened, cooked
>   dried apricot pulp or
>   partly drained pineapple,
>   crushed

with:

>   1½-2 cups sifted
>   confectioners' sugar

Beat in:

>   1-3 tablespoons soft butter
>   ½ tablespoon lemon juice

Add more confectioners' sugar, if needed.

PINEAPPLE ICING

[About 1½ Cups]
Sift:

>   2 cups confectioners' sugar

Beat until soft:

>   ¼ cup butter

Add the sugar gradually. Blend until creamy. Beat in:

>   1 teaspoon lemon juice
>   ⅛ teaspoon salt
>   ½ teaspoon vanilla
>   ½ cup chopped, drained
>   pineapple

Permit to stand for 5 minutes. Beat the icing until creamy. Add more sugar, if necessary.

BANANA ICING

[About 1 Cup]
Put soft bananas through a ricer, until you have:

>   ½ cup banana pulp

Sift:

>   2 cups confectioners' sugar

Stir the sugar into the pulp until smooth.
Beat in:

>   ⅛ teaspoon salt
>   1 teaspoon lemon juice
>   ½ teaspoon vanilla

Add more confectioners' sugar, if needed.

BAKED ICING

[Glaze for an 8 x 8-Inch Cake]
The icing is baked at the same time as the cake. Use it on a thin cake only, one that will require 25 minutes of baking or less—such as spice, ginger or coffee cake.
Preheat oven to 375°.
Sift:

>   ½ cup brown sugar

Whip until stiff but not dry:

>   1 egg white
>   ⅛ teaspoon salt

Fold in the sugar or beat it in slowly. Spread the icing on the cake. Sprinkle it with:

>   ¼ cup broken nut meats

For an exciting new taste, fold in:

>   (2 tablespoons cocoa)

Bake the cake as indicated in the recipe.

BROILED ICING

[For an 8 x 8-Inch Cake]
Combine and spread on a cake, coffee cake or cookies, while they are warm, a mixture of:

>   3 tablespoons melted
>   butter
>   ⅔ cup brown sugar
>   1 to 2 tablespoons cream
>   ⅛ teaspoon salt
>   ½ cup shredded coconut
>   or other nut meats

Place the cake 3 inches below a broiler, with the heat turned low. Broil the icing until it bubbles all over the surface, but see that it does not burn.

QUICK-DIPPING ICINGS

Dip tops and sides of small cakes in icing, see illustration, page 431, then right them on a cake rack to drip. Catch the drippings on a pan and use them to ice other cakes.
I. [About 1½ Cups]
Stir over heat, then boil for 1 minute:

>   1 cup sugar

½ cup butter
½ cup milk
Cool slightly. Add:
1¼ cups sifted confectioners'
    sugar
½ teaspoon salt
½ teaspoon vanilla
    A few drops of vegetable
    coloring
(¼ teaspoon almond flavor)

II. [About 1½ Cups]
Place over hot water and stir
until smooth:
    3 oz. cut-up chocolate
    3 tablespoons butter
Pour:
    5 tablespoons scalding hot
    milk
over:
    2 cups sifted confectioners'
    sugar
    ¼ teaspoon salt
When dissolved, add the chocolate mixture and:
    1 teaspoon vanilla
Beat until of the right consistency to be dipped or spread.

ABOUT ICING SMALL CAKES AND COOKIES

Here are a number of ways to
ice and garnish small cakes
quickly. Some are shown
sketched. I. Place on a hot cup
cake a small piece of semi-sweet
or sweet chocolate. Spread it as
it melts. II. Just before removing cookies from the oven, put
on each one a mint-flavored
chocolate candy wafer and return the cookie sheet to the oven
until the wafer melts. III. To
ice cup cakes or leaf cookies, dip

them rapidly in a dipping icing.
Swirl the cakes as shown. The
cookies are most easily iced if
impaled on a skewer. IV. For
cup cakes, sift confectioners'
sugar over them through a
strainer, below.

QUICK LACE TOPPING

A good, quick decorative effect
can be gained on any cake with
a slightly rough top, see sketch,
page 418. Place a paper doily
or monogrammed cut paper pattern on top of the cake and fill
the interstices with sugar. Be
sure that the sugar, confectioners' or colored, is dusted
lavishly over the doily and filters
down into all the voids. Lift the
doily or pattern off gingerly,
with a straight upward motion,
and you will find a clearly
marked lacy design on your cake
top. Shake into a bowl any surplus sugar left on the pattern.
Reserve it for future use. You
may also follow this principle in
applying finely grated semi-
sweet chocolate on an iced cake.

HARD-SAUCE TOPPING

Soften slightly, then apply a
thin layer of brandied:
    Hard sauce, page 480
to any cooled cake or coffee
cake.

ABOUT MERINGUE TOPPINGS

Pie and pudding meringues are
delicate affairs that ▶ are best
made and added to pastry

shortly before serving. Since meringue is beaten constantly until the moment to spread it, have the ♦ oven preheated to between 325° and 350°. Lower heat will dry the meringue. Higher heat will cause egg protein to shrink or shrivel. The two toppings below differ greatly in volume, texture and method. The first is cooked on the pie or dessert itself. The second is cooked separately and beaten until cool before applying; it may or may not be browned later. As volume in the egg white is essential, please follow these suggestions: ♦ Have the utensils absolutely free of grease, with ♦ egg whites at about 75° and ♦ without a trace of yolk. Add sugar, as specified in each recipe. Excess sugar, beaten into the meringue, will cause it to be gummy and to "bead" out. If you prefer a topping sweeter than these for which the recipe is given, you may glaze the surface, after the meringue is in place, by sprinkling it with additional sugar. This also makes the meringue easier to cut cleanly when serving. You may also top it with a sprinkling of coconut or slivered almonds before baking.

Meringue toppings for small tarts may be baked on foil and slipped onto a cooked or fresh pie filling just before serving. For a large pie, spread it lightly from the edges toward the center of the pie. ♦ Should it not adhere well to the edges at all points, it will pull away during the baking. ♦ To avoid shrinkage, cool meringues in a warm place, away from drafts.

MERINGUE TOPPING

I. [For a 9-Inch Pie]
Preheat oven to 325° to 350°.
Whip until they are frothy:
    2 egg whites

Add:
    ¼ teaspoon cream of tartar
Whip them until they are ♦ stiff, but not dry; until they stand in peaks that lean over slightly when the beater is removed.
Beat in, ½ teaspoon at a time:
    3 tablespoons sugar or
    4 tablespoons powdered
        sugar
♦ Do not overbeat. Beat in:
    ½ teaspoon vanilla
Bake 10 to 15 minutes, depending on the thickness of the meringue.

II. [About 1¼ Cups]
This classic Italian meringue does not require baking, because the egg whites are already cooked by the hot sirup. You may want to brown it lightly in a 350° oven. This is not as stiff a meringue as the preceding one.
Heat in a heavy pan and stir until dissolved:
    ½ cup water
    ¼ teaspoon cream of tartar
    1 cup sugar
When the sirup is boiling ♦ cover and cook for about 3 minutes or until the steam has washed down any crystals which may have formed on the sides of the pan. ♦ Uncover and cook to 238° to 240°. Pour the sirup ♦ very gradually onto:
    3 well-beaten egg whites
beating constantly, until this frosting meringue is cool and ready to be spread on the pie filling or pudding.

TOPPINGS OR STREUSEL FOR COFFEE CAKES, PIES AND SWEET ROLLS, APPLIED BEFORE BAKING

I. Streusel [For an 8 x 8-Inch Cake]
Prepare:
        Any Coffee Cake Dough,
        page 264–268

After spreading it with butter, combine:

2 tablespoons all-purpose flour
2 tablespoons butter
5 tablespoons sugar

Blend these ingredients until they crumble.
Add:

½ teaspoon cinnamon

Sprinkle the crumbs over the cake and bake as directed.
Add:

(¼ to ½ cup chopped nuts)

II. Streusel
[For 9-Inch Pie]
Frequently called Danish or Swedish and much like the topping for Apple Paradise. This is a crumb topping usually served in place of a top crust on apple or tart fruit pie, but which does well for coffee cakes.
Melt:

6 tablespoons butter

Stir in and brown lightly:

1 cup fine dry cake clumbs
¾ teaspoon cinnamon

III. Honey Glaze
[For a 9 x 13-Inch Cake]
Cream:

½ cup sugar
¼ cup butter

Blend in:

1 unbeaten egg white

Add:

¼ cup honey
½ cup crushed nut meats
½ teaspoon cardamon

Spread these ingredients on coffee cakes that are ready to be baked.

IV. Honey-Bee Glaze
[For Two 9-Inch Square Cakes]
Stir and bring to the boiling point over low heat:

½ cup sugar
¼ cup milk
¼ cup butter
¼ cup honey
½ cup crushed nut meats

Spread these ingredients on cof-fee cakes that are ready to be baked.

V. Caramel-Roll Topping
[Enough for 6 Rolls]
This heavy topping is put in the bottom of the pan and when the cake or rolls are reversed it becomes the topping.
Melt:

¼ cup butter

Stir in until dissolved:

½ cup sugar
3 tablespoons packed brown sugar
1 to 2 teaspoons cinnamon
½ teaspoon chopped lemon rind
3 tablespoons chopped nuts

Add:

(2 tablespoons finely chopped citron)

GLAZES APPLIED BEFORE OR DURING BAKING

I. To give color to yeast dough or pastry, brush with:

Milk or butter or a combination of milk and sugar

II. French Egg Wash or Dorure
To give color and gloss to yeast dough or pastry, brush with:

1 egg yolk diluted with
1 to 2 tablespoons water or milk

III. To sparkle a glaze, sprinkle before baking with:

Granulated sugar

IV. For a clear glaze, just before the pastry has finished baking, whisk with brush dipped in:

¼ cup sugar

dissolved in:

¼ cup water or hot strong coffee
(½ teaspoon cinnamon)

and return to oven.

V. To give yeast dough or pastry

a glow and flavor, brush with sweetened fruit juice and lemon rind.

VI. To gloss and harden crust of yeast dough, brush with a cornstarch and water glaze, several times during the baking.

VII. Broiled Icing, page 430.

VIII. Baked Icing, page 430.

GLAZES APPLIED AFTER BAKING

Just after these glazes are applied, decorate with:

> Whole or half nuts, cherries, pineapple bits and citron

When it dries, the glaze will hold the decorations in place on cakes and sweet breads.

I. Milk Glaze

This can be used as a substitute on small cakes similar to petits fours, which are classically iced with fondant.
Sift:

> ½ cup confectioners' sugar

Add:

> 2 teaspoons hot milk
> ¼ teaspoon vanilla

II. ★ Lemon Glaze
[About ½ Cup]

No heating is necessary: Spread it right on the warm cakes or Christmas cookies. It is of a fine consistency for imbedding decorative nuts and fruits. Enough glaze to cover four 8 x 8-inch cakes.
Mix or ⅃ blend:

> 1¼ cups confectioners' sugar

with:

> ¼ cup lemon, orange or lime juice
> 1 teaspoon vanilla

Mix until smooth.

III. ⅃ Blender-Whipped Cheese Topping
[About ⅓ Cup]

Soften:

> 3 oz. cream cheese

with:

> 1 tablespoon cream
> ½ teaspoon vanilla

Blend in and cream well:

> 3 tablespoons confectioners' sugar

IV. Liqueur Glaze
[About ⅔ Cup]

Combine and mix well:

> 2 cups sifted confectioners' sugar
> 3 tablespoons liqueur
> 2 tablespoons melted butter

Spread over cake or cookies.

V. Glaze for Breads

To make a crisp crust, brush with water immediately when taken from oven.

VI. Glaze for Puff Paste

For a crisp crust, brush with a light sugar sirup immediately when taken from oven.

GLAZE FOR FRUIT PIES, TARTS AND COFFEE CAKES

I. Apricot Glaze

For already baked pastries, the following recipe is easy to use:

> Sweetened, cooked dried apricot pulp or preserves or melted currant, quince or apple jelly

However, we like to have on hand the glaze below, which keeps well if refrigerated.
Prepare:

> 3 cups strained apricots, peaches or raspberries

Cooked until the sugar is dissolved with:

> 1 cup sugar
> 1 cup light corn sirup

While the mixture is still warm, glaze the cooled pastry.

II. Fruit Glaze
[Sufficient for Glazing 3 Cups of Berries or Fruit]

Boil to the jelly stage, page 573, then strain these ingredients:

 ¼ cup water
 1 cup sugar
 1 cup cleaned fruit
 2 medium-sized chopped apples
   A little red vegetable coloring
 (1 tablespoon butter)

The butter will keep the glaze supple. Cool. When the jelly is about to set, pour it or spread it over the fruit to be glazed.

III. Strawberry Glaze
[Sufficient for a 9-inch Pie Shell or Six 2½-Inch Tarts]
Hull and crush:

 3 cups strawberries

Strain them first through a ricer, then through a fine sieve. Add to the juice:

 ⅓ cup sugar
 1 tablespoon lemon juice
 1 tablespoon cornstarch
   A little red vegetable coloring

Cook and stir these ingredients over low heat until thick and transparent. Cool. Spread over the fruit to be glazed.

IV. Thickened Fruit Glaze
Glaze may also be made of canned fruit sirups or jellies. Boil the sirup until thick. To each ½ cup, add:

 1 teaspoon cornstarch or arrowroot

blended with:

 1 tablespoon sugar

The cornstarch will give a smooth glaze, the arrowroot a more transparent and stickier one.

CLEAR CARAMEL GLAZE
[About 1 cup]
This brittle topping is used on many European cakes, especially the famous Dobos or Drum Torte, page 367.
Place in a large, heavy skillet over low heat:

 1 cup sugar

Cook and stir with a wooden spoon, using the same kind of gentle motion you use for scrambling eggs. ◗ Keep agitating the pan as this scorches very easily. When the sugar bubbles, remove the pan from the heat. The glaze should be clear and light brown and smooth and have reached a temperature of about 310°. Spread it at once with a hot spatula. ◗ If you work quickly enough, you may score it in patterns for easier cutting later. Use a knife dipped in cold water.

FRESH FLOWERS FOR CAKES

Cake decorations can be made from flowers, if you are sure they were ◗ not sprayed. Place on the cake just before it is served. Choose delicately colored open-petaled flowers like hollyhocks. Remove the stamens. Cut off all but ¾ inch of the stem. Arrange the flowers on an iced cake. Place a small candle in the center of each one. A hemerocallis wreath is good for daytime decorations, but closes at night. Field daisies and African daisies hold up well. ◗ Beware of flowers like lilies of the valley or Star of Bethlehem, which have poisonous properties.

DESSERTS

A family we know had a cook who always urged the children to eat sparingly of the main course, so as to leave a little room for the "hereafter." Desserts can indeed be heavenly. They also give the hostess a chance to build a focal point for a buffet, produce a startling soufflé, or confect an attractively garnished individual plate. See also Filled Cakes, page 369, and Torten that serve as complete desserts, page 366.

ABOUT CUSTARDS

Custard puddings, sauces and fillings accompany the seven ages of man in sickness and in health. Rarely anywhere, however, are these delicacies prepared in ways that enhance their simple charm. To do so, remember some simple precautions. ♦ When pasteurized milk is used in making custards, it is not necessary to scald it; but scalding does shorten the cooking time. If scalded, cool the milk enough afterward to keep the eggs, when added, from curdling. For a baked custard, simply whip the ingredients together well, pour them into custard cups, set them on a rack or on a folded towel in a pan in which you have poured an inch of hot but not boiling water. Bake them at low heat, around 325°, for about 20 to 30 minutes. If you have used homogenized milk, allow about 10 minutes longer. To test for doneness, insert a knife ♦ near the edge of the cup. ♦ If the blade comes out clean, the custard will be solid all the way through when cooled. There is sufficient stored heat in the cups to finish the cooking process. Remove the custards from the pan and cool on a rack. ♦ However, should you test the custard at the center and find it as well done as at the edge, set the custard cups in ice water at once to arrest further cooking.

For softer top-of-the-stove custards and sauces, use a double boiler, cooking ♦ over—not in—hot water. Too high heat will toughen and shrink the albumen in the eggs and keep it from holding the liquid in suspension as it should. Beat the eggs well. Add about ¼ of a cup of the hot liquid to them and then slowly add the rest of it, stirring constantly. Cook until the custard is thick enough to coat a spoon. Remove pan from heat. Strain. Then continue stirring to release steam. If the steam is allowed to condense it may make the custard watery. If you suspect that the custard has become too hot, turn it into a chilled dish and whisk it quickly or put it in the blender at high speed to cool it rapidly. ♦ Always store custards or custard-based dishes like pies and éclairs in a very cool or refrigerated place as they are highly susceptible to bacterial activity although they may give no evidence of spoilage.

CUSTARD
[About 2½ Cups]

◗ This artless confection, often referred to as "boiled" custard, is badly nicknamed as it must not be permitted to boil at any time. ◗ Very slow cooking will help deter curdling.

Beat slightly:

> 3 or 4 egg yolks

Add:

> ¼ cup sugar
> ⅛ teaspoon salt

Scald and stir in slowly in a double boiler:

> 2 cups milk

Place the custard ◗ over—not in —hot water. Stir it constantly until it begins to thicken. Cool. Add:

> 1 teaspoon vanilla, rum or dry sherry, or a little grated lemon rind

Chill thoroughly. This is not as firm as baked custard because stirring disturbs the thickening. It is really more like a custard sauce.

⅄ BAKED OR CUP [5] CUSTARD

Preheat oven to 300° to 325°.

Delicious as is, but better as a summer brunch served over unsweetened dry cereal with fresh berries, or as a company dessert molded over cored pear halves, fresh or stewed, sprinkled with rum, the centers filled with a stewed pitted prune dusted in cinnamon. If you want to unmold the custard, use the larger quantity of egg.

Blend together:

> 2 cups pasteurized milk
> ¼ to ½ cup sugar or ⅓ cup honey
> ⅛ teaspoon salt

Should the milk be unpasteurized, be sure to see About Custards, above. Add and beat well:

> 2 to 3 beaten whole eggs or 4 egg yolks

The greater the proportion of yolk, the tenderer the custard will be. You may even use 2 egg whites to 1 yolk for a quite stiff custard.

Add:

> ½ to 1 teaspoon vanilla (⅛ teaspoon nutmeg)

When this is all well beaten, pour it into a baker or into individual custard cups. Place the molds in a pan of water in the oven for an hour or more. To test, see About Custards. Chill and serve with:

> Caramel Sirup, page 518, fruit juice, or
> Maple Sirup Sauce, page 478

⅄ COFFEE [4] CHOCOLATE CUSTARD

A sophisticated dessert easily made in a blender.

Put in blender:

> ½ to 1 oz. finely cut-up chocolate

Pour over it:

> 1 cup strong, hot coffee

Add:

> 1 cup milk
> 4 to 6 tablespoons sugar
> ⅛ teaspoon salt
> 2 whole eggs or 3 egg yolks

Blend this mixture. To bake, see About Custards, page 436.

CARAMELIZED [4 to 5] CUSTARD, SPANISH CREAM OR CRÈME CARAMEL

Caramelize I:

> ½ cup sugar, page 169

Place it in a 7-inch ring mold or custard cups. Turn the mold to permit the caramel to spread evenly, then push the coating with a wooden spoon until the entire base of the dish is covered. At this point the sirup should be, and should remain, thick if you have caramelized the sugar properly.

> Cup Custard, page 437

Bake as directed. Invert it when cold onto a platter. To be sure the caramel comes out intact, dip the mold to the depth of the caramel quickly in hot water, as you would in releasing a gelatin. Now the center may be filled with:

Whipped cream

Sprinkle the top with:

Shredded toasted almonds or crushed nut brittle

CARAMEL CUSTARD

Prepare:

Cup Custard, page 437

omitting the sugar. Mix with it:

½ cup Caramelized Sugar I, page 169

To bake, see About Custards, page 436.

RICH CUSTARD   [6]

Mix in the top of a double boiler:

¾ cup sugar
2 tablespoons cornstarch
⅛ teaspoon salt

Gradually stir in:

2 cups milk and cream, mixed

Cook covered ◗ over hot water for 8 minutes without stirring. Uncover and cook for about 10 minutes more. Add:

4 well-beaten egg yolks
2 tablespoons butter

Cook and stir these ingredients over hot water for 2 minutes longer. Cool, stirring occasionally to release steam, then add:

1½ teaspoons vanilla

Fold in:

1 cup whipped cream

Chill the custard. It will have the consistency of a heavy whipped cream. It is divine with:

Dampfnudeln, page 322, or
Drained Tutti Frutti, page 583

FLOATING ISLAND   [4]

I.

This is the delicate French des-sert called Oeufs à la Neige or Eggs in Snow.

Whip until stiff:

3 egg whites

Beat in gradually:

¼ cup sugar

Scald:

2 cups milk

Drop the meringue mixture from a tablespoon in rounds onto the milk. Poach them gently with-out letting the milk boil, for about 4 minutes, turning them once. Lift them out carefully with a skimmer onto a towel. Use the milk to make:

Custard, page 436

Cool the custard. Place the meringues on top. Chill before serving.

II.   [4]

This American dessert is a great favorite—our children call it "eating clouds."

Preheat oven to 500°.

Prepare:

Custard, page 436

Flavor it with:

Lemon rind

Pour it in a baking dish.

Whip until stiff:

3 egg whites

Add very slowly, whipping con-stantly:

3 tablespoons sugar
½ teaspoon vanilla or a few drops almond extract

Heap the egg whites on the custard. Place the custard dish in a pan of ice water and put the whole into the hot oven just long enough to brown the tips of the meringue.

CRÈME BRULÉE   [6]

A rich French custard—famous for its hard, caramelized sugar glaze.

Heat in a double boiler until hot:

2 cups whipping or even heavier cream

Pour it slowly over:

4 well-beaten eggs

Beat constantly while pouring. Return the mixture to the double boiler. Stir in:

(2 tablespoons sugar)

Heat until the eggs thicken and the custard coats a spoon heavily. Place the mixture in a greased baking dish or custard cups. Some people insist this custard should be made and chilled the day before it is caramelized. In any case, chill it well. Cover the custard with:

**¼- to ⅓-inch layer of
lump-free light-brown
sugar or maple sugar**

Place the custard cups or dish in a shallow pan. If the custard has been chilled for 12 hours, put it in a cold oven. Turn the heat to 250° and heat until the sugar is caramelized. If the custard has been chilled a shorter time, put the dish in a shallow pan. Surround it with ice. Place it under a hot broiler just long enough to let the sugar form a crust. Keep the oven door open and regularly rotate the dish to even the heating. While the sugar caramelizes, watch carefully as it may scorch. Serve at once. A delicate garnish is:

**A compote of greengage
plums and apricots**

BRULÉE CRUSTS

This is an assembly job, rather than a welded one. Making the brulée crusts separately relieves tensions and assures a professional look. Cut a piece of aluminum foil the exact size of the dish in which you want to serve the brulée.

Grease the foil on one side with:

Butter

Pat onto the buttered side in a firm, lacy disk pattern about ¼-inch thick:

Brown sugar

Put the sugar-covered foil on a cookie sheet. ◗ At this point the operation needs your entire attention. Put the cookie sheet under broiler heat until the sugar is caramelized or glazed. Remove it from the oven and reverse the foil, with sugar disks, onto a cake rack to cool. When slightly cooled, the sugar topping should peel off the foil like a large praline. You may repeat this process and freeze a quantity of these large or small disks. Place them on the custard just the moment before serving, so they do not disintegrate.

FRUIT JUICE CUSTARD

So rich a dessert, this should serve 4.

Mix:

**4 be · n egg yolks
⅔ cup sugar
1 cup fruit juice**

We like a combination of canned pineapple and fresh orange juice. Bake as directed for Cup Custard, page 437.

ZABAGLIONE OR   [6]
SABAYON

Very similar to Weinschaum, below, but somewhat sweeter. It is served as sauce, dessert or beverage. Marsala is the classic wine, but Madeira or sherry are also used. If for a sauce, you might even try a good dry white wine and a little Cointreau. For Sabayon Sauce, which can be made in advance and held, see page 475. Beat until very light:

**8 egg yolks
1 cup confectioners' sugar**

Place these ingredients in the top of a double boiler ◗ over— not in—boiling water. ◗ Do not permit the water to touch the bottom of the double boiler top. Beat the custard constantly with a wire beater. When foamy, add gradually:

**½ cup dry Marsala, Madeira
or sherry**

Continue to beat the custard

until it doubles in bulk and begins to thicken. Remove it from the heat. Sometimes the egg whites are omitted. If you want a fluffier result, whip until stiff:

8 egg whites

Fold in the custard. Serve the Zabaglione at once in sherbet glasses.

WINE CUSTARD OR [6] WEINSCHAUM

Place in the top of a double boiler ♦ over—not into—boiling water:

2 cups dry white wine
½ cup water

Add:

4 unbeaten eggs
½ cup sugar

Beat these ingredients vigorously with a wire whisk. Cook the custard until it thickens. Beat it constantly. Serve it hot or cold.

ORANGE CUSTARD [6] WITH MERINGUE

Preheat oven to 325°.
Grate the rind of:

2 oranges

into:

⅓ cup sugar

Peel:

6 oranges

Separate the sections and remove the membrane, see page 100. Place sections in a baking dish. Scald:

3 cups milk

Pour over:

3 beaten egg yolks

Beat these ingredients until well blended. Combine the sugar with:

2 tablespoons cornstarch
¼ teaspoon salt

Stir this mixture into the custard. Cook and stir in a double boiler until thick, for about 7 minutes. Cool. Pour over the oranges. Top the custard with a Meringue, page 431. Bake for about 15 minutes. Serve chilled.

ABOUT SPONGE CUSTARDS

From a fan came a drawing of an elaborate mold and the question, "Can you tell me how my great-aunt used to make a dessert that had a spongy bottom and a clear quivery top?" Her objective must have been a sponge custard baked and unmolded. This batter holds together when put into the baker, but magically separates while cooking. If you serve it in the baker, the sponge will form a decorative top. If you prefer a meringue-like quality rather than a spongy one, reserve ¼ cup sugar to beat slowly into the stiff egg whites before folding them into the egg-yolk mixture.

PINEAPPLE SPONGE [4] CUSTARD

Please read About Sponge Custards, above.
Preheat oven to 350°.
Combine and stir in the order given:

5 tablespoons sugar
3 tablespoons all-purpose flour
½ cup pineapple sirup
1 teaspoon grated lemon rind
2 tablespoons lemon juice
2 or 3 beaten egg yolks
½ cup milk
1½ tablespoons melted butter

Whip until stiff, then fold in:

2 or 3 egg whites

Place in the bottom of a 7-inch baking dish or in four 3½-inch individual ones:

1¼ to 1½ cups coarsely cut drained pineapple

Pour the custard mixture over the fruit. Place the dishes in a pan in 1 inch of hot water. Bake the custard for about 1 hour for the dish and 45 minutes for the cups. Serve hot or cold.

ORANGE OR   [4 to 6]
LEMON SPONGE CUSTARD

Preheat oven to 350°.
Please read About Sponge Custards, page 440.
Cream:

   ¾ cup sugar
  1½ tablespoons butter
   1 tablespoon grated orange
     rind or 2 teaspoons
     lemon rind

Add and beat well:

  2 or 3 egg yolks

Stir in:

  3 tablespoons all-purpose
    flour

alternately with:

  ⅓ cup orange juice, or
  ¼ cup lemon juice
  1 cup milk

Beat until stiff ◗ but not dry:

  2 or 3 egg whites

Fold them into the yolk mixture.
Place the batter in buttered custard cups, or in a 7-inch ovenproof dish, set in a pan filled with 1 inch of hot water. Bake for about 45 minutes for the cups and about 1 hour for the baking dish, or until set. Serve hot or ice cold with:

    (Thick cream or Raspberry Sauce)

CHOCOLATE CUSTARD
OR POTS-DE-CRÈME

Some custard recipes are perfect for use in lidded antique pots-de-crème. Although the classic procedure is baking, the consistency is easier to control by this top-of-the-stove method.

I.   [6]

Combine and cook over very low heat:

  2 cups milk or cream or
    half milk and half cream
  5 to 8 oz. grated, best
    quality sweet chocolate
  (2 tablespoons sugar)

Cook and stir these ingredients until they are blended and the milk is scalded. Remove from heat. Beat into them:

  6 lightly-beaten egg yolks
  1 teaspoon vanilla or
    grated rind of 1 orange

Strain the custard. Pour into custard cups. Chill well.

II. Pots-de-Crème Café   [4]

Cook and serve as above, using:

  ½ cup heavy cream
  ½ cup sugar
  1 tablespoon instant coffee
  6 egg yolks
  1 tablespoon brandy

RUM CHOCOLATE [8 to 10]
MOUSSE

A phenomenally smooth, rich dessert that is quickly assembled. A specialty of our friend Chef Pierre Adrian.
Cook over very low heat until dissolved but not colored brown:

  ¼ cup sugar
  2 to 4 tablespoons rum

Melt in a double boiler:

  ¼ lb. semi-sweet or sweet
    chocolate

When the chocolate is melted, stir in:

  2 to 3 tablespoons
    whipping cream

Add the sirup to the melted chocolate and stir until smooth.
When the mixture is cool but not chilled, fold into it:

  2 stiffly beaten egg whites

and then fold this combination very gently into:

  2 cups whipped cream

Chill in sherbet glasses at least 2 hours before serving.

FRENCH CHOCOLATE   [6]
MOUSSE

Stir and scald in a saucepan over low heat:

  2 cups milk
  ¼ cup sugar
  3 oz. grated sweet
    chocolate

Pour part of these ingredients over:

4 beaten egg yolks

Return the sauce to the pan. Stir the custard constantly over low heat until it thickens. Strain it. Cool by placing the pan in cold water. In a separate bowl, whip until stiff:

¾ cup heavy cream

Add:

1 teaspoon vanilla
2 tablespoons brandy

Fold the cold custard into the whipped cream mixture until it is well blended. Fill custard cups with the pudding. Chill thoroughly before serving.

CHESTNUT MOUND OR [6] MONT BLANC

Boil in water for 8 minutes:

2 lbs. chestnuts

Remove shells. Cook the hulled nuts until mealy in a double boiler over hot water in:

1 quart milk

Drain, discard milk, then cook in a sugar sirup made of:

1 cup water
1 cup sugar

until the sirup is reduced. Add:

(¼ cup almond paste)

When partially cool, add:

1 teaspoon vanilla or 2 or
more tablespoons brandy,
curaçao, etc.

Put chestnuts through a ricer. Let them fall lightly onto a large plate into a mound. If necessary to touch them, try to do so very lightly, so that they will not be mashed. Whip until stiff:

1 cup whipping cream

Fold in:

1 teaspoon vanilla
2 tablespoons sifted
confectioners' sugar

Place the cream on the mound and let it overflow onto the sides. Chill well before serving. You may cover the top of the cream with a grating of:

Sweet chocolate

And then, as our dear old French friend would have said, "I'd be so pleased, I would not thank the King to be my uncle."

CORNSTARCH   [8]
CUSTARD PUDDING OR
BLANCMANGE

To be really good, this pudding needs loving care. For success, see About Cornstarch, page 155. Mix in the top of a double boiler:

½ cup sugar
3 tablespoons cornstarch
¼ teaspoon salt

Gradually, add while stirring well:

4 cups milk

Place the mixture ◗ over boiling water and stir constantly for 8 to 12 minutes, when it should have begun to thicken. Cover and continue to cook for about 10 minutes more. Stir 1 cup of this thickened mixture, slowly, into:

2 well-beaten eggs

Return it to the milk mixture and continue to cook for 2 minutes, stirring constantly. Do not overcook. The pudding will thicken more as it cools. Remove from heat, and when slightly cooled by gentle stirring, add:

1 teaspoon vanilla

To mold, see About Cornstarch, page 155.

CARAMEL CUSTARD   [8]
CORNSTARCH PUDDING

◗ Please read About Cornstarch, page 155. Heat slightly in the top of a double boiler over direct heat:

3 cups milk

Caramelize I:

1 cup sugar, page 169

Put it gradually into the warm milk and heat to the boiling point. Make a thin paste by stirring and pouring gradually over:

3 to 4 tablespoons
cornstarch
1 cup cold milk

When this is smooth, combine the two mixtures by pouring the hot one ♦ gradually into the cold one, and stirring until smooth again. Place the top of the double boiler ♦ over boiling water and stir constantly for 10 minutes until the mixture begins to thicken. Cover and continue to cook for 10 minutes more. Mix 1 cup of this thickened mixture slowly into:

> 2 well-beaten eggs

Return to the rest and continue to cook for 2 minutes, stirring constantly. Then remove pudding from heat. Stir gently until slightly cooled, then add:

> 1 teaspoon vanilla

To mold, see About Cornstarch, page 155.

CHOCOLATE [4]
CORNSTARCH PUDDING

♦ Please read About Cornstarch, page 155.
Melt in a double boiler:

> 1 oz. chocolate

Stir in slowly:

> ½ cup sugar
> 1¾ cups milk
> ⅛ teaspoon salt

Heat these ingredients to the boiling point.
Dissolve:

> 3 tablespoons cornstarch

in:

> ¼ cup milk

Stir the cornstarch slowly into the hot milk mixture. Cook over boiling water for 10 minutes, stirring constantly. Cover and cook for 10 to 12 minutes more until you can no longer taste the cornstarch. Cool by stirring very gently. When slightly cool, add:

> 1 teaspoon vanilla

To mold, see About Cornstarch, page 155. Serve with:

> Cream

FRIED CREAM OR
CRÈME FRITE

♦ Please read About Cornstarch,

page 155. Place in the top of a double boiler:

> 1 vanilla bean
> 1 cinnamon stick
> 1½ cups milk

Bring to a boil over direct heat and then cool slightly. Mix in a bowl until smooth:

> ¼ cup sugar
> 1 tablespoon flour
> ¼ cup cornstarch
> ½ cup milk

Remove vanilla bean and cinnamon stick from the slightly cooled milk and stir the smooth cornstarch mixture into the milk. ♦ Cook over hot water until it begins to thicken—about 10 minutes. Pour some of this mixture over:

> 3 beaten egg yolks

Return the egg mixture to pan and cook ♦ stirring gently for about 3 minutes more. Beat in:

> 1 tablespoon butter
> ¼ teaspoon salt

Pour the thickened cream into a 9 x 9 inch buttered pan. Cool. Cut into diamonds or squares, about 1½-inches long. Beat:

> 1 egg

Dust cream with:

> Finely crushed bread or
> cake crumbs

Dip the pieces of cream in the egg, then again in the crumbs. Fry in deep fat, heated to 370°. Drain and roll in:

> Powdered vanilla sugar

Serve at once sprinkled with:

> Rum

or with:

> Fruit Sauces, page 473

ABOUT DESSERT
SOUFFLÉS

If you have never made sweet soufflés before, ♦ please read the directions for making and baking them on (I, 196). ♦ To prepare a dish for sweet soufflé, use a straight-sided ovenproof

baker. Butter it and dust the
inside with powdered sugar.

Some fruit and nut soufflés
are very close in texture to omelets and whips, having no bind-
ing sauce. For such soufflés, the
proper beating of the egg whites
and the right baking temperatures are more important than
ever. If the egg whites are
under- or over-beaten or the
baking heat too high, they have
the look and texture of an old
leather belt. If mixed and
baked with care, these same ingredients produce a delicacy and
strength that remind us of dandelion seed puffs just before
they blow. Some soufflés are
made on a cream-puff or choux-
paste base. See Apricot Omelette Soufflé, page 448.

If you decide to add liqueurs
as a flavoring, allow an extra
egg yolk for every 2 tablespoons
of liqueur. Otherwise, the mixture will be thinned too much.

To glaze a soufflé, dust it 2 or
3 minutes before it is to come
from the oven with powdered
sugar. The soufflé should have
doubled in height and be firm
before the glaze is applied.
Watch it closely with the oven
door partially open. The gla-
çage will remain fairly shiny
when the soufflé is served.

Cold soufflés are based on
gelatins and resemble mousses
or Bavarians, see page 450. They
are frequently heightened by
preparing a collar or band of
paper tied around the outside of
the dish in which the soufflé is to
be served, and extending a few
inches above it. Remove the
collar just before serving. We
have never found a collar to be
an asset in making a hot soufflé.

Note carefully the size of the
baker indicated as this affects
the lightness and volume of the
result. A 7-inch baker should
serve 3 to 4; a 10-inch baker 8
to 10.

VANILLA SOUFFLÉ

[A 9-Inch Soufflé Dish]
◆ Please read About Dessert
Soufflés, above, to prepare a
soufflé baker.

This soufflé has a versatile
wardrobe and many aliases. You
may add a very few drops of
oil of anise or a few marrons
glacés; or you may replace the
sugar with ⅓ to ½ cup of sirup
from preserved ginger; also, add
about ¼ cup very finely chopped
candied fruits that have been
soaked in Danziger Goldwasser
or kirsch. In the latter guise, it
is called Soufflé Rothschild. Sift
before measuring:

> ½ cup all-purpose flour

Resift with:

> ¼ cup sugar
> ¼ teaspoon salt

Stir in until smooth:

> ½ cup cold milk

Scald:

> 2 cups milk

with:

> A vanilla bean

Remove the bean and stir in the
flour mixture with a wire whisk.
Cook and stir these ingredients
over low heat until they thicken.
Remove from the heat. Stir in:

> ¼ cup butter
> 4 to 5 beaten egg yolks

You may add:

> (¾ cup chopped nut meats)

Cool the batter.
Preheat oven to 350°.
Whip until ◆ stiff, but not dry:

> 5 egg whites

Fold them lightly into the batter.
Bake soufflé for about 25 minutes. Serve with:

> A fruit sauce
> Maple Sirup Sauce,
> page 478, or
> Rum Sauce, page 476

SOUFFLÉ GRAND MARNIER

[An 8-Inch Soufflé Dish]
Preheat oven to 400°.
◆ Please read About Dessert

Soufflés, page 443, to prepare a soufflé baker.
Beat in a double boiler over hot water:

8 lightly beaten egg yolks
⅔ cup sugar

Continue to beat until the mixture forms a broad ribbon as it runs from a lifted spoon. Add:

½ cup Grand Marnier liqueur

To arrest the cooking, transfer the mixture to a bowl and beat it over ice until cooled. Beat until foamy:

10 egg whites

Add:

¼ teaspoon cream of tartar

Continue to beat until ♦ stiff, but not dry. Fold the egg yolk mixture into the whites, see illustration, page 336. Mound the mixture in a soufflé dish. Bake 12 to 15 minutes and serve at once.

PINEAPPLE SOUFFLÉ

[A 7-Inch Soufflé Dish]
Preheat oven to 325°.
♦ Please read About Dessert Soufflés, page 443, to prepare a soufflé baker.
Melt over low heat:

3 tablespoons butter

Stir in:

3 tablespoons flour

When blended, stir in:

1 cup crushed, drained pineapple

When thick and smooth, stir in:

⅔ cup dry, crushed macaroons
3 egg yolks

Permit the yolks to thicken slightly. Cool the mixture.
Beat until ♦ stiff, but not dry:

3 to 4 egg whites

Beat in gradually:

2 tablespoons sugar
½ teaspoon vanilla

Fold this into the soufflé mixture. Bake in a soufflé dish for about 30 minutes.

CHOCOLATE SOUFFLÉ

[A 9-Inch Soufflé Dish]
♦ Please read About Dessert Soufflés, page 443, to prepare a soufflé baker.
Melt:

2 tablespoons butter

Stir in until blended:

1 tablespoon all-purpose flour

In a separate saucepan, heat but do not boil:

1 cup milk
1 oz. chocolate, cut in pieces
⅓ cup sugar

Add the hot milk mixture to the flour mixture, stirring constantly until well blended. Beat until light:

3 egg yolks

Beat part of the sauce into the yolks, then add the yolk mixture to the rest of the sauce and stir the custard over very low heat to permit the yolks to thicken slightly. Cool the custard well. Preheat oven to 350°.
Add:

1 teaspoon vanilla

Whip until ♦ stiff, but not dry:

3 egg whites

Fold them lightly into the cooled chocolate mixture. Bake in a soufflé dish set in a pan of hot water for about 20 minutes or until firm. Serve at once with:

Cream, Vanilla Sauce, page 480
Foamy Sauce, page 481, or Weinschaum Sauce, page 476

LEMON SOUFFLÉ

[An 8-Inch Soufflé Dish]
♦ Please read About Dessert Soufflés to prepare a soufflé baker, on page 443.
Preheat oven to 350°.
Sift:

¾ cup sugar

Beat until very light:

5 egg yolks

Add the sugar gradually. Beat

constantly until the eggs are creamy. Add:

1 teaspoon grated lemon
rind
¼ cup lemon juice
(½ cup chopped nut meats)

Whip until stiff but not dry:

5 egg whites

Fold them lightly into the yolk mixture. Bake the soufflé in a dish set in a pan of ◗ hot, but not boiling, water, for about 35 minutes, or until it is firm. Serve at once with:

Cream

FRESH FRUIT SOUFFLÉ
[A 7-Inch Soufflé Baker]
◗ Please read About Dessert Soufflés to prepare a soufflé baker, on page 443.
Preheat oven to 350°.
Prepare, by peeling and mashing, ripe fruits to make:

1 cup sweetened fruit pulp:
fresh apricots, nectarines,
peaches, plums or
raspberries

Add:

1½ tablespoons lemon juice
4 beaten egg yolks
⅛ teaspoon salt
(1 tablespoon grated orange
rind)

Beat until ◗ stiff, but not dry, and fold in:

4 egg whites

Bake the mixture in a pan of ◗ hot, but not boiling, water for about 30 minutes. Serve hot with:

Cream

PRUNE OR APRICOT SOUFFLÉ OR WHIP
[A 9-Inch Soufflé Baker]
◗ Please read About Dessert Soufflés to prepare a soufflé baker, on page 443.
Preheat oven to 350°.
Have ready:

1 cup sweetened, thick
dried prune or apricot
purée

Whip until ◗ stiff, but not dry:

5 egg whites

Add:

¼ teaspoon cream of tartar

Fold in the prune or apricot pulp and:

(½ cup broken nut meats)
(1 teaspoon grated lemon
rind)

Place the soufflé in a baking dish set in a pan of hot water. Bake for about 1 hour or until firm. Serve hot with:

Cream or Custard Sauce,
page 475

HAZELNUT SOUFFLÉ
[An 8-Inch Soufflé Baker]
◗ Please read About Dessert Soufflés to prepare a soufflé baker, on page 443.
Preheat oven to 350°.
Put through a nut grinder:

¾ cup hazelnuts

Heat to just below the boiling point and pour over the nuts:

1 cup milk

Beat until light:

3 egg yolks

Beat in gradually:

3 tablespoons sugar
3 tablespoons flour
⅛ teaspoon salt

Stir a small quantity of the hot mixture into the eggs and then return this combination to the rest of the hot mixture. Stir and cook these ingredients over low heat to permit the yolks to thicken slightly. Stir in:

3 tablespoons butter

Cool. Beat in:

½ teaspoon vanilla or
1 tablespoon rum

Beat until ◗ stiff, but not dry:

3 egg whites

Fold them into the cooled custard. Bake for about 30 minutes. Serve hot with:

1 cup whipped cream

flavored with:

Caramel or coffee

NUT SOUFFLÉ
[A 12-Inch Soufflé Baker]
◗ Please read About Dessert

Soufflés to prepare a soufflé baker, on page 443.
Preheat oven to 350°.
Sift:

  1 cup confectioners' sugar

Beat until very light:

  8 egg yolks

Add the sugar gradually. Beat constantly until the yolks are creamy. Fold in:

  2 teaspoons grated lemon rind or 1 teaspoon vanilla
  ½ lb. blanched ground almonds or walnuts

Whip until stiff but not dry:

  8 egg whites

Fold them lightly into the yolk mixture. Place the batter in the baking dish, set in a pan of ♦ hot, but not boiling, water. Bake until firm, about 45 minutes.
Serve with:

  Sabayon Sauce, page 475, or Fruit Sauce, page 473

SOUR CREAM APPLE CAKE COCKAIGNE

[A 12 x 17-Inch Pan or Ten 4-Inch Round Bakers]

We had this, our great-grand-mother's specialty, once served to us in a pie crust, as a re-nowned confection of Lyons. We feel the pie shell makes an attractive container. However, the crust does not greatly im-prove the flavor.
Preheat oven to 325°.
Pare, core, and slice:

  5 to 6 cups tart apples

Melt in a large, heavy skillet:

  ¼ cup butter

Add the apples and cook them uncovered over medium heat, stirring them often until they are tender. Do not let them brown. Combine and pour over the apples:

  ½ cup cultured sour cream
  Grated rind and juice of 1 lemon
  1 cup sugar, scant unless apples are very tart

  2 tablespoons all-purpose flour
  8 egg yolks
  (½ cup blanched shredded almonds)

Stir these ingredients over low heat until they thicken. Cool the mixture. Whip until ♦ stiff, but not dry:

  8 egg whites

Fold them lightly into the apple mixture. Spread the soufflé to a thickness of 1 inch in a large pan or ovenproof dish. Sprinkle the top with a mixture of:

  ¼ cup sugar
  2 tablespoons cinnamon
  ¼ cup dry bread crumbs
  ¼ cup blanched shredded almonds

Bake for about 45 minutes or until firm. The cake may be served hot, but it is best very cold, covered with:

  Whipped cream, flavored with vanilla or with Angelica Parfait, page 492

OMELETTE AUX CONFITURES   [2]

Prepare as for a French Ome-lette (I, 188), using:

  2 egg yolks

Beat them until light. Beat in gradually:

  ¼ cup confectioners' sugar

Add:

  ½ teaspoon vanilla or a grating of orange or lemon rind

Whip until stiff, ♦ but not dry:

  4 egg whites

Fold them lightly into the yolk mixture. Melt in a skillet:

  2 tablespoons butter

When the butter is very hot, pour in the omelet mixture. To cook and fold, see page 335. When done, sprinkle with:

  Confectioners' sugar

Serve with:

  Preserves or jelly

or fold the omelet and spread
with:

Applesauce, prune or
apricot pulp, drained
canned fruit or sugared
berries

BAKED ALASKA, [12]
NORWEGIAN OMELET OR
OMELETTE SOUFFLÉ

This tour de force speaks several
languages and always seems
gala. It needs last minute preparation to be "à point"—the meringue glazed and delicately
colored, the ice cream firm, the
cake not soggy—in other words,
"Just right!" There are either individual, see below, or large
pans, and also ovenproof dishes
made especially for this dessert.
You may even build a "cake
case" on an oval heatproof dish.
Preheat broiler.
Line the dish with a ½-inch
layer of:

Génoise, see page 370, or
sponge or angel cake

Three-day-old cake is suggested,
so it will absorb any liquid from
the ice cream. Sprinkle it lightly
with:

(Brandy)

Have ready:

¾-inch strips of Génoise,
sponge or angel cake
to cover the ice cream
later

Make a meringue as follows.
Beat:

4 egg yolks

Beat in:

¼ cup sugar
½ teaspoon grated lemon
rind

Whip until stiff ◗ but not dry,
and fold in:

6 egg whites

Or use instead a triple portion
of Meringue I or II, see page
432. Quickly form on the cake
base an oval mound made of:

1½ quarts ice cream

◗ softened just enough so you

can shape it. Cover this melon-
mold shape with the cut strips
of cake. Cover it at once with
the meringue, so the cake surface is entirely coated to at least
a ¾-inch thickness. Bring the
meringue right down to the dish

surface. You may use some of
the meringue in a pastry bag to
pipe on fluted edges and patterns and you may accent the
patterns with:

(Candied fruit)

Run this meringue-covered confection under a 500° broiler—
not more than 3 minutes—to
brown. Watch it very closely!
Serve at once.
You may like to try out this
baked meringue covering by
using orange cups as a base to
hold the ice cream. Bring the
meringue well down over the
edge of the orange cup.

APRICOT OMELETTE [6]
SOUFFLÉ

[Two 9-Inch, Round Pans
with Removable Rims]
Preheat oven to 325°.
Blend together in the top of a
double boiler and heat ◗ over—
not in—hot water, until the mass
leaves the sides of the pan:

¼ cup butter
1 cup flour
1 tablespoon sugar
1¼ cups cream
¾ cup milk

Cool the mixture and add one at
a time, beating after each addition:

6 egg yolks
1 teaspoon vanilla

Beat until stiff ▶ but not dry and fold in:

6 egg whites

Pour the omelette mixture into the pans and bake 25 to 30 minutes. While baking, heat in the top of a double boiler:

1½ cups apricot jam

Have ready a heated serving dish, on which to reverse one of the omelet layers. Cover it lightly with the jam. Reverse the second layer over it. Cover second layer with jam and serve at once with:

(Whipped cream)

ABOUT DESSERT MOLDS

Almost any bowl that splays out is suitable for a pudding mold. Be sure the slanted sides allow molded ingredients to slide out easily when the mold is inverted. For straight-sided desserts, use spring forms, see page 185. One of the favorite shapes for Bavarians is the melon mold.

To prepare the mold, rinse it out with cold water. Oil is sometimes used to coat the mold, but may leave an unpleasant finish, especially on clear gelatins.

Dessert molds are often cakelined. To make a pudding mold from a cake itself, see description and illustration below. If the mold is deep and the pudding or cake surface very tender, always use the paper lining as a safety measure. Cut as shown

on the left, page 693. The simplest cake linings are made with thin sheets of Génoise—see page 370—or large areas cut from Jelly Rolls—see page 373—while they are still flat, before filling. Shown on the right is a mold lined with filled jelly roll slices. Macaroons and cookies can also be used in this pattern. In the center, you see ladyfingers, either whole or split, forming the mold. If they are split, be sure to put the curved sides against the form. To make an even top, slice each section to a point by cutting it diagonally, as shown, and placing it with the pointed end toward the middle, until the base is filled. You may want to cut a small round for the very center.

If the ladyfingers are barely moistened with a liqueur or a fruit after placing, they will soften enough to fill any crevices. If moistened too much, they will disintegrate.

For fillings in such molds, see suggestions on page 376. Whatever fillings you choose, be sure to ▶ refrigerate them, preferably 12 hours before unmolding. Garnish the molded food with flavored creams, sauces or fruit and serve at once.

ABOUT CARAMEL-COATED MOLDS

I. Sprinkle a mold with:
Sugar

Heat it in a slow—250° to 300°

—oven or over low heat until the sugar is brown and bubbling. This is a simple method to be used if only the top of the custard or pudding is to be caramelized when the mold is reversed.

II. Spread the mold with:
    Caramelized Sugar I,
    page 169
before the sirup hardens. If necessary, spread the caramel around with a wooden spoon to coat the sides. Then reverse the mold before filling, to let the caramel harden.

ABOUT BAVARIAN CREAMS

You can count on finding eggs as ingredients in a classic Bavarian. In an hors d'oeuvre, the term can mean a Hollandaise base for a fish purée. For desserts, the eggs are usually combined with gelatin and cream. ♦ If Bavarian puddings are to be unmolded, chill them 12 hours or more. If served in sherbet glasses, chill 4 hours. If very heavy in egg and cream content, they may be frozen for a few days. Bavarians are often called "Cold Soufflés."

CABINET PUDDING   [10]
OR BAVARIAN DE LUXE

Whose Cabinet? Cabinet de Diplomate. Where else could you find anything so rich and suave? The classic Cabinet Pudding is baked. We prefer this one, a variation developed by our friend Chef James Gregory.
Heat in a double boiler until lukewarm, about 85°:
    5 whole eggs
Beat at medium speed for 7 minutes; then beat in:
    ¼ cup sugar
until a mayonnaise consistency is reached. Beat in an additional:
    ¼ cup sugar
♦ but do not overbeat. The eggs

should stand in soft peaks. Dissolve over hot water:
    1½ tablespoons gelatin
    ¼ cup cold water
Fold the gelatin very gently into the egg mixture. Chill the mixture, while you beat over a bowl of ice until stiff:
    2 cups whipping cream
♦ Do not overbeat the cream. Let it still have a glistening finish when you combine it with the egg mixture. Dribble onto it:
    2 teaspoons vanilla or
    1 tablespoon kirsch or
        Grand Marnier
You may fold into it:
    ⅓ cup preserved ginger or
    ½ cup sliced candied
        kumquats
Chill this mixture until it is like heavy cream. Line a mold with:
    Ladyfingers, page 449
Build a pattern of rum or lemon sprinkled fruits and berries in layers with ladyfinger crumbs and the Bavarian mixture. Repeat these layers until the mold is complete, with ladyfingers on top. ♦ Refrigerate about 12 hours before unmolding.

CHOCOLATE OR COFFEE BAVARIAN

Add to any of the Bavarians calling for scalded milk, page 451:
    2 oz. melted sweet
        chocolate and/or
    2 teaspoons instant coffee

NESSELRODE PUDDING

Prepare:
    Cabinet Pudding,
    page 450
You may use the fruits or not, as you like. Fold into it, after putting through a ricer:
    2 cups slightly sweetened
        Chestnut Purée
        (I, 283)
    5 oz. crumbled Glazed
        Chestnuts, page 525

Serve it garnished with:
> Crème Chantilly, see
> page 377

BAVARIAN BERRY CREAM [8]

Crush:
> 1 quart hulled strawberries
> or raspberries

Add:
> 1 cup sugar

Permit them to stand ½ hour.
Soak:
> 2 teaspoons gelatin

in:
> 3 tablespoons water

Dissolve it in:
> 3 tablespoons boiling water

Stir this into the berries. You
may add:
> 1 tablespoon lemon juice

Cool the gelatin. When it is
about to set, fold in lightly:
> 2 cups whipped cream

Pour the cream into a wet mold.
◗ Chill for 12 hours if you plan
to unmold it. Serve with:
> Strawberry or Fruit
> Glaze, page 434

HAZELNUT BAVARIAN CREAM [8]

Soak:
> 1 tablespoon gelatin

in:
> 2 tablespoons cold water

Scald:
> ½ cup milk

Beat together:
> ¼ cup sugar
> 4 egg yolks
> ⅛ teaspoon salt

Combine the milk with the egg
mixture ◗ by pouring first a little
of the hot milk over the mixture
and adding the rest gradually.
Stir ◗ over—not in—hot water
until the ingredients begin to
thicken. Stir in the soaked gelatin until dissolved. Grind and
add:
> ¾ cup hazelnuts

Add:
> 1 teaspoon vanilla

Chill these ingredients until they
are about to set. Whip until
stiff:
> 2 cups whipping cream

Fold into the other ingredients.
Place the pudding in the dish
from which it is to be served—
or in a wet mold. Chill thoroughly, if you plan to unmold
it—12 hours or more. Serve
with:
> Raspberry juice

CARAMEL OR MAPLE [8] BAVARIAN CREAM

Soak:
> 1 tablespoon gelatin

in:
> ¼ cup water

Prepare:
> ¾ cup Caramelized Sugar I,
> see page 169, or ½ cup
> maple sirup

When the sugar is slightly
cooled, put it or the maple sirup
in the top of a double boiler
with:
> 1 cup hot milk
> ¼ cup sugar
> ¼ teaspoon salt

Stir over hot water until these
ingredients are dissolved. Pour
part of this over:
> 3 beaten egg yolks

Return the sweetened yolks to
the double boiler. Stir and cook
the mixture over hot water until
it coats a spoon heavily. Stir in
the soaked gelatin until it is dissolved. Cool the custard. Add:
> 1 teaspoon vanilla or
> 1 tablespoon rum

Fold in:
> 1 cup whipped cream

Place the Bavarian in a wet
mold. Chill at least 12 hours or
more before serving—if you plan
to unmold it.

EGGLESS BAVARIAN CREAM [8]

Not classic but pleasant, and
will lend itself to all the varia-

tions in the previous recipes.
Soak:

> 1 tablespoon gelatin

in:

> 2 tablespoons cold water

Scald:

> 1½ cups milk

If a richer pudding is preferred, use instead ½ cup milk and 1 cup whipped cream. Add:

> ⅓ to ½ cup sugar
> ¼ teaspoon salt

Stir the gelatin into this mixture until dissolved. Chill. As it thickens, flavor with:

> 1½ teaspoons vanilla
> (¼ teaspoon almond extract)

Whip it with a wire whisk until fluffy. Beat until stiff:

> 1 cup whipping cream

Fold into gelatin mixture. Place pudding in a wet mold. If desired, alternate the pudding mixture with:

> 6 broken macaroons or
>   ladyfingers soaked in rum
>   or dry sherry and
> ½ cup ground nut meats,
>   preferably almonds

◗ Chill the pudding, at least 12 hours or more if you plan to unmold it. Serve with:

> Whole or crushed berries
>   or stewed fruit and
>   whipped cream

RENNET PUDDING   [4]
OR JUNKET

This favorite English dish is made of milk, coagulated with extract from the lining of un-weaned calves' stomachs. It has a consistency much like that of a tender blancmange. Dioscorides said that rennet had the power to join things that were dispersed and to disperse things that come together. No chemist these days dares match such a claim!
Put into a bowl in which it will be served:

> 2 cups milk

warmed to exactly 98°. Add:

> 2 teaspoons sugar

Stir in:

> 2 teaspoons essence of
>   rennet or 1 teaspoon
>   prepared rennet
> (2 teaspoons brandy)

Let the pudding stand about 1½ hours until it coagulates. Sprinkle with:

> Cinnamon or nutmeg

Serve cold.

MOLDED PINEAPPLE   [4]
CREAM

Soak:

> 1 tablespoon gelatin

in:

> ¼ cup cold water

Combine and stir constantly over very low heat until slightly thickened:

> 2 egg yolks
> ½ cup sugar
> 2 cups unsweetened
>   pineapple juice
> ⅛ teaspoon salt

Add the soaked gelatin. Stir until dissolved. Pour half of this mixture into a wet mold. Chill it. Chill the remaining gelatin until it begins to set. Then fold into it:

> 1 cup whipped cream

Fill the mold. Chill until firm.

ABOUT GELATIN
PUDDINGS

These desserts vary greatly in texture. ◗ For details about handling gelatin, see About Gelatin, page 183. Easiest to prepare are the clear jellies, to which you may add fruit and nuts. If you add puréed fruits, you lose clarity at once and the dessert bears some similarity to a mousse. When gelatins are allowed to set partially and are then beaten or combined with egg whites, they are known as whips, sponges or snows. Whipped gelatins double in volume—snows and sponges, which include egg white, may triple.

Sometimes, a clear and a spongy gelatin are combined in layers in a single mold.

For very rich gelatin puddings, see Bavarians, page 450. For both Bavarians and clear fruit gelatins, you may line the mold with macaroons. Sprinkle them lightly with fruit juice, rum or cordial before adding the pudding or gelatin.

A word of caution: gelatin puddings with uncooked egg whites are often served to children or invalids over protracted periods of time. Since it has been discovered recently that biotin deficiency is occasionally induced by overproportionate quantities of raw egg white, we suggest varying such diets. Substitute instead some of the puddings we describe, in which the egg whites are cooked like meringues.

To get a snow or whip texture, begin as for clear gelatin. Chill to a sirupy consistency. ◗ Work in a cold bowl or over ice. ◗ If the gelatin is not sufficiently chilled before whipping or adding the egg white, it may revert to a clear jelly. Gelatins without cream or eggs ◗ must be refrigerated, but cannot be frozen. Bavarians, mousses and ice creams made in the refrigerator tray and placed in the freezing unit have a gelatin base as a stabilizer. The use of gelatin in these puddings prevents the formation of coarse crystals and produces a lovely smooth texture. ◗ Do not deep freeze this type of pudding longer than four or five days.

LEMON GELATIN   [4]

Soak:
    1 tablespoon gelatin
in:
    ¼ cup cold water
Dissolve it in:
    1½ cups boiling water

Add and stir until dissolved:
    ¾ cup sugar
    ¼ teaspoon salt
Add:
    ½ cup lemon juice
    (1 teaspoon grated lemon
    rind)
Pour the jelly into a wet mold. ◗ Chill for 4 hours or more. Serve with:
    Cream or Custard Sauce,
    see page 475

ORANGE GELATIN   [4]

Soak:
    1 tablespoon gelatin
in:
    ¼ cup cold water
Dissolve it in:
    ½ cup boiling water
Add and stir until dissolved:
    ½ cup sugar
    ¼ teaspoon salt
Add:
    6 tablespoons lemon juice
    1½ cups orange juice
    (1½ teaspoons grated orange
    rind)
Pour jelly into a wet mold. Chill 4 hours or more. Unmold and serve with:
    Cream or Custard Sauce,
    see page 475

FRUIT MOLDED INTO LEMON OR ORANGE GELATIN

Prepare:
    Lemon or Orange Gelatin
◗ Chill it until nearly set. It will fall in sheets from a spoon. Combine it with well-drained:
    Cooked or raw fruit
Add:
    (Nut meats)
    (Marshmallows cut into
    quarters)
◗ Do not use more than 2 cupfuls of solids in all. ◗ Fresh pineapple must be poached before it is added to any gelatin mixture. Pour jelly into a wet mold and ◗ chill for 4 hours or more before serving.

PINEAPPLE GELATIN   [8]

◗ Note that fresh pineapple must be poached before being added to any gelatin. Soak:

    2 tablespoons gelatin

in:

    1 cup cold water

Dissolve it in:

    1½ cups boiling pineapple
        juice

Add:

    1 cup boiling water

Add and stir until dissolved:

    ¾ cup sugar
    ⅛ teaspoon salt

◗ Chill the gelatin until it is about to set—it will fall in sheets from a spoon. Add:

    2½ cups canned, shredded,
        drained pineapple
    3 tablespoons lemon juice

Pour the jelly into a wet mold. ◗ Chill for 4 hours or more. Unmold and serve with:

    Cream or Custard Sauce,
    see page 475

FRUIT-JUICE GELATIN   [4]

Soak:

    1 tablespoon gelatin

in:

    ¼ cup cold water

Dissolve it in:

    ¾ cup boiling water

Add:

    1 cup sweetened fruit juice:
        prune, apricot, peach or
        cooked pineapple
    (2 tablespoons lemon juice)

and if not sweet enough, add:

    Sugar

When gelatin is ◗ about to set, it will fall in sheets from the spoon. Add:

    Drained diced fruit

Pour jelly into a wet mold and chill for 4 hours or more before serving.

QUICK FRUIT   [4]
GELATIN

Dissolve:

    1 package fruit flavored
        gelatin

in:

    1 cup boiling water

Chill rapidly by adding any but pineapple:

    1 can frozen fruit juice:
        6 oz.

Pour jelly into sherbet glasses. Chill further until firm.

WINE GELATIN   [8]

Soak:

    2 tablespoons gelatin

in:

    ¼ cup cold water

Dissolve it in:

    ¾ cup boiling water

The proportions of water, fruit juice and wine may be varied. If the wine is not strong, use less water to dissolve the gelatin and increase the amount of wine accordingly. This makes a soft jelly of a very good consistency, suitable for serving in sherbet glasses or from a bowl. If a stiff jelly is desired for molds, increase the gelatin to 3 tablespoons.

Stir in until dissolved:

    ½ cup or more sugar

It is difficult to give an accurate sugar measurement. One-half cup is sufficient if both the oranges and the wine are sweet. Taste the combined ingredients and stir in additional sugar if needed.

Cool these ingredients. Add:

    1¾ cups orange juice
    6 tablespoons lemon juice
    1 cup well-flavored wine

If this mixture is not a good color, add:

    A little red vegetable
        coloring

Pour the jelly into sherbet glasses. Chill until firm. Serve with:

    Cream, whipped cream
    or Custard Sauce,
    page 475

MOCHA GELATIN   [4]

The subtle flavor of this gelatin

comes from coffee combined with a sirup from canned fruit. Dress it up if you want with nuts or cream, but we like it served simply with a light custard sauce.
Soak:

1 tablespoon gelatin

in:

¼ cup cold water

Dissolve it in:

1 cup very hot
double-strength coffee

Add:

¾ cup canned fruit sirup
(¼ cup sugar)

You may use single or mixed flavors—peach, pear, apricot, pineapple, etc. If you use a mold, be sure to moisten it before filling. ◗ Chill 4 hours or more. Unmold and serve with:

Custard Sauce, page 475

BLANCMANGE   [8]

Blancmange, in America, is often a cornstarch pudding, see page 442, but the true French type is made with almond milk and gelatin.
To prepare almond milk, pound in a mortar:

½ lb. blanched almonds
(3 or 4 bitter almonds
blanched)

adding gradually:

¼ cup water
½ cup milk

Make an effort to extract as much flavor as possible from the almonds and then strain the liquid through a cloth. Soak:

1 tablespoon gelatin

in:

¼ cup water

Heat until scalded:

1 cup cream
½ cup sugar

Dissolve the gelatin in the hot cream mixture. Stir in the almond milk. Add:

1 tablespoon kirsch or
orgeat sirup

◗ Chill it for about 4 hours.

Serve the pudding in sherbet cups with:

Fresh or stewed fruit

PERSIAN CREAM   [6]

Soak:

1 tablespoon gelatin

in:

¼ cup cold milk

Scald:

1½ cups milk

Dissolve the gelatin in it. Beat:

2 egg yolks
⅓ cup sugar

Beat a little of the hot milk into the yolks, then return to saucepan. Cook and stir these ingredients over ◗ very low heat until they begin to thicken. Cool. Add:

1 teaspoon vanilla or rum

Whip until stiff but not dry:

2 egg whites

Fold them lightly into the gelatin mixture. Chill for 4 hours or more. Serve very cold with:

Crushed fruit or
fruit sauce

FRUIT WHIPS   [6 to 8]

◗ Please read About Gelatin Puddings, on page 452. Oranges, raspberries, peaches, strawberries, apricots, prunes, etc.—raw or cooked—may be used alone or in combination. ◗ If fresh pineapple is preferred, it must be poached before being added to any gelatin mixture.
Stir:

1 teaspoon grated lemon
rind

into:

⅞ cup sugar

Soak, according to the juiciness of the fruit:

2½ teaspoons to 1 tablespoon
gelatin

in:

¼ cup boiling water

Stir in the sugar until dissolved.
Add:

3 tablespoons lemon juice
1 cup crushed or riced fruit

If a single kind of fruit is used, add:

1 teaspoon vanilla

Place the pan holding these ingredients in ice water. When they are chilled ◗ to a sirupy consistency, whip them with an egg beater until frothy. Whip until stiff:

4 egg whites

Whip these ingredients into the gelatin mixture until the jelly holds its shape. Pour it into a wet mold. ◗ Chill 4 hours or more. Serve with:

Cream or Custard Sauce, see page 475

☘ BLENDER FRUIT WHIP   [4]

Cut into 16 pieces:

A 10 oz. package frozen fruit

Put into an electric blender:

1 tablespoon gelatin
2 tablespoons lemon juice
½ cup boiling water

Cover and blend for 40 seconds. Add:

2 unbeaten egg whites

Cover and blend 10 seconds. Continuing to blend, uncover the container and drop in, a few at a time, the pieces of still frozen fruit until they are all mixed in. Pour into a wet mold and chill 4 hours or more.

MARSHMALLOW PUDDING   [6 to 8]

Sift:

1 cup sugar

Soak:

1½ tablespoons gelatin

in:

½ cup cold water

Dissolve it in:

½ cup boiling water

Cool these ingredients. Whip until stiff:

4 egg whites

Add the gelatin to the egg whites in a slow stream. Whip the pudding constantly. Add the

sugar, ½ cupful at a time. Whip well after each addition. Whip in:

1 teaspoon vanilla

Continue to whip until the pudding thickens. ◗ Chill 4 hours or more. Serve with:

Custard Sauce, see page 475

Flavor the custard when it is cold with:

Cointreau

or serve the pudding with:

Crushed sweetened fruit

★ PINEAPPLE SNOW   [8]

A pretty Christmas pudding.
Soak:

1 tablespoon gelatin

in:

¼ cup cold water

Heat:

2 cups canned crushed pineapple

◗ If fresh pineapple is used, be sure it is poached before adding it to the gelatin mixture. Stir in:

1 cup sugar
⅛ teaspoon salt

When these ingredients are boiling, add the soaked gelatin. Remove pan from heat and stir in the gelatin until dissolved. ◗ Chill jelly until it is about to set. Whip until stiff:

2 cups whipping cream

Add:

½ teaspoon vanilla

Fold in the pineapple. Place pudding in a wet mold. Chill 4 hours or longer. Unmold and serve with:

(Maraschino cherries)

EGGLESS FRUIT WHIP   [2]

An easy dessert, if canned puréed baby fruits are used.
Soak:

1 teaspoon gelatin

in:

⅓ to ½ cup fruit juice

Dissolve over hot water. Add the contents of:

1 small jar puréed
apricots, prunes,
applesauce or peaches,
etc.
3 tablespoons sugar
½ teaspoon vanilla

♦ Chill these ingredients until they reach a sirupy consistency. Whip in a chilled bowl until the gelatin has doubled in bulk. Chill for at least 4 hours before serving with:

Cream

COFFEE [6]
MARSHMALLOW CREAM

Melt in the top of a double boiler, over boiling water:

1 lb. diced marshmallows

in:

1 cup double-strength
coffee

Stir and cook these ingredients until the marshmallows are dissolved. Chill the mixture until it is about to set. Fold in:

2 cups whipped ceram

Place the jelly in a wet ring mold. Chill at least 4 hours. Invert and cover the top of the cream with:

Slivered toasted Brazil
nuts or crushed nut
brittle

INDIAN PUDDING [8]

This dish is sometimes made with apples. In that case, add 2 cups thinly sliced apples and use, in all, 2 cups milk.
Preheat oven to 325°.
Boil in the top of a double boiler over direct heat:

4 cups milk

Stir in:

⅓ cup corn meal

Place these ingredients over boiling water. Cook them for about 15 minutes. Stir into them and cook for about 5 minutes:

¾ cup dark molasses

Remove from heat. Stir in:

¼ cup butter
1 teaspoon salt

1 teaspoon ginger
3 tablespoons sugar
(1 well-beaten egg)
(½ cup raisins)
(½ teaspoon cinnamon)

Pour the batter into a well-greased baking dish. To have a soft center, pour over the top:

(1 cup milk)

Bake the pudding from 1½ to 2 hours. Serve pudding hot with:

Hard Sauce, see page
480, or cream

It is a barbarous New England custom to serve it with:

Vanilla Ice Cream, see
page 487

FARINA PUDDING [6]

Try this for a finicky breakfaster. Boil:

2 cups milk
¼ cup sugar

Add:

½ cup farina

Stir and cook the farina over low heat until thick. Add and stir until melted:

1 tablespoon butter

Remove pan from heat. Beat in, one at a time:

2 egg yolks

Cool. Add:

1 teaspoon vanilla
(½ teaspoon grated lemon
rind)

Place on a platter and whip until stiff, but not dry:

(2 egg whites)

Fold into the farina mixture. If used as a dessert, serve the pudding cold with:

Cream, tart fruit juice,
stewed fruit, crushed
sweetened berries or Hot
Wine Sauce, page 476,
using claret.

MILK-RICE RINGS [6]

This dessert is frequently served in Europe, where rice puddings are highly appreciated. Steam covered in the top of a double boiler for about 1 hour:

¾ cup rice
3 cups milk
¾ teaspoon salt
When the rice is tender, cool slightly and add:
1½ tablespoons butter
2 teaspoons vanilla or 1 teaspoon vanilla and 1 teaspoon lemon rind, grated
2 teaspoons sugar
Pack the rice into buttered individual ring molds. Chill. Turn out onto plates. Fill the centers with:
Stewed or canned fruit, crushed sweetened berries or Jelly Sauce, page 475, using quinces
or serve with:
Caramel Sauce, see page 479, or with cinnamon and sugar

RICE PUDDING   [6 to 8]

Preheat oven to 325°.
Have ready:
2 cups cooked rice, see (I, 158)
Combine, beat well and add:
1⅓ cups milk
⅛ teaspoon salt
4 to 6 tablespoons sugar or ½ cup brown sugar
1 tablespoon soft butter
1 teaspoon vanilla
2 to 4 eggs
Add:
½ teaspoon grated lemon rind
1 teaspoon lemon juice
(⅓ cup raisins or dates)
Combine these ingredients lightly with a fork. Grease a baking dish. Cover the bottom and sides with:
(Cake or cookie crumbs)
Put rice in dish and cover top with more crumbs. Bake the pudding until set—about 50 minutes. Serve hot or cold with:
Cream, Fruit Sauce, see page 473, fruit juice or

Hot Wine Sauce, see page 476

RICE AND FRUIT   [5]
CREAM

Combine:
1 cup cooked rice
1 cup drained apricots, pineapple, etc.
Whip until stiff:
½ cup whipping cream
Fold in the rice mixture. Add:
12 diced marshmallows
Place the cream in individual dishes. Chill thoroughly. You may top it with:
Crushed nut brittle

RICE PUDDING   [10]
WITH WHIPPED CREAM

Boil, see (I, 158):
⅓ cup rice: about 1 cup cooked rice
Drain off any excess liquid. Soak for 5 minutes:
2 teaspoons gelatin
in:
¼ cup cold water
Dissolve over heat. Add to the rice. Stir in:
6 tablespoons sugar
(½ cup blanched, shredded almonds)
Chill. Whip until stiff:
2 cups whipping cream
Fold into the cream:
2 teaspoons vanilla
Fold the cream into rice. Place in a wet mold. Chill 4 hours or more. Unmold and serve very cold with:
Cold Currant Jelly Sauce, see page 475, or Hot Butterscotch Sauce, see page 478

QUICK TAPIOCA   [4]
CUSTARD

For a fluffy pudding, separate the eggs and add one stiffly

beaten white after the tapioca cools.

Combine and stir in a double boiler:

> 3 tablespoons
> quick-cooking tapioca
> ½ cup sugar
> ¼ teaspoon salt
> 1 or 2 beaten eggs
> 2 cups milk

Cook these ingredients without stirring ♦ over rapidly boiling water for 7 minutes. Stir and cook them 5 minutes longer. Remove from steam. The tapioca thickens as it cools. Fold in gradually:

> ½ teaspoon vanilla or 1
> teaspoon grated orange
> or lemon rind

Chill. Serve with:

> Cream, fresh berries,
> crushed or canned fruit
> or Chocolate Sauce,
> page 477

Additions may be made to this recipe. In that case, the eggs may be omitted. Suggestions:

> ¼ cup or more coconut or
> toasted almonds
> ½ cup or more chopped
> dates
> ½ crushed banana and
> ½ diced banana
> 1 cup sliced, drained,
> cooked apples
> ½ cup fruit, soaked in wine
> or liqueur

If the eggs are omitted, serve with:

> Custard Sauce, page 475

BUTTERSCOTCH [4]
TAPIOCA CUSTARD

Follow the preceding rule for:
> Quick Tapioca Custard

but omit the sugar. Melt:
> 2 tablespoons butter

Stir in until it melts and bubbles:
> ⅓ cup packed brown sugar

Add this mixture to the cooked tapioca.

CRUSHED-FRUIT [8]
TAPIOCA PUDDING

This may be made with pineapple, prunes, berries, etc. It is eggless.

Boil in the top of a double boiler over direct heat:
> 2 cups water

Combine and stir in gradually:
> ⅓ cup quick-cooking
> tapioca
> ½ cup sugar
> ¼ teaspoon salt

When these ingredients are boiling, place them ♦ over—not in —rapidly boiling water. Cook and stir them for about 5 minutes. Remove from heat. Cool slightly. Fold in:

> 2½ cups canned crushed
> pineapple or 2 cups
> cooked prune or apricot
> pulp or 2 cups crushed
> sweetened berries
> 2 tablespoons lemon juice

Chill. This may be served in sherbet glasses with:

> Whipped cream, plain
> cream or custard sauce

PEARL-TAPIOCA [8]
PUDDING

Soak overnight, refrigerated:
> 1 cup pearl tapioca

in:
> 1 cup milk

Add these ingredients to:
> 3 cups milk

and cook them for 3 hours in a double boiler ♦ over—not in— hot water. Cool.
Preheat oven to 325°.
Beat and add:

> 5 egg yolks
> Grated rind of 1 lemon
> Juice of ½ lemon
> ¾ cup sugar

Beat until stiff, but not dry:
> 5 egg whites

Line a baking dish with a layer of the tapioca mixture, a layer of the egg whites, another layer of tapioca and end with the egg whites on top. Bake for about

15 minutes. Serve hot or cold, with or without a sauce such as:

Hot Fruit Sauce, see page 473

BREAD PUDDING [6] WITH MERINGUE

Preheat oven to 350°.
Cut bread into slices and trim away crusts. It should be measured lightly, not packed.
Soak for 15 minutes:

3 to 5 cups diced fresh bread or 3½ cups stale bread, or stale cake

in:

3 cups warm milk or 2 cups milk and 1 cup fruit juice
¼ teaspoon salt

Combine and beat well:

3 egg yolks
⅓ to ½ cup sugar
1 teaspoon vanilla
(½ teaspoon nutmeg)

Add:

Grated rind and juice of ½ lemon
(¼ cup raisins, dates or nut meats or ½ cup crushed, drained pineapple, or ¼ cup orange marmalade)

Pour these ingredients over the soaked bread. Stir them lightly with a fork until well blended. If preferred, the meringue may be dispensed with and the stiffly beaten egg whites may be folded in at this time. Bake the pudding in a baking dish set in a pan of hot water for about ¾ hour. Cool pudding. Cover with:

Hard Sauce, page 480, Fruit Hard Sauce, page 481, or cream, fruit juice or dabs of tart jelly

BROWN BETTY [5]

Who would ever think that this simple old favorite could turn into a sophisticated tea dish?
Preheat oven to 350°.
Combine:

1 cup dry bread or graham cracker crumbs
¼ cup melted butter

Line the bottom of a baking dish with ⅓ of the crumb mixture. Prepare:

2½ cups peeled, diced or sliced apples or peaches, cherries or cranberries

Sift:

¾ cup packed brown sugar
1 teaspoon cinnamon
¼ teaspoon each nutmeg and cloves
½ teaspoon salt

Add:

1 teaspoon grated lemon rind
(1 teaspoon vanilla)

Place ½ of the apples in the dish. Cover the layer with ½ of the sugar mixture.
Sprinkle with:

1 tablespoon lemon juice

Add:

2 tablespoons water

Cover the apples with ⅓ of the crumb mixture and:

(¼ cup raisins or currants)

Add the remaining apples and sprinkle them as before with the sugar mixture and:

2 tablespoons lemon juice
2 tablespoons water
(¼ cup raisins or currants)

Place the last ⅓ of the crumb mixture on top. Cover the dish and bake for about 40 minutes, until the apples are nearly tender. Remove cover, increase heat to 400° and permit pudding to brown for about 15 minutes. Serve hot with:

Hard Sauce, see page 480, or cream or Lemon Sauce, see page 473

PRUNE OR APRICOT BETTY

Follow the preceding recipe for:

Brown Betty

Use only:

2 tablespoons sugar

Substitute for the apples:

1½ cups stewed, drained,
     sweetened prunes or
     apricots

Substitute for the lemon juice
and water:

¾ cup prune or apricot
    juice

BAKED PINEAPPLE [4] BETTY

This may be made in advance.
It is equally good served hot
or very cold.
Preheat oven to 325°.
Cream until light:

½ cup butter
¾ cup sugar

Beat in:

5 egg yolks
¼ cup dry bread crumbs
1 cup crushed, drained
   pineapple
1 tablespoon lemon juice

Whip until stiff, then fold in:

3 egg whites

Place the mixture in a baking
dish. Cover with a meringue,
see page 432, and bake it, set
in a pan of hot water, for about
30 minutes. Serve with:

Cream or whipped cream

★ BAKED FIG [14] PUDDING

Preheat oven to 325°.
Beat until soft:

½ cup butter

Add and beat until fluffy:

2 eggs
1 cup molasses

Add:

2 cups finely chopped figs
½ teaspoon granted lemon
   rind
1 cup buttermilk
(½ cup broken black walnut
    meats)

Sift before measuring:

2½ cups all-purpose flour

Resift with:

½ teaspoon soda
2 teaspoons baking powder
1 teaspoon salt
1 teaspoon cinnamon

½ teaspoon nutmeg

One teaspoon ginger may be
substituted for the cinnamon
and nutmeg. Stir the sifted ingredients into the pudding mixture. Bake in a greased 9-inch
tube pan for about 1 hour. Serve
hot with:

Brown Sugar Hard
Sauce, see page 481,
Sabayon Sauce, page
475, or Hot Wine
Sauce, see page 476

★ BAKED DATE RING [6] OR CHRISTMAS WREATH

You may bake this in a ring
mold. When cold, unmold it
onto a platter, cover it well with
whipped cream and stud it with
maraschino cherries. Surround
it with holly leaves. Although
very effective this way, it tastes
just as good baked in a shallow
pan, cut into squares and served
with Foamy Sauce.
Preheat oven to 350°.
Prepare:

1 cup pitted minced dates
1 cup chopped nut meats

Combine these ingredients with:

½ cup white or brown sugar
1 tablespoon flour
1 teaspoon baking powder
2 beaten egg yolks
1 teaspoon vanilla

Fold in:

2 stiffly beaten egg whites

Bake the pudding in a well-
greased 9-inch ring mold for
about ½ hour. You may sprinkle
over it, while hot, ¼ cup Madeira or sherry or 3 tablespoons
brandy or rum. Permit it to cool
in the pan.
Whip until stiff:

1 cup heavy cream

Fold in:

2 tablespoons powdered
   sugar
1 teaspoon vanilla

Garnish the ring as suggested
above.

★ BAKED PLUM   [10]
  PUDDING

Not for Jack Horner's legendary
thumb, but a rewarding con-
fection just the same.
Preheat oven to 375°.
Beat until soft:
    ½ cup butter
Add gradually:
    1 cup sugar
Blend these ingredients until
creamy. Beat in, one at a time:
    6 eggs
Combine:
    1 cup raisins, currants and
       pecans
Sprinkle lightly with:
    Flour
Add these ingredients to the
butter mixture. Combine:
    2 cups bread crumbs
    2 teaspoons cinnamon
    ½ teaspoon cloves
    ½ teaspoon allspice
Stir these ingredients into the
butter mixture. Bake in a
greased pan or baking dish for
about ½ hour. Serve with:
    Hard Sauce, see page
    480, Lemon Sauce, see
    page 473, or Hot Wine
    Sauce, see page 476

COTTAGE PUDDING   [6]

Preheat oven to 400°.
Follow the recipe for:
    One Egg Cake, see page
    364
For a new fillip, line a greased
8 x 8-inch pan with:
    1 cup heated marmalade
Pour the batter over the marmalade. Marmalade or none,
bake the pudding for about 25
minutes. Serve cut into squares
with:
    Crushed fruit, stewed
    fruit, Fluffy Orange
    Sauce, Raisin Sauce, see
    page 475, Coffee Sauce,
    see page 479, Wine Sauce,
    see page 476, or Hot
    Brown Sugar Sauce, see
    page 479

PANCAKE AND WAFFLE
DESSERTS

Serve:
       Pancakes or waffles
spread with:
       Thick cultured sour
       cream
       Strawberry or other
       preserves
or serve with:
       Crushed sweetened
       berries or fruit or with
       Sauce Cockaigne, see
       page 474

CHOCOLATE FEATHER   [8]
PUDDING

Perhaps this should be placed
among the steamed puddings,
but they are more troublesome
and this one might be neglected
in such surroundings. It is an
inexpensive and delightful dessert.
Preheat oven to 350°.
Sift:
    1 cup sugar
Beat until light:
    1 egg
Stir in sugar, gradually. When
these ingredients are well
blended, stir in:
    1 cup milk or coffee
    1 tablespoon melted butter
    1½ oz. melted chocolate
Sift:
    1½ cups all-purpose flour
Resift with:
    ¼ teaspoon salt
    1½ teaspoons double-acting
       baking powder
Stir these ingredients into the
egg mixture.
Add:
    ½ teaspoon vanilla
Place the batter in well-greased
deep custard cups—about ⅔
full. Cover with foil. Steam in
the oven, by setting cups in a
pan of hot water, for about ½
hour; or place pan over low heat
on top of stove for same length
of time. Remove foil and serve
pudding at once with:

Vanilla Sauce, see page
480, flavored with rum

SWEET-POTATO PUDDING [6]

Preheat oven to 350°.
Combine and beat well:
   2 cups cooked, mashed
     sweet potatoes
   1 cup sugar
   ½ cup melted butter
   6 beaten egg yolks
   1½ teaspoons grated lemon
     rind
   1 cup orange juice
   ¼ teaspoon nutmeg or
     2 tablespoons rum
Fold in:
   2 stiffly beaten egg whites
Bake pudding in a greased baking dish for about 1 hour. The top may be sprinkled before baking with:
   Sliced citron
   Broken nut meats
After the pudding is baked and cooled, it may also be topped with a Meringue, see page 432, made with the remaining egg whites. Bake in a 325° oven for about 15 minutes.

PERSIMMON PUDDING [8]

This can be made with the small native Diospyros virginiana or with the large Japanese Diospyrokaki. Use the greater amount of flour for the Japanese fruit, as it is very juicy. The native fruits give a waxy, but not tough, consistency to the pudding.
Preheat oven to 325°.
Put through a colander:
   Persimmons
There should be about 2 cups of pulp.
Beat in:
   3 eggs
   1¼ cups sugar
   1 to 1½ cups all-purpose
     flour
   1 teaspoon any baking
     powder

   1 teaspoon soda
   ½ teaspoon salt
   ½ cup melted butter
   2½ cups rich milk
   2 teaspoons cinnamon
   1 teaspoon ginger
   ½ teaspoon freshly grated
     nutmeg
One cupful raisins or nut meats may be added to the batter. Bake the pudding in a greased 9 x 9-inch baking dish until firm —about 1 hour. Serve with:
   Cream or Hard Sauce,
   page 480

ABOUT STEAMED PUDDINGS

To steam pudding mixtures in a steamer, use pudding molds or cans with tightly fitting lids —like baking powder tins. First, grease insides of molds well, then sprinkle with sugar. Containers should be ◗ only ⅔ full. Place molds on a trivet in a heavy kettle over 1 inch of boiling water. Cover kettle closely. Use high heat at first, then, as the steam begins to escape, low heat for rest of cooking.

◗ To steam pudding mixtures in a ⊙ pressure cooker, use tightly-lidded molds or cans as described above and ◗ fill only ⅔ full. Place them on a rack in the bottom of the cooker—allowing space both between the molds and the walls of cooker. Add boiling water ◗ until it is halfway up the sides of the molds.

If the steaming period in a regular steamer is supposed to be 30 minutes, steam with vent off for 5 minutes, then pressure cook at 15 pounds for 10 minutes. If steaming for 45 minutes to 1½ hours is called for, steam without closing the vent for 25 minutes, then pressure cook at 15 pounds pressure for 25 minutes. If steaming for 2 to 4 hours is called for, steam without closing the vent for 30 minutes, then pressure cook at 15 pounds pressure for 50 minutes. ◗ After steaming, reduce the heat at once. True steamed puddings need complete circulation of steam, so do not expect good results if you use a greased double boiler. Always ◗ before unmolding, take the lid from the mold and allow the pudding to rest long enough to let excess steam escape. The pudding will be less apt to crack in unmolding.

▲ In high altitudes, reduce the leavening by ½ the required amount.

STEAMED BROWN PUDDING [14]

Combine and blend well:
    1 cup packed light-brown sugar
    ½ cup shortening
Add:
    1 cup milk
    1 cup molasses
    1 cup dry bread crumbs
    2 beaten eggs
    2 cups chopped seeded raisins
Sift before measuring:
    2 cups all-purpose flour
Resift with:
    2 teaspoons double-acting baking powder
    ½ teaspoon soda
    1 teaspoon cinnamon
    ½ teaspoon each ginger, cloves and grated nutmeg
Add sifted ingredients to the molasses mixture. Pour batter into a well-greased pudding mold. Steam for 1½ hours. To steam or ✪ pressure cook and unmold, see About Steamed Puddings, page 463. Serve hot with:
    Hard Sauce, page 480, or Foamy Sauce, see page 481

★ STEAMED FRUIT [12] SUET PUDDING

Less cooking is needed here, as the thickener is bread crumbs. See About Steamed Puddings, page 463.
    1 cup beef suet: ½ lb.
Add gradually:
    1 cup sugar
When these ingredients are well blended, beat in:
    3 egg yolks
Stir in:
    1 cup milk
    3 tablespoons brandy
Put through a grinder and add:
    1 lb. figs or dates or 2 cups peeled sliced apples
    (1 cup chopped pecans or walnuts)
Grate and add:
    2 teaspoons orange rind
    1 teaspoon freshly ground nutmeg or ginger
Combine and add:
    1½ cups dry bread crumbs
    2 teaspoons any baking powder
Whip until stiff, then fold in:
    3 egg whites
Pour the ingredients into a greased mold. Steam slowly for 4 hours. To steam or ✪ pressure cook and unmold, see About Steamed Puddings, page 463. Serve with:
    Hot Sabayon Sauce, page 475, or Hot Wine Sauce, see page 476
Flavor the Sauce with:
    (2 teaspoons or more brandy)

★ STEAMED DATE [8] PUDDING

Not so rich as Steamed Fruit Suet Pudding, but equally good. Sift:
    1 cup brown sugar
Beat until soft:
    ¼ cup butter
Add the sugar gradually. Blend

these ingredients until they are creamy. Beat in:

> 1 egg
> ½ teaspoon vanilla

Sift before measuring:

> 1¼ cups all-purpose flour

Resift with:

> 2⅔ teaspoons double-acting baking powder
> ½ teaspoon salt

Add sifted ingredients to butter mixture in 3 parts, alternately with thirds of:

> 1 cup milk

Beat batter until smooth after each addition. Fold in:

> 1 cup chopped dates
> 1 cup broken nut meats

Pour into a greased pudding mold. Cover closely. Steam for 2 hours. To steam or ✿ pressure cook and unmold, see About Steamed Puddings, page 463. Serve hot with:

> Foamy Sauce, page 481, or Fluffy Hard Sauce, page 481

STEAMED [6]
CHOCOLATE PUDDING

This is richer than Chocolate Feather Pudding, which may also be steamed in a mold. Beat until light:

> 6 egg yolks

Beat in gradually:

> 1 cup sugar

Stir in:

> ¾ cup grated chocolate
> 2 tablespoons finely crushed crackers or toasted bread crumbs
> 1 teaspoon any baking powder
> 1 teaspoon vanilla
> ½ teaspoon cinnamon
> (½ cup grated nut meats)

Beat until stiff but not dry:

> 6 egg whites

Fold them lightly into the batter. Pour into a greased pudding mold. Steam for 1½ hours. To steam or ✿ pressure cook and

unmold, see About Steamed Puddings, page 463. Serve with:

> Hard Sauce or cream

STEAMED CARAMEL [6]
PUDDING

Try this as a company pudding. Melt in a heavy skillet:

> ⅓ cup sugar

When it is light brown stir in ◗ very slowly:

> ¾ cup hot milk.

Cool this sirup. Beat until soft:

> 2 tablespoons butter

Beat in one at a time:

> 5 egg yolks

Add the sirup and:

> 1 teaspoon vanilla
> 1½ tablespoons all-purpose flour
> 1 cup ground, unblanched almonds

Beat batter until smooth. Place on a platter and whip ◗ until stiff, but not dry:

> 5 egg whites

Fold them lightly into the batter. Pour into a greased pudding mold sprinkled with:

> Sugar

Cover closely. Steam for 1 hour. To steam or ✿ pressure cook and unmold, see About Steamed Puddings, page 463. Serve hot with:

> Whipped cream or Sauce Cockaigne, see page 474

STEAMED APPLE [6]
MOLASSES PUDDING

Cream until fluffy:

> ¼ cup butter
> ½ cup packed brown sugar

Beat in:

> 1 egg
> ½ cup molasses
> 1 tablespoon grated orange rind

Measure:

> 1½ cups sifted all-purpose flour

Resift with:

> ½ teaspoon soda

1 teaspoon double-acting
baking powder

1 teaspoon each ginger,
cinnamon

Add these ingredients to the
butter mixture, alternately with:

½ cup buttermilk

Stir in:

1 cup chopped apples

Place the pudding in a greased
mold. Steam it for 1½ hours.
To steam or ✪ pressure cook
and unmold, see About Steamed
Puddings, page 463. Serve with:

> Lemon Sauce, see page
> 473, or Hard Sauce, see
> page 480

★ STEAMED PLUM   [24] PUDDING

A truly festive Christmas dish
that needs patience in the making. ♦ The slow six-hour cooking is necessary, so that all the
suet melts before the flour particles burst. If the pudding cooks
too fast and the flour grains
burst before the fat melts, the
pudding will be close and hard.
Sift:

1 cup all-purpose flour

Prepare and dredge lightly with
part of the flour:

1 lb. chopped suet: 2 cups
1 lb. seeded raisins
1 lb. washed dried currants
½ lb. chopped citron

Resift the remaining flour with:

1 grated nutmeg
1 tablespoon cinnamon
½ tablespoon mace
1 teaspoon salt
6 tablespoons sugar or
½ cup brown sugar

Combine the dredged and the
sifted ingredients.
Add:

7 egg yolks
¼ cup cream
½ cup brandy or sherry
3 cups grated bread
crumbs, white or rye

The latter helps make the pud-

ding light. Place on a platter
and whip until stiff:

7 egg whites

Fold them lightly into the
raisin mixture. Pour the batter
into a greased, covered gallon
mold and steam for 6 hours. To
steam or ✪ pressure cook and
unmold, see About Steamed
Puddings, page 463. Serve with:

> Hot Sweet Wine Sauce or
> Hard Sauce, page 480

UNCOOKED DATE   [12] LOAF

Crush:

½ lb. graham crackers

Remove pits and cut into pieces:

1 lb. dates: 2 cups

Cut into pieces:

½ lb. marshmallows

Chop fine:

1 cup pecan meats

Whip until stiff:

1 cup whipping cream

Fold in:

1 teaspoon vanilla

Combine ½ the cracker crumbs
with the dates, marshmallows,
nuts and whipped cream. Shape
into a roll. Roll it in the remaining cracker crumbs. Chill
for 12 hours. Serve, cut into
slices, with:

> Cream or whipped cream

ABOUT DOUGHNUTS

For tender doughnuts ♦ have all
ingredients at about 75°, so the
dough can be mixed quickly.
This prevents the development
of gluten in the flour, which
would tend to toughen the batter. Keep the mix just firm
enough to be easy to handle.
Chill the dough slightly to shape
it, before cutting, so that the
board won't have to be too
heavily floured. Roll or pat the
dough to about a ½-inch thickness. ♦ Cut with a well-floured
double cutter, or 2 sizes of biscuit cutters. ♦ If you allow the
dough to dry 10 or 12 minutes

on a very lightly floured board or absorbent paper, you will find that the doughnuts will absorb less fat while frying. The richer and sweeter the dough, the more fat they absorb. ♦ To cook doughnuts, please read About Deep Fat Frying (I, 75–79). Bring the fat to 375° unless otherwise stated. Then, one at a time ♦ slide the doughnuts into the fat at the side of the kettle. They will keep their shapes well if you transfer them to the fat with a pancake turner which has already been dipped into the kettle.

Each doughnut takes about 3 minutes to cook. ♦ Never crowd the frying kettle. You can develop a machine-like precision by adding one doughnut at a time to the kettle, at about 15-second intervals for the first six doughnuts. Turn each as soon as brown on one side. It will usually rise at this point. When done, remove with a fork or tongs and place on absorbent paper to drain. Replace it immediately with an uncooked one to keep the fat at an even temperature. When the doughnuts cool, dust them with powdered, spiced or flavored sugar. For an easy method, use a paper bag. Or glaze them with Milk or Lemon Glaze, see page 434.

▲ Yeast-based doughnuts require no adjustment for high altitudes. For quick leavened doughnuts, reduce the baking powder or soda by ¼. ♦ But do not reduce soda beyond ½ teaspoon for each cup of sour milk or cream used.

SWEET MILK DOUGHNUTS

[About 36 Doughnuts]
♦ Please read About Doughnuts, page 466.
Preheat deep fryer to 370°.
Bat:
   2 eggs

Add slowly, beating constantly:
   1 cup sugar
Stir in:
   1 cup milk
   4 to 5 tablespoons melted shortening
Sift before measuring:
   4 cups all-purpose flour
Resift with:
   4 teaspoons double-acting baking powder
   ¼ teaspoon cinnamon or 1 teaspoon grated lemon rind
   ½ teaspoon salt
   (¼ teaspoon nutmeg)
Mix moist and dry ingredients. To fry, see About Deep Fat Frying (I, 75–79).

SOUR CREAM DOUGHNUTS

[About 36 Doughnuts]
♦ Please read About Doughnuts, page 466.
Preheat deep fryer to 370°.
Beat well:
   3 eggs
Add slowly, beating constantly:
   1¼ cups sugar
Stir in:
   1 cup cultured sour cream
Sift before measuring:
   4 cups all-purpose flour
Resift with:
   1 teaspoon soda
   2 teaspoons double-acting baking powder
   ¼ teaspoon cinnamon or ½ teaspoon nutmeg
   ½ teaspoon salt
Stir the sifted ingredients and the egg mixture until they are blended. To fry, see About Deep Fat Frying (I, 75–79).

YEAST POTATO DOUGHNUTS

[About 48 Doughnuts]
Preheat deep fat fryer to 375°.
Prepare:
   Buttermilk Potato Roll, page 257
When ready to shape, pat into ½-inch thickness. Cut into rings

or into strips ½ x 3½ inches.
Twist the strips gently. You
may bring the ends togther to
form twisted wreaths. Allow the
twists to rise ♦ uncovered for
about 30 minutes. Meanwhile,
please read ♦ About Deep Fat
Frying (I, 75–79). To cook,
see About Doughnuts, page 466.

QUICK POTATO DOUGHNUTS

[About 36 Doughnuts]
Preheat deep fat fryer to 370°.
♦ Please read About Doughnuts,
page 466.
Prepare:
    1 cup freshly riced potatoes
Beat well:
    2 eggs
Add very slowly, beating con-
stantly:
    ⅔ cup sugar
Stir in the potatoes and:
    1 cup buttermilk
    2 tablespoons melted
        butter
Sift before measuring:
    4 cups all-purpose flour
Resift with:
    2 teaspoons double-acting
        baking powder
    1 teaspoon baking soda
    ⅔ teaspoon salt
    ¼ teaspoon nutmeg or ¼
        teaspoon cinnamon
Stir in the sifted ingredients and
the potato mixture until they are
blended. Add enough of the
sifted flour to form a soft dough.
Chill the dough until it is
easy to handle. ♦ To fry, see
About Deep Fat Frying (I, 75–
79).

DOUGHNUTS VARIATIONS

I. Molasses Doughnuts
Prepare Sour Cream Doughnuts,
page 467.
Replace ¼ cup sugar with:
    ½ cup molasses
Add
    1½ teaspoons ginger

II. Berlin or Jelly Doughnuts
Prepare Yeast Potato Doughnuts, page 705. Cut the dough
into 2½-inch rounds instead of
rings. Place on one round:
    1 heaping teaspoon jelly or
        preserves
Brush the edges of the round
with:
    Egg white
Cap it with another round. Press
the edges together. Repeat the
process. After allowing the
doughnuts to rise, fry them as
directed in About Doughnuts,
see page 466.

III. Orange Doughnuts
Prepare any of the recipes for
Doughnuts.
Substitute:
    The grated rind of 1
        orange and ¼ cup
        orange juice
for ¼ cup of the milk

IV. Chocolate Doughnuts
Prepare any one of the recipes
for Doughnuts, adding 5 table-
spoons flour.
Melt:
    1½ oz. chocolate
Add it to the melted shortening.
Stir in:
    1½ teaspoons vanilla

V. Pecan or Date Doughnuts
Prepare any recipe for Doughnuts. Add:
    ½ cup broken nut meats or
    ½ cup pitted diced dates

VI. Drop Doughnuts
While devoid of the characteristic hole, these are lighter in
texture.
Prepare any recipe for doughnuts, using ¼ to ½ cup less
flour. Slide a tablespoon of
dough at a time into the hot
fat.

ABOUT CRULLERS AND BEIGNETS

To be good, these must be delicate in flavor, therefore the frying fat must be impeccable. If you fry in a usual bland cooking oil, heat it between 365° to 370° and cook the batter until almost golden. If you use butter, start frying with the fat at 330° and let the heat rise, over about a 7 minute period to 360°. ◗ Be sure to bring the heat of the fat down to 330° again between cookings. Drain on absorbent paper. Beignets may be served hot with a sauce or cold, either dusted with:

> Powder sugar

or frosted with:

> Milk or Lemon Glaze, see
> page 434

Very similar to beignets are Rosettes, see (I, 209), and some fritters, page 125.

BEIGNETS OR   [4 to 6]
FRENCH FRITTERS

I.
These are as light as air.
Heat deep fat to 370°.
Combine in a saucepan and boil and stir over low heat for about 5 minutes:

> 6 tablespoons water
> 1 tablespoon butter
> 6 tablespoons all-purpose
> flour

Remove the pan from the heat. Beat in one at a time:

> 4 eggs

Beat the batter for about 3 minutes after each addition. Add:

> 1 teaspoon vanilla

Drop the batter from a teaspoon into deep hot fat. Cook until golden. Drain. Dust with:

> Confectioners' sugar

Serve at once with:

> Lemon Sauce, see page
> 473

Or fill with:

> Gooseberry Conserve

II. Heat deep fat to 370°.
Prepare dough for:

> Cream Puff Shells, see
> page 305

Add:

> (½ teaspoon grated lemon or
> orange rind)

but instead of baking, drop in deep fat, a teaspoon of dough at a time. As soon as they are cooked enough on one side, they will automatically turn themselves over. Remove when brown on both sides. Drain and sprinkle with:

> Powdered sugar

Serve with:

> Vanilla or Apricot Sauce,
> see page 480

CRULLERS

This recipe makes a lot—hard to gauge the exact amount!
◗ Please read About Crullers, page 468. Heat deep fat to 370°.
Sift:

> ⅔ cup sugar

Beat until light:

> 4 eggs

Add the sugar gradually, blending until the mixture is creamy. Add:

> ¾ teaspoon grated lemon
> rind
> ⅓ cup melted shortening
> ⅓ cup milk

Sift before measuring:

> 3½ cup all-purpose flour

Resift with:

> ½ teaspoon cream of tartar
> ½ teaspoon soda
> ¼ teaspoon salt

Stir the sifted ingredients into the egg mixture. Roll the dough to the thickness of ¼ inch. Cut it into strips of about ½ to 2½ inches with a pie jagger. To make a fancier shape, twist the strips slightly into several convolutions. To cook, read About Deep Fat Frying (I, 75–79).

RICE CRULLERS [4 to 5]
OR CALAS

Prepare:

    1 cup cooked rice

Mix and add to it:

    3 beaten eggs
    ½ cup sugar
    ½ teaspoon vanilla
    ½ teaspoon nutmeg or
      grated lemon rind
    2¼ teaspoons double-acting
      baking powder
    6 tablespoons all-purpose
      flour

◗ Please read About Deep Fat Frying (I, 75–79), and bring the fat to 365°. Drop the batter into the fat from a teaspoon. Fry the calas until they are golden brown—about 7 minutes. Drain on absorbent paper. Sprinkle with:

    Confectioners' sugar

Serve with:

    Tart jelly

RAISED CALAS

These are the famous breakfast delicacies which are hawked on the New Orleans streets in the early morning.

Mash:

    ¾ cup cooked rice

Dissolve in:

    ½ cup water at 85°
    ½ cake compressed yeast

Mix these ingredients together and let stand covered overnight. In the morning, add:

    3 well-beaten eggs
    ⅓ cup sugar
    ½ teaspoon salt
    ¼ cup all-purpose flour
    ¼ teaspoon nutmeg

Let the mixture rise covered for about 15 minutes. Preheat deep fryer to 365°. Drop the batter into the fat from a teaspoon. Fry until golden brown, about 10 minutes, and drain on absorbent paper. Serve the calas hot, dusted with:

    Powdered sugar

ABOUT DESSERT CHEESES

Although in some climates certain types of cheese are cellared for years, like wines, the American housewife, with no comparable storage facilities, is hard put to it to keep cheeses "à point." Cheeses are constantly changing, do not freeze well, refrigerate only on a short-term basis, and if served properly, almost have to be brought to their peak of ripeness in small lots and used at once. There are several cheese-keepers which have platforms elevated above a vinegar base, and a cloche cover. Another device for short-term preservation is to wrap cheeses in cloths which have been wrung out in vinegar. Sometimes storing cheese in covered glass or enameled containers helps. Other expedients include refrigeration and the separate wrapping of each variety of cheese. The most drastic methods—at which true turophiles wince—are to buy canned cheese, or to pot natural cheese in crocks, with a sufficient addition of wine, brandy or kirsch to arrest enzymatic action. If you are interested generally in cheese types, methods of ripening and how to use cheeses in cooking, please read About Cheese, page 175.

Dessert cheeses may be served after the roast, with the same red wine that has accompanied that course, or after the salad. They may also be served following the sweet or with a suitable dessert fruit such as apples, pears, grapes, cherries, plums or melons. Cheeses should always be served at a temperature of about 70°. Some types which are best when "coulant" or runny, should be removed from refrigeration 3 to 6 hours before serving.

Usually some pats of sweet butter are added to the cheeseboard. Toast, crackers, pumpernickel, crusty French bread, page 245, or Sour Rye, page 250, follow the cheese on a separate tray. Salted, toasted or freshly shelled nuts, roasted chestnuts, celery or fennel make pleasant accessories. Try mixing mild cheese with the more highly ripened, aromatic or smoked ones.

Above all, remember that cheeses have their own seasons. And choose varieties that are in season. Below are listed some favorite dessert cheeses.

Soft types include uncrusted, unripened cheeses like Petit Gervais and Petit Suisse, Ricotta and Coulommiers; as well as those which are ripened and have soft edible crusts, such as Brie, Camembert, Liederkranz and Poona.

Among the semihards are the famous "fromages persillés," or mold-ripened blue-greens, in which the mold patterns the cream-colored bases in traceries resembling parsley. The interior mold, which contribute to the characteristic flavor, must be distinguished from green mold on the exterior of the cheese, which may be harmless but should be removed.

The famous blues include Stilton, Gorgonzola, Bleu, Dorset Vinney and Roquefort. Other well-known semihard dessert cheeses are Muenster, Port du Salut, Bel Paese and Gammelost.

Hard types, from which come the very best cheese for cooking, afford many choice ones for dessert: cheddar, Gruyère, Provolone, Gjetost, Emmentaler, Cheshire and Edam, to name a few.

DESSERT CHEESE MIX

Many people like to mix sweet butter with the stronger cheeses in serving them for dessert. The combinations are legion. This one is a favorite of our friend, Helmut Ripperger, who likes to prepare it at the table. However, sometimes these mixtures are made in advance, formed into a large ball, and rolled in toasted bread crumbs.

‣ Have ingredients at room temperature.
Mix:
    2 parts Roquefort cheese
    1 part sweet butter
Add enough:
    Armagnac or your
    favorite brandy
to make a soft spreadable paste.
Serve with:
    Toasted crackers

POTTED CHEESE

[About ¾ Cup]
If you would like to make up a combination of cheeses to keep, try one based on a mixture of:
    4 oz. cheese
    2 oz. butter
    3 tablespoons port, sherry
    or brandy
Correct the seasoning with:
    Pepper or cayenne
    (Mace)

COEUR À LA CRÈME [6] OR FRENCH CHEESE CREAM

When the fruit is prime, this very simple dessert is as good as any elaborate concoction we know or use.
Beat until soft:
    1 lb. rich firm cream cheese
    2 tablespoons cream
    ⅛ teaspoon salt

Have ready:
     1 cup cultured sour cream
        or 1 cup whipped cream
Fold the cheese into the cream.
Place these ingredients in a wet
mold, in individual molds or in
the traditional heart-shaped
wicker basket, lined with moistened cheesecloth. Chill the
cheese thoroughly. Unmold it.
Serve with:
     Fresh unhulled straw-
     berries, raspberries or
     other fresh fruit, or
     Cherry Sauce, see page
     473

YOGURT, COTTAGE OR CREAM CHEESE DESSERT

Sweeten:
     Yogurt, cottage or cream
     cheese
with:
     Sugar
     Vanilla
Sprinkle the top with:
     Cinnamon
Serve the mixture very cold
with:
     Stewed cherries, crushed
     strawberries, apricots or
     peaches

BAR-LE-DUC

[About 1 Cup]
A pleasant summer dish. Serve
it with toasted crackers.
Stir to a smooth paste:
     ¾ cup firm cream cheese
     1 or 2 tablespoons cream
Fold in:
     2 tablespoons Bar-le-Duc
        Preserves, page 576
Refrigerate to firm the dessert,
but serve at about 70°.

LIPTAUER CHEESE

[About 2 Cups]
If you can't buy the real thing,
try this savory cheese made by
mixing together, until well
blended:
     ½ lb. dry cottage cheese
     ½ lb. soft butter
     ½ teaspoon paprika
     ½ teaspoon caraway seed
      1 teaspoon chopped capers
     ½ teaspoon anchovy paste
     ½ teaspoon mild prepared
        mustard
      1 teaspoon chopped chives
Serve within 6 hours of mixing,
as the taste of the chives may
grow strong.

ABOUT SAVORIES

Traditionally English, savories
are a course presented before the
fruit or after the sweet to cut
the sugar taste before the port
is served. They function like an
hors d'oeuvre—see page 66—although they are slightly larger
in size. See Oysters or Chicken
Livers in Bacon; also Sardine,
Caviar and Roe Croûtes or Pancakes, Tomato Tart, Deviled or
Curried Seafish Tarts or Toasted
Cheese Balls. If you are serving wine, choose cheese straws
or cheese-and-cracker combinations rather than the fishy
savories.

To most Americans savories
seem curious desserts. Of course,
ours must also seem strange to
the English—for, to them, the
word "dessert" signifies fruit.
Their term for our cold desserts
is "sweets," and they call our
hot ones "puddings."

DESSERT SAUCES

With pudding sauces, "the object all sublime" is to "let the punishment fit the crime." In fact, unless the sauce can complement the dessert, omit it. Should the pudding be tart, tone it down with a bland sauce; if it is bland, use a sauce to which a tablespoon of liqueur imparts the final sprightly touch. Sauces based on sugar are usually very simple to confect. They have distinct branches similar to those of their unsweetened counterparts. The main things to remember are ◗ don't overbeat cream bases or cream garnishes ◗ do cook egg sauces over—not in—hot water. ◗ Be sure that sauces thickened with flour and cornstarch are free from lumps and cook them thoroughly to avoid any raw taste. See Flour Paste (I, 356), and Cornstarch (I, 356). ◗ In preparing heavy sirups, do not let them turn to sugar, see page 499.

LEMON, ORANGE OR LIME SAUCE

[About 1 Cup]
A lovely, translucent sauce.
Combine and stir in a double boiler ◗ over—not in—hot water until thickened:
    ¼ to ½ cup sugar
    1 tablespoon cornstarch
    1 cup water
Remove sauce from heat. Stir in:
    2 to 3 tablespoons butter
    ½ teaspoon grated lemon or
        orange rind
    1½ tablespoons lemon or
        lime juice or

    3 tablespoons orange juice
    ⅛ teaspoon salt

FRUIT SAUCE

[About 1½ Cups]
Combine, stir and heat to the boiling point, in the top of a double boiler:
    1 cup unsweetened fruit
        juice
    ½ to ¾ cup sugar
Mix, add and cook ◗ over—not in—hot water, until thick and clear:
    1 tablespoon cornstarch or
    2 tablespoons flour
Remove sauce from heat. Stir in:
    2 teaspoons lemon juice
    (2 tablespoons butter)
Cool. You may add:
    (1 cup crushed, shredded
        fruit, fresh or stewed)
Flavor with:
    Sherry or other wine or
        liqueur
Serve hot or cold.

CHERRY SAUCE

[About 2½ Cups]
Drain well:
    2 cups canned cherries,
        red or Bing
Add to the cherry sirup and simmer for about 10 minutes in the top of a double boiler over direct heat:
    ¼ cup sugar
    ¼ cup corn sirup
    1 stick cinnamon: 2 inches
    1 tablespoon lemon juice
Remove the cinnamon. Mix:
    2 teaspoons cornstarch
    1 tablespoon cold water
Stir this mixture into the hot cherry juice. Cook ◗ over—not

in—hot water and stir until it thickens. Add the cherries. Serve hot or cold.

CHERRY JUBILEE SAUCE

[About 1¼ Cups]
This sauce always involves the use of liqueurs. If you do not wish to ignite the brandy, you may soak the cherries in it, well ahead of time. Otherwise, be sure that the fruit is at room temperature. Other preserved fruits may be substituted for the cherries.
Heat well:

>   1 cup preserved, pitted
>   Bing or other cherries

Add:

>   ½ cup slightly warmed
>   brandy

Set the brandy on fire. When the flame has died down, add:

>   2 tablespoons kirsch

You may serve the sauce hot, on:

>   Vanilla ice cream

MELBA SAUCE

[About 1¾ Cups]
Combine and bring to the boiling point in the top of a double boiler over direct heat:

>   ½ cup currant jelly
>   1 cup sieved raspberries

Mix and add:

>   1 teaspoon cornstarch
>   ⅛ teaspoon salt
>   ½ cup sugar

Cook ♦ over—not in—hot water, until thick and clear. Chill before using.

⚘ QUICK AMBROSIA SAUCE

[About 1¾ Cups]
Mix:

>   ¾ cup puréed apricots
>   ¾ cup puréed peaches

Add:

>   ¼ cup orange juice
>   1 teaspoon grated lemon
>   rind

>   2 tablespoons rum or
>   sloe gin

SAUCE COCKAIGNE

[About 8 Cups]
Good with custards, glazed bananas, cottage pudding and waffles, by itself or combined with whipped cream. One of its distinct advantages is the availability of its ingredients at any and all seasons.
Cook gently, in a wide-bottomed, covered pan, until the fruit is pulpy and disintegrates easily when stirred with a wire whisk:

>   2 cups dried apricots
>   1¼ cups water

Add:

>   1½ cups sugar

Stir until dissolved. Add:

>   5 cups canned crushed
>   pineapple

Bring the mixture to a boil. Pour into jars and cover. Keep under refrigeration.

RAISIN SAUCE

[About 1⅔ Cups]
Boil for 15 minutes:

>   1½ cups water
>   ⅓ cup seeded raisins
>   ¼ cup sugar
>   ⅛ teaspoon salt

Melt:

>   2 tablespoons butter

Stir in, until blended:

>   1 teaspoon flour

Add the hot sauce slowly. Stir and cook until it boils. Mix in:

>   A grating of nutmeg or
>   lemon rind

Serve over:

>   Steamed puddings, page
>   463

JELLY SAUCE

[About ¾ Cup]
Expressly for steamed and cornstarch puddings.
Dilute over hot water in double boiler:

¾ cup currant or other jelly
Thin with:
    ¼ cup boiling water or wine
Serve hot or cold. This sauce may be thickened. To do this, melt:
        1 tablespoon butter
Blend in:
        1 tablespoon flour
Add the jelly mixture. Stir over low heat until it thickens. You may spice it with:
        1 teaspoon cinnamon
        ⅛ teaspoon ground cloves
        ⅛ teaspoon grated lemon rind

JAM SAUCE

[About ¾ Cup]
Combine in a small saucepan:
        ¼ cup raspberry, damson, gooseberry, grape or peach jam
        (2 tablespoons sugar)
        ½ cup water
Stir and boil these ingredients for 2 minutes. Remove from heat and add:
        1 teaspoon kirsch or
        ¼ teaspoon almond extract
Serve hot or cold. Use on:
        Bread, farina and other cereal puddings, page 457

CUSTARD SAUCE

Prepare:
        Custard, page 436
You may add:
        (½ cup slivered almonds)

QUICK FRUIT CUSTARD SAUCE

[About 3 Cups]
Cream:
        ¼ cup butter
Add gradually and beat until fluffy:
        1 cup sugar
Beat in, one at a time:
        2 eggs
        (One or two extra eggs will add richness)

Beat in slowly and thoroughly:
        1 cup scalded milk
        1 teaspoon vanilla
        1 teaspoon nutmeg
Fold in:
        (1 cup crushed berries, sliced peaches, etc.)

CLASSIC SABAYON SAUCE

[About 3 Cups]
Prepare:
        Zabaglione or Sabayon, page 439
You may omit the egg white if you prefer a richer and denser texture. If you do, use in all:
        1 cup wine

HOT SABAYON SAUCE

[About 2 Cups]
Excellent with beignets and fruit cake. Marsala is traditional in Italian recipes. We find that it gives the sauce a rather dull color and prefer to use, instead, a sweet white wine—after the French fashion. This mixture should be creamy rather than fluffy. For a fluffy sauce, see the following recipe.
Stir constantly until thick in the top of a double boiler ♦ over—not in—hot water:
        6 egg yolks
        ⅓ cup sugar
        1 cup white wine or ½ cup water and ½ cup Cointreau or Grand Marnier

COLD SABAYON SAUCE

[About 1¼ Cups]
The advantage of this sauce over the classic version is that it will keep under refrigeration. Use it over fresh fruits. Combine, beat and heat in the top of a double boiler ♦ over—not in—hot water:
        4 egg yolks
        ¾ cup sugar
        ¾ cup dry sherry or other dry wine

Beat with a whisk until very thick. Set the double boiler top in a pan of cracked ice and continue to beat the sauce until cold. Add:

    (¼ cup lightly whipped
    cream)

WEINSCHAUM SAUCE

Prepare:
        Wine Custard or
        Weinschaum, page 440

RUM SAUCE

[About 2½ Cups]
Beat:
        2 egg yolks
Add and beat until dissolved:
        1 cup sifted confectioners'
        sugar
Add slowly:
        6 tablespoons rum
Beat these ingredients until well blended.
Whip until stiff:
        1 cup whipping cream
Fold in:
        1 teaspoon vanilla
Fold the egg mixture into the cream.

RED WINE SAUCE

[About 2 Cups]
Boil for 5 minutes:
        1 cup sugar
        ½ cup water
Cool and add to the sirup:
        ¼ cup claret or other red
        wine
        ½ teaspoon grated lemon
        rind

HOT WINE OR
PLUM PUDDING SAUCE

[About 1½ Cups]
Cream:
        ½ cup butter
        1 cup sugar
Beat and add:
        1 or 2 eggs
Stir in:
        ¾ cup dry sherry, Tokay
        or Madeira

        1 teaspoon grated lemon
        rind
        (¼ teaspoon nutmeg)
Shortly before serving, beat the sauce over hot water in a double boiler. Heat thoroughly.

CRÈME-DE-MENTHE
OR LIQUEUR SAUCE

Allow, for each serving, about:
        1½ tablespoons crème de
        menthe or other liqueur
Pour it over:
        Ice cream, ices or lightly
        sugared fruits
Garnish with:
        A few maraschino
        cherries

NESSELRODE SAUCE

[About 4 cups]
Combine and stir well:
        ¾ cup chopped maraschino
        cherries
        ⅓ cup chopped citron or
        orange peel
Add:
        1 cup orange marmalade
        ½ cup coarsely chopped,
        candied ginger
        2 tablespoons maraschino
        juice
        1 cup cooked, chopped
        chestnuts (I, 283)
        ½ cup or more rum, to
        make the sauce of a
        good consistency
Place in jars and seal. Ripen for 2 weeks.

CIDER SAUCE

[About 2 Cups]
Melt over low heat:
        1 tablespoon butter
Stir in, until blended:
        ¾ tablespoon flour
Add:
        1½ cups cider
Add, if needed:
        (Sugar)
        (1 teaspoon cinnamon)
        (¼ teaspoon cloves)
Stir and boil these ingredients

for about 2 minutes. Serve hot or cold on a bland pudding.

CHOCOLATE SAUCE COCKAIGNE

[About 2 Cups]
Dreamy on vanilla, coffee or chocolate ice cream.
Melt in the top of a double boiler ♦ over—not in—hot water:

3 oz. chocolate

Combine, then stir into the chocolate:

1 well-beaten egg
¾ cup evaporated milk
1 cup sugar

Cook for about 20 minutes. Remove from heat and beat with a rotary beater for 1 minute or until well blended. Stir in:

1 teaspoon vanilla

Cool sauce before using. If tightly covered and placed in the refrigerator, it will keep for several days.

⅄ BLENDER CHOCOLATE SAUCE

[About 1 Cup]
Fine for ice cream, puddings, soft frosting or flavoring for milk. Put into an electric blender:

2 squares chopped chocolate
½ cup sugar
6 tablespoons warm milk, cream, coffee or sherry
½ teaspoon vanilla or rum
⅛ teaspoon salt

Blend until smooth.

CHOCOLATE SAUCE

[About 1 Cup]
Stir until dissolved, then cook, without stirring, to the sirup stage, about 5 minutes:

½ cup to 1 cup water
½ cup sugar

Melt in the sirup:

1 to 2 oz. chocolate

Cool. Add:

1 teaspoon vanilla

If the sirup is too thick, thin it to the right consistency with:

Cream, dry sherry or brandy

Serve hot. If made in advance, keep hot in a double boiler.

HOT FUDGE SAUCE

[About 1 Cup]
The grand kind that, when cooked for the longer period and served hot, grows hard on ice cream and enraptures children. Melt in a double boiler ♦ over—not in—hot water:

2 oz. unsweetened chocolate

Add and melt:

1 tablespoon butter

Stir and blend well, then add:

⅓ cup boiling water

Stir well and add:

1 cup sugar
2 tablespoons corn sirup

Permit the sauce to boil readily, but not too furiously, over direct heat. Do not stir. If you wish an ordinary sauce, boil it for 5 minutes. If you wish a hot sauce that will harden over ice cream, boil it for about 8 minutes. Add just before serving:

1 teaspoon vanilla or
2 teaspoons rum

When cold, this sauce is very thick. It may be reheated over boiling water.

CHOCOLATE CUSTARD SAUCE

[About 2¼ Cups]
Heat in a double boiler ♦ over—not in—hot water, until melted:

2 oz. chopped chocolate
2 cups milk

Beat well:

4 egg yolks
¾ cup sugar
⅛ teaspoon salt

Beat the hot mixture gradually into the yolks. Return to double boiler for 5 minutes and cook gently, stirring constantly. Cool. Add:

1 teaspoon vanilla
Serve, hot or cold, over:
> Filled cream puffs,
> puddings or ice cream

CHOCOLATE [8]
NUT-BRITTLE SAUCE

Melt in a double boiler ♦ over—
not in—hot water:
> 3 oz. sweet chocolate

Add:
> 1¼ cups crushed nut brittle

Stir in slowly:
> ½ cup boiling water

Heat until the candy is melted.
Cool slightly. Before serving,
add:
> 1 tablespoon brandy

Serve over:
> Ice cream

MOCHA SAUCE

[About 1½ Cups]
Bring to a boil and cook over
moderate heat for about 3 minutes, stirring occasionally:
> ½ cup cocoa
> ⅛ teaspoon salt
> 1 cup dark corn sirup
> ¼ cup sugar or 16
>   average-sized
>   marshmallows
> ¼ cup water
> 1 teaspoon instant coffee

Swirl in:
> 2 tablespoons butter

When slightly cool, stir in:
> ½ teaspoon vanilla

Serve hot or cold.

CHOCOLATE MINT [6]
SAUCE

Melt in a double boiler ♦ over—
not in—hot water:
> 10 large chocolate
>   peppermint creams

Add:
> 3 tablespoons cream

Stir well.

CHOCOLATE CARAMEL
SAUCE

[About 1 Cup]

Melt over low heat:
> 4 oz. semi-sweet chocolate

Stir in and cook until sauce is
thick:
> 1 cup packed brown sugar
> ½ cup cream
> 1 tablespoon butter

Cool slightly and add:
> 1 teaspoon vanilla

MAPLE SIRUP SAUCE

[About ¾ Cup]
Heat, but do not boil:
> ½ cup maple sirup

Add:
> ½ teaspoon grated lemon
>   peel
> ¼ teaspoon freshly grated
>   nutmeg or ⅛ teaspoon
>   ginger or cloves
> (2 to 3 tablespoons nut
>   meats)

Chill and serve cold. If you
serve it hot, swirl in:
> 1 to 2 tablespoons butter

MAPLE SUGAR SAUCE

[About 2 Cups]
Stir over low heat until dissolved, then boil, without stirring, to a thin sirup:
> 1 lb. maple sugar
> ½ cup evaporated milk

Add:
> ¼ cup corn sirup
> ½ teaspoon vanilla
> ½ cup shredded nut meats

BUTTERSCOTCH SAUCE

[About ¾ Cup]
Boil to the consistency of heavy
sirup:
> ⅓ cup white corn sirup
> ⅝ cup packed light-brown
>   sugar
> 2 tablespoons butter
> ⅛ teaspoon salt

Cool these ingredients. Add:
> ⅓ cup evaporated milk or
>   cream

Serve the sauce hot or cold. It
may be reheated in a double
boiler.

HOT BROWN-SUGAR SAUCE

[About 1½ Cups]
Cook for 5 minutes, stirring occasionally:

    1 cup brown sugar
    ½ cup water

Pour the sirup in a fine stream over:

    1 beaten egg

Beat constantly. Cook and stir in double boiler ♦ over—not in—hot water for 2 minutes.
Add:

    3 tablespoons dry sherry
    ⅛ teaspoon salt

Serve hot.

BROWN-SUGAR BUTTER SAUCE

[About 1 Cup]
Fine with hot puddings or waffles.
Cream in a small saucepan:

    ¼ cup butter
    1 cup closely packed brown sugar

Add gradually:

    1 cup warm thin cream

Stir over low heat until it boils. Remove from heat. Add:

    ¼ cup bourbon or brandy

Beat with an egg beater until smooth. Add and mix in:

    (⅓ cup chopped nuts)

BROWN-SUGAR CREAM SAUCE

[About 1½ Cups]
Place in a double boiler ♦ over —not in—hot water:

    3 beaten egg yolks
    ¾ cup cream
    ¾ teaspoon salt
    ½ cup brown sugar

Stir and cook until thick and creamy. Add a little at a time, stirring constantly:

    3 tablespoons butter
    1½ tablespoons lemon juice

BROWN-SUGAR ORANGE SAUCE

[About 1 cup]
Good for filling coffee cakes or poured over pancakes and waffles.
Combine in a saucepan:

    ¾ cup brown sugar
    ¼ cup butter
    ½ cup orange juice

Stir constantly and heat for 3 minutes, then cool.

CARAMEL SAUCE

[About 1 cup]
Prepare and cool, so as not to curdle the cream:

    ½ cup Caramel Sirup, page 518

Add:

    1 cup cream or strong coffee
    1 teaspoon vanilla
    ⅛ teaspoon salt

If you use coffee, swirl in:

    2 tablespoons butter

You may keep the sauce hot over hot water.

CARAMEL CREAM SAUCE

[About 1½ Cups]
Combine and stir in a double boiler ♦ over—not in—hot water, until melted:

    ½ lb. Caramels, page 509
    1 cup whipping cream or evaporated milk

COFFEE SAUCE

[About 1½ Cups]
Beat:

    2 eggs

Beat into them, very slowly:

    ½ cup strong boiling coffee

Add:

    ¼ cup sugar
    ⅛ teaspoon salt

Cook ♦ over—not in—hot water and stir the sauce in the top of a double boiler until it coats a spoon. Chill.
Shortly before serving, fold in:

    ½ cup whipped cream

(¼ cup chopped candied
ginger)

HONEY SAUCE

[About 1 Cup]
Combine and stir well:
 ¼ cup hot water
 ½ cup honey
 ¼ cup chopped nut meats
 ¼ cup minced candied
   orange or lemon peel or
   candied ginger
Chill.

HONEY MINT SAUCE

[About ¾ Cup]
Recommended for fruit compotes.
Combine:
 ½ cup orange juice
 2 tablespoons lemon juice
 2 tablespoons honey
 ⅛ cup finely chopped fresh
   mint

VANILLA SAUCE

[About 1 Cup]
Prepare:
   Lemon, Orange or Lime
   Sauce, page 473
Use the smaller amount of sugar
and substitute for the lemon
juice:
 1 inch of vanilla bean,
   page 201 or 1 to 2
   teaspoons vanilla or
 1 tablespoon rum

MARSHMALLOW SAUCE

[About 2 Cups]
Stir over low heat until the
sugar is dissolved:
 ¾ cup sugar
 1 tablespoon light corn
   sirup
 ¼ cup milk
Bring to a boil, then simmer
gently for about 5 minutes. Dissolve in top of double boiler by
stirring ♦ over—not in—hot
water:
 ½ lb. marshmallows,
   page 505

2 tablespoons water
Pour the sirup over the dissolved
marshmallows, beating well.
Add:
 1 teaspoon vanilla
Serve the sauce hot or cold. It
may be reheated in a double
boiler. Beat well before serving.

COCONUT DULCIE

[About 4½ Cups]
Good by itself over fruit puddings, or combined as a sauce
with purées of tart fruit such as
guava and currant.
Boil to the thick sirup stage:
 4 cups water
 3 cups sugar
Add:
 1 freshly grated coconut,
   page 193
Cook slowly for about 25 minutes until the mixture is translucent. Pour into sterile jars and
seal.

SWEETENED BUTTERS

I. [About ¼ Cup]
Cream, then chill:
 3 tablespoons butter
 ½ cup sifted confectioners'
   sugar
 ¾ teaspoon cinnamon

II. Honey Butter
[About ½ Cup]
This is delicious on waffles or
toast.
Beat well:
 ¼ cup honey
 2 tablespoons soft butter
 2 tablespoons whipping
   cream

III. See Henri's Butter Sauce,
   page 115.

HARD SAUCE

[About 1 Cup]
The basic ingredients of hard
sauce are always the same, although proportions and flavoring
may vary. In this recipe, the

larger amount of butter is preferable. An attractive way to serve hard sauce on cold cake or pudding is to chill it and mold it with a small fancy cutter —or to put it through an individual butter mold.

Sift:

  1 cup powdered sugar

Beat until soft:

  2 to 5 tablespoons butter

Add the sugar gradually. Beat these ingredients until they are well blended. Add:

  ⅛ teaspoon salt
  1 teaspoon vanilla or 1 tablespoon coffee, rum, whisky, brandy, lemon juice, etc.

Beat in:

  (1 egg or ¼ cup cream)

When the sauce is very smooth, chill thoroughly.

SPICY HARD SAUCE

[About 1 Cup]

Prepare:

  Hard Sauce, above

Beat into it:

  ½ teaspoon cinnamon
  ¼ teaspoon cloves
  1 teaspoon vanilla
  ½ teaspoon lemon juice
  ⅛ teaspoon salt
  (Liqueur, to taste)

Chill.

BROWN-SUGAR HARD SAUCE

[About 1⅔ Cups]

Sift:

  1½ cups brown sugar

Beat until soft:

  ½ cup butter

Add the sugar gradually. Beat these ingredients until well blended. Beat in slowly:

  ⅓ cup cream

Beat in, drop by drop:

  2 tablespoons dry wine or
  1 teaspoon vanilla

Chill well. Add for garnish:

  (¼ cup chopped nuts)

FRUIT HARD SAUCE

[About 1⅔ Cups]

Sift:

  1 cup confectioners' sugar

Beat until soft:

  ⅓ cup butter

Add the sugar gradually. Beat until well blended. Beat in:

  ¼ cup cream
  ⅔ cup crushed strawberries, raspberries, apricots or bananas

Chill thoroughly.

FLUFFY HARD SAUCE

[About 1½ Cups]

Sift:

  1 cup sugar

Beat until soft:

  1 tablespoon butter

Add the sugar gradually and:

  1 tablespoon cream

Beat until well blended. Whip until stiff:

  3 egg whites

Fold them into the sugar mixture. Add:

  2 tablespoons cream
  1 teaspoon or more vanilla, rum or port

Beat the sauce well. Pile it in a dish. Chill thoroughly.

FOAMY SAUCE

[About 2 Cups]

Sift:

  1 cup powdered sugar

Beat until soft:

  ⅓ to ½ cup butter

Add the sugar slowly. Beat until well blended. Beat in:

  1 egg yolk
  1 teaspoon vanilla or
  2 tablespoons wine

Place the sauce in a double boiler ◗ over—not in—hot water. Beat and cook until the yolk has thickened slightly. Whip until stiff:

  1 egg white

Fold it lightly into the sauce. Serve hot or cold.

LIQUEUR CREAM SAUCE

[About 1½ Cups]

So zestful that it will glorify the plainest cottage pudding, cake or gingerbread. Less extravagant, too, than it sounds—only a small amount being needed.

Beat until soft in the top of a double boiler ♦ over—not in—hot water:

    ⅓ cup butter

Add gradually and beat until creamy:

    1 cup sifted confectioners'
        sugar

Beat in slowly:

    3 tablespoons brandy or
        other liqueur

Beat in, one at a time:

    2 egg yolks

Add:

    ½ cup cream

Cook until slightly thickened.

SOUR CREAM SAUCE

[About 1½ Cups]

Use as dressing for berries, or combine berries with it and serve over cake or fruit gelatin.

Combine:

    1 cup cultured sour cream
    ½ cup packed brown sugar
    (1 cup berries)
    (½ teaspoon vanilla)

ICE CREAMS, ICES AND FROZEN DESSERTS

ABOUT CHURNED ICE CREAMS AND ICES

Nowadays, with plentiful ice and electric churning, few people recall the shared excitement of the era when making ice cream was a rarely scheduled event. Then the iceman brought to the back door, on special order, a handsome 2-foot-square cube of cold crystal and everyone in the family took a turn at the crank. The critical question among us children was, of course, who might lick the dasher. A century or so ago the novelist Stendhal knew only hand-churned ice cream and, when he first tasted it, exclaimed, "What a pity this isn't a sin!"

Hand-churning is still tops for perfectionists, for no power-driven machine has yet been invented that can achieve a comparable texture. Even French Pot, the very best commercial method for making ice cream, calls for finishing by hand.

Ice creams are based on ♦ carefully cooked ♦ well-chilled sirups and heavy custards, added to ♦ unwhipped cream. ♦ No form of vanilla flavoring can surpass that of vanilla sugar or of the bean itself, steeped in a hot sirup. If sweetened frozen fruits are incorporated into the cream mixture instead of fresh fruits, be sure to adjust sugar content accordingly.

♦ Make up mixtures for churn-frozen ice creams the day before you freeze, to increase yield and to produce a smoother-textured cream. ♦ In churn-freezing ice creams and ices, fill the container only ¾ full to permit expansion. ♦ To pack the freezer, allow 3 to 6 quarts of chipped or cracked ice to 1 cup of coarse rock salt. Pack about ⅓ of the freezer with ice and add layers of salt and ice around the container until the freezer is full. Allow the pack to stand about 3 minutes before you start turning. Turn slowly at first, about 40 revolutions a minute, until a slight pull is felt. Then triple speed for 5 to 6 minutes. If any additions, such as finely cut candied or fresh fruits or nuts are to be made, do so at this point. Then repack and taper off the churning to about 80 revolutions a minute for a few minutes more. The cream should be ready in 10 to 20 minutes, depending on the quality.

If the ice cream or ice is to be used at once, it should be frozen harder than if you plan to serve it later. Should the interval be 2 hours or more, packing will firm it. ♦ To pack, pour off the salt water in the freezer and wipe off the lid. Remove the dasher carefully, making sure that no salt or water gets into the cream container. Scrape the cream down from the sides of the container. Place a cork in the lid and replace the lid. Repack the container in the freezer with additional ice and salt, using the same proportions as before. Cover the freezer with newspapers, a piece of carpet or other heavy material.

The cream should be smooth when served. If it proves granular, you used too much salt in the packing mixture, overfilled the inner container with the ice cream mixture or turned too rapidly. ✳ If you are making a large quantity with the idea of storing some in the deep-freeze, package in sizes you plan on serving. Should ice cream be allowed to melt even slightly and is then refrozen, it loses in volume and even more in good texture.

GARNISHES AND ADDITIONS TO ICE CREAM MIXTURES

Add to ice cream, when it is in a partially frozen state, allowing the following amounts per quart:

> 1 cup toasted chopped nuts
> 1 cup crushed nut brittle
> ⅓ cup preserved ginger and 1 tablespoon of the sirup
> 1 cup crushed chocolate molasses chips
> 1 cup crushed macaroons plus 2 tablespoons sherry or liqueur
> ½ cup Polvo de Amor, page 194

For fruit additions, see Fruit Ice Creams, page 486.
To garnish ice cream, add just before serving:

> Chopped nuts or shredded coconut
> Candied violets
> Chopped candied citrus peel or other candied fruits
> Crystallized angelica, cut in tiny fancy shapes
> Decorettes
> Shaved or chopped sweet or bitter chocolate

> Marzipan fruits or rosettes

SNOW ICE CREAM

This is the ancestor of all frozen delights and a favorite winter scoop for small fry. Arrange attractively in a chilled bowl, trying not to compact it:

> Fresh, clean snow

Pour over it:

> Sweetened fruit juice

or a mixture of:

> Cream
> Sugar
> Vanilla

VANILLA ICE CREAM I

[About 9 Servings]
Warm over low heat, but do not boil:

> 1 cup cream

Stir in, until dissolved:

> ¾ cup sugar
> ⅛ teaspoon salt

Chill. Add:

> 3 cups cream
> 1½ teaspoons vanilla

To churn-freeze the ice cream, see page 483. Serve with:

> Tutti Frutti, page 583, Cherries Jubilee, page 474, or a liqueur

DELMONICO ICE CREAM OR CRÈME GLACÉE

[About 9 servings]
Scald over low heat, but do not boil:

> 1½ cups milk

Stir in, until dissolved:

> ¾ cup sugar
> ⅛ teaspoon salt

Pour the milk slowly over:

> 2 or 3 beaten egg yolks

Beat these ingredients until well blended. Stir and cook in a double boiler ♦ over—but not in—hot water, until thick and smooth. Chill. Add and fold into the custard:

> 1 tablespoon vanilla

1 cup whipping cream
1 cup cream

To churn-freeze the ice cream, see page 483. Serve with:

Crushed Nut Brittle,
page 515

CARAMEL ICE CREAM

Prepare:

Vanilla or Delmonico Ice
Cream, page 484

Add:

2 to 4 tablespoons
Caramelized Sugar I,
page 169

To churn-freeze and serve, see page 483.

Garnish with:

Chopped pecans or
roasted almonds

PEPPERMINT-STICK ICE CREAM

[About 12 Servings]

Grind or crush:

½ lb. peppermint-stick
candy

Soak for 12 hours in:

2 cups milk

Add:

1 cup cream
1 cup whipping cream

To churn-freeze and serve, see page 483.

Serve with:

Shaved Sweet Chocolate,
page 191, or Chocolate
Sauce Cockaigne,
page 477

CHOCOLATE ICE CREAM

[About 8 Servings]

Dissolve in the top of a double boiler ◗ over—not in—hot water:

2 oz. chocolate

in:

2 cups milk

Stir in:

1 cup sugar
⅛ teaspoon salt

Remove from the heat. Beat

with a wire whisk until cool and fluffy. Add:

1½ teaspoons vanilla
1 cup whipping cream
1 cup cream

Fold the cream into the chocolate mixture. To churn-freeze the ice cream, see page 483. You may serve it in:

(Meringues, page 310)

with:

(Chocolate Sauce,
page 477)

COFFEE ICE CREAM

[About 9 Servings]

Scald over low heat, but do not boil:

2½ cups milk

Stir in, until dissolved:

1½ cups sugar

Pour the milk slowly over:

2 beaten eggs

Beat until well blended. Stir and cook in a double boiler ◗ over—not in—hot water, until thick and smooth. Chill. Add:

½ cup strong cold coffee
½ teaspoon salt
1 cup whipping cream

When almost frozen, add:

1 teaspoon vanilla
3 tablespoons rum

To churn-freeze and serve, see page 483.

Garnish with:

Shaved chocolate

★ PISTACHIO ICE CREAM

[About 9 Servings]

A pretty Christmas dessert served in a meringue tart garnished with whipped cream and cherries.

Shell:

4 oz. pistachio nuts

Blanch them, page 189. Pound them in a mortar with:

A few drops rose water

Add to them:

¼ cup sugar
¼ cup cream
1 teaspoon vanilla

½ teaspoon almond extract
A little green coloring

Stir these ingredients until the sugar is dissolved. Heat, but do not boil:

1 cup cream

Add and stir until dissolved:

¾ cup sugar
⅛ teaspoon salt

Chill these ingredients. Add the pistachio mixture and:

2 cups whipping cream
1 cup cream

To churn-freeze and serve, see page 483.

FRUIT ICE CREAMS

[About 9 Servings]

Delicious fruit creams can be made using:

2 to 2½ cups sweetened
puréed or finely sliced
fruit—greengage plums,
mangoes, peaches,
apricots or bananas

Add:

¼ teaspoon salt
Lemon juice to taste
2 to 3 cups whipping cream
1 cup cream

To churn-freeze the cream, see page 483.

APRICOT OR PEACH ICE CREAM

[About 9 Servings]

Pare, slice and mash:

4 lbs. ripe peaches or
apricots

Stir in:

½ to ¾ cup sugar
⅛ teaspoon salt

Cover the peaches or apricots closely and permit them to stand in the refrigerator until the sugar is dissolved. Combine:

1 teaspoon vanilla
½ cup sugar
2 cups cream
2 cups whipping cream

Partly churn-freeze these ingredients, see page 483. When they are half-frozen, add the fruit mixture and finish freezing.

ORANGE ICE CREAM

[About 9 Servings]

Heat but do not boil:

1½ cups cream

Stir in, until dissolved:

1½ cups sugar

Chill. Add:

1½ cups whipping cream

Churn-freeze the cream, see page 483, until it has a slushy consistency. Add:

3 tablespoons lemon juice
1¼ cups orange juice

Finish freezing. Serve with:

Polvo de Amor, page 194

STRAWBERRY OR RASPBERRY ICE CREAM

[About 9 Servings]

Hull:

1 quart berries

Sieve them. Stir into the pulpy juice:

⅞ cup sugar

Chill thoroughly. Combine with:

2 cups cream
2 cups whipping cream

To churn-freeze, see page 483.

ABOUT STILL-FROZEN ICE CREAMS, ICES, BOMBES, MOUSSES AND PARFAITS

In our family, a richly loaded bombe, even more than a churned ice cream, betokened festivity—the burst of glory which topped off a party dinner. These fancy molds were reserved for winter festivities and we always hoped that they would be buried in the snow. Finding them again was such a lark.

Then, as now, these still-frozen desserts ♦ needed an emulsifying agent—eggs, cornstarch, gelatin or corn sirup—to keep large crystals from forming during the freezing process. Classic French recipes specify at least 8 eggs to a cup of sugar sirup to obtain the requisite smoothness. Here are some good combinations:

> Strawberry ice outside, Delmonico with strawberries in kirsch inside
> Raspberries and pistachios
> Coffee and vanilla praliné
> Coffee and banana mousse
> Chocolate and angelica
> Vanilla, orange and chocolate

♦ To still-freeze creams and ices ♦ whip the cream only to the point where it stands in soft peaks. Any further beating will make the dessert disagreeably buttery. The cream and any solids such as nuts and candied fruits are incorporated when the rest of the mixture is partially frozen, and liqueurs are added almost at the end of the freezing period.

Descriptions of the many desserts that can be made in the ✻ freezer or in the freezing compartment of the refrigerator will follow. When the mixtures are in the mold, rest them in the deep freeze on other packages, not directly on the evaporator shelves. They may be made the day before you plan to use them but do not keep well much longer than this. ♦ Remove them from the freezer about ½ hour before use, leaving them in the mold until ready to serve. Then garnish with meringues, fruits, sauces or cakes. ♦ To make ornamental bombes, put the cream into tall, fancy or melon molds or in the special ones from which they took their playfully sinister name.

Churn-frozen ices or ice creams may form a single or double outside coating. They are applied as a rather thin layer to the inside surface of the mold, each layer being, in turn, individually frozen, see

Gelatin Molds, page 185. The softer, still-frozen bombe, mousse or Bavarian mixtures are then filled into the center and the mold covered before placement in the freezer. To pack in refrigerator trays, cover with foil. ♦ In the absence of a freezer, set the well-covered mold in a bed of cracked ice. Allow from 2 to 4 parts of ice to 1 of salt and use a bucket or a pail that will ensure complete coverage—about 3 inches on top, bottom and sides. Chill the cream from 4 to 6 hours. Serve parfaits in narrow and tall-stemmed glasses or place in layers between preserved fruits, ice creams and sauces, topped with whipped cream and a maraschino cherry.

VANILLA ICE CREAM II

[About 9 Servings]

Soak:

> 2 teaspoons gelatin

in:

> ¼ cup cold water

Scald in a double boiler:

> ¾ cup milk

with:

> 1 vanilla bean

Stir into it, until dissolved:

> ¾ cup sugar
> ⅛ teaspoon salt

Stir in the soaked gelatin. Cool and place this mixture in refrigerator trays until thoroughly chilled. Whip with a wire whisk until thickened, but not stiff:

> 3 cups whipping cream

Fold into the chilled and beaten gelatin mixture. ♦ Still-freeze the cream in a mold, or in a foil-covered refrigerator tray, see above. Serve with:

> Chocolate Mint Sauce, page 478, or Maple Sugar Sauce, page 478

or cover with:

> Shredded coconut
> Chocolate sauce

An attractive way to serve vanilla ice cream in summer is to place balls of cream in the center of a large platter and surround them with mounds of red raspberries, black raspberries and fresh pineapple sticks, using green leaves as a garnish. You may also use any of the additions suggested in Vanilla Ice Cream I, page 484.

VANILLA ICE CREAM   [6]
WITH EGG YOLKS

Beat:

2 egg yolks

Beat in until well blended:

½ cup confectioners' sugar
¼ cup cream

Cook and stir in a double boiler
♦ over—not in—hot water, until slightly thickened. Chill. Add:

1 teaspoon vanilla or 1
   tablespoon or more dry
   sherry

♦ Whip until thickened, but not stiff:

1 cup whipping cream

In a separate bowl, whip until stiff ♦ but not dry:

2 egg whites

Fold the cream and the egg whites into the custard. ♦ Still-freeze the ice cream in a mold, page 486, or in foil-covered refrigerator trays, page 487. Serve with:

Jelly Sauce, page 475

FROZEN EGGNOG

Prepare:

Delmonico Ice Cream,
   page 484, or Vanilla Ice
   Cream and Egg Yolks

When almost frozen, make a funnel-shaped hole in the center. Place in it:

Several tablespoons rum,
   brandy or whiskey

Stir the liquor into the ice cream. Let the mixture continue to freeze.

VANILLA ICE CREAM   [4]
WITH EVAPORATED MILK

Start to make this the day before you need it. During the process of evaporating milk, a caramel overtone develops, which plays hob with the delicate flavor of vanilla. We prefer to accentuate the caramel by adding:

2 to 4 tablespoons or more
   Caramel Sirup, page 518

Or you may transform the caramel flavor with:

1 to 2 teaspoons instant
   coffee

To prepare the ice cream, stir over heat, but do not boil:

⅓ to ½ cup sugar
¼ cup cream

Chill. Add:

1½ teaspoons vanilla

Prepare for whipping by the recipe on page 132:

1¼ cup evaporated milk

Whip. Combine lightly with the sugar mixture. To still-freeze and serve, see page 486.

BISCUIT TORTONI OR   [4]
MACAROON BOMBE

Combine:

¾ cup crushed macaroons
¾ cup cream
¼ cup sifted confectioners'
   sugar
A few grains of salt

Permit these ingredients to stand for 1 hour. ♦ Whip until thickened, but not stiff:

1 cup whipping cream

Fold in the macaroon mixture and:

1 teaspoon vanilla

Place in paper muffin cups set in a refrigerator tray. To still-freeze, see page 486. Either before freezing or when partly frozen, decorate tops with:

Maraschino cherries
Unsalted toasted almonds
Crystallized angelica, etc.

MOCHA ICE CREAM   [8]

In spite of an almost lifelong prejudice against marshmallows, we give the next 2 recipes a more than grudging approval. Melt in a double boiler ◆ over—not in—hot water:

18 average-size marsh-
mallows: ¼ lb.
½ lb. semi-sweet chocolate

Cool slightly and stir in:

2 cup whipping cream
¾ cup strong coffee

Pour this mixture gradually over:

4 well-beaten egg yolks

◆ Be sure that the mixture is not so hot as to curdle the eggs. To still-freeze and serve, see page 486.

CHOCOLATE ICE   [4]
CREAM WITH
EVAPORATED MILK

Chill until ice-cold:

1 cup evaporated milk

Combine:

6 tablespoons cocoa or
1½ oz.
melted chocolate
6 tablespoons sugar
¼ teaspoon salt

Stir in gradually:

½ cup evaporated milk
½ cup water

Stir and cook these ingredients in a double boiler ◆ over—not in —hot water, until smooth. Add and stir until melted:

18 average-size
marshmallows: ¼ lb.

Cool this mixture. Whip the chilled milk until stiff, then fold it in. To still-freeze the ice cream in a mold, see page 486, or in foil-covered refrigerator trays, page 487.

GREENGAGE PLUM   [12]
ICE CREAM

Drain:

3½ cups canned greengage
plums

Put them through a ricer. There should be about 1½ cups of pulp. Soak:

1½ teaspoons gelatin
in:
¼ cup cold water

Heat to the boiling point:

2 cups milk
½ to 1 cup sugar
⅛ teaspoon salt

Dissolve the gelatin in the hot milk. Cool, then add the plum pulp and:

2 tablespoons lemon juice

Chill the mixture until slushy. Add when ◆ whipped, until thickened but not stiff:

2 cups whipping cream

Still-freeze the ice cream in a mold, see page 486, or in foil-covered trays, page 487.

DELMONICO BOMBE

[About 15 Servings]

Soak:

1½ teaspoons gelatin
in:
¼ cup cold water

Stir and bring to the boiling point:

2 cups milk
1½ cups sugar

Dissolve the gelatin in the hot milk. Pour part of this mixture over:

2 beaten egg yolks

Beat until blended. Stir and cook in a double boiler ◆ over—not in—hot water, until the eggs thicken slightly. Cool the custard. Add:

1 teaspoon vanilla

Chill until about to set. ◆ Whip until thickened, but not stiff:

4 cups whipping cream

In a separate bowl whip until ◆ stiff, but not dry:

2 egg whites

Fold the cream and the egg whites lightly into the custard. Have ready:

18 macaroons

Sprinkle them with:

Cointreau or kirsch

Spread them with:

Tart jelly

Place alternate layers of cream and macaroons in a mold or in refrigerator trays. To still-freeze the ice cream, see page 486.

CHOCOLATE BOMBE

[About 10 Servings]

Soak:

1½ teaspoons gelatin

in:

1 cup cold water

Stir and bring to the boiling point:

1 cup milk

1½ cups sugar

2 tablespoons cocoa

Dissolve the gelatin in the mixture. Cool. Add:

1 teaspoon vanilla

Chill until about to set. ◗ Whip until thickened, but not stiff.

2 cups whipping cream

Fold lightly into the gelatin mixture. To still-freeze the bombe in a mold or in foil-covered refrigerator trays, see page 487.

STRAWBERRY OR RASPBERRY BOMBE

Prepare:

Bavarian Berry Cream, page 451

using in all:

1½ cups sugar

To still-freeze the ice cream, see page 486.

BUTTER PECAN ICE CREAM

[About 6 Servings]

Boil for 2 minutes:

1 cup packed light brown sugar

½ cup water

⅛ teaspoon salt

Beat:

2 eggs

Beat in the sirup slowly. Cook in a double boiler ◗ over—not in—hot water, stirring constantly until slightly thickened. Add:

2 tablespoons butter

Cool, then add:

1 cup milk

1 teaspoon vanilla extract

1 tablespoon sherry

Beat until ◗ thickened, but not stiff:

1 cup whipping cream

Fold it into the egg mixture. To still-freeze, see page 486. When partially frozen, fold in:

½ cup broken toasted pecan meats

If the nuts are salted, a very special piquancy results.

FRUIT BUTTERMILK ICE CREAM

[About 5 Servings]

This is a low-fat dish and quite acceptable. Combine:

1 cup sweetened fruit purée: apricot, pecan or strawberry

with:

3 tablespoons lemon juice

⅛ teaspoon salt

1½ cups buttermilk

To still-freeze, see page 486.

PERSIMMON ICE CREAM

[About 6 Servings]

A California creation.

Put through a ricer:

4 ripe Japanese persimmons

Add:

2 tablespoons sugar

6 tablespoons lemon juice

◗ Whip until thickened, but not stiff:

2 cups whipping cream

Still-freeze in a mold, page 486, or in foil-covered refrigerator trays, page 487.

FRUIT MOUSSE

[About 9 Servings]

Prepare:

2 cups crushed fruit— peaches, apricots, bananas, strawberries or black raspberries

Stir in:
  ⅛ teaspoon salt
  ¾ to 1 cup confectioners'
    sugar
Soak:
  1½ teaspoons gelatin
in:
  2 tablespoons cold water
Dissolve it in:
  ¼ cup boiling water
Chill and add:
  2 tablespoons lemon juice
Stir into the fruit mixture.
◗ Whip until thickened, but not
stiff:
  2 cups whipping cream
Fold into the fruit and gelatin
mixture. Still-freeze in a mold,
page 486, or in foil-covered refrigerator trays, page 487.

APRICOT MOUSSE WITH EVAPORATED MILK

[About 6 Servings]
Surprisingly good—the fruit flavor being decided enough to
disguise the evaporated milk
taste.
Prepare for whipping, page 132:
  1¼ cups evaporated milk
Put through a ricer or blend:
  ¾ cup cooked sweetened
    drained dried apricots
We do not like to substitute the
canned ones, as the flavor is not
strong enough. Soak:
  1 teaspoon gelatin
in:
  2 tablespoons cold juice
Dissolve it in:
  2 tablespoons hot juice
Add the gelatin to the apricot
purée. Chill until about to set.
Whip the chilled evaporated
milk and add to it:
  ½ teaspoon vanilla
  ⅛ teaspoon salt
Fold lightly into gelatin mixture. To still-freeze in foil-covered refrigerator trays, see page
487.

COFFEE PARFAIT

[About 6 Servings]

Combine:
  2 tablespoons cornstarch
  ⅔ cup sugar
  ⅛ teaspoon salt
Stir into this:
  2 tablespoons milk
Beat, then add:
  2 egg yolks
  1 cup strong coffee
Stir and cook this custard in a
double boiler ◗ over—not in—
hot water, until it thickens. Chill.
◗ Whip until thickened, but not
stiff and fold in:
  1½ cups whipping cream
To still-freeze in foil-covered refrigerator trays, see page 487.
Serve in tall glasses, topped
with:
  Whipped cream
  (Grated chocolate)

TUTTI FRUIT PARFAIT

[About 6 Servings]
Cover and soak:
  1 cup chopped candied
    fruit
in a combination of:
  Brandy, rum, liqueur and
    sirup from canned stewed
    fruit
Drain well. Reserve liquid for
flavoring puddings. Soak:
  1 teaspoon gelatin
in:
  2 tablespoons water
Dissolve it over hot water. Boil
to the thread stage, page 726:
  ½ cup water
  ½ cup sugar
Beat ◗ until stiff, but not dry:
  2 egg whites
Pour the sirup over the egg
whites in a fine stream, beating
constantly. Add the dissolved
gelatin and continue beating
until mixture thickens somewhat.
Beat in drained fruit. ◗ Whip
until thickened, but not stiff:
  1 cup whipping cream
  1 teaspoon vanilla
Fold into fruit and egg mixture.
Still-freeze in a mold, page 486,
or in foil-covered refrigerator

trays, page 487. Serve topped with:

> Whipped cream
> Candied cherries

CARAMEL PARFAIT

[About 9 Servings]
Soak:

> 1½ teaspoons gelatin

in:

> ½ cup cold water

Prepare:

> ¾ cup warm Caramelized Sugar I, page 169

Beat:

> 2 egg yolks

Beat in slowly:

> ½ cup sugar

Beat these ingredients until well blended. Add the caramel mixture. Stir in a double boiler ♦ over—not in—hot water until the custard coats a spoon. Stir in the soaked gelatin. Cool. Add:

> 2 teaspoons vanilla

Chill until about to set. ♦ Whip until thickened, but not stiff:

> 2 cups whipping cream

Fold lightly into the custard. Still-freeze in a mold, page 486, or in foil-covered refrigerator trays, page 487. Garnish with:

> Toasted slivered almonds

BUTTERSCOTCH PARFAIT

[About 6 Servings]
Stir and melt in a saucepan over low heat, then boil for 1 minute:

> ⅔ cup packed brown sugar
> 2 tablespoons butter
> ⅛ teaspoon salt

Add:

> ½ cup water

Cook the butterscotch until smooth and sirupy. Beat:

> 4 egg yolks

Add the cooled sirup slowly, beating constantly. Cook and stir in a double boiler ♦ over—not in—hot water, until light and fluffy. Chill. ♦ Whip until thickened, but not stiff:

> 1 cup whipping cream

Add:

> 2 teaspoons vanilla

Fold into egg mixture. Still-freeze in a mold, page 486, or in foil-covered refrigerator trays, page 487.

MAPLE PARFAIT

[About 9 Servings]
Cook and stir ♦ over—not in—hot water until thick:

> 6 egg yolks
> ¾ cup maple sirup
> ⅛ teaspoon salt

When the custard coats a spoon, remove it from the heat. Pour into a bowl and beat with a wire whisk until cool. ♦ Whip until thickened, but not stiff:

> 2 cups whipping cream

Fold it lightly into the custard. When partially frozen, add:

> (½ cup crushed Nut Brittle, page 515)

Still-freeze in a mold, page 486, or in foil-covered refrigerator trays, page 487.

RASPBERRY PARFAIT

[About 9 Servings]
Crush and strain through 2 thicknesses of cheesecloth:

> 1 quart raspberries

Boil to the thread stage, page 500:

> ¾ cup water
> 1 cup sugar

Whip until stiff ♦ but not dry:

> 3 egg whites

Pour the sirup over them in a slow stream. Whip constantly until cool. Fold in crushed berries. In a separate bowl ♦ whip until thickened, but not stiff:

> 2 cups whipping cream

Fold lightly into other ingredients. Still-freeze in a mold, page 486, or in foil-covered refrigerator trays, page 487.

ANGELICA PARFAIT

[About 12 Servings]
Try combining layers of angelica, chocolate and lime.

Boil to the thread stage, page 500:

　　1½ cups sugar
　　½ cup water

Whip ♦ until stiff, but not dry:

　　2 egg whites

Pour sirup over them in a slow stream. Whip constantly. When cool, add:

　　1 teaspoon vanilla or
　　1 tablespoon or more
　　　Cointreau

♦ Whip until thickened, but not stiff:

　　3 cups whipping cream

Fold lightly into egg mixture. Still-freeze in a mold, page 486, or in foil-covered refrigerator trays, page 487. Serve with:

　　Raspberry Juice, or
　　Chocolate Sauce,
　　page 477

ABOUT ICES AND SHERBETS

Ices and glaces are made simply of fruit juice, sugar and water. Sherbets have variants, like Italian Graniti and French Sorbets. These may add egg white, milk or cream and are generally less sweet confections. Sherbets may be appropriately served with the meat course, as well as for dessert. Both are best when churn-frozen. Some types may be still-frozen without the addition of gelatin or egg white, but their texture is considerably lighter and less flinty when these modifying ingredients are included.

Freezing diminishes flavoring and sweetening, so sugar your base accordingly. ♦ However, if ices are too sweet they will not freeze: be sure there is never more than 1 part sugar to 4 parts liquid. Stir in any liqueurs after the ices have frozen.

♦ To churn-freeze ices and sherbets, follow the directions for processing ice creams, page 483. Like ice creams, they can be molded, after freezing, into attractive shapes. Pack a mold in salted ice for 3 hours. Remove the ice or sherbet from it about 5 minutes before serving.

♦ To still-freeze ices and sherbets, put them in a covered mold or a refrigerator tray covered with foil and place them in the freezer. While they are still slushy, they should be stirred or beaten from front to back in the tray to reduce the size of the crystals. Repeated beating at ½ hour intervals will give them the consistency of a coarse churn-frozen water ice. Remove them from freezer to refrigerator about 20 minutes before serving. Ices and sherbets are especially delectable when served in fruit shells—fancy-cut and hollowed-out lemons, tangerines, oranges, cantaloupes, even apples—garnished with leaves. See also Frozen Orange Surprise, page 495.

Of course, meringues topped with whipped cream are containers as wonderful as crystal coupe or frappé goblets. Ices and sherbets lend themselves particularly to combinations with fruits—fresh, poached, preserved and candied; to chestnut garnishes with touches of liqueur; and if you are really professional, to veils of spun sugar.

FRUIT ICE

[About 10 Servings]

♦ Be careful not to use more than 1 part sugar for every 4 parts liquid, as too much sugar prevents freezing.

Use:

　　1 cup any fruit purée

Add to taste:

　　(Lemon juice)

Combine with:

　　4 cups water

To churn-freeze, see page 483. If adding:

　　(Liqueur)

♦ have the ice almost completely

churned before you do so, as the high alcoholic content tends to prevent the freezing.

LEMON AND ORANGE ICE

[About 9 Servings]
Combine and stir:

    2 teaspoons grated orange rind
    2 cups sugar

Stir in and boil for 5 minutes:

    4 cups water
    ¼ teaspoon salt

Chill. Add:

    2 cups orange juice
    ¼ cup lemon juice

To churn-freeze, see page 483. Top each serving with:

    1 teaspoon rum or orange marmalade

RASPBERRY OR STRAWBERRY ICE I

[About 10 Servings]
This method makes delicious linings for bombes. The still-frozen method combines well with angelica or Biscuit Tortoni, page 488. Try either ice served in green apple cups, the cut parts of which you have sprinkled with lemon juice to prevent browning.
Cook until soft:

    2 quarts strawberries or raspberries

Strain the juice through 2 thicknesses of cheesecloth. There should be about 2 cups of thick juice. Combine, stir until the sugar is dissolved, then boil for 3 minutes:

    4 cups water
    2 cups sugar

Chill. Add the thick berry juice and:

    1 tablespoon lemon juice

To churn-freeze, see page 483.

PEACH ICE

[About 12 Servings]
Combine:

    2 cups peach pulp: fresh peaches, peeled and riced
    6 tablespoons lemon juice
    ¾ cup orange juice

Boil for 5 minutes:

    3 cups water
    1 cup sugar

Chill. Combine with the fruit pulp and juices. To churn-freeze, see page 483. Top each serving with:

    1 teaspoon cassis or Melba Sauce, page 474

APRICOT ICE

[About 9 Servings]
Put through a ricer or a sieve:

    3½ cups drained canned apricots

Add:

    2¼ cups orange juice
    6 tablespoons lemon juice

Stir in until dissolved:

    1 cup sugar

To churn-freeze, see page 483.

PINEAPPLE ICE

[About 9 Servings]
Boil for 5 minutes:

    1 cup sugar
    4 cups water

Chill and sirup and add:

    1 cup canned crushed pineapple
    6 tablespoons lemon juice

To churn-freeze, see page 483. Garnish with:

    Mint leaves

LEMON MILK SHERBET

[About 9 Servings]
Dissolve:

    1⅓ cups sugar

in:

    7 tablespoons lemon juice

Stir these ingredients slowly into:

    3½ cups milk or milk and cream

If the milk curdles, it will not affect texture after freezing. To churn-freeze, see page 483.

ORANGE MILK SHERBET

[About 10 Servings]
Combine and stir:

1½ teaspoons grated orange
rind
1½ cups sugar

Dissolve the sugar mixtur in:

¼ cup lemon juice
1½ cups orange juice
(1½ riced bananas)

Stir these ingredients gradually
into:

4 cups very cold milk

If the milk curdles slightly, it
will not affect the texture after
the sherbet is frozen. To churn-
freeze, see page 483.

PINEAPPLE MILK SHERBET

[About 10 Servings]
Combine and stir:

1 cup unsweetened
pineapple juice
1 teaspoon grated lemon
rind
¼ cup lemon juice
1 cup sugar
⅛ teaspoon salt

Stir these ingredients slowly
into:

4 cups chilled milk

To churn-freeze, see page 483.

FROZEN ORANGE OR LEMON SURPRISE

This dessert can be made well
in advance. If it is removed from
the freezer and set in place just
before the guests are served—
and if the meal is not a long
one—it may even be used as a
centerpiece or table decoration.
Choose:

Navel oranges or heavy-
skinned lemons

Cut a fancy opening near the
top, which later serves as a lid.
Hollow out the pulp. Use it for
juice or for making fruit ice or
sherbet. Refill the orange with:

Fruit ice or sherbet

or a combination of:

Fruit ice
Ice cream
Partially frozen rasp-
berries, peaches,
strawberries
A touch of liqueur

Serve on fresh green leaves,
garnished with a leaf on top of
the lid. A note of warning: ♦
match bottoms and tops of fruit
shells before you start filling.
Also have all ingredients ready
for filling and work fast, so that
no undue melting takes place.
Wrap individually in foil and
deep-freeze immediately, until
ready to serve. Depending upon
the temperature of the room,
allow about ½ hour or more to
defrost.

LEMON ICE

[About 9 Servings]
Grate:

2 teaspoons lemon rind

onto:

2 cups sugar

Add, stir over heat until sugar
is dissolved, then boil for 5
minutes:

4 cups water or tea
¼ teaspoon salt

Chill. Add:

¾ cup lemon juice

To churn or still-freeze, see page
483 or 486. Serve in a mound or
ring with:

Fruit or canned fruit
used in some attractive
combination, flavored
with curaçao, Cointreau
or rum

RASPBERRY OR STRAWBERRY ICE II

[About 4 Servings]
Strain:

1 quart strawberries or
raspberries

Soak:

1 teaspoon gelatin

in:

1 tablespoon cold water

Boil for 3 minutes:

1 cup water or ½ cup
water and ½ cup
pineapple juice
¾ to 1 cup sugar
Add:
1 to 2 tablespoons lemon
juice
Dissolve the gelatin in the hot
sirup. Chill. Combine juice with
sirup. To still-freeze, see page
486.

LEMON SHERBET

[About 5 Servings]
Soak:
2 teaspoons gelatin
in:
¼ cup cold water
Boil for 10 minutes:
2¼ cups water
¾ cup sugar
Dissolve gelatin in hot sirup.
Chill. Grate:
1 teaspoon lemon rind
Add to it:
¾ cup lemon juice
Add these ingredients to the
sirup. Fold into this chilled mixture:
2 stiffly beaten egg whites
To still-freeze, see page 486.
Serve topped with:
(Finely chopped candied
orange or lemon mind)

ORANGE SHERBET

[About 5 Servings]
Soak:
2 teaspoons gelatin
in:
¼ cup cold water
Boil for 10 minutes:
1 cup water
⅔ to ¾ cup sugar, as
needed
Dissolve gelatin in hot sirup.
Cool. Add to it:
1 teaspoon grated lemon
rind
1 teaspoon grated orange
rind
1½ cups orange juice
⅓ cup lemon juice

Beat ◗ until stiff, but not dry
and add:
2 egg whites
To still-freeze, see page 486.
Garnish with:
Fresh pineapple slices

LIME SHERBET

[About 6 Servings]
Boil for 10 minutes:
⅔ cup sugar
1¾ cups water
Stir in:
1¼ teaspoons gelatin
dissolved in:
¼ cup cold water
Cool slightly. Add:
½ cup lime juice
2 drops green coloring
Beat until ◗ stiff, but not dry
and add:
2 egg whites
To still-freeze, see page 486.
Serve in:
Lemon shells
Garnish with:
Green leaves

GRAPEFRUIT SHERBET

[About 4 Servings]
Soak:
2 teaspoons gelatin
in:
½ cup cold water
Boil for 10 minutes:
1 cup sugar
1 cup water
Dissolve the gelatin in the hot
sirup. Chill.
Add to it:
¼ cup lemon juice
2 cups fresh grapefruit
juice
⅓ cup orange juice
¼ teaspoon salt
Beat until ◗ stiff, but not dry
and add:
2 egg whites
To still-freeze, see page 486.
Serve in:
Grapefruit shells

RASPBERRY OR STRAWBERRY SHERBET

[About 5 Servings]

Soak:

2 teaspoons gelatin

in:

¼ cup cold water

Press through a sieve or a ricer:

1 quart fresh berries

Add to them:

¼ cup lemon juice

Boil for 10 minutes:

1¾ cups water
¾ cup sugar

Dissolve the gelatin in the hot sirup. Cool and add berries. Chill. Beat until ◗ stiff, but not dry and add:

2 egg whites

To still-freeze, see page 486.

BANANA PINEAPPLE SHERBET

[About 8 Servings]

Combine and stir until dissolved:

1½ cups crushed pineapple
¾ cup confectioners' sugar

Add:

1½ cups banana pulp: about 3 large bananas
½ cup orange juice
6 tablespoons lemon juice

Place in refrigerator trays. Freeze until nearly firm. ◗ Beat until stiff, but not dry:

2 egg whites

Add fruit mixture gradually. Beat sherbet until light and fluffy. Return to trays. To still-freeze, see page 487.

★ CRANBERRY SHERBET

[About 8 Servings]

Boil until soft:

1 quart cranberries
1¾ cups water

Strain the juice and put berries through a sieve. Add to them and boil for 5 minutes:

1¾ cups sugar
1 cup water

Soak:

2 teaspoons gelatin

in:

¼ cup cold water

Dissolve the gelatin in the hot juice. Chill. Beat until ◗ stiff, but not dry and add:

2 egg whites

To still-freeze, see page 486. Serve in:

Orange cups

MINT SHERBET OR ICE

[About 9 Servings]

A refreshing alternate for the mint jelly which traditionally accompanies lamb.

Prepare:

Any orange or lemon ice or sherbet

After the sirup reaches the boiling point, pour it over:

½ cup fresh chopped mint leaves

Steep briefly, drain out the mint leaves and add dissolved gelatin, if necessary.

WINE SHERBET

[About 8 Servings]

A dry sherbet—good served after roasted meat or as a garnish for a fruit compote.

Soak:

1 tablespoon gelatin

in:

¼ cup cold water

Boil for 10 minutes:

1 cup water
¾ cup sugar

Dissolve gelatin in hot sirup. Chill. Add:

2 cups dry white wine
1 cup unstrained lime juice
1 tablespoon crème de menthe

Beat until ◗ stiff, but not dry and fold into this chilled mixture:

1 egg white

Serve garnished with:

Fruit

or in:

Lemon cups

CHAMPAGNE SHERBET

[About 8 Servings]
Stir until dissolved and boil for
about 5 minutes until thick:

   1¼ cups sugar
   1 cup water

Cool. Stir in:

   1½ cups champagne
   3 tablespoons lemon juice

Churn-freeze, page 483, until
almost set:
Fold in:

   Meringue I, page 432

When ready to serve, pour over
each portion:

   2 tablespoons champagne

FRUIT MILK SHERBET

Any of the milk sherbets may be
frozen as for Lemon Ice, page
495, but they are somewhat
lighter and less granular if prepared with gelatin.
Prepare:

   Any of the lemon, orange,
   pineapple or banana
   sherbets

Soak:

   2 teaspoons gelatin

in:

   2 tablespoons cold water

Dissolve over heat. Add to the
other ingredients. Add:

   3½ cups milk or milk and
   cream

Stir well. Place in foil-covered
trays in refrigerator. To still-
freeze, see page 487.

PINEAPPLE BUTTERMILK SHERBET

[About 6 Servings]
Combine:

   2 cups buttermilk
   ½ cup sugar
   1 cup crushed pineapple

Freeze these ingredients until
they have a slushy consistency.
Place them in a chilled bowl.
Add:

   1 slightly beaten egg white
   1½ teaspoons vanilla

Beat until light and fluffy. Replace in foil-covered refrigerator
trays. To still-freeze, see page
486.

ORANGE ICE ANGELICA

[About 6 Servings]
Prepare:

   2 cups orange juice

Add:

   ⅓ cup sugar

Dissolve over hot water:

   1 teaspoon gelatin

in:

   ¼ cup cold water

Add the gelatin to the orange
juice. ◗ Whip until thickened,
but not stiff:

   2 cups whipping cream

Fold into it:

   1 teaspoon vanilla
   1 tablespoon or more
   powdered sugar
   (½ cup broken nut meats)

Place orange juice mixture in
bottom of a mold or tray. Pile
the cream on top. Still-freeze in
a mold, page 486, or foil-covered refrigerator trays, page 487.

FROZEN SUCKERS

[Fourteen 1½-inch Suckers]
Quickly made from canned baby
fruits. When these mixtures are
partially frozen in a compart-
mented ice tray or in individual
paper cups, insert a looped para-
fined string or a paper spoon
into each unit to form a handle.
Then freeze until hard.
I. Mix and stir well:

   2 cups sweetened puréed
   fruit
   1 cup orange juice
   2 tablespoons sugar

Freeze as described above.

II. Mix and freeze, as described
above:

   ¾ cup orange or grape juice
   1 cup yogurt
   ½ teaspoon vanilla
   (1 tablespoon lemon juice)

CANDIES AND CONFECTIONS

The fudge pot is responsible for the beginnings of many a good cook. So be tolerant when, some rainy day, your children take an interest in the sweeter side of kitchen life. Weather and altitude play important roles for confectioners, young and old. On humid days, candy requires longer cooking and ingredients must be brought to a heat at least 2 degrees higher than they do on dry .ones. In fact, dry, cool weather is a necessary condition for certain types of confections, such as those made with honey, hard candies, glazes, divinities, fondant and nougats.

To avoid a mess ◗ always choose a pan with about four times as great a volume as that of the ingredients used, so that the candy will not boil over. ◗ To keep from burning the candy see that the pan has a heavy bottom. ◗ To keep from burning yourself, use a long wooden spoon that will not heat up during the prolonged cooking period.

ABOUT SUGARING IN CANDIES

When we were inexperienced, we were constantly baffled by the tendency of smooth, promising candy sirups to turn with lightning speed into grainy masses. We did not realize that one clue to our failure was stirring down the sugar crystals which formed on the sides of the pan into crystals of quite different structure in the candy mass.

Here are other tips to prevent sugaring in making candy: ◗ If the recipe calls for butter—and remember, always use unsalted butter—you may grease the sides of the pan before putting in the other ingredients. Here is a method we have used with never-failing success. ◗ Bring the liquid—whether milk or water—to a boil. ◗ Remove pan from heat and add the required sugar ◗ stirring until it is dissolved. For the addition of other ingredients see individual recipes. ◗ Return the pan to heat, cover it long enough for the candy to boil and to develop enough steam to wash down crystals from the walls of the pan. This is a matter of 2 or 3 minutes only. ◗ Now, uncover the pan to allow for evaporation. ◗ Do not stir after uncovering, but continue cooking until the mixture has reached the desired temperature. Use ◗ medium heat if the liquid is milk ◗ greater heat if the liquid is water. When you test for temperature, be sure to use an absolutely clean spoon or thermometer; the reason being, again, to avoid introducing extraneous sugar crystals. Should the candy start to sugar, add a small quantity of water and begin over again.

Those who make candy frequently will do well to provide themselves for the finishing step with a marble slab of generous proportions. For candies which require rapid cooling, this kind of material absorbs heat quickly and evenly, but not so rapidly as to affect crystallization adversely. The next best thing is a heavy stoneware platter. Both surfaces should be buttered in advance, except for fondant.

ABOUT CANDY THERMOMETER TEMPERATURES

As successful candy making depends largely on the temperatures at which different crystallizations of sugar occur ♦ an accurate professional candy thermometer, properly used, is invaluable. To test your thermometer for accuracy, heat it—in water, gradually to avoid breakage—and keep it in boiling water for 10 minutes. It should register 212°. If there is any variation, add or subtract the number of degrees necessary to make its reading conform to a standard scale.

When actually using the thermometer, warm it as for testing before inserting it into the candy. Place it near the center of the pan and do not let the bulb touch the bottom. Heat rises slowly to 220°, then takes a spurt—so watch carefully. ♦ For true accuracy, read at eye level, which of course means some gymnastics on your part. Have a spoon ready when you remove the thermometer to catch any sirup drops that might fall back into the pan. Clean the thermometer after each use by letting it stand in warm water.

If you have no thermometer, practice can make you expert in recognizing the subtle differences in color, bubbling and threading that correspond to the basic temperatures. Always remove the pot from the heat while testing so as not to overcook, as a few extra degrees can bring the candy up into the next stage of crystallization.

THREAD—230° to 234°

Drop a small quantity of sirup into ice water. This is a coarse-thread stage.

SOFT BALL—234° to 240°

Drop a small quantity of sirup into ice water. It forms a ball which does not disintegrate but flattens out of its own accord when picked up with the fingers.

FIRM BALL—244° to 248°

Drop a small quantity of sirup into ice water. The ball will hold its shape and will not flatten unless pressed with the fingers.

HARD BALL—250° to 266°

Drop a small quantity of sirup into ice water. The ball will hold its shape but is still pliable.

SOFT CRACK—270° to 290°

Drop a small quantity of sirup into ice water. It will separate into hard threads, which, when removed from the water, will bend and not be brittle.

HARD CRACK—300° to 310°

Drop a small quantity of sirup into ice water. The sirup will separate into threads that are hard and brittle.

CARAMELIZED SUGAR— 310° to 338°

Between these temperatures sirup turns dark golden, but will turn black at 350°.

♦ For candy making at high altitudes, adjust for temperatures as follows: If soft ball at 236° at sea level is called for: test for soft ball at 226° at 3000 feet, 223° at 5000 feet and 220° at 7000 feet.

♦ Do not jostle the pan when removing it from heat or during the cooling period. ♦ The candy should never be beaten until it has cooled to at least 110°. There are two ways of cooling. If you are the impatient type, place the pot gently—the minute you take it from the heat—

into a pan of ice-cold water and allow it to remain until you can touch the bottom without discomfort. The other way is to pour the candy onto a marble slab or a buttered heavy platter. If it is taffy, caramel or brittle, hold the pouring edge of the pan away from you and only a few inches above the slab to avoid spattering. With these candies, too, let the mix run out of the pan of its own accord. ▶ Do not scrape the dregs out of the pan. The reason is to avoid sugaring. There is a difference in crystallization rate between the free flowing portion and the other, near the bottom of the pan, which was exposed to greater heat. If you have neglected to use butter to grease the sides of the pan, you may drop it onto the surface of the hot candy and beat it in after the candy reaches 110°.

These are general principles. For particulars, follow the individual recipes carefully. If you substitute honey in part for sugar, remember that honey needs a higher degree of heat and longer beating. Frequently, because honey attracts atmospheric moisture, the candies become sticky.

In gauging the yields for the following recipes, we have not counted in nuts, fruits and other additions where such additions are optional.

ABOUT CANDY WRAPPINGS

For that professional look, wrap candies in attractive foils or buy, at small cost, fancy fluted foil cups into which you can pour directly. Delight the children with lollipop cords or let them package hard candies between a double strip of self-adhesive plastic, which you cut into squares after inserting the candy.

ABOUT FONDANT AND CENTERS

One of the charms of fondant is that a batch can be made and ripened and then used at will over a period of weeks, with varying flavors, colors and shapes to suit the occasion. Basic Fondant also lends itself to variations during cooking. You may replace the water in the recipe with strong coffee or you may use half white and half brown sugar or you may use half white and half maple sugar. But in case you don't want to make up a large batch of Basic Fondant, read the alternate processes given after the basic recipe—or use recipes carrying the word "center" in the title.

BASIC FONDANT

[About 1¼ Pounds]
Bring to a boil in a large, heavy pan:
        1 cup water
Remove from heat and stir in until dissolved:
        3 cups sugar
Return to heat and have ready:
        ¹⁄₁₆ teaspoon cream of tartar
More will make the fondant harder to work later. ▶ Just as the sirup comes up to a boil, add the cream of tartar to the mixture by tapping it from the spoon on the edge of the pan. Be ready to stir, as it will tend to make the sirup boil over. ▶ Cover until the steam can wash down the sides of the pan. ▶ Cook this mixture uncovered, without stirring, until it reaches 238° to 240°. Remove pan gently from heat. Pour sirup onto a wet marble slab or platter. ▶ Do not scrape pan. ▶ Let the sirup cool thoroughly.

Work it with a candy scraper or a wooden spoon by lifting and folding always from edges to center. When the sirup loses its translucency and begins to become opaque and creamy, knead it well with the hands. Dust them with confectioners' sugar if necessary.

Even experts sometimes cook fondant too hard to knead it. If you have done so, add two-thirds of a cup of water. Melt the mixture very slowly in the top of a double boiler ♦ over —not in—hot water, stirring constantly until the boiling point is reached again. Then proceed by covering, letting the steam wash down the sides of the pan and cooking again to 238° to 240°.

After kneading fondant, put it in a tightly covered container. Allow it to remain in a cool place for from 24 hours to a week or more.

To prepare fondant for shaping, put it in a double boiler ♦ over—not in—hot water. Heat it slowly, with the water at 170° to 180°, until you can shape it, then put it on a slab.

If you want to color the fondant, make a depression in the mass and pour in a few drops of food coloring. Gash it in several places but not all the way through to the slab—allowing the color to spread into the candy. Continue chopping and folding to complete the spreading process. Flavoring can be worked in the same way. At this time, you may also incorporate chopped or whole nuts, candied fruits, ginger, coconut or jam. Allow equal portions of these additions to the amount of fondant. Correct to the proper consistency with confectioners' sugar if necessary.

Form fondant by rolling it into one-half inch rods then cut into round or oval pieces. You are now ready to dip them in:

Chocolate Coating, see
page 505

♦ Be sure to have centers at room temperature to keep chocolate from developing gray streaks.

SOFT CENTER FONDANT

[About 1 Pound]
This is the type of fondant often used around a candied cherry in a chocolate coating. It is not allowed to ripen but must be molded and dipped at once. After dipping, the egg white causes it to become liquid inside its coating.
Bring to a boil in a large, heavy pan:

    2 cups sugar
    1 cup water
    ¼ teaspoon glycerin
    1 tablespoon light corn
        sirup

Stir these ingredients until the sugar is thoroughly dissolved. Place the pan over low heat. ♦ When the mixture begins to boil, cover it, so that the steam will wash down any crystals that may have formed on the sides of the pan. Cook the sirup for about 3 minutes. ♦ Uncover and continue cooking sirup without stirring until it reaches the soft-ball stage, 238° to 240°. Remove it gently from heat. Pour onto a wet slab or platter. Cool sirup to 110°. Spread over it with a spatula:

    1 well-beaten egg white
To work, flavor, form and dip, see Basic Fondant, above. These processes must be done as quickly as possible.

UNCOOKED FONDANT

[About 1½ Pounds]
Tempting, opulent-looking—not for reducers. This candy is the specialty of a very clever hostess, whose parties seem incomplete without it. Her son calls them "knockout drops" because he once indulged in 13 and suffered the consequences. This candy must be kept refrigerated.
Beat until soft:

½ cup butter

Add very slowly and cream until very light:

> 1 lb. sifted confectioners' sugar

Add:

> ¼ cup whipping cream
> 1 scant teaspoon vanilla

Work the fondant well with the hands and shape it into 1-inch balls. To roll the balls use about:

> ¼ lb. sifted confectioners' sugar

Raisins, nut meats or a bit of candied fruit may be rolled into the center of the balls. Place balls on foil in the refrigerator, covered, until they are hard. To dip, see Chocolate Coating, page 505.

When coating has hardened, store balls in a covered container in refrigerator until ready to serve.

CARAMEL FONDANT

[About 1¼ Pounds]
Heat in a large, heavy pan:

> ½ cup milk

Remove from heat and stir in until dissolved:

> 1½ cups sugar
> ¼ cup butter

Return to heat and bring very slowly to a boil. Meanwhile, caramelize—see page 169—in a heavy skillet:

> ½ cup sugar

When the sugar and butter mixture boils, stir in the caramelized sugar very slowly. Boil, then ◗ cover about 3 minutes until any crystals on the sides of the pan have been washed down by the steam. Cook candy to soft-ball stage, 238°, without stirring. Cool candy to 110°. Beat it until creamy. Pour it into a pan and mark it into squares or form candy into small balls. Place between them:

> Nut meats

or dip them in:

Chocolate Coating, see page 505

NEWPORT CREAMS OR CENTERS

[About 1½ Pounds]
Much like an opera cream in texture.
Bring to a boil in a large, heavy pan, stirring until the sugar is dissolved:

> ⅔ cup light corn sirup
> 2 cups brown sugar
> 6 tablespoons hot water

◗ Cover about 3 minutes until any crystals on the sides of the pan have been washed down by the steam. ◗ Uncover and cook, without stirring, to the thread stage, 234°. Whip until stiff:

> 1 egg white
> A few grains of salt

Pour sirup slowly into the egg white, whipping constantly. Add:

> 1 teaspoon vanilla
> 1¼ cups nut meats

When you can no longer stir the candy, flatten it out on a buttered tin. When it is cold, cut it into squares.

OPERA CREAMS OR CENTERS

[About 1¼ Pounds]
Bring to a boil in a large, heavy pan, stirring until the sugar is dissolved:

> 2 cups sugar
> ¾ cup whipping cream
> 1 cup milk
> 2 tablespoons light corn sirup
> ⅛ teaspoon salt

◗ Cover and cook about 3 minutes until the steam has washed down any crystals on the sides of the pan. ◗ Uncover and cook over low heat to 238°. Remove from heat. Cool to 110°. Add:

> 1 teaspoon vanilla

Beat the mixture until it is creamy. Pour it into special candy rubber-sheet molds or a buttered pan. When cold, cut into squares. Place in an airtight container. This candy improves if aged at least 24 hours. When it has ripened, you may dip it in a:

Chocolate Coating, see page 505

MAPLE CREAM CANDY

[About 1 Pound]

Who would ever suspect that this delicious confection was just plain maple sirup in a more solid form?

Boil over very low heat without stirring:

2 cups maple sirup

until it reaches the late thread stage, 233°. Allow this reduced sirup to cool to 110°, about 1 hour, without stirring. Add:

(1 teaspoon vanilla)

Beat until it becomes light in color and fluffy in texture and is hard enough to hold its shape for patties or in molds. This candy dries out on exposure to air, so box tightly as soon as cool.

PEPPERMINT CREAM WAFERS

[About 1¼ Pounds]

Stir over low heat in a large, heavy pan until the sugar is dissolved:

2 cups sugar
¼ cup light corn sirup
¼ cup milk
¼ teaspoon cream of tartar

Cook and stir these ingredients slowly until they boil. ◗ Cover for about 3 minutes until any crystals on the sides of the pan have been washed down by the steam. ◗ Uncover and cook without stirring to the soft-ball stage, 238°. Remove from heat. Cool slightly. Beat until creamy. Flavor with:

8 to 12 drops oil of peppermint

Tint lightly with vegetable coloring if desired. Drop the mix-

ture from a teaspoon onto foil to form patties in the size you want. These and the preceding wafers are delightful decorated or initialed for teas. See About Decorative Icings, page 420.

★ ALMOND OR FILBERT PASTE

[About 2 Pounds]

In some parts of Europe this almond confection is traditional at Christmas time. It is molded into fancy shapes or into flat cakes that are pie-shaped and elaborately decorated. A thin wedge is served to visitors, together with a glass of dessert wine. You may also prepare filberts this way for cake fillings. Blanch, see page 189:

1 lb. almonds or filberts

Grind them. All our other recipes for grinding almonds read: "Put through a nut grinder." This is the only recipe that says: "Put them through a meat grinder." This time you want the nuts to be oily. Use the finest blade and grind the nuts at least 4 times. If you use a ⅄ blender, use the orange juice or kirsch called for to start the blending action. Cook to the end of the soft-ball stage, 240°, in a large heavy pan:

2 cups sugar
1 cup water

Add the ground nuts and:

6 to 8 tablespoons orange juice or kirsch
(A few drops rosewater)

Rosewater is the traditional flavoring. Stir these ingredients until they are thoroughly blended and creamy. Permit them to cool until you can knead them. There are 2 things that make kneading easier: put confectioners' sugar on your hands or cover the paste and permit it to rest for about 12 hours. Flatten it on a hard surface dusted with confectioners' sugar, then mold it into any desired shape. Pack in a closely covered tin or jar. Ripen from 6 to 8 days.

★ MARZIPAN OR MARCHPANE

[About ½ Pound]

The Arabs brought this confection to Europe; and at various times since, in tribute to its preciousness, the word which describes it has meant "a sitting king," "a little box," "a stamped coin."

Marzipan cake and dessert decorations made in advance are useful to have on hand, and those by the first method can be ✳ frozen for future use.

I. Whip until fluffy:

　　1 egg white

Work in gradually:

　　1 cup Almond Paste, see
　　　recipe above.

Add:

　　1½ cups sifted confectioners'
　　　sugar

Use more if necessary to make a paste that is easy to handle. Should it become too thick, work in drop by drop:

　　Lemon juice

Should it become too oily, work it in a dish over ice. In either case, knead the paste. Mold it into any desired shape. Small fruit shapes are great favorites. If you wish to color it, use a pastry brush with a little diluted vegetable coloring. Glaze the "fruits" with a solution of:

　　Gum arabic, see page
　　523

Also, you may roll the paste in:

　　Equal parts of cocoa and
　　powdered sugar

or use it as a center for dipping. Wrap each piece separately in foil. Store in a cool place.

II. Use:

　　Equal parts of almond
　　paste and fondant

Knead, mold and color as above.

MARSHMALLOWS

[About 1¾ Pounds]

This recipe requires the use of an electric mixer. Results are also much improved if you can get, at a professional outlet, gelatin of 250 bloom—a more concentrated form than that sold to the housewife.

Put in the mixer bowl and let stand for 1 hour:

　　3 tablespoons gelatin
　　½ cup cold water

Then in about ½ hour start to prepare a sirup. Place in a heavy pan over low heat and stir until dissolved:

　　2 cups sugar
　　¾ cup light corn sirup
　　½ cup water
　　¼ teaspoon salt

When the mixture starts to boil ♦ cover it for about 3 minutes to allow any crystals which have formed to be washed down from the sides of the pan.

Continue to cook ♦ uncovered and unstirred over high heat until the thermometer reaches 240° to 244°. Overcooking will make marshmallows tough. Remove from heat and pour slowly over the gelatin, beating constantly. After all the sirup is added, continue to beat for about 15 minutes. When the mixture is thick but still warm add:

　　2 tablespoons vanilla

Put the mixture into an 8 x 12-inch pan that has been lightly dusted with cornstarch. When it has dried for 12 hours remove it from the pan, cut it into squares with scissors dusted with cornstarch and store the fully dusted pieces in a closed tin.

CHOCOLATE COATING

For a long time our attempts to dip candies attractively were not an unqualified success. We finally sought the advice of Larry

Blumenthal, whose family has been "in chocolate" for generations. He finds our procedure solid, but warns us that when you heat chocolate and cool it to dipping temperature, you have "tempered" it, and that its reactions from this point on are somewhat unpredictable. In the candy trade, dipping is turned over to a "handcoater," who uses no special processed chocolate, although he may thicken his mix adroitly by adding at just the right moment a few drops of water at 65° to 70°— but who, through long practice, develops a "knack."

♦ Choose crisp dry weather for dipping. ♦ Work in a room where the temperature is 60° to 70° and where there are no drafts.

Grate about:

    1 lb. chocolate, sweet,
       bitter, bittersweet or
       milk

Melt it very, very slowly in the top of a 1½ quart double boiler. ♦ over—not in—hot water. ♦ Stir the chocolate until its temperature reaches 130°. If you do not stir constantly at temperatures over 100°, the cocoa butter will separate out. Remove from the heat and cool to about 88°. Heat water to 90° in the bottom of the double boiler. Place chocolate in the upper part of the double boiler.

Before dipping into chocolate be sure the candy centers or fillings are at room temperature. Otherwise, the chocolate may streak with gray. Immerse the centers one at a time in the chocolate— maintaining its temperature. Lift them out with a fork or a candy-dipping fork onto a ¼-inch wire rack, above a pan or tray—to catch chocolate drippings, which may be re-melted and re-used. There is always surplus on the dipping fork—this is lifted directly above the candy to make designs which identify the various fillings.

FUDGE COCKAIGNE

[About 1¼ Pounds]

Bring to a boil in a large heavy pan:

    1 cup, minus 1 tablespoon,
       rich milk

Remove from heat and stir in until dissolved:

    2 cups sugar
    ⅛ teaspoon salt
    2 oz. grated chocolate

♦ Bring to a boil and cook covered 2 to 3 minutes until the steam washes down from the sides of the pan any crystals which may have formed. ♦ Uncover, reduce heat and cook without stirring to soft-ball stage, 238°. When nearing 238°, there is a fine overall bubbling with, simultaneously, a coarser pattern, as though the fine bubbled areas were being pulled down for quilting into the coarser ones. Remove from heat without jostling or stirring. ♦ Cool the candy to 110°. You may hasten this process by placing the hot pan in a larger pan of cold water until the bottom of the pan has cooled. Add:

    2 to 4 tablespoons butter

Beat fudge partially. Add:

    1 teaspoon vanilla

Then beat until it begins to lose its sheen. At this point the drip from the spoon, when you flip it over, holds its shape against the bottom of the spoon. Quickly add:

    ½ to 1 cup broken nut
       meats

Pour the fudge into a buttered pan. Cut into squares before it hardens. To use fudge for centers, beat until thick, knead and shape.

COCOA FUDGE OR CENTERS

[About 1½ Pounds]

We find that when made with dry milk solids this candy has an unusually interesting texture for centers. We like to cut it

into caramel-size cubes for dipping. If you prefer to make it with fresh milk use the same liquid proportions but mix and cook as for Fudge Cockaigne, see page 506. Melt in a large, heavy skillet over medium heat:

    ¼ cup butter
Add:
    1½ cups boiling water
Mix and stir into the hot mixture:
    3 cups sugar
    ⅔ cup cocoa
    ⅛ teaspoon cream of tartar
♦ Continue to stir until the mixture boils. Cover about 3 minutes to allow steam to wash down any crystals that may have formed on sides of pan. ♦ Uncover, lower heat and cook slowly ♦ without stirring to the soft-ball stage, 236°. Do not stir after removing candy from heat. When the mixture has cooled to 110° add:
    6 tablespoons whole or
        skim milk solids
    1 teaspoon vanilla
Beat until creamy. Pour into an 8 x 8-inch buttered pan or, when it becomes firm, knead it into 1-inch balls. If it seems too

stiff to knead, cover with a damp cloth for about an hour.

COFFEE FUDGE

[About 1 Pound]
Bring to a boil in a large, heavy pan:
    1 cup strong coffee
Remove from heat and stir in until dissolved:
    2 cups sugar
    1 tablespoon cream
    1 tablespoon butter
    ⅛ teaspoon salt
    ¼ teaspoon cream of tartar
Cook these ingredients quickly, stirring them constantly until they boil. ♦ Cover and cook for about 3 minutes until the steam washes down any crystals which may have formed on the sides of the pan. ♦ Uncover and cook over moderate heat to 238°. Remove from heat. Cool to 110° Add:
    ½ teaspoon almond extract
        or ½ teaspoon cinnamon
Beat until the mixture begins to harden. Add:
    1 cup broken pecan or
        hickory nuts
Pour onto a buttered surface. Permit the candy to cool and harden before cutting into squares.

COCONUT FUDGE OR CENTERS

[About 1¼ Pounds]
Combine in a deep saucepan:
    1½ cups sugar
    ½ cup corn sirup
    ½ cup top milk
    ¼ cup molasses
    (1 tablespoon vinegar)
    ⅛ teaspoon salt
Stir these ingredients over medium heat until the sugar is dissolved. Bring to a boil and ♦ cook covered for about 3 minutes until the steam has washed down from the sides of the pan any crystals which may have formed. ♦ Uncover and cook slowly to

the soft-ball stage—238°—without stirring. Remove from heat and stir in:

 1¼ cups moist shredded
      coconut
 3 tablespoons butter

Pour candy onto a buttered platter. When cool enough to handle, shape into small balls or centers. Place them on foil to dry.

DIVINITY

[About 1½ Pounds]
Pick a dry day. This candy does not keep well. If you use the brown sugar and vinegar, you may prefer to call this Sea Foam. Bring to room temperature:

 2 egg whites

Bring to a boil in a heavy pan:

 ½ cup water
 ½ cup light corn sirup

Dissolve in it:

 2 cups sugar or brown
      sugar
 (1 tablespoon vinegar)

When boiling ♦ cover pan and cook about 3 minutes until the steam has washed down any crystals that may have formed on the sides of the pan. ♦ Remove lid and cook over moderate heat, without stirring, to the hard-ball stage, 254°. While sirup is cooking, beat egg whites in a large bowl until they just hold their shape. When the sirup is ready, pour it slowly over the egg whites in a steady thin stream, whipping slowly at the same time. Toward the end, add the sirup more quickly and whip faster. ♦ Do not scrape pan. After all sirup has been added, put in:

 1 cup broken nut meats
 (1 cup raisins)

As a variation try omitting nuts and raisins and add:

 (1 cup crushed peppermint
      candy)

Beat until candy can be dropped onto a buttered surface into patties which hold their shape.

CARAMEL CREAM DIVINITY

[About 2 Pounds]
A smooth, rich candy which keeps better than divinity. Bring to a boil in a large heavy pan:

 2 cups cream

♦ Remove from heat and stir in:

 3 cups sugar
 1 cup white corn sirup

Return to heat and cook slowly. When the candy boils ♦ cover and cook for about 3 minutes until the steam washes down any crystals which may have formed on the sides of the pan. ♦ Uncover and cook slowly, without stirring, to the soft-ball stage, 238°. Remove sirup from heat. Cool to 110°. Beat until very stiff. Beat in:

 1 cup pecan meats

Pour the candy into a buttered pan. Cut it when cool.

NOUGAT

[About 1¼ Pounds]
Southern France and Italy are famous for luscious nougats with distinctive flavors due to regional honey variations. So, why is there no honey in our recipe? For the answer, see About Honey, page 167. Pick a dry day. This is a 2-part process and an electric mixer is almost imperative.
First, cook in a 2-quart heavy saucepan:

 6 tablespoons sugar
 1 tablespoon water
 ⅓ cup light corn sirup

Blend over low heat and stir until boiling. ♦ Cover and cook for about 3 minutes until the steam has washed down any crystals which may have formed on the sides of the pan. Cook ♦ uncovered over medium heat, without stirring, to the soft-ball stage, 238°. Remove pan from heat and let stand while you beat in a mixer until very stiff:

    ¼ cup egg whites

Add the hot sirup gradually to the whites, continuing to beat for at least five minutes until the mass thickens.

Blend in a heavy 1-quart pan and stir over low heat until it boils:

    1 cup light corn sirup
    1 cup sugar

Stop stirring ♦ cover again for 3 minutes, then uncover and boil rapidly, without stirring, to 285°. Remove from heat and let stand until sirup stops bubbling. Now pour the second mixture into the first and beat until well combined. Beat in:

    2 tablespoons butter cut in small chunks

Add:

    1 cup blanched almonds
    ½ cup blanched pistachio nuts
    (½ cup chopped candied cherries)

Pour into an 8 x 8-inch buttered pan dusted with confectioners' sugar or lined with baker's wafer paper. Let set in a cool place 12 hours. If hard to get out of pan, release sides with a knife. Then hold bottom of pan briefly over heat and reverse the block onto a board for slicing.

VANILLA CREAM CARAMELS

[About 2½ Pounds]
Dissolve over low heat in a large, heavy pan, stirring until mixture boils:

    2 cups sugar
    2 cups dark corn sirup
    1 cup butter
    1 cup cream

Cook over moderate heat, stirring constantly, to 240°. Remove from heat and add very gradually:

    1 cup cream

Return to heat and cook to 244° to 246°. Pour the mixture at once, without stirring, into a buttered pan. When firm, about 3 hours later, invert the candy onto a wooden board and cut into squares with a thin-bladed knife. Use a light sawing motion.

MAPLE CARAMELS

[About 1½ Pounds]
Stir in a large, heavy pan over quick heat until the sugar is dissolved:

    2 cups brown sugar
    1½ cups maple sirup
    ½ cup cream

Stir and cook these ingredients slowly to the firm-ball stage, 242°. Add:

    1 tablespoon butter

Pour candy onto buttered tin. Cut into squares as it hardens. Nuts may be added to the candy just before removing it from the heat or they may be sprinkled on the buttered tin before pouring the candy. When cool, about 3 hours later, invert onto a board and cut into squares.

CHOCOLATE CARAMELS

[About 1½ Pounds]
Stir over quick heat until the sugar is dissolved:

    3 cups sugar
    1 cup light corn sirup
    1 cup milk
    1½ tablespoons butter

Cut into small pieces and stir in:

    3 oz. chocolate

Stir and boil these ingredients slowly to the firm-ball stage, 248°. Add:

    1 teaspoon vanilla

Pour candy into lightly buttered tins. When firm—about 3 hours later, invert onto a board and cut into ¾-inch squares.

CHOCOLATE CREAM CARAMELS

[About 1 Pound]
Stir over quick heat until the sugar is dissolved:

1 cup sugar
¾ cup light corn sirup
3 oz. chocolate
¼ teaspoon salt
½ cup cream

Over moderate heat bring the ingredients to the soft-ball stage, 238°. Stir constantly. Add:

½ cup cream

Cook candy until it again reaches the soft-ball stage, 238°, Add:

½ cup cream

Cook the candy until it reaches the firm-ball stage, 248°. Remove candy from heat and pour into an 8 x 4-inch buttered pan. Do not scrape pan. When candy is firm, about 3 hours later, invert onto a board and cut into squares.

FILLED CARAMELS

Prepare:
Chocolate Cream
Caramels, above

Pour the candy into two 4 x 8-inch buttered pans. When it holds its shape, remove the two layers from pans. Slice a ¼-inch layer of:

Basic Fondant, page 501

Place it over the surface of one layer. Cover it with the other layer. Cut the caramels in ½- or ¾-inch squares, using a sharp knife and a sawing action. Wrap individually.

OLD-FASHIONED BUTTER-SCOTCH

[About 1 Pound]
Place in a heavy pan, large enough to allow for foaming:

2 cups brown sugar
¼ cup molasses
½ cup butter
2 tablespoons water
2 tablespoons vinegar

Stir these ingredients over quick heat until the sugar is dissolved. Boil quickly—stirring frequently—to the hard-crack

stage, 300°. Drop candy from a teaspoon onto a buttered slab or foil to form patties.

BUTTERSCOTCH

[About 1¾ Pounds]
Stir in a large, heavy saucepan until dissolved:

2 cups sugar
⅔ cup dark corn sirup
¼ cup water
¼ cup cream

Cook these ingredients to just below the hard-ball stage—260°—then stir constantly until they almost reach the hard-crack stage 288°. Pour candy into a buttered pan. When cool and almost set, mark into squares or bars. When cold, cut or break apart.

COFFEE DROPS

[About 1¼ Pounds]
Use same ingredients as in above recipe for Butterscotch, but cook to 295°. Have ready an essence made of:

6 to 8 tablespoons coffee
⅔ cup water
1 tablespoon vinegar

Simmer slowly until about three tablespoons or less of liquid remain. Drain from the grounds and add:

½ teaspoon glycerin

Remove sirup from heat. Sprinkle coffee essence over the surface. Stir it in very gently. Drop sirup into ¾-inch patties from the edge of a spoon onto a buttered surface. When cool, wrap individually and store in a tightly covered container.

ABOUT TAFFIES

If you have a hankering to recreate an old-time "candy pull," be sure you have a reasonably stout pair of arms or an adolescent in the family who wants to convert from a puny weakling to a strong man. This way, taffy

pulling is fun and seems easy. However, should you lack these advantages and wish to pull taffy often, you will find that a candy hook is well worth the investment.

When the sirup has cooked to the indicated temperature ◗ pour it slowly onto a buttered slab. ◗ Hold the pouring edge of the pan away from you and only a few inches above the slab, so you won't be spattered with the dangerously hot sirup. Allow the sirup to cool briefly. ◗ This is the moment to flavor the taffy. Because of the great heat, use flavoring essences based on essential oils. See flavoring of Hard Candies, page 513. Sprinkle these over the surface of the hot sirup. Go easy, as they are very strong. If chocolate is to be added, grate it on the buttered slab before pouring. Nuts, fruits and coconut can be worked in during the pulling process.

Begin to work the sirup up into a central mass, turning it and working it with a candy scraper until it is cool enough to handle with your oiled fingertips. ◗ Take care in picking up the mass. It may have cooled on the surface and still be hot enough to burn as you press down into it. Taffy cooked to 270° should be pulled near a source of heat. When you can gather it up, start pulling it with your fingertips, allowing a spread of about 18 inches between your

hands. Then fold it back on itself. Repeat this motion rhythmically. As the mass changes from a somewhat sticky, side-whiskered affair to a glistening crystal ribbon—see illustration above—start twisting, while folding and pulling. ◗ Pull until the ridges on the twist begin to hold their shape, see center illustration, this page.

The candy will have become opaque, firm and elastic but will still retain its satiny finish. Depending on proper cooking, the weather and your skill, this pulling process may last from five to twenty minutes.

◗ Have ready a surface dusted with confectioners' sugar or cornstarch. Then form the candy into a ball in your hands and press it into a narrow point at the finger-tip end. Grasping the narrow point in one hand, pull it away from the rest of the ball into a long rope about one-inch thick. Let the rope fall out onto the dusted board like a snake. Cut it into the size you prefer with well-buttered shears. Let it cool. If you do not want to wrap separately, put it in a tightly covered tin, dusting and all. Some taffies, especially those heavy in cream, will, of their own accord, turn from a pulled chewy consistency to a creamy one. This happens sometimes a few minutes after cutting, sometimes as long as 12 hours later. After creaming takes place, be sure to wrap the taffies in foil and store them in a closed tin. They dry out readily on exposure to air.

VANILLA TAFFY

[About ½ Pound]

If you allow this candy to become creamy, it rivals the very rich Cream Pull Candy, next page. Combine and stir over slow heat until the sugar is dissolved:

    1¼ cups sugar
    ¼ cup water
    2 tablespoons mild vinegar
    1½ teaspoons butter

Cook these ingredients quickly, without stirring, to just between the very-hard-ball and the light-crack stages, 268°–270°. Add:

    ½ teaspoon vanilla or other flavoring

Pour candy on buttered platter or marble slab and let cool until a dent can be made in it when pressed with a finger. Gather it into a lump and pull it with fingertips until light and porous, see page 511. Pull any desired flavoring or coloring into the candy. Roll it into long thin strips and cut into 1-inch pieces. Place candy in a tightly covered tin if you wish it to become creamy.

MOLASSES TAFFY

[About 1 Pound]

Stir over quick heat until the sugar is dissolved and stir until boiling:

    1 cup molasses
    2 teaspoons vinegar
    1 cup sugar
    ⅛ teaspoon salt

◗ Cover pan and, without stirring, cook sirup rather quickly to just below the firm-ball stage, 240°. Add, by dropping in small pieces:

    2 tablespoons butter

Boil sirup slowly—just past the very-hard-ball stage, 270°. Holding the pouring edge of

the pan away from you and a few inches above the slab allow sirup to spread over slab. ◗ Do not scrape pan. Sprinkle surface of taffy with:

    4 drops oil of peppermint

To work, pull and form, see About Taffies, page 510. To make chips, pull in long, very thin strips. For coating with:

    Chocolate, see page 505

PULLED MINTS

[About 1 Pound]

Like the old-fashioned cushion ones we used to buy in tins. Combine in a large, heavy pan and stir until it again reaches a boil:

    1 cup boiling water
    2 cups sugar
    ¼ teaspoon cream of tartar

◗ Cook covered about 3 minutes until the sides of the pan are washed free of crystals. ◗ Uncover and cook without stirring to hard-ball stage, 262°. Remove from heat and pour onto buttered marble slab.

Sprinkle with:

    A few drops oil of peppermint

To work, pull, form and cream, see about Taffies, page 510.

SALT WATER TAFFY

[About 1½ Pounds]

Combine and stir over low heat until sugar is dissolved:

    2 cups sugar
    1½ cups water
    1 cup light corn sirup
    2½ teaspoons salt
    2 teaspoons glycerin

Cook the sirup without stirring to the hard-ball stage, 265°. Remove it from the heat. Add:

    2 tablespoons butter

Holding the pouring edge of the pan away from you, and a few inches above the oiled slab, allow the sirup to spread. ◗ Do not scrape pan. To work, pull, flavor and form, see About Taffies, page 510.

CREAM PULL CANDY

[About 1½ Pounds]

Do not try this in damp, hot weather.

Combine in a heavy saucepan and stir over low heat until dissolved and boiling:

    3 cups sugar
    1 cup boiling water
    ⅛ teaspoon soda
    ½ teaspoon salt

◊ Cover about 3 minutes until steam has washed crystals from sides of the pan. ◊ Uncover and cook without stirring to 236°. ◊ Reduce heat—but not below 225°—while adding gradually:

    1 cup cream
    (¼ cup butter cut in small
    bits)

Cool: over moderate heat ◊ without stirring, to 257° and pour sirup at once over buttered marble slab. Hold the pouring edge away from you, and a few inches above the slab. Allow sirup to spread over the slab. ◊ Do not scrape pot. To work, pull, flavor, form and cream, see About Taffies, page 510.

HARD CANDY OR LOLLIPOPS

[About 1½ Pounds]

Bring to a boil in a large, heavy pan:

    1 cup water

Remove from heat. Add and stir until dissolved:

    2 cups sugar
    ¾ cup light corn sirup
    1 tablespoon butter

Return to heat. When boiling ◊ cover for about 3 minutes so the steam can wash down any crystals on the sides of the pan. ◊ Uncover and cook at high heat without stirring until the thermometer reaches 310°. Prepare a slab or molds by brushing them well with butter or oil.

If you are going to make lollipops, have stiffened lollipop cords on the oiled slab ready to receive patties. Remove candy mixture to low heat and add:

    A few drops coloring
    matter

Choose a vegetable color suitable to the flavor you have decided to use. An alcohol-based flavor like vanilla will evaporate in the intense heat. So be sure to use a flavor based, instead, on essential oils. For the above recipe, for instance, we suggest one of the following:

    ¼ teaspoon, or less, oil of
    peppermint or
    1 teaspoon, or less, oil of
    orange, lime or
    wintergreen
    ¼ teaspoon or less oil of
    cassia or cinnamon
    ⅛ teaspoon oil of anise

ROCK CANDY

Broken into small pieces and piled in an open bowl, this makes a sophisticated looking sugar substitute for coffee. Small clumps clustered on ⅛-inch dowels make attractive swizzle sticks for drinks. Whether the candy be on sticks or on strings, the process of making it is a fascinating experiment in crystallization. Produce it, first, on a very small scale by letting a supersaturated heated sirup cool undisturbed in a test tube into which you have previously sunk a weighted string. Make it on a larger scale by punching holes at the top edge of a thin 8-inch square pan and lacing about seven strings from one side to the other. Place the laced pan in a deeper pan to catch excess sirup.

Dissolve:

    2½ cups sugar

in:

    1 cup water

and cook without stirring to

247°–252°. Pour sirup into pie pan. It should reach a level about ¾ of an inch above the strings. Cover the surface with a piece of foil. Watch and wait. It sometimes takes a week to crystallize. Lift the laced pan out. Cut the strings and dislodge the rock candy. Rinse quickly in cold water, and put on racks in a very low oven to dry.

HOREHOUND CANDY

[About 2½ Pounds]
Make an infusion of:

6 cups boiling water
1 quart loosely packed horehound leaves and stems

Steep for 5 minutes. To 2 quarts of this bitter dark brew add:

4 cups sugar
1¼ cups dark cane sirup
1 tablespoon butter

Cook these ingredients until they reach the hard-crack stage, 300° to 310°. Skim off any scum. Pour into a 15 x 10 x 1-inch pan and score into pieces before it sets. Allow to cool.

NUT CRUNCH

[About 2 Pounds]
Sliver large, dense nuts like almonds and Brazil nuts. Others can be left whole. You may add them at once to the mixture if you like a roasted quality in the nut. If not, spread them on a buttered slab or pan and pour the sirup over them after cooking. Heat in a large, heavy skillet:

1 cup sugar
1 cup butter
3 tablespoons water

Cook rapidly and stir constantly for about 10 minutes or until the mixture reaches 295°. Add:

1 to 1½ cups nuts

Turn the candy quickly onto the buttered slab. Form into a shape about 1-foot square. When almost cool, brush with:

¼ lb. melted semi-sweet chocolate

Before the chocolate hardens, dust with:

¼ cup finely chopped nuts

Break into pieces when cold.

ENGLISH TOFFEE

[About 1½ Pounds]
Combine in a large, heavy saucepan and stir over quick heat until the sugar is dissolved:

1¾ cups sugar
⅛ teaspoon cream of tartar
1 cup cream

Stir and boil these ingredients for about 3 minutes. Add:

½ cup butter

Cook and stir the sirup until it is light colored and thick to the soft-crack stage, 285°–290°. Remove from heat. Add:

1 teaspoon vanilla or
1 tablespoon rum

Pour candy onto a buttered pan. When cool, cut into squares. To cover it with semi-sweet chocolate and nuts, see Nut Crunch, opposite.

ABOUT PENUCHE AND PRALINES

The taste of these candies is very similar. Penuche is often cut in squares, like fudge, while pralines are usually made into 3- to 4-inch patties. Why so large, we wonder? We prefer small sugared nuggets made by separating the nuts as the sugar begins to harden. They are best when freshly made with nuts of finest quality. Sometimes raisins or coconut are added. Pralines do not keep well unless wrapped in foil and stored in tightly covered containers.

PENUCHE AND PRALINES

[About 1 Pound]

I. Dissolve in a large, heavy pan and stir constantly until boiling:

3 cups brown sugar
¼ teaspoon salt
1 cup milk or cream

◗ Cover and cook about 3 minutes until the steam has washed down any crystals from the sides of the pan. ◗ Uncover and cook slowly, without stirring, to the soft-ball stage, 238°. Remove candy from heat and add:

1 to 2 tablespoons butter

Cool to 110°. Beat until smooth and creamy. Add:

1 teaspoon vanilla
1 cup nut meats

In summer try adding instead:

(½ cup grated fresh
  pineapple)
(1 teaspoon lemon juice)

Drop candy from a spoon onto a buttered surface.

II. [About 2 Pounds]

Dissolve in a large, heavy pan over low heat until boiling:

1⅓ cups sugar
⅔ cup brown sugar
⅔ cup water
⅔ teaspoon vinegar
⅛ teaspoon salt

◗ Cover and cook for about 3 minutes to allow the steam to wash down any crystals from the sides of the pan. ◗ Uncover and cook to the soft-ball stage, 236°. Remove pan from heat and add:

2 to 3 tablespoons butter

◗ Cool candy to 110°. Beat until it begins to lose its gloss and thickness. Quickly stir in:

2 cups pecans

Drop candy in patties from a spoon onto a buttered platter. When hardened, wrap them individually in foil.

PEANUT OR NUT BRITTLE

[About 2 Pounds]

Have ready a pair of clean white cotton gloves. It is best to use raw nuts and cook them in the sirup. Should only roasted nuts be available, add them after the sirup is cooked. In this case the candy is best if aged 24 hours. If the nuts are salted, rub them between paper towels and omit salt from the recipe. This recipe makes a tender clear brittle. For a porous one, combine ¼ teaspoon cream of tartar with the sugar, and sprinkle ½ teaspoon of soda all over the hot sirup just before pouring. Bring to a boil in a large heavy pan:

1 cup water

◗ Remove from heat and stir in until dissolved:

2 cups sugar

Then add and stir in:

1 cup corn sirup
2 cups raw Spanish
  peanuts, pecans, Brazil
  nuts or some other nut
  combination
1 teaspoon salt

Stir occasionally to keep any exposed nuts submerged, so they cook thoroughly and the candy does not burn. Cook to 295°. Remove from heat. Stir in lightly:

1 to 2 tablespoons butter
¼ teaspoon baking soda

Pour onto a well-buttered slab at once, scraping out bottom of pan. Spread mixture rapidly with a spatula. At this point, do the cotton gloves. Loosen the mass from slab with a scraper, reverse it and, discarding the scraper, stretch and pull the brittle so thin that you can see through it. When cool, crack into eating-size pieces and store in a tightly covered tin.

NUT BRITTLE, GLAZED NUTS AND PRALINÉ FOR GARNISH

I. [About ½ Pound]

This clear candy when ground or crushed is called praliné. Delicious over ice cream or when added to icings and dessert sauces. Melt in a skillet over low heat:

>   1 cup sugar

Stir constantly. When the sirup is light brown, 310°, stir in until well coated:

>   1 cup toasted almonds or
>   hazelnuts or toasted
>   benné seeds

Pour the candy onto a buttered platter. When it is cool crack into pieces.

II. For another sirup to use over nuts, see:

>   Glazed Fresh Fruits,
>   pages 523–526

ALMOND CREAMS

Blanch and toast lightly:

>   Almonds or hazelnuts

Cover them first with:

>   Basic Fondant, page 501,
>   or Uncooked Fondant,
>   page 502

Then dip them at once in:

>   Chocolate Coating,
>   page 505

Place them on a wire rack to dry.

SPICED CARAMEL NUTS

Have ready:

>   Toasted, blanched
>   almonds, hazelnuts or
>   pecans, see page 189

Prepare:

>   Chocolate Cream
>   Caramels, page 509

Add to the dissolved ingredients:

>   1 teaspoon cinnamon

When the candy has cooked to 248°, remove it from heat and spread to a ¼-inch thickness on a marble slab. Score the candy in 1-inch squares. Place a whole toasted nut on each square. Before candy hardens, enclose each nut in its candy square, shaping it to the nut.

SUGARED OR BURNT ALMONDS

[About 2 Pounds]

Cook over slow heat, stirring constantly:

>   2 cups sugar
>   ½ cup water
>   1 teaspoon or more
>   cinnamon

Boil the sirup rapidly. When it is clear and falls in heavy drops from a spoon, add:

>   1 lb. unblanched almonds,
>   hazelnuts or peanuts

Stir the nuts until they are well coated. Remove candy from heat and stir on a marble slab until nuts are dry. Sift them to remove the superfluous sugar. Add a very little water to the sifted sugar, a few drops of red vegetable coloring and as much additional cinnamon as is desired. Boil sirup until it is clear, then add the nuts and stir them until they are well coated. Drain and dry.

SPICED NUTS

[About ¼ Pound]

Preheat oven to 250°.

Sift into a shallow pan:

>   ½ cup sugar
>   ¼ cup cornstarch
>   ⅛ teaspoon salt
>   1½ teaspoons cinnamon
>   ½ teaspoon allspice
>   ⅓ teaspoon each ginger nad
>   nutmeg

Combine and beat slightly:

>   1 egg white
>   2 tablespoons cold water

Dip in this mixture:

>   ¼ lb. nut meats

Drop them one at a time in the sifted ingredients. Roll them about lightly. Keep nut meats separated. Place them on a cookie sheet. Bake for about 1½ hours. Remove from the oven and shake off excess sugar. Store tightly covered.

CHOCOLATE TRUFFLES

[About ⅓ Pound]
Not a hot weather dish—it is definitely a brisk weather confection.
Coarsely grate:
    3 oz. chocolate
Melt it with:
    ¼ cup butter
Add:
    2 tablespoons cream
Gradually stir in until lump free:
    7 tablespoons sifted confectioners' sugar
    2 tablespoons grated hazelnuts
Let the mixture stand covered in a cool place 12 to 24 hours. Make individual balls by rolling a small teaspoonful of the mixture in the palm of the hand. This friction and warmth will cause chocolate to melt slightly, so that final coating will adhere. Roll balls in:
    Cinnamon-flavored cocoa
    or Chocolate pastilles
    or shots
This covering will stick to them very satisfactorily. Keep refrigerated, but remove 2 hours before serving for best flavor.

★ BOURBON BALLS

[About ⅓ Pound]
Sift together:
    2 tablespoons cocoa
    1 cup powdered sugar
Combine and stir in:
    ¼ cup bourbon whisky
    2 tablespoons light corn sirup
Add and mix thoroughly:
    2½ cups crushed vanilla wafers
    1 cup broken pecans
Roll mixture into small balls. Dredge in:
    ½ cup powdered sugar

HEAVENLY HASH CANDY

[About 1¼ Pounds]
Surely, at least, a child's idea of heavenly!

Dice:
    12 marshmallows
Chop:
    1 cup nut meats
Boil water in bottom of a double boiler. Turn off heat. Place in top:
    1 lb. milk chocolate
Stir occasionally. Line a tray with waxed paper. Pour in ½ the chocolate when melted. Cover with marshmallows and nut meats. Pour rest of chocolate over this. Cool and break candy into pieces.

CHOCOLATE CLUSTERS

[About ¾ Pound]
Melt over hot water:
    ½ lb. semi-sweet chocolate
Stir in slowly:
    ¾ cup sweetened condensed milk
When well blended, add:
    1 cup nut meats or unsweetened ready-to-eat cereal, sesame seed or wheat germ
Drop candy from a teaspoon onto foil.

PEANUT BUTTER FUDGE OR CENTERS

[About 2 Pounds]
Mix and stir until blended:
    1 cup peanut butter
    1 cup corn sirup
    1¼ cups nonfat milk solids
    1¼ cups sifted confectioners' sugar
Mix, then knead. Form into balls.

ABOUT POPCORN

One-half cup corn equals about 1 quart when popped. If popcorn has the right moisture content, you will hear it in a minute—popping gently. It will be completely fluffy and ready in another minute. If it does not respond in this way, put it in a closed jar with 2 tablespoons of water, shake well and let stand for several days. For best results, never overload popper. Wire ones, used over coals, will process about ¼-cup popcorn at a time. A heavy lidded, or electric, skillet or a 4-quart pressure pan will pop ½-cup corn at a time. With an electric popper, follow the manufacturer's directions. Unless you are using an open popper, add to the preheated pan for each cooking:

    1 tablespoon peanut or
      corn oil

◗ Cook over high heat. ◗ Keep pan moving constantly. When corn stops popping, discard all imperfect kernels. For each 4 cups of hot popcorn, sprinkle with:

    ¼ to ½ teaspoon salt
    2 tablespoons or more
      melted butter or grated
      cheese

CANDIED POPCORN

Besides making a tasty confection, candied popcorn lends itself well to large, but mostly inedible, decorations. For a smaller decoration, use a well-oiled or buttered fancy two-piece cake mold, such as a lamb or rabbit form, ramming the corn tightly into all the nooks and crannies after you have coated it with sirup. If you want to color popcorn, use plenty of coloring matter to counteract the whiteness of the base over which it is spread. To prepare popcorn for shaping, have ready in a large bowl:

    6 cups popped corn

Prepare any of the sirups below. When the sirup has been taken from the heat, pour it over the popped corn. Stir corn gently with a wooden spoon until well coated. Then, when you are sure the corn is cool enough to handle with lightly buttered fingers, press it into balls or lollipops as illustrated below, left.

WHITE SUGAR SIRUP

Stir until the sugar is dissolved:
    ⅔ cup sugar
    ½ cup water
    2½ tablespoons white corn
      sirup
    ⅛ teaspoon salt
    ⅓ teaspoon vinegar

Bring to a boil. ◗ Cook covered for about 3 minutes until steam washes down sides of pan. Uncover and cook without stirring, nearly to the hard-crack stage, 290°.

MOLASSES SIRUP

Melt:
    1 tablespoon butter
Add:
    ½ cup molasses
    ¼ cup sugar

Stir these ingredients until sugar is dissolved. Bring to a boil. ◗ Cover and cook for about 3 minutes until the steam has washed down the sides of the pan. ◗ Uncover and cook without stirring, nearly to the hard-crack stage, 290°.

CARAMEL SIRUP

Melt:
    1½ tablespoons butter
Add:
    1½ cups brown sugar
    6 tablespoons water

Stir these ingredients until sugar is dissolved. Bring to a boil.

◆ Cover and cook for about 3 minutes until the steam has washed down the sides of the pan. ◆ Uncover and cook without stirring to the soft-ball stage, 238°.

PASTILLAGE OR GUM PASTE

[About 3 Cups]

This is a favorite mixture for decorations, especially on wedding cakes, and makes lovely molded leaves and flowers. The shapes are separately formed and held together later with Quick Decorative Icing, see page 426. Gum paste can be rolled out like pie crust, but never roll more at a time than you plan to shape immediately because it dries rapidly and becomes cracked and grainy.

Dissolve in the top of a double boiler:

    1 tablespoon gelatin
    ½ cup water
    1 teaspoon cream of tartar
    1 tablespoon powdered
        gum tragacanth

To keep paste white, add:

    1 or 2 drops blue coloring

If you want different colors, work them later into separate portions of the paste as you knead it. Knead the above mixture as you would pastry into:

    4 cups confectioners' sugar

Store it in a bowl covered with a damp cloth and let it rest at least one-half hour. When you are ready to use the gum paste, dust a board, a roller and your hands with cornstarch. Roll as much paste as you will immediately use to the desired thickness. Cut into shapes. Large flat ones are allowed to dry on the cornstarch-covered board for at least 24 hours. Cover tops also with cornstarch. Petals, leaves, etc., are shaped and stored in cornstarch or cornmeal until dry and ready to assemble.

TURKISH FRUIT PASTE, TURKISH DELIGHT, OR RAHAT LOUKOUM

[About 1½ Pounds]

Called "Peace Candy" in Turkey, this sweet is served with coffee to friends who drop in for a visit. It calls for simultaneous cooking and stirring in 2 pans. Have everything ready before you turn on the heat.

Put in a very heavy 2-quart pan:

    2 tablespoons water
    ¾ cup liquid fruit pectin

Stir in:

    ½ teaspoon baking soda

The soda will cause foaming. Do not be alarmed. Put in another pan:

    1 cup light corn sirup
    ¾ cup sugar

Put both pans on high heat. Stir alternately from 3 to 5 minutes or until foaming has ceased in the pectin pot and boiling is active in the other. Then, still stirring the corn sirup mixture, gradually and steadily pour the pectin mixture into it. Continue stirring and boiling and add during the next minute:

    ¼ cup any jelly: apple,
        currant, raspberry, peach
        or quince

Remove from heat and stir in:

    1 teaspoon lemon juice
    (1 teaspoon grated lemon
        rind)
    (½ cup broken pistachio or
        other nut meats)

If the color of the jelly is not a pleasant one, add:

    A few drops of vegetable
        coloring

Pour the mixture into an 8 x 8-inch pan. Let stand at room temperature for about 3 hours. When it is very firm, cut in shapes or squares. Dust well with confectioners' or powdered sugar or cornstarch. If you plan packaging these candies, let them stand sugared 12 hours or more on a rack. Re-dust on all sides and pack.

MEXICAN ORANGE DROPS

[About 2 Pounds]

Heat in the top of a double boiler:

    1 cup evaporated milk

Melt in a deep saucepan:

    1 cup sugar

When the sugar is a rich brown, stir in slowly:

    ¼ cup boiling water or
        orange juice

Add the hot milk. Stir in until dissolved:

    2 cups sugar
    ¼ teaspoon salt

◗ Bring to a boil and cook covered for 3 minutes until the steam washes down any crystals on the sides of the pan. ◗ Cook uncovered over low heat, without stirring, to the soft-ball stage, 238°. Add:

    Grated rind of 2 oranges

Cool these ingredients. Beat until creamy. Stir in:

    1 cup nut meats

Drop the candy from a spoon onto foil.

GINGER CANDY OR CENTERS

[About 1¾ Pounds]

Bring to a boil in a large, heavy pan:

    ¾ cup milk

◗ Remove from heat. Add and stir until dissolved and cook until boiling:

    2 cups white sugar
    1 cup brown sugar
    2 tablespons white corn
        sirup

◗ Cover and cook for about 3 minutes until the steam washes down any crystals which may have formed on the sides of the pan. ◗ Uncover and cook to 238°. Remove from heat and drop on surface of sirup:

    2 tablespoons butter

Cool to 110°. Beat until it begins to thicken. Add:

    1 teaspoon vanilla
    ¼ lb. finely chopped ginger

If preserved ginger is used, drain it well. If candied ginger is preferred, wash the sugar from it in the milk, then dry ginger in paper towels and chop it.

Pour candy onto a buttered platter. Cut into squares before it hardens. These candy squares may be dipped in:

    Chocolate Coating, page
    505

HAWAIIAN CANDY OR CENTERS

[About 1 Pound]

A fine combination—the tart flavor of pineapple with the spicy taste of ginger.

Bring to a boil in a large, heavy pan:

    1 cup cream

◗ Remove from heat and stir until dissolved:

    ½ cup brown sugar
    1 cup sugar
    ½ cup crushed drained
        pineapple

Stir constantly until these ingredients boil. ◗ Cover and cook for about 3 minutes until the steam washes down any crystals which may have formed on the sides of the pan. ◗ Uncover and cook over low heat, stirring only if necessary, to the soft-ball stage, 238°. Remove from heat and add:

    1 tablespoon butter
    1 teaspoon preserved
        ginger
    ½ cup broken pecan meats
    1 teaspoon vanilla

Cool to 110°. Beat until creamy. Pour into a shallow buttered pan. Cut into squares before it is cold.

★ CANDY FRUIT ROLL OR CENTER

[About 5 Pounds]
Bring to a boil in a large, heavy pan:

    1 cup cream
    ¼ cup water

◗ Remove from heat and stir in until dissolved:

    5 cups light brown sugar
    ¾ cup light corn sirup
    1 tablespoon butter
    ¼ teaspoon salt

Bring these ingredients slowly to a boil, stirring constantly. ◗ Cover and boil about 3 minutes until the steam has washed down any crystals which may have formed on the sides of the pan. ◗ Uncover and cook without stirring to the soft-ball stage, 238°. Remove from heat and add:

    1 lb. blanched shredded almonds
    ¼ lb. chopped figs
    1 lb. seeded chopped raisins

Cool to 110°. Beat mixture until it begins to cream. Shape into a roll. Cover with foil. Roll in, when almost firm:

    (Melted semi-sweet chocolate)

When the candy is cold and firm, cut into slices and roll in:

    (Finely chopped nuts)

★ PERSIAN BALLS OR CENTERS

Some or all of the fruit ingredients may be used. Put through the coarsest cutter of a meat grinder:

    ½ lb. pitted dates
    1 lb. dried figs with stems cut off
    1 lb. seeded raisins
    1 lb. pecan meats
    ½ lb. crystallized ginger or candied orange peel

If the mixture is very stiff, add:

    1 or 2 tablespoonfuls lemon juice

Shape these ingredients into balls or centers for dipping or make a roll to be sliced. Roll in:

    Confectioners' sugar

Then wrap in foil.

★ DATE ROLL OR CENTERS

Boil to the soft-ball stage, 238°:

    3 cups sugar
    1 cup evaporated milk

Stir in:

    1 cup chopped dates
    1 cup chopped nut meats

When cool enough to handle, form these ingredients into a roll with buttered hands. Wrap the roll in foil. Chill and slice later.

★ STUFFED DRIED FRUITS

Steam over hot water in a covered colander for 10 to 20 minutes:

    1 lb. apricots, prunes, dates or figs

Stuff fruits as soon as cool with one or two of the following:

    Fondant, see page 501
    Hard Sauce, see page 480
    Nut meats
    Candied pineapple
    Candied ginger
    Marshmallows, etc.

I. After steaming, the fruits may be rolled in:

    Granulated or powdered sugar or grated coconut

II. Or, you may coat the fruits in a meringue glaze. Preheat oven to 250°. Beat until stiff:

    2 egg whites

Add gradually, beating steadily:

    ½ cup sugar
    ½ teaspoon vanilla

Place the stuffed fruits on a fork. Dip them in the egg mixture until well coated. Place on a wire rack with a baking sheet underneath. Sprinkle tops with:

    Grated coconut

Bake for about ½ hour.

★ APRICOT ORANGE BALLS

[About 2 Pounds]

Placed in Christmas cookie boxes, these confections keep the tougher cookies from drying out. Use best quality, slightly soft, dried apricots. Steam any that are too dried out. Grind twice in a meat grinder using the finest knife:

    1 lb. apricots
    1 whole seedless orange or
      5 seeded finely ground
      preserved kumquats

You may also grind with them a choice of:

    (¼ lb. candied lemon rind)
    (¼ lb. candied citron)
    (½ cup shredded coconut)
    (½ cup nut meats)

Shape into balls or patties. Dust in:

    Granulated sugar

Store closely covered.

★ APRICOT OR PEACH LEATHER

[About 2 Pounds]

An old-time Southeast Seaboard favorite. Cover with:

    1 cup boiling water

and soak for 12 hours in a glass dish:

    1 lb. dried apricots or
    ¾ lb. dried apricots and
    ¼ lb. dried peaches

If tenderized fruit is used, omit soaking. Grind fruit with finest blade. Mix in:

    (2 teaspoons grated lemon
    rind)

Sprinkle on a board:

    Powdered sugar

You will need about 2 cups sugar in all. Start rolling a small quantity of the fruit pulp with a rolling pin. Sprinkle powdered sugar on the surface if the mass sticks. Continue to roll and to add sugar, as necessary, until you have a very thin sheet resembling leather in texture. This amount should make about a 12 x 16-inch sheet, ⅟₁₆-inch thick. Cut it into 1¼ x 2-inch strips and roll the powdered strips very tightly. Store closely covered.

ABOUT CANDIED, CRYSTALLIZED OR GLAZED FRUITS, LEAVES AND BLOSSOMS

There are a number of different methods suggested in the following recipes and the "keeping" qualities of the product vary. Some fruits and leaves are glazed for temporary decorative effects, which involve a ◆ superficially applied covering of sirup or egg and sugar. Unless used on very thin leaves and blossoms, they will hold for only a day. If the leaves or blossoms are thin and are stored ◆ after thorough drying, in a tightly covered container, they will keep for several months.

The other methods described call for ◆ sugar penetration as well as glazing, and the fruits will keep for about 3 months. Different sirup weights and different time intervals of drying are suggested, but the principles in these recipes demanding sugar penetration remain the same.

There is a third hot sirup method for blossoms, especially the imported violets, Viola odorata, which is much like the sirup for Candied Kumquats, page 525. Our native violets are too tender to use.

◆ In every operation keep the fruit or other material covered with the sirup to avoid any hardening or discoloration. To begin with, the fruit is dropped into a thin sirup, which can penetrate the skins and cells. Then the sirup is reduced or replaced with a heavier one. This also penetrates, after the thin sirup has opened the way, and finally sugars out or dries into a crystal coating.

GLAZED FRESH FRUITS

[Enough to Cover About
1 Cup of Solids]
The beauty of these sparkling confections depends on sparkling weather and last minute preparation. They must be eaten the very day they are prepared. Use only fresh fruits that are in prime and perfect condition. If you are covering a large quantity of fruit, divide it into several batches for successive sirup cooking. All fruit must be at room temperature and very dry. Orange sections must be dried for at least 6 hours in advance. Work very quickly to keep the sirup effective. Stir in a heavy saucepan, over low heat, until dissolved:

      1 cup sugar
      ½ to ¾ cup boiling water
      ¹⁄₁₆ teaspoon cream of tartar
Bring sirup to the boiling point. Cover and cook without stirring for about 3 minutes. The sirup should reach the hard-crack stage, 300°. Remove pan from heat and place over hot water. Dip fruits or nuts a few at a time and remove them with a fork. Place them on a wire rack until the coating hardens. Should sirup in the pan harden, reheat it over hot water and repeat the dipping. If reheated more than once, the sirup is apt to burn.

EGG-GLAZED BLOSSOMS, LEAVES OR FRUITS

For an alternate method, which stores better, see Glazed Mint Leaves, below.
Pick while still dewy:
      Borage and violet
      blossoms, rose petals,
      mint leaves, johnny
      jump-ups, grapes

Allow them to dry on paper towels. Stir:
      1 egg white
Causing as little foam as possible, beat in:
      1 to 2 tablespoons cold
      water
Hold the leaf or flower in your fingers and paint this mixture over it with a very soft brush. Dust the sticky leaf or flower thoroughly with:
      Granulated sugar
Let the sugar fall into a bowl beneath for reuse. Put blossom on a screening rack to dry. When dry, store in a tightly-closed container.

GLAZED MINT LEAVES

Have ready the following solution.
Dissolve and cook over low heat until clear:
      1 cup sugar
      ½ cup water
Cool the sirup slightly, before blending in thoroughly:
      4 teaspoons powdered
      acacia
This mixture is called gum arabic. ◆ Refrigerate it until chilled, before using. The mint leaves should be freshly picked and kept cold, so as not to wilt. Prepare by carefully stripping from the main stem individual leaves, with their small stems attached. Wash and dry thoroughly. Put on a napkin over ice. Dip each leaf in the gum arabic and sugar solution. Run your forefinger and thumb gently over each leaf to make a smooth, thin coating. ◆ Be sure every bit of leaf is covered, for any uncoated area will turn brown later. Place leaves carefully on a rack. Turn with a spatula after 12 hours. When the coated leaves become thoroughly dry, store them in tightly-covered containers.

CANDIED APPLES

I. Cook the sirup used for:
  Glazed Fresh Fruits,
    above
Add:
  A few drops of red
    vegetable coloring
After cooking glaze, keep it in
a double boiler ▶ over—not in—
hot water. Now, work quickly.
Dip in:
  Apples on skewers
Place them on a well-buttered
surface or on a metal flower
holder to harden, see sketch
below.

II. Wash, dry and stick a skewer
in the stem end of:
  5 medium-sized apples
Place in the top of a double
boiler:
  1 lb. caramels
  2 tablespoons water
Heat and stir these ingredients
until they melt into a smooth
coating. Dip the skewered apples into the sauce, twirling
them until completely coated.
Dry as above. They will harden
in a few minutes, if refrigerated.

GLAZED PINEAPPLE

Drain and reserve juice from:
  3½ cups sliced canned
    pineapple
Dry slices with a cloth or paper
towel. Add to the juice:
  2 cups sugar
  ⅓ cup light corn sirup
Stir and bring these ingredients
to a boil in a large, heavy pan.

Add the fruit, but do not crowd
it. Simmer until the fruit is
transparent. Lift pineapple from
sirup. Drain it on racks until
thoroughly dry. Place between
waxed paper and store tightly
covered.

★ CANDIED CITRUS PEEL

This is good eaten as candy, or
it can be grated for zest in cakes
and desserts.
A moist peel.
Grate fruit slightly to release oil
from cells. Cut into thin strips
and place in a heavy pan:
  2 cups grapefruit, orange,
    lime or lemon peel
Cover it with:
  1½ cups cold water
Bring slowly to the boiling point.
Simmer 10 minutes or longer if
you do not like a very bitter
taste. Drain. Repeat this process
3 to 5 times in all, draining well
each time. For each cup of peel
make a sirup of:
  ¼ cup water
  ½ cup sugar
Add peel and boil until all sirup
is absorbed and the peel is transparent. Roll it in:
  Powdered sugar
Spread on racks to dry. When
▶ thoroughly dry, dip in:
  Chocolate Coating, see
    page 505

II. This quicker process makes
a softer peel which does not
keep as well as the one prepared
according to the first method.
Cut into strips:
  Grapefruit or orange peel
Soak for 24 hours in:
  Salt water to cover
Use 1 tablespoon salt to 4 cups
water. Drain peel. Rinse and
soak for 20 minutes in fresh
water. Drain, cover with fresh
water and boil for 20 minutes.
Drain again. Measure in equal
parts with the peel:

Sugar

Cook the peel. Add a very little water—only if necessary—until it has absorbed the sugar. Shake the pot as the sirup diminishes, so that the peel does not burn.
◗ Dry thoroughly and store tightly covered.

★ CANDIED OR PRESERVED KUMQUATS OR CALAMONDINS

These miniature oranges should first be washed well in warm soapy water. Then cover with fresh water and boil 15 minutes:

   1 lb. kumquats or
      calamondins

Drain well and repeat twice. Make a sirup of:

   1½ cups sugar
   4 cups water

Boil for 5 minutes. Place drained kumquats in hot sirup and bring sirup to 238° or let boil gently until the kumquats are transparent. To plump up the fruit, cover pan just before heat is turned off and allow fruit to remain covered in hot sirup for about half an hour. At this point, you have Preserved Kumquats or Calamondins. Pack in sterile jars. Serve as a meat garnish or with desserts. If you chop them, be sure to slit them to take out the seeds.

To candy the kumquats, drain from the sirup. Prick a hole in the stem end. Bring to a boil a heavier sirup of:

   1 part water to
   1 part sugar
   (⅛ teaspoon cream of tartar
      for every quart of liquid)

Reboil the kumquats for 30 minutes. Remove them from heat but allow them to stand in the sirup 24 hours. Bring them to a boil again. Cook for 30 minutes more. Drain, dry on a rack and roll in:

   (Granulated sugar)

★ GLAZED CHESTNUTS OR MARRONS GLACÉS

Prepare:

   Chestnuts II, see
      (I, 283)

Soak overnight, covered with cold water, to which you have added:

   Juice of 1 lemon

Next morning, drain and drop into boiling:

   Water or milk

Simmer until tender but firm. Drain chestnuts and discard water or milk. For every cup of nuts, make a sirup by cooking to 238°:

   1 cup sugar
   1 cup water
   ¼ teaspoon cream of tartar

Drop nuts into boiling sirup and simmer for about ten minutes. Remove from heat and let stand, covered, for 24 hours. Drain nuts, reserving sirup. While preparing the sauce, put nuts in a 250° oven to dry. Reduce the sirup until it is very thick. Place nuts in jars. Add to each jar:

   1 to 2 tablespoons cognac

Fill jars with the heavy sirup and seal. To candy the nuts they must be dried not once but three times, dipping them between dryings in the reduced sirup. After the final drying roll them in

   Granulated sugar

Store in tightly-covered tins.

CANDIED CRANBERRIES

Because of their innate keeping qualities cranberries can be candied by a rather simple method. They will remain good during about 3 months' storage if kept covered.
Stir until dissolved and bring to a boil:

   2½ cups sugar
   1½ cups water

Have ready in a heat-resistant bowl:

   1 quart cranberries

Pour the boiling sirup over the berries. Put the bowl in a steamer for 45 minutes. Remove and cool without stirring. Leave in a warm, dry room for 3 to 4 days. Stir at intervals. When the sirup reaches a jelly-like consistency, remove berries and let them dry 3 days longer—out of the sirup. Turn them for uniform drying. When the fruit can be handled easily, store in a tightly covered container. Use the berries on toothpicks to stud a ham or for other garnishing.

FRUIT PASTE

You find this delicacy in Italy, Spain, the American tropics, and in Germany where it bears the quaint name of Quittenbrod or Würste because quince is a favorite flavor. The trick is to reduce, until they are stiff, equal parts of:

> Fruit pulp—guava,
> quince, apricot, etc.
> Sugar

◗ The real trick, of course, is to find the patience and time to watch this mixture so it won't scorch. When stiff, spread the mixture to a ½-inch thickness in pans that have been dipped in cold water. Cut into squares and dry on racks in a cool place, turning once a day for 3 to 4 days. Dust the squares with:

> Granulated sugar

Or, stuff the stiff pulp without drying into cellophane sausage casings. Before pouring or stuffing, you may add at the last minute:

> Ground cinnamon,
> cloves, citron or almonds

Slices or squares look attractive when served on a green leaf.

CANDIED OR CRYSTALLIZED ROOTS AND STALKS

[About 1 Pound]

Wash:

> 2 cups angelica roots and
> young stalks or cleaned
> scraped acorus calamus
> roots

Place them in a crock. Pour over to cover:

> ⅓ cup salt
> 2 cups boiling water

Cover crock and let the angelica soak for 24 hours. Drain, peel and wash in cold water. Cook to 238°:

> 2 cups sugar
> 2 cups water

Add the cleaned angelica roots and stems. Cook for 20 minutes. Drain the angelica, but reserve sirup. Put the angelica on a wire rack in a cool, dark place for 4 days. Then bring the sirup and roots to 238° and cook 20 minutes or until the sirup candies the roots. Drain on a rack until ◗ thoroughly dry. Store tightly covered.

THE FOODS WE KEEP

This section divides into those foods we freeze, can, salt, smoke and preserve. It also includes those items with both long and short keeping-tolerance that we buy at rather frequent intervals and store briefly. On the whole we take greater care with the former, perhaps because of the effort we personally put into processing them.

Most purchased staples come under state and local laws; and any that are in interstate commerce are covered by Federal Food and Drug legislation. A special and recent subject of federal concern is additives—those extra substances which are present in food as a result of the manufacturers' determination to boost nutritive content or of special conditions growing out of processing, packaging or storage. Some additives are time-honored, like seasonings and salts. Some provide enrichment, such as vitamins. Some are chemicals which improve flavor, color, consistency and keeping quality. An entirely different kind of additive is the unintentional or accidental kind—the one which results from improper processing, contamination, imperfect sealing, careless storage. In this area, again, there is a whole series of federal rulings.

A change in the nature of legal concepts during the past few years now puts the burden of proof for the safety of additives on the manufacturer and thus provides more immediate and positive protection for the consumer. It is the business of each and every one of us to support further legislation controlling amounts and kinds of food additives—so that we may be sure they will not increase beyond human tolerance. ◗ Read the labels and carefully note both contents and weight of all the packaged food you buy.

For most of us, the responsibility for keeping food in good condition starts as we roll our baskets past the checker. And what a lot we push! In one week, one normally well-fed American uses a minimum of 3½ quarts of milk, ½ pound of fat, 4½ pounds of meat, poultry, fish, cheese, beans or nuts, 3 pounds of cereals and ½ pound of sugar. Add fruits and vegetables and multiply by 52, then by the number of persons in your family. If there are four of you, the total will stand at something like a ton and a half a year. This is an impressive investment in hard currency: an item, in fact, amply huge to warrant protecting your market purchases to the very best of your ability.

But all of us are guilty on occasion of picking up Junior at the swimming and tennis club after shopping and getting involved in some friendly gossip —while the lettuces back in the car wilt down and the frozen foods begin disastrously to thaw. Remember that heat and moisture encourage spoilage, bacteria, insect-infestation and mold. And sunlight may destroy vitamin content, as in milk; or cause flavor deterioration, as in spices.

Many molds need no light and thrive on acids; some may only occur on the surface but give off gases which may adversely affect the rest of the food. ◗ Store most foods in a cool, dark, dry place, preferably with a constant temperature around 70°; or, if indicated, refrigerate. Throughout this book, we have listed ideal storage suggestions with individual types of food, but following is a quick rundown on storage standards and the keeping life of typical larder items. ◗ Any stockpiled food should be kept on a rotating system. Place the new food at the back of the shelves and use the older purchases from the front for the day to day needs of the household. Although we know canned foods may not spoil for years, flavor and nutritive qualities, as the months roll by, are progressively lessened.

Once again we urge you to ◗ use a preponderance of fresh foods whenever possible. Build your menus around government "best buys" on produce that appear regularly in the newspapers. These items are apt to be both reasonable in price and fresh, because they are seasonal. After buying, store them as suggested later and cook them carefully, following the "pointers" ◗ so as to assure topmost nutritive and taste value.

ABOUT LONG TERM STORAGE

You may store in an area that ◗ stays around 70°:
◗ For about 2 years: Salt, sugar, whole pepper.
◗ For about 18 months: Canned meat, poultry and vegetables—except tomatoes and sauerkraut —alone or mixed with cereal products. Canned fruit—except citrus fruit and juices and berries. Dried legumes, if stored in metal.
◗ For about 12 months: Canned fish, hydrogenated fats and oils, flour, ready-to-eat dry cereals stored in metal, uncooked cereal in original container, canned nuts, instant puddings, instant dry cream and bouillon products, soda and baking powder.
◗ For about 6 months: Evaporated milk, nonfat dry whole milk in metal containers, condensed meat and beef soups, dried fruit in metal container, canned citrus fruit and juices, canned berries. To store water, see page 148.
If temperatures are lower than 70° but still above freezing, the permissible storage period for most of these items is longer.

STAPLES FOR THE AVERAGE FAMILY

Beverages: coffee, tea
Bacon
Cereals: breakfast foods, rice, macaroni, spaghetti, noodles, farina, corn meal, tapioca
Cottage and other cheeses
Chocolate, cocoa
Coconut
Butter, lard, cooking oil or other shortening
Flour: whole-grain, all-purpose, cake flour
Sugar: granulated, confectioners', brown, loaf, maple
Bread, crackers
Fruits: fresh, dried, canned
Fruit and vegetable juices: canned, frozen
Potatoes: white, sweet
Onions, garlic, shallots, chives
Sirups: corn, molasses, maple
Mayonnaise and French dressing
Salad oils, vinegars
Milk, cream, eggs
Milk solids, evaporated and condensed milk
Canned meats, fish

Beef, chicken and vegetable cubes

Nuts

Vegetables: fresh, canned, frozen

Honey, preserves, marmalade, jellies

Soups: frozen, canned, dried

Raisins, currants

Peanut butter

Debittered brewers' yeast

Worcestershire and hot pepper sauce

Gelatin: flavored, unflavored

Catsup, chili sauce, horseradish

Flavorings: vanilla, almond, etc.

Baking powder, baking soda

Cornstarch

Ground and stick cinnamon

Ground and whole cloves

Ground ginger

Allspice

Whole nutmeg

Bay leaves

Salt

Celery seed

Celery salt

Dry and prepared mustard

Black and white peppercorns

Paprika, cayenne

Curry powder

Garlic and onion salt

Chili powder

Dried herbs: tarragon, basil, savory, sage, etc. See Herbs, page 202

Monosodium glutamate

KITCHEN HINTS

Glasses, to wash: Glasses may be safely washed in very hot water if slipped in edgewise. For hard water use a low sudsing detergent rather than soap.

Glasses or pitchers with milk residue: Rinse with cold water, then warm water.

Refrigerator: Wash inside with a mixture of 1 tablespoon powdered borax to 1 quart water.

Bread Box: To deter mold, wash with a mixture of 2 tablespoons vinegar to 1 quart water.

Pots and Pans: Lime deposits may be removed by boiling vinegar in the pan.

Food Chopper: To fasten securely, place a potholder under the foot before tightening the screw.

Mixing Bowls: To keep steady when mixing or whipping, place on a wet folded cloth.

Broken Glass: To remove small slivers from a rug, press sticky tape against it. To remove from a smooth surface, use wet paper tissues.

STAIN REMOVAL

Gum, Adhesive Tape, etc.: Lemon juice will remove it from hands and clothes. It will also remove ink, fruit and other stains.

Wax or Paraffin: Scrape cloth to remove hardened wax. Place blotting paper under the cloth and press with warm iron. Cool and sponge with cleaning fluid.

Chocolate and Cocoa: For washable material, use soap and hot water. Otherwise, scrape off and apply cleaning fluid.

Coffee: Boiling water poured from a height of 2 feet is good for fresh stains.

Fruit: Boiling water as for coffee stains, or try bleaching in sun after moistening with lemon juice and salt.

For other stains, we recommend the Home and Garden Bulletin No. 62 of the U. S. Department of Agriculture, Washington, D.C.

CANNING, SALTING AND SMOKING

It is a thrill to possess shelves well stocked with home-canned food. In fact, you will find their inspection—often surreptitious —and the pleasure of serving the fruits of your labor comparable only to a clear conscience or a very becoming hat.

In fact, you must carry a clear conscience right with you through the processing itself, making absolutely sure that the food you keep is safe to eat. Great care must be exercised in the canning of all foods to avoid spoilage. Even greater care is required in the canning of non-acid foods—see page 538—to prevent the development of *Clostridium botulinum*, a germ so deadly that "1 oz. could theoretically kill 100 million people." The spores of botulinus may resist 212°, or boiling temperature, even after several hours of processing, and produce a fatal toxin in the canned product. Botulinus poisoning may be present even if no odor, gas, color changes or softness in food texture indicate its presence.

Whether or not your suspicions are aroused, ◗ do not test home-canned, non-acid food by tasting it out of the container. Instead, follow the recommendations of all reputable authorities, and cook home-canned vegetables, meat and fish—without exception—for 15 minutes in boiling liquid, uncovered, stirring frequently before serving. By this means—high heat in the presence of air—botulinus toxin is positively destroyed.

Don't let the botulinus bogey haunt you when you use commercially canned foods, for in the last thirty years botulism cases reported from commercial sources have been extremely rare.

◗ For maximum nutritional value only the freshest and best food should be canned. Inspect it with an eagle eye, discarding all blemished or rotted portions and washing or scrubbing the selected remainder to remove spray, soil or insects. Produce which is imperfect before processing may spoil the rest of the food in its container afterwards, producing color changes and encouraging the formation of mold or gases. Obviously if, as a result of careless preliminary handling, your jars, when opened, show these evidences of spoilage, their contents should be discarded at once.

◗ Good organization and proper equipment simplify canning and give you, with a minimum of effort, gay-looking shelves of glistening, jewel-like jars, filled with canned fruits and vegetables, all labeled and dated and ready to use.

Seasonal heat and heat from the stove inevitably accompany canning. Hot fluids in hot jars and heavy pans have to be handled carefully. ◗ Have a funnel, plenty of dry pot-holders, strong tongs or a jar lifter, and paraffin at hand.

ABOUT CANNING PROCESSES

◗ Remember that all nonacid vegetables and all meats and fish must be pressure-processed.
◗ The boiling-water bath is not recommended for any nonacid foods.
◗ Oven canning is not recommended under any cirmustances. The open-kettle method has been abandoned by officialdom but is still used by some housewives for acid fruits. Work quickly on those steps in the canning process which involve the exposure of food to air. To can specific foods, see alphabetical listings in this chapter.

In canning, follow these general steps.
◗ Line up your equipment and read below about the type you are using. If the lids call for separate rubbers, test the rubbers even though they may be newly purchased. Unused leftover rubbers may deteriorate from one canning season to another. ◗ To test rubbers, bend them into small pleats. If they crack, discard them. Or stretch them to see if they will return to their original shape. If not, they are worthless.
◗ Should you be using a pressure canner—see illustration, page 533—make sure that the jars are the type which can stand 240° or more of heat. ◗ In any case, check all jars against chipping, cracking or other defects.

Next, check the closures between the jars and lids. If using screw types, first place them on sound jars without a rubber. Screw them tight. They are usable if it is impossible to insert a thin penknife blade or a thumbnail between the jar and the lid. Unscrew them. Put the rubbers in place and fill the jars with water. Screw down the lids. Invert the jars. If there is no seepage, the jars and lids are safe to use. This test may also be applied to the clamp or wire-bail type of closure.

Lids are of two main types—those which need separate rubbers and adjustment both before and after processing, and those which have an attached rubber and are adjusted once before processing and then close automatically by vacuum when cooling. The vacuum type is sketched first on the left. Lids with attached rubbers should never be sterilized. Merely pour boiling water over them.
◗ Unless you are pressure canning, other jars and lids shown with separate rubbers should be sterilized for 15 minutes in boiling water. The rubbers should be washed in soap and hot water, well rinsed, and then placed in a pan. Cover them with boiling water and leave them there until ready to use.

The first three types sketched above fit on the regular grooved-top canning jars, whether of pint, quart or half-gallon size.

The zinc- and glass-disk tops, shown second and third on page 531, are placed on the rubber ring, screwed clockwise as tight as possible, and then turned counterclockwise ¼ inch.

The jar with the all-glass lid shown next has a wire-bail or clamp closure. While processing, the longer wire rests in the groove of the lid. The shorter wire is not snapped down in its final position until after processing. ♦ The slight openings provided by all these adjustments are temporary. They allow excess air to be forced out of the jars during processing, and thus avoid possible explosion.

ABOUT PREPARING FOOD FOR CANNING

♦ To prepare food for canning, wash, clean, pare and cut up food just as you would if planning to cook it for immediate use. ♦ Remember that vitamins escape quickly, so prepare only small batches of food, about 1 quart at a time. The size in which pieces are cut may depend on convenience in packing. When making sirups for fruit, allow about 1 cup of sirup for each quart of fruit, see page 535.

♦ To blanch or precook foods for canning, put large fruits and all vegetables in a wire basket and immerse them, about 1 quart at a time, in boiling liquid for 5 minutes, counting from the time the water begins to boil again after immersion. Then dip them up and down quickly in cold water 2 or 3 times to reduce the heat quickly. This will keep the food shapely and make handling easier. Blanching shrinks food and drives out air so that produce may be packed more closely. Its most important role, however, is to arrest some undesirable kinds of enzymatic action.

Berries, soft fruits and tomatoes may be canned without blanching. ♦ The liquid in which the foods were precooked or steamed should be used to fill the jars, thus saving valuable minerals. Meat may be partially cooked (about two-thirds done) by simmering or roasting. For more details about meat, see page 541.

♦ To steam foods for canning, use a steam basket or a cheesecloth bag. Steam only a small quantity at a time. ♦ Do not crowd the food, as the steam must penetrate all of it. Use a kettle with a tightly fitting lid. Have in the kettle several inches of boiling water. Suspend the steam basket or bag over it and close the lid tightly. Steam food the length of time given in individual recipes for fruit or vegetables.

ABOUT PACKING JARS

♦ In canning, pack containers firmly, but not so tightly that the material is crushed. ♦ Pack fruits and vegetables to within ½ inch of jar-tops, with the exception of Lima beans, dried beans, peas and corn, which swell considerably more than other vegetables. ♦ These and meats canned under pressure should be packed to within 1 inch of jar tops, and the jars filled with boiling water to within ½ inch of the top. You may add salt to meats and vegetables at the rate of 1 teaspoon per quart.

Fill jars of fruit with sugar sirup to within ½ inch of top. For sugar sirup formulas, see page 535. ♦ Before putting on lids, make sure that any air which may be trapped in the liquid is expelled. Run a long thin spatula down between the inside of the jar and the produce, changing the position of the contents enough to release the trapped air as shown on page 533. Then carefully wipe the top of the jar.

♦ When jars are packed, it is always wisest to follow the manufacturer's directions in adjusting the lids. If the type of lid you are using requires a separate rubber, be sure it is wet.

ABOUT PRESSURE CANNING

♦ Pressure canning or cooking is the only method recommended for nonacid fruits and vegetables. ♦ A pressure canner or cooker is in any case a necessity for those who plan to do a lot of canning. Detailed directions for the use of such appliances are furnished by the manufacturer and should be followed carefully—especially the checking of pressure gauges. ♦ Be sure also to exhaust the air from the canner for at least 10 minutes so that no cold spots develop and cause the food to be underprocessed. ♦ If using a small steam pressure saucepan, keep the heat constantly at 10 pounds pressure, and be sure to add 20 minutes to the processing time. For vegetable pressure canning, see page 538.

▲ If canning at high altitudes in a pressure canner ♦ add ½ pound to the pressure gauge for each additional 1000 feet. For instance, if processing requires 5 pounds pressure at sea level, use 7 pounds at 4000 feet, 9 pounds at 7500 feet; if 15 pounds at sea level, use 17 pounds at 4000 feet, 19 pounds at 7500 feet.

ABOUT CANNING IN A BOILING WATER BATH

♦ The boiling-water bath process is used only for acid fruits and brined vegetables. A regular hot-water canner or a clean wash boiler or lard can may be used if it has a tight-fitting lid.

An important utensil in canning is a rack for the bottom of the boiler to keep the jars from cracking when they come in contact with heat. A wire rack may be bought for this purpose, or one may be made of coarse wire mesh at home. Have ready a holder for lifting jars out of boiling water. Fill the boiler with water to about jar height. When the water is boiling, lower the jars into the boiler. ♦ The jars must not touch one another or the sides of the container. Leave a 2-inch space between them. ♦ The jars should rest on the rack. Add more boiling water to cover them at least 1 inch above the tops. Continue to add boiling water as the water in the boiler evaporates. Process the required length of time for the particular food chosen—see pages 535–537—counting from the time the water begins to boil after the jars have been added.

▲ Canning at high altitudes in a boiling-water bath ♦ requires a 1-minute increase in

processing time for every 1000 feet above sea level if the total time is 20 minutes or less, and 2 minutes per 1000 feet if the total time is more than 20 minutes. ◗ To remove the jars from the boiling water, use tongs or a jar lifter as soon as the time is up. ◗ Do not lift the jars by the lids. ◗ Place the jars on wood, a paper pad, or a cloth surface, allowing several inches between them. See that there is no draft on the hot jars, as sudden cooling may cause the glass to crack.

ABOUT SEALING AND LABELING JARS

◗ Seal all jars according to manufacturer's directions. With the types of lids described above, the rubber-attached metal lid is self-sealing and should not be touched. The zinc screw type and the glass-disk and metal-ring lid should be turned clockwise as far as possible. Be sure to screw lids with a slow, steady turn, so as not to displace the rubbers. The shorter wire on the bail or clamp type should be snapped down into place. ◗ Whatever type you use, be sure to leave the jars upright and undisturbed for 12 hours. With the first and third lids from the left on page 531, you may remove the metal ring, for when the jar is cold the thin top should be tight enough to hold by itself. While the jars are still hot after sealing, you may see active bubbling going on. If it ceases as the contents cool, it was merely continued boiling due to the lowered boiling point produced by the vacuum in the jar. ◗ Test-seal the metal tops by tapping the lids lightly with a metal spoon or knife. A ringing

note indicates a safe seal. If the contents touch the inner side of the lid, the sound may be dull but not hollow. ◗ If the note is both dull and hollow, reprocessing with a new lid is in order. Or, if you prefer, use the food right away. ◗ Label and store the jars in a cool dark place. Storage temperatures between 45° and 60° maintain good color and are generally suitable for all properly heat-processed foods.

ABOUT FRUIT CANNING

◗ Choose fresh, firm fruit that is not overripe. Imperfect fruit may be used, but it must be carefully gone over and all blemishes removed. Wash the fruit. Prepare as for table use. If it is to be pared, it may be dipped in boiling water until the skins loosen, and then dipped for a moment in cold water. It is best to process a small quantity—about a quart of fruit at a time. ◗ To keep fruit from discoloring until you can pack it, mist it over with lemon juice or ascorbic acid solution, see page 555, or one of the following solutions, as you would sprinkle clothes. Allow to 1 quart water 3 tablespoons lemon juice or ½ teaspoon dissolved ascorbic acid crystals.

APPROXIMATE YIELD OF TYPICAL FRUITS

FRUIT	POUNDS PER QUART	QUARTS PER BUSHEL
Apples	2½	28
Berries	1⅓	24
Cherries	1⅓	20
Peaches	2¼	21
Pears	2¼	30
Plums	2	28
Tomatoes	3	18

ABOUT SIRUPS FOR CANNING

Sirup for canned fruit varies in consistency, depending upon the fruit or the use to which it will be put. The following formulas will help you decide on the most appropriate blend of sugar and water. ‣ For choicest results make the sirup from the water in which the fruit was cooked or cook some of the cut-up fruits and use the liquid as your sirup base instead of water. Allow ¾ to 1 cup sirup for each quart jar.

THIN SIRUP

[About 2¼ cups]
One cupful sugar to 2 cupfuls water. Stir well before heating and bring slowly to a boil, 236°. Use for naturally sweet fruits and to approximate the quality of fresh fruits.

MEDIUM SIRUP

[About 2¾ cups]
1½ cupfuls sugar to 2 cupfuls water. Prepare as for thin sirup. Good for canning fruits that are not highly acid.

HEAVY SIRUP

[About 1¼ cups]
Use 1 cupful sugar to 1 cupful water. ‣ Dissolve and boil very carefully to prevent crystallization and scorching. Use for very sour fruits like rhubarb; also suitable for dessert use. If too heavy a sirup is used the fruit may rise to the top of the jar during processing.

SYNTHETIC SWEETENER

Use a sodium cyclamate base type: 1 tablespoon or 24 tablets to each cup boiling water. Sour cherries require 2 tablespoons or 48 tablets; large fruits like pears, applesauce and berries, 2 teaspoons or 16 tablets. Do not use this substitution con-stantly without a doctor's consent.

ABOUT PROCESSING NON-ACID FRUITS

Use a pressure canner. Place jars as described on page 534. Vent canner for 10 minutes. Process fruits 5 minutes at 5 lbs. pressure.

ABOUT PROCESSING ACID FRUITS

The following directions are for quart jars processed in a boiling-water bath. Start counting time when the water surrounding the lidded jars reaches a fast boil. Reduce the processing time by 10% if pint jars are used, by 25% for tomatoes. Increase the processing time by 15 minutes for half-gallon jars. ‣ Do not use iron, copper, aluminum or tin pans in fruit processing, as these may produce discoloration. ‣ See that all jars and lids are sterile.

APPLES

Select firm, sound, tart varieties. Wash, pare and core; cut into quarters or halves. Drop into discoloration solution, see page 555. Drain. Boil 1 minute in thin or medium sirup. Pack in jars, cover with boiling sirup and process 20 minutes in boiling-water bath. Apples may also be baked, packed, covered with boiling sirup and processed 15 minutes in a boiling-water bath.

APPLESAUCE

Prepare applesauce, pack boiling hot. Process at once for 10 minutes in a boiling-water bath. To prevent darkening at top of jar, add at the last moment before sealing 1 teaspoon lemon juice.

APRICOTS

Select ripe, firm fruit. Blanch to

remove skins. Pack whole or halves into jars and cover with boiling medium sirup; process 25 minutes in a boiling-water bath.

BERRIES

Pick over, wash if gritty, stem, pack closely in jars, fill with boiling medium sirup and process 15 minutes in a boiling-water bath. For strawberries, the following more complicated procedure will yield plump, bright-colored fruit. Wash if gritty, then hull. Add 1 cup sugar to each quart prepared berries, placing in alternate layers in shallow pans, and let stand 2 hours. Simmer them for 5 minutes in their own juice. Fill jars full and add boiling thin sirup if additional liquid is needed. Process at once 15 minutes in a boiling-water bath.

CHERRIES

Wash and stem. Can whole or pitted. To seed, use a cherry pitter or the rounded end of a paper clip. If not seeded, prick with a pin. Use heavy sirup for sour cherries; medium sirup for sweet. Pack, cover with boiling sirup and process at once 15 minutes in a boiling-water bath.

CRANBERRIES

Wash and stem. Boil 3 minutes in heavy sirup. Cover with boiling sirup. Process 3 minutes in a boiling-water bath.

CURRANTS

Same as for berries, above.

GRAPES

Use only sound, firm grapes. Wash and stem. Bring to a boil in medium sirup. Cover with boiling sirup. Process 20 minutes in a boiling-water bath.

GRAPE JUICE

Wash sound, ripe grapes. Cover with boiling water and heat slowly to simmering. ◗ Do not boil. Cook slowly until fruit is very soft, then strain through a bag. Let stand 24 hours refrigerated. Strain again. Add ½ cup sugar to each quart juice. Reheat to simmering and pour into hot sterile jars. Seal and process for 20 minutes in a water bath held at 180°.

OTHER FRUIT JUICES

Select sound, ripe fruit, crush and heat slowly to simmering point. Strain through several layers of cheesecloth. Heat again and simmer for 10 minutes. ◗ Do not boil, as it ruins the flavor. Pour into clean hot jars, seal, and process in a water bath held at 180° for 20 minutes. Do not allow water to boil.

Juices from uncooked fruit may be pressed out in a cider press and heated to lukewarm before being poured into jars and processed as above. Peach, cherry, apple juice and cider canned this way are less likely to taste flat. The addition of sugar to tart fruit juices before canning is more satisfactory than sweetening after canning. One cup sugar to 1 gallon juice is a moderate proportion.

PEACHES

Use firm, ripe fruit. Scald to remove skins. Halve peaches. Pack in jars, cover with boiling medium sirup and process at once for 20 minutes in a boiling-water bath.

PEARS

Pare, core, halve, quarter or slice. Drain. Boil gently about 5 minutes in medium sirup. Pack into jars, cover with boiling sirup, process for 20 minutes in a boiling-water bath.

Hard pears are best if cooked in water only until nearly tender. The sugar is then added in the same proportions as for a medium sirup and the whole brought to a boil. Pack into jars, cover with boiling medium sirup and process at once for 20 minutes in a boiling-water bath.

PINEAPPLE

Slice, pare, core, remove eyes. Shred or cut into cubes. Pack, cover with boiling thin or medium sirup, depending on sweetness of fruit. Process at once for 20 minutes in a boiling-water bath.

PINEAPPLE JUICE

Discarded eyes, cores and skins of fresh fruit can be used in making pineapple juice. Cover with cold water. Cook slowly in covered kettle from 30 to 40 minutes. Strain through a jelly bag. Measure juice, heat. For each cup of juice add ⅛ cup sugar. Boil rapidly 10 minutes and process for 5 minutes in boiling-water bath. Juice may also be extracted from pineapple by putting the pared fruit through the fine blade of a food chopper with a large bowl beneath to catch the liquid.

PLUMS

Use moderately ripe fruit. Wash and prick skins. Pack firmly, but do not crush, into jars. Cover with boiling sirup, thin for sweet plums, medium for tart varieties. Process at once for 25 minutes in a boiling-water bath.

PUREES AND PASTES

Use ripe, soft, unblemished fruit. Simmer until it can be forced through a fine strainer or food mill. You can want to reduce the liquid by further cooking. You may add sugar to taste, unless you are puréeing tomatoes. Reheat the purée, fill the jars, seal and process for 20 minutes in a boiling-water bath.

QUINCES

"Preserved," notes an herbalist, optimistically, in 1562, "they do mightily prevail against drunkenness."

Use well-ripened fruit. Pare, cut into convenient-size pieces and boil gently in a medium or heavy sirup about 1½ minutes. Or, for easier handling, wipe the fuzz from the quince, cut out the stem and blossom ends and cook the fruit gently in several inches of water, covered, for 20 minutes. Drain the water for use in the canning sirup. Pare or simply cut the fruit from the core unpared. Pack into jars, cover with boiling sirup, and process at once for 60 minutes in a boiling-water bath.

RHUBARB

Wash stalks and cut into ½-inch pieces. Pack, cover with boiling heavy sirup, process at once for 10 minutes in hot-water bath.

TOMATOES

Use firm, fresh tomatoes, scald 1 minute and then dip 1 minute in cold water to remove skins. Cut out cores. Leave whole, halve, or quarter. Pack closely in jars, fill with boiling water or tomato juice. Process at once for 45 minutes in a boiling-water bath.

TOMATO JUICE

Use soft but perfect tomatoes. Wash, remove stem ends and cores. Chop or cut into small pieces. Heat in a covered kettle until the juice flows freely. Put through a fine sieve. Pack hot into jars to within ½ inch of top. Process in a boiling-water bath for 10 minutes. Flavor just before serving.

APPROXIMATE YIELD OF TYPICAL VEGETABLES

RAW VEGETABLE	POUNDS PER QUART	QUARTS PER BUSHEL
Beans, Lima in the pod	2	7
Beans, snap	1¾	17
Beets	2¾	18
Carrots	2¾	18
Corn cut off cob	7 ears	8
Greens	2	7
Okra	2	17
Peas in the pod	2	6
Squash, summer	2	18
Sweet potatoes	2½	20

Tomatoes, see Fruits, above.

ABOUT VEGETABLE PRESSURE CANNING

♦ Pressure canning is the only process recommended for vegetables. Vegetables must be very carefully and quickly washed, through several waters if necessary or under running water, to remove all soil. Prepare only one pressure canner load at a time and work quickly.

Great care must be exercised in the canning of nonacid foods to prevent the development of *Clostridium botulinus*, a deadly germ which may be present even though no odor or color changes indicate its presence. The U.S. Government warns that all nonacid home-canned vegetables should be boiled in an open pan for 15 minutes before tasting or serving. They should be stirred frequently during cooking.

The Department of Agriculture does not recommend home canning the following vegetables:

> cabbage, except sauerkraut
> cauliflower
> celery
> cucumbers
> baked beans
> eggplant
> lettuce
> onions
> parsnips
> turnips
> vegetable mixtures

The following directions are for 1-quart glass jars, unless otherwise specified, processed in a steam pressure canner at 10 pounds pressure.

ARTICHOKES

Wash well, precook 5 minutes in brine of ¾ cup vinegar or lemon juice and 3 tablespoons salt to 1 gallon water. Pack in hot jars. Fill brine to ½ inch of top. Process 25 minutes at 10 pounds pressure.

ASPARAGUS

Wash, remove loose scales and tough ends. Grade for uniformity. Place upright in wire basket. Hold in boiling water which reaches just below tips for 3 minutes. Or cut in 1-inch lengths and boil 2 to 3 minutes. Pack and fill jars with boiling water. Process 40 minutes at 10 pounds pressure.

BEANS, GREEN, SNAP OR WAX

Wash, remove strings and tips. Break into small pieces. Precook 5 minutes. Reserve water. Pack and fill jars with boiling reserved water. Process 40 minutes at 10 pounds pressure.

BEANS, FRESH LIMA

Sort and grade for size and age. Boil young beans 5 minutes, older beans 10 minutes. Pack loosely, allowing 1 inch head space. Cover with boiling water. Process 55 minutes at 10 pounds pressure.

BEETS

Boil for 15 minutes small whole beets with 1 inch stem and all the root. Trim off roots and stems. Slip off skins. Pack in jars. Add boiling water. Process 45 minutes at 10 pounds pressure.

CARROTS

Sort and grade for uniformity. Wash and scrape. Boil 5 minutes. Reserve water. Slice or pack whole. Fill jars with boiling reserved water. Process 45 minutes at 10 pounds pressure.

CORN, WHOLE-KERNEL

Use tender, freshly gathered corn. Cut from cob. Do not scrape cobs. To each quart of corn add only 1 pint boiling water. Heat to boiling. Pack at once, adding no more water. Process for 75 minutes at 10 pounds pressure.

CORN, CREAM-STYLE

Pack in pints only. Cut off the tops of kernels, scrape cobs with back of knife or corn scraper—see (I, 284)—to remove all pulp. Add half as much boiling water as corn, by weight. Heat to boiling. Pack at once. Process pints for 75 minutes at 15 pounds pressure.

GREENS

Use fresh, tender greens. Wash thoroughly, discard any decayed leaves and tough stems. Steam about 8 minutes, or until wilted. Pack quickly and loosely. Fill jars with boiling water. Process for 1¾ hours at 10 pounds pressure.

HOMINY

Pack loosely, boiling hot. Leave 1½ inches head space. Cover with boiling liquid. Process at once for 60 minutes at 10 pounds pressure.

MUSHROOMS

Wash well. Peel if wilted or old. Drop into hot water with 1 tablespoon vinegar or white wine per quart. Cover and pre-cook 3 to 4 minutes. Drain. Pack hot, covering with freshly boiled water. Process 40 minutes at 10 pounds pressure.

OKRA

Use tender pods only. Wash and remove caps without cutting into pod. Cover with boiling water and bring to a boil. Pack hot. Cover with boiling liquid. Process 40 minutes at 10 pounds pressure.

PEAS

Pack only in pint jars because they overcook and become mushy if packed in quarts. Shell, sort for size. Cover with boiling water, boil 5 minutes. Pack loosely into jars. Cover with boiling cooking liquid to within 1 inch of top of jars. Process 45 minutes at 10 pounds pressure.

PUMPKIN AND SQUASH

Peel and cut into 1-inch cubes. Add enough water to prevent sticking. Cook or steam until tender. Mash and pack hot in jars. Process 90 minutes at 10 pounds pressure.

SWEET POTATOES

Wash well. Boil about 15 minutes or until skins will slip off easily. Skin and cut into pieces. Pack hot. Cover with fresh boiling water. Process 1 hour and 50 minutes at 10 pounds pressure.

TOMATOES

See directions under Fruits, page 537.

ABOUT MEAT, POULTRY, GAME AND FISH PRESSURE CANNING

Methods for canning fish are not

given in this book because the various recommended processes are controversial. Government bulletins call for long processing and, in addition, before the food is served, for prolonged cooking of home-canned fish and sea food. This causes great loss of flavor and food value. ♦ The freezing of fish is recommended as an alternative for better retention of both qualities, see page 562. But the canning of meats, poultry and game in homes can be both a safe and economical procedure and a much more convenient one than the old-fashioned method of preserving by salting and smoking, although again not nearly so satisfactory as freezing, see page 545. **The Government warns that all home-canned meats should be boiled in an open pan for 10 minutes before tasting or eating.**

For safe serving of home-canned meat products, process all these nonacid foods in a pressure canner. ♦ Make sure that the temperature reaches at least 240°.

ABOUT PREPARING GAME

The hunter must almost of necessity learn to clean, cut and store his meat, since most states forbid the use of packing plants or butcher shops for this purpose. Quick cooling, scrupulous cleaning and careful preservation greatly enhance that deliciously and legitimately gamey flavor which derives from the fruit, the seeds, the berries or the grasses on which the animal has fed. All too often, gaminess is just the unpleasantly exaggerated result of improper care and manipulation before cooking.

Immediately after the kill, the animal must be bled. If it is a bird or small mammal, place it in a funnel that has an opening wide enough so that the head can hang through. For details about handling birds, see About Wild Birds (I, 590). Behead the animal or cut the jugular vein at the base of the neck, slightly to the left of center. Have a bowl ready underneath to keep the blood, which you may want to use later for blood sausage—see (I, 533)—or as a thickener for gravies, see (I, 357). To store see (I, 357).

If the animal is large, place it on a slope with its head at the lowest point. Cut the vein as described above and make sure the blood is flowing freely. Should the animal have been shot in a vital organ, the blood may not be released through the neck but inwardly. It will then be necessary to gut the carcass as quickly and as cleanly as possible to avoid taint from the bullet-ruptured organs.

Whatever procedure you use ♦ clean and cool the meat as rapidly as possible. Leaving the animal with its head lower than the body, you may cut off the feet, pierce the legs and turn it on its back. Tie a rope or wire to each leg and attach them to a shrub or tree nearby, so that, when you split the breast bone and cut all the way down the center, the animal will be steadied. You may prefer to brace the animal by putting rocks or logs on either side of it.

A good way to start the center cut is to slit the skin for about three or four inches at the breast bone. Insert your free hand and press the inner organs down out of the way as you continue to cut. In doing this ♦ being very careful, of course, not to pierce the intestines, turn the blade of the knife upward and rip the skin all the way to the vent.

Continue to press downward with your free hand as you go.

When the long slit is made, roll the skin back about three or four inches on either side of the cut, keeping the loose hairs away from the flesh. Cut the breast bone and pull the ribs apart. Cut all the organs loose for removal after tying off both the colon and the bladder, which are removed through the anal cavity. The colon will need a double tie before removal. To make it, grasp the colon near the center and squeeze it, clearing a four- or five-inch section as well as possible. Tie it tightly at each end of the cleared area. Then cut between the ties so none of the feces can contaminate the meat. With deer, the musk sacs will have pulled off with the skin.

Work if possible in such a way that after removal of the internal organs you will merely have to wipe the cavity with a dry cloth. If internal bleeding has taken place, however, and fluids from the organs have touched the flesh, scrape or cut the flesh as clean as possible and wipe the areas with salted water. Dry carefully. If the weather is warm, dust the entire cavity with black pepper or powdered charcoal.

To shorten the cooling time of large animals, prop the cavity open with sticks. Separate the heart and liver from the entrails, being careful not to pierce the gall. Don't be surprised, incidentally, if you do not find the gall in deer. They have none.

Use the edible variety of meats at once in camp cooking. Skin furry animals as quickly as possible. Over large areas the skin can be pulled free rather than cut. ▶ Allow no hairs to remain on the meat. Scrape and wash thoroughly any bullet-pierced areas. Keep the meat as cool as possible.

Before canning or freezing soak meat for 24 hours in water to remove all traces of blood. Any blood allowed to remain in the meat may produce "fishy" off-flavors. After killing, meats, game and poultry should be well bled and cooled to below 40°, preferably for 24 hours, before canning. Beef is better if allowed to age for a week or 10 days at 34° to 38°. Large game animals are prepared and processed like beef; small game, like poultry. Copper or iron utensils may produce discoloration. Meat should not be left in galvanized utensils for more than ½ hour, or it may take up harmful quantities of zinc.

▶ Spices should be used sparingly in this type of preservation, and vegetables omitted altogether. White pepper retains a better flavor than black pepper in meat products. If you like, you may place 1 teaspoon salt in each empty quart container. It flavors, but does not help to preserve the meat.

ABOUT PRECOOKING, PACKING AND PROCESSING MEATS FOR CANNING

To bake, preheat oven to 350°. Cut the meat into pieces about 1 pound each. Place in the oven. Roast until the red or pink color of the meat has almost disappeared at the center, about 20 to 40 minutes. Cut the meat into pieces small enough to fit the jars. Pack closely while still hot into hot, sterile jars, at least 2 pieces to a pint jar. Skim fat from drippings. Add enough boiling water or broth to them to cover the meat, leaving ½ inch head space. Remove air bubbles, see page 534.

To stew, cut meat in uniform pieces about 1 pound each, drop in boiling water and simmer 12 to 20 minutes or until the raw color has disappeared at center. Cut meat into smaller serving pieces, salt, pack closely, cover with boiling broth. ♦ To remove air bubbles, see page 534.

Frying is the least desirable method of precooking. It makes the surface of the meat hard and dry and often gives an undesirable flavor to the finished product.

♦ Meat that is not covered with liquid will discolor and lose some flavor in storage. Depending on the shape of the pieces, 1 to 1½ pounds of meat will fill a pint jar and still remain submerged. ♦ Pint jars are preferable to larger containers, as the heat penetrates more readily to the center of the container.

♦ Most meat is processed at 10 pounds pressure. Process for the length of time given below. ▲ For high altitude processing, see page 533.

ROASTS AND STEAKS

Remove all large bones, gristle and excess fat, leaving just enough fat for flavor. Precook in oven or hot water except for pork, which has a better flavor when precooked in an oven. Pack hot and cover with boiling liquid in which the meats were cooked. Process pints for 75 minutes, quarts for 90 minutes, in a pressure cooker at 10 pounds pressure.

GROUND BEEF

Be sure the meat is fresh and is kept clean and cold. Grind lean meat, using plate with ⅛-inch holes. Form into flat cakes that can be packed without breaking. Precook in moderate oven 350° until medium done. Pack hot. Skim fat from drippings. Cover cakes with drippings and boiling water. Leave 1-inch head space. Process for

same length of time as for roasts or steaks, above.

MEAT FOR STEWS OR HASH

Use less tender cuts and small pieces. Cut meat into 1 inch cubes. Add boiling water to cover. Simmer until raw color is gone. Pack hot. Cover with boiling broth. Process pints for 75 minutes, quarts for 90 minutes in pressure canner at 10 pounds.

LIVER

Wash, remove veins and membranes, slice or cut as desired. Drop into boiling salted water, simmer about 5 minutes. Pack. Cover with boiling water. Process as for stews, above.

HEART

Wash, remove thick connective tissue. Precook by stewing, as above. Pack, salt and add boiling broth to cover. Process as for stews, above.

TONGUE

Wash, place in boiling water and simmer about 45 minutes or until skin can be removed. Skin, slice or cut into pieces. Reheat to simmering in broth. Pack. Add broth to cover. Process as for stews, above.

SOUP STOCK AND BROTH

Crack or saw bones. Simmer them in salted water until the meat is tender. Strain stock to remove bones. Skim off excess fat. Meat may be returned to stock. Reheat to boiling and pour into jars. Process pints for 20 minutes, quarts for 25 minutes at 10 pounds pressure.

SAUSAGE

Make country-style sausage— (I, 531)—according to your favorite recipe, but omit sage. One-fourth beef may be used. Form into flat cakes. Brown in moderate oven, 350°, or on top of stove in heavy skillet over moderate heat, pouring off fat as it accumulates. Pack hot. Cover with boiling pan gravy and water. Leave 1-inch head space. Process as for stews, above.

POULTRY AND SMALL GAME

Chickens should be dressed, cut as for frying and cooled at 40° or lower for at least 8 hours—preferably 24—before canning. Mature chickens yield a more flavorful canned product than do younger ones, though either may be used.

Trim off all lumps of fat. Separate the meat into 3 piles—the meaty pieces, the bony pieces and the giblets. The giblets discolor the meat and are best canned alone.

To precook the chicken, first prepare a broth by simmering the bony pieces until tender. Add broth to meaty pieces and simmer until medium done. Skim fat from broth. Pack meaty pieces with or without bone and add boiling broth to cover, leaving 1-inch head space. Work out air bubbles, see page 534. Remove meat from bone, cut in uniform pieces and can, covered with boiling broth. Process pints for 65 minutes, quarts for 75 minutes at 10 pounds pressure.

It is desirable to can livers separately, gizzards and hearts together. Cover giblets with boiling chicken broth or water. Cover and cook until medium done. Pack hot. Cover with boiling broth. Leave 1-inch head space. Work out air bubbles, see page 534. Process pints for 75 minutes at 10 pounds pressure.

ABOUT SMOKING AND BRINING HAM

Somebody has defined eternity

as a ham and two people. But one may while away the time more tolerably if he remembers to serve the choicer parts of a ham first; then to slice, chop and grind the rest for emergency storage in the refrigerator where —if covered—it will remain in good condition up to three weeks. For other suggestions, see Economical Use of Large Cuts of Meat (I, 461 and 463).

The distinctive flavor of a ham depends on what the animal has been fed: corn, acorns, peanuts, peaches or table scraps. We have always been incensed that there is no universal legislation which could reduce the incidence of trichinosis to a minimum by requiring that refuse fed to hogs be presteamed. Since it is not, it is imperative for you to be sure that the hams you buy are processed long enough and at a high enough temperature to kill the dangerous trichina parasite. The internal heat should reach at least 140°. ◗ Smoking (I, 92), alone, will not suffice. But any ham marked with the round purple U.S. Inspection stamp should be safe to eat; although even if marked "fully cooked" it will probably need ◗ further cooking, for palatability, up to 160° to 180°.

There are two chief ways to salt hams: brining and dry-curing. When hams are soaked in brine or, in the more modern technique, when brine is forced through the arterial system under pressure, temperatures must be very carefully controlled. Neither type of brining is recommended for the amateur. The arterial method, plus steam-smoking, gives us the commercially processed ham usually encountered in the meat market. So prepared, it needs neither soaking nor simmering before baking. Dry-cured hams include "old hams" like Smith-field, Virginia, Kentucky and Dijon—the last being imported from France. Very salty, they need 12 hours of soaking, as well as long simmering, before they are ready to bake with their final garnish. Two especially interesting foreign varieties of aged hams are Westphalian and the Italian Prosciutto. The Italian porkers during their happy lifetime are fed on a diet of chestnuts and the ones native to Perma get whey from the local cheese. The Westphalians thrive on sugar-beet mash. With their succulent translucence, they are very close in texture to smoked salmon. Both are painstakingly aged. Unlike the "old" hams previously mentioned, they are ready to eat without further preparation or cooking.

Dry-cured hams are more tolerant of fluctuating temperatures under processing than those treated with brine. And, while they are less salty than brined, they will still profit by a six-hour soaking before cooking. Ideally, the curing and storing of hams should take place in a 36° to 40° temperature. Even considering the somewhat inconveniently higher temperatures in which most of us are obliged to work, we still recommend dry-curing rather than brining in home-processing. This way is more certain to win the race between salt-penetration and bacterial growth.

♦ To dry-cure ham, allow the meat to cool as naturally and rapidly as possible after butchering. Spread the pieces out on racks, never allowing them to overlap. Sprinkle them at once ♦ very lightly with salt. Do not blanket them at this time with the salt, as this would retard cooling. When cool, rub them repeatedly with the following salt mixture, being sure to cover the entire surface well in the process. Then pack them in salt. Allow for every 10 lbs. of ham a mixture of:

    1 cup salt
    ¼ cup sugar
    2 teaspoons saltpeter

with:

    (2 bay leaves)
    (2 coriander seeds)
    (3 cloves)
    (6 peppercorns)

which you have crushed in a mortar.

The salt and pepper are preservatives, the sugar adds flavor and the saltpeter will help the meat hold a good color. To secure effective salt-penetration, allow three days for each pound of meat per piece. Boned hams and small pieces will of course cure more rapidly. If the temperature should go below 36° at any time, be sure to add an equal length of time to the curing period, as salt-penetration is slowed to a standstill in freezing temperatures.

Salting takes perseverance, but smoking takes skill. For directions to build a smoke oven and fuel it, see (I, 93). Our farm neighbors always leave a piece of skin on the meat they smoke. This is because the weight of the meat will not tear it in hanging where a loop of wire or string goes through it. The hams must be hung so they do not touch each other at any point, for they will not "take" the smoke where they do. Dry-curing requires longer smoking than brining. For this reason, allow at least 36 hours to drive out any excess moisture. Try not to let the temperature rise over 120° at any time.

When the hams are cool, wrap them in a densely woven cloth and bury them in wooden boxes in the cooled ashes which have been retrieved from the smoking-fire. The ashes will deter moisture and insects and add an increasingly good smoked flavor to your hams. Sometimes, in carving even professionally cured ham, an odor is detectable as you get near the bone. This means that the ham was insufficiently smoked. If a rainbow iridescence appears on sliced ham, it is merely due to light refraction on the fat film. Ham should be served warm or cool, but never chilled. Many people freeze ham, page 561. We find it retains good flavor for only a relatively short time—especially if it has been brined arterially and reprocessed with tenderizing enzymes.

SALT OR PICKLED PORK

◗ Please read About Pickling Ingredients and Equipment, page 584.
Cut into pieces 6 inches square:

Fat back or other thin pieces of fat pork
Rub each square well all over with:

Pickling salt
Pack the salted pork tightly in a clean crock and let stand 12 hours. For each 25 lbs. of meat, mix and cool the following brine:

2½ lbs. salt
½ oz. saltpeter
4 quarts boiling water
Pour the ◗ cooled brine over the meat to cover. Store the pork ◗ weighted and covered at 35° to 38° temperature until ready to use.

HARD SAUSAGE

After smoking, hang in a cool dry place, about 1 to 2 months, to cure.
Have ready:

2½ lbs. peeled potatoes
Cook 12 minutes, drain, cool overnight covered. Grind three times:

2½ lbs. of top round of beef
2½ lbs. lean pork
2½ lbs. small-diced pork fat
Mix with:

2 tablespoons salt
1 teaspoon saltpeter
2 teaspoons coarsely ground pepper
Grind the cooked potatoes once and add to the meat. Work together until well mixed. Put into sausage casing and smoke, (I, 92).

ABOUT SMOKING FOWL

If birds are to be smoked for preservation, they must be brined as for ham. If the smoke flavor is your aim and you plan using them just as you would fresh fowl, roast them (I, 573), for ¾ the normal cooking time. Then smoke at 140° from 6 to 8 hours. This smoking period will both flavor and finish the cooking.

To smoke wild birds, cut off meat in strips, dust with salt and pepper. Smoke as for ham, page 543.

◗ To cook smoked birds, steam for a few minutes to remove excess salt. Then cook as for ham (I, 488).

ABOUT SMOKING OR KIPPERING FISH

For fish suitable for smoking, see (I, 393). Prepare a Smoke Oven (I, 93). Use a nonresinous wood or sawdust. The smoking period and temperatures will depend on the length of time you want to preserve the fish. To keep them 2 weeks under refrigeration, smoke at least 24 hours. If they are to be kept longer than 2 weeks, use method II, or a 5-day or longer smoke period—longer if the weather is not clear and dry. Or use a Chinese Smoke Oven (I, 93).
I. For small whole fish, we suggest a dry salting, cold smoke

method. The best temperature is 70° to 80°. Be sure it does not go above 90°. It is easier to handle small fish with the heads on. E:th:r split them for cleaning or make a small incision just under the gills and pull them out as well as the viscera with the thumb and forefinger. Prepare a brine of:

1 gallon water
1 cup salt

Immerse the thoroughly cleaned fish for 30 minutes. Drain, rinse in fresh ♦ cold water. Drain again to remove all excess moisture. Have ready a wooden box lined with a ½-inch layer of pickling salt and a tub or large pan filled with enough fine-grained salt in which to dip the fish, allowing them to pick up as much of it as will cling to them. Pack the fish in single layers in the salt-lined box, with layers of salt between the layers of fish. Leave it in 6 hours if split, 12 hours if whole. Remove from salt, rinse and arrange fish on grill or rods just as they will hang or be racked in the barrel. ♦ Be sure not to crowd them so the smoke can circulate freely. Hang them first in a shady spot for about 3 hours until a shiny casing forms over their surface. Place them without disturbing this surface in the preheated smoke can, as indicated previously—depending on the time you plan keeping the fish before use.

II. For smoking large salt water fish fillets, try this hot smoke method. Fillet the fish, but do not remove the skin. Cut into 3- to 4-inch chunks. Wash carefully to remove all blood and viscera. Let chunks stand refrigerated 14 to 18 hours in a brine made of:

1⅛ cups granular pickling
   salt to each gallon of
   water

Rinse well: Place on racks, skin side down, leaving a space between pieces so smoke can circulate well. Place rack in preheated Smoke Oven (I, 93). Smoke with a nonresinous wood 3 to 4 hours. During this period never let the smoke get over 90°. Then raise heat to 165° to 170° for 45 to 50 minutes. This both cooks the fish and gives it a lovely golden brownish sheen. Cool fish. Refrigerated, they will keep 3 to 5 weeks. For a longer period, pressure can, page 533, at 10 lbs, in sterile ½-pint jars, 60 minutes for boned fish, 90 minutes if the bones are still left in.

ABOUT PREPARING ROE FOR CAVIAR

Remove from very fresh fish, as soon as possible:

Roe

Tear the egg masses into small-size pieces. Work them through a ¼-inch or finer screen to free the eggs from the membrane. Place them for 15 to 20 minutes in a cold water brine made of:

1⅛ cups pickling salt, page
   196, to every quart of
   cold water

If you use a salinometer, the reading should be 28.3. There should be twice as much brine as roe in volume. Remove from liquid and drain thoroughly by allowing to drip through a strainer for about 1 hour. Keep refrigerated during this operation. Place in an airtight non-metal container and store at 34° for 1 to 2 months. Remove, drain and repack, storing at 0° Fahrenheit until ready to use.

FREEZING

We are indebted to an Arctic explorer for the following Eskimo recipe for a frozen dinner: "Kill and eviscerate a medium-sized walrus. Net several flocks of small migrating birds and remove only one small wing feather from each wing. Store birds whole in interior of walrus. Sew up walrus and freeze. Then two years or so later, find the cache if you can, notify clan of a feast, partially thaw walrus. Slice and serve." Simplicity itself.

Simple, too, are the mechanics of home freezing, a comparatively easy method of food preservation which has been advertised as all things to all cooks. The result is that some frozen food enthusiasts toss any type of food into the poor freezer and expect fabulous results. Yes, some foods can be preserved by freezing more successfully than in any other way, but quality produce comes out only if quality produce goes in. There are other important factors, too. Suitable foods must be chosen and given ♦ quick and careful preparation. They must be sealed in ♦ moisture-vapor-proof wrappings and kept at ♦ constant zero or lower temperatures during storage. Then, of course, they must be properly thawed and cooked.

In spite of necessary precautions, meats, fish, poultry, fruits and precooked foods are quite easy to freeze. Vegetables, because of the necessity of blanching, require both more time and care. But even so, freezing takes a third to a half the amount of time and labor as compared with canning. And the yields per bushel of produce are about the same, see pages 534–538.

ABOUT THE FREEZER AND ITS CONTENTS

The economics of keeping a well-stocked freezer presents what we have heard called a "mooty" point. Unless you are a strong-willed planner and dispenser, it may lead to extravagance. Faced with an emergency, it is a great temptation to use that choice cut of meat reserved for company, and children love to draw on the seemingly unlimited freezer resources of ice cream and desserts. ♦ It is often only by sharp-eyed husbanding of supplies and by raising your own meat and vegetables that the satisfactions as well as the cash savings from a freezer are realized. ♦ You may also profit, as a quick-witted trader, when markets are glutted with raw vegetables and fruits or meat and poultry specials. But avoid bargain frozen foods that have been stored a long time—for they will not have a full complement of vitamins and flavors.

In any case, the freezer is not meant for miserly hoarding but ♦ should be managed on an over-all, continuously shifting plan—a seasonal plan—geared to your family's food needs and preferences. But keep the freezer stocked with favorites, so the

family will continue to ask:
"What's thawing?"

Space estimates differ, depending on family appetites, but a minimum allowance of 3 cubic feet per person is average if you schedule a turnover every six months.

ABOUT FILLING THE FREEZER

♦ Neither overload your freezer ♦ nor add, at one time, more than 2 to 3 lbs. for each cubic foot of freezer space, during any 24 hour period. Either procedure will cause damage to the food you are storing. ♦ Until the new packages are frozen, keep them against the freezer plates or the walls of the freezer, unless the manufacturer directs otherwise. ♦ Exceptions are sandwiches and baked items, which attract moisture to themselves if placed there. These items should be put upon other frozen packages away from the walls. When you finally use these frozen treasures ♦ allow enough time for proper thawing and cooking.

ABOUT DEFROSTING THE FREEZER

Your freezer operates most economically if it is located in an area where the temperature is between 50° to 70°. It is hard to specify just how often a freezer will need defrosting. The number of times it is opened, the state of loading, and how carefully food is wrapped all affect the buildup of condensation. ♦ Defrost whenever there is ½ inch of frost on the plates or sides. If frost has not solidified into ice, scraping is a good method. ♦ Turn off the current first, though. Remove all food from the freezer and refrigerate it immediately. Pans of hot

water are sometimes used, but must be elevated on racks so that they are not in direct contact with freezer walls or plates. No matter how often you have to defrost ♦ be sure to clean up any spillage when it occurs and ♦ to wipe out your freezer at least once a year with a cloth that has been dipped in a solution of 1 tablespoon baking soda to 1 quart of lukewarm water. ♦ Dry the freezer well, either with a cloth or a hair dryer. ♦ Be sure the lining is thoroughly dry before you turn the current on again. It is wise to let the freezer run for one-half hour before returning food to it.

ABOUT POWER BREAKS

The seriousness of a power break should not be underestimated because a 25° rise in temperature over a 24-hour period is ruinous to nutritive values. So, if a prolonged break is indicated call your local dealer or ice cream company for a source of dry ice. This ice has a temperature of 110° below zero F. A 50 lb. cake, if placed in the freezer soon after the electricity fails, will prevent thawing for 2 or 3 days. ♦ Handle dry ice with heavy gloves. Do not attempt to chip or cut it, as a stray chip might cause injury. If you use dry ice in the freezer, do not lock the box or fasten the clamp. However, actual thawing, if the ♦ freezer is kept closed, is not likely to occur in even 4- or 6-cubic-foot freezers within the first 15 to 20 hours. After 48 hours, the temperature will just reach 40° to 45°—the normal refrigerator range. Food that still retains ice crystals can be refrozen, but meats, poultry and fish registering more than 50° must be cooked and used at once.

ABOUT TYPES OF FOOD
SUITABLE FOR FREEZING

If you have rushed to this chapter to learn what discoveries in home freezing we have made since the last edition of "The Joy," we must report that the methods previously described are still the recommended ones —and will be until major changes in principle are introduced into household freezing equipment.

It is true that you will find a host of new ready-cooked frozen items in the shops. Among them are potatoes and other watery foods processed with recently developed machinery which removes harmful excess moisture. But such freeze-dry vacuum-processing is beyond the scope of the home-freezing equipment presently available. And, although its proponents claim much for it, the foods it preserves cannot be regarded as equal in flavor to those freshly prepared. There are on the market, however, several ♦ waxy corn and rice flours which do help in stabilizing frozen sauces, see pages 155 and 157.

Beware of using the freezer for certain types of processing. ♦ Freezing, for example, will ruin gelatins. In yeast and some other refrigerator doughs, the leavening action that should continue to take place is often stopped by the lower temperature of the freezer. ♦ In general, most cooked foods can be frozen, but some do not justify the amount of preparation required. Always balance original preparation time against the time it takes to prepare properly for freezing, and omit quick broils, quick-cooking pastas or quick sautés. Freezing techniques, as described later, have settled down into a practice as reliable as canning. But keep in mind

that the storage life of frozen food is not in the least comparable.

This principle bears repetition. ♦ The retention of nutritional values and flavors depends on the speed with which food can be processed after harvesting, the favorable temperatures at which it is held until frozen and the manner in which it is thawed. Work quickly with small quantities of fruits and vegetables and keep the rest chilled in the refrigerator.

ABOUT QUALITY

Whatever quantity you freeze, the quality of the food you use is of first importance. ♦ Quality cannot be created in the freezing process itself. It is sometimes lost even though well-fed animals, and fruits and vegetables from rich soils are used. For example, the keeping qualities of varieties of the same fruit or vegetable differ. Elberta peaches grown in New York are considered tops for freezing, but Elberta peaches grown in Virginia are often reported poor for that purpose.

Time and conditions of harvest or slaughter are also factors to reckon with. ♦ Crops are prime when they have sun just before maturing. Undue rain before harvest may cause the entire pack to be mediocre. Crops such as ♦ early apples, the first asparagus, etc., keep their flavor best.

Because new discoveries are being made constantly, it is wise, if you are barging into freezing in a big way, to ♦ consult your county agricultural agent about the best varieties of fruits and vegetables to grow and to buy from your neighborhood. Watch government bulletins and state experimental station publications, too, for these agencies continue to make discoveries in the science of home-freezing.

♦ The retention of nutritional values and flavors depends on the speed with which food can be processed after cropping. From then on ♦ it must be kept at such favorable temperatures that microbial and enzymatic activities are held to a minimum, see page 527. Should they have begun before freezing, the freezing process will not destroy the resultant contamination, but only arrest it temporarily. Therefore ♦ you are courting danger to allow perishable frozen foods to thaw for any length of time before cooking. Modern once-a-week marketing is feasible if the transfer of food packages from commercial compartment to home-freezer is effected with all speed. Remember ♦ once thawed—do not refreeze.

♦ Any frozen foods stored in the ice cube compartment of the refrigerator should be used within 1 week, as the temperature range in this section is between 10° and 25° in most refrigerators, not the required 0° or minus of a freezer. ♦ Permitting the temperature of frozen food to rise to 25° or 30° for even 1 day does more damage to its eating quality and nutritional value than holding it at zero for a year.

ABOUT WRAPPING, PACKAGING AND SEALING

After selecting quality food, decide how to package it. ♦ Excess air within the frozen food package is a real enemy. Choose only those wrappings which will insure an absolutely moisture-proof and vapor-proof seal, both to protect the food from drying out and to keep odors from penetrating into the freezer and

causing off-flavors in other food. Air left in the containers dries out the food during the inevitable temperature variations of storage, drawing moisture from the food itself to form a frost in the package—a frost made from the juices and seasoned with the flavors of the food itself. ♦ So, try always to exclude as much air as possible from the package.

♦ Liquid foods must be stored in leak-proof containers and enough space allowed for the expansion of the liquid during the freezing process. Allow ½ inch in pint and ¾ inch in quart cartons. If you use glass, allow 1 inch for a pint and 1½ inches for a quart container. Always choose vapor- and moisture-proof containers of convenient size and shape. ♦ Cubical containers conserve a good deal more storage space than cylindrical ones of the same dimensions.

Meats and irregularly formed foods are wrapped in aluminum foil or special laminated papers. ♦ The foil, which should have a weight of .0015 or thicker, needs no sealing, but profits from an overwrap of stockingnet which helps to hold the wrapping close to the food and also protects against tearing of the foil. For economy, old nylon stockings may be used in place of stockingnet.

Plastics and papers vary in quality and it is often difficult to judge their efficiency. They need careful sealing with tapes adapted to low temperatures. Some may be sealed with heat. A special iron is available for heat sealing, although a not-too-hot curling or pressing iron will do.

♦ All sheet wrappings should be applied with a lock-seal or drugstore wrap shown on page 551 or, where size demands,

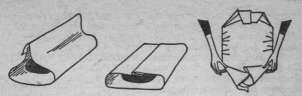

with the costlier butcher wrap shcwr. below. To make the drugstore or lockseal wrap, place the food in the center of a piece of paper large enough so that when the ends are brought together they can be folded into an interlocking seam, as shown on the left. Make the seam and draw the paper down against the food to enclose it tightly, as shown in the center. Reverse the pacakage, so that the seam lies on the table. Now turn the package, so that the closed ends are at right angles to your body. Pleat-fold the end farthest from you and make an extra fold in the end, before pressing the folded end against the package. Spin the package around, so that the doubly folded end can be braced against your body, as shown on the right. Now very carefully force any excess air from the package. Then fold the remaining open end. Seal the package with ◗ a tape that is adapted to low temperature.

To make the butcher wrap, the food is placed on a large square of paper on the diagonal. One corner is brought over it generously, as shown on the left, below. The adjoining corners are then folded over, as shown in the center, and the entire package folded over in turn, as shown on the right. This wrap requires great care if excess air is to be excluded from the package and the food kept flat. ◗ Easiest to handle are polyethylene bags made of a plastic which can be heat-sealed, but it is equally good practice and simpler to twist them tightly into a goose neck and secure them closely with a rubber band. These bags remain pliable even at zero temperature, need no overwrap and can be re-used. Pliofilm bags may also be reused if handled carefully, but an overwrap of stockingnet is advisable.

Some frugal housewives keep their old butter and ice cream cartons and line them with pliofilm bags, but such cartons must be considered as merely protective overwraps for a moisture- and vapor-proof liner. Plastic boxes and heavily waxed cartons are good for liquids, but watch for a tight seal. Both may be used again. Before reusing, wash the wax cartons with a

detergent and cold water to keep the wax firm. ◗ Aluminum foil cartons particularly are satisfactory for foods that can be served with a mere reheating. Be extremely careful to seal them tightly. They are also satisfactory for rapid chilling before storage and can go from freezer to oven without further handling or loss of contents.

If packing vegetables in cartons, size them carefully. A device such as the one shown on the right below can be made out of a wooden box. Adjusted to your carton size, it is a great aid for quick, close packing. ◗ Should several servings of meat, cookies or other small items be combined in 1 package, they separate more easily when 2 thicknesses of moisture-proof paper are placed between each 2 units, as shown on the left below, or when they are slid into folded foil, as shown in the center below, before the outside wrapping is put on. ◗ In packaging your foods, wrap in convenient serving or meal-size quantities. Holding over or recooking thawed leftovers is not advisable. Since good results depend so much on the speed with which the fresh foods are prepared and put into the freezer, it is wise to have all filling, wrapping and labeling equipment ready at hand. Use proper funnels for filling cartons, to keep liner edges dry for a perfect seal. Rectangular ones can be bought or they can be made by removing both ends from tin cans and compressing the lower end to fit the carton.

ABOUT LABELING AND DATING

Soft wax or china marking pencils or marking pens do well for cartons. Labels may be slipped between stockingnet and other wrappings or under transparent wrap. Small, tough different-colored tags with string attached are helpful for quick identification of stored opaque packages. ◗ Keep a master record of dates of freezing, as well as poundage on meats and of portions of other foods. ◗ The labeling and dating of the packages themselves, needless to say, is essential. While many foods keep satisfactorily for months, there are some exceptions, which are noted in detail later ◗ such as fat meats, poultry, prepared doughs and precooked foods. ◗ You may find our storage-limit recommendations short compared to others, but we believe you also prefer optimum standards for food flavor and texture to merely edible ones. Whatever you are processing, remember to start with quality food, have it properly prepared, well cooled, wrapped and labeled before storing it.

ABOUT FREEZING, THAWING AND COOKING RAW FOODS

Certain changes take place in

frozen foods during storage that call for distinctive handling before and during cooking. A tendency to mushiness in vegetables and dryness in meat and fish can be lessened by proper thawing and heating.

Always thaw frozen foods in their original containers. When time allows, it is preferable to thaw them on a refrigerator shelf, with the exception of unbaked doughs, page 566. Thawing food, still packaged, at room temperature, takes about half as long and, if the package is put before a fan, about one third as long as the refrigerator method. For emergencies, if the package is absolutely waterproof, it may be immersed in cool—not warm—water. This procedure should be adopted only when you are pressed for time, as the result is poor with fragile foods or those with high water content—like melons. Use all frozen items as soon as possible after thawing, for growth of bacteria can occur rapidly in thawed foods left at room temperature ♦ especially pot pies, TV dinners and foods containing gravies, sauces and stuffings. Rapid use after thawing is especially important with blanched products whose oxygen-resisting enzymes have been destroyed and whose further exposure to air and heat causes rapid adverse changes in quality and nutritional value. Speed in serving helps prevent these disappointing changes.

ABOUT FREEZING AND THAWING FRUITS

Choose almost any firm, sound, uniformly sun-ripened fruit. Exceptions are pears, which seldom freeze well, but do somewhat better if ripened off the tree, and bananas, which had better be kept out of the freezer. It is not essential to use sugar in freezing fruit, but it is often preferable, see below. Freshly grated, unsweetened coconut may be frozen by adding one part sugar to eight parts coconut. Mix it with its own milk, page 193, before freezing. Leftover packaged coconut may also be frozen and used as needed.

ABOUT AMOUNTS OF SUGAR FOR FREEZING FRUITS

♦ To sugar fruit, place it on a shallow tray. ♦ Just before you are ready to pack, sift the sugar over it until evenly coated. The longer you allow the fruit to stand with the sugar before freezing, the more juice it will draw. When the fruit is coated, pack it gently into suitable cartons, allowing space for expansion. Seal, label and freeze.

Use 1 pound sugar to the pounds of fruit indicated below

*5 lbs. apples
4 to 5 lbs. blackberries
**4 lbs. blueberries
*3 to 5 lbs. sour cherries
3 lbs. currants
4 to 5 lbs. dewberries
3 to 4 lbs. gooseberries
*3 lbs. peaches, sliced
3 lbs. pineapple
*3 to 4 lbs. plums
4 lbs. raspberries, whole or crushed
4 to 5 lbs. rhubarb, diced
†4 lbs. strawberries, whole or crushed
*Mix ½ teaspoon dry ascorbic acid crystals with every 5 lbs. of dry sugar.
**Steam-blanch, page 557, ½ to 1 minute to keep skins tender. Shake well to coat with sugar to keep them from clumping.
†After washing, prick whole strawberries with fork to re-

lease excess air before combining with sugar.

No sugar is required for these fruits.

°Apples
°Apples, sliced
°°Blueberries
  Cranberries
  Currants
°Figs
  Gooseberries
  Loganberries
  Melons
  Pineapple
°Plums
  Prunes
  Rhubarb
  Raspberries
  Youngberries
°Immerse briefly in a solution of 3 tablespoons lemon juice or ¼ teaspoon ascorbic acid to 1 quart water, then drain dry on paper toweling.
°°Steam-blanch, page 557, ½ to 1 minute to keep skins tender.

ABOUT SIRUP FOR FREEZING FRUIT

◗ These sirups may be made several days in advance and stored in the refrigerator, so as to be well chilled when combined with the fruit.

For light or 40% sirup, use 1¾ cups sugar to 1 pint water
For medium or 50% sirup, use 2½ cups sugar to 1 pint water
A heavier sirup is not recommended

Some people prefer to combine sugar with corn sirup. If this combination is desired, never use more than ⅓ cup corn sirup to ⅔ cup sugar. Any of these sirups may be made by merely dissolving the sugar and corn sirup in water, but it is preferable to boil the mixture until the sugar is dissolved. Chill well before using.

◗ Use enough sirup to cover the fruit well. When using sirup with small or sliced fruits or berries, allow about 1½ cups of fruit and ⅓ to ½ cup of sirup for a pint container. Halved fruits require about 1½ cups of fruit and ¾ to 1 cup of sirup to a pint container.

If the fruit tends to rise above the sirup, crush a piece of moisture-proof paper lightly and put it on top to keep the fruit submerged until the expansion of freezing makes the sirup fill the carton. Leave the paper in the carton.

In the list below, the L stands for light sirup; the M stands for a medium one. For relative amounts of fruit and sirup, see opposite.

°‡L Apples
°L-M Apricots, peeled or unpeeled
  L Blackberries
  L Blueberries
  L-M Boysenberries
°M Cherries, sweet
  M Dewberries
°L-M Figs
  L Grapefruit
  L Guavas, pulp and rind
  L Grapes
  L-M Loganberries
°L Nectarines
  L Oranges, sections
°L Peaches
°L Pears
  L-M Pineapple
  L-M Papaya, ½-inch cubes
  L-M Pomegranate
°L-M Plums
  L-M Prunes
  L-M Raspberries, whole or crushed
  L-M Strawberries
  L-M Youngberries
°Use lemon juice or ascorbic acid opposite.
‡Blanch 1½ minutes in sirup.

ABOUT FREEZING SMALL FRUITS

People who grow their own berries may freeze them successfully without washing—provided they have not been treated with toxic spray. It is safer to wash berries which are not home grown. Fragile fruits like berries or cherries should be washed twice in cold or ice water to clean and firm them. Drain fruit well, then spread it out on several thicknesses of paper toweling and cover it lightly with additional toweling to absorb as much surface moisture as possible. To avoid crushing or bruising the fruit, use very gentle movements. After the fruit is picked over and hulled or stemmed, it is ready for packaging with or without the addition of sugar. For different methods of preparation, see page 553. Blueberry skins remain tender if the fruit is blanched, page 558, before sugar is added. Since, during cooking and cooling, the waxy bloom on blueberries becomes somewhat adhesive, shake the container now and then to avoid clumps. If whole strawberries are to be packaged without sugar, prick them with a fork to release the air. Unsweetened raspberries may be frozen by placing them unwrapped, in a single layer, on trays in the freezer until solidly frozen. Then they can be packaged closely, sealed and stored. They may be wrapped and frozen in small packages for garnishes, but should be used for this purpose ◗ while still frozen, otherwise they will "weep."

Some fruits keep better packed in dry sugar or in Sirup, page 554. The dry method of sweetening is preferable, as the addition of water tends to weaken the flavor of the fruit.

Sugar just before packaging and freeze as soon as possible, so the sugar will not draw juices from the fruit. It is sometimes suggested that fruits and berries be served only partially thawed and while still slightly icy, so they do not "weep." While this is a practical approach for garnishes, we so dislike biting into a glassy texture that we suggest ◗ frozen berries be fully thawed and used for sauces and flavorings, where their taste is superb and their "weeping" not a liability. Thaw fruits on a refrigerator shelf.

ABOUT FREEZING LARGE FRUITS

Sort them carefully. Remove pits, cores and stems and pare when necessary. Treat fruits that tend to discolor before freezing and during thawing, such as apples, peaches, apricots, pears, with one of the following **Discolorations Solutions:**

I. Do not slice fruit into a bowl, but drop it, prepared, directly into a solution of 3 tablespoons lemon juice or 2 tablespoons of vinegar to 1 quart of water, or ¼ teaspoon ascorbic acid crystals or 1 crushed tablet dissolved in 1 quart water. One quart of either of these mixtures is enough for about 4 quarts of fruit. Drain the fruit well before adding it to the sirup. It is advisable to Blanch, page 558, sliced apples and other light-colored fruits.

II. Drop the prepared fruit directly into the sirup in which it is to be frozen, adding 1½ teaspoons lemon juice or ¼ teaspoon of the ascorbic acid to each 2 cups of sirup. To distribute the acid evenly, dissolve ¼ teaspoon of the ascorbic acid crystals or powder in 1 teaspoon of water. Do this in a small bottle and shake the contents until dissolved before adding it to each 2 cups sirup. Add the lemon juice or acid to the sirup shortly before putting in the fruits. If those which tend to discolor are packed in combinations which include citrus fruits, the lemon juice or acid may be omitted.

ABOUT FREEZING PURÉES

Some fruits, such as plums, prunes, avocados, papayas, mangoes, persimmons and melons, keep better in uncooked purée form. Bananas should not be frozen. Applesauce is one of the most delicious of cooked frozen purées, especially if made with early apples. All may, if necessary, be packaged without sugar, but when packaging with sugar allow about 1 cup of it per pound of fruit.

ABOUT FREEZING FRUIT JUICES

Juices such as apple, raspberry, plum, cherry and grape, as well as fruit ciders, freeze very well. For each gallon of cherry or apple juice, add ½ teaspoon ascorbic acid or 2 teaspoons lemon juice. Peaches for pressing can be steamed to 150° to keep color clear without tasting cooked. Cherries, plums, prunes and grapes have a better flavor if slightly cooked, as some of their characteristic flavor is extracted from the skin. Raspberries are best if the whole berries are mixed with one pound of sugar to each 10 pounds of fruit and frozen. Extract the juice when ready to use. In freezing citrus juices, it is difficult to retain their vitamin content without an elaborate vacuum process. Fruit for jelly and jam may be frozen unsugared and the juice extracted

later without any cooking. To make the jelly, proceed as usual, see page 573. Fruit sauces or cobbler fillings made from seedy berries, especially blackberries, are smoother if the frozen berries are broken apart and put unthawed through a meat grinder. Use a fine blade.

ABOUT FREEZING RAW VEGETABLES

Vegetables such as peas, asparagus, green beans, lima beans, broccoli and corn, take well to freezing. If the produce was garden-fresh and properly processed, its taste, when served, is hardly distinguishable from that of fresh vegetables. Kale, New Zealand spinach, white potatoes and salad materials—tomatoes, cucumbers and onions —are distinct failures. Certain other vegetables, such as sweet potatoes, the squashes, celery and cabbage are eligible for freezing only when precooked. The processing list on pages 558–560 includes some vegetables which, under normal circumstances, are more successfully kept by canning or root storage.

ABOUT BLANCHING VEGETABLES

Enzymes continue to be active in vegetables even after harvesting and, unless arrested, will bring about changes which lead to nutritional loss and off-flavors. Therefore, blanching is imperative before freezing, as it lessens such activity. There are 2 methods of blanching: boiling and steaming. Both may be used more or less interchangeably, although steam-blanching takes 30 seconds to 1 minute longer. Exceptions are the blanching of leafy vegetables, which must be boiled if the heat is to penetrate quickly, and watery vegetables like squashes and cut sweet corn, which lose flavor badly through leaching and must be steamed. Since blanching is not meant to be a cooking process, but merely a preparatory one, it should be carefully timed to avoid textural and nutritional breakdowns. Removal of excess moisture after blanching, and proper chilling before packaging, are two extremely important steps.

Choose young, tender vegetables. The starchy ones, such as peas, corn and lima beans, are best when slightly immature. If not prepared and frozen at once, vegetables should be kept fresh by remaining chilled between harvesting and processing. Prepare them quickly, as for regular cooking. In order to blanch them evenly and pack them efficiently, sort the vegetables for size. Several handy devices for sizing and cutting are available and a corn scraper (I, 284), is a great asset for preparing corn cream-style. Better food values and flavor are retained if vegetables are not shredded or frenched.

◆ To blanch by boiling, allow 6 to 10 quarts of boiling water to 1 pound of vegetables. The larger amount of liquid is preferable, as boiling resumes more rapidly after the vegetables are added and tends to leach them less. Put 1 pound of vegetables in a wire basket. Submerge them completely in the boiling water and wait until it again reaches a boil. Begin to time the blanching, see next page. Shake the wire basket several times during this period to allow even penetration of heat. When finished, lift vegetables from boiling water and put at once into a pan of ice water. Chill until the vegetables are cool to the center. Remove, drain and package.

◆ To steam-blanch, bring 6 quarts of water to an active boil in a kettle. Put the vegetables, not more than a pound at a time, in a wire basket and suspend them above the water. Cover the kettle. When the steam starts escaping under the lid, begin to time for blanching. Shake the basket several times during this period to make sure that all the vegetables are uniformly exposed to the steam. Whether you have used the boiling or steam method, when the time is up, remove the vegetables from the heat at once. Since the blanching process is not meant to cook them, but merely to halt the enzymatic action, they must be chilled at once to stop further softening of the tissues by heat. If your tap water is 60° or less, hold the vegetables under it. If not, immerse them in ice water or chill them over it, as directed in the chart. Drain the vegetables well and spread them on several thicknesses of paper toweling. Also cover them with paper toweling to absorb as much of the surface moisture as possible

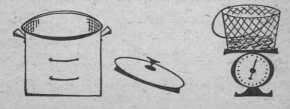

before packaging. Except for greens like spinach, which should have a ½ inch head space, the containers should be closely and completely filled, but not stuffed. Some vegetables keep best as purées. If frozen vegetables toughen consistently, the water used ◗ may be too hard for good results.

ABOUT BLANCHING EQUIPMENT

Whether you parboil or parsteam, the equipment consists preferably of a special blanching kettle with a tight-fitting lid and a wire basket. In either case, handle no more than 1 pound of produce at a time.

BLANCHING CHART FOR VEGETABLES
Showing preferred method

Vegetable	Minutes to parboil	Minutes to parsteam	Minutes to chill in ice water
†Artichoke, whole	8 to 10		12 to 15
Asparagus, medium size	3 to 12		3 to 5
Bamboo Shoots	7 to 13		3
Beans, French		2	5
Beans, Lima	1½		3
Beans, Shell	1¾		3
Beans, Green	2		5
Beans, Soy and Broad	4, in pod		Cool, shell and pack
*Bean Sprouts	4 to 6		Cool over, not in, cold water
Beans, Wax	2		5
Beet Greens	2		5
Beets, small	Until tender		Cool over, not in, cold water
Broccoli, split		3 to 5	4 to 5
Brussels Sprouts	4 to 6		8 to 12
*Cabbage, leaf or shredded	Until tender	3 to 4	Cool over, not in, cold water
Carrots, scrubbed	3		5
Cauliflower, florets		3	4
*Celery, diced	Until tender		Cool over, not in, cold water
Chard	2		5
Chayote, diced	2		5
*Chinese Cabbage, shredded	1½		Cool over, not in, cold water

BLANCHING CHART FOR VEGETABLES Cont.

Vegetable	Minutes to parboil	Minutes to parsteam	Minutes to chill in ice water
Collards	2		5
Corn, cream-style, white or yellow		3 to 5	
		off the cob	Cool over, not in, cold water
		8 on cob	15
Corn, medium size, cut, yellow			15 on cob, then cut off for packing
Corn on Cob (I, 284)			
Corn, scraped for pudding (I, 285)			
*Dasheen	2½		5
†Eggplant, 1½-inch slices	4		‡4 in ascorbic acid solution
*Kale	4 to 6		4 to 5
Kohlrabi, diced		1¾	5
*Mushrooms, medium, whole	3½		5
*Mustard Greens	Until tender		Cool over, not in, cold water
Okra, medium, whole	2		5
Parsnips		3	5
Peas, Black-eyed	2		5
Peas, Green		1⅓ to 3¾	2 to 5
Peppers	2		2 to 5
*Potatoes, Sweet, purée	Until tender		Cool over, not in, cold water Add 1 teaspoon ascorbic acid to every quart potatoes
*Pumpkin, purée	Until tender		Cool over, not in, cold water
Rutabaga	2		5
Spinach	2½		3
*Squash, Winter, purée	Until tender		Cool over, not in, cold water

BLANCHING CHART FOR VEGETABLES Cont.

Vegetable	Minutes to parboil	Minutes to parsteam	Minutes to chill in ice water
Turnip Greens	2½		4
Turnips, sliced, peeled		1½	5
Vegetables, mixed	Blanch separately, as directed above; combine after chilling		

*Cook before freezing
†Add 1 teaspoon ascorbic acid to each quart of water used in blanching
‡Ascorbic acid solution—2 teaspoons acid to 2 pints of ice water

ABOUT THAWING AND COOKING FROZEN VEGETABLES

Most frozen vegetables, because of previous blanching and a tenderizing process induced by temperature changes during storage, cook in from one-third to one-half the time that fresh vegetables require, see page 252. Uncooked frozen vegetables may be substituted in recipes calling for fresh vegetables, but shorten their cooking time. Example: add them to stews for the last minutes of cooking. As with fresh vegetables, it is imperative, if flavor and food values are to be retained, not to overcook them, especially if you use a pressure pan, see (I, 82).

The question of thawing or not thawing before cooking vegetables is a controversial one. If you do thaw, cooking must follow immediately, otherwise adverse changes take place. To unfreeze a 12- to 16-ounce package of vegetables, allow about 6 hours in the refrigerator, 3 at room temperature or 1 before a fan. Broccoli and spinach profit by partial thawing and ♦ corn on the cob should always be completely thawed. It is delicious if buttered and rewrapped in the aluminum foil in which it was frozen, then baked at 400° for 20 minutes. Frozen corn on the cob may also be prepared first by pressure cooking without previous thawing for 1 minute at 15 lbs. pressure, cutting off kernels, adding salt and butter and heating in an ovenproof dish under moderate broiler heat for 2 minutes. Do not thaw frozen mushrooms before cooking as they will become pulpy.

When cooking unthawed vegetables, break them apart into 4 or 5 pieces before removing from the carton to allow the heat to penetrate rapidly and evenly. To cook them, use the smallest possible amount of boiling water—¼ cup is enough for most vegetables. However, lima beans take almost a cup and sowbeans and cauliflower about ½ cup. They should be covered ◆ at once with a lid. Once the boiling has begun again ◆ simmer the vegetables until tender. They will take from one-third to one-half the time required for fresh vegetables. As the addition of water is ruinous to the flavor of some frozen vegetables, steaming or pressure cooking on a rack over hot water, double boiler cooking or baking, is recommended. This is especially true for corn cut from the cob, or squash.

ABOUT FREEZING MEATS

Meats, both domestic and game, should be slaughtered, chilled and aged as for canning, page 539. Then they should be divided into meal-size quantities for packaging, see page 550. ◆ The reheating of once-thawed and cooked meats does not make for very tasty, nutritious or safe eating. Serve such leftovers cold or heat them immediately in a hot sauce.

The same advice as for all frozen produce applies to the choice of meats: watch quality. Storage at low temperatures does not induce enough change to make tough meats tender. If you usually buy quality cuts over the counter, make sure you can trust a new source which sells in quantity.

Beef, lamb and mutton must be properly aged in a chill-room before being frozen, but not too long, see below. ◆ Pork and poultry should be frozen as soon as they cool, after slaughtering, to forestall the tendency of the fat to turn rancid.

Although some frozen meats may be held over a year, it is a questionable economic or gastronomic procedure. Hold corn-fed beef, lamb and mutton a year if necessary; pork, veal and young chicken no more than 8 to 9 months; old chickens, turkeys and variety meats 3 to 4 months. Game storage depends, in part, on the type of game and, in part, on the laws of your state, which may limit holding time. For large game, see directions for meat above. For birds, see directions for poultry below. ◆ Ground and sliced meats do not keep as well as solid cuts. ◆ Do not hold meat loaves over 3 months, as the seasonings deteriorate. Salted or fat meats, such as fresh sausage, should never be held longer than a month, as the salt tends to make the fats rancid. Smoked meats, like bacon and ham, will keep 2 to 4 months, but ◆ extra precautions should be taken in wrapping smoked meats ◆ to keep the odor from penetrating other foods. Bones, which add flavor to meats during cooking, take up considerable locker space and may also cause wrappings to tear. Even though removal of bones requires both skill and time, it is worth it. Cook bones, thus removed, with meat trimmings to make a concentrated stock, see page 138. This is valuable for soups, gravies ◆ or for packaging precooked meats, page 541. Freeze stock in ice-cube-sized trays, remove and wrap for storage. These concentrates make quick gravy or soup.

ABOUT THAWING AND COOKING FROZEN MEATS

Frozen meats may be cooked thawed or unthawed. ◆ But partial or complete thawing helps retain juiciness in thick cuts. Thin cuts and patties may toughen if left frozen and ◆ variety meats or meats prepared by breading or dredging must be completely thawed. ◆ Always defrost in the original wrappings and, when possible, on a refrigerator shelf. Allow 5 hours for each pound of thick cuts, less for thinner ones. Defrosting wrapped meat at room temperature takes about half as long as the refrigerator method and about a third as long when put before a fan. ♦ Cooking unthawed large cuts of meat takes one and a half times as long as fresh ones. Small, thin cuts take one and a quarter times as long. ♦ Thawed cuts are cooked as for fresh ones. ♦ In any roasting process, use only the slow method, see (I, 456). A meat thermometer is a reassuring aid, see (I, 458).

ABOUT FREEZING AND THAWING POULTRY

Uncooked broilers, fryers and roasting chickens are most desirable for freezing. For stewers, see About Freezing and Thawing Precooked Foods, page 563. If you raise your own, starve the chickens for 24 hours before slaughtering, but give them plenty of water. Then bleed them well. Clean and dress (I, 568 and 572), immediately. Be careful not to tear or bruise the flesh. Chill not longer than 2 hours. ♦ Do not age them, unless you are fortunate enough to have wild duck or pheasant, which should be aged 2 or 3 days. For details, see directions listed under recipes for each kind of wild fowl. Remove excess cavity fat. ♦ Wrap giblets separately in moisture-proof wrappings and store in the cavity. Wrap and seal ♦ being careful to expel as much air as possible from the package. One helpful method is to put the bird in a freezer bag and plunge it quickly into a deep pan of cold water—keeping the top of the bag above the surface

of the water. Twist the top and fasten.

When preparing several birds, storage space is saved if chickens are halved or disjointed before packaging. Freeze halves, breasts, thighs and drumsticks separately and wrap with double moisture-proof paper between them or store in cartons. Cook the backbones, wings and necks, remove the meat and freeze in the chicken broth. Store young chickens no more than 9 months, older ones 3 to 4 months. Keep ducks and turkeys 6 to 9 months. A slight discoloration of the bones may occur during storage. It is harmless.

♦ It is not advisable to freeze stuffed poultry, as frequently the stuffing does not freeze fast enough to avoid spoilage. Freeze the stuffing separately.

Poultry is always best when thawed before cooking, unless used for fricassee, see (I, 577). The usual methods is to thaw in the original wrappings and allow 2 hours per pound on the refrigerator shelf, 1 hour per pound, wrapped, at room temperature, 20 minutes per pound if the package is placed before a fan. Cook immediately after thawing. Although we do not recommend it ♦ unthawed fowl needs about one and one-half the time to cook that nonfrozen fowl requires. ♦ Treat thawed fowl like nonfrozen fowl.

ABOUT FREEZING, THAWING AND COOKING FISH

Fish, shellfish and frog legs freeze most successfully when cleaned and frozen immediately. If this is impractical, keep fish under refrigeration from catching to freezing, but in no case over 24 hours. Fish weighing 2 pounds or less, minus viscera, head, tails and fins, are frozen whole. For fish weighing 2 to 4 pounds, filleting is advised (I, 394). Larger fish are usually cut into steaks (I, 395). Separate fillets or steaks with a double thickness of water-proof paper, page 552.

Fish heavy in fat, like salmon, should be used within 2 months. Lobster and crab freeze best if cooked first as for the table, but without salt. Shrimp, minus head, are best frozen uncooked, as they toughen if frozen after cooking. In fact, most shellfish are apt to toughen, cooked or uncooked, if held over 2 months. Types like lobster and shrimp may be closely dry-packed. Oysters, clams and scallops should be shelled. The liquor is saved. Scallops may be washed after shelling, but not the other shellfish. Package all of these in their own liquor to cover and freeze. Hold no longer than 6 months.

Fish and shellfish are often packed commercially in an ice glaze to seal from oxygen. This is a good method, but hard to do at home.

Slowly thawed fish loses less juice and is more delicate when cooked than fish quickly thawed. Thaw fish in the original wrappings and allow about 8 hours per pound if placed on a refrigerator shelf, 4 hours per pound wrapped at a room temperature, 2½ hours per pound if the package is put before a fan. Lobster takes slightly more, scallops, oysters, shellfish and uncooked shrimp slightly less time than given above. Shrimp need not be thawed before cooking, unless it is to be deep-fat fried.

Unthawed fish must be cooked both longer and at much lower temperatures than fresh fish—usually about one and one-quarter times as long.

ABOUT FREEZING AND THAWING EGGS

Eggs must be removed from the shell before freezing. For short periods, shelled eggs may be frozen individually in an ice-cube tray, then packaged and stored. Usually, yolks and whites are stored separately. The whites are simply packaged in vapor-proof, small recipe-size containers, perhaps in the exact amount for your favorite angel cake. Whole eggs or yolks should be stabilized or they become pasty and hard to mix after freezing. Stabilization is accomplished as follows: If yolks are to be used for unsweetened foods, add 2 teaspoons of salt to each pint. If for desserts, add 2 tablespoons of sugar, honey or corn sirup to each pint. You will, of course, do well to label the yolks accordingly. To use ♦ thaw in the refrigerator for 8 to 10 hours; at room temperature for 4 to 5 hours.

If you prefer to package whole eggs, stir in with them 2 tablespoons of sugar or corn sirup or 1 teaspoon of salt to each pint. In packaging, allow a small head space for expansion during freezing. Thaw all eggs before using in recipes. To reconstitute a whole egg from your separately packed whites and yolks, allow 1 tablespoon of yolk and 2 tablespoons of white.

ABOUT FREEZING BUTTER, CREAM AND MILK

Unsalted butter stores well, but if salt is added, 3 months should be the limit of storage. ♦ Cream, whether in butter or stored separately, should be pasteurized first, page 130. When thawed, the uses for thick cream are limited mainly to whipping or making frozen desserts. Its oil rises on contact with coffee and the texture is not good for cereals. If making ice cream or frozen desserts for the freezer, choose a recipe which calls for heating the cream first. ◗ If milk is frozen, pasteurize first, page 130, and allow 2 inches for expansion in freezing. To use ◗ thaw butter about 3 hours on a refrigerator shelf and milk or cream about 2 hours at room temperature.

ABOUT FREEZING CHEESES

Cheeses of the hard or cheddar type may be stored for 6 months. Cream cheese, but not creamed cottage cheese, may be stored for 2 weeks. Dry cottage cheese can be frozen only before the curds are washed free of whey, see page 178. It is then washed after thawing, and drained. To thaw, rest cheese for about 3 hours on a refrigerator shelf.

ABOUT FREEZING AND THAWING PRECOOKED FOODS

The precooked frozen meal, for better or for worse, is a reality. The following suggestions present increments for labor saving. Bake several pies, cakes or batches of bread at one session and store the extras; or double a casserole recipe and store half. Prepare school lunches in advance. We urge you, though, to read about the kinds of products really suitable for freezing, page 549, about quality, page 549, and to remember ◗ to cool the cooked dishes you plan to freeze through and through before you pack them. If you do not cool them sufficiently, the outside edges may freeze hard and the interior may not cool quickly enough to prevent spoilage. ◗ Also, do not try to freeze too much at one time, for overload-

ing your freezer raises the temperature to the detriment of your already-stored frozen foods. Be just as careful with packaging cooked foods, page 550, as with raw ones. Do not hold them too long before using and in reheating be sure to thaw properly or reheat slowly.

Perhaps the most important thing to consider in precooking frozen foods is not to overcook foods that are to be reheated later. ◗ Also, watch seasonings carefully. Baffling changes take place. Onion and salt tend to vanish, as do herb flavorings, even the indomitable sage. Garlic and clove grow stronger and curry acquires a musty flavor. Do not use synthetic flavorings of any kind, including substitutes for true vanilla.

Sauces have their own peculiar reactions. Avoid freezing all sauces based on egg. Sauces heavy in fat have a tendency to separate on reheating, but often recombine with stirring, while those with much milk or cheese tend to curdle. Thickened sauces may need thinning. The best thickeners so far available for frozen sauces are waxy corn and waxy rice flours. Use them in the same amounts as you would all-purpose flour or use half the waxy type and half all-purpose.

ABOUT FREEZING CANAPÉS AND SANDWICHES

Canapés and sandwiches should not be stored longer than a few weeks. Make them up quickly to keep the bread from drying out. For mass production methods, see page 50. Be sure to spread all bread well and make the fillings rather heavy in fats, so that the bread will not become saturated. Or you may prefer to prepare and freeze sandwich spreads for use later with fresh bread. As a corollary, bread for canapés can be cut into fancy shapes, frozen and then thawed slightly just before spreading. ♦ In choosing recipes for fillings, avoid mayonnaise and boiled salad dressings, hardcooked egg whites, jellies and all crisp salad materials. Garnishes like cress, parsley, tomato and cucumber cannot be frozen, so add these the last moment before serving. Ground meats, fish, butter, cream and cheddartype cheese, sieved egg yolk, peanut butter, nut meats, dried fruits and olives are all suitable for freezing.

You may freeze canapés on trays first or wrap them carefully and then freeze them. In either case, keep the different kinds separated from one another and away from the interior walls of the freezer, as this contact makes the bread soggy. Canapés and sandwiches should always be thawed in the wrappings. They take from 1 to 2 hours to thaw on a refrigerator shelf and from 15 to 45 minutes at room temperature—depending on size.

ABOUT FREEZING SOUPS

To freeze soups, prepare them as for regular use. Chill them rapidly over ice water. Store in any containers suitable for liquids, page 550, allowing head space of ½ inch in pint and 1 inch in quart containers. Concentrated meat or fish stock, the stock simmered until reduced to one-half or one-third its original quantity, see Soup Stock, page 144, are the most space-saving soups to store. Freeze them first in ice-cube trays for additions to gravy and sauces. If a soup or chowder calls for potato, it is preferable to add freshly cooked

potato just before serving. If you do freeze the potato, undercook it. Fish and meat stock thawed and combined in a ⅃ blender with fresh vegetables make delicate soups in short order. To serve frozen soups, bring them to a boil in a saucepan, unless they are thick or on a cream base, when a double boiler is necessary. For cold soups, thaw until liquid and serve while still chilled.

ABOUT FREEZING MAIN DISHES

Main dishes of the creamed type, stews, casseroles, meat pies, rissoles, croquettes and sphagetti sauces are among the most convenient of precooked foods for freezing. Fried foods almost without exception tend to rancidity, toughness and dryness when frozen. There is no time saving in freezing such starchy foods as macaroni, noodles, rice. And potatoes should not be frozen.

Prepare main dishes as usual —following your favorite recipes. But, in all instances, undercook the vegetables involved. Chill precooked foods rapidly over ice water and package closely and carefully, see page 550, before freezing.

Reheat stews and creamed dishes in a double boiler or in the oven at 350° in a heatproof dish that has been placed in hot water. Stir as little as possible. Allow 1½ times as long as normal to heat a frozen casserole at the usual temperature. Put frozen meat pies into a 350°–375° oven until brown.

Thaw croquettes or ♦ any breaded food that is to be sautéed or deep fried ♦ uncovered, at room temperature, so moisture does not form. If the food is already fried, thaw ♦ uncovered, at room temperature and bake in a 400° oven. Oven-prepared meats, fish and fowl hold much better than fried ones, which tend to rancidity.

Stewed meats keep best in heavy sauces. If they are to be used for salads, freeze them in clear concentrated stock.

Chill rapidly to room temperature. Cut in meal-sized portions; package closely and freeze. Hold no longer than 3 months. Thaw in original wrappings on a refrigerator shelf, allowing about as much time as for uncooked meats. Reheat in a double boiler or in the oven, in a pan of hot water at 350°.

ABOUT FREEZING VEGETABLE DISHES

A number of vegetables such as squash, boiled and candied sweet potatoes and creamed celery are best cooked before freezing and good to have on hand. See Chart, page 558, for these and other suggestions. All such vegetables may be heated in a double boiler or in a 400° oven without thawing.

Corn Pudding (I, 285) was once a seasonal treat but is now available in frozen form at any time. Prepare the pudding as for immediate use. Put it into aluminum cartons, heat it in a moderate oven at 325° for 10 minutes. Cool over cold water. Cover, seal when thoroughly cool and freeze at once. To serve, heat in a 250° oven for about 1 hour until brown. If you plan keeping the corn longer than 4 months, merely scrape it, heat, chill and seal it as above. Then when ready to serve it, thaw in a 250° oven until soft, add butter, cream and salt and continue to heat the pudding until brown. For an attractive way to serve corn on the cob, see (I, 284).

ABOUT FREEZING SALAD INGREDIENTS

The materials that the word salad brings to mind—fresh crisp greens, tomatoes, cucumbers and aspics—are impossible to freeze, but some of the foods traditionally served with them freeze well and will shorten salad preparation time. For instance, frozen precooked meats and fish —whole, diced or sliced and covered with concentrated stocks —are welcome ingredients for a salad. Precooked green beans, evenly sized and unsliced, may be packaged, frozen and later coated with French dressing. And almost any fruit mixture, excluding bananas and pears, may be frozen for use in fruit salads later.

ABOUT FREEZING UNBAKED PASTRY AND DOUGHS

▶ Doughs, batters and unbaked pastry on the whole respond less favorably to freezing than do the finished products. ▶ We do not recommend the freezing of cake doughs and batters. For one thing, the spices and condiments used in their preparation have a disconcerting tendency to "zero out" during the freezing process. For another, all leavens are highly variable under frozen storage, particularly those incorporated in the moister kinds of dough.

Unbaked yeast bread dough is most acceptable when frozen and stored for only a week or ten days. It is made up in the usual way, see page 239, kneaded and allowed to rise once until double in bulk, then kneaded again and shaped before packaging into loaves not more than 2 inches thick. Thin loaves, of course, will thaw with much greater rapidity than thick ones. Frozen bread dough is a notable exception to the rule that frozen foods are best when slowly thawed. Place the dough in a 250° oven for 45 minutes, then bake it as usual, cool and serve. "Serve soon" would be a timelier suggestion, because thawed and baked bread dough dries out very rapidly. Partially baked breads in the brown-and-serve category may be put into the oven without thawing.

Unbaked dough for yeast rolls should not be held frozen for more than one week. Follow the procedure for frozen dough, above. Grease all roll surfaces; freeze them 2 to 4 hours on trays. Set them away from interior walls of the freezer and package them within 24 hours after freezing, or wrap them before freezing, separating the rolls with sheets of moisture-vapor-proof material. To serve, remove the rolls from the package, cover them with a cloth, put them in a warm place to rise until doubled in bulk, 2 to 4 hours, and bake as usual.

Unbaked biscuits may also be frozen on trays or packaged before freezing. They, too, rise well and thaw quickly if rolled thin. Thaw them wrapped at room temperature for 1 hour and bake as usual. Pastries heavy in fat, like pies, tarts, filled rings and rich cookies, whether frozen baked or unbaked, come through zero storage rather well; but whenever possible, it is good practice to store all but the cookies in the same containers in which they will ultimately be baked. If you want to cut cookies before freezing, put them on trays until hard. Then package for freezing. But if you want to cut them after freezing, make a roll of the dough and wrap it in moisture-vapor-proof material in batch sizes and seal. These uncooked cookie doughs keep about 2 months. Bake cookies in a 350°–375° oven for 10 to 12 minutes.

ABOUT FREEZING BAKED PASTRY, CAKES, COOKIES AND DOUGHS

Doughs previously baked are quicker and easier to freeze than the corresponding raw material and, generally speaking, yield more satisfactory results. Careful packaging for either category is imperative. ▶ Always plan to unfreeze just the amount of baked articles needed, for they dry out rapidly after thawing.

Precooked pastries heavy in fats are the most successful "freezers" of all. Their storage limit is about 3 months. Baked yeast bread and rolls have the longest storage potential—6 months or more—but they do begin to lose flavor after eight weeks. Bake all of these varieties in the usual way and, before packaging, let them cool for 3 hours, page 239. If bread is to be used for toast, it is not necessary to thaw it. Otherwise thaw it wrapped, at room temperature, for 1 hour before serving. Should you freeze "boughten" bread, leave it in its original wrapper and slip it into a plastic bag or wrap it in foil as well.

▶ Baked cakes will keep 3 to 4 months unfrosted, but only 2 months if frosted. Filled cakes tend to sogginess and any filling with an egg base is to be avoided. Actually, it is a better policy to wait and add fillings just before serving. Spice cake should not be stored over 6 weeks, as the flavors change in the freezing process. Use a minimum of spices and omit cloves. If frosted cakes are frozen, use icings with a confectioners' sugar and butter base. Brown sugar icings and those containing egg whites or sirups tend to crystallize and freeze poorly. Boiled frosting becomes sticky on thawing. Do not wrap any iced cakes until the icing has been well firmed by chilling, unwrapped, in the freezer. Place waxed paper over iced portions before putting on the outer wrap. Seal. Protect cakes with an extra carton to avoid crushing. Thaw cakes, unwrapped, in a covered cake dish at room temperature for 2 hours before serving.

♦ When cookies are baked before freezing, they will keep about 3 months. Bake as usual, cool and package closely, separating each cookie with moisture-vapor-proof material. To avoid breakage, store in an extra carton after wrapping. Let the cookies thaw wrapped in the refrigerator. ♦ Freshen them with a quick run in a 350° oven.

ABOUT FREEZING UNBAKED PIES

Use foil pans or pans in which you are willing to store the pies so they can be frozen and then baked in the same container. You will get better results with frozen pie crust if it has ♦ a high shortening content. Pie crust may be frozen ready for rolling or be rolled and cut ready to be put in the pan, but ♦ unrolled dough must be handled while it is still chilled so it will remain tender. Freeze shells to be filled later, unwrapped in the pan, then remove and stack them in a box before wrapping or store them wrapped in disposable foil pans. In making complete pies for freezing, brush the inside of the bottom crust with shortening to keep it from becoming soggy. After filling, wipe the top crust also with shortening. Never use

water, egg or milk for these glazes.

The best pie fillings for freezing are fresh fruits or mincemeat and their storage limit is 4 to 6 months. Use pumpkin pie within 6 weeks for the best flavor. Fruits, like peaches and apricots, which darken on exposure to air, should be treated with ascorbic acid, page 553 and 554, or scalded in sirup, page 554, 2 minutes. Cool before using. The fillings for unbaked pies should have about 1½ times more cornstarch or tapioca than usual or, if possible, use waxy starches, page 155 and 158. ♦ Never freeze a cream or custard pie.

Allow at least 1 pint of filling for an 8-inch pie. ♦ Freeze the pie before wrapping if the filling is a wobbly one. Then package closely. Seal and protect against weight of other objects in the freezer until frozen hard.

Bake uncooked pies unthawed in a 450° preheated oven 15 to 20 minutes on the lowest shelf. Reduce heat to 375° until done, about 1 hour in all.

ABOUT FREEZING BAKED PIES

Use foil pans or containers you are willing to store, so the ♦ pie can be cooked, stored and reheated in the same pan.

Use a high proportion of shortening in the crust. After lining the pan with the crust, brush the inside with melted shortening to keep it from becoming soggy when filled and, after the pie is covered, wipe the top also with shortening. ♦ Never use water, egg or milk for these glazes.

♦ Unfilled baked pie shells are one of the most convenient of all frozen items for filling quickly before serving with creamed foods or fruits. Freeze them unwrapped in the pan, then remove and stack them in a box before wrapping or store them wrapped in disposable foil pans. If you are freezing any precooked fillings with starch, be sure to ▶ cook them very thoroughly and, if possible, use waxy starches, page 155 and 158.

The best pie fillings for freezing are fresh fruit and mincemeat. Store 4 to 6 months. Use pumpkin pie within 6 weeks for best flavor. Fruits like peaches or apricots which darken on exposure to air should be treated with ascorbic acid, page 553 and 554, or scalded in sirup, page 554, for 2 minutes. Cool before using. Allow about 1 pint of filling for an 8-inch pie. Freeze wobbly filling before packaging or be very careful to keep them level during packaging and freezing. Package pies closely, seal carefully and protect with carton or tin against the weight of other objects in the freezer.

Thaw a baked pie at room temperature for 8 hours if it is to be served cold. If it is to be served hot, place it unthawed in a 400° preheated oven for 30 to 50 minutes, depending on size.

▶ Never freeze a cream or custard pie. Chiffon pies can be frozen in a baked shell if, before freezing, the filling has at least ½ cup of whipping cream incorporated into it. ▶ Defrost unwrapped at room temperature for 1 to 2 hours. Garnish with whipped cream before serving, if preferred.

ABOUT FREEZING DESSERTS

The same principles apply to desserts made in zero storage cabinets as to those which are still-frozen in refrigerators. Whipped cream, whipped egg white or a gelatin base are necessary to prevent the formation of undesirable graininess or crystals. If these stabilizing ingredients are not used, the dessert mixture must be beaten several times during the freezing to break up these crystals. ▶ Such desserts should be used shortly after being frozen and not stored for any length of time.

Churned ice cream is best for freezing when the recipes call for beating the cream. A final beating and refreezing may be necessary if these creams have been stored longer than 3 weeks. For safety, do not store in the freezer longer than 3 months. Remove all frozen desserts from storage 10 to 15 minutes before serving.

Fruit and steam puddings may be made, baked, cooled and then frozen. These may be kept in the freezer for as long as one year. Thaw at room temperature for 6 hours, then steam to heat them through.

ABOUT FREEZING DRIED FRUITS, NUTS AND JELLIES

Dried fruits and nuts meats can be successfully frozen whole, chopped or ground. Wrap them in convenient quantities, taking the usual precautions to exclude air from the packages. Jellies and jams, especially raspberry and strawberry, retain that fresh taste and clear color they have just after preserving, for many months.

JELLIES, JAMS, PRESERVES
AND MARMALADES

Have you ever tried to raise money for your church or club at a food stand? It's the home-made breads and old-fashioned cooked-down jellies that get snapped up first, for neither of these is likely to be duplicated commercially. With jams, jellies and preserves, flavor is largely a matter of sugar percentage. ♦ The less sugar you use, the greater the impact of the fruit flavor. It has been proved that ♦ cane and beet sugars produce equally good jellies. Only the amount of sugar, not the type, is important here. ♦ But if honey is substituted, there is a distinct flavor change, delicious if the honey is a good one. ♦ Jellies or jams made with honey must be cooked longer than those based on sugar. If you try preparing jellies with artificial sweeteners, see warning, page 169, use only the cyclamate type, and follow the processors' directions for jelly making. The texture of jellies made with synthetic sweeteners is quite different from that of those prepared with either honey or sugar. ♦ Cooked-down jellies, the type we recommend, in which the juice is extracted by the open kettle method, usually contain about 60% fruit and 40% sugar. The open kettle method is not so apt to destroy the natural pectins in the fruit.

♦ Commercial jellies according to law must have at least 45% fruit and 55% sugar. The juice is extracted by pressure cooking, and although as much as ¼ more juice can be extracted than in the open kettle method, the natural pectins in the fruit are destroyed by the higher heats and must be replaced. ♦ These added pectins demand a greater percentage of sugar to fruit in order to make the fruit juices jell. In fact, pectin manufacturers suggest for homemade jellies a proportion as high as 60% sugar to 40% juice if commercial pectins are used. They point out, of course, the advantage of greater yield, because with the use of commercial pectins there is little loss of liquid. Only a minute or two of cooking is necessary after the sugar is added. ♦ No recipes for the use of commercial pectins are given here, for, whether this substance comes in liquid or powdered form, the processor always gives specific recommendations.

Although it is both more time-consuming and expensive ♦ we prefer to stick to the old-fashioned jelly-making traditions described below, combining, where necessary, fruits rich and low in pectin but keeping a basic relationship of about 60% fruit to 40% sugar in jellies, jams, fruit butters and conserves.

Just what is the difference between these categories? Jelly has great clarity. Two cooking processes are involved. First, the juice alone is extracted from the fruit. Only that portion, thin and clear enough to drip through a cloth is cooked with sugar until ◗ firm enough to hold its shape, but never stiff and never gummy. ◗ Jams, butters and pastes are purées of increasing density. ◗ Preserves, marmalades and conserves are bits of fruit cooked to a translucent state in a heavy sirup. These and the jams, all of which need only one cooking, take patience and ◗ careful stirring, so that they reduce without any taint of scorching. For these thicker types, some oven and double-boiler techniques are suggested in the recipes.

Let us come back to the importance of pectins in all jelly and jam making. ◗ With high-pectin fruits, such as apples, crabapples, quinces, red currants, gooseberries, plums, and cranberries, you need have no worries about jelling. If you should get a sirupy jelly with any of these fruits, either you have used too much sugar or did not cook the juice long enough after the sugar was added.

Low-pectin fruits, such as strawberries, blueberries, peaches, apricots, cherries, figs, pears, raspberries, blackberries, grapes and pineapples, or plants, such as rhubarb, have to be combined either with one of the high-pectin fruits above— or, of course, with commercial pectins.

◗ To determine if fruit juice contains a sufficient amount of pectin to jell, put 1 tablespoon of the cooled fruit juice in a glass. Add the same quantity of grain alcohol and shake gently. The effect of the alcohol is to bring the pectin together in a jelly. If a large quantity of pectin is present, it will appear in a single mass or clot when poured from the glass. This indicates that equal quantities of sugar and juice should be used. If the pectin does not slip from the

glass in a mass, less sugar will be required. If the pectin collects in 2 or 3 masses, use ⅔ or ¾ as much sugar as juice. If it collects in several small particles, you may use ½ as much sugar as juice, unless the fruit is very tart. ◗ Get your equipment ready before you begin to cook the jelly or jam. If you are making jelly, have a bag ready for straining the juice, see page 573 in About Jelly Making. ◗ Have ready, too, sterilized jelly glasses. To do this, fill glases or jars ¾ full of water and place them, well apart, in a shallow pan partly filled with water. Simmer the glasses 15 or 20 minutes. Keep hot until ready to fill. If the lids are placed lightly upon the glasses, they will be sterilized at the same time.

In jelly or jam making ◗ use a heavy enamel or stainless-steel pan in preference to aluminum, copper or iron, which may discolor the product and even prove dangerous. ◗ Again, to retain flavor, unless fruit is very acid, when sugar can be used cup for cup with fruit ◗ we recommend ¾ cup sugar to 1 cup fruit or juice. Preheat the sugar while the juice comes to a boil by spreading it in baking pans and just warming it in very low oven heat. ◗ Be sure the jars are sterile and seal tightly at once after filling to avoid spoilage. ◗ In making up jellies and jams, the best flavor results if you work in small quantities. ◗ Prepare not more than 6 cups of fruit or juice at a time, preferably only about 4 cups. ◗ If the fruit is one that discolors easily, see remedy under About Fruit Canning, page 534. ✳ Jellies and jams may be frozen to advantage, see page 569, but do not keep them in the refrigerator, as they may "weep." ◗ Keep them in a cool, dark, dry place. If stored in over 70° temperature, deterioration may be rapid.

ABOUT MAKING JAM

Jam is the easiest type to make —and the most economical—as it needs only one cooking step and utilizes the fruit pulp. Measure the fruit. In putting it into the pan, crush the lower layers to provide moisture until more is drawn from the fruit by heat; or, if necessary, add about ½ cup of water. ♦ Simmer the fruit until it is soft before adding the warmed sugar. ♦ Stir until the sugar is well dissolved. ♦ Bring to a boil and continue to stir, making sure no sticking occurs. ♦ Reduce the heat and cook until the mixture thickens. To keep the heat diffused, you may even want to use an asbestos pad. Sometimes it takes as long as half an hour for jam to thicken.

ABOUT MAKING PRESERVES AND CONSERVES

These, like jams, need only one cooking and can be made by several methods. The fruit can be placed in a crock or stainless steel pan in layers with equal parts of sugar, ending with the sugar layer on top, and allowed to rest covered for 24 hours. It is then brought slowly to a boil and is ♦ simmered until the fruit is clear. Or, the fruit can be placed with a very small quantity of water in a heavy stainless or enamel pan with sugar. Allow ¾ to ½ cup sugar per cup of fruit, depending on the sweetness of the fruit. The sugar and fruit are then brought slowly to a boil and ♦ simmered until the fruit is translucent. In either case, should the sirup not be thick enough, the fruit may be drained, put into sterile jars and kept hot while the sirup is simmered to the desired thickness. It is then poured over the fruit. Seal and store in a dark cool place.

ABOUT MAKING JUICE FOR JELLY

♦ To prepare juice for jelly by the open kettle method, wash the fruit well and drain. To accent flavor ♦ add water only if you must. Prick or crush the fruit that forms the bottom layer in the preserving kettle. Less juicy fruits, such as apples and pears, require relatively large amounts of water. Add it to the kettle until you can see it through the top layer of fruit, but ♦ never use enough so that the fruit floats. Cook over low heat until more moisture is drawn from the fruit and then increase the heat to moderate. Cook ♦ uncovered until the fruit is soft and has begun to lose its color. ♦ Have ready a jelly bag. This should be made of a material similar to flannel or of several thicknesses of cheesecloth. If well enough sewn, the bag may eventually be suspended, if not, it can be held in a strainer. Wet the bag and wring it out before you pour the jelly into it, as a dry bag can absorb a lot of the precious juice. If you want a sparklingly clear and well-flavored jelly ♦ do not squeeze the bag. Squeezing not only muddies the jelly, but may leave a bitter and unpleasant taste. After using the bag, rinse it in boiling water.

♦ Never prepare juice in a pressure cooker unless you are willing to forego prime flavor and are willing to use added commercial pectins. ♦ The higher heat destroys the natural pectin in the fruit. This method of juice extraction will, however, yield about ⅕ to ¼ more juice than the open kettle

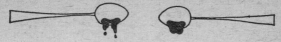

method. Wash and drain the fruit. ◗ Never fill the pressure cooker more than ⅓ full, as the vent may clog with pulp. Add the necessary amount of water, using manufacturer's directions and remembering that the less water used, the more concentrated the flavor. ◗ Adjust the cover and bring the pressure up to 15 lbs. ◗ Remove at once from the heat and let the pressure recede of its own accord. Strain the juice through a jelly bag ◗ without squeezing and proceed to make jelly as described below.

If not utilized at once ◗ the fruit juices, whether cooked by the open kettle method or by pressure, will keep for about 6 months and can be made into jelly at your convenience. ✳ You may freeze it, page 569, or you may reheat the strained juice, pour it boiling hot into sterilized jars, page 532, cover with screw tops and cook in a hot water bath, page 533, at 185° for at least 20 minutes. ◗ Seal the jars completely and keep them ◗ stored in a cool dark place.

ABOUT MAKING JELLY

Measure the strained fruit juice and put it into ◗ a large enamel or stainless steel pan. Simmer the juice about 5 minutes. ◗ Skim off any froth that forms. ◗ Measure and add the warmed sugar. ◗ Stir until the sugar is dissolved. To guard the pectins, the color and the flavor ◗ keep the heat at simmer. Because of the addition of the sugar, the boiling point of the mixture will have been raised and the jelly will seem to be boiling at this heat. Keep the heat at a simmer and stop stirring.

Cook it just long enough to bring it to the point of jelling. ◗ Begin to test the juice 10 minutes after the sugar has been added. Place a small amount of jelly in a spoon, cool it slightly and let it drop back into the pan from the side of the spoon. As the sirup thickens, 2 large drops will form along the edge of the spoon, 1 on either side. ◗ When these 2 drops come together and fall as a single drop, as shown at the right above, the "sheeting stage," 220° to 222°, has been reached. This makes a firm jelly. For a somewhat softer jelly or sirup for preserves, cook the sirup only until it falls in 2 heavy drops from the spoon, as shown at left above. The jelly is then ready to be taken from the heat. The required time for cooking will range from 8 to 30 minutes, depending upon the kind of fruit, the amount of sugar and the amount of juice in each pan.

Shortly before you are ready to use the jars, take them from the hot water, empty them and reverse them onto a cake cooler. Pour the jelly into them when they are ◗ still hot, but dry. Fill to within ¼ inch of the top. Cover the jars with paraffin, unless you use the jelly glasses described on page 574. ◗ Melt paraffin over very low heat or over hot water. If the paraffin becomes very hot, it is apt to pull away from the sides of the jelly glass. Pour it from a small pitcher, so that it covers the jelly with a very thin coating. To make it easy to remove, you may, on the second day, place a string across the top, allowing it to project somewhat beyond the edge of the glass. Cover the jelly again with a thin film of paraffin, tilting the glass to permit it to cover every bit of the surface. The second coating should not be more than ⅟₁₆ inch thick. A heavier coating is apt to pull away from the sides of the glass. ◗ If the jelly you are covering has ◗ an added pectin base, the paraffin should be applied while the jelly is still hot, because added pectin jellies are not cooked as long as the others and therefore may tend to mold more rapidly unless they are quickly covered.

◗ With cooked-down jellies and preserves, let the jelly cool to the point of setting before covering with a coating of melted paraffin ⅛ to ³⁄₁₆ inches thick. If you allow jellies to remain unsealed for any length of time, you may find that they may mold later, even under the paraffin. If you use a pint or a half-pint all-purpose canning jar with a two-piece metal screwtop lid, shown first in the illustration on page 531, you will need no paraffin. Pour jelly immediately into hot jars to the top; wipe the rims. Place a clean, hot metal lid so that the sealing compound is next to the jar. Screw the metal band on firmly. ◗ Cool on a metal rack or folded dry cloth; then ◗ store in a cool, dry place. ◗ Do not remove the metal screw band until ready to use.

CURRANT JELLY

◗ Please read About Making Jelly, page 573.
Wash:

> Red, white or black
> currants

Drain and place in a stainless-steel kettle. It is not necessary to stem currants, and they may be cooked with or without water.
If water is used, allow about ¼ as much water as fruit. If no water is used, crush the bottom layer of currants and pile the rest on top of them. Cook the currants first over low heat for about 5 minutes, then over moderate heat until soft and colorless. Drain through a jelly bag, page 572. Allow to each cup of juice:

> ¾ to 1 cup sugar

Cook only 4 cups of juice at a time.

CURRANT AND RASPBERRY JELLY

◗ Please read About Making Jelly, page 573.
Prepare currants, as for Currant Jelly, above.
Crush:

> Raspberries

Add from 1 to 1⅛ cups raspberries for every cup of currants. Cook the fruit until the currants are soft and colorless. Strain the fruit through a jelly bag, page 572. Allow to each cup of juice:

> ¾ to 1 cup sugar

Cook only 4 cups of juice at a time.

BLACK RASPBERRY AND GOOSEBERRY JELLY

◗ Please read About Making Jelly, page 573.
Wash and drain fruit. Place in a saucepan and stew until soft:

> 4 quarts black raspberries
> ¼ cup water

Place in a separate saucepan and stew until soft:

> 2 quarts gooseberries or
> about 2 cups sliced green
> apple with peel and core
> ½ cup water

Combine the fruits and strain through a jelly bag, page 572. Allow to each cup of juice:

> ¾ to 1 cup sugar

Cook only 4 cups of juice at a time.

APPLE, CRABAPPLE OR QUINCE JELLY

Good in itself, especially if made with tart fruit. Apples, crabapples or quinces are also extremely useful in combination with fruits whose pectin content is low, such as blueberries, blackberries, raspberries and grapes, whether fresh or frozen. In apples, the greatest amount of pectin lies close to the skin. Apple peelings and cores can be cooked up and strained through a jelly bag for addition to low-pectin juices.

◗ Please read About Making Jelly, page 573.

Wipe, quarter and remove stems and blossom ends from:

Tart apples, crabapples or quinces

Place in a saucepan. Add water until it can be seen through the top layer of fruit. Cook ◗ uncovered, until fruit is soft. Put the juice through a jelly bag, page 572. Allow to each cup of juice:

¾ to 1 cup sugar

Cook only 4 cups at a time.

HERB AND SCENTED JELLIES

◗ Please read About Making Jelly, page 573.

Prepare:

Apple or Crabapple Jelly, above

After testing for jelling and before removing the jelly from the heat, bruise the leaves and tie a bunch of one of the following ◗ fresh, unsprayed herbs:

Mint, basil, tarragon, thyme, lemon verbena or rose geranium

Hold the stem ends and pass the leaves through the jelly repeatedly until the desired strength is reached. Add a small amount of:

(Vegetable coloring)

PARADISE JELLY

◗ Please read About Making Jelly, page 573.

Wash and cut into quarters:

3 quarts apples

Peel and cut into quarters:

3 pints quinces

Remove seeds. Place the apples in a pan with:

1 quart cranberries

Barely cover the water. Boil until soft. Follow the same procedure with the quinces. Strain the juices of all the fruits through a jelly bag. Allow to each cup of juice:

1 cup sugar

Cook only 4 cups at a time.

GRAPE JELLY

◗ Please read About Making Jelly, page 573.

Wash:

Slightly underripe Concord or wild grapes

They are preferable to ripe or overripe grapes because of their tart flavor and higher pectin content. Remove stems. Place fruit in a kettle with a small quantity of water—about ½ cup of water to 4 cups of grapes. Add:

1 quartered apple

If you wish to spice the jelly, add at this time:

⅓ cup vinegar
1 inch stick cinnamon
½ teaspoon whole cloves without heads

Boil grapes until soft and beginning to lose color. Strain through a jelly bag. Allow to each cup of juice:

¾ to 1 cup sugar

Cook only 4 cups at a time.

WATERLESS GRAPE OR BERRY JELLY

◗ Please read About Making Jelly, page 573.

Try this recipe when slightly underripe fruits are available.

It is superlative when it works, but everything depends on the condition of the fruit.
Wash:

> Concord grapes or berries

Mash them in a large pot. Cook until soft. Strain the juice. Measure it. Bring juice to a rolling boil. Remove from heat. Add 1½ times more:

> Sugar

than you have juice. Stir it over heat until dissolved. Pour the jelly into sterilized glasses and seal. ◗ Should the liquid not jell, nothing but time is lost. Allow 1 apple and ¼ cup water to every 4 cups original fruit used. Cook the apple and water until the apple is soft. Strain off the juice, add it to the unjelled jelly, and recook as for any other jelly.

GUAVA JELLY

◗ Please read About Making Jelly, page 573.
Wash and cut in quarters:

> Slightly underripe guavas

Cover with water and boil, then ◗ simmer for about ½ hour. Put the juice through a jelly bag, page 572, but do not press, as the juice will become bitter. Allow to each cup of juice:

> 1 cup sugar

Bring again to a boil and add for each cup of juice:

> 1 teaspoon lime juice

Cook only 4 cups at a time.

PLUM JELLY

Goose plums make delicious jelly or jam. ◗ Please read About Making Jelly, page 573.
Wash:

> Small red plums

Place in a saucepan. Add water until it can be seen through the top layer. Boil plums until soft. Put the pulp through a jelly bag. Allow to each cup of juice:

> ¾ to 1 cup sugar

Boil only 4 cups at a time.

RED RED STRAWBERRY JAM

◗ Please read About Making Jam, page 572.
Wash, dry well and stem:

> 1 quart ◗ perfect strawberries

Put them in a 10-inch ◗ very heavy cooking pot, cutting into a few of the berries to release a little juice. Cover with:

> 4 cups sugar

Stir the mixture ◗ very gently with a wooden spoon ◗ over low heat until it has "juiced up." Then raise the heat to moderate and stop stirring. When the whole is a bubbling mass, set your timer for exactly 15 minutes (17, if the berries are very ripe). From this point do not disturb. You may take a wooden spoon and streak it slowly through the bottom to make sure there is no sticking. When the timer rings, tilt the pot. You should see in the liquid at the bottom a tendency to set. Slide the pot off the heat. Allow berries to cool ◗ uncovered. Sprinkle surface with:

> (Juice of ½ lemon)

When cool, stir the berries lightly and place in sterile jars.

BAR-LE-DUC PRESERVES

For use with Bar-Le-Duc, page 472.
Wash and Stem:

> Red or white currants

If you are a classicist, pierce the bottom of each berry and force the seeds through the opening. For 1 cup of currants, cook to the soft-ball stage, 238°:

> 1½ cups sugar
> ½ cup honey
> 1¼ cups water

Drop the berries into the boiling sirup. Bring the sirup up to the boiling stage again and cook for 1 minute. Pour into sterilized glasses and seal.

BLUEBERRY JAM

If blueberries are picked early in the day and are only half ripe, at the red instead of blue stage, the result is a jam far more flavorful than usual—almost like the one made with Scandinavian lingonberries.
◗ Please read About Making Jam, page 572.
Pick over, wash and measure:
    Blueberries
Put in a heavy stainless-steel pan. Crush the bottom layer. Add:
    (½ cup water)
Cook over moderate heat ◗ simmering until almost tender. Add, for each cup of blueberries:
    ¾ to 1 cup heated sugar
Stir and cook over low heat until a small amount dropped on a plate will stay in place. Place in hot sterilized jars.

SPICED PEAR JAM WITH PINEAPPLE

[About 2 Quarts]
◗ Please read About Making Jam, page 572.
As it is hard to gauge the acidity of the pear used, taste the jam as it cooks. Add sugar or lemon juice, as needed. Peel and core:
    3 lbs. firm cooking pears
Wash well:
    1 seeded orange
    1 seeded lemon
Put the fruit through a grinder, using a coarse blade. Save the juices. Add to the pulp with:
    1 cup crushed pineapple
    4 to 5 cups sugar
    3 or 4 whole cloves
    About 6 inches of stick cinnamon
    1 one-inch piece ginger
Stir the mixture while heating it. Boil for about 30 minutes. Pour into hot sterilized glasses.

RASPBERRY, BLACKBERRY, LOGANBERRY OR ELDERBERRY JAM

◗ Please read About Making Jam, page 572.
Crushing a few berries, combine:
    4 cups raspberries, blackberries, elderberries or loganberries
with:
    3 cups sugar
If the berries are tart, use a scant cup of sugar to 1 cup of fruit. Stir and cook over low heat until sugar is dissolved. ◗ Simmer and stir frequently from the bottom, to keep them from sticking. Cook until a small amount dropped on a plate will stay in place. Pack while hot in hot sterilized jars.

FIVE-FRUITS JAM COCKAIGNE

On the whole, we like food to retain its natural flavor. Our sympathy goes out to the cowboy movie actor who is reported to have said, after his first formal dinner: "I et for two hours and I didn't recognize anything I et, except an olive." However, this jam is both mysterious and delicious.
◗ Please read About Making Jam, page 572.
Hull and place in kettle, in layers:
    Strawberries
pound for pound with:
    Sugar
End with a layer of sugar on top. Allow this mixture to stand, covered, for 12 hours. Now bring strawberries quickly to the boiling point and ◗ simmer with as little stirring as possible until the juice thickens, about 15 minutes. As strawberries usually appear a little in advance of the other fruits, these preserves may be placed in sterilized and

sealed fruit jars and set aside until the other 4 fruits are available. Stem and seed:

Cherries

Stem:

Currants

Pick over:

Raspberries

Stem and head:

Gooseberries

The first 4 fruits are best used in equal proportions, but gooseberries have so much character that it is well to use a somewhat smaller amount, or their flavor will predominate. Bring the fruits separately or together to the boiling point. Add to each cup of fruit and juice:

¾ cup sugar

◗ Simmer the jam until thick, about 30 minutes. Combine with the strawberry preserves which have been reheated to the boiling point.

QUICK APRICOT PINEAPPLE JAM

Prepare Sauce Cockaigne, page 474.
Keep under refrigeration.

ROSE-HIP JAM

Wait to collect the hips until after the first frost. Do not use any which have been sprayed with poison insecticides.
◗ Please read About Making Jam, page 572.
Place in a heavy stainless-steel pan and ◗ simmer until fruit is tender. Allow:

1 cup water

to:

1 lb. rose hips

Rub through a fine sieve. Weigh the pulp. Allow, to each pound of pulp:

1 lb. heated sugar

◗ Simmer until thick.

APPLE BUTTER

[About 5 Pints]

Use Jonathan, Winesap or other well-flavored apples for good results.
Wash, remove the stems and quarter:

4 lbs. apples

Cook slowly until soft in:

2 cups water, cider or cider vinegar

Put fruit through a fine strainer.
Add to each cup of pulp:

½ cup brown sugar

Add:

1 teaspoon cinnamon

½ teaspoon cloves

¼ teaspoon allspice
(Grated lemon rind and juice)

Cook the fruit butter over low heat, stirring constantly until the sugar is dissolved. Continue to cook, stirring frequently until the mixture sheets from a spoon. You can also place a small quantity on a plate. When no rim of liquid separates around the edge of the butter, it is done. Pour into hot sterilized jars. To store, see page 573.

BAKED APPLE BUTTER

[About 5 Quarts]
A more convenient method than the above, as stirring is not necessary.
Wash and remove cores from:

12 lbs. apples: Jonathan or Winesap

Cut them into quarters. Nearly cover with water. Cook gently for about 1½ hours. Put the pulp through a fine strainer. Measure it. Allow to each cup of pulp:

½ cup sugar

Add:

Grated rind and juice of 2 lemons

3 teaspoons cinnamon

1½ teaspoons cloves

½ teaspoon allspice

Bring these ingredients to the boiling point. Chill. Stir into them:

1 cup port, claret or dry
white wine

Place about ¾ of the purée in a large heatproof crock. Keep the rest in reserve. Put the crock in a cold oven. Set oven at 300°. Permit the apple butter to bake until it thickens. As the purée shrinks, fill the crock with reserved apple butter. When the butter is thick, but still moist, put into sterile jars. To store, see page 573.

PEACH OR APRICOT BUTTER

[About 5 Pints]
Wash, peel, pit and crush:
    4 lbs. peaches or apricots
Cook very slowly in their own juice until soft. Stir. Put the fruit through a fine strainer. Add to each cupful of pulp:
    ½ to ⅔ cup sugar
Add:
    2 teaspoons cinnamon
    1 teaspoon cloves
    ½ teaspoon allspice
        (Grated lemon rind and
        juice)
Cook and store as for Apple Butter, page 578.

DAMSON PLUM BUTTER

Wash, peel and quarter:
    Damson plums
Put them in a heat-proof crock, in a pan of boiling water, over direct heat. Cover the whole container and cook until the fruit is soft enough to purée. To each cup purée allow:
    1 cup sugar
Place in a heavy pan and ◗ stir over low heat at least 45 minutes or until the fruit butter is quite stiff. To store, see page 573.

SUNSHINE STRAWBERRY PRESERVES

Like the recipe for Waterless Jelly, page 575, this method is

risky, but well worth taking the chance if it succeeds.
Arrange in a large kettle:
    2 layers of washed, hulled,
        perfect strawberries
Sprinkle the layers with an equal amount of:
    Sugar
Permit to stand for ½ hour. Heat over low heat until boiling, then ◗ simmer for 15 minutes. Pour the berries onto platters. Cover loosely with glass or plastic dome, out of the reach of insects. Permit the berries to stand in the sun for 2 or 3 days, until the juice forms a jelly. Turn the berries very gently twice daily. These preserves need not be reheated. Place in hot sterilized glasses and seal.

STRAWBERRY AND PINEAPPLE PRESERVES

◗ Please read About Making Preserves, page 572.
Combine:
    1 quart hulled berries
    4 cups sugar
    1 cup canned pineapple
        Rind and juice of ½
        lemon
◗ Simmer these ingredients for about 20 minutes. Stir frequently. When thickened, place in sterile jars.

STRAWBERRY AND RHUBARB PRESERVES

◗ Please read About Making Preserves, page 572.
Cut into small pieces:
    1 quart rhubarb
Sprinkle over it:
    8 cups sugar
Permit these ingredients to stand for 12 hours. Bring quickly to the boiling point. Wipe and hull:
    2 quarts strawberries
Add to the rhubarb. ◗ Simmer the preserves until thick, about 15 minutes.

CHERRY PRESERVES

◗ Please read About Making Preserves, page 572.
If cherries are very sweet, ¾ pound sugar will suffice.
Wash, stem, seed and place in pot, in layers:

> Cherries

pound for pound with:

> Sugar

End with a layer of sugar on top. Allow the cherries to stand covered for 8 to 10 hours. Then bring this mixture slowly to a boil, stirring frequently. ◗ Simmer until tender—about 20 minutes. If the juice seems too thin, skim off the cherries and place them in sterile jars. Simmer juice until it thickens, then pour over cherries.

PEACH OR APRICOT PRESERVES

◗ Please read About Making Preserves, page 572.
Use firm, slightly underripe, well-flavored fruit.
Peel and cut into lengthwise slices:

> Peaches or apricots

Dip the fruit briefly in boiling water to facilitate the removal of skins. Reserve and crack some of the stones. Remove and discard the kernels. Measure the fruit. Allow to each cup:

> ¾ cup sugar
> 2 tablespoons water
> 1½ teaspoons lemon juice

Stir this sirup and cook it for 5 minutes. Add the fruit. (If preferred, omit the water and just pour the sugar over the peaches and permit them to stand for 2 hours before preserving them.) ◗ Simmer until transparent. Place in glasses or jars. If the fruit is juicy and the sirup too abundant, place the peaches in jars and reduce the sirup until thick. Pour over peaches. Add to each glass 1 or more peach or apricot stones. This is optional, but they give the preserves a distinctive flavor. Add to the sirup:

> (Lemon juice—about 2 teaspoons to every cup of fruit)

DAMSON, ITALIAN PLUM OR GREENGAGE PRESERVES

◗ Please read About Making Preserves, page 572.
Wash, cut into halves and remove the seeds from:

> Damsons, Italian plums or greengages

Stir into the plums an equal amount of:

> Sugar

The sugar may be moistened with a very little water or the fruit and sugar may be permitted to stand for 12 hours before cooking. Bring the preserves to a boil, then ◗ simmer until the sirup is heavy. Add:

> (2 minced seeded unpeeled oranges)
> (½ lb. walnut meats)

QUINCE PRESERVES

◗ Please read About Making Preserves, page 572.
Scrub:

> Quinces

Slice them into eighths. Core and seed. Pare and put the peelings in a pan with just enough water to cover. To each quart of liquid, add:

> 1 sliced seeded lemon
> 1 sliced seeded orange

◗ Simmer this mixture until the peelings are soft. Strain, reserving the liquid. Now weigh and add the quince slices. Weigh same quantity:

> Warmed sugar

Bring quince slices to a boil and add the sugar. Bring to a boil again. Then ◗ simmer until the fruit is tender. Drain off the sirup and reduce it until heavy. Place the fruit in sterile jars. Cover with the reduced sirup and seal.

HARVEST PRESERVES

◗ Please read About Making Preserves, page 572.
Pare, core, seed and quarter equal parts of:

> Tart apples
> Pears
> Plums

Prepare as for Quince Preserves, above.

TOMATO PRESERVES

◗ Please read About Making Preserves, page 572.
Scald and skin:

> 1 lb. tomatoes

Yellow tomatoes may be used with especially fine results. Cover tomatoes with:

> An equal amount of sugar

Permit to stand for 12 hours. Drain the juice. Boil until the sirup falls from a spoon in heavy drops. Add the tomatoes and:

> Grated rind and juice of
> 1 lemon or 2 thinly sliced seeded lemons
> 2 oz. gingerroot or preserved ginger or
> 4-inch stick cinnamon

Cook the preserves until thick.

FIG PRESERVES

[About 1 Quart]
◗ Please read About Making Preserves, page 572.
Wash and combine:

> 1 lb. finely cut unpeeled rhubarb
> ¼ lb. chopped stemmed figs
> 3 tablespoons lemon juice

Cover with:

> 1 lb. sugar

Let stand 24 hours in a cool place. Bring to a boil in a heavy stainless-steel pan and ◗ simmer until thickened.

GOOSEBERRY PRESERVES

◗ Please read About Making Preserves, page 572.
These, being tart, are good with a meat course, soft cream cheese or a sweet cake. Wash:

> 1 quart gooseberries

Remove stems and blossom ends. Place in a heavy saucepan. Add:

> ¼ cup water

Place over quick heat. Stir. When boiling, add:

> 3 to 4 cups sugar

◗ Simmer preserves until the berries are clear and the juice thick, about 15 minutes.

KUMQUAT OR CALAMONDIN PRESERVES

[About 3 Pints]
◗ Please read About Making Preserves, page 572.
Weigh the fruit. This recipe is for 3 lbs. Separate pulp from skins. Cover skins with:

> Cold water

Cook until tender. If you do not like the bitter taste, drain several times during this process and replace with fresh water. When tender, slice fine or grind the skins. Meanwhile, cover the pulp with:

> 3 cups water

and simmer for 30 minutes. Strain the pulp and add to the juice:

> 3 cups water

Discard the pulp. Allow to each cup juice:

> ¾ cup heated sugar

Heat the juice and ◗ stir in the sugar until dissolved. Add the cut-up skins and cook until sirup jells.

ORANGE MARMALADE

[About 8 Jelly Glasses]
Fully ripe oranges may still have a greenish peel, especially in the spring, but this has nothing

to do with their minimum sugar content, which the government checks before oranges are shipped for sale. Scrub well, cut into quarters and remove the seeds from:

> 2 large Valencia oranges
> 2 large or 3 small lemons

Soak the fruit for 24 hours in:

> 11 cups water

Remove fruit. Cut into very small shreds. Return to the water in which it was soaked. Boil for 1 hour. Add:

> 8 cups sugar

Boil the marmalade until the juice forms a jelly when tested, see page 573. To store, see page 574.

ORANGE, LEMON AND GRAPEFRUIT MARMALADE

[About 18 Jelly Glasses]

Scrub, cut in halves, remove the seeds and slice into very small pieces:

> 1 grapefruit
> 3 oranges
> 3 lemons

Measure the fruit and juice and add 3 times the amount of water. Soak for 12 hours. ♦ Simmer for about 20 minutes. Let stand again for 12 hours. For every cup of fruit and juice, add:

> ¾ cup sugar

Cook these ingredients in small quantities, about 4 to 6 cups at a time, until they form a jelly when tested, see page 573. To store, see page 574.

LIME MARMALADE

[About 3 Jelly Glasses]

Cut the thin outer rind from:

> 6 small limes or 2 Persian limes
> 3 lemons

Prepare and store as for the above, Orange, Lemon and Grapefruit Marmalade.

TAMARIND MARMALADE

Wash:

> 1 quart tamarinds

Cover with:

> 1½ cups water

♦ Simmer until soft. Put through sieve to remove fibers and seeds. Heat the pulp and allow for each cup:

> 1 cup heated sugar

♦ Simmer, stirring constantly until the mixture thickens. To store, see page 574.

BLUE PLUM CONSERVE

[About 20 Jelly Glasses]

Peel and chop:

> The thin yellow rind of 2 oranges and 1 lemon

Add:

> The juice and seeded, chopped pulp of 3 oranges and 1 lemon
> 1¼ lbs. ground seeded raisins
> 9 cups sugar

Seed and add:

> 5 lb. blue plums
> 4 pared, cubed peaches

Cook the conserve slowly until fairly thick. Stir frequently. Add:

> ½ lb. broken walnut meats

♦ Simmer the conserve 10 minutes longer. To store, see page 574.

BLACK CHERRY CONSERVE

[About 8 Jelly Glasses]

Cut into very thin slices:

> 2 seeded oranges

Barely cover with water. Cook until very tender. Stem, seed and add:

> 1 quart black cherries

Add:

> 6 tablespoons lemon juice
> 3½ cups sugar
> ¾ teaspoon cinnamon

♦ Simmer the conserve until thick and clear. To store, see page 574.

SPICED RHUBARB CONSERVE

[About 8 Jelly Glasses]
Cut into very thin slices:
  1 seeded orange
  1 seeded lemon
Tie in a small bag:
  1 oz. gingerroot
  ¼ lb. cinnamon candy: redhots
  1 blade mace
  2 whole cloves
Add the spices to the fruit with:
  ½ cup water
  ¼ cup vinegar
♦Simmer these ingredients until the fruit is tender. Add and cook, until the conserve is thick:
  1½ cups strawberry rhubarb
  1½ cups strawberry rhubarb
  3 cups sugar
  (¼ cup white raisins)
To store, see page 574.

TUTTI FRUTTI COCKAIGNE OR BRANDIED FRUIT

A sort of liquid hope-chest, the contents of which may be served with a meat course or over puddings and ice cream. Be sure that during its preparation ♦ your container is big enough to hold all the ingredients you plan putting into it and, just as important, that ♦ you can store it in a consistently cool place, not above 45°, to prevent runaway fermentation. Place in a sterile stoneware crock with a closely fitting lid:
  1 quart brandy
Add, as they come into season, five of the following varieties of fruit—perfect fruit only:
  1 quart strawberries
  1 quart seeded cherries
  1 quart raspberries
  1 quart currents
  1 quart gooseberries
  1 quart peeled sliced apricots
  1 quart peeled sliced peaches
  1 quart peeled sliced pineapple
Avoid apples, as too hard; bananas and pears, as too mushy; blackberries, as too seedy; and seeded grapes, unless skinned, as their skins become tough. With each addition of fruit, add the same amount of:
  sugar
Stir the tuiti frutti every day until the last of the fruit has been added, securing the lid well after each time. The mixture will keep indefinitely.

PICKLES AND RELISHES

Peter Piper proved a pretty pampered pepper picker. Less priveleged persons—such as you and we—are expected to pick produce unpickled and process it promptly ourselves. Pickling can be accomplished in several ways, some of them lengthy, but none of them difficult. Granted that a considerable number of vitamins and minerals leach away in liquid residue during the pickling process, it remains a piquant and important method of food preservation.

ABOUT PICKLING EQUIPMENT

◗ Because of the acid factor involved in pickle making, be sure your equipment for brining is stoneware, pottery or glass, and that your pickling kettles are stainless steel or enamel. For stirring use long-handled spoons and, for transferring the pickles, a stainless, enamel-covered or slotted wooden spoon or glass cup. Pack pickles in perfect sterile glass jars with glass lids, page 531. All equipment should be absolutely clean and grease-free.

ABOUT PICKLING INGREDIENTS

For best results it is ◗ imperative that vegetables and fruits for pickling are in prime condition and were harvested no longer than 24 hours in advance. If cucumbers have been held longer, they tend to become hollow during processing.

Black-spined varieties are the usual choice for cucumber pickles. They may be slightly underripe but must be ◗ unblemished. ◗ Scrub them well to remove any dirt which might spark bacterial activity later, and trim to retain ⅛ to ¼ inch of stem.

If using garlic as a seasoning, blanch it 2 minutes before adding it to other ingredients, or remove it before sealing. ◗ Water used should be soft, page 147. If you are in a hard water area, try to get distilled water, or trap some rainwater. If the water contains iron or sulphur compounds, the pickles will become dark.

◗ Use only pickling or dairy salt, free from additives which might deter processing, see About Salt, page 195.

◗ Vinegar should test 5% to 6% acetic acid. Distilled white vinegar gives the lightest color. Cider-based malt and herb-flavored vinegars, although they yield a richer flavor, will darken pickles. You may want to make up and have ready to use one of the spice vinegars, page 151. Homemade wine vinegars of uncertain strength should not be used, as the vinegar will "mother," page 150.

Since spices vary so greatly in strength, page 198, the amounts given are only approximate. Taste before bottling and correct the seasoning. ◗ Spices should be both fresh and whole. Ground spices darken the pickle, old spices impart a dusty flavor. Tie spices in a cloth bag for easy removal. If left in, they may cloud the liquid. Distillates, like the oils of cinnamon and of clove, are available at drug stores. They give a clearer pickle than steeped condiments, but the flavor is not so lasting.

♦ To make pickles crisp, use grape or cherry leaves during brining. Or, in short-brine pickling, after the brining period, soak the pickles for 2 hours in enough of the following lime solution to cover.

Allow:

>1 tablespoon calcium oxide

to:

>1 quart soft water, page 147

Stir well, and after stirring allow the solution to settle. Use only the clear portion of the liquid to cover the pickles. After the 2 hour soaking, drain and cover with the hot pickling liquid as directed. Alum is not recommended for crisping, as just a trifle too much may make the pickles bitter.

ABOUT SHORT-BRINE PICKLING

Most homemade pickles are of the less exacting short-brined type. They are soaked in a salt solution only 24 hours or so. This brining period is sufficiently long to draw out moisture, ♦ but not long enough to induce the fermentation needed for adequate keeping. An essential further step, after draining off the brine, is to pour over the produce a hot vinegar solution which penetrates the softened vegetable tissue and so preserves it.

Although in the short-brine process, the hot vinegar also tends to firm the produce, it is advisable, for greater crispness, to add to the jar a few fresh grape or cherry leaves, or to use the lime water process described above. Firmness in pickled produce contributes both to its keeping and its eating qualities.

In the short-brine process, unless lime water is used, the produce is packed as soon as the brine is drained off, and just before the addition of the vinegar. Pack closely in sterile jars —the type which have glass lids. Heat the vinegar solution to the boiling point, and fill the jars full to the top. Wipe the rims, adjust and seal the lids and process in a boiling water bath for 15 minutes, page 533. By this time the interior of the jars should have reached 180°, enough to inhibit destructive enzymes. Sometimes, even if this final precautionary treatment has been used, further fermentation takes place which shows up in the form of small bubbles or leakage from the container.

Keep an eye on your pickles after you have stored them away, and if you detect evidences of fermentation make up a fresh boiling pickling solution. Wipe the jars clean, refill them to overflowing again with boiling vinegar solution, and reprocess for 15 minutes in a boiling water bath. The flavor of almost all pickled produce is improved if it is stored for 6 weeks before using.

YELLOW CUCUMBER PICKLES

[About 14 Quarts]

♦ Please read About Pickling Equipment and Ingredients, page 584.

These large, luscious, firm, clear slices are served very cold with meat. Pare, cut into strips of about 1½ x 2½ x ¾ inches, and seed:

>1 bushel large yellow cucumbers

Soak the strips for 12 hours in a:

10% Brine, page 196

Drain well. Sterilize 14 one quart jars, page 532. Place in each one:

> A slice of peeled horse-radish: 1½ by ⅓ by ⅓ inches
> A ½-inch piece long hot red pepper
> 4 sprigs dill blossom with seeds
> 1 tablespoon white mustard seed
> 2 white peppercorns

Combine:

> 3 cups water
> 1 cup sugar
> 1½ gallons white distilled vinegar

Cook about 3 cupfuls at a time, enough to cover the bottom of a large saucepan to the depth of about ½ inch. Keep several pans going to hasten the process. Immerse in the ◗ boiling vinegar sufficient cucumber strips to cover the bottom of the pan. Let them come to the boiling point. Remove them at once to the jars. Do not cook the strips longer, as it will soften them. When a jar is filled with cucumber strips cover them with boiling vinegar. Seal the jars. Process in a boiling bath, page 533, for 15 minutes. Permit the pickles to ripen for at least 6 weeks before serving.

SWEET-SOUR YELLOW CUCUMBER PICKLES OR SENEGURKEN

[About 9 Quarts]

◗ Please read About Pickling Equipment and Ingredients, page 584.

Peel, cut into strips about 1½ x 2½ x ¾ inches, and seed:

> 12 large yellow cucumbers

Soak them for 12 hours in:

10% Brine, page 533

Drain. Have ready 8 or 10 steri-lized quart jars, page 532. Prepare the following mixture:

> 1 gallon pickling vinegar, page 150
> 8 cups sugar
> ¼ cup mustard seed

Place in a cloth bag and add:

> ¾ cup whole mixed spices

◗ Boil about 5 cupfuls of the mixture at a time, enough to cover the bottom of a large stainless steel or enamel pan to a depth of about ½ inch. Place bag of spices in pan. Immerse in the boiling vinegar sufficient strips to cover the pan bottom. Bring vinegar to boiling point. Remove strips at once. Place them in jars. Fill jars with boiling vinegar mixture. Seal and process for 15 minutes in a boiling water bath, page 533.

SWEET-SOUR SPICED CUCUMBER PICKLES

[About 12 Quarts]

◗ Please read About Pickling Equipment and Ingredients, page 584.

These are wonderfully good. Scrub:

> 20 lbs. very small cucumbers

Soak for 24 hours in brine made of:

> 1 cup coarse salt
> 3 quarts water: 12 cups

Remove from brine and add boiling water to cover. Drain quickly in a colander and pack closely while hot in sterilized jars, page 532. Cover at once with the following vinegar mixture, ◗ just at boiling point:

> 1 gallon cider vinegar
> 11 cups sugar
> 2 oz. whole mixed spices
> 1 oz. stick cinnamon
> 1 teaspoon cloves
> 4 tablespoons lime water

Seal jars at once. Process for 15 minutes in boiling water bath, page 533.

BREAD AND BUTTER PICKLES

[About 6 Quarts]

◗ Please read About Pickling Equipment and Ingredients, page 584.

Wash well:

    1 gallon medium-sized
        cucumbers: 4 quarts

Parblanch for 2 minutes, see (⁖, 88), and add:

    6 to 12 large onions or
        3 cups or more small
        white ones
    2 green or red peppers with
        seeds and membrane
        removed

Proportions for this recipe may vary, as onion fanciers use the larger amount, and even more, of their beloved vegetable. Cut the unpared cucumbers and the peeled onions into the thinnest slices possible. Remove seeds and fibrous membranes from peppers. Shred or chop them. Place vegetables in a bowl. Pour over them:

    ½ cup coarse salt

Place in refrigerator for 12 hours with weighted lid over them. Drain vegetables. Rinse in cold water. Drain again thoroughly. A cloth bag is frequently used to let all the moisture drip from them. Prepare the following sirup:

    5 cups mild cider vinegar
    5 cups white or brown
        sugar
    1½ teaspoons turmeric or
        allspice
    2 tablespoons mustard
        seed
    1½ teaspoons celery seed
    ½ teaspoon ground cloves
        or 1 inch stick cinnamon

Bring these ingredients ◗ just to the boiling point. Add vegetables gradually with very little stirring. Heat to the scalding point but do not let them boil. Place pickles in hot sterile jars. Seal jars and process in boiling water bath, page 533, for 15 minutes.

SACCHARIN PICKLES

[4 Quarts]

◗ Please read About Pickling Equipment and Ingredients, page 781.

Scrub, dry and pack in sterile jars:

    16 cups small cucumbers

Mix but ◗ do not heat:

    1 teaspoon saccharin
    3 tablespoons mixed spices
    1 tablespoon powdered
        alum
    1 gallon cider vinegar
    2 tablepoons dry mustard
    ¾ cup salt

Pour this mixture over pickles and seal and store in a dark place.

MUSTARD PICKLE OR CHOW CHOW

[About 6 Quarts]

◗ Please read About Pickling Equipment and Ingredients, page 584.

This formula meets with such enthusiastic approval that we are often tempted to abandon all other mixed pickle recipes. Slice, unpeeled if tender:

    1 quart or more green
        cucumbers

Cover for 12 hours with:

    10% Brine, page 196

Drain well. Slice to make 4 quarts, including cucumbers, but keep all the vegetables separate:

    Green vegetables: green
        tomatoes, snap or wax
        beans, etc.

If the vegetables are not very young, parblanch them (I, 88). Pour over the vegetables to cover:

    Boiling salted water: I
        teaspoon salt to 1 quart
        water

and bring to the boiling point.

Drain well. Peel and slice:
   2 dozen small onions
Break into florets:
   1 large cauliflower
Slice:
   2 dozen or more small
      pickled gherkins
Keep them separate. Pour boiling salted water over them. Bring to the boiling point. Drain well. Combine all vegetables. Prepare the following mustard sauce in an enamel pan.
Combine and stir until smooth:
   1½ cups flour
   6 tablespoons dry mustard
   1½ tablespoons turmeric
   2 cups mild cider vinegar
Bring ▶ just to the boiling point:
   2 quarts malt cider vinegar
   2½ cups sugar
   3 tablespoons celery seed
Slowly add the flour mixture, stirring constantly. When the sauce is smooth and boiling combine it with the drain vegetables. Add if needed:
   Salt
Place pickles in sterile jars and seal. Process in boiling water bath, page 533, for 15 minutes.

CURRY SAUCE PICKLE

[About 8 Quarts]
▶ Please read About Pickling Equipment and Ingredients, page 584.
Peel and chop fine:
   12 large green cucumbers
   6 large onions
   2 sweet red peppers
Sprinkle these ingredients with:
   ¼ cup coarse salt
Let stand refrigerated for 3 hours. Drain, rinse, and drain again. Peel and stew until soft:
   12 large tomatoes
Combine vegetables and tomatoes. Tie in a bag, add to the above, and ▶ simmer for 30 minutes:
   4 teaspoons curry powder
   2 teaspoons celery seed
   2 tablespoons brown sugar

   2 cups cider vinegar
Remove bag and pack pickles into jars, seal and process for 15 minutes in boiling water bath, page 533.

PICCALILLI

[Approximately 5 Quarts]
▶ Please read About Pickling Equipment and Ingredients, page 584.
Remove core and seeds and cut into very thin slices or dice:
   4 quarts small green
      cucumbers
Seed, remove membrane and slice:
   4 medium-sized green
      peppers
Skin, parblanch for 2 minutes (I, 88), and slice:
   4 medium-sized onions
Place these ingredients for 12 hours in:
   10% Brine, page 19C
Drain well. Bring ▶ just to the boiling point:
   1 quart cider vinegar
   4½ cups sugar
Place in a bag and add:
   2½ tablespoons whole mixed
      spices
   ½ tablespoon celery seed
   ½ tablespoon mustard seed
Add the drained vegetables. Bring to the boiling point. Remove spices. Place pickles in sterile jars, seal and process for 15 minutes in boiling water bath, page 533.

GREEN TOMATO PICKLE OR RELISH

[About 6 Quarts]
▶ Please read About Pickling Equipment and Ingredients, page 584.
Wash and cut into thin slices:
   1 peck green tomatoes
Peel, cut into thin slices and add:
   12 large onions
Sprinkle with:

1 cup coarse salt
Let mixture stand for 12 hours.
Wash in clear water and drain.
Heat to the boiling point:

3 quarts cider vinegar

Seed, remove membranes and add:

12 green peppers, sliced thin
6 sweet diced red peppers

Add:

12 minced cloves garlic
4 lbs. brown sugar

Add the tomatoes and onions.
Tie in a cloth bag and add:

2 tablespoons dry mustard
2 tablespoons whole cloves
2 sticks cinnamon
2 tablespoons powdered
  ginger
1 tablespoon salt
1 tablespoon celery seed

◗ Simmer until tomatoes are transparent, about 1 hour. Stir frequently. Place pickles in sterile jars and seal. A fan writes that he puts the finished product in his ⅄ blender for a second or two to make his favorite relish.

TART CORN RELISH

[About 6 Pints]
◗ Please read About Pickling Equipment and Ingredients, page 584.
Cut the kernels from:

18 ears corn

Or, if you should want to make this in winter, use canned or frozen kernel corn. Put through a food grinder:

1 head green cabbage
8 white onions
6 green peppers, seeds
  and membranes removed
6 small hot red peppers

Combine these ingredients with the corn and:

2 teaspoons celery seed
2 teaspoons mustard seed
2 quart vinegar
¼ cup salt
2 cups sugar
(1 cup flour)

(⅓ cup minced pimiento)
Bring ◗ just to the boiling point and simmer the relish for 35 minutes. Place in sterile jars, seal, and process for 15 minutes in boiling water bath, page 533.

PICKLED ONIONS

◗ Please read About Pickling Equipment and Ingredients, page 584.
Cover with water:

Small white onions

Add:

1 tablespoon coarse salt
to every quart water

Let the onions soak for 2 hours. Remove outer skins. Soak onions for 48 hours in:

10% Brine to cover, page 196

Drain well. Bring ◗ just to the boiling point:

White vinegar

To each gallon vinegar add:

1 cup sugar

Add onions and ◗ simmer for 3 minutes. Place at once in sterile jars. Cover with the vinegar. Add to each quart jar:

½ inch long red hot pepper
  pod
⅛ bay leaf
(3 cloves without heads)

Seal and process for 30 minutes in boiling water bath, page 533.

CHILI SAUCE

[About 4 Quarts]
◗ Please read About Pickling Equipment and Ingredients, page 584.
Wash, peel and quarter:

1 peck tomatoes: 8 quarts

Put through a food grinder:

6 green peppers with
  membranes and seeds
  removed
1 tablespoon dried hot
  pepper pods
6 large skinned white
  onions

Add the tomatoes and:

2 cups brown sugar

3 cups cider vinegar
3 tablespoons coarse salt
1 tablespoon black pepper
1 tablespoon allspice
1 teaspoon ground cloves
1 teaspoon each ginger,
    cinnamon, nutmeg and
    celery seed
(2 tablespoons dry mustard)

◗ Simmer these ingredients slowly until thick, about 3 hours. Stir frequently to prevent scorching. Add salt if needed. Put sauce in ◗ small sterile jars. Seal tightly and store in cool, dark place.

TOMATO CATSUP

[About 5 Quarts]
This condiment originated in Malaya, and its name derives from the native word for "taste." No other as familiar an American food seems to have so many variations in spelling.
◗ Please read About Pickling Equipment and Ingredients, page 584.
Wash and cut into pieces:
    1 peck tomatoes: 8 quarts
Add:
    8 medium-sized sliced
      onions
    2 long red peppers without
      seeds or membranes
◗ Simmer these ingredients until soft. Rub through a food mill. Add:
    ¾ cup brown sugar
Tie in a bag and add:
    1 tablespoon each whole
      allspice, cloves, mace,
      celery seed and
      peppercorns
    2 inches stick cinnamon
    ½ teaspoon dry mustard
    ½ clove garlic
    1½ bay leaves
The spices may be varied. Boil these ingredients quickly, stirring often. ◗ Continue to stir until the quantity is reduced to ½. Remove the spice bag. Add:
    2 cups cider vinegar

    (Cayenne and coarse
      salt)
◗ Simmer the catsup for 10 minutes longer. Pour at once into sterile bottles. Cork bottles and seal with sealing wax.

PICKLED HORSERADISH

Wash well in hot water:
    Horseradish roots
Scrape off the skin. Have ready in a glass or stainless steel bowl a combination of
    2 cups vinegar
    1 teaspoon salt
Grate or mince the scraped roots and pack into sterile jars. Cover well with the vinegar mixture. Seal and store in a cool place.

PICKLED NASTURTIUM PODS

◗ Please read About Pickling Equipment and Ingredients, page 584.
Use these as a variation for capers.
After the blossoms fall, pick off the miniature:
    Nasturtium seed pods
For 3 days, changing daily, soak them covered with:
    10% Brine, page 196
Drain and drop them into boiling:
    Pickling vinegar, page
      150
Store covered in sterile jars in a cool place.

CHILIS PRESERVED IN SHERRY

Make up this combination and use either the chilis or the sherry for flavoring. The mixture will keep for years if sherry or peppers are replenished as needed.
Wash well:
    Long thin red chili
      peppers
Pack tightly into sterile jars.

Cover with:

> Dry sherry

Store covered in a cool dark place.

PICKLED WATERMELON RIND

[About 5 Quarts]

Good used in fruit cakes, if drained. ◖ Please read About Pickling Equipment and Ingredients, page 584.
Cut before peeling and remove the green skin and pink flesh from:

> Rind of 1 large water-
> melon: about 5 quarts

Dice the rind in 1 inch cubes. Parblanch it (I, 88), until it can be pierced with a fork, ◖ but do not overcook. Drain. Make and bring ◖ just to a boil a sirup of:

> 7 cups sugar
> 2 cups vinegar
> ¼ teaspoon oil of cloves
> ½ teaspoon oil of cinnamon

When just boiling, pour it over the rind, ◖ making sure the rind is covered. Let stand overnight. Remove rind. Reboil sirup and pour over rind. Let stand overnight as before. On the third morning pack the rind in sterile jars. Boil sirup again and pour over rind to overflowing. Seal and store in a cool place. The flavor of each pickle may be varied by placing in each jar:

> (A star anise)
> (1 to 2 teaspoons
> chopped preserved ginger
> or Candied Lemon Peel,
> page 524)

PICKLED DUTCH CHERRIES

◖ Please read About Pickling Equipment and Ingredients, page 584. During processing this method needs an even temperature under 80°.
Stem, seed and put in a heavy crock:

> Sour cherries

Cover with:

> Distilled white vinegar

Let stand 24 hours. Drain. Measure cherries and have ready an equal amount of:

> Sugar

Arrange in the crock alternate layers of cherries and sugar. Let stand 1 week, covered and weighted. ◖ Stir well daily. Ladle into sterile jars and process in boiling water bath, page 748, for 15 minutes. Store well covered in a cool dark place.

PEACH OR MANGO CHUTNEY

[6 or 7 Quarts]

◖ Please read About Pickling Equipment and Ingredients, page 584.
Rub the fuzz from, wash, pit, and dice:

> 30 firm peaches

or use a combination of:

> 15 peeled tropical mangoes
> and
> 8 medium papayas

Mix with:

> 3 tablespoons chopped
> preserved ginger
> ¾ cup chopped citron
> ¼ cup chopped candied
> lemon peel or ½ cup
> chopped preserved
> kumquats

Tie in a bag the following whole spices:

> 2 cinnamon sticks
> 30 whole cloves
> ¾ teaspoon coriander seeds

Make a sirup of:

> 6 cups sugar
> 4 cups cider vinegar

When the sirup ◖ just boils add the chopped fresh and candied fruits and the spice bag. Simmer for 5 minutes. Remove spice bag. Put mixture into sterile jars, seal and process for 15 minutes in boiling water bath, page 533.

INDIAN RELISH

[About 4 Quarts]
▶ Please read About Pickling
Equipment and Ingredients,
page 584. Put through a food
chopper or chop until very fine:
    12 green tomatoes
    12 peeled cored tart apples
    3 peeled onions
Boil:
    5 cups vinegar
    5 cups sugar
    1 teaspoon red pepper
    3 teaspoons ginger
    1 teaspoon turmeric
    1 teaspoon salt
Add the chopped ingredients. ▶
Simmer for ½ hour. Pack the
relish in sterile jars. Seal and
process for 15 minutes in boiling water bath, page 533.

APPLE OR GREEN
TOMATO CHUTNEY

I. [About 1½ Quarts]
▶ Please read About Pickling
Equipment and Ingredients,
page 584.
▶ Simmer until the fruit is ten-
der:
    1 seeded chopped lemon
    1 skinned chopped clove
      garlic
    5 cups firm peeled chopped
      apples or green tomatoes
    2¼ cups brown sugar
    1½ cups seeded raisins
    3 oz. chopped crystallized
      ginger, or ¾ cup fresh
      ginger root
    1½ teaspoon salt
    ¼ teaspoon cayenne
    2 cups cider vinegar
    (2 chopped red peppers,
      seeds and membranes
      removed)
Put the chutney in sterile jars
and seal them.

II. [About 1½ Quarts]
Similar to the preceding recipe
—but with onions and tomatoes
added.

Combine, and ▶ simmer slowly
for 3 hours:
    2 cups chopped seeded
      raisins
    2 cups chopped slightly
      underripe green apples
    1 cup minced onions
    ¼ cup coarse salt
    6 medium-sized ripe,
      skinned, quartered
      tomatoes
    3½ cups brown sugar
    1 pint cider vinegar
    4 oz. white mustard seed
    2 oz. preserved ginger
    3 chili peppers
Place in sterile jars, seal and
store in a cool dark place.

SPICED PEARS

[About 3 Pints]
▶ Please read About Pickling
Equipment and Ingredients,
page 584.
If you are using Bartlett or
similar soft pears, choose rather
underripe fruit, and prepare as
for Brandied Peaches, below. If
you are using Kiefer, Seckel or
other hard pears, prepare as follows:
Wash, peel and core:
    3 lbs. pears
Cook them ▶ covered until they
begin to soften in:
    1½ cups boiling water
Tie in a cloth bag:
    6 cinnamon sticks, 3 inches
      long
    2 tablespoons whole cloves
    2 teaspoons whole ginger
and ▶ simmer for 5 minutes
with:
    2 cups sugar
    1 cup pickling vinegar,
      page 150
Add the partially tenderized
pears and the liquid in which
they were cooking. Simmer with
vinegar sirup for 3 minutes. Remove and discard spice bag.
Pack fruit into sterile jars and
cover with the sirup. Seal jars
and process in boiling water

bath for 15 minutes, page 533.
Store in a cool dark place.

BRANDIED PEACHES

Select ripe, firm:
>   Peaches
Weigh them. Rub away fuzz
with a coarse towel.
Make a thick sirup of equal
parts of:
>   Sugar and water—allow
>   1 cup sugar and 1 cup
>   water for every lb. of
>   fruit
♦ Simmer the peaches in the
sirup for 5 minutes. Drain and
place in sterile jars, page 531.
Pour over each jar:
>   2 to 4 tablespoons brandy
Pour the sirup over the fruit,
filling the jars. Seal and process
in boiling water bath for 15
minutes, page 533. Store in a
cool dark place 3 months before
using.
For other liqueur-flavored fruits,
see page 90.

ABOUT LONG-BRINE AND
SOUR PICKLING

If produce is soaked for a long
enough period at proper temperatures, a mere brine will
suffice to preserve it. The salt
solution draws from the vegetables soaked in it both moisture
and certain natural sugars; and
these combine to form an acid
bath which "cures" the produce,
making it friendly to beneficial
ferments and strong enough to
resist the organisms that cause
spoilage in food. Pickles sub-
jected simply to the long-brine
process and held at 86° from 2
to 6 weeks, turn, after appropriate seasoning, into "dill" types:
"kosher" and non-kosher, see
below. They may be desalted
and further processed in a vinegar solution at 126° for 12 hours
to make sour pickles and then
in a sugar solution to become
sweet-sours.

To learn the details for these
long and exacting processes,
read "Making Fermented Pickles," in the U.S.D.A. Farmer's
Bulletin, 1438.

DILL OR KOSHER DILL
PICKLES

[About 7 Pints]
This dill pickle-making procedure differs from that for
long-brined pickles. The brine
is weaker and the curing more
rapid; but the pickles do not
keep as well, especially if home
processed. We suggest using a
heated brine. Garlic, like all
members of the onion family, is
very susceptible to bacterial
activity, so be sure to remove
the garlic cloves before sealing
the jars. Wash thoroughly and
cut in half lengthwise:
>   4 lbs. cucumbers
Combine and heat to the boiling point:
>   3 cups white vinegar
>   3 cups water
>   1/3 cup salt
If you want Kosher Dills, add:
>   12 peeled sliced garlic cloves
When the boiling point is
reached ♦ remove the garlic
cloves. Pack the cucumbers into
hot sterile jars. Add to each
jar:
>   2 tablespoons dill seeds
>   3 peppercorns
Fill the jars to within 1/2 inch of
the top with the hot pickling
liquid. Immediately adjust lids.
Be sure to use a glass-disked
top, see page 532. Seal and process in boiling water bath for
10 minutes, see page 533.

ABOUT BRINING
VEGETABLES

If sufficient salt is used to brine
vegetables, no fermentation occurs, and no further processing
is necessary. But in brining vegetables the United States Government recommends, without

exception, a final processing for 30 minutes in a boiling water bath, page 533.

Before tasting or eating non-acid brined vegetables, follow the same precautions as for non-acid canned vegetables. ◗ Boil uncovered for 15 minutes. Stir frequently during this period.

SAUERKRAUT

◗ Please read About Pickling Equipment and Ingredients, page 584.
A 2 gallon crock holds about 15 pounds of kraut. Choose sound, mature heads of:
Cabbage
Use:
1 lb. salt for 40 lbs.
cabbage or 2 teaspoons
salt for 1 lb. cabbage
Remove outside leaves, quarter heads, and cut out cores. Slice the cabbage fine into 1/16 inch shreds and mix with salt. Pack firmly in stone crocks to within 2 inches of top. Cover with clean cloth and a plate, or any board except pine. Place a weight on the plate—heavy enough to make the brine come up to the cover and wet the cloth. When fermentation begins remove the scum daily and place a clean cloth over the cabbage. Wash the board daily, too. The best quality kraut is made at a temperature below 60°, re-

quiring at least a month of fermentation. It may be cured in less time at higher temperatures, but the kraut will not be as good. If sauerkraut turns tan, too much juice has been lost in the fermenting process. When fermentation has ceased, store the kraut in a cool place after sealing by either of the following methods:
Simply pour a layer of hot paraffin over the surface of the crock; or, for greater effectiveness, ◗ heat kraut to simmering temperature, about 180°; pack firmly in hot jars; add sufficient kraut juice or a weak brine, 2 tablespoonfuls salt for 1 quart water, to cover, leaving 1/2 inch head space; and process in boiling water bath, page 533, 25 minutes for pints, 30 minutes for quarts. ◗ Cook the sauerkraut, uncovered, 15 minutes before serving, page 530.

ABOUT DRY-SALTING VEGETABLES

Pack in a crock:
Mushrooms, beans, herbs
or other vegetables
in very thin layers well separated between 1/2 inch layers of:
Rock salt
Cover the crock tightly and store in a cool dark place. ◗ Cook the vegetables uncovered 15 minutes before serving.

INDEX

"Knowledge," said Dr. Johnson, 'is of two kinds. We know a subject as our own, or we know where we can find information on it." Below we put into your hands the second kind of knowledge—a kitchen-door key which will help to open up the first.

If you want information on a certain food you will find that the initial listing is often an "About": giving characteristics, peculiarities of handling, tests for doneness, storage needs and serving quantities. The titles which follow usually indicate how that particular food may be cooked: Sweetbreads, braised, or Fish, broiled.

In using the Index look for a noun rather than an adjective: Torte, almond, not Almond Torte; unless the modifying term is a foreign one, in which case it will be listed and lead you to an explanation. Foreign terms are frequently translated in an alternate title, thus: Pickled Fish or Escabèche, revealing a process; or, as in Senegalese or Chicken Curry Soup, showing the ingredients mainly responsible for the term. Or the recipe itself will clear your doubts—for "à la mode" used with a savory food like beef will describe a stew, whereas with a sweet one, like pie or cake, it will indicate the expected scoop of ice cream. Since cooking terms, both foreign and domestic, are dealt with at the point of use, as described above, we have dispensed with a separate glossary.

Remember, too, that the book as a whole divides into three sections: The Foods We Eat, The Foods We Heat and the Foods We Keep, with Know Your Ingredients at the center of things. And that many "convenience" recipes are grouped under Lunch, Brunch and Supper Dishes. Within chapters, too, initial text or recipes often cover basic methods of preparation, and are followed, as in Fruits, Fish and Vegetables by alphabetical listings of varieties—from Apples to Rhubarb, Carp to Whale, Artichokes to Water Chestnuts. Under Meats you will find in the Index general comments and processes, with further references to Beef, Veal, Lamb, Pork, Ham, Ground and Variety Meats and Game. In this chapter a further differentiation is made between those cuts cooked by dry heat—often a quick process—and those cooked by moist heat which, to be effective, are always slower. Note, too, that in the listings below, illustrations can be found immediately by looking up the boldfaced numerals.

As you familiarize yourself with the "Joy" you will need the Index less and less and will become, in Dr. Johnson's fullest sense, a know-it-all. Meanwhile, happy hunting!

Acid Foods, canning of, 530–539
Additives, 527
Akee, puréed, 92, 93
A la Mode, defined, see Apple Pie, 311
Alaska, Baked; in orange cups, 448, 448
ALCOHOLIC BEVERAGES, 25–48; see Drinks
Ale, to serve, 37
Allergy Substitute Flour, 159
Allium or Onion, 209–212, 213
Allspice, 199
Almonds, 186; also see Cakes, Cookies
 blanching, 189
 creams, 516
 filling, and fig or raisin, 381
 milk, about, 138
 oil, 187; paste, 187, 504
 Orgeat sirup, 187
 sugared or burnt, 516
 types: bitter; sweet, 186
Ambrosia, 86; sauce, 474
Ammonium Carbonate, 231
Anadama Bread, 251
Anchovy, cheese, 72
 paste; Pesto, 218
 rolls, 81
 seasoning, as, 218; to desalt, 218
Angel Cakes, 339–341; also see Cakes
 pie, 330; slices, 408
Angelica, herb, 204
 orange ice, 498; parfait, 492
Anise, 204
 drop cookies, 394
Antipasto, 69
Aperitif, to serve, 32
Appetizer, see Canapés; Hors d'oeuvre
Apple, also see Fruit, and individual names
 about, 93
 baked, 95; with sausage, 95
 butters, 578
 cake Cockaigne, 319
 cake, French, 320
 cake, sour cream, Cockaigne, 447
 candied, 524
 canning, 535
 chutney, 592
 cinnamon, 94
 dried, to substitute, 91
 filling for coffee cakes, 270
 honey, 94
 jelly, 575
 molasses pudding, steamed, 465
 pie, see Pies and Tarts
 rings, 94
 sautéed and bacon, 94
 stuffed with sauerkraut, 95
 texture in commercial pies, 93
 to store, 94
Applejack, 30
Applesauce, 95; and cranberry, 96
 cake, 354
 canning, 535
Apricot, fresh, 96; dried, 96
 bread, quick, 271
 cake, chocolate, 352
 candies, 522
 canning, 535

filling, 380; for coffee cake, 270
glaze, 434
ice, 494; ice cream, 486
icing, 430
jam, and pineapple, quick, 578
mousse with evaporated milk, 491
pie, 316
preserves, 580
soufflé, 446; omelette, 448
Aquavit, 31
Arrowroot Flour or Starch, 158
Artichokes, canning, 538
Asparagus, canapés or sandwich rolled, 60
 canning, 538
 spears, garnished, 75
Aspic, shrimp, glazed, 82
 to clarify, 140
Au Gras, defined, 139
Au Maigre, defined, 138
Austrian Pancakes or Nockerl, 116
Avocados, about, 92, 96
 chutney, and, 75
 Guacamole or spread, 61
 stuffed with creamed food, baked, 96
 to prevent discoloration, 96
 to store, 96

Baba au Rhum, 371
Bacon, apples, sautéed and, 94
 canapés and cheese, 59
 corn meal waffles, 121
 seasoning, as, 222
 tidbits in, 78
Baker's Cheese, 176; cake, 327
Baking Powder, about, 164;
 homemade, 164
 to test for freshness, 164
Baking Soda, 165
 with acid ingredients, 165
Banana, about, 97; baked, 97
 breads, quick, 272, 273
 cake, 355
 Caribbean, 97
 icing, 430
 in blankets, 97
 ripeness for cooking, 97
 sherbet, pineapple, 497
Banbury Tarts, 317
Barbadoes Sugar, 166
Bar-le-Duc, 472; preserves, 576
Barley, flour, 158
Barquettes for Canapés, 54
Bars, also see Cookies
 brownies, butterscotch, 389
 chocolate Cockaigne, 390
 Christmas chocolate Cockaigne, 390
 date, fig or prune, 391
 honey, German, 390
 molasses, 389
 nut, 408
 pan size affects texture, 388
 pecan or angel slices, 408
 Scotch shortbread, 404
 to store, 389
 to wrap, 389
 topping for, 427
Basil, 204; Pesto, 218
Batter, blooms in, 128
 fritter, about, 125; for fruit, 126

Batter (*cont.*)
 fritter, for meat, vegetables and fish, 125
 griddle cakes, or, 111
 to mix for cake, 335
Bavarian Creams, 450–452; defined, 185, 450
 berry, 451
 caramel or maple, 451
 chocolate or coffee, 450
 de luxe, 450
 eggless, 451
 hazelnut, 451
 Nesselrode, 450
 pineapple, molded, 452
 to unmold, 450
Bay Leaf, 198, 204
BEANS, canning, green, snap or wax, 538
 flour, 158
 garbanzo or flageolets, 64
 green, canning, 69
 Lima, canning, 538
 marinated, 75
Beating, method of, 335, 335, 336
Bee Balm, 204
Beechnuts, 187
BEEF, ground, canning, 542
 juice, 145
 roast, canning, 542
 steak, canning, 542
 steak, Tartare, 78
 tenderloin canapé and caviar, 62
Beer, about serving, 37
 Bock, 38
 in fritter batters, 126
 steins, 37, 38
Beet, canning, 539
 stuffed, Cockaigne, 75
Beignets, or French Fritters, 469
Benne Seed, 215; wafers, 413
Berry, *also see* individual fruits
 about, 97; canning, 536
 Bavarian cream, 451
 cones, 98, 554
 freezing, 555
 fresh, self-garnished, 98
 jams, 576, 577
 jelly, waterless, 575
 pies, 312–314; *see* Pies
 with cream, 98
BEVERAGES, see individual names
Birds, see Game Birds, Poultry
Birthday Bread Horse, 291, 291
BISCUIT, about, 283; additions to, 284
 beaten, 287
 buttermilk, 285
 drop, quick, 285
 Easter Bunnies, 286, 287
 fluffy or shortcake dough, 286
 griddle, 287
 pineapple, 285
 rolled, 284; pinwheel, 286
 Scones, 288
 Ship's, 288
 sticks, 285
 sweet potato, 288
 whipped cream, 286
Biscuit Tortoni, 488
Black Bottom Gelatin Pie, 332
Blackberry, 97; jam, 577
Blanching, for canning, 532; equipment, 532

 for freezing, 556; chart, 558
 nuts, 189
 vegetables, for freezing, 556
Blancmange, 455; cornstarch, 442
Blender, look for blender symbol, ⅃
Blini or Russian Raised Pancakes, 116
Blintzes, 114
Blood, to prevent clotting, 540
Blossoms, candied and glazed, 522
 in batter, 128
Blueberries, about, 99; freezing, 554
 jam, 577
 muffins, 282
 tart, 314
Boiling, in high altitudes, 148
 water bath, 533
Bologna Cornucopias or Triangles, 78
Bombes, 486; *see* Ice Creams
Bones for Stocks, 139
Borage, as vegetable, 205
Boston Brown Bread, steamed, 274
Boston Cream Pie or Cake, 372
Botulinus Toxin, to destroy, 530, 538
Bouchées, 304
Bouillon, Court, 146
Bouquets Garnis or Faggots, 220
Bourbon, balls, 517
 drinks, 29
Bran, *also see* Bread, Rolls, Muffins
 flour, 154
Brandy, drinks, 30–31, 45
 fruit, Tutti Frutti, 583
 peaches, 593
 punch, 45
 snaps, 411
Brazil, nuts, 187
BREAD, 239–291
 all-rye flour, 250
 Anadama, 251
 apricot, quick, 271
 banana, quick, 272; wheat germ, 273
 bases for canapés, 53
 Birthday Horse, 291, 291
 biscuits, see Biscuits, 283
 bran, almond, 274
 bran, date, quick, 274
 bran with molasses, quick, 273
 breadbox, to wash, 529
 breading, 160–161
 Brioche loaf Cockaigne, 245
 brown, baked, quick, 274
 brown, Boston, steamed, 274
 cheese, 244
 cinnamon loaf, 289
 coffee cakes, see Coffee Cakes
 corn, see Corn Meal Breads
 corn meal, or Anadama, 251
 corn meal salt-rising, 247
 cracked-wheat, 249
 cranberry, quick, 271
 crumbs, see Crumbs
 crusts, varieties of, 243
 date, quick, 271
 dough, sponge, 240; straight, 240
 flour, 153; Cornell Formula, 243
 French, 245, 246
 frozen for canapés, 564
 garlic, 289, 289
 ginger, see Cakes
 glaze for, 433

gluten, 252
griddle, 277
Grissini, 246
Health, 252
honey, all rye, eggless, 276
honey, see Cockaigne, 249
Irish soda, quick, 273
loaf, garlic, 289, 289; cinnamon, 289
muffins, see Muffins, 279
nut, 243; quick, 271
oat, steel-cut, 251
orange, quick, 272
pans, 242
popovers, see Popovers, 283
potato salt rising, 247
pretzels, 252
puddings, see Puddings
prune, 243; quick, 271
quick; in high altitudes, 271
raisin, 244
rolls, see Rolls
rye, sour dough, 250
rye, Swedish, 249
Sally Lunn, quick, 271
salt-rising, 247
sandwiches, about, 50
skillet or griddle, 277
sponge, 240
Spoon, 279
steamed, to cut, 275
sticks, 246, 264, 289
tea, quick, 271–275
temperature for rising, 241
to achieve a fine crumb, 241
to cool, 243, 243
to form a loaf, 241, 242
to knead, 240, 240
to mix, 240, 240
to proof, 241, 241, 242
to serve with hors d'oeuvre, 70
to store, 242
to test for doneness, 242, 242
to test rising of, 241, 241
toasted, 289–290
Torte, 366
use of fermented milks in, 134
white, 243; white plus, 244
whole-grain, 248; Cockaigne, 249; plus, 248
whole-wheat, sweet, quick, 273
yeast, 239–268
Zwieback or twice-baked, 290
Breading, 160, 161; seasoned, 160
Brewer's Yeast, 163
Brine, 196, 543, 585, 593
to test for a 10% brine, 196
vegetables, 593
Brioche, 258; to shape, 259
loaf Cockaigne, 245
yeast starter for, 258
Broths, see Soups
canning, 542
Brottorte, 366
Brown Betty, 460
Brownies, butterscotch, 389
chocolate, Cockaigne, 390
Brulée, crusts, 439
fruits, 90
Brussels Sprouts, stuffed, 75
Bûche de Noël, 374
Buckwheat Cakes, 118
Buffet Service, about, 9–10, 10
Bundkuchen, 266

Buns, 252; see Rolls
Burnet, 205; vinegar, 151
Butcher Wrap, 551, 551
BUTTER, 171; also see Seasoned Butters
balls and curls, 56, 57
creamery, 171
expanded, 171
freezing, 563
processed, 171
salt, 171
sauces, see Sauces
shapes and molds, about, 56, 57
spreads, 56
sweet, 171
to make, 171
to measure bulk, 226
unsalted in candies, 499
BUTTER, SEASONED, dill, 206
mushroom, blender, 57
nut, 57
seafood, 57
sweetened, 480; honey, 480
Buttermilk, 134
biscuits, 285
corn bread, crackling, 277
ice cream, fruit, 490
rolls, 255; muffins, 281
sherbet, pineapple, 498
waffles, 120
Butternuts, 186
Butterscotch, brownies, 389
cake, spice roll, 373
candies, 510
cookies, 397, 399
filling, 379; icing, 428
parfait, 492
pie, 326
sauce, 478
tapioca custard, 459

Cabbage, as sauce container, 67, 68
salads, mound, 75
Cabinet Pudding, 450
CAKES, CUP CAKES, TORTEN, AND FILLED CAKES, 334–385;
also see Cakes, High altitude
angel, 339–341
angel, almond, 341
angel, cocoa, 341
angel, flavored, 341
angel, marble, 341
angel, pan types for, 339
angel, roll, 340, 374
angel, to cool, 340, 340
angel, to mix, 339
apple, peach or plum Cockaigne, 319
apple Cockaigne, sour cream, 447
apple or peach, French, 320
applesauce, 354
Baba au Rhum or Savarin, 371
banana, 355
batter, for oddly shaped pans, 337
Boston cream pie or, 372
brown sugar spice, 353
burnt sugar, 353
butter or shortening, about, 343
butter for, 343
butter, to mix in mixer, 337
caramel cornflake ring, 363

CAKES, CUP CAKES, TORTEN AND FILLED CAKES (*cont.*)
caramel Hurry-Up, 363
Charlottes, 375
cheese, *see* Cheesecakes, 326
chiffon, 361
chocolate apricot, 352
chocolate cream roll, 374
chocolate filled roll, 374
chocolate, quick oil, 362
chocolate, "Rombauer Special," 350
chocolate spice with citron, 351
chocolate sponge, 343
cocoa, Hurry-Up, 363
coconut loaf or layer, 349
coconut-milk, 346
coffee, *see* Coffee Cakes
cornstarch puff, 359
cream meringue tart, Cockaigne, 372
cup, about, 358
cup, angel, 359
cup, caramel, 360
cup, chocolate, 360
cup, coconut, 360
cup, jam, 359
cup, Madeleines, 359
cup, one-egg, 358
cup, pans for, 358
cup, sour milk spice, 360
cup, sponge, or Marguerites, 358
cup, yellow, 358
currant, 356
Daffodil, 343
date spice, 354
decorations, fresh flowers, 435
devil's food Cockaigne, 351
dough, to beat, 335; to fold, 335, 336
dough, to cream, 335; to stir, 335, 335
eggless, milkless, spice, 365
eight-yolk, 349
enlargement of, 346
fig spice, 354
filled, *also see* Charlottes and Torten
filled, about, 369, 376
filling, 376–381
flour, 152
four-egg, 348
freezer, quick mocha, 376
frozen, about, 567
fruit, about, 355
fruit, Cockaigne, 356
fruit, dark, 357
fruit, white, 356
fudge layer, 351
fudge meringue, 351
Génoise, 370
gingerbread, 364; wheatless, 364
gluten, to prevent development, 344
glazes, 434–435
gold layer, 348
griddle, *see* Griddle Cakes
honey, eggless, all rye, Cockaigne, 276
houses, and cookie, 391
Hurry-Up, 362
icings, *see* Cake Icings
jam, Rombauer, 365

jelly roll, 373, **373**
Lady, 350; Lady Baltimore, 346
Ladyfingers, 359
Lamb, Bunnies, Santas, 345, **345**
Langue de Chat or Cat's Tongue, 360
large or wedding, about, 346, 346
lemon roll, 373
Lightning, or whipped tea, 363
Linzertorte, 316
Madeleines, 359
making hints, 334–340, **335**, **336, 337**
marble, 347
mixes, about, 338
molds, about, 345; to ice, 345, 346
molds, to line with paper, 449, 449
Moors' Heads or Mohrenkoepfe, 370
Mystery, 365
oil, chiffon; Mocha, 361
one-bowl in electric mixer, 337
one-egg, 364
orange-filled, 371
pans sized for recipes, 336–337, 337
Parkin, 364
pastries, *see* Pastries
Petits Fours, 360, **360**
pound, 349; pans for, 349
prune, chocolate, spiced, 352
quick, about, 362
raspberry rum or Trifle, 370
refrigerator, 370
roll, 372, **373**
seed, 350
shortcakes, individual, 376; large, 376
skillet or Upside-Down, 320
sour cream, 347
spice, Hurry-Up, 363
spice, quick, oil, 362
spice roll, butterscotch, 373
spice, Velvet, 352
sponge, 341, chocolate, 343
sponge, rice or potato flour, 342
sponge, riser for, 341
sponge, roll, almond, 374
Sunshine, 342
tea, Lightning or whipped, 363
to cool, 336; before icing, 418
to handle iced, 418
to test for doneness, 336
to dust with confectioners' sugar, 418
Torten, see Torten, 366
tube, for secret filling, 377, **377**
Tutti Frutti, 355
wedding, 345, **345**
whipped cream, 347
white, 344; quick oil, 362
CAKE, HIGH ALTITUDE, 381–385
angel, 382; chocolate, 383
angel, spice, 383
baking powder in, 382
cocoa, 384
fruit, hints, 356
fudge, 383
gingerbread, 385
sponge, 384
two-egg, 384

white, 383
CAKE FILLINGS, 376–381; *also see*
  Coffee Cake Fillings
    almond and fig or raisin, 381
    butterscotch, 379
    chocolate fruit, 379
    cream, whipped, or Crème
      Chantilly, 377
    Crème Patissière or custard
      cream, 378
    custard, almond or hazelnut,
      381
    custard, apricot, 380
    custard, lemon and orange, 379
    custard, orange, 380
    Frangipane cream, 379
    ginger fruit, 380
    lemon, 379
    mocha, 379
    orange cream, 380
    ricotta chocolate, 379
    toasted walnut or pecan, 381
CAKE ICINGS, 418–435
  apricot, 430
  baked, 430
  banana, 430
  boiled, about, 418; high
    altitude, 418
  boiled, thread stage defined, 419
  broiled, 430
  brown sugar marshmallow, 426
  brown sugar, quick, 428
  butterscotch, 428
  cakes, small, 360, 431, 431
  caramel, 425; roll topping, 433
  chocolate butter, 428
  chocolate coating over white,
    423
  chocolate cream cheese, 428
  chocolate, easy, 429
  chocolate, European, 428
  chocolate fudge, 425
  chocolate marshmallow, 425
  chocolate, quick, 429
  coconut, 420, 420
  coffee or mocha, 429
  cream cheese, 427
  cup cakes, decorating, 431, 431
  decorations, 423
  decorative, about, 420–423
  decorative: bag types; to make,
    420–423, 421, 422, 423
  decorative, quick, Royal Glaze
    or Swiss Meringue, 426
  decorative or twice-cooked, 423
  dipping, quick, 430
  fondant, to apply, 360, 424
  freezing, 567
  French, 427
  glazes, 433–435
  hard-sauce topping, 431
  honey glaze topping, 433
  honey peanut-butter, quick, 429
  lace topping, quick, 431
  lemon, quick, 427
  lemon topping for cookies or
    bars, 427
  maple, quick, 429; sugar, 425
  meringue topping, about, 432
  nut, 420
  orange, Luscious, 424; quick,
    428
  pineapple, 430
  quick, about, 426

raisin, 420
  seven-minute, 424; lemon, 424;
    orange, 424, seafoam, 424
  small cakes and cookies, about,
    431
  Streusel topping for coffee cakes,
    pies, and sweet rolls, 432–433
  substitutes for, see Cake Fillings,
    376
  three-minute, 427
  toppings, applied before, during,
    and after baking, 431–432
  white, boiled, 419
  White-Mountain, 420
  white, quick, 426
  yields, about, 418
Calamondins, 101; candied or
  preserved, 525
  preserves, 581
Calas or Rice Crullers, 470; raised,
  470
Calvados, 30
Camomile, 205
CANAPES, 49–65; *also see*
  Sandwiches
    defined, 49
    amounts and ways to serve, 66
    Angels on Horseback, 64
    asparagus, rolled, 60
    avocado spread or Guacamole,
      61
    bacon and cheese, 59
    barquettes for, 54
    bread bases, about, 53
    butters and butter spreads,
      56–58, 57
    caviar and cucumber, 62
    caviar and onion, 62
    Cheese Dreams, 59
    cheese puffs, 58
    cheese rolls or logs, toasted, 59
    chicken spread, 62
    Christmas, 52
    chutney and cheese, 59
    clam puffs, 63
    crab, hot, 64; puff ball, 63
    cream cheese spreads for, 58
    cucumber, 61; cream cheese, 58
    egg spreads, 60
    fillings, 55
    flower, 51
    Foie Gras for, 63
    fried pies, 54
    frozen, about, 564
    glazed, 55
    ham salad spread, 62
    herbs, dried, for butter spreads,
      56
    herring, marinated, on toast, 63
    liver paste for, 63
    liver sausage, 63
    lobster, hot, 64
    lobster puff balls, 63
    lobster spread, 64
    mushroom, 61; mushroom
      butter, 57
    nut butters for, 57
    onion and parsley, 61
    oyster, creamed, 64
    pastry, fillings for, 55
    Pizza, small, 62
    puff paste shells, stuffed, 54
    Quiche, cocktail, 53
    radish, black, 61

CANAPES (*cont.*)
  ribbon, 51
  Rissoles, 54
  rolled sandwiches, 51
  Roquefort spread, 58
  Roquefort sticks, puffed, 59
  salmon, smoked, 64
  sardine rolls, 65
  shapes of, 49, 50, 51
  shrimp puffs, 65
  snails, 55
  spreads, sweet tea, 60
  Tacos, 55
  tart, rich cocktail, 53
  tarts and tartlets, 53
  tenderloin and caviar, 62
  tomato, 61
  tuna, hot, 64
  turnovers, 54
CANDIES AND CONFECTIONS,
  499–526
  almond creams, 516
  almond or filbert paste, 504
  almonds, sugared or burnt, 516
  altitude, effect on, 500
  apples, candied, 524, 524
  apricot leather, 522
  apricot orange balls, 522
  bourbon balls, 517
  butterscotch, 510; old-fashioned,
    510
  calamondins, candied or
    preserved, 525
  caramels, chocolate, 509;
    chocolate cream, 509
  caramels, filled, 510
  caramels, maple, 509
  caramels, vanilla cream, 509
  chestnuts, glazed, or Marrons
    Glacés, 525
  chocolate clusters, 517
  chocolate coating and dipping,
    505, 507
  citrus peel, candied, 524
  coffee drops, 510
  cranberries, candied, 525
  date roll or centers, 521
  Divinity, 508; caramel cream,
    508
  fondant, basic, 501; caramel,
    503
  fondant and centers, about, 501;
    soft, 502
  fondant, uncooked, 502
  fruits, leaves, and blossoms,
    glazed and candied, 522
  fruit paste, 526
  fruit paste, Turkish Delight or
    Rahat Loukoum, 519
  fruit roll or centers, 521
  fruit, stuffed dried, 521
  fudge Cockaigne, 506
  fudge, cocoa or centers, 506
  fudge, coconut or centers, 507
  fudge, coffee, 507
  ginger or centers, 520
  hard or lollipops, 513
  Hawaiian or centers, 520
  Heavenly Hash, 517
  honey, cooking and storage of,
    168
  horehound, 514
  kumquats, candied or preserved,
    525

  making, marble slab for, 499
  maple cream, 504
  marshmallows, 505
  Marzipan or marchpane, 505
  mint leaves, glazed, 523
  mints, pulled, 512
  Newport creams or centers, 503
  nougat, 508
  nut brittle, 515
  nut crunch, 514
  nuts, glazed, 515; spiced, 516;
    spiced caramel, 516
  Opera creams or centers, 503
  orange drops, Mexican, 520
  pan sizes for, 499
  Pastillage or gum paste, 519
  peach leather, 522
  peanut or nut brittle, 515
  peanut butter fudge or centers,
    517
  Penuche, 514
  peppermint cream wafers, 504
  Persian balls or centers, 521
  pineapple, glazed, 524
  popcorn, about, 517; candied,
    518
  Pralines, about, 514; pralines,
    514
  Praliné, 515
  pull, cream, 513
  rock, 513
  roots and stalks, candied, 526
  sirups, caramel, 518; molasses,
    518; white sugar, 518
  sirups, stages of, 500
  sugaring, 499
  taffy, about, 510, 511; molasses,
    512
  taffy, salt water, 512; vanilla,
    512
  thermometer, temperatures; to
    use, 500–501
  to cool for beating, 500
  toffee, English, 514
  Truffles, chocolate, 517
  unsalted butter in, 499
  weather, effect of, 499
  wrappings, about, 501
  yields, how counted, 501
Cane Sirup, 168
Canned Goods, sizes, 231; storage,
  528
CANNING, 530–546; *also see*
  individual names of Fruits,
  Vegetables, Meat, Poultry, and
  Game
  acid foods in boiling water bath,
    535; in high altitudes, 533
  blanching of foods for, 532
  boiling water bath, 533
  canner, pressure, with, 538, 539
  equipment, 530–534
  fruit; acid, 535
  fruit juices, 536
  fruit yields, 534
  game, 539, 540
  jars for, sealing, testing, filling,
    530–534, 531, 533
  lids for, 531, 531; to seal, 534
  meat, 539; processing time,
    542–543
  non-acid foods, 535; vegetables,
    538
  open kettle method, 531

oven, 531
pressure: fish, game, meat, and poultry, 539
pressure: vegetables, about, 538
processes, about, 531
purées and pastes, 537
rubbers, to test, 531
sirups for fruit, about, 535
soup stock and broths, 542
spoilage, 530
synthetic sweeteners for, 535
to prepare food for, 532
to preserve nutritional values, 530, 532
to steam food for, 532
vegetable yields, 538
Capers, English, 205
Caramel, Bavarian cream, 451
buns, 258
cake, Hurry-Up, 363
candies, 508–510
cookies, curled, 411
cornflake ring, 363
cup cakes, 360
custard, 438, 442; pie, 325
glaze, clear, 435
ice cream, 485; parfait, 492
icing, 425
molds, coated, about, 449
pudding, steamed, 465
sauces, 479; chocolate, 477
sirup for candies, 518
topping for rolls, 433
Caramelized, custard or Brulée, 438
sugar, 169
Caraway, 205
Cardamon, 199
Carob Flour, 158
Carrots; canning, 539
drop cookies, 396
marinated, 75
Cases, food, 52–54
Cashew Nuts; need to roast, 187
Cassia, see Cinnamon, 199
Cat's Tongue Cakes, 360
Catsup, tomato, 590
Caviar, about, 79; preparing roe, 546
barquettes, 54
canapés, and cucumber, 62
canapés, and onion, 62
canapés, and tenderloin, 62
dip, 84
Celery; as an herb, 205
curls, 76, 76
stuffed or logs, 76, 76
CEREALS, also see individual names
cooked, substituted for flour, 159
muffins, 282
puddings, 457, 458
puffed for cocktails, 71
waxy, in frozen foods, 564
Cerfeuille, Pluches de, see Chervil, 205
Champagne Drinks, 31, 34, 45
fountain, 37, 37
sherbet, 497
to open, 34
Chantilly, Crème, 377
Charlotte, chocolate, 375; maple, 375; Russe, 375
CHEESE, 175–178
anchovy, 72
bacteria-ripened, 176

balls Florentine, 73; pastry, 73; nut, 72
Bar-le-duc, 472
bread, 244
cake, see Cheesecake
canapés, 58–59
Carrots, 73
Coeur à la Crème, 471
cottage, see Cottage Cheese
cream, see Cream Cheese
croquettes, 123; and rice, 123
dessert, about; to serve, 470
dessert mix, 471
dips, 83
Dreams, 59; fried, 73
Edam, filled, 72; nuggets, 72
frozen, 564
heat sensitivity, 175
Liptauer, 72, 472
mold, gelatin, 72
muffins, 282; popovers, 283
natural, 175
Neufchâtel, 178
potted, 471
processed, 176
rennet for, 175
rolls, 256; toasted, 59
sauces, see Sauces
seasonal character, 175, 471
soft; pasteurized milk for, 176
spreads, 58; long-keeping, 83
to store, 470; whole, 176; cut, 176; soft, 177
Vicksburg, 72
waffles, 120
Cheesecake, about; additions, 326
Baker's, or pie, 327
crust, 298
gelatin, 328; fruit, 328
sour cream, 327; whipped cream, 327
Ricotta, or pie, 329
Cherimoya, 93, 99
Cherries, about, 100
canning, 536
conserve, black, 582
Crunch, quick, 321
pie, 312–314; see Pies
preserves, 580
sauce, 473; Jubilee, 474
Chervil, 205
Chess Tarts, 318
Chestnut, 188
glazed, 525
mound or Mont Blanc, 442
roasted, 188; skewered, 189
to reconstitute dried, 188
to shell, 188
to substitute, 188
varieties of, 188
Water, 188
CHICKEN, also see Poultry
croquettes, 123; oyster and, 124
livers, chopped, 79
sherried, bits, 79
spread, 62
stock, 142
Chiffon cakes, 361
Chiffon pies, 330–333
Chiffonade, of fresh herbs, 219
Chili Con Carne, peppers, to prepare, 213; preserved in sherry, 590
powder, 213, 219
sauce, 589; vinegar, 152

Chipped Beef, cornucopias, 78
Chives, 210, 213
CHOCOLATE, about, 191; for
  candy, 505
    Bavarian, 450
    bitter or cooking, 191
    Bombe, 490
    Brioche, 260
    cakes, *see* Cakes
    cases, semi-sweet, 376
    Charlotte, 375
    clusters, 517
    coating, candy, 505, 507; over
      icing, 423
    cookies, *see* Cookies
    curls, to make, 192
    custard, 437, 441; sauce, 477
    dipping, 505, 507
    doughnuts, 468
    Éclairs, 306
    filling, ricotta, 379
    fudge, *see* Cakes, Candies, etc.
    German, 192
    ice cream, 485, 489
    icings, 423, 425
    mousses, 441
    pies, 325, 331
    puddings, 375, 462, 465
    roll cakes, 374
    sauces, 477, 478
    seasoning, as, 192
    soufflé, 445
    sweet and semi-sweet, defined,
      192
    to grate, 192
    to melt, 192
    to substitute, 192
    Torten, 367, 368, 369
    truffles, 517
    waffles, 121
Choux Paste, 305, 305
    fritters, unsweetened, 127
    shells, stuffed, 54, 307
Chow Chow, 589
Chowder, *see* Soups
Christmas, watch for symbol ★
Chutney, apple or green tomato, 592
    avocado, and, 75
    canapés, and cheese, 59
    mango or peach, 591
Cicely, sweet, 215
Cider, sauce, 476
    vinegar, 150
Cilantro, *see* Coriander, 206
Cinnamon, apples or pears, 94
    buns or snails, 257
    loaf, 289
    spices, 199
    Stars, 415
    sugar, 170
    toast or sticks, 289
Citrus, flavor for sugars, 170
    flavor, from rind, 427, 428
    fruits, about, 100
    peel, candied, 524
    peel for drinks, 220
    zests and juices, 219
Clabber, 134
CLAMS, dip, 84
    puffs, 63
Clostridium Botulinum, 530, 538
Clover Leaf Rolls, 253, 254
Cloves, 199
Cobbler, fruit, 319

Cockles, 80, 80
COCKTAILS, 25–32; *also see* Drinks
    equipment, 25–26, 26
    glasses, 26, 26; to frost, 30
    servings, 26
    sugar sirup for, 25
COCOA, about, 191
    "butter" from, 191
    cakes, 341, 363, 384
    fudge or centers, 506
    kisses, 398
    to substitute for chocolate, 233
COCONUT, about, 193; to open,
    193
    butter, to make, 194
    cakes, 346, 349
    cream, 193
    cup cakes, 360
    dry, grated; to reconstitute, 194
    Dulcie, 480
    Extravaganza, 41
    fudge or centers, 507
    grating, 193, 193
    macaroons, 398
    milks, about, 138, 193
    shells, as containers, 194, 194
    to apply to cake, 420, 420
    to substitute flaked for grated,
      194
    waffles, 120
Coeur à la Crème, 471
COFFEE, *also see* Mocha
    drops, 510
    service, 10, 11; at table, 4
COFFEE CAKES, 264–276
    about yeast, 264
    Bundkuchen or Kugelhopf, yeast,
      266
    fillings, seasonings, toppings,
      268–270
    fruit-topped yeast, 266
    glazes for, 432–435
    kneaded for filled braids, rings
      or Vanocka, 265, 265
    Kugelhopf, 266; quick, 275
    no-knead yeast or Panettone,
      264
    quick, 275; about, 271
    quick, rich, moist, 276
    quick sour cream, 275
    quick, with oil, spice, 276
    Scandinavian or Danish, 267,
      268
    stollen or Christmas loaf, 265
    Streusel or toppings for,
      432–433
Coffee Cake Fillings, 268–270
    about, 268
    apple, 269
    apricot, 270
    crumb fruit, 269
    date, 270
    fig, 270
    nut, 269
    poppy seed, Cockaigne, 270
    poppy seed or Mohn, 270
    pot-cheese or Ricotta, 270
Cognac, defined, 31
Color in Food, about, 146, 223
Cones, ice cream or Gaufrettes, 410
Conserves, about, 572
    cherry, black, 582
    plum, blue, 582
    rhubarb, spiced, 583

Consommé, double strength, *see*
  clarifying, 141
CONVERSIONS AND
  EQUIVALENTS, 226–237
COOKIES, 386–417
  about, 386
  almond meringue rings, 415
  almond pretzels or
    Mandelplaettchen, 404
  anise drop, 394
  bars, *see* Bars
  brandy snaps, 411
  butter thins, 402; wafers, 392
  butterless drop, 392
  butterscotch nut, 397
  butterscotch refrigerator, 399
  caramel, curled, 411
  carrot drop, 396
  chocolate almond shells, 405
  chocolate chip drop, 393
  chocolate cracker kisses, 398
  chocolate refrigerator, 400
  Christmas, about, 386, 386; *also*
    see Christmas symbol ★
  cinnamon stars, 415
  cocoa kisses, 398
  coconut meringue, 397
  cookie-press or Spritz, 406
  crusts, 298, 300
  curled, about, 409; iron for, 409,
    409
  cutters for, 401, 401
  drop or hand-shaped, about,
    392, 393
  egg white in, 386
  filled, about, 406; to shape, 406,
    406
  Florentines, 414
  Fortune or almond curls, 411
  Frankfurter Oblaten, 409
  freezing, 567
  frozen, to freshen, 386
  ginger snaps, 403; thins, 393
  gingerbread men, 403, 403
  Gaufrettes, 410
  hazelnut wafers, 413
  Hermits, 394
  high altitude, 388
  honey, German, 395
  houses, 391
  jelly tots, 407
  Jubilee wafers, 400
  Krumcakes, 410
  lace refrigerator, 400
  leaf wafers, 414
  macaroons, 416; coconut, 398;
    chocolate-coconut, 398
  macaroon jam tarts, 407
  maple curls, 411
  molasses crisps Cockaigne, 400
  molasses nut wafers, 413
  nut and date, 416
  nut balls, flourless, 413
  nut tarts, individuals, 408
  nut wafers, 412; curled, 412
  oatmeal, quick, 396; Gems, 396
  oatmeal wafers, glazed or
    flourless, 396
  orange marmalade drops, 397
  pans for, 387
  peanut butter, 397
  pecan or benne wafers, 413
  pecan drop, 412; puffs, 414;
    slices, 408

  Pfeffernüsse, 395
  pinwheel, refrigerator, 399, 400
  plum Bombs, 409
  refrigerator, about, 399; to form,
    399, 399
  rocks or fruit drops, 394
  roll, rich, 402
  rolled and molded, 401, 401
  rum drops, uncooked, 415
  sand tarts, 402
  Scandinavian Krumcakes, 409
  Scotch shortbread, 404
  Speculatius, 406
  Springerle, 405
  sugar drop, to shape, 393, 393
  sugar drop, with oil, 393
  tea wafers, 416
  thumb print, to form, 406, 406
  to avoid toughness, 387
  to bake uniformly, 387
  to beat honey and molasses, 387
  to color, 388
  to crisp, 386; to cool, 388
  to ice, 431; lemon topping, 427
  to pack, to store, 386
  Tortelettes, 392
  vanilla, refrigerator, 399
  yolk, 404
Cordials, 38
Coriander, 206
Corn, breads or cakes, *see* Corn Meal
  canning, 539
  croquettes, ham and, 122
  flour, 155
  fritters, and ham, 128
  pudding, frozen, 566
  relish, 589
  sirup, about, 167
Corn Meal, as flour, 155
  bread, buttermilk, crackling, 277
  bread, muffins or sticks, 277
  bread or Anadama, 251
  bread, salt rising, 247
  bread, skillet, 277
  crackles, 278
  dodgers, 278
  flapjacks, crisp, 117
  griddle cakes, rice, 117
  hush puppies, 279
  pancakes, 117
  puffs, golden, 278
  spoon bread, 279
  waffles, bacon, 121
  zephyrs Cockaigne, 278
Cornell Flour Formula, 243
Cornstarch, introduction to, 155
  puddings and custards, 438, 440,
    442, 443
  puff cakes, 359
Cottage Cheese, dessert, 472
  pancakes or blintzes, 114
  to make, 177
Cottage Pudding, 462
Cottonseed Flour, 158
Country, ham, 543
Court Bouillon, about, 146; à Blanc,
  146; for fish, 146
CRAB, balls, puff, 63
  canapés, hot, 64
  meat dip, 84
Crabapple Garnish, 74
Cracked-wheat Bread, 249
Cracker, for hors d'oeuvre, 70
Cracklings, defined, 174

Cranberry, bread, quick, 271
candied, 525
canning, 536
jelly, spiced, 99
muffins, 282
relish, uncooked, 99
sauce, 99; whole, 99
sherbet, 497
vitamin C content, 99
CREAM, 129–134; *also see* Sour
  Cream
about, 129; freezing, 563
Bavarian, 450
candies, *see* Candies
cheese, *see* Cream Cheese
Crème Chantilly, 377; Fraîche,
  136
Devonshire or clotted, 136
fermented, 134
Frangipane, 379
fried or Crème Frite, 443
half-and-half, 132
pasteurization of, 130
Persian, 455
pie, *see* Pies
pineapple, molded, 452
pudding, coffee marshmallow,
  457
puff shells, 305; fillings for, 307
rice and fruit, 458
rolls, 304
sour, 134; cultured, 136
Spanish, 437
substitutions, 133
sweet, 132
whipped, 132; equivalents, 233;
  substitutions, 133
whipped, sweetened, 377
whipped, to freeze garnishes of,
  133
whipping, 132
Cream Cheese, dessert, 471
Bar-le-Duc, 472
French or Coeur à la Crème,
  471, 471
icing, 427
rich, to make, 178
spreads, 54, 58, 60
topping, sweet, 434
Creaming Methods for Cakes, 335,
  343
Crème Brulée, 438
Crème Caramel, 431
Crème Chantilly, 133, 377
Crème de Menthe Sauce, 476
Crème Fraîche, 136
Crème Frite or fried cream, 443
Crème Glacée, 484
Crème Patissière, 378
Crêpes, Gâteau, 113
Suzette, 114; sauce for, 115
Crescents, sweet, filled, 261
French or Croissants, 261, 261
Croquembouche, 305, 307
CROQUETTE, 121–125
about, 121
cheese and rice, 123
chicken or veal, 124
cooked food, 122
freezing, 565
ham and corn, 122
mushroom, 123
oyster and chicken, 124
rice, sweet, 123

salmon, 124
Crullers, about, 468
rice or Calas, 470
Crumb, bread: dry, soft, browned,
  159
bread and cake, to use, 289
crumbing foods, 160–161
crusts, 299, 300
pie, 317
Crumpets, 261
Cucumber, lily, 76
pickles, 585–588
sandwiches, 61
spread, cream cheese, 58
Cumin, 206
Cup Cakes, 358–360; *see* Cakes
Currant, cake, 356
canning, 536
jellies, 574
to plump, 191
Curry, fruit, 90
nuts, 70
powders, 199
sauce, pickle, 588
CUSTARD, 436–443; *also see*
  Puddings
about, 436
baked or cup, 437
caramel, 437, 442
caramelized, Spanish cream or
  Crème Caramel, 437
chocolate, coffee, 437
chocolate or Pots-de-Crème, 441
cornstarch or Blancmange, 442
Crème Brulée, 438
fillings, pastry, 378–381
Floating Island, 438
fruit juice, 439
orange with meringue, 440
pies, 323–325
rich, 438
sauce, 475; chocolate, 477; fruit,
  quick, 475
sponges, 440–441
tapioca, quick, 450; pearl, 459
tarts or Flan with fruit, 324
to test for doneness, 436
Torte, poppy seed, 368
wine or Weinschaum, 440
Zabaglione or Sabayon, 439
Cyclamate Sweetener, 169

Daffodil Cake, 343
Daiquiri, 30
Dampfnudeln or Raised Dumplings,
  322
Damson, preserves, 580; plum butter,
  579, *also see* Plums
Danish pastry, 267, 268
Date, bars, 391
bread, quick, 271
cake, spice, 354
cookies, nut and, 416
doughnuts, 468
filling for coffee cake, 270
loaf, uncooked, 466
pudding, steamed, 464
ring, baked or Christmas wreath,
  461
roll or centers, 521
Torte, chocolate, 368
Deep-dish Pies, 319
Defrosting, 548

Deglazing, with wine, 150
Delmonico, Bombe, 489; ice cream, 484
DESSERT, 436–472
    Bavarians, 450–452
    Bombes, 488, 489, 490
    cakes, 334–375
    candies and confections, 499–526
    cheeses, 470–472
    cookies, 386–417
    creams or Crèmes, 437, 438, 441, 443, 452, 455, 457, 458
    crullers, Beignets and doughnuts, 466–470
    custards, 436–443
    frozen, storage period, 569
    frozen, to prevent graininess, 569
    fruits, 85–110
    gelatin and gelatin puddings, 452–457
    ices, ice creams, sherbets, 483–498
    molds, about, 449–450
    omelets, sweet, 447–449
    pancakes and waffles, 111–121
    pies and pastries, 292–333
    puddings, 442–443, 450–466
    sauces, 473–482
    savories; defined, 472
    soufflés, sweet, 443–447
    Torten, 366–369
Devil's Food Cake Cockaigne, 351
Devonshire or Clotted Cream, 136
Dhuma, see Coriander, 206
Dill, seeds, 206
    pickles, 593
Dips for Hors d'Oeuvre, 83–84
Divinity, 508
Dobos Torte, 367
Dorure or French Egg Wash, 433
Dough, bread, 239–280
    freezing, 566–568
    pie, basic, 292–300, 292, 293, 294
    puff paste, 300–304, 301, 302
    refrigerator, about, 262
    sour, 163
    yeast, additions to, 243
Doughnuts, about, 466
    chocolate, 468; drop, 468
    high altitude, 467
    jelly or Berlin, 468
    molasses, 468
    orange, 468
    pecan or date, 468
    potato, quick, 468; yeast, 467
    sour cream, 467
    sweet-milk, 467
    variations, 468
DRINKS, Alcoholic, 25–48
    ale, about serving, 37
    Alexander, 27
    aquavit, about, 31
    bar equipment, 25–26, 26
    beer, 37; glasses and mugs, 38
    Benedictine, 30
    Bloody Mary, 31
    Bobbie Burns, 29
    Bowle, 45
    brandy and brandy cocktails, 30
    brandy cup, 45

brandy sour, 27
Bronx, 27
champagne cocktail, 31, 37; punch, 45
claret cup, 46
cocktails, 25
Coconut Extravaganza, 41
cooler, 39
cordials, about, 38
Cuba Libre, 41
Cubana, 30
cup, defined, see Champagne, 45
Curaçao cocktail, 31
Daiquiri, 30
eggnog, 43; in quantity, 46
El Presidente, 30
Fish House Punch, 45
flip, 43
fruit, plugged, about, 41
Gibson, 27
Gimlet, 27
gin and gin cocktails, 27
gin bitter, 27; sour, 27
gin fizz, 40
glasses for tall, 38; mixed, 38; wine, 35; beer, 37
grog, 42
highballs, 39
Horses' Neck, 39
Jack Rose, 31
Knickerbocker, 30
liqueurs, about, 38
Manhattans, 29
Margarita, 32
martinis, 27
May wine, 46
measurements, about, 26
mint julep, 40, 40
mixed, about, 39
negus in quantity, 47
old-fashioned, 29
Orange Blossom, 27
party, about, 43
Pineapple Tropic, 42
Pink Lady, 28
Planter's Punch, 41
posset or hot milk punch, 42
punches and toddies, 41–48, 44
Rhine wine cup, 46
rickeys, 39
Rob Roy, 29
rum and rum cocktails, 29
rum, buttered, 48
rum cassis cup, 45
rum punch, 41
rum sour, 27
Sazerac, 29
sherry types, 32
short, 42
Sidecar, 31
Spritzer, 39
Stinger, 31
syllabub or milk punch, 42
tall, about, 39
to heat, 47
toddy, 42
Tom and Jerry, 42; in quantity, 47
Tom Collins, 39
tonics, 41
vermouth cassis, 39
vodka, about, 31
Wassail, 47

DRINKS (*cont.*)
   whisky and whisky cocktails, 28
   whisky bitter, 27
   whisky cup, 45
   whisky sour, 27
   White Lady, 28
   wines, 32–37; mulled, 47
   Zombie, 41
Drippings, as flavor re-enforcers, 174
   to substitute, 174
Drugstore Wrap, for freezing, 550, 551
Dumplings, fruit, 322
   raised or Dampfnudeln, 322
Duxelles, 220

Easter Bunnies, biscuit, 286, 287
Éclairs, chocolate, 305, 306
Edam Cheese, filled, 72; nuggets, 72
EGG AND EGG DISHES, 179–183
   about, 74, 179
   apples, hors d'oeuvre, 74
   beating, about, 180–182, **181**
   binder, as, 179
   cooking, about, 179
   decorations, as, 74, **74**
   dishes, storage of, 182
   dried, to reconstitute, 183
   duck, bacteria in, 179
   fertile, 179
   freezing and thawing, 563
   freshness, importance of, 179
   glaze, for baking, 433; for blooms, 523
   hard-cooked, spreads, 60
   hors d'oeuvre, about, 74
   in snow, 438
   stains, to remove, 183
   storage of, 182
   to avoid curdling, 180
   to measure for baking, 179
   to preserve at home, 182
   to separate, beat and fold, 180, 181
   to substitute, 183
   wash, French, 433
   whites, to beat, 180; in electric mixer, 339
   whites, to fold, 182
   yolk, fat content, 180
   yolk, to add to hot liquid, 180
   yolk, to store, 182
Eggless, Bavarian cream, 451
   cakes, 463; honey rye, 276
   cookies, 390, 400, 403, 414, 415
   muffins, whole wheat, 281
   pie, lemon or lime cream, 330
Eggnog, 43; in quantity, 46
   frozen, 488
Elderberry, jam, 577
Endive, stuffed, 76
English Muffins, 261, **261**
ENTERTAINING, 1–13
Entrée, defined, 5; fruits for, 91
Entremets, defined, 5
Equipment, blanching, 557, 558
   self-service, 9–11
EQUIVALENTS, SUBSTITUTES AND CONVERSIONS, 226–237

Faggots, 220
Falernum, sirup, 201
Fan Tans or Buttermilk Rolls, 255, **255**

Farina, 153
   pudding, 457
Farls, Irish, *see* Skillet Bread, 277
FATS AND OILS, about, 170–175
   bulk displacement, measuring, 226, **226**
   butter, about, 171
   clarifying, about, 174
   drippings, about, 174
   hydrogenation of, 172
   hidden, 170
   lards and pork fat, about, 173
   margarines, about, 172
   poultry, about, 173
   removing excess salt from, 174
   rendering, about, 174
   saturated, 170
   solid, to measure, 226, **226**
   polyunsaturated, 171
   vegetable shortenings, about, 172
Fennel, as seasoning, 206
Fenugreek, 206
Fig, about, 92, 102; dried, 102
   bars, 391
   cake, spice, 354
   filling, and almond, 381
   filling for coffee cake, 270
   fresh, stuffed, 102
   preserves, 581
   pudding, baked, 461
Filberts, 186; paste, 504
Filé Powder, 206
Fillings, *see names of;* also see
   Cake Fillings, 376–381
   Coffee Cake Fillings, 268–270
Fines Herbes, 220
Finger Bowl Service, 8
Finocchio or Fennel, 206
FISH, *also see* Seafood, Shellfish
   canning, about, 539
   caviar, about, 79
   freezing, thawing, 562
   fritter batter for, 125
   Fumet or stock, 143
   hors d'oeuvre, 79–83
   kippering, 545
   roe and milt, about, 79
   sea tidbits, 80, **80**
   Seviche, 80
   smoking, about, 545
   stock, 143
   to serve, 6
Flambéing, fresh fruits, about, 90
Flan, or Custard Tart, with fruit, 324
Flapjacks, crisp corn, 117
Flavoring, effect of cold; to heighten, 216
   for hard candies, 511
Floating Island, 438
Florentines, 414
FLOUR, about, 152–159
   all-purpose, 152
   arrowroot or starch, 158
   barley, 158
   bean, 158
   bran, 154
   bread, 153
   browned, to substitute, 153
   cake, 152
   carob, 158
   cereal, cooked, substitute for, 159

corn meal, 156
corn or cornstarch; waxy, 155
Cornell Triple Rich Formula, 243
cottonseed, 158
enriched, 153
farina, 153
gluten, 154
graham, 154
measuring, 224, 224
moisture content, 152; variable, 226
non-wheat, about, 155
nut, meal, 158
oat, oatmeal, 158; rolled oats, 158
pastry, 153
patent, 152
peanut, 158
potato, 157
presifted, 153
rice, 157
rye, 157; rye meal, 157
seasoned for flouring, 160
self-rising and phosphated, 153
semolina, 153
sifting, 225, 225
soy, 157
substitutions, see individual flours
tapioca and sago, 157
to flour foods, 160–161, 160
wheat, about, 152–155, 154
wheat, allergy, substitute, 159
wheat, cracked, 154
wheat-germ, 155
whole-grain or graham, 154, 154
Flower, canapés, 51
decorations, for cake, 435
table placement, 2–13
Foam Cakes, 334
Foie Gras, 63
Fondant, 501–503
Fonds or Stock Bases, 138
Food Chopper, to secure, 529
FOODS WE EAT, perishable, warning, 12
serving chilled; hot, 9
FOODS WE KEEP, 527–529
storage, 527, 528
to stockpile, 528–529
Fools, fruit, 86
Foreign Measurements, 229–231
Formal Entertainment; place settings, 4–8, 6, 7, 8
Fowl, also see Poultry and Game Birds
smoking; to cook. 545
Frangipane Cream, 379
Frankfurter, Oblaten, 409
Freezer, contents and management, 547
defrosting, 548
power breaks, 548
Freezing, see Frozen Foods
French, bread, 245, 246
cake, apple or peach, 320
cream cheese mold, 471, 471
crescents or Croissants, 260, 261
egg wash or Dorure, 433
fritters or Beignets, 469
mousse, chocolate, 441
pancakes; stuffed, 113
toast, 290

toast, waffles, 121
Fried Pies, canapé, 54
FRITTER, 125–128
batters, about, 125; for fruit, 126; meat, 125; vegetables, 125; fish, 125
calf brain, 128
Choux paste, unsweetened, 127
corn and ham, 128
eggplant, 127
flower, 128
French or Beignets, 469
fruit, 126
high altitude, 125
meat, cooked, 128
vegetable, puréed, 127
FROZEN FOODS, 547–569; see individual names of; watch for symbol ✳
baked goods, storage periods, 567–568
blanching equipment, 557, 558
breaded, to thaw, 565
economic advantages of, 547
freeze-dry vacuum processing, 549
freezing principles, 547
fried foods, 565
labeling, dating, 552
main dishes, 561–563
packaging for, 550, 551
pre-cooked, 564
quality of, 549
raw, freezing, thawing, and cooking of, 552
sealing, 550, 551
seasoning of, 564
thawing; adverse changes, 552, 560–563
to fill containers, 550
types suitable for freezing, 549, 553, 556, 561, 562, 563
wrapping, 550, 551
FRUIT, 85–110; also see individual names of
acid, thickeners for, 295
Ambrosia, 86
baked, additions to, 89
brandied, 583
broiled, 89
Brulé, 90
butters, 578, 579
cakes, 355–358; also see Cakes
cakes, to decorate, 356
cake, to store, 356
candied and glazed, 522–526
candy roll or centers, 521
canned, spiced sirup for, 88
canning, about, 534–537
citrus, about, 100
cobblers and deep-dish pies, 319–321
compote, fresh, baked, 88
cooked, about, 87
cookies, 394
cream and rice, 458
crisp, fresh or Paradise, 321
cups, 86
curried, 90
dried, 191; cooked, 91; frozen, 569
dried, stuffed, 521; appetizers, 71

FRUIT (*cont.*)
  dried, sulphured, 191
  dumplings, 322
  egg-glazed, 523
  exotic, 92, 92, 93
  filling, 380
  flambéed, 90
  for jellies and jams, 570
  for meats and entrées, about, 91
  Fools, 86
  formal service, 8
  freezing and thawing, 553–556
  fresh, 85; spiced sirup for, 87
  fritters, about, 126; batter, 126; glaze, 126
  gelatin cheesecake, 328
  gelatin molds, in, 452
  glazed, fresh, 523
  glazes, 434
  ices, 493–498; ice creams, 486–493
  juices, canning, 536
  juice custard, 439
  juice, freezing, 556
  juice for jelly making, 572
  juice gelatin, 454
  kebabs, fresh, 89
  Macedoine, 86
  mousse, 490
  pancakes, 113
  pared, poached; "stewed," 88
  paste, 526; canning, 537
  pastries, 319–322
  pectin content test, 571
  pies, 310–317, 329–330; glazed, 314; glazes for, 434–435
  plugged, 41, 104
  pressure cooking of, 89
  pudding, suet, steamed, 464
  puréed; garnishes for, 89
  purées, canning, 537; freezing, 556
  sauces, dessert, 473–482
  sautéed, 90
  sherbets, 496–498
  sirups for, 87; for canning, 535
  soufflé, fresh, 446
  soups, about, 91
  soup Cockaigne, 91; orange, 92
  spiked, 41, 104
  storage of, 85
  thick-skinned, poached; "stewed," 88
  thin-skinned, poached; "stewed," 88
  to place evenly in dough, 243
  to reinforce flavor in, 85
  to wash, 86
  waffles, 120
  whips, 456; eggless, 456
  yields in canning, 534
  zests, 219
Fudge, cakes, 351; *see* Cakes
  candy, 506, 507, 517
  sauce, hot, 477
Fumet, 143

Galette Dough, about, 297; coffee cake, 266
GAME BIRDS, canning, 539–543
  freezing and thawing, 562
  smoked, 545
  stock, 143

GAME, canning, about, 539–543
  preparing, about, 540
  stock, 143
  to bleed and hang, 540
  to clean, cut, and store, 540
Garlic or Ail, about; types, 211
  bread, 289, 289
  to blanch, 211
  to press, 211
  vinegar, 151
Garnishes, citrus fruit, 100, 101, 101
  for fruits, 89
  for ice cream, 484
Gâteau Crêpe, 113
GELATIN, 183–186
  aspic glaze, to make, 185
  Blancmange, 455; cornstarch, 442
  cheese mold, 72
  cheesecakes, 328
  effect of pineapple on, 453, 454
  fruit, for desserts, 452–457
  fruit juice, 453–454
  fruit, molded in, about, 185
  fruit whips, 455–457
  molds, fancy, to make, 185–186, 186
  pies, 331–333
  puddings, about, 452
  to dissolve, 184
  wine, 454
Génoise, 370
Geranium Leaves, 206
German, honey bars, 390; cookies, 395
  pancakes, 115
Giblets, canning, 542
Ginger, about; Canton; root, 200
  candy or centers, 520
  fruit-filling, 380
  snaps, 403; crust, 299
  thins, 393
Gingerbread, 364; high altitude, 385
  house, 391; men, 403, 404
Glass, to remove broken, 529
Glasses, beer, 37, 38; cocktail, 26, 26; for mixed drinks, 38, 39
  frosted, 40; sugar frosted, 30
  to wash, 529
  water, placement and filling, 4, 5
  wine, 35, 35; placement of, 2, 4, 5
GLAZE, 433–435
  applied after baking, 434
  applied before or during baking, 433
  apricot, 434
  arrowroot, 158
  caramel, clear, 435
  for bread, 434
  for canapés and sandwiches, 55
  for fruits, fresh, 523
  for fruits, leaves and blossoms, to candy, 523
  for pies, tarts and coffee cakes, 434
  for puff paste, 434
  French egg wash or Dorure, 433
  fruit, thickened, 435
  honey for coffee cake, 433
  lemon, 434
  liqueur, 434
  meat stock, 145

  milk, 434
    puff paste, 434
    Royal or decorative icing, 426
    strawberry, 435
Gluten, bread, 252; flour, 154
  to prepare, 154
Goose, liver, chopped, 79
Gooseberry, jelly, 574; preserves, 581
Graham, cracker crust, 299
    flour, 154
    griddle cakes, 112
    muffins, 281
Grand Marnier Soufflé, 444
Grape, about, 103; canning, 536
    jelly, waterless, 575
    juice, canning, 536
    pie, 315
Grapefruit, about; to section, 100
    cup, 101
    peel, candied, 524
    sherbet, 496
    sweetened, 101
Gravel Pie, 317
Greengage Plum ice cream, 489;
    preserves, 580
Greens, canning, 539
Gremolata, 222
Grenadine, flavoring, 201
Griddle Breads and Biscuits, 277
Griddle Cakes, see Pancakes, 112
Grissini, 246
Grog, 42
Guacamole, 61
Guavas, about, 93, 103; jelly, 576
Gum Arabic, defined, 523
Gum Paste, 519

HAM, about, 543
    aged, to prepare, 543
    brining of, 543
    country, 543
    croquettes, and corn, 122
    dry cured, 543
    fritters, corn and, 128
    odor near bone, 545
    processing of, 543–545
    Prosciutto and Westphalian, 544
    seasoning as, 222
    smoking, about, 543
    spread, 62
    tidbits in, 78
    trichinosis, 543
HAMBURGER, freezing, 561; to
    wrap, 551
Hard Sauces, 480
Harvest Preserves, 581
Hash, canning, 542
Hazelnuts, 186
    Bavarian cream, 451
    custard filling, 381
    soufflé, 446
    Torte, 367
    wafers, 413
Heart, canning, 542
Heavenly Hash, 517
HERBS, 202–216; also see individual
    names
    about, 202, 202
    Bouquets Garnis or faggots,
      220
    butters, 57
    chiffonade of, 219
    dried, to reconstitute and
      substitute, 203

Fines Herbes, 220
    freezing, 203
    growing and drying, about, 202,
      202
    jelly, 575
    salts, to make, 197
    to cut, 218
    to preserve in salt, 197, 204
    vinegars, 151
Hermits, 394
Herring, hors d'oeuvre, 80–81
    marinated, on toast, 63
    rolls, 81
Hickory Nuts, 186
HIGH ALTITUDE COOKING,
    watch for symbol ▲
    baking, about, 381
    baking soda reactions, 165
    bread, quick, 271; corn, 277;
      yeast, 241
    cakes, 335, 381–385; cookies,
      388
    candies, 500
    canning, 533
    doughnuts, 467
    icings, see Candy, 500
    pancakes and waffles, 111, 119
    pies, 292
    puddings, steam, 464
Hints, Kitchen, 529
Hominy, canning, 539
Honey, about, 167; to reliquefy, 167
    apples, 94
    butter, 480; toast, 290
    cake Cockaigne, eggless, all-rye,
      276
    cookies, German, 395; bars, 390
    glaze, cake, 433
    icing, with peanut butter, 429
    in candy making, 168, 499–501
    sauce; and mint, 480
Horehound, 207; candy, 514
HORS D'OEUVRE, 66–84
    about, 67
    anchovy, cheese, 72; rolls, 81
    Antipasto, 69
    asparagus spears, garnished, 75
    avocado and chutney, 75
    beans, marinated, 75
    beets, stuffed Cockaigne, 75
    bologna cornucopias, 78
    breads to serve with, about, 70
    brussels sprouts, stuffed, 75
    cabbage mound, spiced, 75
    cannibal mound, 78
    carrots, marinated, 75
    caviar, about, 79; dip, 84
    celery curls, 76, 76; logs, 76
    cereals, puffed, 71
    cheese balls, fried, 73;
      Florentine, 73; nut, 72;
      pastry, 73
    cheese carrots, 73
    cheese mold, gelatin, 72
    chicken bits, sherried, 79
    chicken or goose livers, chopped,
      79
    chipped beef cornucopias, 78
    crabapple garnish, 74
    crackers to serve with, about, 70
    cucumber lily, 76
    deep-fat fried, about, 73
    dips, 83–84
    Edam nuggets, 72

HORS D'OEUVRE (*cont.*)
Edam or Gouda cheese, filled, 72
egg apples, 74
eggs as, about, 74, 74
endive, French, stuffed, 76
fish balls, hot, 81
fruit, dried, stuffed, 71
herring; rolled, 81
Kleiner Liptauer, 72
leeks, stuffed, 76
marrow, 78
meatballs, hot, 78
mushrooms, marinated, 76
nut creams, 73
nuts, 70; curried, 70
nuts, toasted in shell, 70
olives, about, 77; garlic, 77
onions, marinated, 77
oyster, cold, 81; pickled, 82
pepper, 77
popcorn, seasoned, 71
Prosciutto and fruit, 78
radish, 77; black, 77
roes, about, 79
Rollmops, 81
Rumaki, 79
salmon rolls, smoked, 81
sardine, 81
sausages, broiled, 79
seeds, toasted, 71
Seviche or raw fish, 80
shrimp aspic, glazed, 82
shrimp balls, fried, 82
shrimp, broiled, 82; pickled, 82
Smorgasbord, 69
steak Tartare, 78
tidbits, sea, 80; skewered, 71–72; in ham or bacon, 78
to serve, 66
tongue cornucopias, 78
turkey and olive, 79
Vicksburg cheese, 72
Horseradish, about, 207
pickled, 590
Huckleberry, 99; tart, 314
Hush Puppies, 279
Hydrogenated Fats, 172
Hyssop, 207

Ice, molds, decorative, 43, 44
punch bowl, 44, 44
ICE CREAM, CHURNED, 483–486
about, 483
additions and garnishes, 484
apricot, 487
caramel, 465
chocolate, 485
coffee, 485
cones or Gaufrettes, 410
Delmonico or Crème Glacée, 484
freezer, to pack, 483
French pot, 483
frozen, storage period, 569
fruit, 486
orange, 486
peach, 486
peppermint-stick, 485
pistachio, 485
raspberry, 486
strawberry, 486
vanilla I, 484

ICE CREAM, STILL-FROZEN, 486–493
about, 486
apricot mousse with evaporated milk, 491
Biscuit Tortoni, 488
butter pecan, 490
chocolate Bombe, 490
chocolate with evaporated milk, 489
Delmonico Bombe, 489
eggnog, frozen, 488
fruit buttermilk, 490
fruit mousse, 490
greengage plum, 489
Macaroon Bombe, 488
mocha, 489
parfaits; *see* Parfaits
persimmon, 490
snow, 484
strawberry or raspberry Bombe, 490
vanilla II, 487; with egg yolk, 488
vanilla with evaporated milk, 488
ICES, 493–498; *also see* Sherbets
about, 493
apricot, 494
fruit, 493; as containers, surprise, 495
lemon, 495; and orange, 494
mint, 497
orange, Angelica, 494
orange or lemon surprise, frozen, 495
peach, 494
pineapple, 494
raspberry or strawberry I, 494; II, 495
suckers, frozen, 498
ICINGS, 418; *see* Cake Icings
Indian, nuts, 187
pudding, 457
relish, 592
Informal Entertaining, 9, 11, 11, 12
INGREDIENTS, 129–238; *see* individual names
optional, watch for symbol, ( )
Italian, meringue, 432

JAM, 570–580
apricot pineapple, quick, 578
Bar-le-Duc, 576
berry, 576, 577
blueberry, 577
cake, Rombauer, 365
cup cakes, 359
defined, 571; making, 572
elderberry, 577
five-fruits Cockaigne, 577
loganberry, 577
pear, with pineapple, spiced, 577
rose-hip, 578
sauce for dessert, 475
strawberry, red red, 576
tarts, macaroon, 407
Jars, canning, to pack, 530–534, 531, 533
for pickles, 584
for pressure canner, 531
JELLY, 570–576
about, 570
apple, 575

bag, to prepare, 572
berry, waterless, 575
black raspberry and gooseberry, 574
crabapple, 575
cranberry, 99
currant, 574; and raspberry, 574
equipment for making, 570–573
freezing, 569
fruit juice for, 572
glasses, to sterilize, 571; to paraffin, 574
grape, 575; waterless, 575
guava, 576
herb and scented, 575
making, about, 573
Paradise, 575
pectin, to test for, 571
plum, 576
quince, 575
raspberry and currant, 574
roll cakes, 372, 373; to line a mold, 449
sauce for desserts, 474
sugar proportions in, 570
sweeteners for, 570
to store, 573
to test for doneness, 573, 573
Tots, 407
Juices, fruit, citrus, 219
fruit, canning, 536–537
fruit, for jelly, 572
fruit, freezing, 556
Juleps, 40, 40
Juniper Berries, 207
Junket, 452

Kebabs, fresh fruit, 89
Keeping Foods, 527–529
Kippering, see Smoking, 545
Kitchen, hints, 529
Kleiner Liptauer, 72
Kolatchen, 255
Kosher, pickles, dill, 593
salt, 196
Kothamille or coriander, 206
Krumkakes, Scandinavian, 409, 409
Kugelhopf, 266; quick, 275
Kumquats, 101; candied or preserved, 525
preserves, 581

Lace, cookies, refrigerator, 400
topping, quick, 431, 431
Lady, cake, 350; Baltimore, 346
fingers, 359; to line a mold, 449
Langue de Chat, 360
Lard, about, 173
seasoned, 222
Lavender, 207
Leavens, about, 161–165
Leaves, candied and glazed, 522, 523
Leeks, seasoning, 212
stuffed, 76
wild, 212
LEFTOVERS, 237
breads, cakes and crackers, 288
Lemon, about, 101, 219
filling, pastry, 379; orange custard, 380
gelatin, 453
glaze, 434
ices, 494, 495

icings, 427
peel, and juices for zests, 219
pies, see Pies
roll cake, 373
sauce, dessert, 473
sherbet, 496; milk, 494
soufflé, 445
sponge custard, 441
sugar, 170
to buy, 219
to cut for garnish, 101
verbena, 207
Lenten Dishes, see au Maigre, 138
Lichee Nuts, 189
Lima Beans, see Beans
Lime, marmalade, 582
pies, see Pies
sauce, 473
sherbet, 496
to buy, 219
Limpet, 80
Liptauer Cheese, 72, 472
Linzertorte, 316
Liqueur, about, 38
glaze, 434
sauce, 476; cream, 482
Liquid, measure, volume, 226–229
Liver, canning, 542
chicken or goose, chopped, 79
pastes, 63
sausage canapés, 63
Lobster, canapés, hot, 63, 64
spread, 64
Loganberry Jam, 577
Lollipops, 513
Lovage, 207

Macadamia Nuts, 187
Macaroon, Bombe, 187
cookies, 398, 416
jam tarts, 407
Mace, 200
Macédoine of fresh fruits, 86
Madeleines, 359
Mandelplaettchen, 404
Mandeltorte or Almond Torte, 366
Mango, tropical, 92, 103
chutney, 591
Mangosteen, 93, 103
Manhattan, cocktails, 29
Maple, candy, cream, 504
Charlotte, 375
curls, 411
gelatin chiffon pie, 333
icing, quick, 429; sugar, 425
parfait, 492
sauce for dessert, 478; sugar, 478
sirup, about, 168; to reliquefy, 168
sirup, to substitute for sugar, 168
sugar, 167; sauce, 478
Marble Cake, 347
Marchpane or Marzipan, 505
Margarines, about, 172
Marguerites, 358
Marigold, 208
Marjoram, 207
Marmalade, 581–582
lime, 582
orange, 581
orange, lemon, and grapefruit, 582

Marmalade (*cont.*)
tamarind, 582
Marrons or Chestnuts, 188–189
glacés, 525
Marrow, hors d'oeuvre, 78
Marshmallow, 505
cream, coffee, 457
Heavenly Hash candy, 517
icings, chocolate, 425
pudding, 456
sauce, 480
Martinis, 27
Martynia, seeds; capers, 205
Marzipan, 505
Mass Cooking, 11–13
Matignon, 221
May Wine, 46
Meals, tray, 11
Measuring, about, 224
comparative U.S. and British,
229, 229
ingredients, dry, 224–226, 224,
225
equivalents and conversions,
226–237
fat, 226–227, 226
fractions in recipes, 228
MEAT, *also see* Beef, Ham, Pork,
Veal, etc.
balls, hors d'oeuvre, 78
canned, boiling before tasting,
540
canning, about, 539–545
color in, 223
drippings, about, 174
freezing and thawing, 561, 565
fritters, 128
fruits for, about, 91
glaze, to make, 145
pastries, about, 297
stocks and stock substitutes,
141–142
Medlars, 103
Melba, sauce, 474
toast, 290
Melons, about, 103
fruit cups or baskets, 104, 104
rounds, filled, 104
spiked, 104
MENUS, 14–24
Meringue, about, 309; paste, 309
cake, fudge, 351
cookies, coconut, 397
Italian, 432
pie, lemon, 329
rings, almond, 415
Swiss, 426
tart, cream Cockaigne, 372
toppings, about, 431
Mexican, orange drops, 520
MILK, 129–138; *also see* Cream,
Sour Cream
about, 129
almond, about, 138
buttermilk, 134; *also see*
Buttermilk
coconut, about, 138
condensed, sweetened, 131
daily requirements, 129
eggnog, quantity, 46
evaporated, 131; frozen
desserts, 488, 489, 491
fermented, 134
for stock, 146

freezing, about, 563
glaze, 434
homogenized, 131; in custards,
436
nut, about, 138
pasteurization of, 130
punches, 42, 43
rice rings, 457
scalding, 137; for bread, 240
sherbets, 494, 495, 498
skim, 131
solids, dry, 131
sour, 135; *also see* Sour Milk
sour and fermented, 134
soy bean, 137
substitutions, 133
sweet, 130
to store, 129
vegetable, 137
whole, 130
Mincemeat, 315
Mince Pie, 315
Mint, candy, pulled, 512
herb or spice, 207
Julep, 40, 40
leaves, glazed, 523
sauce, chocolate, 478
sherbet or ice, 497
Mirepoix, 221
Mixer, electric, for cake batters, 344
Mixing Bowls, to steady, 529
Mocha, blends, 201
cake, chiffon oil, 361
cake, quick, freezer, 376
filling, 379
gelatin, 454
gelatin chiffon cream pie, 332
ice cream, 489
sauce, 478
Mohn or Poppy Seed Filling, 270
Mohrenkoepfe, 370
Molasses, about, 168
bars, 389
blackstrap, 168
crisps Cockaigne, 400
doughnuts, 468
nut wafers, 413
pudding, apple, steamed, 465
sirup for candies, 518
to substitute in baking, 168
Molds, cake, about, 345, 346, 449
caramel-coated, about, 449
dessert, about, 449, 449
gelatin, fancy, to make, 185,
186
gelatin, fruit, 452–456
ice, decorative, to make, 43, 44
to line with macaroons, 449,
449
Mollusks, 80
Monosodium Glutamate, 197
Mont Blanc or Chestnut Mound, 442
Moors' Heads, 370
Mousse, about, 185, 486
apricot, 491
French chocolate, 441
fruit, 490
rum chocolate, 441
Muerbeteig, 297
MUFFINS, 279–283
about, 279, 280
additions to, 278
blueberry, 282
bran, 281; date, quick, 274

buttermilk, 281
cheese, 282
cooked cereal, 282
corn, 277
cranberry, 282
English or raised, 261, 261
graham, eggless, 281
rice, flour, 282
sour cream, 280
whole-grain, eggless, 281
Mulled, wine, 47
Mushroom, butter, blender, 57
canapé or sandwich, 61
canning, 539
croquettes, 123
dried, to reconstitute, 221
frozen, to cook, 560
marinated, 76
seasoning, as, 221
spores, 221
Mussels, hors d'oeuvre, cold, 81
Mustard, about, 208
pickle, 587
types, seasoning, 208

Napoleons, 305
Nasturtium, 209
pods, pickled, 590
Nectarines, about, 104
Negus, 47
Nesselrode Pudding, 450
sauce for desserts, 476
Neufchâtel, 178
Newport Creams, 503
Nockerln or Austrian Pancakes, 116
Nougat, 508
NUT, also see individual names
about, 186–190
balls, flourless, 413
bars, 408
blanching, 189
bread, 243; quick, 271
brittle, 515
brittle, chocolate sauce, 478
butters, 57, 190
cheese balls, 72
cookies, see Cookies
creams, 73
crunch, 514
curried, 70
fillings for coffee cakes, 269
freezing, 569
glazed, 515
grinding, 190, 191
hors d'oeuvre, as, 70
icing, 420
meal, 158
milk, about, 138
soufflé, 446
spiced, 516; caramel, 516
storing and preparing, about, 189
tarts, individual, 408
to apply to cake, 420
to chop, 190
to roast and toast, 70, 189
wafers, 413; curled, 412
waffles, 120
Nutmeg, 200
NUTRITION, 527–528, 530, 549–550

Oat, bread, steel-cut, 251
flours and oatmeal, 158
rolls, molasses, 258

Oatmeal, cookies, quick, 396; Gems, 396
flour, 158
griddle cakes, 117
wafers, glazed or flourless, 396
Oeufs, à la Neige, 438
Oils, about, 173; also see individual names
to substitute in baking, 173, 360
Okra, canning, 539
Olive, about, 77; stuffings for, 77
garlic, 77
oil, cloudiness in, 173
Omelet, dessert, 447–449
Norwegian, 448
soufflés, dessert, 443–449
Onions, about, 209–213, 213
canapés, 61, 62
culture, 209–213
dry, about, 212
griddle cakes, 118
marinated, 77
odor, to remove, 209
pickled, 589
seasoning, as, 209
to blanch, 209
to destroy bacteria, 210
Opera Creams, 503
Orange, about, 100
balls, and apricot, 522
bitter or Seville, 100
bread, quick, 272
cake, filled, 371
custard, sponge, 441
drops, Mexican, 520
fillings, cream or custard, 380
gelatin, 453
ice cream, 486
ices, 494, 498
icings, 424, 428
marmalade drops, 397
marmalades, 581
pie, chiffon, 331; cream, 326
poached, 101
rolls, tea, 262
sauce, 473; brown sugar, 479
sherbets, 495
soup, fruit, 92
sugar, 170
surprise, frozen, 495
to section, 102
toast, 290
Orégano, 207
Orgeat Sirup, 187
Oven, canning, dangers, 531
Oysters, canapés, creamed, 64
croquettes, and chicken, 124
hors d'oeuvre, cold, 81
pickled, 82
Ozmazome, 217

Palm, leaves: rolls, 255, 255; pastry, 304
Panadas, about, 289
PANCAKES, 111–118, 112
about, 111; additions to, 112
Austrian or Nockerl, 116
Blini or Russian raised, 116
Blintzes or cottage cheese, 114
buckwheat, 118
corn meal, 117; flapjacks, 117
corn meal rice, 117
Crêpes Suzette, 114
desserts, as, 112, 462

PANCAKES *(cont.)*
  French, 112; stuffed, 113
  fruit, 113
  Gâteau Crêpe, 113
  German, or Pfannkuchen, 115
  graham, 112
  oatmeal, 117
  onion, 118
  rice flour, 118
  sour milk, 116
  to keep warm, 111
  whole-grain, 112
Panettone, 264
Pans, about, cake size, 336–337,
  337
  spring form, 366, 366
Papaya, about, 92, 105
  in chutney, 591; *see* Mango
Paprika, *see* Red Peppers, 213
Paradise Jelly, 575
Paraffin, for jelly glasses, 573
Parfait, about, 486
  angelica, 492
  butterscotch, 492
  caramel, 492
  coffee, 491
  maple, 492
  raspberry, 492
  to freeze, 487
  Tutti Frutti, 491
Parker House Rolls, 255
Parkin, 364
Parsley, Chinese, see Coriander, 206
  seasoning, as, 213
Parsteaming, 556–558
Parties, *see* Entertaining, 1–13;
  Drinks, 25–48
Paste, canning, 537
  Choux, 305
  gum or Pastillage, 519
  liver, 63
  meringue, 309
  puff, 300, 301, 302
  puff, half or rough, 303
Pasteurization, 130; for cheese, 177
Pastillage, 519
PASTRIES, 292–333
  Beignets, 468
  canapé fillings, 55
  cream puffs, 305, 305
  cream rolls or Schillerlocken,
    304
  Croquenbouche, 305, 307
  Danish or Scandinavian, 267,
    268
  dough, about, 293–304
  dough, frozen, about, 566–568
  éclair, 305, 306
  fillings for, 268–270, 307,
    376–381
  for meats, 297
  fruit, 319–322; dumplings, 322
  Linzertorte, 316
  meringue paste, 309
  Napoleons, 305
  Palm Leaves, 304
  Pâte à Choux, cream puff dough,
    305
  patty shells or Bouchées, 304
  Profiteroles, 307
  Strudel, 307, 308
  Swan, to make, 305, 306
  tarts, *see* Tarts

  turnovers, 54, 321
  Vol-au-vent, 304
Pâte, à Choux, 305, 305
  Brisée, 297
  Feuilletée, 300, 301, 302; demi,
    303
  Sucrée, 297
Patty, shells, 304
Pawpaws, 105
Peas, canning, 539
Peach, about, 105
  brandied, 593
  butter, 579
  cake Cockaigne, 319; French,
    320
  canning, 536
  chutney, 591
  filled, 105
  ice, 494; ice cream, 486
  pie, 312
  preserves, 580
Peanuts, about, 187
  brittle, 515
  butter, to make, 190
  butter cookies, 397
  butter fudge or centers, 517
  butter icing, and honey, quick,
    429
  flour, 158
Pears, about, 105
  canning, 536
  cinnamon, 94
  in liqueur, 106
  jam, spiced with pineapple, 577
  prickly, 108
  spiced, 592
  stuffed, 105
Pecans, 186
  cookies and bars, 408, 412, 413
  filling, toasted, 381
  ice cream, butter, 490
  pie, 318
  Torte, 366
Pectins in Jellies, 571
Penuche, 514
Pepper, about, 201
  black and white, 201
  Cayenne, about, 213
  white, in meat canning, 541
Peppers, chili, dried, to prepare, 214
  chilis preserved in sherry, 590
  hors d'oeuvre, 77
  red and green as spices, 213
  sauce, base for chili, 214
  sweet or pimientos, about, 213
  to peel, 213
  to remove seeds and
    membranes, 213
Peppermint, cream wafers, 504
  pulled mints, 512
  seasoning, as, 207
  stick ice cream, 485
Persian, balls or centers, 521
  cream, 455
Persimmon, about, 92, 106
  ice cream, 490
  pudding, 463
Pesto, Basil and Anchovy, 218
Petits Fours, 360
Pfannkuchen or German Pancakes,
  115
Pfeffernüsse, 395
Piccalilli, 588

PICKLE AND RELISH, *also see*
Chutney
  boiling water bath for, 533
  bread and butter, 587
  cucumber, 585
  curry sauce, 588
  dill, 593
  equipment and ingredients,
    about, 584
  Kosher, dill, 593
  long-brined, about, 593
  mustard or Chow Chow, 587
  Piccalilli, 588
  relish, corn, 589
  relish, green tomato, 588
  relish, Indian, 592
  saccharin, 587
  salt for, 196, 584
  Senfgurken, 586
  short-brined, about, 585
  to make crisp, 585
  vinegar and water for, 584
Pickled, fruits, *see* individual fruits
  horseradish, 590
  nasturtium pods, 590
  onions, 589
  pork, 545
  watermelon rind, 591
PIES, 292–333; *also see* Pastries
  à la mode; *see* Apple Pie, 311
  angel, 330
  apple, 311
  apricot, 316
  baskets, 295
  berry, with cooked fruit, 313
  berry, with fresh fruit, 312
  berry, with frozen fruit, 313
  Black Bottom gelatin, 332
  Boston cream, 372
  butterscotch, 326
  cheese, baker's, 327
  cheese, ricotta, 329
  cherry, fresh, 312; German, 313
  cherry, sour cream, 313
  cherry, with cooked fruit, 313
  cherry, with frozen fruit, 313
  Chess, 318
  chiffon, about, 330
  chiffon, to freeze and thaw, 569
  chocolate, 325; cream, 325
  chocolate gelatin chiffon, 331
  coffee, 325
  cream, 324, 325, 326
  crumb or Gravel, 317
  crusts, additions to, 299
  crusts, cereal, 300
  crusts, cheese cake, 298
  crusts, cookie and Kuchen,
    298, 300
  crusts, crumb, bread or cake,
    299–300
  crusts, crumb, luxury, 299
  crusts, flour paste, 296
  crusts, frozen, unfilled, 568
  crusts, graham cracker, Zwieback
    or ginger snap, 299
  crusts, hot water, 296
  crusts, Pâte Brisée, 297
  crusts, puff paste or Pâte
    Feuilletée, 300, 301, 302
  crusts, quick and easy, 296
  crusts, rich egg, Muerbeteig or
    Pâte Sucrée, 297
  crusts, wheatless, 296
  custard or cream, 324; about,
    323, 324
  custard, caramel, 325
  custard, chocolate-topped, 324
  dough, basic, 293
  dough, freezing, 568
  dough, frozen, baked and
    unbaked, about, 567–568
  dough, Galette, 297
  dough, lattices of, 294, 294
  dough, to crimp, 294, 294
  dough, to cut, 293, 294
  dough, to place top crust, 293,
    294, 294
  dough, to roll, 292, 293
  dough, to vent, 295
  dough, Vienna pastry, 298
  fillings, amounts, 295
  fried, as canapés, 54
  frozen, baked and unbaked,
    about, 566–569
  frozen, fillings, about, 568–569
  frozen, glazes for, 568
  fruit, about, 310
  fruit, deep-dish, 319
  fruit, glazed, 314
  fruit, thickening for, 311, 312
  grape, 315
  Jefferson Davis, 317
  juices, to prevent spillage,
    294–295
  lemon meringue, 329
  lemon or lime chiffon, 331
  lemon or lime Cockaigne, 329
  lemon or lime cream, eggless,
    330
  lemon or lime cream, frozen,
    330
  Linzertorte, 316
  maple gelatin chiffon, 333
  meringue paste, about, 309
  mince, 315; Flambé, 315; Mock,
    316
  mocha gelatin chiffon cream, 332
  orange chiffon, 331
  orange cream, 326
  peach, 312
  pecan, 318
  pinch, *see* Meringue Paste,
    309–310
  prune, 316
  pumpkin, 319
  pumpkin, gelatin chiffon, 333
  raisin, 316
  raspberry cream, 314
  rhubarb, 315
  rum gelatin cream, 331
  shells, individual, to form, 295
  shells, unfilled, 295
  squash, 319
  strawberry cream, 314
  tarts, *see* Tarts
  to seal, 294–295
  toppings for, 431–435
  transparent, 318
Pine Nuts, 187
Pineapple, about, 106, **106**
  Betty, baked, 461
  biscuits, 286
  canning, 537
  cream, molded, 452
  cup, fresh, 107

Pineapple (*cont.*)
  custard, sponge, 440
  effect on gelatins, 454
  filled, 107
  gelatin, 454
  glazed, 524; quick, 107
  grilled, 107
  ice, 494
  icings, 430
  jam, 577, 578
  juice, canning, 537
  preserves, and strawberries, 579
  sherbets, 495, 498
  Snow, 456
  soufflé, 445
  tidbits, 106, **106**
  Tropic, 42
Pistachio, ice cream, 485
  nuts, 187
Pizza, canapé, small, 62
Place Settings, 1–12, **2, 6, 7, 8**
Plums, about, 107
  Bombs, 409
  butter, 579
  cake Cockaigne, 319
  canning, 537
  conserve, 582
  ice cream, greengage, 489
  jelly, 576
  preserves, 580
  pudding, baked, 462; steamed,
    466
  pudding, sauce, or hot wine, 476
Pointers to Success, watch for
  symbol ▶
Polvo de Amor, see Coconut, 194
Pomegranates, 92, 108
Popcorn, about, 517; candied, 518
  seasoned, 77
Popovers, cheese, 283; whole-grain,
  283
Poppy Seed, 201
  fillings, 270
  Torte, custard, 368
PORK, fat, about, 174
  pickled, 545
  salt, 545
  salt, as seasoning, 222
Posset, 42
Pot Liquor, see Vegetable Waters
POTATO, bread, salt-rising, 247
  doughnuts, quick, 468; yeast,
    467
  flour or Fecula, 157
  flour, sponge cake, 342
  rolls, buttermilk, 257;
    refrigerator, 263
  sweet, biscuits, 288
  sweet, canning, 539
  sweet, pudding, 463
  sweet, waffles, 120
Pot-Cheese Filling, 270
Pots-de-Crème, 441
Potted Cheese, 471
POULTRY, see Chicken, Turkey, etc.
  canning, about, 539, 543
  fats, about, 173
  freezing, about, 562
  frozen, thawing and cooking,
    562
  smoking, 545
  stock, 142, 143
  to bleed, 540
Pound Cake, 349

Praliné, 515
Pralines, 514
PRESERVES, 570–583
  apricot, 580
  calamondin, 581
  cherry, 580
  defined, 571
  fig, 581
  gooseberry, 581
  Harvest, 581
  kumquat, 581
  peach, 580
  plum, Damson, Italian or
    greengage, 580
  quince, 580
  strawberry and pineapple, 579
  strawberry and rhubarb, 579
  strawberry Sunshine, 579
  tomato, green, 581
  Tutti Frutti Cockaigne, 583
Pressure Cooking, watch for
  symbol ⊙
  canning, 533, **533**, 538–543; in
    high altitudes, 533
  canning, non-acid foods, 535
  stocks and soups, 145
Pretzels, almond, 404
  bread, 252
Prickly Pears, 108
Profiteroles, 307
Prosciutto, 544
Prune, bars, 391
  Betty, 460
  bread, 243; quick, 271
  cake, spiced chocolate, 352
  chestnuts and, 108
  dried, 108
  filling for coffee cakes, 270
  in wine, 108
  pickled, 108
  pie, 316
  soufflé or whip, 446
PUDDING, SWEET, 436–466; also
  see Custards, Bavarian Creams
  apple molasses, steamed, 465
  Bavarian creams, 450–452
  Betty, Brown, 460; fruit, 460,
    461
  Blancmange, 455
  bread, with meringue, 460
  Cabinet or Bavarian de luxe,
    450
  Charlotte, chocolate, 375; Russe,
    375; maple, 375
  chocolate Feather, 462
  coffee marshmallow cream, 457
  cornstarch, 442, 443
  Cottage, 462
  cream, fried or Crème Frite, 443
  date loaf, uncooked, 466
  date ring, or Christmas wreath,
    461
  English, defined, 472
  farina, 457
  fig, baked, 461
  gelatin, about, 452–456
  Indian, 457
  marshmallow, 456
  milk-rice ring, 457
  molds, 449–450
  Nesselrode, 450
  persimmon, 463
  pineapple snow, 456
  plum, baked, 462; steamed, 466

rennet or junket, 452
rice, 458; fruit, 458; cream, 458
sauces, 473–482
steamed, about, 463; freezing, 569
steamed, brown, 464; caramel, 465
steamed, chocolate, 465; date, 464
steamed, fruit suet, 464
sweet potato, 463
tapioca, 458, 459
whips, fruit, 455, 456; eggless, 456
Puff, canapé, 58, 63, 65
shells, cream, 305, 305; fillings, 307
Puff Paste, 300, 301, 302
glaze for, 434
half or Pâte Demi-Feuilletée, 303
shapes, to make, 303, 304, 305
Pumpkin, about, 318
canning, 539
pie, 319; gelatin chiffon, 333
pie, freezing, 568
totem pole, to carve, 318, 319
Punch, bowl, ice, to make, 44, 44
Bowle, 45
champagne, 45
claret cup, 46
eggnog, 46
Fish House, 45
May wine, 46
milk or Syllabub, 42
mulled wine or Negus, quantity, 47
Planter's, 41
Posset or hot milk, 42
Rhine wine cup, 46
rum, 41
rum cassis cup, 45
Tom and Jerry, in quantity, 47
Wassail, 47
whisky or brandy cup, 45
Purée, canning, 537; freezing, 556

Quantity Cooking, 11–13
Quatre Épices, 221
Quiche, canapé, 53
Quince, 108; canning, 537
jelly, 575; preserves, 580

Rabbit, mold, cake, 345, 345
stock, 143
Radish, canapé, 61; hors d'oeuvre, 77
Rahat Loukoum, 519
Raisin, about; to plump, 191
bread, 244
filling, and almond, 381
icing, 420
pie, 316
sauce, dessert, 474
Ramps, 212
Raspberry, Bombe, 490
cake, rum, 370
ice, I, 494; II, 495
ice cream, 486
jam, 576
jelly, 574
parfait, 492
pie, cream, 314

sherbet, 497
vinegar, 152
Recipes, to increase and decrease, 12, 228
Refrigerator, cakes, 370
cookies, 399, 399
rolls, 263, 264
to wash, 548
Reheating Food, frozen main dishes, 565
Relevés, defined, 5
Relish, see Pickle
Removes, defined, 5
Rennet, for cheese, 177; pudding, 452
Rhubarb, baked, and jam, 109
canning, 537
conserve, spiced, 583
leaves, oxalic acid in, 109
pie, 315
preserves, strawberry and, 579
steamed, 109
RICE, crullers, quick, or Calas, 470
flour; waxy, 157
flour griddle cakes, 118
flour muffins, 282; sponge cake, 342
griddle cakes, corn-meal, 117
puddings, 458
spoon bread, 279

Ricotta, cheese pie or cake, 329
chocolate filling, 379
filling for coffee cakes, 270
Rissoles, 54; sweet, 321
Roast, also see Beef, etc.
canning, 542
Rock, candy, 513; cookies, 394
salt, 196
Roe, about, 79, 546
Rollmops, 81
ROLLS AND BUNS, 252–264
bran, 264
bread sticks, 264
Brioches, 258, 259, 260
buttermilk or Fan Tips, 255, 255
buttermilk potato, 257
caramel or Schnecken, 258
cheese, 256; toasted, 59
Clover Leaf, 253, 254
cinnamon or Snails, 257
crescents or Croissants, 260, 261; sweet, 261
Crumpets, 261
English or raised muffins, 261, 261
fillings, sweet, 270
hard or Vienna, 262
No-knead, light, 253
oat-molasses, 258
orange tea, 262
Overnight, 256, 256
Palm Leaf, 254, 254
Parker House, 254
Pinwheel, filled, 256, 256
refrigerator, 263, 264
refrigerator, no-knead, 263
refrigerator, potato, 263
refrigerator, whole grain, 263
rye, 258
sour cream or Kolatchen, 255
sweet toppings for, 432–435
Versatile, 257
whole-grain, 258
yeast, about, 252

Roquefort, spread, 58
  sticks, puffed, 59
Rose Hips, jam, 578
Rosemary, 214
Rote Gruetze, see Fruit Soup, 91
Royal Glaze, 426
Rue, about, 214
Rum, about, 29
  Baba au or Savarin, 371
  drinks, 29, 41–48
  drops, uncooked, 415
  mousse, chocolate, 441
  pie, gelatin cream, 331
  punch, 41
  sauce, dessert, 476
Rumaki, 79
Russian, pancakes or Blini, 116
Rye, bread, sour dough, 250
  bread, Swedish, 249
  cake, honey, Cockaigne, eggless,
    276
  flour and meal, 157
  rolls, 258

Sabayon, 439; sauces, 475
Saccharin, 169; pickles, 587
Sachertorte, 369
Saffron, 214
Sage, 215
Sago, 157
SALAD, cranberry sauces, 96, 99
  frozen ingredients, 566
  to serve, 8
Sally Lunn, quick, 271
Salmon, croquettes, 124
  smoked canapés and hors
    d'oeuvre, 64, 81
SALT, about, types, 195–198
  brine, 196
  celery, 205
  coarse or Kosher, 196
  cooking or table, 196
  effect in candy making, 195
  effect on gluten formation, 195
  excess, to remove, 174
  foods heavy in, 196
  herb, to make, 197
  iodized, 196
  monosodium glutamate, 197
  pickling or dairy, 196
  rock, 196
  seasoned, to make, 197
  smoked; smoky, 197
  sour, 197
  substitutes, 198
  vegetable, 197; dry salting, 594
Salt Pork, 174, 545
  to remove excess salt, 174
Salt Water Taffy, 512
Salt-Rising Bread; potato, 247
Sand Tarts, 402
SANDWICH, also see Canapés
  about tea and canapé, 49
  asparagus, rolled, 60
  bread for, about, 50
  canapés, for, 49–65
  cheese spreads for toasted, 59
  cucumber, 61
  fillings, see Canapé Fillings,
    55–61
  frozen, about, 564
  glazed, 55
  loaf, 52, 52

  rolled, 51
  shapes, about, 49, 50, 51
  tea, 49–65
  to keep, 50
  to make in quantity, 49, 49
  tomato, 61
  Zoo, 52
Sapodilla, 109
Sapota, white, 109
Sardine, canapés, 65; hors d'oeuvre,
  81
Sassafras, see Filé, 206
SAUCE, also see Dessert Sauces
  chili, 589
  color in, about, 223
  commercial, about, 222
  freezing, 565
  stocks in, 155
SAUCE, DESSERT, 473–482
  Ambrosia, quick, 474
  brown sugar butter, 479; cream,
    479
  brown sugar, hot, 479; orange,
    479
  butter, Henri's, 115
  butters, sweetened, 480
  butterscotch, 478
  caramel, 479; cream, 479
  cherry, 473; cherry Jubilee, 474
  chocolate, 477; blender, 477
  chocolate caramel, 478
  chocolate Cockaigne, 477
  chocolate custard, 477
  chocolate mint, 478
  chocolate nut-brittle, 478
  cider, 478
  Cockaigne, 474
  coconut Dulcie, 480
  coffee, 479
  Crème de Menthe, 476
  custard, 475; and fruit, 475
  foamy, 481
  fruit, 473; custard, 475; hard,
    481
  fudge, hot, 477
  hard, 480; topping, 431
  hard, brown sugar, 481; fluffy,
    481
  hard, fruit, 481
  hard, spicy, 481
  honey, 480; and mint, 480
  honey butter, 480
  jam, 475
  jelly, 474, 573–576
  lemon, 473
  lime, 473
  liqueur, 476; cream, 482
  maple sugar, 478; sirup, 478
  marshmallow, 480
  Melba, 474
  mocha, 478
  Nesselrode, 476
  orange, 473
  plum pudding, or hot wine, 476
  preserves, 579–581
  raisin, 474
  rum, 476
  Sabayon, classic, 439, 475
  Sabayon, cold and hot, 475
  sour cream, 482
  vanilla, 480
  Weinschaum, 476
  wine, hot, 476; red, 476
  Zabaglione, 439, 475

Sauerkraut, 594
  apples stuffed with, 95
SAUSAGE, apples, filled with, 95
  canapés, 63
  canning, 542
  hard, to make and smoke, 545
Savarin, 371; *also see* Bundkuchen, 266
Savory, as dessert, 472
  to serve, 8; herb, 215
Scalding, milk, 137
Scallions, 212
Scallops, about, 80, 80
Scandinavian, coffee cake or pastry, 267
    Krumkakes, 409
Schmierkaese, 177
Schnecken, 258
Scones, 288
Scotch, shortbread, 404
  whisky, 28
Sea Tidbits, 80, 80
SEAFOOD, *also see* Fish and Shellfish
  butter, 57
  canapés, 63–65
  dips, 84
  hors d'oeuvre, 79–83
  to serve, 6, 6, 7, 7
Seasonings, 216–222; *also see* individual names
  about; correcting, 216
  amounts to use, 218
  frozen foods, in, 564
  herbs, 202–216
  salts, 195–198
  spices, 198–202
Seed, cake, 350
  pumpkin, squash, melon, sunflower, 187; sesame or benne, 215
Semolina Flour, 153
Senfgurken, 586
Sesame, oil, 173; seed, 215
Seviche, 80
Shallot, about, to substitute, 211
SHELLFISH, *also see* individual names
  freezing, 562
Sherbet, Churned, about, 493
  champagne, 498
  lemon milk, 494
  orange milk, 495
  pineapple milk, 494
Sherbet, Still-Frozen, about, 493
  banana pineapple, 497
  cranberry, 497
  fruit milk, 498
  grapefruit, 496
  lemon, 496
  lime, 496
  mint, 497
  orange, 496
  pineapple buttermilk, 498
  raspberry or strawberry, 497
  wine, 497
Sherry, about, 32
Ship's Biscuits, 288
Shortbread, Scotch, 404
Shortcake, dough, 286
  individual and large, 376
Shortening, bulk, to measure, 226
  oil-based, 172

vegetable, about, 172
Shrimp, aspic-glazed, 82
  balls, fried, 82
  broiled, 82
  dip, 84
  pickled, 82
  puffs, 65
Sifting, flour, sugar, 225, 225
Silver, Placement, 3–10, 2–10
Sirup, for freezing fruits, 554
  sugar, for candies, 518
  sugar, for canning, 535
  sugar, liquid, about, 167
  sugar; spiced for fruits, 87
Skewer Cooking, tidbits, cold, 71
Skillet, Breads, 277
  cake, Upside-down, 320
Smoke Cookery, 543–546
  fish, 545
  fowl, 545
  ham, 543
  sausage, hard, canning, 545
Smorgasbord, 69
Snow, ice cream, 484
  pineapple, 456
Soda, baking, about, 164–165
  bread, Irish, quick, 273
  for high altitudes, 165
Sorghum, 169
Sorrel, seasoning, as, 215
SOUFFLÉ, see Dessert Soufflés
SOUFFLÉ, DESSERT, 443–449
  about, 443
  Alaska, baked, 448, 448
  apricot, 446; omelette, 448
  chocolate, 445
  fruit, fresh, 446
  Grand Marnier, 444
  hazelnut, 446
  lemon, 445
  nut, 446
  omelet, Norwegian, 448
  Omelette aux Confitures, 447
  Omelette Surprise, 448
  pineapple, 445
  prune, 446
  Rothschild, see Vanilla, 444
  sour cream apple cake Cockaigne, 447
  to glaze, 444
  vanilla, 444
SOUP, *also see* Stock
  freezing, about, 565
  Panades, for, 289
  pressure cooked, about, 145
  stocks, see Stocks, 138
  vegetables for, 144
Sour Cream, about, 134, 137
  apple cake Cockaigne, 447
  berries with, 98
  cake, 347; cup cakes, 360
  cheese cake, 327
  coffee cake, quick, 275
  dips, 83–84
  doughnuts, 467
  muffins, 280
  pie, cherry, 314
  rolls or Kolatchen, 255
  sauce for desserts, 482
  substitutes, 137
  waffles, 120
Sour Dough, about, 163
  rye bread, 250
  to substitute for yeast, 162

Sour Milk, 135
    cup cakes, spice, 360
    pancakes, 116
    substitutions, 135
Soursops, 109
Soy, flour, 157
    sauce, 222
Soybean, milk, 137
Spanish, cream, 437
Spearmint, 207
Speculatius, 406
Spice, 198–201; see individual names
    cakes, see Cakes, Coffee Cakes
    in frozen baked foods, 567
    in quantity cooking, 198
    Parisienne or Quatre Épices, 221
    pickling, for, 584
    to cook with, 198
Spirits for Cooking, about, 149
Spoilage in Canning, 530, 538, 539
Sponge, cakes, see Cakes
    custards, about, 440
    orange, 441; lemon, 441;
      pineapple, 440
Spoon Breads, 279
Spreads, see Canapés and Sandwiches
Springerle, 405
Spritz Cookies, 406
Squares, cake or cookie, about, 388
Squash, canning, 539
    freezing, 556
    pie, 319
Stains, removal of, 529
Staples, household; storage of, 528
Starches, waxy, in frozen pies, 568
Steaming, puddings, 463
    table, 12
STEWS, MEAT, canning, 542
STOCK, 138–147
    about, 138; stock pot, 139, 140
    brown, 141
    canning, 542
    chicken or light, 142
    clarifying, 140
    concentrates, frozen, 565
    Court bouillons, 146
    faggots for seasoning, 220
    fish or Fumet, 143
    fowl, rabbit, game, 143
    glazes, about, 145
    household, quick, 142
    light, 142
    making, 139
    pressure-cooked, 145
    quick, 142
    reinforcers, 145
    scum on, 140
    seasonings for, 140
    substitutes, about, 138, 145
    to retain flavoring, 138–141
    to store, 141
    veal, 142
    vegetable, 145; vegetables for,
      144
Stollen, 265
Storage of Food, 527–529
Strawberry, Bombe, 490
    freezing, 553–555
    fresh, variations, 97–98
    glaze, 435
    ice I, 494; II, 495
    ice cream, 486
    jam, red red, 576
    pie, cream, 314

preserves, 579
Romanoff, 98
sherbet, 497
Streusel Toppings, 432–433
Strudel, about, 307, 308
SUBSTITUTIONS AND
    EQUIVALENTS, 226–238; also
    see individual names
Suckers, frozen, 498
    candy, 513
Suet Pudding, fruit, steamed, 464
SUGAR, 165–170
    brown or Barbadoes, 166; to
      measure, 225, 225
    brown, sauces, 479
    caramelized for color, 169; for
      glazes, 169
    confectioners', 166; powdered,
      166
    cookies, see Cookies
    corn sirup, 167
    crystallized, see Rock Candy,
      513
    equivalents, 226–238
    granulated, 166
    honey, 167
    in jelly and jam, 570–572
    liquid, about; to substitute, 167
    lump, 167
    maple, 167; sirup, 168
    raw, 166
    seasoned, about, 169
    sirup for freezing, 554
    sirup, white, 518
    solid, about, 165; to measure,
      165, 225, 225
    synthetic, 169
    to substitute, 226–241
    to unlump, 225; brown, 166
    volumes vs. weights, 227
Sunshine Cake, 342
Swan Pastry, 305, 305
Swedish, rye bread, 249
Sweet Cicely, 215
Sweet Woodruff or Waldmeister,
    215
Sweeteners, synthetic, 169
    in jellies, 570; canning, 535
Sweets, English definition, 472
Swiss Meringue, 426
Syllabub, 42
Symbols, see Foreword

Tabasco Sauce, 223
Table Décor and Service, 1–13
Tacos, 55
Taffy, 510–513, 511
Tamarind, 110
Tapioca, flour for glazes and frozen
    foods, 158
    puddings, 458, 459
Tarragon, about, 215
    to store in vinegar, 215
    vinegar, 151
Tart, apple, 311
    Banbury, 317
    blueberry or huckleberry, 314
    canapés, tartlets for, 53–54
    Chess, 318
    coffee, 325
    cream meringue, Cockaigne, 372
    custard, with fruit, 324
    glaze for, 434

macaroon jam, 407
nut, individual, 408
Quiche, 53
Sand, 402
shells, 295
Tartare, steak, 78
Taste, 216
TEA, breads, 271–276
cakes, *see* Cakes
sandwiches, 49–65
service, about, 10, 12
spreads, sweet, 60
wafers, 416
Tehina, *see* Sesame Seed, 215
Temperature Conversion Table,
230–231
Tenderloin, canapé and caviar, 62
Tequila, 31
Thawing Frozen Foods, 552,
560–569
Thermometer, candy, 500–501
Thyme, 216
Tisanes and Infusions, to serve, 12
Toast, bread loaf, buttered, 289
cinnamon, or sticks, 289
French, 290
French, waffles, 121
honey butter, 290
Melba, 290
orange, 290
Zwieback, 290
Toddy, 42
Toffee, English, 514
TOMATO, canapés, 61
canning, 537
catsup, 590
juice, canning, 537
pickle, green, 588; chutney,
592
preserves, 581
sandwiches, 61
seasoning, as, 222
Tongue, canning, 542
cornucopia hors d'oeuvre, 78
TOPPINGS, *also see* Cake Icings,
Garnishes, Pie Toppings
for coffee cakes, pies, rolls,
432–435
Tortelettes, 392
Torte, about, 366
almond, Cockaigne, 366
bread or Brottorte, 366
chocolate date, 368; walnut, 368
Dobos or Drum, 367
hazelnut, 367
pans for, 366
pecan, 366
poppy seed custard, 368
Sacher, 369
Toushi, *see* Capers, 205
Transparent Pie, 318
Tray Dining, for buffets, 11, 66–69,
68
invalid, 11
Treacle or Golden Sirup, 169
Trifle, 370
Truffles, candy, 517
Tuna Fish, canapés, hot, 64
TURKEY, soup, 143
Turmeric, 201
Turnovers, 54
Tutti Frutti, cake, 355
conserve, Cockaigne, 583
parfait, 491

Upside-down Cake, 320
Urchins, 80

Vacherin Rings, *see* Meringue Paste,
310
Vanilla, bean and extract, 201
cookies, refrigerator, 399
ice cream, I, 484; II, 487; with
eggs, 488
ice cream with evaporated milk,
488
sauce, 480
soufflé, 444
sugar, 170
Vanocka, 265, 265
VEAL, croquettes, 124
stock, 142
VEGETABLE, *see* individual names
blanching for freezing, and
chart, 556–560
brining, about, 593
canning, 532–534, 538–539
canning, pressure, about, 538
for Court Bouillon Blanc, 146
for stock or soup, 144
freezing, thawing, cooking,
556–561
freezing, 556; to size for, 552,
552
fritter batter for, 125
fritters, puréed, 127
milks, 137
pressure cooked, for soups, 145
salting and brining, about, 593,
594
salts, 197
seasonings, 220–222; *also see*
Mirepoix, Matignon
shortenings, about, 172–173
stock, 145
waters or pot liquors, 138
yields in canning, 538
Velvet Spice Cake, 352
Vinegar, about, 150
chili, 152
cider and malt-based, 150
for pickling, 584
garlic, 151
herb, fresh, 151; quick, 151
raspberry, red, 152
spiced, 151
tarragon or burnet, 151
white, distilled, 150
wine, 150
Vodka Drinks, 31, 41
Vol-au-Vent, 304

Wafers, *see* Cookies
Waffles, 118–121
about, 118
bacon, corn meal, 121
buttermilk, 120
cheese, 120
chocolate, 121
desserts, as, 462
French toast, 121
fruit, 120
iron, care of, 119, 119
raisin, nut or coconut, 120
sour cream, 120
yam, golden, 120
Waldmeister or Sweet Woodruff, 215
Walnut, 186
filling, toasted, 381

Walnut (cont.)
    Leaves or cookies, 414
    Torte, chocolate, 368
Wassail, 47
Water, 147–148
    about; for cooking, 147
    acidulated, 148
    daily intake, 148
    purification, 148
    seasoned, 147, 148
Water Chestnuts, 188
Watermelon Rind Pickles, 591
Weather, effect on cooking, 224
    effect on candy, 499; smoking,
      544
Wedding Cakes, 345, 345
Weinschaum Custard, 440; sauce,
    476
Wheat, breads, see Breads
    flour allergy substitute, 159
    flours and grains, 152–155, 154
Whip, fruit, 455; eggless, 456
    prune or apricot, 446
Whips for Egg Beating, 335, 335
Whisky, about, types, 28
    drinks, 28–29, 45–47
Whole-grain, breads, see Breads and
    Rolls
    flour, 154, 154
    griddle cakes, 112
    muffins, 281; popovers, 283
Wild Birds or Fowl, see Game Birds
Wines, about, 32
    champagne, about, 34, 37
    classifications, 33
    cooking with, 149–150
    custard or Weinschaum, 440
    for aspics and jellies, 150
    for cooking, about, 149
    for soup, 150

    formal pouring of, 5, 35
    fortified, defined, 32
    gelatin, 454
    glasses, 35, 35
    mulled, 47
    sauce, hot, as dessert, 476
    sauce, red, dessert, 476
    savories to serve with, 472
    sherbet, 497
    sherry, about, 32
    to serve, 34; chart, 35–36
    to store, 33
    vinegar, 150
    vintages, about, 36
Winkle, 80
Woodruff, Sweet, 215
Worcestershire Sauce, 223

Yam, see Potatoes, Sweet
    waffles, golden, 120
YEAST, 161–163
    about, 161
    breads, 239–252
    brewer's, debittered, 163
    coffee cakes, 264–268
    compressed, 163
    doughnuts, potato, 467
    doughs, additions to, 243
    dry, 163
    paste for Brioche, 258
    rolls and buns, 252–264
    to substitute, 162, 163
    to test for freshness, 163
Yogurt, dessert, 472
    to make, 135–136

Zabaglione, 439; sauce, 475
Zests as Flavorings, 219
Zwieback, 290; crust, 299